1984

PUBLIC RELATIONS: CONCEPTS AND PRACTICES

PUBLIC RELATIONS: CONCEPTS AND PRACTICES

Third Edition

Raymond Simon
Utica College of Syracuse University

John Wiley & Sons

New York   Chichester   Brisbane Toronto   Singapore

For Lyn, Melissa, Karen, and Lillian
with love and affection

Library of Congress Cataloging in Publication Data:

ISBN 0-471-84122-6

Printed in the United States of America

10 9 8 7 6 5 4 3 2 1

CONTENTS

PREFACE

That old refrain about the bride's attire kept running through my mind as I mulled over this preface to *Public Relations: Concepts and Practices*. To borrow from the refrain, this book consists of:

> Something old,
> Something new,
> Something borrowed,
> Something blue.

Something old is found in the basic core of this third edition of a textbook that has been adopted by more than 140 colleges and universities throughout the United States, Canada, and abroad. The main purpose of this book continues to be its use as a teaching tool in the introductory course in public relations and as a reference resource for practitioners who seek to be reminded of the roots of their calling. This third edition re-emphasizes that there is a solid body of knowledge within the public relations field and a discernible pattern of core concepts, activities, and procedures in the public relations function and the public relations process.

Acting on this premise, I have divided this text into three major sections. The first two explore in depth key concepts and factors concerning the public relations function and the public relations process. The last deals with matters of contemporary concern to public relations students and practitioners.

In order to understand public relations today, it's important that one understand what public relations is, where it comes from, its role and place in our society, and the manner in which it is carried out and managed. Therefore, the seven chapters in Part 1 define public relations; explore its relationship to the management and policies of organizations; relate it to the dual concepts of social responsibility and the public interest; examine historical antecedents and the current status of the field; explain why public relations has assumed an important role in modern society; and detail the role, structure, and activities of internal and external public relations practitioners.

Part 2, which deals with the public relations process, continues to form the main section of the text. The eight chapters in this section focus on public opinion; public relations research; planning and programming; communication; and evaluation, measurement, and reporting. In dealing with these key elements of the public relations process I have developed the text material as applied to all public relations practice. Although it's true that public relations is most widely known for its use by business and industry, it's also true that thousands of practitioners work in the field in government, social agencies, hospitals, colleges, and the armed forces. Therefore, I have sought to set forth basic principles and to apply them to the public relations process in its broadest sense. Given the basic principles, the student and practitioner can then apply them to a wide variety of situations and organizations.

Examples and practical exercises and assignments help bring to life concepts and principles. Therefore, this third edition follows the pattern of its predecessors by its use of illustrations from actual public relations practice and by inclusion at the end of each chapter of projects, assignments, and mini-cases, mini-examples, mini-situations, and mini-problems. Several of the classic mini-cases have been retained from the previous two editions, but most of the projects, assignments, and mini-cases are new to this edition. Intended to bring students face-to-face with reality, the "minis" challenge students to utilize their verbal and writing abilities, to sharpen their perceptions and communication skills, and to form sound judgments and propose reasonable solutions and actions.

Something new in this third edition is the inclusion of important new and timely developments in the field, updated information, new mini-cases, and three chapters in Part 3 dealing with legal aspects of public relations practice, corporate political expression, and communications technological changes as they relate to public relations.

Every decade seems to bring a new focus within public relations practice. It's for this reason that I have dealt in Part 3 with such contemporary concerns as the impact of law on various aspects of public relations practice; on legal rulings in the early 1980s affecting corporate political expression; and on such communications technological developments as public access television, the coming-of-age of cable television, the use of word processors, teleconferencing, narrowcasting, and similar changes which have had important implications for public relations practice and practitioners.

Something borrowed are the concepts, words, and insights of numerous public relations practitioners and teachers who have written about and discussed public relations in articles, books, speeches, talks, and seminars. I have indeed borrowed from and am therefore indebted to these men and women who have influenced my vision of public relations and are bound to influence those who use this text.

Something blue should really be colored true blue because it reflects those who have been an integral part of my life and work through the three editions of this textbook. I remain deeply indebted and wish to express my love and appreciation to my wife, Lyn, and daughters Melissa and Karen for their patience, encouragement, and support. I am similarly in debt to and appreciate the continued help of former students, teaching colleagues, practitioners, editors, publishers, and professional societies who graciously granted me permission to use much of the material which made up the mini-cases, examples, situations, and problems.

Raymond Simon

Utica, New York
April, 1984

Part

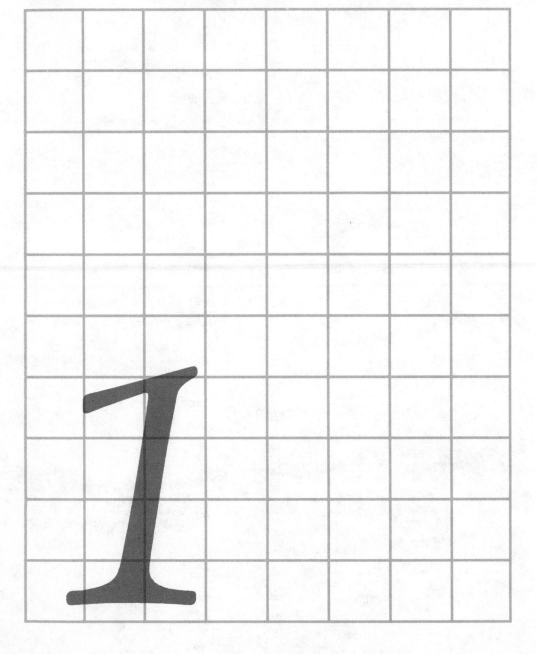

1

PART 1
THE PUBLIC RELATIONS FUNCTION

This first section of the book, consisting of seven chapters, examines the essential nature of public relations and its role in American society as a staff function of organizations.

In order to understand public relations, one must first understand the term itself and the concept. Chapter 1 therefore explores various definitions of public relations and discusses differences between that term and other terms and activities that are frequently confused with it. In amplifying the public relations function the next two chapters deal with the relationship between public relations and management and with the two concepts known as social responsibility and the public interest.

Chapter 4 takes us back through American history to demonstrate some early uses of the public relations function and to link these with current, organized public relations practice. Set forth in Chapter 5 are major trends in American society that have brought about the need for public relations and have affected the way in which public relations is practiced today.

Functions are handled by functionaries, and so in Chapters 6 and 7 public relations practitioners are described and their roles and responsibilities are set forth and analyzed. The major share of Chapter 7 explains the structure and management of internal public relations departments and counseling firms.

1

THE FUNCTION DEFINED: WHAT IS PUBLIC RELATIONS?

The ancient poet stated a simple truth when he wrote that "a journey of a thousand miles must begin with a single step."

Applying that precept to public relations means coming to grips with the term. Taking this first "single step" is important because the term has been used, and mis-used, in so many ways. Some examples:

"The company's action was just a public relations move."

"The hospital has good public relations."

"The former *Time* magazine writer now does public relations."

The above examples were all taken from newspaper articles, and they demonstrate that journalists consider the term public relations to be as versatile as an all-purpose cleanser. Compounding the confusion is the fact that those in the public relations field aren't sure whether they consider themselves to be in a field, business, calling, or profession. Some practitioners are so worried about the negative connotations of the term, they've changed their titles. Instead of directors of public relations, we now find directors of public affairs, communications, or public information. Unlike Shakespeare's Juliet, these practitioners seem to believe that a rose would smell sweeter if it were called by another name. Whatever we call it, however, we ought to recognize that the proper way to commence a study of public relations is to understand the term, concept, process, and activity known as public relations.

SOME DEFINITIONS

Years ago, when life was comparatively simple, a commonly accepted definition of public relations ran something like this: "Doing good and telling people about it." In an increasingly complex world, we have learned this definition could just as well apply to show-and-tell in the first grade. The literature of the field now bears witness to a more thoughtful analysis of the term, and we will try to deal with several definitions because it's important to understand clearly what we mean by *public relations* as we consider it throughout this book. In analyzing the definitions that follow, keep in mind similarities and differences; do not attempt to memorize the definitions in their entirety, but rather sort out recurring ideas and phrases and come to an understanding of public relations as a *process* and *function*.

One of the earliest definitions of public relations was developed by the *Public Relations News*, pioneer weekly public relations newsletter, and has stood the test of time as well as changes in the field. Professor John Marston added two words—"and communication"—to the *Public Relations News* definition and they are cited in parentheses in the statement below:

> Public relations is the management function which evaluates public attitudes, identifies the policies and procedures of an organization with the public interest, and executes a program of action (and communication) to earn public understanding and acceptance.[1]

In the mid-seventies, Dr. Rex Harlow conducted a study under the sponsorship of the Foundation for Public Relations Research and Education to seek consensus among public relations leaders of an accepted definition of public relations. After analyzing the many diverse contributions, Dr. Harlow offered the following definition:

> Public relations is a distinctive management function which helps establish and maintain mutual lines of communication, understanding, acceptance, and cooperation between an organization and its publics; involves the management of problems or issues; helps management to keep informed on and responsive to public opinion; defines and emphasizes the responsibility of management to serve the public interest; helps management to keep abreast of and effectively utilize change, serving as an early warning system to help anticipate trends; and uses research and sound and ethical communication techniques as its principal tools.[2]

A final definition, somewhat briefer than that of Dr. Harlow, is the one adopted by representatives of various public relations groups and societies from throughout the Western world in August, 1978. Called "The Statement of Mexico," the resolution is really a definition of public relations:

> **The Statement of Mexico**
> Public relations practice is the art and social science of analyzing trends, predicting their consequences, counseling organization leaders, and implementing planned programs of action which will serve both the organization's and the public interest.

Though they may differ in their emphasis on certain elements, the three definitions have much in common. Public relations, as seen in these definitions and as underscored in this book, involves the following elements:

1. **A management function which utilizes research and a planned effort and follows ethical standards**

2. **A process involving the relationship between an organization and its publics**

3. **Analysis and evaluation through research of public attitudes and opinions and societal trends and communicating to management**

4. Management counseling so as to insure that an organization's policies, procedures, and actions are socially responsible and in the mutual interests of the organization and its publics

5. Implementation and execution of a planned program of action, communication, and evaluation through research

6. The achievement of goodwill, understanding, and acceptance as the chief end result of public relations activities

A CONTINUING PROCESS

In reviewing the six elements above keep in mind that public relations in action is a continuous process. Figure 1.1 shows the public relations process in graphic form.

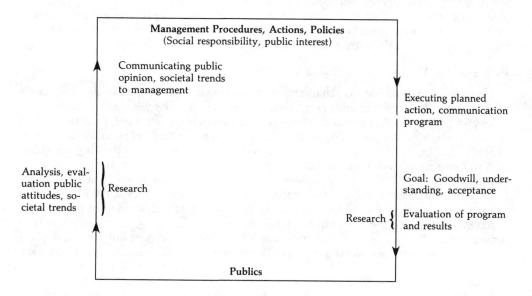

FIGURE 1.1   *The public relations process.*

As seen by the chart, the public relations function/process is carried out through research which evaluates public attitudes/opinions and societal trends and communicates them to organizational leaders/management. The organization's procedures, actions, and policies are measured against these public attitudes/opinions and societal trends. When necessary, these procedures, actions, and policies may well have to be changed or modified if they do not meet the public interest and/or are not socially responsible. Those responsible for the public relations function then carry out a planned program that includes actions, activities, and communication to an organization's publics to bring about goodwill, understanding, and acceptance. Monitoring of public relations effectiveness is carried out through research by various evaluative methods which demonstrate how well or how poorly the public relations program and process has served the organization.

Professor Marston's R-A-C-E formula[3] provides an acronymic description of the public relations process which helps recall its key elements:

> **R** esearch . . . .   the initial step, vital in securing information and data about the organization, issue or situation, audience, and public attitudes and opinion

---

Action . . . . the second step, including advice to management and a planned program

Communication . . . . . the third step, which involves the means whereby elements of the planned program are transmitted to various publics

Evaluation . . . . the fourth step, the means whereby, through research, the effectiveness of the process is monitored and judged

Frank W. Wylie, a past president of the Public Relations Society of America, has charted the public relations process in linear form to show the individual elements and the nature of the process in action (Figure 1.2). Wylie's chart shows the process starting on the left with "inputs" from various publics, the media, trend data, research, and so forth. These are analyzed and evaluated as they reach management. After discussion and consideration of alternatives, an action program is developed and fed as "outputs" in the form of stories, speeches, press releases, and so on. The process, a continuous one, then repeats itself with further, continual "inputs."

Beware the Variables

The continuing process that characterizes public relations in action is also a dynamic process, and therefore it is seldom the neat and orderly one described in the definitions. Those who maintain that public relations is an art and not a science point out that public relations activities and programs do not take place in the controlled situation of the laboratory. Rather, they occur in real-life situations amidst constantly changing variables.

A simple example will demonstrate why the dynamics of a situation make it difficult if not impossible to bring about a cause-and-effect laboratory relationship in public relations programming. Practitioner A drafts a carefully prepared message which aims to calm public fears about a shortage in the products of A's organization. The practitioner sends the message to the media in the form of a press release. The day the release is to appear an earthquake occurs, hundreds are killed, and millions of dollars of property lost. The story of the earthquake makes page one news, and the release is lost in the back pages. Natural disasters not only bury people and property, but all other news as well.

Countless other examples abound to prove the point that the best laid (public relations) plans "gang aft a-gley," as Robert Burns noted more than two hundred years ago. Organizational infighting can often sidetrack sound public relations proposals. Although few nonlegal and nonfinancial personnel would dare to argue the merits of advice and proposals set forth by legal and financial departments, a great many nonpublic relations personnel have little hesitation to contest advice and proposals set forth by public relations departments.

Numerous variables outside the purview of public relations practitioners work to scuttle and vitiate programs which are sound in concept, but which fail in execution for reasons beyond the control of the practitioners. Competition for public attention is fierce, and messages aimed at the public often get detoured down unexpected byways. Only the most skillful are able to get their story across in a form and manner to bring about the desired public understanding, goodwill, and acceptance. Achieving desired public relations goals calls for a clear understanding of the fundamental component parts which comprise the public relations process and function. Such an understanding can be brought about in two ways: by recognizing the difference between public relations and terms sometimes mistakenly associated with it, and by raising questions about some of the essential elements of the process of public relations too often taken for granted.

TERMS CONFUSED WITH PUBLIC RELATIONS

Several terms and activities—advertising; marketing and product promotion; press agentry and publicity; and public affairs—are often confused with public relations. At

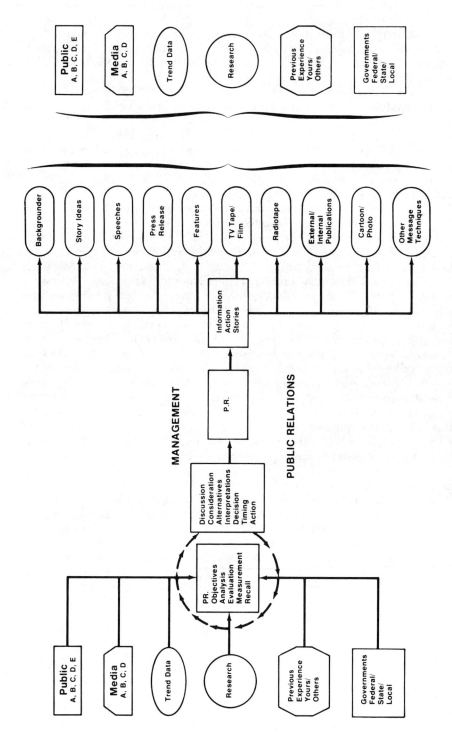

FIGURE 1.2 *Wylie's public relations process.*

Reproduced with permission of Frank W. Wylie.

times public relations involves each of these aforementioned activities, but it should not be considered synonymous with them.

Advertising is concerned chiefly with the sale of products and/or services and involves the use of paid media space or air time. Advertising may be used in the communications phase of the public relations process, not to sell an organization's product, but to create a certain image of the organization. Such advertising is most commonly called "image," "public service," or "institutional" advertising. When it argues a point of view, it's called "advocacy" advertising. Thus, when advertising is used for public relations purposes it aims to "sell"—using the term in its most direct form—an organization; to communicate specific aspects of an organization's activities; or to deliver, intact as written, special messages that aim to bring about clear understanding by the public.

Marketing and product promotion are concerned directly with the distribution and sale of goods and/or services. Their target audience is the ultimate consumer, but they are also involved with other publics in the distribution channel, such as wholesalers, dealers, and retailers. The efforts of marketing/product promotion specialists are often directed at the same publics as those of public relations specialists, sometimes for different and sometimes for similar reasons. It is not surprising, therefore, to find product promotion specialists reporting to a marketing executive in one organization, to a public relations executive in another organization, and to both in a third organization. In some organizations public relations activity is expected to have a direct and verifiable effect on sales, whereas in other organizations it is expected that public relations will support and assist the sales effort but will have many other objectives and responsibilities.

The distinction between marketing and public relations has been difficult to make because the two functions increasingly overlap in numerous organizations. Professors Philip Kotler and William Mindak note that both are the major external functions of the firm and both share common ground in regard to product publicity and customer relations. At the same time, however, they operate on different levels and from different perspectives and perceptions. The traditional view, note Kotler and Mindak, is that "marketing exists to sense, serve, and satisfy customer needs at a profit. Public relations exists to produce goodwill in the company's various publics so that these publics do not interfere in the firm's profit-making ability." Though the use of the verb *interfere* seems ill-advised, the distinction between the two functions seems clear enough. "No one model will be appropriate for all enterprises," state Kotler and Mindak. "The environmental pressures facing the individual enterprise, as well as its own history, will dictate whether to strengthen its marketing function or public relations function or even whether to start a new pattern of meeting and coping with external opportunities and threats."[4]

Press agentry and publicity are terms that are often used synonymously, but there are differences between the two. **Press agentry** is chiefly concerned with gaining attention through imaginative—and often rather bizarre—stunts and events which induce media to write about or air them. Press agents have mainly been associated with show business and the entertainment field, either representing organizations associated with the field or individuals who thrive on having their celebrity status kept constantly in the public eye. The philosophy of the press agent's client was probably best summed up by the one who was reputed to say, "I don't care what they print about me so long as they spell my name right."

> In April, 1983, fifty years after he was machine-gunned off his perch atop the Empire State Building, **King Kong** was back up there trying to scare the daylights out of everyone but not quite succeeding. Old Kong got there thanks to a California manufacturer of display balloons. Weighing in at 3,000 pounds, the eight-story inflatable Kong didn't fare too well. He managed to hang on for one day of glory, but high winds, tangled cables, and rips in his heavy nylon skin left him hanging "like an old brown garbage bag," as *Time* put it.
>
> Was Kong's vinyl reincarnation a failure? Consider it from a press agent's point of view. For a full week Kong was not only a quarter mile up in the sky, but his picture and story were carried for days by newspapers, wire services, radio, television, and magazines

such as *Time* and *Newsweek*. It was a story the media couldn't resist, and most of them even carried the name of Kong's manufacturer![5]

Publicity, which might well be considered to be the more legitimate son or daughter of press agentry, involves providing information, news, and feature material about an organization or person. Publicity can be and often is linked to newsworthy events, but in a manner generally less bizarre than press agent stunts. Whereas press agents usually work as individuals, publicity men most often operate within the framework of public relations departments and counseling firms. Publicity is used as one of the tools in public relations programming and activity, but it's not unusual to find that entire programs are built on publicity. For the latter reason—that is, because some public relations programs are composed chiefly of publicity—the public frequently confuses the part with the whole and thinks of publicity as being public relations. However, important as publicity may be in the framework of some public relations programs, it should be considered an effective public relations tool, but only a tool.

Public affairs is that area of organizational activity which is concerned with government. However, there has been no universally-accepted agreement about the public affairs function, and thus the term has been taken to include political education for employees, community relations, external relations, corporate communications, and public relations. Most of the armed service units and many government agencies prefer to label their public information/public relations activities as public affairs, thereby accentuating the confusion concerning public relations and public affairs.

Richard Armstrong of the Public Affairs Council notes that public affairs and public relations share and claim many similar activities and responsibilities, but he stresses that the essential difference between the two is that the public affairs specialist "is an expert in government" while government is *one* of the many publics with which public relations has to deal.

"The trend in larger corporations today is to centralize all of the external relations of the company under one very high-level person, though not with any uniformity of title at present," Armstrong reports. "Some of those heading such combined departments are identified as vice-presidents for public affairs, some as vice-presidents for corporate relations, others as vice-presidents for external affairs or public relations. And that, quite simply, means that public affairs people and public relations people are going to be working more closely together in the future, whether they want to or not."[6]

When a new Public Affairs Section was formed within the Public Relations Society of America, the new Section defined public affairs as "that public relations function in which an institution copes with the changing social and political environment combining public-policy issues and government relations." Joseph Awad, the 1982 president of the PRSA, took the position that public affairs is one of the sub-specialties of public relations, just as community, invester, and media relations, employee communication, corporate communications, and such are sub-specialties. "Viewed in this light," stated Awad, "public affairs is that function or specialty of public relations which deals with public policy and government relations at the international, Federal, state, and local levels."[7]

ENDNOTES

1. Definition from *Public Relations News,* edited and published by Denny Griswold, as amplified in John Marston's *Modern Public Relations* (New York: McGraw-Hill, 1979), p. 6.
2. Rex F. Harlow, "Public Relations Definitions through the Years," *Public Relations Review,* Spring 1977.
3. Marston, p. 186.
4. Philip Kotler and William Mindak, "Marketing and Public Relations," *Journal of Marketing,* October 1978.
5. For examples of King Kong coverage see *Newsweek,* April 25, 1983, p. 75, and *Time,* April 25, 1983, p. 107.
6. Richard Armstrong, "Public Affairs vs Public Relations," *Public Relations Quarterly,* Fall 1981, p. 26.
7. Joseph Awad, "The President's Report," *PRSA Newsletter,* March 1982, p. 2.

PROJECTS, ASSIGNMENTS, AND MINIS

1. LOCAL PERCEPTIONS OF PUBLIC RELATIONS: A MINI-SURVEY

Your instructor will divide the class into teams of two, and each team will conduct a mini-survey of adults in your community to determine their knowledge of and attitudes and opinions about public relations. Each team member will interview ten adults in your community, and the report of the team will detail the results of the total of twenty interviews.

The basic purpose of the survey is to ascertain respondents' conception of public relations and to measure it against the conception described in the early pages of this text. The first section of your report should summarize your findings in reportorial style, utilizing quotes wherever you believe they will help to highlight the comments of the respondents. The second part of the report should provide your analysis of the results and your conclusions about them. By all means have a point of view.

It is suggested that each team member utilize the same basic findings, achieving this end by exchanging photocopies of the ten interviews, but each write a separate report and analysis.

Raw interview data stemming from each interview should be included as an appendix to each report.

Following are some suggested points you may want to detail in writing your report:

1. What seems to be the general view of public relations as shown by the responses?

2. What basic themes or threads seem to run through most of the responses?

3. What conclusions can you draw from this mini-survey?

4. Do you agree or disagree with the views expressed by the majority of the respondents? Why?

(Note: Instead of having you survey twenty adults in your community, your instructor may want you to survey students at your institution who are majoring in disciplines other than public relations and journalism.)

2. THE UNSINKABLE BOAT THAT SANK: A MINI-CASE

Getting the London *Times* to run on its front page a picture and caption dealing with your product is about as difficult as breaking into the Bank of England. That it can be done, even if inadvertently, was demonstrated by the case of the unsinkable boat that sank.

The publicist/press agent who was given the task of gaining publicity for a rowboat whose manufacturer claimed would not sink came up with what he considered a great stunt idea. He decided he would hire some pretty and curvaceous models, stack them so tightly into the boat they would have to stand, and let the boat move down the Thames while the press took pictures of the great event.

Came the big day. To the delight of the publicist, the press showed up in force, including the prestigious *Times* of London. Into the boat went the models, out into the Thames went the unsinkable vessel, and while cameras clicked noisily the overloaded boat slowly but definitely sank out of sight.

The publicist had his picture all right, and it appeared in a place where pictures seldom appear: right on the front page of the London *Times!* Taken just as the boat went under the water, the picture showed the group of very unhappy models trying desperately to maintain their balance while the waters of the Thames rose above their knees. The accompanying caption explained the tale of the unsinkable boat that sank and even included the name of the manufacturer. The press agent, like all good press agents, remained anonymous.

Questions for Discussion

1. Is there anything the publicist could have done when his carefully staged event went under?
2. If you were the publicist, what would you say to the client if his reaction to the front page picture and caption was negative?
3. What is your reaction to the front page picture and caption?
4. What lessons do you learn from the entire affair?

3. PROJECTS AND ASSIGNMENTS

a) Compile from newspapers or newsmagazines of the past month five examples of the use of the term *public relations* in stories, articles, columns, or editorials. Write a report describing how the term was used in each instance and present your conclusions regarding said usage.

b) Compile from newspapers or newsmagazines of the past month two examples of the use of corporate image or institutional advertising. Write a report describing and comparing the two examples, and include your evaluation of the advertisements' relative effectiveness.

2

THE FUNCTION AMPLIFIED: RELATIONSHIP TO MANAGEMENT AND POLICIES

Four of the elements of the public relations function described in Chapter 1 deserve analysis and discussion because they raise questions which call for responsible and thoughtful answers. The four are: the management function concept; the relationship of public relations to an organization's policies, procedures, and actions; the social responsibility concept; and the relationship between private and public interests. The first two will be discussed in this chapter, and the last two in the next chapter.

THE MANAGEMENT FUNCTION CONCEPT

The statement "public relations is a management function" rolls rather smoothly off one's tongue, but just what does it mean? Does it mean that top management of profit- or nonprofit-making organizations is responsible for carrying out the public relations function? Or does it mean that the head of the public relations department should be on a top-management level? If the former, then why have public relations personnel? If the latter, on what grounds do public relations practitioners stake their claim for being on a top-management level?

This last question demands a sound answer because in any large organization—and public relations departments and personnel are found mainly in rather large organizations—other functional areas also stake out their claim to be on a top-management level. Marketing, legal, financial, and other staff functional people raise the question: why do public relations people feel they must operate on a top-management level to carry out their responsibilities and duties? If the public relations practitioner can't supply the answer, chances are he won't find himself operating on a top-management level. He doesn't get there simply because he claims he must be there, but because he's able to come up with cogent reasons for being in a top-management position.

The literature of the field—including this book—places great stress on the advisability of having public relations report as directly as possible to top management. Why? **Because virtually all actions and activities of an organization have public relations ramifications.** Thus, **the public relations executive can perform most effectively when he's in a position to provide input when top management decisions are being made.** Obviously, this can best be done when the line between the head of public relations and the operating head of the organization—be it a hospital, college, or corporation—is a direct one. The need for this linkage is expressed in the following comments:

> The best public relations person is impotent and wasted unless used and supported by the company. The way to do this is to bring public relations to the heights of management where public relations advice can be regularly and easily inserted into the development and evolution of the company's policies and practices. **The public relations executive can't explain, interpret or defend company policy unless he has seen it at its conception and birth, and participated in both.**[1] (William E. Wall, president, Kansas Power and Light Company)

> Today, public relations is widely recognized as a management function, entrusted not only with speaking **for** management, but **with** management. Top officials in the corporate and non-profit sectors alike are calling on practitioners to participate fully and actively in management.[2] (Engelina Jaspers and A. George Gitter)

> We can no longer afford to view the public relations staff as merely the messengers, the disseminators to the world of management's decisions. Instead, CEOs now need to place the company's public relations personnel as full participating members of management councils. There must be a voice in the management forums which is attuned to the pulse rate and heartbeat of all those groups that affect us. **We'll subject the corporation to far less criticism if our actions are molded with a view—in advance—about how those actions will be perceived.** It is the public relations executive, whose mandate it is to be sensitive to external perceptions, who will enable you to do that.[3] (David Simon, public relations executive)

Agreed, the foregoing are reasonable arguments for having public relations report directly to top management. However, we find many instances where the line is far from direct. Here are some reasons:

1. As organizations grow in size, so do organizational policies. Within large organizations there is as much jockeying for position as there is in the first 100 yards of the Kentucky Derby.

2. As a relative newcomer to the staff field, public relations has to compete with such veteran staff activities as legal, financial, and personnel. The veterans have been there first, hence they occupy choice positions and aren't too likely to open ranks for the newcomer.

3. In order to maintain their sanity, top operating executives restrict their personal contact to as few subordinates as possible. There's little room at the top of the organizational triangle.

4. Some chief executives don't seek or want public relations advice and counsel because they don't consider it important or they consider themselves to be public relations experts.

5. It takes time and *proven* expertise to gain the confidence of top management. Sometimes the opportunity to provide such proof is not given, sometimes it's given but muffed, and sometimes the practitioner is satisfied with his lower management role.

THE LINE-STAFF RELATIONSHIP

A generally reliable way to ascertain the role of a particular public relations department is by noting to whom the head of the department reports. If the department head reports to top management—whether the president, executive director, or similar functionary; to the chairman of the board or board of directors; or to an executive vice-president—the public relations department is a highly regarded staff function. If the public relations department head reports to someone lower down on the organization scale, the public relations department may have difficulty carrying out effectively all of its key staff functions.

Of paramount importance in considering the public relations role within organizations are the parameters of its authority and responsibility. No matter where public relations fits into an organization it is generally a *staff* rather than a *line* function. But just what does this mean?

Briefly, management theorists state that line people are those who are concerned with the basic objectives of a company. Staff people have been described as those experts in techniques who aid the line management to do a better job of reaching an organization's objectives. One authority sees the line-staff dichotomy in terms of "activities." He states that the structure of every organization contains "central" (substitute "line") and "supporting" (substitute "staff") activities.

Central activities in a manufacturing firm are described as those concerned with engineering, producing, and selling a product, while supporting activities include personnel, accounting, quality control, and public relations. Staff positions in a manufacturing firm are not involved directly with either the production or sale of the organization's products or services. Such positions do not possess command authority, but are usually classified as advisory, service, or administrative in nature.

Central or line activities in a college are carried out by professors who teach the students. As staff people the public relations specialists assist the line people by counseling the academic dean and the president in dealing with matters having public relations ramifications and by providing the media with information about college personnel and activities.

Thus, as staff people public relations practitioners have no direct authority over line people but they are expected to assist the line people in carrying out the basic work and purposes of the organization. This assistance applies particularly to those areas of line authority that have a bearing on the organization's relationship with various publics, and obviously this can cover a considerable amount of ground. It also gives rise to some interesting questions and problems.

Take, for example, this simple statement: public relations is a staff function and as such assists the line people in carrying out the work and purposes of an organization. Who takes the initiative in involving public relations with line activities that have bearing on an organization's relationship with its publics? Does public relations wait for line people to come to it? What if a problem develops but is not brought to the attention of public relations until it is too late to do anything except clean up the mess as well as possible? And what if public relations sees the problem developing but is rebuffed when it offers aid and assistance? If the public relations department has no authority over line departments—and it usually does *not* have this authority—then how can public relations have its advice, counsel, and skills effectively utilized if the line departments don't want to use them?

How far the public relations staff can and should go in pressing or opting for a certain public relations stance or viewpoint becomes a matter of mature judgment. Who should and will prevail when the public relations staffer and the line department staffer disagree depends on so many variables it's impossible to set down ground rules. Public relations staffers, to be successful, have to be sensitive to the nuances of power within their organizations and to the fact that they can't order line people to do anything they don't want to do.

POLICIES, PROCEDURES, AND ACTIONS

The model public relations program postulates that after evaluating public attitudes and opinions, the public relations practitioner then checks these against organizational policies, procedures, and actions. If public attitudes and opinions are negative or hostile regarding organizational policies, procedures, and actions, four alternatives present themselves:

Alternative 1:
Public relations can **utilize its skills and resources in an attempt to change or modify public attitudes and opinions.**

Alternative 2:
Public relations can **inform line authorities** and top management about the negative or hostile public attitudes and opinions and subsequently **utilize its skills and resources in an attempt to change** or **modify public attitudes and opinions.**

Alternative 3:
Public relations can **inform line authorities** and top management about the negative or hostile public attitudes and opinions; **suggest changes or modifications** of policies, procedures, and actions so as to conform to public expectations; and subsequently **utilize its skills and resources in communicating** such changes or modifications to the public.

Alternative 4:
Public relations can **inform line authorities** and top management about the negative or hostile public attitudes and opinions; **play an active role in seeking to change or modify** policies, procedures, and actions so as to conform to public expectations; and subsequently **utilize its skills and resources in communicating** such changes or modifications to the public.

Alternative 1 is based on the concept of public relations as a communication activity whose main purpose is to communicate with an organization's publics. It assumes that words and deeds are not necessarily compatible, and that negative attitudes and opinions can be changed through the skillful use of public relations techniques without need for a corresponding change in policies, procedures, and actions. Indeed, there are on record countless case studies of public relations campaigns based on communications programs that were divorced from actual organizational practices or had but minimal relationship to actual practices. The record in regard to such campaigns actually *changing* attitudes and opinions from negative to positive is a spotty one, however. Questions related to Alternative 1 come readily to mind:

- Are words more important than deeds? Are they of equal importance?

- Does the public "buy" words separately from deeds?

- Are we demanding too much of public relations when we ask that it do more than communicate?

- Can you cite illustrations of instances where words or communication programs were not compatible with actual organizational practices?

Alternative 2 is based on the assumption that public relations serves as an intelligence-gathering and communicating agency in regard to public attitudes and opinions. It postulates that the basic role of public relations is to gather intelligence and to communicate, but not to be involved with basic policies, procedures, and actions. The alternative does not intend to downgrade the importance of public relations, because it recognizes that evaluation of public attitudes and opinions and subsequent communication with the public are important duties that can best be carried out by public relations. The alternative asserts that public relations has justified its value and existence simply by carrying out the tasks of intelligence-gathering and communicating. Questions related to Alternative 2 come readily to mind:

- How valid is the above contention?
- Are there advantages to the practitioner in being satisfied with the intelligence-gathering and communicating role and in not becoming involved with policies, procedures, and actions?
- What about the disadvantages?

Alternatives 3 and 4 seem initially to be similar, but there is a significant difference between the two. Both assert that public relations has the responsibility to inform line authorities and management about negative or hostile public attitudes and opinions, and to communicate subsequent changes or modifications in policies, procedures, and actions. Alternative 3 proposes that public relations has the responsibility to *suggest* changes or modifications of policies, procedures, and actions. Alternative 4 proposes that public relations should play *an active role* in seeking such changes and/or modifications.

Both alternatives thus see public relations as taking a more active role than the first two alternatives. The philosophical underpinning of Alternatives 3 and 4 is that words and deeds are inseparable. To say one thing and to be doing another, state the alternatives, is to invite public doubts about the credibility of the organization involved. Thus, in order to be credible—and hence effective—public relations must of necessity be involved in some fashion with an organization's policies, procedures, and actions. How involved forms the difference in approach between Alternatives 3 and 4.

Making a choice between the two alternatives seems to boil down to a matter of authorization, areas of responsibility and competency. Questions that need to be answered:

- Does public relations have the authority to seek or to merely suggest changes or modification in policies, procedures, and actions?
- What's the relationship between public relations and the person or department responsible for the specific policies?
- Is the area one in which public relations people have competency?
- What about jurisdiction and the natural tendency of everyone to guard one's own turf?

There are no "right" or "wrong" answers to the questions posed by the four alternatives. The questions are raised to emphasize that public relations people are often called upon to be problem solvers. Among the many problems facing public relations people are those relating to the core function of public relations **within** an organization. Deciding on sensible and realistic answers to the questions is therefore an important step which should not be taken lightly.

The Function Expressed in Print

Although public relations as a function of the management of organizations has been practiced for several decades now, by 1984 one could count on one's fingers the number of valuable books dealing with public relations and its practices. Of textbooks, as will be

EXHIBIT 2.1

Ten for Your Reading Pleasure

Edward L. Bernays, *Biography of an Idea* (New York: Simon and Schuster, 1965). Subtitled "Memoirs of Public Relations Counsel," this hefty book of personal and professional reminiscences by America's most prolific public relations counselor sums up a professional life that spanned more than six decades. Bernays seems to have almost perfect recall as he discusses clients and the programs he developed for them.

Daniel Boorstin, *The Image: A Guide to Pseudo-Events in America* (New York: Atheneum, 1962). A historian examines certain public relations practices and finds them to be all too deceptive and antisocial. Recommended for those who recognize the importance of seeing ourselves as perceptive critics see us.

John F. Budd, Jr., *An Executive's Primer on Public Relations* (Philadelphia: Chilton Books, 1969). John Budd, who has been a public relations counselor and is currently a public relations executive of the Emhart Corporation, has written a primer which explains public relations in practical terms for the busy non-PR executive. What's of value to such an executive is certainly of value to those who hope to become counselors to him.

L. L. L. Golden, *Only by Public Consent* (New York: Hawthorn Books, 1968). Golden has written a "must" book for anyone who wants to know how four of the largest corporations in America established and handled the public relations function. Here are behind-the-scenes details about the communications activities of the American Telephone and Telegraph Company, Standard Oil of New Jersey, General Motors, and du Pont.

Ray E. Hiebert, *Courtier to the Crowd* (Ames, Iowa: Iowa State University Press, 1961). Hiebert's courtier is Ivy Lee, and his biographical account is about the man who has been termed the father of public relations practice. A meticulous researcher, Hiebert traces Lee's life from his early days at Princeton to his years as public relations counselor to some of America's best-known businesses and their executives.

Walter Lippmann, *Public Opinion* (New York: The Macmillan Co., 1965). This reissue of a classic, originally published in 1922, has merit and value today for those seeking insights about the nature of public opinion and its role in a democratic society. Lippmann's references are, of course, very much outdated but his ideas meet the test of time. You should have such good ones.

William A. Marsteller, *Creative Management* (Chicago: Crain Books, 1981). Here's a very personal book by the founder of Burson-Marsteller. Bill Marsteller recalls fascinating stories about communicators and the clients they serve, told by a stylist who could write about cow turd (see p. 5 of his book) and make it interesting.

Kenneth G. Patrick, *Perpetual Jeopardy* (New York: The Macmillan Co., 1972). Details about the "insider trading" story of Texas Gulf Sulphur as told by a former public relations executive. Patrick's account is of special value to those seeking to know more about the ethical, legal, economic, and professional aspects of the Texas Gulf Sulphur case.

Irwin Ross, *The Image Merchants* (New York: Doubleday, 1958). This book had its origins as a series of full-page newspaper features about public relations counseling firms and leaders. Though now dated, the book provides a lively account of some leading public relations personalities and agencies.

Carlton E. Spitzer, *Raising the Bottom Line* (New York: Longman, 1982). Drawing on his years of public relations experience in counseling, business, and government, Spitzer explores the practical and societal aspects of corporate social involvement. Having served on both sides of the social responsibility fence, he writes with perception of the roles played by business and government.

mentioned in a forthcoming chapter, there has been a sufficiency in the past decade. Of trade books, however, there has been a paucity.

Such books about public relations and its practitioners are valuable, however, because they tend to deal with matters which are beyond the purview of the usual textbook. They are also usually much more interesting to read. Whether read for sheer pleasure or because assigned by a professor, these books broaden one's knowledge and view of the public relations field. Exhibit 2.1 lists ten such books with a brief description of their contents. You can browse at will or upon assignment.

ENDNOTES

1. Cited in Craig E. Aronoff and Otis W. Baskin, *Public Relations, The Profession and the Practice* (St. Paul: West Publishing Co., 1983), p. 41.
2. Engelina Jaspers and A. George Gitter, "Are Public Relations Graduate Students Learning What They Should?", *Public Relations Quarterly*, Summer 1982, p. 13.
3. David A. Simon, "External Pressures on the CEO: Worse Than an Excedrin Headache," *Public Relations Quarterly*, Winter 1981-82, p. 11.

PROJECTS, ASSIGNMENTS, AND MINIS

1. JUSTIFYING THE FUNCTION'S PLACE: A MINI-SITUATION

When Karen Brooke Wilcoming was named president of the Mid-American Life Insurance Company she decided to streamline the headquarters operations of the organization. Under her predecessor a total of fourteen executives reported directly to the president, and Wilcoming concluded that such an arrangement was too cumbersome. Having decided to trim the fourteen to six, Wilcoming took steps to group related departments and functions under a single head instead of under multiple heads, thereby reducing the Executive Committee to six members.

Among the related departments to be affected by the change were those of advertising, marketing, and public relations. Each department was headed by a director, and by a very unusual coincidence the directors of advertising, marketing, and public relations were the same age (42); had the same educational background (either MBA or MS degrees in their specialties); and had been with the company the same number of years (12).

Having interviewed each of the three directors, Wilcoming concluded that their individual positive and negative qualities balanced out. Because the three seemed to have equal qualifications, the president decided on a final test before making her decision. She requested that each director submit a memorandum responding to the following challenge: "As cogently as you can, present reasons to support the argument that your function, rather than the other two under consideration, should be represented on the president's Executive Committee."

Assignment

You are the director of public relations of the Mid-American Life Insurance Company. Write the memorandum requested by the president. In so doing, feel free to make use of any source material you consider valuable in supporting your case.

Alternate Assignment

You are the director of public relations of the Mid-American Life Insurance Company. The president has not asked you to submit a memorandum. Instead, she requests that you present orally the reasons to support the argument that your function, rather than the other two under consideration, should be represented on the president's Executive Committee. In so doing, feel free to make use of any source material you consider valuable in supporting your case.

2. A MATTER OF FEDERAL GUIDELINES: A MINI-CASE FOR DISCUSSION

Joshua Mouldoon is a plant-community relations specialist working for a large national corporation which has its public relations headquarters in Boston. Mouldoon reports indirectly to Walter Cragnolin, manager of plant-community relations for the corporation, but he actually works at the Peachtree Plant of the company in a rural Georgia community. His direct supervisor there is Rip Sturgiss, director of personnel at the plant.

At the yearly meeting in corporation headquarters of all plant-community relations specialists, Mouldoon is brought up to date on recent developments in the company affecting his work. Among other things, Mouldoon and the other specialists are told by

Cragnolin that the company is particularly sensitive about meeting new federal non-discrimination guidelines in hiring and promotions. Cragnolin warns the group that since the company has many federal contracts it is imperative that the federal guidelines be met. He says that the plant-community relations specialists are being involved in the compliance matter because the company recognizes that compliance will be a sensitive matter in some plant locations. Finally, he asks that the specialists send him a report in two weeks advising him what they've done since returning to their plants.

On his way back to Georgia, Mouldoon reflects on the fact that although the Peachtree Plant has 400 blacks out of a work force of 1,200, only two are in a supervisory position and 60 percent of them are in the lowest pay category. He also knows that about 40 of the black employees are college graduates.

The day after Mouldoon gets back, Sturgiss calls him into his office and asks him what he's learned at Boston that might be of some help. Mouldoon thereupon advises Sturgiss about Cragnolin's talk about federal guidelines and suggests that something ought to be done at Peachtree to meet them.

"Listen, Josh," says Sturgiss, "we're in the middle of Georgia, not in Boston, Massachusetts. Why don't you start working on that United Way report and just let me take care of the hiring and promotions, right?"

Questions for Discussion

1. What factual data or information about the people or the situation cited above would you like to have before coming to a decision about the case?

2. Assuming you now have the factual data and information you seek, what do you suggest that Mouldoon *say* in response to Sturgiss? What do you suggest he *do*? What do you suggest he say in his report to Cragnolin?

Written Assignment

You are Joshua Mouldoon and it is ten days later. Write the report requested by Walter Cragnolin.

3. PROJECTS AND ASSIGNMENTS

a) Select and read one of the ten books listed in Exhibit 2.1 and be prepared to give an oral report to the class at a time designated by your instructor. You may be paired off with a classmate on this assignment. Discuss such elements as the following: a summary of the contents; relationship of the material to the course; the most and least valuable aspects of the book; your overall evaluation of the writing and contents.

b) Select from print media—newspapers and/or magazines—an article or articles dealing with a public relations situation or activity which involves any of the important considerations set forth in Chapter 2. Write a report explaining the connection between the situation or activity and the relevant considerations set forth in Chapter 2. Evaluate and draw conclusions about the manner in which the concerned organization or person has handled the situation or activity.

At the end of your report append the originals or photocopies of the article or articles dealing with the situation or activity you've selected.

3

THE FUNCTION AMPLIFIED: SOCIAL RESPONSIBILITY AND PUBLIC INTEREST

*A*t the core of the relationship between public relations and an organization's policies, procedures, and actions are the dual concepts of **social responsibility** and **the public interest.** There are very few instances where organizations have *openly* admitted or made it part of organizational policy to be socially irresponsible or to operate in a manner not in the public interest. However, there are numerous instances of organizations adopting and following practices not socially responsible, not acceptable to the public, and not in the public interest. Such instances pose a dilemma for the public relations practitioner because they raise serious ethical and moral problems.

The student who hopes to make a career in public relations should first realize that such problems are not the unique province of the public relations practitioner. Accountants, lawyers, comptrollers, engineers, salesmen, advertising and marketing executives, and production managers are also faced with such problems and dilemmas.

Second, such problems are not the kind to be dealt with frequently (if they were, we'd have to conclude the entire fabric of our society is rotten).

Third, and probably most important in connection with public relations practice, when problems involving social irresponsibility and nonpublic interest do arise, they are especially relevant to public relations practice for two reasons. As already noted, public relations practitioners stress the importance of the activity as a management function, and the ultimate responsibility for actions, policies, and procedures rests on management and on the public relations practitioner who aspires to counsel management. Thus, those who shoulder ultimate responsibility must also shoulder the task of resolving the

110,252

problems being discussed. The second reason is that practitioners are responsible for relationships that are public, not private, and hence are responsible for the manner in which actions, policies, and procedures will be communicated (or not communicated) to various publics.

At various times in their careers public relations practitioners must face up to the resolution of organizational actions that may be socially irresponsible and not in the public interest. In such instances, do practitioners serve as the "conscience" of their organizations and fight the internal battle needed to have these actions modified or reserved? Do they merely point out possible or probable long- and short-range consequences of following such actions? Do they consider themselves strictly as organizational "advocates" whose first, foremost, and perhaps only responsibility is to the organizations they serve? Do they form their judgments about their roles in terms of the magnitude and scope of the particular issue or problem being faced? Is there an imaginary line which the practitioner will not cross when dealing with issues and actions concerning social responsibility, performance, and the public interest? If the answer is affirmative, where does one draw this line and is one willing and able to handle the consequences of not crossing it?

More than a half century ago two men, Edward L. Bernays and Harwood Childs, faced these questions in the early twenties and late thirties, and their ideas concerning them are worth consideration today. Decades later, it's acknowledged that Bernays and Childs were light-years ahead of their time.

PUBLIC RELATIONS AS SEEN BY BERNAYS

Author of a score of books about public relations, Edward L. Bernays had an active career of more than forty years, and as recently as 1983 was contributing a regular column to the *Public Relations Quarterly.* Starting his professional life after World War I as an admitted press agent, Bernays was the first to refer to himself subsequently as a "public relations counsel." He was also one of the first to recognize that the core of the practice is in establishing "a common meeting ground for an entity (whether a business, an individual, a government body, or a social service organization) and society."

Because public opinion is of paramount importance in a democratic society, Bernays said, the public relations practitioner must be alert to changing societal conditions and be prepared to advise modifications in policy in accordance with changes in the public point of view.

"Perhaps the chief contribution of the public relations counsel to the public and to his client is his ability to understand and analyze obscure tendencies of the public mind . . . ," said Bernays. "It is his capacity for crystallizing the obscure tendencies of the public mind before they have reached definite expression, which makes him so valuable."[1]

The above statements cover but briefly the Bernays view of public relations, but they are cited specifically to indicate his awareness of the close relationship between public relations and the society in which it operates. Political scientist Harwood Childs of Princeton University amplified this relationship when he delivered a series of lectures in the late 1930s and then expanded his remarks in a book called *An Introduction to Public Opinion.* His views, particularly when analyzed in the light of today's heightened interest in social responsibility, are worthy of careful consideration.

PUBLIC RELATIONS AS SEEN BY CHILDS

Disdaining what he called "the antics, stunts, tricks, and devices by which individuals and corporations often seem to obtain goodwill without actually trying to remove the real cause of ill will," Childs stated that he was not interested in the many ways to win friends and influence people. He foresaw that interest in public relations would continue and increase because, as he put it, public relations reflects one of the fundamental problems of the times. His view of the intrinsic nature of public relations is set forth here:

Public relations may be defined as those aspects of our personal and corporate behavior which have a social rather than a purely private and personal significance.[2]

Childs understood that public relations would gain in importance chiefly because an increasing number of private and corporate activities would have social and public significance.

"Public relations as such," he declared, "is not the presentation of a point of view, not the art of tempering mental attitudes, nor the development of cordial and profitable relations. . . . It is simply a name for activities which have a social significance.

"Our problem in each corporation or industry is to find out what these activities are, what social effects they have, and if they are contrary to the public interest, to find ways and means for modifying them so that they will serve the public interest."

In setting forth this analysis of public relations, Childs stressed that the public relations executive is not primarily a publicist or propagandist. To meet Childs' standards the public relations executive has to be "a student of the social effects of personal and corporate conduct" and has to have a thorough understanding of society from a political, economic, cultural, and sociological point of view. Summed up, therefore:

The starting point in working out a public relations policy is a careful analysis of our personal and corporate behaviour in the light of social change generally. Without knowing the basic economic, cultural, political, and social trends of our times, we cannot ascertain, much less anticipate, the public implications of what we are doing. It is the lag between social trends that gives rise to our problems, and the search for answers must be a search for the reasons why these lags exist, where they exist, and what can be done to synchronize social movement.

The business of producing and distributing goods and services must be studied in relation to the total situation, the total environment in which we are functioning. Executives of corporations cannot afford to devote all or even the major portion of their energies solely to technological considerations. They must raise their eyes to the level of wider horizons. The public relations counsel must be something more than a publicist, a journalist or a statistician. He must be a social scientist capable of advising management regarding the environment in which it is operating.[3]

OBSERVATIONS CONCERNING THE CHILDS THESIS

A caveat is in order before proceeding with a discussion of the thesis of public relations expounded by Harwood Childs. Most readers of this textbook will be students who hope to make a career of public relations or who hope to use it in other careers where public relations has an important bearing. Young people entering the field will not generally be given an executive position in public relations and expected to serve as elder statesmen. On the contrary, they will most likely be engaged in tasks which Childs claims are not public relations: helping with "the presentation of a point of view" and in "the development of cordial and profitable relations." In time, however, as the neophyte becomes expert in his field he will be given broader and more significant responsibilities and duties. The time to think about and to understand these broader areas is now, for tomorrow may be too late. Consider, therefore, that you were among the business leaders and professionals to whom Childs addressed himself back in the late thirties. Certain observations and questions should then come more readily to mind.

First, a question about Childs' basic premise. Do you agree or disagree with his contention that public relations is "not the presentation of a point of view, not the art of tempering mental attitudes, nor the development of cordial and profitable relations"? What arguments can be raised *against* this viewpoint? Is it possible that in his desire to underscore the importance of the societal approach to public relations Childs may have overstated his case? What do other authorities say about the issue?

Second, what does Childs mean when he says that public relations is "simply a name for activities which have a social significance"? What about activities having a political, economic, and cultural significance? Do you think Childs meant to incorporate these three—political, economic, and cultural—when he stressed only socially significant activities? How about "societal" as an adjective to describe the activities to which Childs referred?

The word "significance" also brings to mind certain key questions. When is an activity socially *significant*, when is it of moderate importance, and when is it insignificant? Childs does not answer these questions; in fact he leaves the matter up to the individual practitioner. Note, for example, that he states that "our problem" is to ascertain what activities have a social significance, to figure out what social effects they have, and to find ways and means for modifying them if they are contrary to the public interest.

Assuming that Childs' basic premise is correct, we find that he has formulated a conception of public relations which poses innumerable challenges to the competence, wisdom, and judgment of the public relations practitioner. Bernays saw these challenges clearly in 1962 when he told a New York *Times* interviewer that the task of the public relations man should be to study public opinion and social psychology and to "counsel his company on how to adjust to . . . societal forces and to enlist public support for services, products and ideas." One can scarcely counsel if one has little understanding of societal forces. Put another way: "Public relations advice, to be worth anything, must be grounded on a comprehensive knowledge of the past, of trends and relationships in the field of social change," said Childs, and his challenge to the public relations practitioner thus becomes one of being able to cope with the past, the present, and the future of our society.

Coping with the challenge posed by Childs may seem like an academic exercise to some, but relating to problems is a key element in public relations programming. One must first recognize public relations problems before one can hope to solve them. Such recognition comes from understanding past and noting present socially significant activities posing public relations problems and foreseeing future socially significant activities that will bring about public relations problems at some time beyond the present.

Recognition, however, is but one step in the public relations process. What to *do* about these problems is another matter. What to do is often a choice from among three alternatives: what is permissible, what is possible, and what is prohibited. Internal, rather than external, factors generally govern the choice to be made because higher authority in the management of organizations and institutions has the final word over public relations' freedom of action and activity. This is particularly true in the area known as social responsibility.

SCHOOLS OF THOUGHT CONCERNING SOCIAL RESPONSIBILITY

The concept of social responsibility is one that few people dare to challenge. It's akin to God, mother, and apple pie. It takes an agnostic to challenge the idea of God, a Philip Wylie to challenge the institution of motherhood, and a peach pie enthusiast to challenge the virtues of apple pie. Who among us are willing to stand up and say we are socially irresponsible, and what organizations and institutions are willing to contend they are not socially responsible? Everyone, it seems, is socially responsible, but in *varying degrees.* The two major views concerning social responsibility have probably been best expressed by Dr. Milton Friedman and by the Committee for Economic Development.

THE FRIEDMAN VIEW

At one extreme in the debate over social responsibility—particularly as the concept applies to business—is Dr. Milton Friedman, noted professor of economics at the University of Chicago. A staunch defender of the free-enterprise, private-property system, Friedman says that those who contend that business should be concerned not "merely" with profit but also with promoting desirable social ends are "preaching pure and unadulterated socialism."

Friedman's view reminds us that corporate executives are employees of the owners of their business and have a direct responsibility to their employers.

"That responsibility," says Friedman, "is to conduct the business in accordance with their desires, which generally will be to make as much money as possible while conforming to the basic rules of society, both those embodied in law and those embodied in ethical custom."

Friedman observes that the corporate executive is also a person in his own right and as such he may want to devote part of his income to causes he regards as worthy. However, says Friedman, when we talk of the social responsibility of the corporate executive as a businessman we ask him to act in some way not in the interest of his employers. As one example, Friedman says that when we ask the businessman to refrain from increasing the price of his product in order to gain the social objective of preventing inflation, such a decision may not be in the best interests of the corporation. Similarly, he adds, it may be at the expense of corporate profits to ask the businessman to hire "hardcore" unemployed rather than better-qualified workers in order to gain the social objective of reducing poverty.

Professor Friedman sums up his argument in the following words:

> There is one and only one social responsibility of business—to use its resources and engage in activities designed to increase its profits so long as it stays within the rules of the game, which is to say, engages in open and free competition without deception or fraud.[4]

THE COMMITTEE FOR ECONOMIC DEVELOPMENT VIEW

Another view of social responsibility was set forth in the seventies in a 74-page statement by the Research and Policy Committee of the Committee for Economic Development (CED), titled "Social Responsibilities of Business Corporation." Addressing itself primarily to the large, publicly owned, professionally managed corporations—though noting its remarks apply as well to smaller enterprises and to businessmen as individuals—the CED cited some negative attitudes toward business expressed by the public in nationwide public opinion polls. It concluded from these statistics that a clear majority of the public believes that corporations have not been sufficiently concerned about societal problems and that "two-thirds believe business now has a moral obligation to help other major institutions to achieve social progress, even at the expense of profitability. . . . Business is being asked to assume broader responsibilities to society than ever before and to serve a wider range of human values. Business enterprises, in effect, are being asked to contribute more to the quality of American life than just supplying quantities of goods and services."

Four basic questions raised by business in response to the above-mentioned demands, said the CED, are as follows:

1. Why should corporations become substantially involved in the improvement of the social environment?

2. How can they justify this to their stockholders?

3. How can companies reconcile substantial expenditures for social purposes with profitability?

4. What are the limitations on corporate social responsibility?[5]

Agreeing that these are legitimate concerns, the CED said the answer to them is found

EXHIBIT 3.1

General Motors Explains Its Social Responsibilities

Roger B. Smith, chairman of General Motors, explained the corporation's commitment to social responsibility in the preface to the firm's 37-page 11th annual *Public Interest Report* in 1981. Smith first noted that GM will spend $40 billion between 1980 and 1984 to reshape its vehicles, build new plants, and introduce new manufacturing processes. He then stated:[7]

> While committed to the success of this unprecedented capital spending program, General Motors also recognizes its obligations as a responsible corporate citizen outside the boundaries of the marketplace, and that building a better world requires social progress as well as technological advancement. To this end, the Corporation continues its programs of support to minority groups and businesses and its philanthropic activities in educational, social, cultural, and medical areas which benefit the public at large.
>
> All this must be done, while at the same time earning a profit. Only the successful business can exercise a full community role, but to do good it must first do well. Not one of GM's goals can be accomplished unless it prospers. Profits fuel both the growth of the nation and the future of our business.
>
> *Roger B. Smith*
> *Chairman*

* * *

As noted above, one of GM's social responsibility support areas concerned minorities. Here are excerpts from GM's 1983 *Public Interest Report* updating a number of ongoing programs for minorities and women in 1982:[8]

Motor Enterprises, Inc.

Since 1970, Motor Enterprises, Inc. (MEI), GM's Minority Enterprise Small Business Investment Company (MESBIC), has made loans totaling almost $5 million to 146 minority firms. During 1982, MEI approved nine new loans and investment applications, including one to a women-owned and operated firm. An experienced GM employee is assigned as business advisor to each minority entrepreneur.

Auto Dealerships

GM's determination to increase the number of minority and women-owned dealerships is underscored by recent improvements in the GM Dealer Development Academy Program. The Academy, which trains minorities and women in all aspects of the operation and management of a dealership, is being upgraded . . . to make the Academy responsive to the practical needs of its students. . . . To date, the Academy has graduated 100 candidates. Of these, 48 have been appointed dealer-operators, 30 have been qualified and are awaiting appointments, and 22 are not currently qualified as dealer-operators due to either insufficient

in recognizing that business is a basic institution in American society and has a vital stake in the general welfare as well as in its own public acceptance.

Amplifying Harwood Childs' doctrines, the CED then set forth social responsibilities in terms of self-interest:

> There is broad recognition today that corporate self-interest is inexorably involved in the well-being of the society of which business is an integral part, and from which it draws the basic requirements needed for it to function at all—capital, labor, customers. There is increasing understanding that the corporation is dependent on the goodwill of society, which can sustain or impair its existence through public pressures on government. And it has become clear that the essential resources and goodwill of society are not naturally forthcoming to corporations whenever needed, but must be worked for and developed. . . .

EXHIBIT 3.1 (cont.)

personal capital or hands-on work experience. . . . As of December 31, 1982, there were 159 GM minority-owned dealerships in the United States and 96 women named as dealer-operators.

Banking Program

The GM Minority Banking Program, formally established in 1969 with the utilization of 12 minority banks, continues to include deposits with every bank known to be owned by minorities or women. Represented are 95 banks in 64 communities nationwide as well as in Hawaii and Guam.

Media Support

GM regularly schedules advertising in minority-oriented publications. Corporate ads are created and scheduled by a leading minority-owned ad agency, the Uni-World Group in New York City. In the 1982 model year, $3.7 million was spent on Corporate and Divisional ads in minority-owned media.

Minority Suppliers

Despite the depressed condition of the automotive industry in 1982, GM's Minority Supplier Program exceeded $200 million in purchases from minority businesses for the third consecutive year. By providing managerial, technical, and financial assistance to potentially qualified suppliers, the General Motors Minority Supplier Program grew from a modest $1 million in purchases in 1968 to $224 million in 1980, $292 million in 1981 and $255 million in 1982.

Minority Contracting

In 1982, payments for Corporate construction contracts to minority-owned businesses totaled $33.1 million, down $21.2 million from 1981. This reflects the completion of several new assembly facilities in 1980, and the decreasing need for new plant capacity as sales volumes remain low. The $33.1 million represents 12% of all construction completed, up 1% from 1981.

Insurance Programs

GM has two basic programs designed to encourage the participation of minority businesses in the area of insurance. . . . During 1982, $350 million of GM group life insurance was reinsured with four minority-owned companies. At the end of the year, $10.7 billion of GM's property damage insurance was placed through minority brokers.

Minority Communications

At the national level, GM continued its active involvement with a number of minority- and women-oriented organizations which held conventions, convocations, and conferences during 1982. At these meetings, GM executives discussed ongoing activities and programs designed to increase opportunities for these groups.

Communities where GM has at least one plant have Public Affairs Committees which . . . provide speakers for minority organizations, assist local minority firms, and arrange donations of equipment to vocational programs at local Opportunities Industrialization Centers.

Indeed the corporate interest broadly defined by management can support involvement in helping to solve virtually any social problem, because people who have a good environment, education, and opportunity make better employees, customers, and neighbors for business than those who are poor, ignorant, and oppressed. It is obviously in the interest of business to enlarge its markets and to improve its work force by helping disadvantaged people to develop and employ their economic potential. Likewise, it is in the interest of business to help reduce the mounting costs of welfare, crime, disease, and waste of human potential—a good part of which business pays for.

Experience with governmental and social constraints indicates that the corporation's self-interest is best served by a sensitivity to social concerns and a willingness, within competitive limits, to take needed action ahead of confrontation. By acting on its own initiative, management preserves the flexibility needed to conduct the company's affairs in a constructive, efficient and adaptive manner.[6]

Recognizing the cost factor in its analysis of social responsibility, the CED noted that business obviously cannot be expected to solve all the problems of society. The report pointed out that various internal constraints limit corporations in their approach to societal problems. "No company of any size can willingly incur costs that would jeopardize its competitive position and threaten its survival. While companies may well be able to absorb modest costs or undertake some social activities on a break-even basis, any substantial expenditure must be justified in terms of the benefits, tangible and intangible, that are expected to be produced."

The analysis of the two views of social responsibility cited above is obviously a truncated one. On the one hand we have Dr. Friedman's view that the business of business is just business; that management has neither the right nor the qualifications to undertake activities to improve society or to tax its constituents for these purposes; and that society's general welfare is a matter for the government, not business. On the other hand we have the CED view that it's in the self-interest of business to accept a fair measure of responsibility for improving society because "insensitivity to changing demands of society sooner or later results in public pressures for governmental intervention and regulation to require business to do what it was reluctant or unable to do voluntarily."

SOME LAST WORDS BY JOHN W. HILL

In the last year of a long and fruitful life—one that spanned half a century in public relations—John W. Hill summed up his views about the erosion of public trust in business. Agreeing that most Americans believe in our economic system, Hill said that there are growing public expectations of business leadership in helping to solve social problems. However, he added, very few corporations have developed effective means of relating their policies to societal expectations and of explaining these policies in forthright and understandable terms.

A major share of the problem, Hill noted, is that corporate leaders have been insulated from the people. Another reason cited by Hill is the public's distrust of all established institutions, including business.

"Even before the post-Watergate disclosures of illegal political campaign gifts," he declared, "a slow-burning resentment had been building up against some companies for shoddy products, careless service, abuse of warranties, alleged foot-dragging in clearing up pollution, and other matters."

In Hill's opinion, every American corporate management faces two tests: to maintain profitability, and to meet the expectations and demands of society. Stating that business must take a closer look at its operations and ethical standards, Hill issued this challenge:

> What is desperately needed is not more money spent on "communications," but a revised philosophy and a new concept of external relations—of social issues—in the minds of corporate managements in this country. Words alone are useless if not fully supported by policies and performance.

> . . . Unless corporations are willing to examine their decisions and performance, correct any flaws they find, and adopt a policy of candor on matters of public interest, they will never regain the public's confidence. And without that confidence and credibility, business can never effectively rebut its militant critics, never successfully defend itself in the court of public opinion.[9]

THE PUBLIC INTEREST

As we have seen, coming to grips with corporate social responsibility is not a simple matter, but it is even more difficult to come to grips with the concept of the public interest. On its face, the public interest concept has the solid ring of immutable dictum and truth. Public relations practitioners continually define their activities in terms of being in the public interest, the literature of the field is replete with references to the public interest, and there exist few if any public relations experts with soul so daring that they would contend their work is *not* in the public interest.

But some disturbing questions come to mind, and they demand answers:

- What is the public interest? Obviously you can't see, hear, or feel it, so how can you tell what it is?
- Can the public interest be measured, weighed, and assessed?
- Who is to be the judge of the public interest?
- What if an organization's policies, procedures, and actions are in the interests of one public but not of another?
- What if an organization's private interests and the public interest are in obvious conflict?
- What if an organization's policies, in order to be in the public interest, can be modified or changed only at an unbearable cost to the organization?

Of course there are answers to the above questions, just as there are answers to almost any question. But the value of the questions is not in their answers, but in the perceptions, insights, and depth of thought that go into seeking the answers. It is hoped the discussion that follows will assist readers in coping with the questions.

THE CHILDS AND GALLUP VIEW

Harwood Childs defines the public interest in these words:

> It is my thesis that *the public interest, so far as the United States is concerned, is and can only be what the public, what mass opinion, says it is.* By mass opinion, I mean the collective opinions of the American people as a whole.[10]

Childs cites data from many years of the Gallup poll to support his belief that *over reasonably long periods of time public opinion is as safe a guide to follow as the opinions of smaller and select groups.* He also cites Gallup himself as follows:

> The sampling surveys of recent years have provided much evidence concerning the wisdom of the common people. . . . And I think that the person who does examine it (the evidence) will come away believing as I do that, collectively, the American people have a remarkably high degree of common sense. These people may not be brilliant or intellectual or particularly well read, but they possess a quality of good sense which is manifested time and again in their expressions of opinion on present-day issues. . . .[11]

Childs recognized defects in stressing the virtues of mass public opinion as a guide to public interest. In his own words:

> The competence of the masses is, of course, conditioned by the environment and by the opportunities they have to acquire information, to listen to different points of view, to discuss and express their opinions freely—and to use their reasoning powers.[12]

Nonetheless, he said, public relations practitioners do have on hand tangible criteria for finding out what the public interest is, and he rests his case by emphasizing that "on broad questions of social, political, and economic policy the opinions of the masses seem to show a remarkably high degree of common sense."

Let us, for the sake of argument, accept Childs' concept of the public interest as expressed in his remarks and those of George Gallup. There will still remain the difficult and expensive task of measuring mass opinion. National polling organizations, such as Gallup's, have a highly creditable record in this area of opinion measurement, but their results are fixed in time. They reveal what mass opinion was at the time opinion was measured. Further, it would be enormously costly, and often impossible, to take a measurement of the public pulse every time a public relations policy, action, or statement is to be put into effect.

LIPPMANN'S VIEW

There are also those who take direct issue with Childs and Gallup. No less an authority on public opinion than Walter Lippmann believes that in normal circumstances voters can't be expected to transcend their particular, localized, and self-regarding opinions. Lippmann adds:

> I am far from implying that the voters are not entitled to the representation of their particular opinions and interests. But their opinions and interests should be taken for what they are and for no more. They are not—as such—propositions in the public interest. . . .

> The Gallup polls are reports of what people are thinking. But that a plurality of the people sampled in the poll think one way has no bearing upon whether it is sound public policy. For their opportunities of judging great issues are in the very nature of things limited, and the statistical sum of their opinions is not the final verdict on an issue. It is, rather, the beginning of the argument. In that argument their opinions need to be confronted by the views of the executive, defending and promoting the public interest. In the accommodation reached between the two views lies practical public policy.[13]

Lippmann's references to the public interest were made in regard to political affairs, but they could just as well apply to corporate and other institutional affairs. His ideas about the public mind will be more fully discussed in a later chapter, but it is sufficient to say at this point that Lippmann felt the public is often misinformed, ill-informed, and poor judges of great issues.

If he had been alive at the time, Lippmann could have proved his point by citing the results of a New York *Times*/CBS News national survey, taken in mid-1983. As the *Times* reported in a front-page story on July 1, 1983: "Despite months of controversy over United States policies on Central America, most of the American public does not know which side the Reagan Administration supports in either El Salvador or Nicaragua, according to the latest New York *Times*/CBS News Poll. Only 25 percent of those surveyed knew that the Administration supports the Government in El Salvador, only 13 percent knew that it sides with the insurgents in Nicaragua and only 8 percent knew both alignments."

HILL'S VIEW

The veteran public relations counselor John W. Hill was so concerned about the public interest he devoted two chapters of his book *The Making of a Public Relations Man* to a discussion of the public interest concept. Where the public interest lies in given circumstances, said Hill, seems to be a matter of opinion and judgment. Hill surveyed fifty leaders in education, government, theology, and labor and came up with these two general answers:

1. A sizeable body of opinion exists that *no precise definition of the public interest is possible.* (One out of three responses.)

2. A majority of those who said a definition was possible settled for the phrase *"the greatest good for the greatest number."* However, some provided qualifications, and the essential qualification was that *the interests of the minority must be protected.*[14]

From the thoughts about the public interest expressed by his fifty opinion leaders Hill distilled some *criteria* for determining what is in the public interest. The criteria are in the form of questions, and they seem to be sound ones to ask of policies, actions, and statements:

1. How many people will be affected?
2. How many will be harmed?
3. How many people will be benefited?
4. How significant are the effects going to be?
5. What are the probable long-range effects?[15]

PUBLIC RELATIONS PROBLEMS ASSOCIATED WITH THE PUBLIC INTEREST

John Hill's fifty opinion leaders didn't cite answers to the above-listed questions, because the answers depend on the issues under consideration and the many variables associated with these issues. Managements, however, expect answers from their public relations men and women, but it's very difficult to come up with answers when an organization's private interests and the public interest conflict or when an organization is caught in the middle between the conflicting interests of different publics. Consider, for example, the following:

> A private four-year college, established 25 years ago in a metropolitan area of 225,000 residents, has been financially and academically successful despite having no endowment. Its revenues have come from tuition and a thriving evening division. Recently a group of community leaders—including local bankers, industrialists and the publisher of the city's two daily newspapers—has mounted a drive to get the state university to establish a four-year undergraduate college in the area. Such a college would, of course, be an economic boon to the area, but because of its much lower tuition it would pose tough competitive problems to the established private four-year college. Suggest the public relations stance of the private institution where its private interest collides with the public interest.

The example cited above is duplicated daily in numerous ways in American society and is indicative of the difficult public relations problems organizations and institutions face when dealing with public interest. In such instances there are no real answers, and very often the questions that astute practitioners raise about circumstances are more important than are the answers. Shooting from the hip may have been the only way to handle a show-down with a gunslinger in a dusty Western town. In today's modern society, though, it's usually wiser to avoid that show-down by asking the right questions and by applying sound, professional advice to management caught in the bind of the private-public interest conflict.

T. J. Ross, veteran public relations counselor, sized up the problem in terms of *balance* when he declared:

> In a corporation of size, decisions affecting public interest are often difficult. In striving to carry out its job with public consensus and in the public interest, the best it can achieve is what might be called *an acceptable balance of interests*. It has to deal with a number of groups, each of which seeks something for its own benefit and possibly at the expense of another group within the corporation.

> It is in these areas (balancing of interests) that one role of public relations is performed; namely, that of assisting managements in arriving at policies and practices that will be reflected favorably within the family, in the market-place, in the government, in the press and so forth. . . . The other part of our role has to do with communication. . . .[16]

Observations about the public interest made by men like Ross, Hill, and other veteran practitioners suggest the following guidelines for public relations in dealing with the public interest:

1. **Don't use the term "public interest" loosely.** People are not fools, especially when it comes to matters affecting their own interests. Just because an organization claims its actions are in the public interest does not mean that the claim will automatically be accepted by the public. An action that is all-too-obviously a private interest action will be seen as such even though it's wrapped in a pretty package and labeled *public interest*. Use the term carefully, judiciously, and with a sense of discrimination for the nuances of interests.

2. **Explain why your policy or action is in the public interest.** The public is interested in more than mere labels and would be more likely to support you if you explain *why* your organization's position, proposal, or action is in the public interest. At the same time, however, complex explanations are difficult for the public to assimilate and understand, so keep explanations simple. This, of course, is easily said, but hard to carry out if the issue itself is complex.

This leads to an obvious conclusion: if your explanation has to be so complex that it's hard for the public to understand, then you had better restudy the issue to see if it's really in the public interest. And that leads to the next point:

3. **Make sure you're being reasonable and honest.** When an action is taken, you should make sure it's a sound one that will be accepted as reasonable and fair under the circumstances. Most people recognize that the primary purpose of an organization is to sustain itself. They can therefore accept the fact that it may not be possible to act in the public interest if, in so doing, an organization's existence or interests will be seriously impaired. What they may not so readily accept is an attempt to pass off one's purely private interests as being in the public interest.

4. **Emphasize congruous aspects.** There are very few situations that are clearly in the public interest or clearly in an organization's private interests. You can take almost any organization's policy, procedure, or action and chart the degree in which it will be in the public interest and the degree in which it will be in the private interest of an organization. Within a range from zero to ten you will find that one aspect of the situation will rate *two* in terms of being in the public interest and *ten* in terms of being in the private interest of the organization. Another aspect of the same situation, however, might rate *six* in terms of both public and private interests. By all means, therefore, stress the degree of agreement rather than the degree of disagreement:

> Your college decides to raise its tuition by $500 (so what else is new?). The financial aspects of the action would rate *zero* in terms of the interests of the student body and *eight* in terms of the interests of the college. But in respect to being able to maintain and attract an excellent faculty, the action would rate *eight* in terms of the interests of both the student body and the school. In making the announcement, therefore, the public relations department would be advised to emphasize the second point rather than the first.

A cautionary note is in order regarding congruous interests. When rating interests as they apply to various aspects of a situation, don't overemphasize what is relatively unimportant. It would clearly not be advisable to stress an aspect that is of minor importance within a situation merely because it meshes with both public and private interests.

5. **Keep in mind Ross's concept of an acceptable balance of interests.** Many times in your professional life you will be dealing with a situation that affects diverse groups. What will benefit one group will not benefit another, and therefore the best that can be achieved is what Ross terms an acceptable balance of interests. Compromise may not be

the ideal solution, but it may well be the only realistic solution when trying to mesh public and private interests.

The above guidelines, of course, are predicated on the assumption that your organization's policies, actions, and statements are somehow tuned to the public interest. When they clearly are *not* in said interest, don't try to pass them off as being so. If you are in a position to do anything about them, bring your weight to bear in modifying or changing policies, actions, and/or statements so that they *will* meet the public interest in some degree of importance and will be so perceived by the public. Above all, keep your personal involvement in check when trying to judge the public interest in a given situation. It's usually the disinterested person who can best judge what is and what isn't in the public interest.

ENDNOTES

1. Edward L. Bernays, *Crystallizing Public Opinion,* rev. ed. (New York: Liveright, 1961), p. 173.
2. Harwood Childs, *An Introduction to Public Opinion* (New York: John Wiley & Sons, 1940), p. 2.
3. Ibid., p. 21.
4. Milton Friedman, "The Social Responsibility of Business Is to Increase Its Profits," *New York Times Magazine,* September 13, 1970.
5. The Committee for Economic Development, *Social Responsibilities of Business Corporations* (New York: Committee for Economic Development, 1971).
6. Ibid.
7. From introduction, *1981 General Motors Public Interest Report,* April 15, 1981.
8. *1983 General Motors Public Interest Report,* May 2, 1983, p. 39.
9. John W. Hill, "Corporations—The Sitting Ducks," *Public Relations Quarterly,* Summer 1977.
10. Childs, *An Introduction to Public Opinion,* p. 24.
11. Ibid., p. 30.
12. Ibid., p. 33.
13. Walter Lippmann, *The Public Philosophy* (Boston: Little, Brown & Co., 1955), p. 39.
14. John W. Hill, *The Making of a Public Relations Man* (New York: David McKay, 1963).
15. Ibid.
16. T. J. Ross, "The Public Relations Function: What It Is . . . And What It Is Not," talk given at the New School for Social Research, New York City, February 4, 1963.

PROJECTS, ASSIGNMENTS AND MINIS

1. PRIVATE/PUBLIC INTEREST EXAMPLES: A PROJECT

This assignment requires you to report and analyze two relatively recent situations showing how an organization's private interests—as demonstrated in its reported policies, actions, or statements—either meshed or conflicted with the public interest.

Your examples should come from news stories in daily newspapers or magazines. The stories should deal only with private organizations or their representatives, not with government or political agencies and/or people. The organizations you select can be either profit or nonprofit organizations.

Your report should summarize the situation or issue concerning each organization; explain the nature of the private/public interest connection; and evaluate how well or how poorly the organization did in meshing its interests with the public interest. Include in your report an appendix containing copies of the stories upon which your report is based.

2. CHILDS' THESIS PUT TO THE TEST: A PROJECT

As noted in this chapter, Harwood Childs maintains that a major task of the public relations practitioner is to delineate those policies, activities, or actions of an organization that have societal significance. Listed below is a sampling of some major American organizations and institutions:

commercial airlines	your favorite labor union
hospitals	major oil companies
private colleges and universities	the television networks
public colleges and universities	automobile companies
your favorite conglomerate	

Select any three of the above and for each of them cite and describe:

a) A **current** socially significant policy, activity, or action of said organization or institution that poses public relations problems for the organization or institution.

b) A **future** socially significant policy, activity, or action of said organization or institution that will, in your opinion, pose public relations problems for the organization or institution.

3. THE FOUNDATION LECTURE: A REPORT

Each year the Foundation for Public Relations Research and Education honors an outstanding public relations practitioner by inviting him or her to deliver the Foundation Lecture at the Foundation's annual meeting. The lecture is subsequently reprinted in an issue of the *Public Relations Review*, quarterly publication of the Foundation.

Select any one of the Foundation Lectures of the past decade and prepare a report which summarizes the major points made by the lecturer and your evaluation—positive or negative—of these points. In short, summarize the lecture and have a point of view about it.

Your instructor will decide whether your report should be written or oral.

THE FUNCTION
THROUGH HISTORY

Professor Ray E. Hiebert has pointed out that the definitive history of public relations has not yet been and may never be written. He notes, however, that the Foundation for Public Relations Research and Education sponsored a series of lectures by eminent historians "for the purpose of exploring the historical antecedents of what is now termed public relations." The six lectures, reproduced in a special issue of the *Public Relations Review*, provide a fascinating mosaic about the role of public relations in the past 200 years and are recommended reading for public relations students.[1] The discussion of public relations antecedents in this chapter will be brief, but it should provide some understanding of the use of public relations throughout our history.

REVOLUTION THROUGH CIVIL WAR PERIOD

Most high school students give little thought to public relations as they study the Revolutionary War period, but it's intriguing to recognize the degree to which modern public relations techniques and practices were utilized by **Samuel Adams** and his fellow revolutionaries. They did not put the title "public relations" on their activities and work on behalf of the revolution, but they could well have done so. Among the modern techniques and practices they made use of were:

> **an organization,** achieved by setting up the Sons of Liberty and the Committees of Correspondence in 1766 and 1772;

symbols, achieved by such identifying devices as the Liberty Tree;

slogans, achieved by such catch phrases as "taxation without representation is tyranny";

staged events, such as the Boston Tea Party, to arouse and crystallize public opinion;

timing in getting their story to the public first so that their interpretation of an event, such as the Boston Massacre, becomes the accepted one; and

saturation campaigns to make sure the public receives the message through all available means of communication.[2]

Just as Adams used public relations techniques to involve us in a war with England, so did Alexander Hamilton and James Madison use the power of communication to establish a Constitution once the war was won. Because the Constitution had to be accepted by Congress and ratified by the States, a massive public relations effort was required. Historians agree that the authors of *The Federalist Papers*—chiefly **Hamilton** and **Madison**—produced one of the finest public relations documents in history. Declares Allen Nevins: "Obtaining national acceptance of the Constitution was essentially a public relations exercise, and Hamilton, with his keen instinct for public relations, took thought not only to the product but to the ready acquiescence of thoughtful people; and he imparted his views to others." Through their essays and the eloquence of their debating techniques, the Federalists, in Nevins's view, carried out "the greatest work ever done in America in the field of public relations."[3]

Although relatively unknown today—even among public relations people—**Amos Kendall** performed so many public relations tasks for President Andrew Jackson he has been termed "the first presidential public relations man."[4] Joining the Jackson administration in 1829 as Fourth Auditor of the Treasury, Kendall soon impressed Jackson with his abilities and became a member of that influential advisory group known as the "Kitchen Cabinet." Kendall's talents and abilities were put to good use by Jackson in performing public relations tasks associated today with White House press assistants. In addition to ghostwriting State of the Union messages and speeches for the President, Kendall served as a political advance man on presidential trips; wrote articles and stories which served as press releases; contributed pamphlets for use during campaigns; and gave advice and counsel to the President on matters political and governmental. Kendall's constant goal was to depict and reinforce an image of Jackson as a resourceful, bold, and humanitarian leader of the common man. Modern presidents rely on dozens of specialists to perform the tasks that one man, Amos Kendall, did for President Jackson from 1829 to 1837. "By the time Jackson left office in 1837," writes Professor Fred Endres, "Kendall rightly had earned the title of the first presidential public relations man."[5]

More than seventy years after the adoption of the Constitution, the country split in half as the Confederacy and the Union fought a Civil War that historian Frank E. Vandiver describes as "a war of opinion, a war to win people's approval, a truly public war." As spokesman for the Confederate cause, **Jefferson Davis** sought indefatigably to present the cause of the South as "the bulwark of constitutional government in America." Speaking just as indefatigably for the Union, **Abraham Lincoln** used speeches, textbooks, and newspapers to rally public opinion to the Union side. Terming Lincoln a "master of public relations," Vandiver ranks him as one of "the most effective fashioners of public opinion in American history."[6]

POST-CIVIL WAR PERIOD

The end of the Civil War brought many profound changes to American life, and one of the most significant was the rise of large-scale business and industry. In the last quarter of the nineteenth century the utilities, railroads, and other industries expanded across the country in a profusion of monopolies and powerful concentrations of power and wealth. The years at the end of the century proved to be the age of the "robber barons" who made up their own rules and who felt they were beholden to no one and certainly not to the public. It was an era when "the public be damned." As one historian noted: "Big business was committed to the proposition that the less the public knew of its operations, the better. . . . Demands for publicity were further lessened by the esteem, almost awe in which the big businessman was held by large segments of the population."[7]

An important segment unawed by the industrial captains was a group of writers who came to be known as the "muckrakers." Through the written word, and especially via magazines and books, these writers proceeded to rake up the muck that existed in certain industries, in the cities, and in politics. Among the most famous were Ida Tarbell (*History of the Standard Oil Company*), Thomas Lawson (*Frenzied Finance*), Upton Sinclair (*The Jungle*), and S.S. McClure, whose magazine (*McClure's*) carried most of the articles written by the muckrakers. With *McClure's* showing the way, *Collier's*, *Cosmopolitan*, *Munsey's*, the *Independent*, the *American Magazine*, and other mass-circulation publications joined the exposure trend. Business leaders reeled from the attack and from the reform legislation that followed, but for the most part they simply did not know how to respond. Into the gap stepped the forerunners of the public relations practitioners of today.

The public relations men who came to the fore in the early decades of the twentieth century differed in one significant way from those of the two preceding centuries. Samuel Adams, Alexander Hamilton, and James Madison, for example, used public relations **techniques** to achieve their purposes, but they did not carry out organized public relations. The new men of the early decades of the twentieth century established the first public relations and publicity counseling firms and the first public relations departments within businesses. One can therefore say that the organized practice of public relations began in the current century.

Most of the public relations activities by business in the period 1900 to 1914 were defensive in nature. However, one business leader—Theodore N. Vail, president of the American Telephone and Telegraph Corporation—proved to be far ahead of his time in recognizing that sound service to the public, clearly explained to the public, was the road to growth and stability for his company. His organization was one of the first to establish a public relations department—called at the time an Information Department—and to consider that the public interest and the corporation's self-interest were inseparably linked.

Operating as a "publicist" at this time was Ivy Ledbetter Lee, often called the "father of public relations." Lee formed one of the country's earliest public relations firms and also served as advisor to the Pennsylvania Railroad and the Rockefeller interests. In 1906, while representing the anthracite coal interests, Lee wrote his "Declaration of Principles" and sent it to city editors.

Ivy Lee's Declaration of Principles

This is not a secret press bureau. All our work is done in the open. We aim to supply news. This is not an advertising agency; if you think any of our matter ought properly to go to your business office, do not use it. Our matter is accurate. Further details on any subject treated will be supplied promptly, and any editor will be assisted most cheerfully in verifying directly any statement of fact. . . . In brief, our plan is, frankly and openly, on behalf of the business concerns and public institutions, to supply to the press and public of the United States prompt and accurate information concerning subjects which it is of value and interest to the public to know about. . . . I send out only matter every detail of which I am willing to assist an editor in verifying for himself. I am always at your service for the purpose of enabling you to obtain more complete information concerning any of the subjects brought forward in my copy.[8]

Lee, of course, was not the sole practitioner of public relations at the time, and, as Hiebert notes in *Courtier to the Crowd*, "Ivy Lee was never quite sure of the title of his

TEN TO BE REMEMBERED

In alphabetical order below are brief sketches of ten public relations pioneers whose work and activities have had a significant effect on modern public relations practice.

Leone Baxter   Teaming up in 1933 with husband Clem Whitaker, she formed the first public relations firm specializing in political campaigns. Operating out of their San Francisco headquarters, the firm handled scores of primary and election campaigns in California and later widened their activities to take on political public relations activities on a national scale. Among other programs carried out by Whitaker and Baxter was the extensive national campaign the firm waged on behalf of the American Medical Association to head off President Truman's proposed Compulsory Health Insurance program.

Edward L. Bernays   A member of the Creel Committee during World War I, Bernays was one of the first "Creel alumni" to establish his own counseling firm at war's end. His *Crystallizing Public Opinion* was the first book to explain public relations concepts, and he has certainly been the most prolific writer on public relations subjects. He retired from active practice in 1962, but was still writing a regular column and giving talks in 1983. Among his firm beliefs are the need for a social science approach to public relations problems and some form of licensing procedure for practitioners.

George Creel   Selected by President Wilson to head the Committee on Public Information, Creel assembled a talented group of editors, writers, artists, and publicity experts who utilized all forms of mass persuasion to mobilize American public opinion in support of the war effort. Many of the men who subsequently established the early public relations counseling firms gained their experience from service on the committee headed by Creel.

Paul Garrett   As a one-man department in 1931, Garrett established public relations as a management function at General Motors. He sold top management at GM on the concept that public acceptance is gained when an organization's policies are seen as being in the public interest. By the time he retired in 1957, public relations at General Motors was a well-established department with ready access to the major operating executives of the corporation.

Denny Griswold   Publisher and owner of the country's oldest public relations newsletter, she and her husband Glenn, now deceased, founded the *Public Relations News* in 1944. Griswold's weekly newsletter has provided over the years a continuing chronicle of

profession, confessing toward the end of his life that even his children did not know what to call him."[9] Others, spurred particularly by the highly successful use of public relations techniques in World War I by the Creel Committee on Public Information, established themselves as independent practitioners or started public relations departments within corporations and other institutions. Some of these pioneers were Edward L. Bernays, John Hill, Paul Garrett, Carl Byoir, William Baldwin, and Pendleton Dudley. By the end of World War II the term "public relations counselor" had come into current usage, and most of the practices in use today were developed and put into motion.

THE MODERN ERA

The modern era in public relations dates from the end of World War II in 1945 to the present. Within that four-decade period public relations developed into its own as a field the important events, activities, and personalities of the public relations field and has been an invaluable research resource for four decades.

Rex Harlow   Educator, editor, publisher, and consultant, Dr. Harlow began his public relations career in 1912 and was still active writing about public relations in 1983. During his long professional life this Californian taught social science and public relations at Stanford University; founded the American Council on Public Relations; was first editor of the *Public Relations Journal* and one of the founding fathers of the Public Relations Society of America; and was editor and publisher of the *Social Science Reporter*, a newsletter designed to bridge the gap between social science research and the public relations field.

John W. Hill   A former newspaperman, Hill was the founder of Hill and Knowlton, presently the world's largest public relations firm. Hill's professional life spanned half a century, 1927-1977, and during this period he built his firm into an international public relations company with headquarters in New York City and offices in major U.S. cities and abroad. In two books, written near the end of his active career, Hill summed up decades of experience as one of the country's most respected public relations practitioners.

Ivy Lee   Considered to be the father of modern public relations practice, Lee set up his firm in the first decade of this century. At the time he set precedent by his "Declaration of Principles," cited in this chapter. Lee operated on the principle that publicity has to be supported by good performance. Although he was a public relations counselor by virtue of his actions, he did not call himself one and was not certain what to call the work he did.

Earl Newsom   Highly regarded by his contemporaries, Newsom established his firm in 1935 and limited much of his activities to counseling such large corporations as Standard Oil Company of New Jersey, Ford Motor Company, and General Motors Corporation. Newsom deliberately kept his firm small, but he and his partners were highly respected for their ability to help solve major public relations problems and anticipate future ones.

Arthur W. Page   A writer and editor in the first quarter of this century, Page became vice president of public relations for the American Telephone and Telegraph Company in 1927. A firm believer in the importance of public opinion in a democratic society, Page stressed the need for company performance to match company words, and he insisted on having a voice and input into company policy.

of activity with recognizable practices, techniques, skills, codes, and boundaries. Seven major elements coalesced during the period to bring about the maturation of public relations as a broadly-accepted activity and managerial function.

Recognition of Perceived Need

During this modern period not only business and industry—the two prime users of public relations—but most organizations and institutions of size recognized the need to establish public relations as an important staff function to assist management in carrying out its tasks. Thus, we now find public relations departments in unions, colleges and universities, social service and health organizations, religious bodies, government agencies, politics, and the courts. Why is this so? Because these organizations have discovered they have the same public relations needs as business and industry, and that the same public relations techniques and skills can be used to meet these needs.

Growth in Number of Practitioners

The need for specialized services usually begets the specialists to provide the services, hence it's not surprising to find the increase in the number of those practicing public relations. The U.S. census is considered to be the most reliable source of data concerning occupations, though even the census is not entirely accurate because it has only one occupational heading for the public relations field, "Public Relations and Publicity Writers." There are many public relations people who are not writers, hence they may not be listed by the census under the public relations heading. Table 4.1 shows the trend of public relations employment according to the U.S. Census under its "writers" designation.

TABLE 4.1

Public Relations Employment

U.S. Census	Public Relations and Publicity Writers
1950	19,000
1960	31,141
1970	75,852

An additional source of government information regarding public relations employment is the *Occupational Outlook Handbook* issued by the Bureau of Labor Statistics of the U.S. Department of Labor. According to the 1981 edition of the handbook, there were 87,000 public relations practitioners in 1980. Given the fact that it is not uncommon to find professional people carrying out public relations duties but under a different name—hence missed in the normal count—it is safe to assume that **there are at least 87,000 and probably 100,000 public relations specialists** in the United States today (1984). Both the handbook and the census figures thus show a steady increase in the number of people in the public relations field during the modern era.

Formation and Growth of Professional Organizations

The Public Relations Society of America (PRSA), formed in 1948 by the merger of the American Council on Public Relations and the National Association of Public Relations Counsel, has been an important influence in the public relations field. With an ever-increasing membership and a full-time professional staff in New York City, the PRSA in 1983 had 11,500 members and active chapters in all parts of the country. Through its four-day annual conference; regional conferences, seminars, and meetings; various publications; Silver Anvil awards program; and central office activities, the PRSA serves as a unifying body for the public relations field and a means for advancing professionalism.

Another national organization—the International Association of Business Communicators (IABC)—was mainly concerned with business communication in its early days, but in recent years its membership has expanded to include public relations professionals in all kinds of institutions and organizations. Its full-time professional staff is located in San Francisco and the association has an annual conference, regional meetings and seminars, an awards program, several publications, and continuing extensive research projects. As with the PRSA, these IABC programs and activities serve as a unifying force for the public relations field and a means for developing professionalism. Other public relations groups and associations, many of them specialized in nature, are listed in Figure 4.1. They attest to the fact that the modern era is characterized by functional specialization as well as growth by the field as a whole.

Major Public Relations Associations

Academy of Hospital Public Relations
418 N. Glendale Avenue
Glendale, CA 91206
(213) 244-4548

Agricultural Relations Council
18 South Michigan Avenue
Chicago, IL 60603
(312) 346-1387

American Association of Minority
   Consultants
C/O Charles A. Davis & Associates
2400 South Michigan Avenue
Chicago, IL 60616
(312) 326-4140

American Jewish Public Relations Society
515 Park Avenue
New York, NY 10022
(212) 752-0600

American Society for Hospital Public
   Relations Directors
840 North Lake Shore Drive
Chicago, IL 60611
(312) 645-9467

Bank Marketing Association
309 West Washington Street
Chicago, IL 60606
(312) 782-1442

Baptist Public Relations Association
460 James Robertson Parkway
Nashville, TN 37219
(615) 244-2355

Canadian Public Relations Society, Inc.
Suite 640, 220 Laurier Ave. W.
Ottawa KIP 5Z9, Ontario, Canada
1613-232-1222

Council for Advancement and Support of
   Education
One DuPont Circle, N.W.
Washington, D.C. 20036
(202) 293-6360

International Public Relations Assoc.
Sam Black
50 Pine Grove
Totteridge, London, Great Britain
N20 8LA
(01) 445-5256

International Association of Business
   Communicators
870 Market Street, Suite 928
San Francisco, CA 94102

Library Public Relations Council
C/O Alice Norton
Box 516
Ridgefield, CT 06877
(203) 438-4064

National Association of Government
   Communicators
7204 Clarendon Road
Washington, D.C. 20014
(202) 656-3544

National Investor Relations Institute
1629 K Street N.W.
Washington, D.C. 20036
(202) 223-4725

National School Public Relations Association
1801 N. Moore Street
Arlington, VA 22209
(703) 528-5840

New York Airlines Public Relations
C/O Harvey Berman
National Airlines
219 E. 42nd Street
New York, NY 10017
(212) 697-8181

New York Financial Writers Association
Box 4306
New York, NY 10017
(212) 737-4033

Public Affairs Council
1220 16th Street, N.W.
Washington, D.C. 20036
(202) 872-1790

Public Relations Society of America
845 Third Avenue
New York, NY 10022

Publicity Club of Chicago
1945 N. Hudson
Chicago, IL 60614
(312) 337-1501

Publicity Club of New York
404 Park Avenue South
Suite 1207
New York, NY 10016
(212) 685-8220

Railroad Public Relations Association
American Railroads Building
Washington, DC 20036
(202) 293-4194

Religious Public Relations Council
475 Riverside Drive-Room 1031
New York, NY 10027
(212) 870-2013

Women Executives in Public Relations
C/O Ms. Retha Odom
Shell Oil
50 W. 50th Street
New York, NY 10020
(212) 262-6983

Women in Communications, Inc.
8305-A Shoal Creek Boulevard
Austin, TX 78758
(512) 452-0119

FIGURE 4.1

Solidification of the Education Base

The higher education base provides the foundation for every profession or field of professional activity. Prior to the modern era there was very little educational foundation to the public relations field. Bernays taught the first public relations course in an institution of higher education in 1923 (New York University), and other universities and colleges offered a course or two. However, it wasn't until the end of World War II that sequences and majors in public relations began to be offered on the university level. Public relations teachers organized themselves into divisions and sections of the Association for Education in Journalism and of the Public Relations Society of America. Slowly but surely, education for public relations began to establish itself, grow, and expand. Several studies, conducted under the auspices of the PRSA and by the Foundation for Public Relations Research and Education, showed that the number of collegiate institutions offering public relations courses grew from 30 in 1946 to more than 300 in 1970. A 1970 survey by Dr. Ray Hiebert identified 89 schools offering complete sequences or degree programs, and a 1980 study by Dr. Albert Walker showed that 96 schools offered such programs. After reviewing all the data from his study, Dr. Walker concluded that "public relations education has come of age in America."[10]

Strengthening the educational foundation has been the phenomenal growth of the Public Relations Student Society of America (PRSSA). Chiefly through the initiative of Professor Walter Seifert of Ohio State University, the PRSSA was established in the late sixties under the auspices of the PRSA, quickly grew to more than 60 chapters, and was formally incorporated into the PRSA a few years later. By 1983 the student group had grown to 123 chapters with a total membership of 4,000 organized into districts, with district and national conferences, an information exchange program, and a quarterly publication.

Solidification of the Research Base

Research, as well as education, provides an important foundation for any profession and field of professional activity. Although public relations research on the higher educational level has not kept pace with education on the same level, the amount and degree of research activity has been on an ever-increasing scale. Prior to the modern era virtually no research was carried out, and only a small amount was evidenced in the 1950s and 1960s. Commencing in the 1970s and continuing in the 1980s, the pace of research activity has quickened for several reasons.

In this period a new group of public relations teachers, many of them trained in the social sciences and holding Ph.D. degrees, entered the teaching field. Research studies, many if not most of them funded by the Foundation for Public Relations Research and Education, were undertaken and reported at regional meetings of public relations teachers and practitioners and at the national conferences of both groups. The *Public Relations Review*, published by the Foundation, began and continued to carry an ever-increasing number of articles reporting research findings. Practitioners, particularly in the early 1980s, commenced making sizable contributions to the Foundation and this enabled the organization to fund more studies. Thus, by 1984 one could discern the outlines of a body of knowledge for the public relations field brought about by the proliferation of research studies and reports. Compared to that of other, older fields the public relations field's research activity on the higher educational level is still in its infancy, but has been maturing at a pace which promises to grow in the future.

Growth in the Literature of the Field

The literature of the public relations field is found in its articles in magazines and journals; trade and text books; masters' theses and Ph.D. dissertations; and occasional reports. As with the other areas discussed in this section, the growth of public relations literature has been speedy and substantive in the past four decades.

Public Relations Journal, monthly publication of the PRSA, was started in 1944 by Dr. Rex Harlow and is the oldest publication in the field. Under the editorship of Leo Northart, the *Journal* features six to eight articles per issue, carries such standing features as professional book reviews and columns on consumerism, environmentalism, the Washington scene, and people in the field. Northart supervised a complete graphics overhaul of the *Journal* in 1982 and set a policy of featuring a specific topic or area of interest in each issue.

Public Relations Review, started in 1975 by the Foundation for Public Relations Research and Education, has proven to be the preeminent research findings home for public relations studies and reports. Editor Ray E. Hiebert, assisted by a very capable group of associate editors, publishes four to five well-documented articles in each issue of the quarterly. In addition, the journal carries a solid book review section and, as of 1984, was devoting one issue a year to an update of the *Public Relations Bibliography.* The first annotated *Public Relations Bibliography,* prepared by Dr. Scott Cutlip in 1957, was subsequently updated by Dr. Robert L. Bishop, and has been issued on an annual basis as compiled and edited by Dr. Albert Walker since 1976. The tenth edition, appearing in the Winter, 1982, issue of *Public Relations Review,* contained titles published the previous year and compiled from more than 200 periodicals, books, abstracts, and book review digests. Included were relevant titles of dissertations and theses. Another listing of theses and dissertations about public relations subjects was first prepared in the mid-seventies by Professor Raymond Simon and has been periodically updated since under the direction of Dr. Frederick Teahan of PRSA.

Public Relations Quarterly, first published in 1954 as *PR Quarterly* by the American Public Relations Association, has been privately published since 1961 when APRA merged with PRSA. It has been edited since its inception by Howard Hudson, a Washington-based public relations counselor, and it carries articles, regular columns, and book reviews.

Three weekly newsletters which serve the public relations field are *Jack O'Dwyer's Newsletter, pr reporter,* and *Public Relations News.* Each is a four-page publication carrying news about the field and its practitioners and each serves as an important source of current information about the state of public relations activity.

Communication World, monthly publication of the International Association of Business Communicators, published its first issue in November, 1983. The initial issue contained nine articles, six columns, and a score of departmental features on communication and public relations.

The most dramatic change in the literature of public relations has taken place in the textbook field, and this change has been most evident in the period from 1970 to 1984. When Cutlip and Center's *Effective Public Relations* was published in its first edition in 1952, it was one of two texts dealing solely with public relations. Teachers selecting a text for a public relations course now have a choice from among eight to ten texts, at least half of which keep up to date by revisions every four to five years. The increase in such texts is clear evidence of the increase and interest in public relations courses taught on the college and university level and is another demonstration of the maturation of the public relations field.

Proliferation of Public Relations Departments and Firms

Public relations as a management function and as a professional activity has been evidenced by the growth and spread of public relations departments and of counseling firms and agencies. Detailed treatment of public relations departments and counseling firms will be given in a succeeding chapter, but it's pertinent to note here the degree of sophistication in structuring and managing such departments and firms in the 1970s and 1980s. In trying to keep abreast and ahead of a changing society, practitioners have developed new specialties and refined old ones. As an example, the concept of issue management was still so new in 1984 those engaged in dealing with it were still debating what the term and concept entailed. Public relations departments were being established in 1984 within organizations that previously had not thought such departments were needed. Some counseling firms were seeking to become all-purpose firms while others found it profitable to place their strength in special areas of public relations. And a final significant change was the merging of some of the oldest and most successful public relations firms with some of the country's largest advertising agencies.

Call public relations what one may—a field, a business, a profession, or a calling—there is no doubt that the modern public relations era we now find ourselves in is an exciting and challenging one. By exploring the nature of the field and the public relations process, this book aims to help those who seek to meet the challenges.

ENDNOTES

1. Ray E. Hiebert, "Foundation Lectures on Public Relations in American History," *Public Relations Review*, Fall 1978, p. 3.
2. Scott Cutlip and Allen Center, *Effective Public Relations*, rev. 5th ed. (Englewood Cliffs, N.J.: Prentice Hall, 1982), p. 68.
3. Allan Nevins, "The Constitution Makers and the Public: 1785-1790," *Public Relations Review*, Fall 1978, p. 5.
4. Fred F. Endres, "Public Relations in the Jackson White House," *Public Relations Review*, Fall 1976, p. 5.
5. Ibid.
6. Frank E. Vandiver, "The First Public War: 1861-1865," *Public Relations Review*, Fall 1978, p. 36.
7. Eric F. Goldman, "Public Relations and the Progressive Surge: 1896-1917," *Public Relations Review*, Fall 1978, p. 54.
8. Sherman Morse, "An Awakening on Wall Street," *American Magazine*, September 1906, p. 460.
9. Ray E. Hiebert, *Courtier to the Crowd: The Story of Ivy L. Lee* (Ames, Iowa: Iowa State University Press, 1966), p. 6.
10. Albert Walker, "End-of-Decade Survey Shows Academic Growth in Public Relations," *Public Relations Review*, Summer 1982, p. 46.

PROJECTS, ASSIGNMENTS, AND MINIS

1. STARTING A PUBLIC RELATIONS LIBRARY: A PUBLICATIONS SURVEY

You are to assume that you are a member of a newly-formed public relations department of a manufacturing firm whose wide variety of consumer products are sold throughout the United States and abroad. The firm is listed on the New York Stock Exchange, and it has 64,000 employees who work in twenty-four locations in all parts of the country. The head of the department is a vice-president and she reports to the chief executive officer.

Your superior informs you that she wants to start a departmental public relations library, but budgetary considerations require making choices among publications. She has therefore asked you to prepare a memorandum in which you should recommend one publication from each group cited below:

Group A: *Public Relations Journal* or *Communication World*

Group B: *Public Relations Review* or *Public Relations Quarterly*

Group C: *Jack O'Dwyer's Newsletter, pr reporter,* or *Public Relations News*

It is expected that in preparing the memorandum you will read several recent issues of each publication; summarize the sections and contents of each publication, paying special attention to the major articles; and cite the reasons for your choice of publication in each of the three groups.

2. QUESTIONS FOR A PUBLIC RELATIONS PIONEER: A PROJECT

A national monthly publication whose readers include a large number of public relations practitioners has assigned you to write a 2500-word profile of one of the ten public relations pioneers cited in this chapter under the heading "Ten to Be Remembered."

You are to select one of the ten and to assume that you are writing the profile at the time when the subject was actively engaged in public relations work. You have researched the important factual data about the subject and are now preparing to interview the subject.

Your task on this project is twofold:

a) To set forth, exactly as you would ask them, five questions whose answers would provide you with perceptive and interesting insights about the subject and the subject's views of the public relations field and public relations practice.

b) To explain, in a paragraph after each question, why you asked the question.

Because the interviewee has granted you a limited amount of time for the interview, it has been agreed that you will keep questions to a minimum. For this reason, the five that you ask should be those you consider to be most important in meeting the objectives of your assignment.

In summation, the paper you submit to your instructor should consist of the five questions, worded exactly as they will be asked of the interviewee, and the reason(s) why you are asking each question.

5

SOME KEY CAUSAL TRENDS OF THE FUNCTION

B y 1984 the public relations function was firmly established in the United States and, to an increasing extent, internationally. Given the changes that have occurred in American society, one could safely say this was inevitable. Says Dan J. Forrestal, a veteran public relations practitioner: "Public relations in its current concept and nomenclature, was invented simply because a wide variety of organizations simply couldn't afford not to have it. They recognized that merited understanding and acceptance by their principal constituencies were prerequisite for successful survival. They acknowledged the concept that performance/behavior plus communication/interpretation equals reputation. They acknowledged that somewhere in this mix a need existed for specialists with specific skills. . . ."[1]

The recognition that Forrestal speaks about demands a close look at those facets of society which have brought about the **need** for public relations and which, in turn, have created particular **problems** for the public relations specialist. These two elements—need and problems, cause and effect—comprise what one might call the climate for the public relations function in American society.

Two public relations teachers and authors have linked the term "ecology" to public relations practice in answering the question "Why public relations?"[2] Biologically, ecology refers to the mutual relationship between organisms and their environment. Ecology in a public relations sense relates to *those aspects of American society which have brought about the need for and the utilization of public relations* in America today and which, in turn, *have created particular problems for the practitioner*.

To bring ecology into focus, therefore, this section will outline and explore the nature of certain fundamental societal trends or aspects to clarify why they've caused the need for public relations practice. In a society as complex as America's, there are many trends which have wide societal significance. Five of them, however, seem to have special pertinence for public relations practice and will therefore be discussed in some detail. They are:

1. Population changes and movements
2. Large and complex components
3. Growth in the power of public opinion and the swiftness of opinion change
4. Changes in the technology, role, and impact of the mass media
5. Consumerism and environmental sensitivity

FUNDAMENTAL TRENDS IN AMERICAN SOCIETY CAUSING THE PRACTICE OF PUBLIC RELATIONS

POPULATION CHANGES AND MOVEMENTS

The first fundamental trend in American society that needs to be understood in considering the ecological nature of public relations is that dealing with population changes and movements. Of key importance is the change from a rural to an urban to a suburban society.

In 1910, when there were 92 million people in the United States, more than 54 percent of the population was classified as rural and 46 percent as urban. By 1920 the figures had changed to 51 percent urban and 49 percent rural, and the urban population has increased and the rural decreased in every decade since 1920. By 1980, 73.7 percent of the population was urban and 26.3 percent was rural. Figure 5.1 shows the dramatic change of population in the period 1910 to 1980.

	1910	1920	1930	1940	1950	1960	1970	1980
Urban:	46%	51%	56%	56.5%	64%	70%	73.5%	73.7%
Rural:	54%	49%	44%	43.5%	36%	30%	26.5%	26.3%

FIGURE 5.1 *Percentage of urban and rural population.*

Source: U.S. Bureau of the Census, *U.S. Census of the Population,* 1910-1980.

Equally revealing are the data in Figure 5.2 showing the United States population for 1960, 1970, and 1980 in terms of those living in central cities, urban fringes of central cities, urbanized areas outside central cities, and rural areas.

The data in Figure 5.2 demonstrate that we are definitely an urban society. Most of us live either within the central cities or in the urban fringes of these cities.

Of interest are the percentages as they apply to central city/urban fringe living. Commencing in the seventies the rich and the affluent started a movement back to the cities. Urban specialists referred to this process as inner-city "gentrification," and they cited as the most noted examples Boston and Baltimore, where rebuilt inner-city decaying areas

	Population (in thousands)			Percent of Total Population		
	1960	1970	1980	1960	1970	1980
Urban	125,269	149,325	167,051	69.9	73.5	73.7
Inside urban areas	95,848	118,447	139,171	53.5	58.3	61.4
Central cities	57,975	63,922	67,035	32.3	31.5	29.6
Urban fringe	37,873	54,525	72,135	21.2	26.8	31.8
Outside urban areas	29,420	30,878	27,880	16.4	15.2	12.3
Rural	54,054	53,887	59,495	30.1	26.5	26.3

FIGURE 5.2   *Urban area and rural population, 1960, 1970, 1980.*

Source: U.S. Bureau of the Census, 1980 *Census of the Population.*

were turned into much sought-after townhouse developments and high-finance, high-culture centers.[3] It was believed there would be a growing trend back to central city living. The 1980 census figures show, however, that this movement did not attract large enough numbers to make a dent in the trend away from central city living.

What the data do show is that the population living in the central cities declined from 32.3 percent of the total population in 1960 to 31.5 percent in 1970, and to 29.6 percent in 1980. Where did the people go? Certainly not to rural areas or to small towns outside urban areas, because the population of these areas also declined.

The answer is found in the percentages of those living in urban fringe areas, that is, in the suburbs contiguous to central cities. A total of 21.2 percent of the total population lived in the suburbs in 1960, 26.8 percent in 1970, and 31.8 percent in 1980. Thus, in 1980 those living in the suburbs of central cities were the largest single group in the population in terms of where people live.

The Meaning for Public Relations

Whether we consider the wave of the future as city growth by itself or a combination of city-suburban satellite growth, the trend is obviously towards an urban society. What does this mean vis-a-vis public relations? Compare life in the not-so-distant past with that today (and tomorrow) and the answer becomes a bit more clear.

When most Americans lived on farms or in small isolated communities, life was relatively uncomplicated. People knew their neighbors and were somewhat independent of external forces. There was a sense of community, of belonging. There were problems, plenty of them, but one had the feeling these problems were manageable and within one's ability to solve.

Now that most of us live in cities or suburbs, life is complicated. Neighbors are often the people who moved in last week (or was it the week before?). We are almost totally dependent today on external forces for mere sustenance. There is little sense of community and a great many maladjusted people. Viewed from this perspective, the movement from rural to urban to suburban sprawl has manifold implications for public relations. In our more leisured, easy-going days the gap of understanding between organizations and their publics was as narrow as the streets of small-town America. Today's gap is broad and wide.

By no means should we look upon public relations as a panacea for the better life for all of us, nor as some sort of magical cure-all for the ills of urban life. *But public relations can help bridge the gap of understanding* brought on by the ecological trend towards an urban society. Whether consciously and by plan or unconsciously in random fashion, more and more organizations are utilizing public relations as a means of gap-bridging and the building of goodwill and understanding. They're doing so because the urbanization trend has the causal effect of bringing on the felt need for public relations assistance and practice.

LARGE AND COMPLEX COMPONENTS

A second fundamental trend which needs to be considered in understanding the ecological basis for public relations in American society is the fact that *the chief components of that society are both large and complex.* The Hupmobile and Stutz cars long ago vanished into such giant enterprises as General Motors, Ford, Chrysler, and American Motors. Working men and women have joined together to form the United Auto Workers, the Teamsters, and the United Steelworkers of America. Small state colleges in California and New York have become units of the massive University of California and the State University of New York. Young people may still dream about leading adult lives as individuals controlling their own destinies, but the reality belies the dream. Through large and complex organizations and components most Americans now receive their education, spend their working lives, join together for collective bargaining purposes, are provided with government services, and receive the goods and other services necessary to sustain life.

We accept as routine the fact that large and complex organizations dominate the national scene in industry, labor, government, the military, farming, education, and all other key areas. We also accept as routine the many benefits that size and complexity bring to the average American, but large organizations cannot simply ride with the fact that they bring benefits, because these same benefits bring serious problems that affect all of us.

By their very nature large organizations become bureaucracies, and these in turn cause maladjustments and indifference. Today's highly organized society, says Professor Robert Presthus, has created what he terms "the indifferents" and he describes them this way:

> The indifferents are those who have come to terms with their environment by withdrawal and by redirection of their interests towards off-the-job satisfactions. They have also been alienated by the work itself which has often been downgraded by machine processing and assembly-line methods. . . . [The indifferents] are found among the great mass of the wage and salaried employees who work in the bureaucratic situation. By a rough estimate we can say that . . . just about half the wage-earning labor force now work in big organizations. Moreover, this vast reservoir of potential indifferents is steadily increasing.[4]

Max Scheler, a European social scientist, calls the current condition *ressentiment*. More powerful than just resentment and indifference, *ressentiment* means pervasive, pent-up anger that can best express itself by exploding. Daniel Yankelovich, public opinion authority, states that opinion surveys taken during the Vietnam War and the Watergate crisis revealed national unhappiness with the state of the nation, but he notes that the public was basically able to express its frustrations. More recently, however, polls have revealed that people feel *personally* victimized by institutions over which they have little or no control.

The Meaning for Public Relations

Thus, we not only have vast numbers of indifferents in today's society, but we've got mistrustful indifferents who are deeply resentful when they perceive they are being ripped off by large organizations and institutions. There is in the American character a traditional, almost ingrained mistrust of size. We value competition because we know that competition is a weapon to cut large organizations down to size and to provide us with some sort of individuality and choice, some way to allow us to exercise a small amount of independence.

Many large organizations take pains to show that they care for the individual. Far too many don't, and the individual reacts accordingly. An increasing number turn to protests. Others see to it that their elected representatives pass antitrust, zoning, and antipollution laws; establish the Securities and Exchange Commission, the Federal Trade Commission, Consumer Product Safety Commission, Environmental Protection Agency, Occupational Safety and Health Administration, and the Equal Employment Opportunity Administration. Little wonder that astute managements of large and complex organizations call on public relations assistance to measure the national mood, to suggest changes in corporate policy and actions to meet public expectations, and to communicate that size can be trusted (when it *deserves* to be trusted). The causal effect of the trend toward large and complex organizations is the same as the effect of the trend toward urbanization and suburbanization: that is, it has brought about the need for professional public relations assistance and practice.

GROWTH IN THE POWER OF PUBLIC OPINION AND SWIFTNESS OF OPINION CHANGE

A third fundamental trend in American society relates to public opinion. In a later chapter in this book public opinion will be analyzed and discussed in more detail, but our concern at the moment is with two factors: first, there has been a steady growth in the power of public opinion, and second, changes in public opinion can often be swift, sudden, and drastic.

Public opinion in America is a powerful force for the very basic reason that ours, for the most part, is an open society. There are times, of course, when a curtain hides from the general public the policies and actions of important elements of our society. During periods when we are at war, either "hot" or "cold," information is kept from the public while deliberate steps are taken to mold the public's opinion to support the nation's efforts to achieve victory. In peacetime the curtain of "national security," sometimes used properly and sometimes improperly, is lowered to prevent numerous government decisions and information from reaching the public and permitting an informed public opinion. In times of negative or bad news and actions, the reaction of many business managements is to hide the news, again because of concern about public opinion.

History teaches, however, that efforts to close off information fail to survive over the long run, and sometimes even in the short run. The reach and impact of mass media is too all-embracing to permit for long the retention of negative news and information. Insiders "leak" information to the media; the press uncovers information on its own; word get about, and public opinion begins to solidify. Once solidified, whether in a negative or positive direction, public opinion is difficult to change except through some dramatic event or action.

Astute students of the public psyche understand full well the power of public opinion in all elements of American society. Large business organizations that sell consumer products take pains to insure that products sold under their brand names achieve a deserved reputation for reliability. Why? Because about the only guide available to consumers about the worth of the product is the reliability of the brand. Veteran senators and representatives are reelected not because of their votes on a particular bill, but because the public in their states and districts are of the opinion that they can be relied upon to serve the public's interests. Without having even the slightest knowledge of the kind of education they provide, parents send their offspring to certain institutions of higher education because general public opinion holds that they are excellent institutions. Without the slightest knowledge of the services they provide, millions of Americans support certain health foundations because general public opinion holds that they perform highly valuable services. We vote for certain candidates, buy certain products, and support certain institutions because public opinion holds them worthy of our trust and confidence. Not without reason, then, does one state that public opinion has great power in American life. Achieving favorable public opinion, maintaining it over the years, and solidifying it is the basic reason why such institutions as Harvard and Yale, such corporations as General Electric, General Motors and Ford, and such personalities as Dwight D. Eisenhower and Walter Cronkite have been held in high esteem for decades.

Yet dramatic events and actions can with sudden swiftness change and modify the public's opinion of even the most sanctified institutions and people. Marshall McLuhan makes the following point: "In the mechanical age now receding, many actions could be taken without too much concern. Slow movement insured that the reactions were delayed for considerable periods of time. Today the action and the reaction occur almost at the same time. . . . As electronically contracted, the globe is no more than a village."[5]

Accepting the premise that public opinion is all-powerful in American life and that dramatic events and actions can swiftly change and modify opinions, what does this mean for public relations? The answer is that there is a need for experts who have solid insights and understanding of the nature of public opinion, the manner in which it is formed, ways in which to measure it, and realistic means for anticipating its future course. Managements have turned to public relations because its successful practitioners have proved themselves to be experts in the area of public opinion. Dealing with public opinion is as essential to the public relations practitioner as the scalpel is to the surgeon, knowledge of the law to the lawyer, and mathematics to the physicist. The expertise the public relations practitioner brings to the handling of public opinion is one of his chief assets and reasons for existence.

CHANGES IN THE TECHNOLOGY, ROLE, AND IMPACT OF THE MASS MEDIA

Legend has it that when Paul Revere wanted to arouse the Minutemen he got on his horse, rode through the countryside, and shouted at the top of his voice to arouse the sleeping citizenry. Result: a grim band of Minutemen showed up at Lexington commons. Today he would either hold a press conference or telephone the Associated Press and United Press International, the four major radio and the three major television networks; they'd put the story on the air immediately or send it via satellite. The news would be all over America in a matter of minutes.

This exemplifies the fourth fundamental trend in American society—the changes that have taken place in the technology, role, and impact of the mass media in the United States. In two of the areas—*technology* and *impact*—the changes have been dramatic; the *role* played by the mass media remains virtually the same as in Paul Revere's day.

Technology

For almost two-thirds of the history of our country the major media force in society was the print media, and for a considerable period of that time, changes in the technology of the print media were of a limited nature. Newsmen wrote their stories by hand, printers set them in type by hand, and slow presses turned the stories into printed newspapers. The telephone and Western Union wire speeded up the reporting process; the typewriter speeded up the writing process; and the Linotype and rotary presses speeded up the printing process. Dramatic technological change occurred in the print field in the last decade as newspapers and wire services switched to all-electronic writing, editing, and printing through the use of the cathode ray tube (CRT), the video display terminal (VDT), the optical character reader or scanner, and the master control computer.

By 1984 typewriters were disappearing from newsrooms at an ever-increasing pace to be replaced by VDTs and computers complete with pagination capability for makeup purposes. Satellite transmission of copy and printed pages made possible the introduction of *USA Today*, Gannett's national newspaper, and of national editions of the *Wall Street Journal* and the New York *Times*. Earth receiving dishes atop newsroom buildings were becoming a common sight as the wire services made use of satellites for the swift transmission of copy. Although newspapers still lag behind the electronic media in the speed race, the gap has been considerably narrowed. Videotex and teletex in 1984 held out promise of meshing the newspaper with television, though at the time these two new uses of television were still in the nascent stages.

Speed continued to be on the side of the electronic media in transmitting news in 1984. Radio has been the fastest way of getting across messages to the largest number of people in the country, chiefly because radio deals only with sound. Television involves a team effort between newsman and cameraman, and the process has been speeded up by the use of hand-held, portable cameras, videotape, and satellite transmission. In addition, by 1984 cable television was reaching 38 percent of U.S. TV homes (31,766,550 homes)[6] and opening up innumerable news channels and additional ways of bringing news and entertainment to the nation. The technological revolution was in full swing by the early eighties. It was reshaping our traditional media, but the final form was not yet fully developed.

Impact

For more than a century and a quarter the daily newspaper served as the primary source of news for the vast majority of adult Americans, but with the advent of the electronic media—especially television—there has been a significant change. The primary source of news, according to continuing trend studies conducted for the Television Information Office by the Roper polling organization, is now television, followed by the daily newspaper, radio, and magazines. Figure 5.3 tells the story.

The data in Figure 5.3 are not surprising when one considers the "reach" of the electronic media. As of January, 1983, there were 1,000 television and more than 8,000 radio

Response of a national sample of 2,000 to the question *"First, I'd like to ask you where you usually get most of your news about what's going on in the world today—from the newspapers or radio or television or magazines or talking to people or where?"*

Source of most news:	1959 %	1964 %	1968 %	1972 %	1976 %	1982 %
Television	51	58	59	64	64	65
Newspapers	57	56	49	50	49	44
Radio	34	26	25	21	19	18
Magazines	8	8	7	6	7	6
People	4	5	5	4	5	4
All mentions	154	153	145	145	144	137

FIGURE 5.3

Source: Burns W. Roper, *Trends in Attitudes Toward Television and Other Media: A Twenty-Five Year Review* (New York: Television Information Office, 1983).

stations in the United States. More than 83 million homes, representing 99 percent of all U.S. homes, had one or more television sets, and there were more than 443 million radio sets in use in homes and cars. At that same time the 1,730 daily newspapers in the country had a total combined circulation of 62.2 million.

One has to be cautious in dealing with the above figures and with survey results such as those shown by the survey sponsored by the Television Information Office. For example, a survey sponsored by a newspaper group, the Newsprint Information Committee, showed that 78 percent of a national sample said they had read a newspaper the day before the survey, 60 percent said they watched one or more television newscasts, and 55 percent said they heard one or more radio newscasts. Note that the Roper question in the television-sponsored survey refers to "what's going on in the world today," and this implies national and international news.

Except in our largest cities, where television stations have large and competent staffs with a great deal of financial backing for their news-gathering efforts, local television newscasts don't come anywhere near matching the work of the local daily newspaper. By their own admission, network television commentators barely scratch the surface with their daily half-hour news show.

Television viewers seem well satisfied with the way the medium is handling the news function. Figure 5.4 shows the response to a new question asked in the 1982 Roper study of television viewing.

Response of a national sample of 2,000 in 1982 to the question *"In terms of meeting your overall needs for news, would you say television is doing an excellent, good, not very good, or poor job?"*

Job television is doing of meeting overall news needs: %

Excellent	21
Good	67
Not very good	8
Poor	2
DK/NA	2

FIGURE 5.4

Source: Burns W. Roper, *Trends in Attitudes Toward Television and Other Media: A Twenty-Five Year Review* (New York: Television Information Office, 1983).

The newspaper remains the main source of local news and for national and international news and interpretative commentary in depth. For those millions who want the news brought into focus, the three national newsmagazines—*Time, Newsweek,* and *U.S. News and World Report*—are powerful molders of public opinion. Specialized magazines flourish because of their strong appeal and interest to special groups in the population. Ben Bagdikian, author and journalist, sums up the situation: "Even conflicting and competing surveys make clear that there has been no large-scale preemption of one medium by another, that each is used for a different set of reasons. Certain kinds of news continue to be dominant in print, other kinds in radio and television. In most kinds of news the media seem to reinforce each other—more and more people use both—rather than cancel each other out."[8]

Further, the media monitor each other carefully and often feed on each other's output. A local daily in Peoria, for example, runs an unusual feature story. The story catches the eye of the U.P.I. bureau man in a nearby city, and he rewrites it and sends it to the U.P.I. bureau in the state capital. They put it on the national wire. Two weeks later the New York *Times* sends a reporter to Peoria, and after a day or so on the scene he writes his updated version of the same feature story. It runs on the front page and is also sent out to subscribers to the *New York Times News Service*. Someone on the *Today* show reads about the story, and as a result the show carries a five-minute segment the following week. Because of one local reporter's curiosity and ability with words, millions of Americans learn about a purely local feature.

Role

From its earliest beginnings in America the role of the daily newspaper has been as a supplier of news, entertainment, and opinion. Radio and television have primarily served as entertainment vehicles, but their role as suppliers of news has become increasingly important. When the unblinking eye of the television camera is focused on an unfolding event—such as happened when television carried gavel-to-gavel coverage of the Senate Watergate hearings—television's role as a molder of public opinion becomes of highly significant importance.

With the exception of the two newsmagazines *Time* and *Newsweek*—which have built their readership through skillful editing and a combination of interpretation and news—the mass media stick for the most part to straight objective reporting and separation of the news and opinion functions. But when a major story or event breaks; when the story carries implications for millions of people; and when it involves controversy and builds momentum, the usual rules go out the window. To the beleaguered organization or individual caught in the vortex of the event, the media assume the role of a thousand Paul Reveres riding about the national countryside arousing the citizenry. A few examples should suffice to establish the point: stories following the Bay of Pigs disaster in the Kennedy administration; stories following the My Lai massacre in the Johnson administration; stories about the major oil companies during the Carter administration; and stories about automobile defects and massive recalls during any administration.

Considering, therefore, the role and effect of mass media in American society, one need not wonder why amateurs should not be entrusted with the task of dealing with the media. *With each passing year as the mass media increase in importance as purveyors of information and molders of opinion, so does it become obvious that organizations and individuals which rely on public support for their very existence turn to public relations practitioners for guidance and assistance in dealing with the media.* It takes skilled public relations professionals to understand and keep up with technological changes in the mass media which require new approaches for those who rely on the mass media to carry messages to the mass public and to special publics. It takes skilled public relations professionals to understand that each of the mass media is unique and has uniquely different advantages and disadvantages in impacting on its audience and fulfilling its role in American society. Dealing with the mass media, in short, is a matter for professionals, not amateurs.

CONSUMERISM AND ENVIRONMENTAL SENSITIVITY

Consumerism and environmental sensitivity—the fifth major trend in American society causing a need for public relations—have been around for a long time, but they assumed heightened significance as recently as the late sixties and seventies. While in no way meaning to downgrade the importance of the new sensitivity to the environment, this section will deal chiefly with consumerism because of its across-the-board appeal to all segments of the population; its long history as recognized by established government agencies and by newly formed ones; the staying power and strength of broad-based national, regional, state, and local activist groups; and its obvious concern to a wide variety of organizations with direct dealing with the consumer. Further, the term "consumerism" will include concern with numerous environmental aspects of our society as well as concern for the quality and performance of goods and services.

Consumers have always been considered an important public by public relations practitioners, and especially by those whose organizations have had direct contact with consumers. When an organization's chief source of income is through sales to consumers, its relationship with customers is of key importance to profit or loss. With good reason, therefore, such organizations have long-established customer relations departments, and the public relations function has been used in establishing, maintaining, and solidifying good customer relations.

Consumerism, however, is to customer relations what this year's model cars are to the Model T. Just as it would be unwise to try to sell the Model T in today's marketplace, so is it unwise to try to sell the old customer relations platitudes in today's *consumer activist* marketplace. Commencing in the mid-sixties as virtually a one-man movement led by Ralph Nader, consumerism built up an astonishing head of steam in a few short years, and by the mid-seventies had become a force that had to be reckoned with by all major corporations. *U.S. News and World Report*, generally considered to be the most conservative of the three major newsmagazines, described the movement succinctly in a full-page ad in the *Public Relations Journal*. Headed "A New Breed of Activist Has Emerged in the Seventies," the ad declared in part:

> Today's corporation faces a new public interest activism. A new breed of activist has emerged in the Seventies among corporate constituencies which traditionally have looked with favor upon the business community. Skepticism is on the rise, even among shareholders. . . .

> Primarily middle class, today's activists bear little resemblance to those of the Sixties. Well above average in income, education and awareness, they speak out for different goals: consumer protection, automobile and airplane safety, pure food, air and water, and (most crucial) corporate accountability. Their radiating influence on the thoughts and actions of millions of others threatens to hit corporations where they live—in the profit and loss statement. . . .

Perceptive analysts of the American scene trace the swift rise of the new consumerism to a combination of factors. In part, it resulted from the general unhappiness with many forms of American life in the late sixties; the political and social activism which found voice in the massive dissent to our continuing involvement in Vietnam; and with what Arthur H. White of the Daniel Yankelovich organization called the "galloping psychology of entitlement." White summed up the essentials of this psychology in the following words:

> One of the most boat-rocking social trends in the United States is a phenomenon we have called "the galloping psychology of entitlement," and it has profound implications for the future of American business. It is the psychological process whereby a person's wants or desires become converted into a set of presumed rights.

> An American who once said, "I would like to be sure of a secure retirement," now says, "I have a right to a secure retirement." A view expressed not long ago as "my job would mean more to me if I had more to say about how things are run" changes to "I have the right to take part in decisions that affect my job." From "If I could afford it, I would have the best medical care," to "I have the right to the best medical care whether I can afford it or not." From "I hope this cottage cheese is fresh," to "I have the right to know when it was made and how long it will stay fresh."

> The consumer movement, as it exists today, has enormous strength. Its public support is massive. In our own surveys and others, an unswerving average of 80-90 percent of the public supports consumerism—virtually a consensus. Furthermore, the support is strongest in mainstream America. It is not a function of liberal politics, but cuts across ideo-

logical and class lines. The core of support is the middle and upper middle income housewife—a force to be reckoned with. Of equal significance, the consumer movement has great appeal to political leaders. They see, as we do, that it is an issue people care about. . . .[9]

White's emphasis on the broad-based nature of consumerism is particularly important because it was addressed to public relations practitioners, and unfortunately many of them viewed the burgeoning consumer activist movement as being forced on Americans by the government and/or politicians.

This viewpoint was typified in an address given by a leading counselor in the mid-sixties to a group of television advertising executives and summed up in these words:

This country didn't just discover the consumer with the help of Esther Peterson or Betty Furness. We built a successful economy and an unrivaled standard of living on the philosophy that says consumer is king. I argue that business, not bureaucracy, discovered the consumer. And I say that business by and large has served him very well.

And yet business—including your business—is now being told that it can't possibly do the job without a legion of helping hands. Who wants it? Obviously not the consumer.

. . . One thing is sure. If you and I don't speak up, we can't expect others to protect us from the protectors. Even as our fellow consumers, we can be smothered by too much loving attention or drown in the overflow from bleeding hearts. . . .

The difference between White's view of the consumer movement and that of the unnamed public relations counselor cited above is clearly one of perception, but it's a difference that is highly important. White sees consumerism as "the major single cause of erosion of public confidence in business" and involving "the mainstream of American business." The counselor sees consumerism as stemming chiefly from "bleeding hearts" and politicians and being directed at a few dishonest businessmen. It should be obvious that the perception one has of consumerism will affect the response to the movement.

Meanwhile, consumerism has continued to flourish through the various Nader groups; other national and state-wide consumer groups; and such agencies of the government as the Consumer Product Safety Commission, the Food and Drug Administration, the Office of Consumer Affairs, and the Agency for Consumer Advocacy. In a 1978 study the Council on Economic Priorities, a public interest group that makes detailed studies of corporate practices and their impact on consumers, profiled eighty-three major public interest groups. The Council reported that the dominant issue among such groups at that time was energy and the environment. The Council reported that other key issues then were community and consumer affairs, minority rights, fair representation and advertising practices in the media, health and nutrition, and peace and disarmament.

Introducing an issue of *Public Relations Quarterly* dealing entirely with consumer affairs, Editor Howard P. Hudson reported that there were in 1980 more than 100 state and 500 to 600 local public interest groups. Hudson also noted that there has been growing concern within the media for identifying and reporting consumer problems plus better reporting of consumer issues and the establishment of new beats dealing with consumerism and the environment. "Consumerism as a movement," stated Hudson, "is a way of life."[10]

The Love Canal and the dioxin scares, the concern about acid rain and other kinds of air pollution showed the public's heightened interest in the early eighties with environmental matters. These were instances where people were directly affected by an environmental matter. Although environmental issues do not generally have as direct and immediate an impact on the average person as consumerism factors, there is widespread concern and sensitivity about air, soil, and water pollution, waste disposal, depletion of natural resources, oil spills, and potential shoreline hazards. This concern resulted in 1970 legislation such as the National Environmental Policy Act, the Clean Air Act, and the establishment of the U.S. Environmental Protection Agency. Within five years the

EPA mushroomed into the country's largest regulatory agency with 9,000 employees, a two million dollar daily budget, and jurisdictions and responsibilities in air and water pollution, solid waste, noise, pesticides, and radiation. Direct citizen concern with the environment has been evidenced by the strong stands taken by conservation and citizen activist environment groups that fought the Alaskan pipeline project, the building of atomic power plants, and leases for off-shore drilling purposes. When such issues reach the action stage, their handling calls for public relations judgment and skills. In too many instances, however, those handling such sensitive environmental issues have called public relations professionals into play *after* rather than *before* the decisions are made.

Public relations should play the same role in regard to the environment as it does to consumerism, and one of the chief tasks and responsibilities of the practitioner should be to serve as an "early warning system" concerning public attitudes, opinions, and activities relating to environmental factors. When an organization's actions, activities, products, or services have a serious effect on the environment, advice and counsel about expected public relations are clearly needed. No matter what the final decision, communication skills are needed. Thus, at each step in dealing with matters bearing on the environment there is an obvious need for the kinds of skills that public relations practitioners should be able to provide.

FUNDAMENTAL TRENDS IN AMERICAN SOCIETY AND THEIR EFFECT ON PUBLIC RELATIONS PRACTICE

If we want to make an analogy between the ecology of public relations and a phonograph record, then we have heard one side of the record: the causal side. That is, we have heard why certain fundamental trends in American society have brought on the need for public relations. The flip side of the same record tells us why these same trends have brought about difficult problems for public relations practitioners.

URBANIZATION AND SUBURBANIZATION

Urbanization and suburbanization have had several major effects on the practice of public relations.

On the one hand, the movement from a rural to an urban society has brought about a concentration of the population into large urban centers and has thus made it easier for practitioners to reach people through a smaller number of key mass media than if the population were spread evenly throughout the country. Various media in our largest cities reach millions of people, and it is theoretically possible to reach anywhere from ten million to sixty million people by means of a handful of carefully selected media.

On the other hand, however, these media are not simply open to the highest bidder, but are managed by experienced and sophisticated journalists careful to guard their pages and their air time from intrusion by outsiders. Veteran public relations practitioners know they must gear their messages and approaches so that they *first* meet the high demands of the media "gatekeepers," and this means a skillful meshing of one's private interests with the wider public interests serviced by the media managers.

At the same time, the move to the suburbs has brought about a further dispersion of the population and conflict between people's allegiances. Though millions of wage earners *gain* their living from the city, they *do* their living in the suburbs. As a result, conflicts arise in regard to such areas as taxes, municipal and suburban services, and the like. The astute practitioner has to be keenly aware of the nature of one's loyalties in such conflict situations and use judgment in seeking to resolve what may often seem to be irreconcilable differences.

The trend towards urbanization and suburbanization has thus had the interesting effect of concentrating the population and at the same spreading it out miles beyond the reaches of the inner city. The result has been a significant change in living patterns, social groupings and political affiliations, and attitudes and opinions about a wide variety of issues. All of these call for a wise understanding of the differences existing among people who live and work in our cities; people who work in the city and live in the suburbs; and people who live and work in the suburbs.

LARGE AND COMPLEX ORGANIZATIONS

Any student who attends a large university of 10,000, 20,000, or 30,000 enrollment knows what it means to exist within a large and complex organization. The perceptive student of public relations can immediately recognize the kind of problems that such an organization poses.

One of the first problems is in providing people with some sense of "belonging." A second problem is in attempting to resolve conflicts in needs and demands that inevitably arise in large and complex organizations. When the hourly worker seeks an eight percent increase, he's not really interested in learning that he can't have it because it might mean a decrease in dividends to shareholders. When customers complain about the poor quality of the products they buy, they're not really interested in learning that it resulted from a deliberate action by disgruntled workers. When students complain about constantly increasing tuition, they're not really interested in learning it resulted in part from a drying up of outside giving. Thus, attempting to resolve conflicts in needs and demands calls for astute and carefully designed explanations, and all too often the explanation will satisfy one constituency but not another.

A final problem facing practitioners who deal with large and complex organizations is the sheer distortion of messages that arises when communication has to move through the many layers that make up such organizations. The problem becomes particularly acute when the central headquarters and its public relations staff is in one city, and the constituency is spread out across the entire country. What seems clear-cut in an office in Chicago's Loop can become cloudy and murky in a plant community in the Deep South. The public relations staffer reporting to the chancellor on the main campus of a multi-university finds it difficult to understand what's really going on at a branch campus several hundred miles away. Maintaining contact, keeping in touch, and understanding the diverse nature, needs, wants, and desires of people existing within large and complex organizations inevitably affect public relations practice and procedures.

GROWTH IN THE POWER OF PUBLIC OPINION AND THE SWIFTNESS IN OPINION CHANGE

Public relations practitioners use primary-direct and secondary-indirect methods in dealing with the vital tasks of assaying and attempting to influence public opinion.

When public relations practice was in its infancy, practitioners relied on relatively primitive methods of measuring public opinion. Just as many small newspapers today measure public opinion by sending a reporter out to do man-woman-on-the-street interviewing, so the early practitioners conducted similar interviews with "average" people and "opinion leaders." Today, however, most practitioners recognize the need for a scientific approach to public opinion measurement and hence turn to national, regional, and state polling organizations to handle both long-range and individually-commissioned, cross-section, in-depth interview polls. These polls—described in more detail in a later chapter—are carefully designed for a variety of purposes. They're used to measure long-range trends in public attitudes and opinion, to judge consumer reaction to products and services, to ascertain general public or special public moods and attitudes, and to test an organization's reputation among the public at large or among individual publics.

There is also general recognition that a poll is able to measure public opinion only at the time it is taken. Because events and actions can swiftly change the nature of public opinion, practitioners must be cautious in their assessments and constantly alert to the sudden dips in public moods, attitudes, and opinions. This calls for constant monitoring, by means of secondary-indirect methods, of certain weathervanes of opinion change. Long before they become too obvious, changes in public opinion can be detected from trends in news stories and features, articles in national news and opinion magazines and in specialized publications, and books by men and women who have the deserved reputation for sizing up the public scene.

Through such means, practitioners treat the power of public opinion by analyzing it to provide "intelligence" data and information for the organizations they serve. They also use their other skills in attempting to influence public opinion in meeting predetermined public relations goals and objectives. These skills and techniques—described in detail in the chapters on planning, programming, and communicating—make up the core of public relations practice. They've been refined and developed because dealing with public opinion requires the highest degree of public relations competence.

CHANGES IN THE TECHNOLOGY, ROLE, AND IMPACT OF THE MASS MEDIA

Although, as noted earlier in this chapter, there have been technological breakthroughs within the mass media in the past decade, basic concepts about news have remained surprisingly constant. News can be transmitted much more swiftly than in the past and television has brought instant history into the living room, but the elements that make one story of national significance and another of only local interest remain the same.

Thus, the practitioner should be on top of technological changes in the mass media, but it's more important that the practitioner know when the media will be interested in a particular story or feature. Equally important, the practitioner has to be aware of changes in editorial policy, format, and personnel; to know, for example, the varying deadlines and technical imperatives of differing media; to understand how to ride the crest of the wave of mutual interest shown by all media in certain kinds of stories and events; and to be attuned to the justified criticisms leveled by the media against the amateurs who flood their offices with material that has little interest to readers and viewers.

Practitioners keep track of mass media changes by maintaining personal contact with mass media personnel and by careful reading of publications which reflect developments in the mass media. These include *Editor and Publisher, Broadcasting, Variety*, the *Columbia Journalism Review*, various major city and statewide journalism reviews, *Journalism Quarterly*, the AP and UPI internal organs, *ASNE Bulletin*, the press sections of *Time* and *Newsweek*, and the numerous books about the mass media which have been published in increasing numbers in recent years. The hack keeps sending out releases en masse to hundreds of outlets which can have little interest in the material; the skilled practitioner knows the value of keying material to the needs and interests of different media and of keeping abreast of changing media developments.

CONSUMERISM AND ENVIRONMENTAL SENSITIVITY

This trend presents both an internal and external problem to the public relations practitioner. The internal problem arises because the criticisms and complaints of the consumer and those sensitive to the environment are directed at areas of organizational activities which are not directly in the control of the public relations practitioner. The practitioner does not make or produce the products or services or engage in organizational activities and actions which fail to measure up to the expectations of the consumer or the environmentalist. These are the provinces of other functions within organizations: the marketing department which distributes and sells the product through high-pressure methods; the advertising department which extolls products far beyond normal belief; the executive who directs or countenances price-fixing, strip-mining, and carefully "washed" contributions of money to bring about large contracts. Handling and dealing with these internally produced and managed activities and factors calls for the wisdom of Solomon, the patience of Job, and the skill of Moses.

But the external problem connected with consumerism and environmental sensitivity is equally difficult and taxing. When consumer and environmental activists and/or the government target in on an organization's transgressions—or alleged transgressions—the matter becomes one of public interest and display. All too often, in such cases the practitioner is called upon to work some sleight of hand and magically disarm the dragon slayers. Unfortunately, in recent years the shafts and slings of consumer and environmental activist organizations and the government are frequently a justified reaction to products, services, and actions that do not measure up to expectations.

Thus, handling the challenges raised by consumerism and environmental sensitivity calls for ways and means of handling the dilemma posed by the internal-external demands placed on the practitioner. The following basic recommended procedures, organized by Richard A. Aszling of General Foods for PRSA chapter workshops on consumerism, suggest that the practitioner:

> Be on top of developments by staying informed about legislative developments and activist actions. Know the literature and the reliable information sources
>
> Seek to provide realistic forecasts of trends and developments
>
> Develop effective communication upwards to boss or client and thus help him stay sensitive and to sort out fact from fancy
>
> Be familiar with the successful programs of response to consumer pressures carried out by other companies
>
> Advise employer or client on effective methods of responding to expressions of consumer dissatisfaction
>
> Develop and carry out effective internal and external communication programs designed to make publics aware of steps taken on behalf of consumers[11]

ENDNOTES

1. Dan J. Forrestal, "Placing Public Relations in Perspective," *Public Relations Journal*, March 1974, p. 6.
2. Scott Cutlip and Allen Center, *Effective Public Relations*, 4th ed. (Englewood Cliffs, N.J.: Prentice-Hall, 1971), p. 100.
3. T. D. Allman, "The Urban Crisis Leaves Town and Moves to the Suburbs," *Harpers*, December 1978, p. 41.
4. Robert Presthus, *The Organizational Society* (New York: Random House, Vintage Books, 1965), pp. 205-208.
5. Marshall McLuhan, *Understanding Media* (New York: McGraw-Hill, 1965), p. 4.
6. A.C. Nielsen figures cited in *Broadcasting*, June 20, 1983, p. 8.
7. Data from *Editor and Publisher Yearbook* and *Broadcasting Yearbook*.
8. Ben Bagdikian, *The Information Machines* (New York: Harper and Row, 1971), p. 61.
9. Arthur H. White, "Changing Rules of the Game in the American Marketplace," *Public Relations Journal*, October 1973, p. 6.
10. Howard P. Hudson, "Consumer Affairs in Perspective," *Public Relations Quarterly*, Fall 1980, p. 5.
11. John R. O'Connell, "What Should the Public Relations Practitioner Be Doing?" *Public Relations Journal*, December 1972, p. 30.

PROJECTS, ASSIGNMENTS, AND MINIS

1. RELATING A POPULATION CHANGE TO PUBLIC RELATIONS PRACTICE: A POSITION PAPER

As noted in Figure 5.2, one of the significant population changes in the United States between 1970 and 1980 was the increase among those living in the urban fringe of central cities and the decrease of those living in central cities. As stated in the text, those living in the suburbs of central cities in 1980 were the largest single group in the population in terms of where people live.

You are to consider that you work as a research assistant in the public relations department at the national headquarters of a nonprofit social agency that has branches and units throughout the country. You have been given the assignment of exploring the current (at the time you are using this text) extent of the movement from a rural to an urban-suburban society and of a population that resides mainly in the urban fringe of central cities. You are to set forth a position paper answering the following questions:

1. How and in what ways do the above-mentioned changes affect your organization's basic **programming** and **activities**?

2. What are the special **public relations problems** the above-mentioned changes cause for your organization? Be sure to explain these problems in some detail.

In handling this assignment, select a nonprofit social agency you know something about. By all means utilize a variety of resources in researching and handling the assignment.

2. PREDICTING SOCIAL AND POLITICAL CHANGES: A RESEARCH REPORT

In a talk to a group of public relations counselors, George Hammond of Carl Byoir & Associates, Inc., emphasized the need to meet client expectations in the decade of the eighties:

"Our clients know that they're not going to enjoy the luxury of the status quo," Hammond told the counselors. "They want and expect help from us in dealing with large-scale social and political changes that are coming at mind-boggling speed. It will take hindsight and the particular kind of broad experience we bring to the client/agency relationship to spot some of these changes and invent the most effective ways to deal with them."

Among Byoir clients at the time were A&P (The Great Atlantic & Pacific Tea Company); Eastman Kodak; F.W. Woolworth; Hallmark Cards; and Toyota Motor Sales, U.S.A.

You are to assume you work for the Byoir organization. Hammond has asked you to select one of the above-mentioned Byoir clients and, through library research, ascertain key data bout the company relative to its products, sales, and important publics.

Your assignment is to write the draft of a two- to three-page memorandum, addressed to the client, setting forth some of the major large-scale social and political changes that you predict will take place in the country in the next five years. Try to be specific in assessing these predicted changes in American life and in relating them to the client's major goals and purposes. Wherever possible, cite data from reliable sources to buttress the wisdom of your predictions, insights, and judgment.

(*Note:* Do *not* assume that the five fundamental trends cited in this chapter are *the* answer to this assignment, but rather see them as illustrative of the type of societal and political changes you may want to deal with in your memorandum.)

3. THREE MAJOR MEDIA DEVELOPMENTS: A RESEARCH REPORT

Each year significant developments occur that involve the ownership, management, operation, and status of the mass media. Such developments, of course, have important consequences for the practice of public relations.

You are to assume that you are on the public relations staff of one of America's largest national corporations. You have been given the assignment of researching and reporting *three major developments* occurring this past year and involving either the ownership, management, operation, or status of one or more of the mass media. Your source can be news stories in the daily press, articles in news and/or trade publications, court decisions, and other such items.

In a memorandum to your department head, cite each development in detail, cite the source for your information, and include an explanation of how each development may affect public relations practice.

6

THE PRACTITIONERS (1): ADVANTAGES/ DISADVANTAGES, ROLES, AND RESPONSIBILITIES

 herever there's a function, there are bound to be functionaries. So it is with the public relations function. This chapter and Chapter 7 will deal with the two major types of practitioners: those who operate internally within public relations departments and those working externally within counseling firms. Both internal and external systems of handling public relations have their advantages and disadvantages.

THE FUNCTION HANDLED INTERNALLY THROUGH DELEGATION TO A DEPARTMENT OR STAFF

In most sizable organizations that deal with many publics, the task of utilizing public relations principles, talents, and techniques is entrusted to a department or staff—and sometimes to a single person—specifically empowered and assigned to carry out the public relations function.

In such instances the public relations job is considered important enough and of such magnitude to justify the need for a specialized staff organized into a separate department or integrated with another department. An example would be the public relations department of a large university or business, the public relations staff of a large hospital, or the advertising/public relations department of a large industrial organization or trade association.

It's within this system and the one which follows that most public relations practitioners operate in the United States. The internal staff might be just one person or it might be many people, but the common feature is that the public relations function is entrusted to professionals.

THE FUNCTION HANDLED EXTERNALLY BY A COUNSELING FIRM OR ADVERTISING AGENCY

Large organizations often assign the public relations task, by contract, to a public relations counseling firm or to the public relations department of an advertising agency.

In such instances the managements of large organizations believe that the public relations task can best be carried out by outside firms who represent a wide variety of clients and have proven expertise which may not be possible to achieve through an internal staff or department. An example would be a contract signed with a public relations counseling firm to handle all or certain specific public relations tasks of a national concern whose stock is publicly owned and traded, or a similar contract made with the advertising agency that handles the concern's national advertising and is capable of carrying out specified public relations tasks.

As will be explained later, there are sound reasons why organizations seek outside counsel to handle the public relations function. Proof that this arrangement works satisfactorily is found in the fact that numerous large companies have been served by the same public relations counseling firm for many years, some for periods ranging between fifteen and twenty-five years.

THE FUNCTION HANDLED BY INTERNAL DEPARTMENT AND OUTSIDE COUNSEL

Though many large organizations have their own public relations departments, they also retain public relations counseling firms or the public relations departments of advertising agencies. Thus, we have a *combination of the internal staff or department and the outside firm* working together to achieve desired public relations results.

In such instances the managements of large organizations utilize the inside-outside arrangement. An example would be a large midwestern manufacturing concern which has its own public relations department at the concern's headquarters/plant site, but which utilizes a New York City-based counseling firm or ad agency public relations department in an adjunct capacity.

Though one may wonder why organizations with internal public relations departments would also find it advisable to employ outside counsel, the arrangement is a common one. Counseling firms, for example, may be able to provide certain services that the internal department is not geared to handle. An outside firm may be more objective and free from certain political restraints that inhibit the internal staffer. For these and many other reasons, the internal-external combination is on the increase in American public relations activity.

Each of the three methods of handling public relations has advantages that the others either do not possess or cannot equal. Yet, given proper circumstances, what may on the surface seem to be an advantage can just as easily turn out to be a disadvantage. It's therefore of value to consider both the advantages and disadvantages of each system.

INTERNAL STAFF OR DEPARTMENT: ADVANTAGES

Although there are many advantages to having the public relations function carried out by an internal staff or department, authorities in the field believe that the three major advantages are:

1. Knowledge of the organization
2. Availability
3. Team membership

Each of these, ranked in no particular order of importance, is discussed below.

KNOWLEDGE OF THE ORGANIZATION

Any competent public relations person working on the public relations staff o organization ought to have an intimate working knowledge of the entire organization for which he or she works. This should include knowledge of the key *people, products,* and *activities* of the organization; the *"politics"* of the organization; and forthcoming and upcoming *changes* affecting people, products, and activities.

Most organizations publish nice, tidy charts which indicate where everyone belongs and the role assigned to each. But the charts often mask reality, and the astute public relations man or woman should know what really goes on. To do the job properly the practitioner ought also to have advance knowledge of important changes affecting people, products, and activities. There are three basic reasons behind this necessity of having an insider's knowledge:

1. Public relations functions at the optimum when its advice and counsel is sought *in advance,* not after the event.
2. The output of public relations staffs and departments is most effective when it accurately reflects an organization's activities and policies.
3. The public relations department ought to be the department most available to the media when they seek information about an organization. If the department cannot provide this information or aid the media in securing it, then the media will get their information by other means.

AVAILABILITY

Though a large share of public relations activity involves such routine duties as preparing brochures and publishing periodic newsletters, reports, and magazines, every organization has moments when the unexpected demands immediate public relations action. Being on the spot at such moments is of inestimable value in providing the right kind of advice, suggesting the most effective action, and following through with the proper response.

Sometimes the situation will call only for the giving of advice, but advice given by people who are on the scene has an advantage over advice given from afar. The same applies to the action to be taken and the response to be made. The hospital with its own internal public relations department has a great advantage over one without such a department when a national figure is seriously injured and brought to its emergency room or wing. The college with its own internal public relations department has a great advantage over one without such a department when its faculty or staff suddenly go out on strike. The large research complex with its own internal public relations department has a great advantage over one without such a department when an explosion takes place in one of its laboratories.

Proper timing is so often the key to successful public relations that its role cannot be overestimated. Timing, in turn, relies on the availability of public relations personnel, and the internal public relations person has the advantage of being always available.

TEAM MEMBERSHIP

The very fact that a public relations department has been established within an organization makes the members of that department part of the management team. Most public relations functions and activities are related to other departments and their activities, so the relationship should be cordial, friendly, and cooperative. As an insider who is called upon to interact almost daily with personnel in other departments, the internal public relations man or woman has many opportunities to develop a cooperative working relationship with those in other departments. The more the public relations person demonstrates his or her value and worth to the organization and particularly to other departments in the organization, the more solid becomes the relationship and the more valuable the factor of team membership.

INTERNAL STAFF OR DEPARTMENT: DISADVANTAGES

Two of the three factors which comprise the major advantages of the internal staff or department—availability and team membership—can prove to be dysfunctional in certain circumstances.

There is such a thing as being *too available.* In many organizations there is either no clear understanding of public relations or else there is a tendency to dump on the department many duties and responsibilities which do not belong in the department or which are peripheral to the department's main duties. There is no great mystery about why this happens. Public relations, by its very nature and name, involves relations with the public. Many of an organization's activities do not fall clearly within the province of any single department, but do involve the public. The organization has a public relations department; ergo, dump the matter into the lap of the public relations department.

Availability and interpersonal relationships within an organization have a great deal to do with how much and how often the public relations department will be saddled with peripheral public relations matters. The head of the personnel department, for example, ordinarily wouldn't think of asking outside public relations counsel to assist in a personal matter that might touch on public relations activity. But he might very well make that same request of the public relations department if it's right in the next office headed by someone he lunches with every day. If the request is made by the chief executive or other high official of the organization, it's even more difficult to turn it down.

> Responsibility for all social and health agency fund drives carried out in the main plant of a large industrial concern is assigned to the plant personnel department. This year the plant manager has been elected president of the city's United Way organization. He is so busy running the plant he needs someone to do most of his work for the United Way. Both the personnel manager and the public relations manager have more than enough to do handling their own work, but the plant manager asks the public relations manager rather than the personnel manager to help him with his United Way duties for the year. As he explains it: being president of the United Way brings goodwill to the plant, and the development of goodwill is a public relations function.

Team membership can be as dysfunctional as availability. *Being a member of the team can cloud one's objective vision,* yet at all times the public relations practitioner needs a clear-eyed view of what's going on. When such a view indicates that one's fellow "teammate" is responsible for product flaws uncovered by an inquiring journalist, what responsibility does the public relations man have to the truth, to his organization, and to his fellow member of the team? When such a view indicates a "teammate's" clear incompetence, which in turn can lead to a loss of public confidence in the organization, it becomes difficult to expose such incompetence within the councils of the organization. The ultimate in professional frustration and dysfunction occurs when top management itself is incompetent but expects the public relations practitioner team member to present the executive to the public as highly competent and able. At such a time the practitioner would gladly trade the so-called advantage of team membership for a job on the assembly line.

THE COUNSELING FIRM: ADVANTAGES

The major advantages of the public relations counseling firm (or the public relations department of an advertising agency) are seen by most authorities to be fourfold:

1. Objectivity
2. Wide range of experience and talents
3. Flexibility
4. Economy

Each of these, ranked in no particular order of importance, is discussed below.

OBJECTIVITY

The outside public relations counselor is not a member of the inside organization or team, and this is a virtue because the counselor brings an objective view to public relations problems. The outside counselor calls the shots as he sees them, not as management thinks he *ought* to see them. He is usually retained with the expectation that he will be objective. If he tells some hard truths, gives advice and counsel which causes him to lose the account, the world doesn't come to an end as a result. (That is, unless the counseling firm has only a few accounts and this is a major one.) The outside counselor does not wear rose-colored glasses which cast a euphoric glow over every perceived problem, but bifocals which allow a realistic, *objective* look at problems.

WIDE RANGE OF EXPERIENCE AND TALENTS

Counseling firms which have been in business for any appreciable length of time have dealt with almost every conceivable type and kind of public relations problem and situation. The longer the firm has been in business, the more its experience in handling a wide diversity of problems and situations can be taken for granted. A new problem to the client has probably been handled by the counseling firm many times in the past.

Further, the well-established counseling firms have on their roster not only account executives with wide experience but also specialists in educational, media, and financial relations; consumerism; pollution; graphics; photography; and a host of other areas. These specialists are there to serve the account executive (and the client) when the situation calls for their expertise.

FLEXIBILITY

Public relations counseling firms have great flexibility chiefly because they can move their personnel around when there is need. At any one time, as the demand requires, these firms can move staff personnel from old Account X to new Account Y or assign an account executive to take on the supervision of a new account as part of her nominal responsibilities.

ECONOMY

Counseling firms are not inexpensive entities, but they can prove to be economical in certain circumstances. For example, when an organization has a limited but definite amount of public relations work to be achieved, it's more economical to utilize a counseling firm rather than to set up a permanent staff with salaries, equipment and supply needs, adjunct salaried personnel, and overhead costs. When an organization runs into a public relations problem which may last only one or two years, again the counseling firm route would be less expensive than to employ full-time staff. Finally, when an organization has certain special needs—such as the need to reach the financial community or the New York City media outlets—it's more economical to utilize a counseling firm rather than hire a financial relations expert or establish a New York City office.

THE COUNSELING FIRM: DISADVANTAGES

Advantages which counseling firms hold can prove to be dysfunctional under certain circumstances.

The outside counseling firm can generally be more objective than the internal practitioner, but it becomes difficult to maintain such objectivity when the counseling firm has had the same account and dealt with the same people for ten, twenty, or thirty years. At such times the nominal outsider virtually is looked upon as a member of the "inside" team.

The larger the account, the more sizable the yearly fee, and the greater the role of a client in the counselor's roster, the greater the likelihood of loss of objectivity if such objectivity can lead to loss of the account. Counselors have resigned accounts when their objective advice is constantly ignored by the client. However, such account resignations become increasingly difficult and economically painful when the account is a very large one, the yearly fee is very sizable, and the account represents half of the counselor's total yearly billing.

Getting to know you—as the song went in "The King and I"—is a pleasurable experience when one is governess to the king's children. It becomes more difficult to bring about when one is outside counsel to a large and complex organization which has difficult public relations problems. Clients become very edgy in the early stages of the counselor-client relationship. They desire immediate results, but results are not usually brought about until the counselor has a close and intimate grasp of the client's organization, personnel, policies, practices, and problems. Impatience on the part of the client; the geographical distance between the client and the counselor; internal political maneuvering; innate distrust of strangers; unwillingness to give up one's turf—all these provide stumbling blocks as the counselor seeks to obtain a close and intimate grasp of the client's organization, personnel, policies, practices, and problems.

Counseling firms provide Cadillac public relations service, but unfortunately most small and medium-sized organizations can only afford medium-priced cars. The most prestigious counselors are located in New York City, Chicago, and other large cities, which means they have to pay high salaries and rent and incur high overhead costs which in turn have to be reimbursed through fees which, though reasonable, are still high to many would-be clients. Though the relatively small would-be client may not agree, he is fortunate when he is told at the outset by the large, prestigious counseling firm: "Look, you really can't afford to retain us. Why not try Firm X, they're more in your price range."

INTERNAL-EXTERNAL COMBINATION: ADVANTAGES

As has already been noted, certain advantages accrue to organizations having their own public relations departments, and there are certain other advantages to utilizing a counseling firm. It would seem logical to assume that the combination of the two would provide the best of all possible worlds. Burson-Marsteller underscores the combination advantages in the description of the firm's role and resources given in Figure 6.1.

In effect, the combination provides a balance, and when the tandem operation is working well it's hard to fault. The internal staff, for example, may be too close to the problem to be objective, but the counselor is sufficiently removed to provide objectivity.

The internal public relations director may be too much a member of the "team" to be critical of a colleague when criticism is justified, but the counselor as an outsider is not so bound by organizational politics. In certain situations it may be more economical to use internal staff to handle certain public relations tasks, and in other situations more economical to use the outside counseling firm.

Another advantage of the combination system, not often mentioned because it is mainly psychological and subsurface, is that the utilization of an outside counseling firm lends weight and substance to the internal department. When the internal director proposes a certain line of action and is backed up by a reputable counseling firm, the proposal seems to gain stature (even though it's still the same proposal).

INTERNAL-EXTERNAL COMBINATION: DISADVANTAGES

The chief disadvantage of the combination system is that it entails additional expenditures for public relations services. Two may be able to live as cheaply as one in popular mythology, but not in the world of public relations. There's no problem when management recognizes or agrees that the additional expenditures are essential and justified. There's a definite problem, though, when management is uncertain whether the additional expenditures are essential in terms of the end results. Legend has it that a newcomer to wealth thought he might want to buy a yacht so he asked J.P. Morgan how much it cost to maintain his yacht. Whereupon Morgan replied: "If you have to worry about the cost you can't afford a yacht." The same might apply to the cost of public relations counsel; if you have to worry about cost, you probably shouldn't retain outside counsel.

THE PRACTITIONER'S ROLE AND RESPONSIBILITIES

Whether they work internally or externally the practitioners carry out a wide variety of tasks. In describing these tasks and responsibilities, some authorities take a broad approach while others zero in on specific, more narrow duties. The views of the authorities are not necessarily inconsistent because a practitioner's perceived duties and responsibilities may well depend on the position held by the practitioner. One would certainly

---

not expect a vice-president of public relations to have the same job responsibilities as a recent graduate in an entry-level position. Keep in mind, therefore, that the discussion that follows deals first with higher-level roles and responsibilities and then with lower-level ones.

THE BROAD PICTURE

In a recent study, senior executives representing banks, hotels, utilities, colleges, health institutions, government agencies, and trade associations were asked for their views of the public relations role and function in their institutions. Those interviewed listed the following five job characteristics as the major responsibility of the public relations staff:[1]

1. Communicating and defending management actions to the public.

2. Keeping management informed about public reactions to what an organization does.

3. Identifying for top management social or political problems, needs, and issues that may be of importance to the organization.

4. Helping top management to develop and execute a constructive response to key issues affecting the organization.

5. Setting goals and priorities in deciding what communications programs to recommend to senior management.

(It's instructive to compare the above five to the duties and responsibilities of the practitioner cited in Exhibit 6.1, the **Official Statement on Public Relations** adopted by the Assembly, governing body of the Public Relations Society of America, November 1982.)

In summing up the results of the study, Walter Lindenmann and Alison Lapetina of Hill and Knowlton's Group Attitudes Corporation said it shows that the greatest perceived strength of the public relations professional is in serving as an interpreter for management. Of interest is that the senior executives felt that the public relations *field* shows great promise for the 1980s, but that the practitioners do not know enough about the fields they are in. The administrator of a large hospital commented in these words in analyzing professional weaknesses: "Public relations people need a broader knowledge of problems and issues. Continuing education is essential to keep up with the issues. Public relations people also lack good management skills. More development is needed in the areas of budgeting, proper use of time, and the ability to look at the big picture."

The "big picture" must certainly have been on the mind of Harold Burson, chairman of Burson-Marsteller, when he set forth the following four roles for the public relations professional:[2]

> **The Early Warner:** Public relations executives serve as the sensor of social change. They perceive those rumblings at the heart of society that augur good or ill for their organizations. And, after detecting the yearnings and stirrings, they interpret the signals for management.

> **The Conscience:** The second role the public relations professional must fulfill is that of corporate conscience. One should not infer from this that public relations people behave in ways more moral and ethical or more in the public interest than executives with different titles. . . . But being the professional corporate conscience is not part of the job description of other executives. It is part of the job description of the chief public relations officer.

> **The Communicator:** The third major role of the public relations professional is that of communicator—internally and externally. Internal communications must do more than tell or inform. Its primary function is to bring about understanding. . . . Communicating with the public outside the corporation is an equally critical undertaking. The problem for the public relations professional is to convince the public that the corporation is, indeed, being responsive.

EXHIBIT 6.1

OFFICIAL STATEMENT ON PUBLIC RELATIONS
(Formally adopted by PRSA Assembly, November 6, 1982.)

Public relations helps our complex, pluralistic society to reach decisions and function more effectively by contributing to mutual understanding among groups and institutions. It serves to bring private and public policies into harmony.

Public relations serves a wide variety of institutions in society such as businesses, trade unions, government agencies, voluntary associations, foundations, hospitals and educational and religious institutions. To achieve their goals, these institutions must develop effective relationships with many different audiences or publics such as employees, members, customers, local communities, shareholders and other institutions, and with society at large.

The managements of institutions need to understand the attitudes and values of their publics in order to achieve institutional goals. The goals themselves are shaped by the external environment. The public relations practitioner acts as a counselor to management, and as a mediator, helping to translate private aims into reasonable, publicly acceptable policy and action.

As a management function, public relations encompasses the following:

- **Anticipating, analyzing and interpreting public opinion, attitudes and issues which might impact, for good or ill, the operations and plans of the organization.**

- **Counseling management at all levels in the organization with regard to policy decisions, courses of action and communication, taking into account their public ramifications and the organization's social or citizenship responsibilities.**

- **Researching, conducting and evaluating, on a continuing basis, programs of action and communication to achieve informed public understanding necessary to the success of an organization's aims. These may include marketing, financial, fund raising, employee, community or government relations and other programs.**

- **Planning and implementing the organization's efforts to influence or change public policy.**

- **Setting objectives, planning, budgeting, recruiting and training staff, developing facilities—in short, *managing* the resources needed to perform all of the above.**

- Examples of the knowledge that may be required in the professional practice of public relations include communication arts, psychology, social psychology, sociology, political science, economics and the principles of management and ethics. Technical knowledge and skills are required for opinion research, public issues analysis, media relations, direct mail, institutional advertising, publications, film/video productions, special events, speeches and presentations.

In helping to define and implement policy, the public relations practitioner utilizes a variety of professional communication skills and plays an integrative role both within the organization and between the organization and the external environment.

Source: "Society Adopts Official Statement on Public Relations," *PRSA Newsletter,* November/December 1982, pp. 1 and 3. Reprinted with permission. (Boldface added.)

The Monitor: The fourth function of the public relations professional is to serve as a corporate monitor. Since public relations is involved with public issues, there is a need for constant monitoring of corporate policies and programs to make sure that they match public expectation. If the programs are not functioning or if they fall short of expectations, it is the professional's job to agitate for new programs and new policies. If the professionals fail to do so, they fail to live up to the requirements of their job.

Four seems to be a popular number with those assessing the role of public relations practitioners. Like Burson, Glen M. Broom of the San Diego State University public relations teaching staff perceives four conceptual role models for the public relations professional. He cites them as follows:[3]

The Expert Prescriber: In this role, the practitioner operates as the authority on both public relations problems and their solutions. . . . The practitioner researches and defines the problem, develops the program and takes major responsibility for its implementation.

The Communication Technician: These practitioners are typically hired on the basis of their communication and journalistic skills—writing, editing, and working with the media. Rather than being part of the management team, practitioners in this role are primarily concerned with preparing and producing communication materials for the public relations effort.

The Communication Facilitator: In this role the practitioner serves as a liaison, interpreter and mediator between the organization and its publics. The emphasis is on maintaining a continuous flow of two-way communication. Another major concern is with removing barriers to the exchange of information to keep the channels of communication open.

The Problem-Solving Process Facilitator: As members of the management team, practitioners operating in this role collaborate with others throughout the organization to define and solve problems. The public relations practitioner helps guide other managers and the organization through a rational problem-solving process that may involve all parts of the organization in the public relations planning and programming process. Likewise, the practitioner maintains a high level of management involvement in implementing all phases of the program.

Broom found in his study of PRSA members that most of the respondents saw themselves as expert prescribers. A distant second was the problem-solving facilitator. The communication technician and the communication facilitator were virtually tied for third. Broom's study also showed that men and women in public relations differ significantly in regard to the four roles. Half of the women see themselves primarily as communication technicians, while close to 60 percent of the men report that their dominant role is that of the expert prescriber. Table 6.1 shows the distribution of dominant roles for men and women.[4]

TABLE 6.1

Perceived Dominant Roles by Sex

	Men (n = 300)	Women (n = 117)
Expert Prescriber	58%	34%
Communication Technician	21	51
Communication Facilitator	5	4
Problem-Solving Facilitator	16	11

$(x^2 = 36.7, \text{d.f.} = 3, p > .001)$

SPECIFIC ACTIVITIES

The broad, generalized description of the practitioner's role, cited in the previous section, becomes more specific when explained in terms of work that the practitioner actually does. Authorities generally agree that most public relations positions involve one or more of the following activities:

- **Advice and counsel:** Providing advice and counsel on organizational policies and actions which have public relations ramifications. Given to both top management and to line departments when situations and problems indicate the need for public relations input and expertise.

- **Media relations:** Setting up and maintaining open channels of communication with mass media personnel.

- **Programming:** Analyzing problems and opportunities, defining goals, objectives, publics, strategies, and plans.

- **Production:** Producing publications, brochures, flyers, reports, films, and slide-sound presentations.

- **Relations with publics:** Establishing and maintaining two-way communications with those publics deemed important to the organization.

- **Research and evaluation:** Carrying out or sponsoring studies of key publics, issues, and trends. Used both for intelligence-gathering and evaluation of work carried out.

- **Special events:** Planning and handling special showings, convention exhibits, anniversary and new facility celebrations, awards programs, tours, and special meetings.

- **Speaking:** Preparing speeches for others and also delivering speeches and talks to groups and organizations.

- **Writing and editing:** Generating all forms of publicity, written reports, scripts, items

---

TABLE 6.2

Public Relations Activities Reported by 4,500 PRSA Members

Activity	Percent
Media relations	64.0
Public relations management or administration	60.4
Publicity	60.0
Community relations	45.8
Public relations counseling	40.9
Editor of publications	33.9
Employee relations	27.8
Government relations	24.3
Invester relations	16.3
Consumer affairs	14.2
Public relations teaching	7.9
Advertising/sales promotion	4.4
(Multiple responses were invited on the question)	

---

for magazines and newsletters, stockholder reports, product information and technical reports. Though last in alphabetical order, perhaps the most crucial of public relations' roles.

In one of the most comprehensive surveys ever of public relations people, 4,500 PRSA members reported that the activities most often carried out are those involving the media, public relations management/administration, and publicity.[5] The survey results, cited in Table 6.2, represent the responses from more than half the then-existing total membership of the society. Nearly two-thirds of the respondents, 64 percent, see themselves first, and foremost, involved in media relations. Virtually tied for second were the 60.4 percent citing "Public relations management or administration" and the 60 percent citing "Publicity" as main activities.

Summing up and making sense of the work activities of public relations people requires that one recall the description of the public relations function and process cited

---

EXHIBIT 6.2

**Positions Held by a Random Sample of
Graduates of One Institution, 1974-1983**

A random sampling of graduates of one institution offering a public relations major shows the variety of tasks carried out by public relations workers.

Marlene W, '83: Public relations assistant in a 300-bed hospital. Writes press releases, arranges photo opportunities, writes copy and edits internal monthly publication.

Paul McK, '82: Director of public relations, regional cultural/arts institute. Responsible for media relations, publicity, promotional literature, and a limited amount of advertising.

Stacy B, '81: Editorial assistant, international drug firm. Writes articles for monthly, high-quality publication.

John R, '80: Assistant account executive, large New York City counseling firm. Helps service two accounts. Most of work is in product promotion and includes writing and media contacts.

Susan J, '79: Director of public relations, small liberal arts college. Reports to the president. Most of daily work involves publicity, media relations, and graphics.

Laurie C, '78: Publicist, major television network. Writes press releases, arranges press tours and conferences, works with the media.

Peter L, '77: Public relations manager, medium-sized bank with eight branches. Supervises two assistants, reports to bank vice president. Does little writing, but supervises the work of a public relations agency which handles the bank account.

Sol P, '76: Public relations administrator, national trade association. Responsible for national publicity and media relations as well as promotion of the association's two major trade shows. Reports directly to the president of the association.

Kim M, '75: Account executive, medium-sized New York City counseling firm. Handles two accounts, working with marketing director of one and with the public relations director of another. Arranges major press conferences, serves as contact with national media, has major responsibility for promotion of national trade shows.

Stanley D, '74: Vice-president of public relations and advertising, national financial services corporation. Reports to the president, serves as his counsel, and oversees the work of a 60-person department.

---

in Chapter 1. Public relations practitioners serve to link organizations with their environment and the society in which they exist. How this linkage is achieved depends on many variables. Included among these variables are the nature of the organization; the people who manage it; the products it produces and the services it renders; the nature of the various publics important to it; and so forth and so on. The list is long, the variables many, but the core of the work remains in counseling; writing, production, and speaking; and managing the function. Experience and length of time in the field are also key determinants of position responsibilities. Exhibit 6.2 shows positions held and work responsibilities of a random sample of public relations graduates of one institution over a ten-year period.

ENDNOTES

1. Walter Lindenmann and Alison Lapetina, "Management's View of the Future of Public Relations," *Public Relations Review*, Fall 1981, p. 6.
2. Harold Burson, "The Role of Public Relations," Burson-Marsteller brochure, 1982.
3. Glen M. Broom, "A Comparison of Sex Roles in Public Relations," *Public Relations Review*, Fall 1982, p. 17.
4. Ibid.
5. James A. Morrissey, "Will the Real Public Relations Professional Please Stand Up," *Public Relations Journal*, December 1978, p. 25.

PROJECTS, ASSIGNMENTS, AND MINIS

1. WALTER DRAGO ASSESSES HIS AVAILABILITY: A MINI-CASE FOR DISCUSSION

Upon graduation with a degree in public relations, Walter Drago was given a job as director of public relations of a local manufacturing concern with an employee force of 980 in a city of 54,000. The position was a new one and the president of the firm told Drago that his chief responsibility would be to write, edit, and produce a semimonthly internal publication of six to eight pages. Drago was given to understand there would be other duties, but the nature of these was not clearly defined. As the president explained: "Of course, I expect that you will be doing other public relations things, but we'll see about them as they develop. I'm mainly interested in having you produce a fine publication."

Drago found little difficulty in producing the first issue of the new internal publication because there was a backlog of material available for the initial issue. Commencing with the second and third issues, however, he found that a good deal of his time was taken up not only with writing and editing, but with gathering news and exploring story ideas with various department supervisors. Drago began putting in ten-hour days and shortly found himself hard put to meet his publication deadline.

As he reviewed the situation in his own mind two months after starting work as director of public relations, Drago set down on paper some of the activities—other than those connected with the publication—in which he had been engaged. They consisted of the following items:

1. Helping the personnel manager for two days, at his request, produce four advertisements designed to attract much-needed trained machinists for a government contract project the company had suddenly secured.

2. Serving as a tour guide, at the request of the president, when four Japanese industrialists inspected the plant as part of their two-day trip sponsored by the United States Department of State.

3. At the request of the company's vice-president, writing a story announcing the engagement of his daughter to a member of one of Virginia's most prominent families.

4. Answering a variety of letters originally directed to various managers of the company and rerouted by them to Drago for reply. They came from a college student assigned to write a term paper and requesting detailed information about the company; a disgruntled customer who had many complaints; the local newspaper, which was planning a special industrial edition and which asked for a 1,000-word story about the company; and ten members of a sixth-grade class, each of whom said he or she was entered in an essay contest entitled "What Industry Does for Our Community" and would appreciate information about Drago's company.

In reviewing the above activities, Drago found they had substantially interfered with his major responsibility of producing the semimonthly internal publication, but he was not sure what, if anything, he should do about the situation.

Questions for Class Discussion

1. What information, other than that cited in the case fact pattern, would you like to have before answering questions about the case? (Your instructor will provide assumed answers.)

2. Do you consider that Drago has made himself too available, and is this good or bad?

3. What options does Drago have?

4. What do you suggest that Drago do, and why should he do what you suggest?

2. MONDAY MORNING POLICY GROUP: A MINI-CASE

When Pauline Strong was named director of public relations of Rawley College, the school was a medium-sized liberal arts institution with a predominantly white, middle-class student body of 2,500 students; a faculty of 135 full-time teachers; and a non-academic staff of 35 professionals. At the time the president's top management staff consisted of the vice-president of operations; the dean of the faculty; and the dean of student activities. Strong reported directly to the president, but she was not a member of the above-mentioned presidential top management group—known by some on campus as the Hatchetmen—which met every Monday morning to discuss and act on overall college plans, policies, and problems.

Strong's predecessor had devoted the major share of his time to writing news releases and photography. Though Strong wrote major stories from time to time, she assigned the bulk of release writing to the news bureau manager, and she hired a student to take care of photography needs.

During her first six months on the job, Strong spent half her time in her office and the rest of her time becoming personally acquainted with leaders among the faculty, student body, and staff and observing how matters were handled by the Faculty Senate, the Student Assembly, and committees of both groups. In the following year Strong—

- assisted several senior faculty members by editing article manuscripts with which they were having trouble;

- helped the vice-president of operations run a very successful regional conference on college management, and provided the vice-president with guidance and direct assistance in handling statements to the press during a dispute with the maintenance staff;

- aided the dean of faculty by editing a revision of the Faculty Manual, compiling a report updating trends in unionization among faculty in institutions the size and nature of Rawley, and writing several of the dean's speeches to alumni groups around the country;

- upon request, wrote a five-page memorandum to the dean of student activities outlining steps which could be taken to ease racial tension that occurred when the college enrolled a significant number of minority students; and

- volunteered to take on for the president many tasks which did not fall within anyone's special area, but which had important ramifications for the college.

Strong performed the major share of these tasks capably and responsibly.

A year and a half after Strong became director of public relations the president had a long talk with her one Friday afternoon. The president told her that he and the other members of the Monday morning policy group were pleased with her work, and the president especially singled out for praise most of the activities previously cited in this case fact pattern. The president then said that he was somewhat concerned because the other three men had also expressed the opinion that Strong—

- was out of her office too much of the time, hence was not available when public relations matters demanded immediate action;

- became unduly involved at times with matters that were not truly public relations matters; and

- should have made at least one major media placement in the year and a half she had been with the college but had not achieved this objective.

"I've mentioned these things because I had been considering whether to suggest to the Monday group that you become a regular member of it," said the president. "However, when the others cited their reservations in regard to time out of the office and such, I decided to have this talk with you first.

"To be perfectly frank, I've had different reservations. As you may or may not know, the average age of the members of the Monday group is 52 and each member has been with Rawley anywhere from 20 to 24 years. You, on the other hand, are in your late twenties and have been with us less than two years. Furthermore, despite the fact that other senior management people have sought from time to time to be included in the Monday group, I've resisted enlarging the number because I've been most comfortable with the group as it's now constituted.

"On the other hand, I've been favorably impressed with your work and your approach to problems. I think you can contribute to the group, and I have an idea that the person holding your position ought to be included in it.

"We might well discuss this the rest of the afternoon, but what I would like you to do is to think about what I've said and to prepare a reaction memorandum over the weekend. Leave it with my secretary Monday morning, and I'll get back to you sometime during the week."

Assignment

You are to consider yourself to be Pauline Strong. Write the reaction memorandum requested by the president of Rawley College.

Questions for Discussion

1. What other information would you like to have in addition to that provided in the case fact pattern? (Your instructor will provide it if you ask appropriate questions.)

2. Given the information available to you, what's your opinion about the manner in which Pauline Strong has been carrying out her job?

3. If you were Strong, would you make a strong pitch in your reaction memorandum to be included in the Monday morning policy group? Why or why not?

7

THE PRACTITIONERS (2): STRUCTURE AND MANAGEMENT OF INTERNAL DEPARTMENTS AND COUNSELING FIRMS

*I*n continuing this discussion of those who practice public relations, one should recognize that the bulk of public relations practitioners in the United States and Canada work internally within organizations rather than in counseling firms. Sizable numbers are found in government, health, social service, higher education, and similar nonprofit bodies. The largest number of practitioners work for business and industrial concerns and for trade and professional associations.

THE INTERNAL DEPARTMENT

The 1983 *O'Dwyer's Directory of Corporate Communications*—described by its publisher as "the most complete tabulation of corporate PR departments ever assembled" —listed 2,600 companies, 500 major trade associations, and more than 6,000 individual corporate and association public relations people. The listing for each organization contains the name and title of the top executive in charge of public relations, the individual to whom he or she reports, and the number of professionals in the department. The 2,600 companies listed in 1983 compare with 1,293 listed in the first O'Dwyer directory, issued in 1975. According to the directory, more than fifty different names were in use in 1983 to distinguish what America's biggest companies were calling their communications functions.[1]

No matter what the title given to the public relations function, there was clear evidence in the late seventies and early eighties that the status of the function was increasing in the eyes of management. In a special report, *Dun's Review* concluded that "the seventies have introduced a new seriousness to public relations activities. For the first time, public relations campaigns deal with major public policy issues and are managed on a businesslike basis. And some public relations practitioners believe that sobriety may impel management to accept public relations as an essential business function."[2] Despite the weak economic environment public relations held its own in the 1982 recessionary period. In its eighteenth annual survey of the public relations profession, the weekly newsletter *pr reporter* noted that the number of professionals, clerical staff, and budgets had either remained the same in 1982 or increased more than decreased compared with 1981 (see Table 7.1).

TABLE 7.1

Changes in Employment and Budget Items since Last Year

Item	More	Less (In Percentages)	About the Same
Number of professionals	29.0	18.5	52.5
Number of secretarial/clerical workers	17.2	14.7	68.1
Total public relations budget	48.6	21.1	30.3
Use of outside consultants	34.0	26.9	39.1
Use of word processing equipment	76.1	1.1	22.8

Source: "Eighteenth Annual Survey of the Profession," *pr reporter*, October, 18, 1982. Reprinted with permission.

STRUCTURE

There are no definitive guidelines for structuring an internal public relations department, though as a general rule departments are organized in such a manner as to best facilitate the carrying out of their main activities and functions. Where the department is a small one—such as in the case of a social service organization or a hospital—one or sometimes two professionals will be expected to carry out all departmental tasks. As organizations increase in size, so do internal public relations departments. Major industrial organizations, for example, have departments with several hundred professional public relations staffers headed almost invariably by a vice-president in charge of public relations, or public relations and advertising, or communications, or public affairs.

Departments which consist of more than one or two people are usually organized according to one or more of the following:

Publics—consumer relations; stockholder relations; government relations; employee relations; dealer relations; community relations; etc.

Functions—graphics; press and media relations; special events; institutional advertising; internal communications; product publicity; research; trend/issues analysis; public affairs.

Geography—eastern division manager; Washington office; New York City office; international.

Divisions—western division; corporate headquarters; plastics division; Texas division.

Combination—parts or all of the above, as in the case of large industrial and business organizations.

Though public relations is a staff function, the department itself is managed as though it were a line unit. Reporting to the head of the department will be a limited number of managers; each manager in turn supervises the activities of staffers with skills and experience in the specific area for which the manager is responsible.

In Figures 7.2 through 7.4—showing typical small, medium-sized, and large public relations departments—we note how the line relationship expands as the department expands. In the small public relations department we find only a public relations director and three managers. In the medium-sized department, however, there's a vice-president of public relations, four managers, and scores of specialists reporting to these managers. In the large department the vice-president has an administrative assistant and a plans board to aid him, six managers, and scores of specialists—some at division and plant localities—to carry out the many assignments and tasks needed to fulfill the function in a large and complex organization.

FIGURE 7.1 *A small public relations department.*

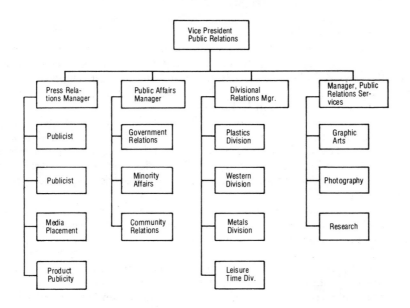

FIGURE 7.2 *A medium-sized public relations department.*

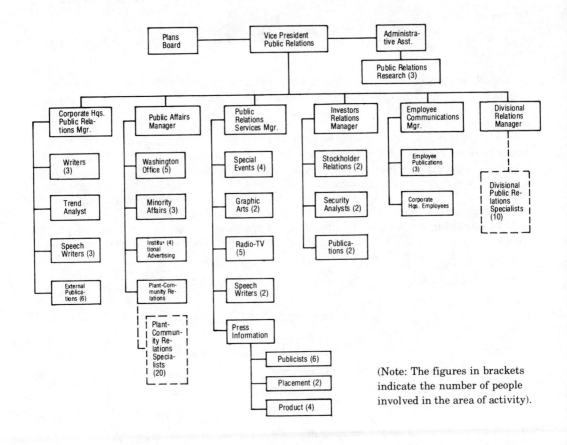

FIGURE 7.3 *A large public relations department.*

(Note: The figures in brackets indicate the number of people involved in the area of activity).

Very large corporations have found it advisable to establish a central, relatively small corporate headquarters public relations staff, and to have public relations activities handled on the division, plant, and/or installation level by staff who report directly to the heads of divisions, plants, and/or installations. Exemplifying this type of public relations organization is that of Litton Industries.

A major electronics company serving worldwide markets with high-technology products and services designed for commercial, industrial, and defense-related applications, Litton Industries had total sales in 1982 of close to $5 billion and an employee force numbering 75,000. Its products include military electronics systems, naval ships, seismic exploration services, machine tools, microwave ovens, electrical equipment, and material handling systems.

Corporate communications at Litton is headed by a vice-president who reports to the chairman and chief executive officer and who supervises a staff of eighteen professionals (see Figure 7.4). Each of the more than ninety divisions of the company is responsible for its own public relations and advertising activities. At the divisional level marketing/sales is usually responsible for marketing communications (product advertising, publicity, sales promotion, and trade shows), while industrial relations is usually responsible for employee communications, local news media, and community/local/state government relations. Outside agencies are retained by many divisions for both product publicity and advertising.

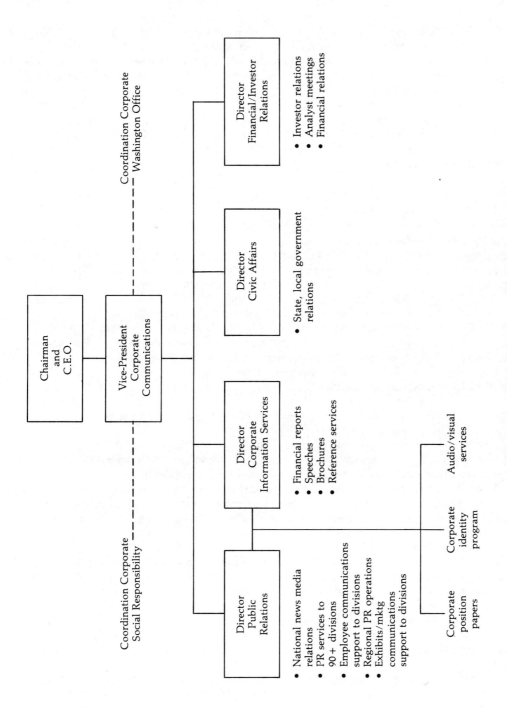

Chairman
and
C.E.O.

Vice-President
Corporate
Communications

Coordination Corporate
Washington Office

Coordination Corporate
Social Responsibility

Director
Public
Relations

- National news media
  relations
- PR services to
  90+ divisions
- Employee communications
  support to divisions
- Regional PR operations
- Exhibits/mktg
  communications
  support to divisions

Corporate
position
papers

Corporate
identity
program

Audio/visual
services

Director
Corporate
Information Services

- Financial reports
- Speeches
- Brochures
- Reference services

Director
Civic Affairs

- State, local government
  relations

Director
Financial/Investor
Relations

- Investor relations
- Analyst meetings
- Financial relations

Courtesy Litton Industries.

FIGURE 7.4 *Corporate communications department, Litton Industries.*

Five regional offices in Washington, New York, Chicago, Beverly Hills, and Zurich, Switzerland, are manned by corporate communications professionals who provide advice and counsel and frequent on-site assistance to operating units in their regions on every communications matter imaginable. The corporate regional offices are also the general conduit for all information to national news media in their regions.

"We find it very practical and effective to work on a regional basis," explains Robert Knapp, director of public relations for Litton Industries. "[For example,] if we get a call anywhere from the Atlanta *Constitution*, our Washington office will respond. Our regional offices are well acquainted with the media in their regions, as well as with the operations of the Litton divisions in their regions. We're in on securities analyst meetings and business plan meetings. We read business operations reports regularly and exchange information tapes, transcripts, etc., constantly. We've a working relationship with the divisions that their responsibility is direct product publicity to the trade and market-place, and our responsibility is the national news media and events or anticipated events that can be of consequence to the corporation."

RELATIONSHIPS WITH LINE, PLANT, AND DIVISION PERSONNEL

In the previous chapter, while discussing "Knowledge of the Organization" as being an advantage to the internal public relations staffer, it was pointed out that nice tidy organization charts often mask the reality of what goes on within the organization. Dangerous medications usually include the notice "Warning, do not keep within the reach of children." Organization charts ought to include the notice "Warning, do not entrust this function to those who lack sensitivity to the nuances of organizational power."

The internal public relations staffer has to be acutely aware of the nuances of organizational power in two particular instances: in his or her relationship with line people; and especially in his or her relationship with plant and/or divisional people.

The three charts denoting the structure of small, medium-sized, and large internal public relations departments indicate that almost every staffer reports on a direct line to someone else in the public relations department. Thus, for example, the staff specialists cited in the chart of the medium-sized department are responsible to one of the four managers who direct their activities.

However, in carrying out these public relations activities, almost all staffers have to interact with line people in other departments of the organization. In so interacting there inevitably come times when the public relations staffer and the line department staffer will not see eye to eye on the handling of a particular situation, stance, or action.

The public relations staffers who ought to be most sensitive to the nuances of power within an organization are those who handle either plant-community relations or division relations. A glance at the chart indicating the structure of a large public relations department provides a hint why this holds true.

According to the chart, under the public affairs manager is a staffer responsible for plant-community relations, and under this staffer are twenty plant-community relations specialists. The chart also shows there is a divisional relations manager, and under this manager are ten divisional public relations specialists. In both instances, there is a dotted line between the twenty plant-community relations specialists and the plant-community relations staffer, and a similar dotted line between the ten divisional public relations specialists and the divisional relations manager. The specialists in both instances are boxed in by dotted lines.

The English translation of this chart language means that so far as plant-community and divisional relationships are concerned this organization operates under a *decentralized system*. The dotted lines indicate that the public relations managers responsible for these two public relations staff functions *have only indirect control* over the specialists under them. The plant-community relations specialists are directly controlled by someone in the line organization of the plant-community to which they are assigned. The divisional public relations specialists are also directly controlled by someone in the line organization of the division to which they are assigned.

This arrangement can and often does work well but can also lead those involved to ulcer gulch. The public relations staffer most likely to find himself in the direct line of a possible cross fire between two superiors is the specialist. Further, the same cross fire can take place if we reverse the situation; that is, if we have this specialist report directly to the public relations staff manager above him and indirectly to someone in the line organization for whom he or she carries out public relations tasks.

BUDGETING

Every organization, even the very smallest, utilizes a budget as a means of predetermining what its anticipated costs, income, and profit will be. Within organizations each individual department—such as the public relations department—is asked in advance of the coming fiscal year to provide a financial forecast. As the public relations department is not an income or profit center, its forecast will set forth the expenses it expects to incur in the coming year. This forecast will receive a certain number of checks and changes as it moves up the organizational ladder towards final approval. Once approved, the department's budget is expected to be adhered to carefully. The department that exceeds its approved budget midway through the fiscal year is going to run into considerable trouble; in fact, it could well come to a standstill.

Thus, budgeting is more than a game played on a ouija board or the future seen murkily through a clouded crystal ball. Budgeting is the financial plan which the department follows in pursuing and achieving its objectives. When objectives, plans, and programs are carefully worked out in advance, then budgeting is not a particularly difficult task. "Catch-22" becomes commonplace, however, when the unforeseen occurs, because how can one budget in advance for the unforeseen and yet how does one secure the money necessary to meet the unforeseen if one hasn't received budget approval in advance? (As will be soon demonstrated, the wily public relations executive finds answers even to this dilemma.)

In handling the department's budget the public relations executive deals with two essential costs:

- **Administrative costs.** These are costs of salaries of the professionals, secretaries, and clerical workers, plus the benefits they receive and such overhead costs as telephone, space, light, heat, office equipment, and others of a similar nature.

- **Program costs.** These are the costs of carrying out the public relations program, and they include costs for research, publications, special events, films, press conferences and media relations in general, and others of a similar nature.

Program costs, which form the key basis for budget-making, fall within three categories: (1) carry-over or continuous programs; (2) projected or new programs; and (3) the unexpected or contingencies.

Carry-over or Continuous Programs

Unless the head of the public relations department is starting entirely from scratch, he or she has the benefit of past experience in setting up the budget for the coming fiscal year. Further, most departments have programs which are of a continuous and more or less permanent nature, and these will usually form the bulk of the department's total program for the coming year. Budgeting for these continuous programs and activities becomes a matter of projecting expected increases (or decreases in case of a dip in prices) over and above (or below) current costs.

Projected or New Programs

Budgeting for projected or new programs which have been approved for the coming year involves figuring out what the administrative and program costs will be. Arriving at cost figures means researching the expected expenses which will be incurred in carrying out elements of the program, and also figuring out the administrative costs. As a hedge, it's also advisable to base cost figures on the "high" side in case prices go up between the time the budget is planned and the program put into effect.

Example. Assume the department plans to institute a new external monthly publication commencing with the next fiscal year. To budget for this the department head would need to know the size and press run of the publication; paper and printing costs; and mailing costs. In addition, the department head would have to cover the costs of department staffers and overhead expense. As a hedge, he would be wise to add six percent to the aforementioned program costs.

The Unexpected or Contingencies

There are three ways in which a department head can handle the troublesome budget problem of the unexpected or contingencies.

Budget for them. In short, include a specific line item in the budget to take care of the unexpected. Label this item either "contingencies" or "miscellaneous," and keep one's fingers crossed. If the line item is too large, those responsible for approving the budget will probably suggest the line figure be for an approved program item. Most budget approvers have an instinctive dislike for "miscellaneous" line figures, hence it's wise to keep the line figure within reasonable limits.

Use other line items. If management will permit the practice, the department head can use, for the unexpected expenses, money that has already been approved but not expended for other line items in the budget. Some managements, recognizing that no one can reasonably be expected to predict the unexpected in advance, will permit the use of unexpended funds from other line items. The problem becomes difficult to solve when this practice is not allowed.

Ask for the funds. When the unexpected or contingencies occur, the most direct way to secure the necessary money is to go to management and ask for it. An understanding management knows one can't fight fires without water and one can't handle unexpected developments without money.

THE COUNSELING FIRM

The closest analogy to the public relations counselor and the public relations counseling firm is the legal counselor and the law firm. Both are retained to give counsel and advice and to provide a variety of services; one does so on public relations matters and the other on legal matters. In both fields there are small, single-member; medium-sized, multi-member; and large counseling firms. In both fields we find counsels situated all over the United States, and in both fields counsels make their living representing a variety of clients.

There are, of course, significant differences between the two. To practice law one needs to be licensed, but you don't need a license to practice public relations. Legal counseling is a much older field of activity, and one finds legal firms—generally single-member entities—in even the smallest towns. Public relations counselors are located chiefly in our larger cities because the bulk of their clients are not single individuals but large organizations. Further, the major share of these clients are in business and industry, and as their headquarters are generally located in our large cities the public relations counselors find it advisable to locate where the clients and media are.

Small towns and cities are not receptive locations for a public relations counseling firm because there is usually not enough potential business for such a firm. Graduating seniors who have majored in public relations sometimes talk about opening and sometimes do open their own counseling firms in a small town or city, but the chances of succeeding in such a milieu are dim. One might pick up a client or two, but they are generally on the basis of single projects involving a political campaign or the production of print material for a fund drive. To succeed, however, a counseling firm needs clients who are willing to pay for public relations services over a period of time, and such clients are not generally found in small towns or cities.

NUMBER

There are no definitive figures for the number of public relations counseling firms in the United States, but the most reliable estimates place the number somewhere between 1,600 and 1,700. The firms range in size from one- or two-member operations to the top two firms, which each have over 1,000 employees.

Jack O'Dwyer, publisher and editor of the weekly newsletter bearing his name, compiles an annual list of the fifty largest United States-based public relations operations. His listing, which includes independent counseling firms and those affiliated with or owned by advertising agencies, ranks firms by net fee income (fees and mark-ups minus any reimbursed expenses) and includes total number of employees (see Exhibit 7.1).

O'Dwyer reported that most of the larger public relations operations performed very well in 1983. Only two of the fifty largest firms showed declines from the previous year, and twenty-three had gains of 20 percent or more. Burson-Marsteller took the number one spot from Hill and Knowlton with net fee income of $63,771,00 compared to H&K's net fee income of $60,807,000. B-M's staff rose to 1,335 while H&K's rose to 1,100. Both public relations firms are subsidiaries of larger advertising agencies, as are four other firms among the top ten. Leading the independents in terms of both net fee income and number of employees were Ruder Finn & Rotman (a merger of two independent firms) and Daniel J. Edelman.

The merger of public relations firms with advertising agencies is a relatively recent development and has mostly involved very large advertising agencies and relatively large public relations counseling firms. The trend started in 1978 when Foote, Cone & Belding acquired Carl Byoir & Associates. It was followed in the next two years by Young & Rubicam's acquisition of Burson-Marsteller; Benton & Bowles's acquisition of Manning, Selvage & Lee; J. Walter Thompson's buyout of Hill and Knowlton; and Batton, Barton, Durstine, and Osborne's acquisition of Doremus & Company. In 1983 Ogilvy & Mather acquired the public relations firm of Dudley-Anderson-Yutzy. In virtually all cases of merger-purchase, the public relations firm has retained its own identity and, to varying degrees, its own operating independence and autonomy. That's how matters stood in 1984 when the public relations subsidiaries were performing well. What will happen when and if they don't perform up to expectations remains to be seen.

STRUCTURE

Counseling firms are basically organized according to (1) *the size and scope of their operations*, but their structure is also affected by (2) *the accounts they service* and by (3) the *kinds of services they emphasize.*

Items 2 and 3 are not major reasons for the structuring of counseling firms, but they occur often enough to warrant explanation. At times a counseling firm will handle a major client that requires a specific type of servicing, and if the client is retained a suffi-

EXHIBIT 7.1

50 LARGEST U.S. PUBLIC RELATIONS OPERATIONS, INDEPENDENT AND AD AGENCY AFFILIATED

FOR YEAR ENDED DECEMBER 31, 1983.   *DENOTES ADVERTISING AGENCY SUBSIDIARY

	1983 Net Fee Income	Employees as of Oct. 15, 1983	% Change from 1982 Income
1. Burson-Marsteller*[1]	$63,771,000	1335	+ 26.2
2. Hill and Knowlton*	60,807,000	1100	+ 12.3
3. Carl Byoir & Associates*	23,800,000	473	+ 8.7
4. Ruder Finn & Rotman	17,650,000	400	+ 8.3
5. Ogilvy & Mather PR*[2]	13,020,000	235	+ 19.7
6. Manning, Selvage & Lee*	10,758,000	178	+ 27.8
7. Daniel J. Edelman	10,120,397	221	+ 21.2
8. Doremus & Company*	9,680,328	163	+ 16.4
9. Booke Communications Incorporated Group	8,784,328	112	+ 60.8
10. The Rowland Company	8,417,500	131	+ 14.2
11. Ketchum PR*	8,411,096	125	+ 8.4
12. Rogers & Cowan	7,980,669	146	+ 31.4
13. Fleishman-Hillard	7,933,125	110	+ 29.6
14. Gray and Company	7,000,000[3]	82	—
15. Robert Marston and Associates	6,093,000	75	+ 19.4
16. Creamer Dickson Basford*[4]	5,435,000	94	+ 1.5
17. Regis McKenna	5,248,000	77	+ 78.8
18. Bozell & Jacobs PR*	4,500,000	70	+ 5.4
19. Golin/Harris Communications	4,206,475	79	+ 23.5
20. Baron/Canning and Company	3,876,100	47	+ 3.2
21. Ayer Public Relations Services*	3,573,000	42	+ 1.9
22. Financial Relations Board	3,357,000	61	+ 23.7
23. Kanan, Corbin, Schupak & Aronow	3,202,110	38	+ 24.2
24. The Strayton Corporation	3,133,000	66	+ 30.0
25. Aaron D. Cushman and Associates	3,026,000	55	+ 16.3
26. Dorf/MJH	2,850,000	68	+ 40.3
27. Richard Weiner	2,850,000	49	+ 49.1
28. Hank Meyer Associates	2,733,512	30	+ 25.4
29. Porter, Novelli and Associates*	2,535,300	51	+ 6.6
30. Anthony M. Franco	2,525,000	50	+ 24.3
31. Lobsenz-Stevens	2,488,000	42	+ 43.4
32. John Adams Associates[5]	2,294,709	36	+ 7.5
33. The Rockey Company	2,220,000	43	+ 4.1
34. Padilla and Speer	2,217,308	30	+ 17.3
35. Gibbs & Soell	2,153,800	37	+ 17.4
36. Mallory Factor Associates	2,101,000	35	+ 30.1
37. The Hannaford Company	2,024,747	35	− 4.2
38. Public Relations Board	1,807,089	49	+ 9.3
39. Geltzer & Company	1,795,345	30	even
40. Simon/Public Relations Inc.	1,772,638	32	+ 39.6
41. Porter, LeVay & Rose	1,658,348	26	+ 45.1
42. ICPR	1,600,504	32	+ 10.5
43. Franson & Associates Public Relations	1,524,387	30	+128.1
44. Charles Ryan Associates	1,507,335	23	− 6.8
45. Kamber Group	1,401,669	33	+ 27.6
46. Woody Kepner Associates	1,342,059	18	+ 9.9
47. Holder, Kennedy & Co.	1,341,791	32	+ 16.3
48. Brum & Anderson	1,321,177	35	+ 51.1
49. The Bohle Company	1,310,415	37	+ 66.9
50. Edward Howard & Co.	1,242,687	22	+ 1.3

1 Does not include Cohn & Wolfe, with net fee income of $2,124,529 in 1983, acquired Jan. 3, 1984.
2 Includes Dudley-Anderson-Yutzy PR, billing $3,449,000 in 1982, acquired May 1, 1983. O&M PR's 1982 fees adjusted to include D-A-Y.
3 Estimate based on preliminary prospectus filed with the Securities & Exchange Commission Dec. 23, 1983.
4 Includes Glick & Lorwin, billing around $700,000, acquired in 1983, for both years.
5 Includes Gray Consulting Group, acquired in 1983.

Copyright 1984 by J.R. O'Dwyer Co. Inc.

Source: O'Dwyer's Directory of Public Relations Firms, 1984 (New York: J.R. O'Dwyer Company, 1984). Reprinted with permission.

cient length of time this service department becomes a feature of the firm's operation. Given sufficient time to prove itself, the service department attracts other clients and becomes a permanent part of the firm's structure.

At one time in its past a major counseling firm had a client that needed assistance in its relationship with the world of education. This need was of sufficient scope to justify the setting up of an education department in the counseling firm. Other clients came along with need of similar assistance, and by this time the education department had proven its worth. The department today is considered one of the most valued service arms of the counseling firm.

Some counseling firms have found it advisable and profitable to concentrate on special areas of public relations competence. Rather than expand into full-service firms they prefer to maintain their limited size, capitalize on their special expertise, and prove thereby that size alone doesn't make for success. A few firms, for example, concentrate on straight counseling and very personalized service, hence keep themselves deliberately small. Others specialize in the nonprofit field or in financial or labor relations.

The major share of the counselors, however, opt for full-servicing, and the distinguishing factor among them is size. As with internal departments, these firms are divided among small, medium-sized, and large firms, size being dependent on the number of clients served.

Though almost every counseling firm stresses its individual virtues, there is a great deal of similarity in the way firms are structured. In the small firm where there are a limited number of professionals, members of the professional staff serve as both account executives and specialists. Each member of the professional staff is expected to advise and counsel and also to handle the myriad of specialized tasks demanded by the nature of client accounts. This would include writing releases, handling press conferences and media contacts, conducting studies, writing and preparing publications, and similar tasks.

As firms grow in size and take on more accounts and employees the structure of the firm takes on added dimensions. At the top of the structure will be the senior members of the firm: the chairman of the board; president; one or more senior or executive vice-presidents. Each senior member of the firm takes under his wing a group of account executives, and usually these will be given vice-president status after suitable service with the firm. If an account is large enough, the account executive vice-president will have one or more professionals working with him on the account. In a large number of instances account executives will be handling more than one account unless an account is of sufficient substance and billing to warrant the full-time attention of one account executive.

To provide quality control and integration of talents, skills, and judgment, counseling firms add various forms of committees or boards to the above basic structure. Some firms call these plans boards, audit review committees, program review committees, or account performance review committees. Such groups provide a pooling of talents and resources which are called upon either at the onset or during a client relationship, and they serve to assist in planning and programming for the client or to measure, assess, and improve performance by those primarily responsible for the account (see Figure 7.5).

Thus, the medium and large counseling firms have the senior executive and account executive tier to handle accounts, and various committees or boards to backstop the primary, front-line team. The third element in the firm's structure is provided by the specialized departments common to all medium-sized and large counseling firms. These departments are not responsible for accounts as such, but are available for use by all account supervisors as the occasion warrants. If the account executive handling Client A, for example, decides to hold a press conference, he calls on the publicity department to help him plan and run it. If the account executive for Client B decides to produce a four-color brochure, he calls on the graphics department for assistance. At any one time, each specialist department could be providing assistance for a wide variety and number

FIGURE 7.5 *Creative task force.* Meetings are one problem-solving technique used by Carl Byoir & Associates, Inc., a New York-headquartered public relations firm. At a typical session, such as the one here, an account executive calls several colleagues together either to help solve a client problem or to program future activities for the account. The pooling of information, insights, and experiences benefits each account.

Source: Courtesy of Carl Byoir & Associates.

of clients retained by the firm. How many and what kind of specialized departments the counseling firm will have varies with the firm. Exhibit 7.2 exemplifies the specialized departments of three major firms.

The final structural element of the medium-sized and particularly of the large firms is geographical in nature. To provide on-the-spot national and international service these firms either establish their own offices in major U.S. cities and abroad or work out arrangements with other U.S. and foreign counseling firms. Through such arrangements the larger firms are able to provide local, regional, national, and international service when such service is needed.

Hill and Knowlton, for example, has offices in nineteen cities in the United States and Canada as well as twenty-five offices in cities all over the world. Burson-Marsteller has offices in thirteen U.S. and Canadian cities as well as twenty-six offices in cities all over the world.[3] Ruder Finn & Rotman has major offices in New York, Chicago, Los Angeles, Washington, D.C., and Toronto. In addition, the firm provides added resources for client assignments in more than seventy-five local and regional markets through its Field Network, an exclusive affiliation with independent public relations firms throughout North America.[4] Similar national and international branch offices and network affiliations are in effect at Carl Byoir & Associates, Manning, Selvage & Lee, and other firms among the top fifty on the O'Dwyer list.

METHOD OF OPERATION

Clients who retain public relations counsel can be assured they are buying a service tailored to their measurements. In fact, public relations counseling firms operate very much like custom tailors. When you have a fine suit made to order by a custom tailor, you don't go into his shop and pick your suit off the rack. Rather, you'll be greeted by the owner of the shop, have your measurements taken, be shown some swatches of material, come to agreement about the kind of suit you want, come back another time or two to try on the suit while it is being made by skilled craftsmen, and finally end up with a garment that meets your objectives and is fit only for your frame.

Counseling firms work in similar fashion. Most counselors do not sell prepackaged programs but rather get to work tailoring a program only after the client has agreed to retain counsel. The "swatches" the client is shown are usually testimonials from other clients who have recommended the counseling firm. Most counseling firms do not sign lengthy, formal contracts with their clients but rather have relatively simple letters of agreement and, in some cases, verbal agreements. These outline the general nature of the work to be accomplished, the basic elements of the fee involved, and the stipulation that either party can terminate the contract by giving thirty, sixty, or ninety days' notice. (Two typical letters of agreement are shown at the end of the chapter.)

The counselor "measures" his client by conducting a careful and systematic study of the client's organization, policies, strengths and weaknesses, competitive position, needs and problems. The account team responsible for handling the client then gets to work setting objectives and goals and developing an overall public relations plan and budget to meet them. Some counseling firms then have the plan and budget reviewed by standing or special review committees within the organization before it is submitted to the client for approval. Once the client approves the program, the account team puts it into effect utilizing the members of the team, senior management, and the specialized departments. Further, in order to insure quality control during the contract period many firms conduct periodic account reviews or "audits" to check on account team performance, measure the program's effectiveness, and make revision when necessary.

The operating procedures described above are illustrated in actual practice by Burson-Marsteller and by Carl Byoir & Associates in the brochures published by both firms and reprinted in Exhibits 7.3 and 7.4.

FEES

In the early days of public relations counseling there was so little mention of fees in the professional literature one might have concluded that a fee was some sort of social

---

EXHIBIT 7.3

Burson-Marsteller Explain How They're Organized to Serve

We tailor our relationships with each client to accommodate that client's specific needs. For some, our responsibility spans the total public relations/public affairs spectrum. For others, it is well-defined—investor relations, corporate counsel, marketing support, public affairs, media relations, for example.

For some clients, we work in one geographic area. For others, we have multiple-office assignments, nationally, regionally or internationally.

Most clients hire us on a continuing basis (we have client relationships that have endured for more than a quarter century); others assign us specific programs of finite duration.

Most of our clients employ sizable internal public relations/public affairs staffs; others have smaller staffs that plan and manage the public relations function and call on us for program implementation.

Our goal is to provide the service the client needs—where it is needed—either a total package or a specific service in one or more of our offices. Varying needs prohibit a single approach to client relationships, yet there are common principles we follow.

Management Responsibility: A senior member of Burson-Marsteller management has overall responsibility for planning, monitoring and maintaining contact with each client to ensure satisfaction with the work entrusted to us.

Within each office, a Planning and Creative Review Board adds broad perspective to a client's account programming. Additionally, a corporate review process assures performance to company-wide standards. Internal and client reporting systems keep all key parties continually apprised of program status and effectiveness.

Account Groups: Each client program is assigned to an account group—group manager, account supervisor and account executives, as needed. The account group has primary responsibility for planning and implementing activity and for direct contact with the client.

Support Services: While the account group is the core of client service, no single group contains all the specialized talents required to meet today's public relations/public affairs needs. The account group draws on the required special support services (of the firm).

Working Procedures: Burson-Marsteller adapts its operating procedures to the needs of the individual client. Working relationships, therefore, vary. Basic to most are:

- A written program, with established objectives and, where appropriate, measurable goals.
- A firm understanding of budget, both for account services and out-of-pocket expenses.
- A detailed monthly report of activities—what has happened over the previous 30 days; the priorities for the next 30 days.
- A detailed monthly invoice, in understandable form.
- Conference reports, distributed to all concerned, each time a substantive action is taken or decision made.
- Periodic program reviews to reaffirm or adjust priorities and activities.

Source: Burson-Marsteller brochure, 1982. Reprinted with permission.

EXHIBIT 7.4

The Byoir Systems Approach

Just as successful businesses today rely on a complex and orderly organization of systems . . . , public relations, as we view it, must be responsive to similar discipline.

In any area, an efficient and effective system is one in which all elements are related to each other and to stated objectives. And that characterizes the Byoir systems approach to public relations.

In developing a comprehensive program, it is our practice to work in close, daily contact with a client in undertaking a series of methodical steps:

1. **Systematic study** and analysis of all elements of the company's present situation, including its management's policies, relationships with various publics, organizational attributes and opportunities, competitive position, outside trends (social, political, environmental) and goals (financial, marketing, social).

2. **Planning and programming** of a system of specific projects and actions, related to each other and to goals determined by the preceding analysis.

3. **Implementation** of the program through systematic application in all communication media to achieve the stated objectives with maximum impact.

4. **Regular review** to measure the program's effectiveness, with revisions to meet any change of conditions or objectives . . .

. . . The most important result of the Byoir systems approach is: (a) to identify a company's true objectives and (b) to help it achieve them by projecting a strong, clear and consistent picture of the company's activities to its various publics. Another result, though less important, is to increase the efficiency of the money spent by the company on its public relations.

Typical Systems Flow
Carl Byoir & Associates

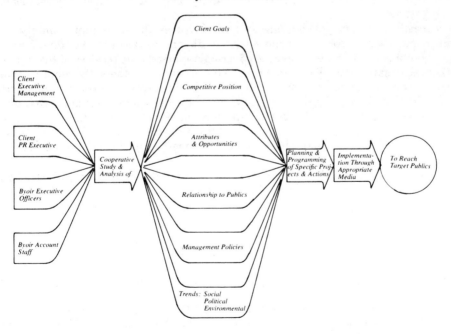

Source: The Byoir Way, undated brochure. Reprinted with permission of Carl Byoir & Associates.

disease not to be mentioned in polite company. In the past decade, on the other hand, there have been so many confusing articles about fees one might just as well conclude that a fee is one of the mysteries of the Far East.

Boiled down to its bare essentials, a fee is what the counselor charges the client in order to cover the following four elements:

1. The cost of servicing the client

2. The counselor's overhead costs

3. The counselor's margin of profit

4. Reimbursement for the counselor's out-of-pocket expenses

To cover the *cost of servicing the client,* the firm's billing system must provide for the salaries of everyone working on the account, and this includes reimbursement for top-level management as well as professional and secretarial staff time spent working on the account.

Overhead costs include the client's share of the firm's total overhead items including rent, telephone, heat, lighting, and so on.

As for *profits,* most counseling firms aim for a target gross profit before taxes of 25 percent of gross billings less out-of-pocket costs. Such a 25 percent gross profit will normally produce a net profit of approximately 5 percent to 6 percent after provision is made for annual contribution to employee profit sharing and federal and state income taxes.

Included in out-of-pocket expenses—which are almost always billed separately—are the cost of printing, postage, messenger service, press clippings, radio and television reports, travel, and entertainment expended by the firm in servicing the account.

There are various systems of billing the client, but the most common is to bill monthly in advance to cover an agreed-upon minimum fee or retainer, and to bill at the end of the month for all out-of-pocket and other expenses. It is still common for counseling firms to charge out-of-pocket expenses at cost. However, many firms now apply an additional percentage—usually 17.65 percent—for handling such out-of-pocket expenses as printing and artwork.

The basic difference in charging systems involves the minimum monthly fee or retainer and charges for staff people who work on the account. In some firms, the monthly retainer is an all-inclusive fee covering not merely the services of the top executives of the firm but also all others servicing the account. In others, the monthly retainer only covers consultation, planning, supervision by the executive officers, and overhead and profit. In addition, the client is also charged for the salaries—usually two and one-half to three times their hourly rate—of the account executives and staff working on the account. Work performed on the account by the special services departments is also charged separately on the same basis of two and one-half to three times the hourly rate of those in the departments.

The examples that follow illustrate weekly expense and time report forms used by Burson-Marsteller, and two sample letters of agreement.

ENDNOTES

1. *O'Dwyer's Directory of Corporate Communications, 1983* (New York: J.R. O'Dwyer Company, 1983).
2. Arlene Hershman, "Public Relations Goes Public," *Dun's Review,* September 1977.
3. *O'Dwyer's Directory of Public Relations Firms, 1983* (New York: J.R. O'Dwyer Company, 1983).
4. From Ruder Finn & Rotman brochure, 1983.

EXHIBIT 7.5

BURSON-MARSTELLER/MARSTELLER INC. WEEKLY EXPENSE REPORT

EMPLOYEE NAME: T. GREEN
EMPLOYEE NUMBER: 1234   WEEK ENDING (SUNDAY): 2 / 12 / 19 84 (Mo. / Day / Year)

SEC. 1 PERSONAL

DATE	MON 2/6		TUES 2/7		WED 2/8		THUR 2/9		FRI		SAT		SUN	
LOCATION	SF		SF/NY		NY		CINN							
CAB-LIMOS														
PARK-TOLLS							28 00 C							
HOTEL	88 00 A													
TIPS (OTHER)	1 00 A		2 95 A											
BRKFST. & TIPS			3 80 A											
LUNCH & TIPS					5 00 B									
DINNER & TIPS					5 00 B									
TOTALS	89 00		6 75		5 00		28 00							

SEC. 2 ENTERTAINMENT (Includes Meals for Others)

DATE	NAMES	COMPANY AFFILIATION	PLACE	BUSINESS REASON	AMOUNT	J/R CODE
2/6	A. HAY / B. CLAY	DEF CO.	ERNIE'S, SF	CLIENT ENT.	73 62	A
2/7	C. JAY / D. RAY	GHI CO. / B-M	CRICKET, CINN	NEW BUSINESS	65 48	C
2/8	E. MAY / F. KAY	GROCERY MKTG.	J.D.'S NEW YORK	EDITORIAL CONTACT	23 30	D

SEC. 3 TRANSPORTATION

MODE OF TRAVEL	AIR	CAR RNTL	AIR	PRSNL CAR
FROM	NY	NY	NY	
TO	SF/NY	NJ	CIN/NY	NWRK
CASH				
CHARGE	458 00 A	36 10 A	152 00 C	4 80 C

SEC. 4 EXPENSE SUMMARY (Detail Exactly As It Is To Appear For Billing)

CLIENT NUMBER / JOB NUMBER	DETAIL	AMOUNT		Billable Yes/No
222-05	TRAVEL EXPENSES 2/3-4, SAN FRANCISCO	664 17	A	✓
021-33	SUPPER MONEY	5 00	B	✓
021-92 52227	NEW BUSINESS GHI CO.	250 23	C	✓
333-05	EDITORIAL CONTACT – F. KAY, GROCERY MKTG.	23 30	D	✓

TOTAL (Sum of Secs. 1, 2 & 3): 942 70   T. Green

SEC. 5 BALANCE

	CASH	CHARGE	TOTAL
EXPENSES THIS WEEK	295 90	646 80	942 70
LESS ADVANCES	300 00		
TOTAL DUE EMPLOYEE OR			
TOTAL DUE COMPANY			4 10

DATE PAID   VOUCHER #   CHECK #
MGMT. APPRVL   ACCTG. APPRVL   EXT. OK

EXHIBIT 7.6

BURSON-MARSTELLER/MARSTELLER INC. WEEKLY TIME REPORT

EMPLOYEE NAME **CAROL SMITH**   EMPLOYEE NO. 3 2 1 4   WEEK ENDING SUNDAY* 0 5 | 8 | 19 8 3
                                                                                          Mo.   Day   Year

INSTRUCTIONS: 1) Print legibly; 2) Reports must be submitted weekly; 3) *BM billing period ends 15th of mo., MI ends last day of mo. If cutoff falls on a weekday, complete 2 time sheets—one through cutoff, and one subsequent to that date; 4) Use latest client code list for correct client #s when recording intercompany/interoffice time; 5) MI <u>must</u> use job #s for billable time; 6) Do not break time down in units smaller than 0.25 hr.; 7) Do not report hours for paid holidays; 8) Report religious holidays when office is opened, jury duty, etc. as absence; 9) Total each line and day; each day must total at least 7 hours.

Client Code	Client Name	Job No.	MON Hours	TUES Hours	WED Hours	THURS Hours	FRI Hours	SAT Hours	SUN Hours	TOTAL HOURS
357-05	GILLETTE PCD				4	2				6 .
357-05	" "	74236				3.25	.50			3 . 75
357-05	" "	52641					4.50			4 . 50
357-25	GILLETTE SILKIENCE			5						5 .
232-05	COLT				L75		2			3 . 75
-										.
-										.
-										.
-										.
-										.
-										.
-										.
-										.
-										.
-										.
-										.
-										.
-										.
-										.
-										.
-										.
-										.
-										.
-										.
-										.
021-32	New Business	55169			2	3				5 .
021-33	Administrative			2	1					3 .
-34	Company Meetings (Non-Client)									.
-35	Outside Meetings, Conventions, etc. (Non-Client)									.
-38	Company Promotion									.
-90	General									.
-91	Absence									.
021-92	Vacation		7							7 .
	TOTAL HOURS		7	7	8.75	8.25	7			38

Courtesy of Burson-Marsteller. Reprinted with permission.

EXHIBIT 7.7

Sample Letter of Agreement for Firm Using a Minimum Charge

Dear Mr. _____ :

This is to summarize the arrangement under which _____(counsel)_____ will serve _____(client)_____ Company as public relations counsel.

As counsel,_____(counsel)_____ will:

(a) Advise the management of _____(client)_____Company on public relations aspects of the company's policies and problems.

(b) Develop for approval and implementation, a program designed to achieve the company's public relations objectives.

(c) Provide professional staff services as may be required to help the company carry out its program.

The financial arrangement will be as follows:

Charges for the services of _____(counsel)_____ will be made at standard hourly rates for participating officers and staff assistants as they are required to carry out the programs and activities approved. _____(client)_____Company will pay _____(counsel)_____a minimum of $_____ per month for services under this agreement. Any staff time charges incurred in any month for the _____(client)_____Company account will be applied against this minimum, and any staff time charges incurred above the minimum will be billed at the regular rates.

_____(client)_____ Company will reimburse _____(counsel)_____ for all reasonable out-of-pocket disbursements made in the performance of its duties under this arrangement.

_____(counsel)_____ will maintain accurate records of all staff time and all out-of-pocket expenditures incurred in behalf of the company, and will be prepared to supply any supporting detail required by the company's auditors or yourself. Authorization for projects and operating activities will be obtained in advance before commitments are made.

_____(client)_____Company agrees to indemnify and hold harmless from and against any and all losses, claims, damages, expenses or liabilities which _____(counsel)_____ may incur based upon information, representations, reports or data furnished by_____(client)_____ Company to the extent such material is furnished or prepared by or approved by _____(client)_____Company for use by _____(counsel)_____ .

This arrangement is to extend from _____ 19__ , with either party having the right to terminate the agreement at the end of one year by 60 days' advance notice.

Sincerely yours,

(counsel) _____

By _____

Title   Date

Accepted by:

_____ Company

By _____

Title   Date

Source: Primer of Public Relations Counseling, The Counselors Academy, Public Relations Society of America. Reprinted with permission.

EXHIBIT 7.8

Sample Letter of Agreement for Firm Using a Counseling Fee

Dear Mr. _____ :

This letter is to summarize the arrangement under which _____(counsel)_____ will serve as public relations counsel for the _____ Company. The financial arrangements will be on the following basis:

Counseling. A total annual retainer fee of $_____ will be paid by the _____ Company to _____(counsel)_____ at the rate of $_____ per month for the term of this agreement. This fee covers the counseling and supervisory service of the firm's principals at the New York headquarters of the firm, and access to all of its services and physical facilities.

Staff Operations. Charges for services of account executives and such staff assistants as may be required to carry out the programs and projects as developed by _____(counsel)_____ management and approved by the _____ Company will be at the standard _____(counsel)_____ per diem rates covering direct salary and applicable overhead.

Out-of-Pocket Expenditures. The _____(client)_____ Company will reimburse _____(counsel)_____ for all reasonable out-of-pocket disbursements made in the performance of its duties under this arrangement.

_____(counsel)_____ will maintain accurate records of all staff time work and all out-of-pocket expenditures incurred in behalf of the Company, and will be prepared to supply any supporting detail required by Company's auditors or yourself. Budgets for projects and operating activities will be cleared in advance before commitments are made.

_____(client)_____ Company agrees to indemnify and hold harmless _____(counsel)_____ from and against any and all losses, claims, damages, expenses or liabilities which _____(counsel)_____ may incur based upon information, representations, reports or data furnished by _____(client)_____ Company to the extent such material is furnished or prepared by or approved by _____(client)_____ Company for use by _____(counsel)_____.

This arrangement is to extend from _____ 19__, with either party having the right to terminate the agreement at the end of one year by 60 days' advance notice.

Sincerely yours,

_____
(counsel)

By: _____
Title   Date

Accepted by:

_____(client)_____ Company

By: _____
Title   Date

Source: Primer of Public Relations Counseling, The Counselors Academy, Public Relations Society of America. Reprinted with permission.

PROJECTS, ASSIGNMENTS, AND MINIS

1. INVITATION FROM A PROSPECTIVE CLIENT: AN ASSIGNMENT

Due to declining birth rates in the mid-sixties, colleges and universities in the mid-eighties found themselves dealing with a diminished pool of college-bound high school seniors. Many institutions of higher education increased their publication and public relations budgets, and in addition some sought help from advertising agencies in order to attract potential students. Your institution decided on a different approach: it sought to augment the work of the institution's public relations staff by contracting for the services of a public relations counseling firm.

As a preliminary step the governing board of your school requested that your instructor carry out a screening of counseling firms. He, in turn, contacted a limited number of firms in two groups:

1. Small to medium-sized firms composed of from ten to fifteen professionals and located close enough to your college to know its key characteristics. The client list of each firm in this group numbers less than twenty-five. Most of the clients are located within your state. None of the counseling firms in this group has a college or university as a client, but all of the firms have clients in the educational field.

2. Large, full-service counseling firms composed of from 20 to 200 professionals and located in a major metropolis situated at some distance from your college. The client list of each firm in this group numbers in the hundreds and includes both national and international organizations. None of the counseling firms in this group has a college or university as a client, but all of the firms have clients in the educational field.

In his letter to the firms in the two groups your instructor advised them that the school has budgeted $80,000 for outside counseling services for the coming year and that he is carrying out an initial screening. He concludes as follows: "If you are interested in being considered for the account, we would like to hear from you within the next ten days. We do *not* expect you to present to us a public relations program at this time, but we do expect you to let us know why you feel that your firm, more so than any other, can carry out an eminent public relations program. Please restrict your letter to two pages of single-spaced type."

Assignment

Your instructor will first divide the class into teams of two, each team to belong to one of the two groups of firms cited in the case fact pattern.

In writing your letter you can make up certain characteristics of your firm that would be expected to apply to it because of its size and client list. However, the emphasis in your letter should be on the kind and quality of service the client could expect from your firm.

In addition to writing the letter, your firm should be prepared to make an oral presentation if so requested by the instructor.

2. GETTING TO KNOW YOU COSTS MONEY: A MINI-CASE FOR DISCUSSION

A medium-sized Illinois firm seeking to expand its market regionally retained a major Chicago counseling firm at a monthly retainer fee of $5,000 plus out-of-pocket costs.

The letter-of-agreement was signed after two exploratory sessions between the executive head and public relations director of the client and the president and executive vice-president of the counseling firm. It was agreed that the $5,000 retainer fee would be paid monthly in advance, and out-of-pocket expenses would be billed at the end of each month in which they were incurred. Each party to the contract had the option of canceling out by giving thirty days' notice.

On September 1, the first month of the contract, the client PR director was billed for $5,000 and subsequently paid the bill. On September 10 he was visited by P. Lawrence Platt, an account executive whom he had briefly met at an exploratory session in Chicago. Platt made another visit on September 20, and on September 30 he sent the client a five-page program proposal.

On October 1, the second month of the contract, the client was billed for $5,000 and subsequently paid the bill. Along with the payment the client's director of public relations sent a detailed letter of response to the five-page program proposal citing serious reservations about some of the proposed ideas and projects. The client also expressed some concern because, as he put it, he had not seen "any action on the account," and he suggested that the account executive concentrate his activities at the moment on the handling of an upcoming trade show. On October 14 he received a reply from the counseling firm, signed by Joseph Munster and notifying him that Platt was being replaced on the account by Munster but assuring him of immediate service and attention to the trade show project. A telephone call from the client brought Munster to the client's headquarters, where he spent the day getting acquainted with the client and its director of public relations.

On October 31 the client received a revised proposal from Munster and Munster's ideas about handling the trade show. Attached was a bill for $850 for out-of-pocket expenses for the months of September and October. The next day the client received his retainer bill of $5,000 to cover the month of November. Two days later, after reviewing Munster's program proposal and deciding it wasn't much better than the original, the client notified the counseling firm he was exercising his thirty-day option and canceling the contract effective December 3.

(All names and places have been disguised.)

Questions for Discussion

What seems to have gone wrong here, could it have been anticipated, and what could have been done to prevent it?

3. A COUNSELOR EXPLAINS HIS FEE SYSTEM: A MINI-EXCERPT FOR DISCUSSION

When counselors write proposal letters—whether they be general letters outlining the counselor's competence or more specific letters outlining the proposed program—they usually end up discussing their fee. Here is how one counseling firm explained the proposal fee:

> Our fee for professional services is $48,000 annually. This covers the professional side of the budget in Los Angeles, which would be the center of account activity.
>
> At this point we can only estimate the 'out-of-pocket' part of the budget for such things as publications, travel, telephone calls, photography, and so forth. We're sure we'd be well covered if you would budget $25,000-$30,000 for the year for these items. With the exception of petty cash items, disbursements from this fund would be made only with your prior approval.
>
> We would also like to suggest that you set aside a contingency fund of $10,000 so we could have on-the-spot support for the market-by-market program from our regional

offices located in New York, Washington, Chicago, and Houston and supplemented by our Field Network in the next 25 most important cities in the country. We can use the regional office people as we need them for specific support of special promotions.

Thus, the total cost should be in the neighborhood of $83,000-$88,000 for the year. We would want a firm one-year agreement, cancellage either way thereafter by sixty days' notice. . . .

Questions for Discussion

1. In what way does the above fee system protect the counseling firm? The client?

2. If you were the client-to-be, what questions might you have about the above fee system?

3. If you were the counseling firm, what answers would you give to the questions?

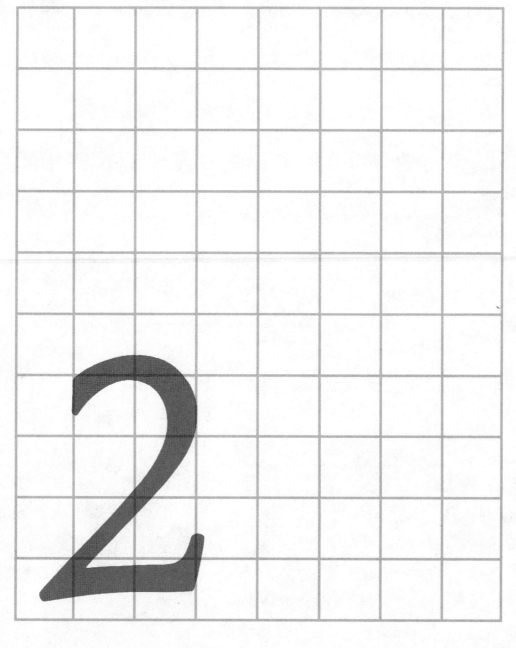

Part

2

PART 2
THE PUBLIC
RELATIONS PROCESS

The basic premise of this book is that public relations is a dynamic process involving a series of interlocking elements constantly interacting. In the preceding chapters we have analyzed the broad nature of public relations and discussed its role as a function of the management of profit and nonprofit organizations. We have also described how public relations relates to American society and we have discussed the role and nature of its major practitioners.

The chapters in this section deal with the elements that comprise the dynamics of public relations in action. To achieve a clear understanding of the process, we have treated each key element separately, but the reader should keep in mind that as an action process public relations is constantly in motion. This section, forming as it does the core of the book, describes, discusses, and analyzes the following key elements:

PUBLIC OPINION

Prerequisite to all public relations activity is an understanding of the nature of public opinion. Analyzed in detail here are publics, attitudes, mores, stereotypes, opinion formation, and public opinion guideposts.

RESEARCH

In dealing with research we first provide an overview of research by discussing its meaning, benefits, and use in public relations programming. The audit as a research tool is described, and the environmental and social audit is discussed as a means of dealing with emerging public issues. A second chapter concentrates on the application of research techniques, particularly public opinion polling, as a means of aiding the public relations process.

PLANNING AND PROGRAMMING

Though public relations in action is not always an orderly procedure, there are certain steps that should be taken in programming public relations activities. These steps are set forth to provide a blueprint for action.

COMMUNICATION

Communication, which is considered by many to be the basic skill of the most proficient public relations practitioners, is treated in three chapters. The first sets forth some basic elements and theories of communication. The second dissects a simple communication model and analyzes the four major elements in that model. The third communication chapter emphasizes communication techniques and stresses media relations and publicity.

EVALUATION, MEASUREMENT, AND REPORTING

Feedback by means of evaluation, measurement, and reporting closes the public relations circle. Thus, the last of the eight chapters in this second section of the book explores the various ways in which the practitioner evaluates and measures progress and reports the results of public relations activities.

Some words of reminder are called for at this point. Public relations is a dynamic activity involving forces in motion, hence the reminder that the public relations process is not static but continuously in action. At any one time the busy practitioner may be planning a new program while carrying out an old one or evaluating its effectiveness. The practitioner may also be involved in several steps in the public relations process at the same time. An orderly discussion of the dynamics of public relations should be a first step in understanding the whole as well as its parts.

8

PUBLIC OPINION

The authors of a survey of 139 public relations executives of *Fortune 500* firms summarized their findings as follows:

> The executives . . . overwhelmingly endorsed a functional mode of public relations. They see their job as that of not only conveying a favorable corporate image to sundry publics, but also of sensing, interpreting, and conveying the views of these publics to corporate management. Perhaps even more importantly, respondents feel that their job is one of making certain that public opinion and social responsibility are properly considered in the formulation and implementation of corporate decisions. Thus, practitioners tend to see themselves as the eyes, ears, voice, and conscience of the company.[1]

As with all public relations practitioners, the above-cited executives recognize the crucial role that public opinion plays in the public relations process. They see their role as assessing and interpreting public opinion to management, making certain that management considers it in implementing corporate decisions, and "conveying a favorable corporate image" to publics. Like an invisible cloud of oxygen, public opinion permeates and gives life to the public relations scene. However, trying to capture and bottle it is no simple task, as shown by the scenes below.

SCENES FROM A TELEVISION PLAYLET

Scene 1: The plaza in front of the administration building at Roscoe College. Students mill about as a group of thirty faculty members with hand-painted signs walk up and down in front of the main entrance chanting, "No Contract, No Teaching." The signs tell us that the faculty is on strike.

Scene 2: The president's office in the same building. The president is reviewing the situation with her top assistants: the strike is one week old; no classes are being held; students are tossing Frisbees and planning a rally; a score of students have packed up and gone home; the bursar reports a potential loss of $90,000 in tuition income. The president tells the group that the trustees refuse to reopen negotiations. She turns to her director of public relations and asks: "Just how strong is faculty feeling on this strike business? Do you think they're united and behind their leaders? What about the students, how do they feel about all this?"

Scene 3: The office of the director of public relations, half an hour later. He is being interviewed by the education writer for the local newspaper. The writer asks: "How do the trustees feel about the strike? Will the students support the faculty? How solidified are the teachers?"

Our brief television drama ends with a close-up shot of the director of public relations. He is peering at a little crystal ball that he keeps on his desk, and at the same time he is playing with a ouija board he keeps within easy reach. He looks like a man who hopes to find the answers to the questions about public opinion that have been directed at him by the president and the education writer, but he knows that neither the crystal ball nor the ouija board will be of much help. He also knows that he doesn't have the time—given the situation—to conduct a scientific poll of public opinion. Finally, and most important, he's aware that because he's the director of public relations the president expects him to know the state of student and faculty opinion. It's obvious to the director, as it should be to those reading this book, that his ability to assess public opinion is directly linked to his ability to function as a public relations practitioner.

Exactly how important is public opinion to public relations practice? Socrates would probably answer that question with some questions of his own: How important are the lungs to breathing? How important are the ears to hearing? How important is the nose to smelling?

The answers to the questions are self-evident. Without an understanding of the nature of public opinion and how it operates there can be no meaningful public relations practice. It's with good reason that the word "public" is an integral part of both terms; in the one case we are dealing with the *opinions* of the public and in the other we are dealing with *relations* with the public. Thus the tie that binds the two is the public, and it's the public's opinion with which the practitioner is concerned when he or she plans and carries out a public relations program. The details of the program, in turn, depend on the specific concern the practitioner has with public opinion. Is he concerned merely about the *essence* of public opinion? Does he want simply to *measure* public opinion? Does he want to *create* favorable public opinion? Does he want to *neutralize* unfavorable public opinion? These are some of the basic questions which have to be faced and answered by the practitioner.

DIFFERING PERSPECTIVES

Dealing with questions and answers about public opinion first involves recognition of the relative place of public relations as compared to other fields of study whose standing and research are more firmly established. Public relations practitioners are relative newcomers to the study of public opinion and hence have relied on the findings of other disciplines, primarily political science, sociology, and psychology. As one goes through the literature of the three fields he discovers studies dealing with the formulation of basic theories of public opinion as well as empirical studies describing research in public opinion formulation. Some authorities have gone so far as to formulate so-called rules of public opinion, but a close analysis of these "rules" reveals that they hold true only under certain circumstances. Unfortunately, these circumstances have a disconcerting tendency to occur only once in their pristine state and are not much help.

Analysis of the theories of public opinion and the empirical studies also reveals that there is not a great deal of agreement among the political scientist, the sociologist, and the psychologist when it comes to public opinion. This is due partly to the fact that the authorities in each of the three fields approach public opinion from the unique perspective of their specialties. The political scientist is primarily concerned with public opinion in the framework of politics and governance; the sociologist's primary concern is in the framework of society; and the psychologist approaches public opinion in the framework of the individual. There is nothing wrong with any of these concerns—but the fact remains that each perceives only part of the picture.

There's a final significant difference between the approach to public opinion taken by the public relations practitioner and that taken by the political scientist, the sociologist, and the psychologist. The practitioner is concerned with *practical* aspects of public opinion whereas the other three are concerned chiefly with theoretical and academic aspects. In no way should we consider theory and academic perspectives to be inferior; on the contrary, it's from them that most of what is practical in today's world is derived.

If the practitioner were dealing with tangible objects, his search for answers would not be so difficult. Public opinion, however, is not a tangible object. We know that it exists, we know that it's all-powerful in a democratic society, but our problem is in defining it, measuring it, trying to influence it, and above all, understanding it. This chapter aims to examine these problematic aspects of public opinion and to relate them to the practice of public relations. As a preliminary warm-up for this examination the student should consider the questions which follow and discuss them in dialogue with his fellow classmates.

1. Under what circumstances would the public relations practitioner be concerned merely about the *essence* of public opinion? About the *measurement* of public opinion? About wanting to create *favorable* public opinion? About wanting to *neutralize* unfavorable public opinion?

2. How would you rate the four public opinion goals or concerns in terms of their degree of difficulty of achievement? Justify your selections.

3. Why do you think it's so difficult to *define* public opinion? To *measure* public opinion? To *influence* public opinion? To *understand* public opinion?

4. Can you cite any organization which has little or no need to be concerned about public opinion? Justify your selection.

5. How do you think students feel about the college in which you are enrolled? How about the alumni? How about the public at large? What's the reason(s) for the similarities or differences in these views? Justify your conclusions.

6. How well do you think you are able to judge the opinions of your classmates about the kind of job the president of the United States is doing? A little experiment should give you the answer.
   In advance of actual measurement, jot down on a piece of paper your assessment of the percentage of the class who you think judge the president as doing an excellent, good, fair, or poor job. The instructor will now have each of you jot down your own judgment of the job the president is doing, and the total percentages will be tabulated. Now compare your prior estimate with the actual percentages.

7. In his editorials dealing with public issues the editor of a daily newspaper in a city of 125,000 invariably concluded with the remark that "rank and file Americans" or "rank and file residents" felt thus-and-thus about the particular issue. What's your reaction to this usage of public opinion?

THE PUBLIC

From Roman times to the present the phrase *vox populi* has been used as a way of saying that the people have spoken. The Romans used the phrase to mean "the voice of the people," and today *the public* is used to mean anything from the entire United States population to an alderman's ward constituency. Two parties in a conflict, taking opposite sides of an issue, frequently base their claim to legitimacy on the allegation they are doing so because this is what the public wants. No term should be used so loosely, and certainly not by public relations practitioners who claim expertise in the area of public opinion. Clarification rather than obfuscation should be the goal of those who deal with the opinions of people, and one way to achieve such clarification is to recognize the following key ramifications about the word *public:*

1. There is no such entity as "the public" because "the public" is a myth.
2. There is not one, but many publics.
3. Issues create their own publics.
4. The nature of an organization usually dictates its publics.

"THE PUBLIC" IS A MYTH

Politicians, news and editorial writers, columnists, and others refer constantly to the mass audience as *the public,* but they do so because necessity is the mother of invention. Plainly stated, there is no such entity as the public, even though the term seems to suit the needs of those who use it indiscriminately. Sometimes they do so because of ignorance. More often, they do so because it's convenient and helpful to contend that their point of view has the support of the American public. Reality, however, tells us that the so-called American public is made up of innumerable subpublics, some of whom may support organizations strongly, some weakly, and some not at all. Two examples should suffice to demonstrate misuse of the term:

> The American public firmly believes that our military establishment should be second to no one. I support the MX Missile because the public demands that we be Number One.
> —A United States Senator

> We are building this nuclear plant because the American public demands we meet the energy challenge and because the American public insists that we be less dependent on foreign oil imports.
> —Utility executive

The important point to keep in mind is that only in exceptional circumstances can one speak of an American public united in its views on an issue. For the most part, the American public is amorphous, transitory, ever-changing, and virtually infinite in numbers. To lump together 230 million people under the umbrella term *the public* is to misconstrue and oversimplify the term.

THERE IS NOT ONE, BUT MANY PUBLICS

All of us, at one and the same time, belong to an almost infinite number of publics. At this very moment you may well be a Protestant, union member, Elk, youth, a voter, football fan, bird-watcher, and a Democrat. Or you may be a Catholic, an entrepreneur, Knights of Columbus member, chess player, hunter, and a Republican. If you want to complicate matters, consider that you and your neighbor are Protestants but you are a Methodist who goes to church every Sunday and your neighbor is a Congregationalist who attends church only on Easter Sunday. First and foremost you're Methodist and Congregationalist; second, regular and irregular church-goers; and third, members of that vast body of people who call themselves Protestants.

For the sake of convenience, practitioners prefer to deal with publics in broad, general terms by referring to the employee, stockholder, customer, and community publics. Harwood Childs, however, warns against the danger of such easy generalizations. He points out that if you want to analyze a firm's actions on employees you should examine not merely broad publics but also subpublics. In seeking to predict employee reactions to company actions it's important to distinguish between employees who belong to unions and those who don't; employees who have been in the work force for decades and those who have but recently been employed; employees who hold two jobs and those who hold but one.

Further, to be successful in reaching people one must be cognizant of the fact that *the multiplicity of publics to which all of us belong can cause internal conflicts of loyalties not easy to resolve.* Examples of those who face loyalty conflicts due to multipublic membership are the professor who believes firmly in independence of mind and in professionalism and yet joins with his colleagues in a union; the young Catholic mother who is an ardent believer in feminist rights, including the right to abortion; the son of a Marine colonel who is torn between duty to country and fighting in an undeclared war which he believes is immoral. Sorting out primary loyalties for such individuals becomes a soul-wrenching experience, and should teach all of us to heed the road sign which reads: warning, publics ahead, proceed with all due caution.

That road sign should serve as a warning that the large public is always a combination of smaller publics, that individuals usually belong to different publics simultaneously, and that one of the most difficult tasks in the world is to figure out which public has an individual's loyalties when two or more of his publics are on a collision course.

ISSUES CREATE THEIR OWN PUBLICS

Though members of a public are usually not in direct physical contact with each other, there are times and circumstances when such members get together to form an audience. There are also times when a loosely organized public is activated by an issue which is of prime importance to those making up said public. At such a time, when an issue activates a public, the effectiveness of such a public as an action group becomes a matter of real concern to the public relations practitioner. Individuals who previously had an unstructured relationship to each other may join together or tie themselves to other groups with a more institutionalized structure. The result is a public which has found its voice to make its weight felt, and in such instances attention must be paid.

Issues that are perceived by members of a public to be of key importance to them are the ones which trigger a public to coalesce into an action group. Unfortunately, there is no magic means whereby the practitioner can predict with certitude that such-and-such issue will activate a hitherto nascent public to become an active public. Nor is there any magic method of predicting the degree of intensity of feelings which an issue can arouse in a particular public. The astute practitioner:

1. Keeps careful watch as issues arise.

2. Tries to anticipate which individuals in society are affected by issues.

3. Notes whether these individuals are either in an organized grouping or are in the process of becoming an organized grouping.

4. Takes steps to deal with statements or actions that he or she anticipates to be forthcoming from that particular public.

5. Provides answers to questions that people may have but that they may often not express.

THE NATURE OF AN ORGANIZATION
USUALLY DICTATES ITS PUBLICS

Probably because he didn't have to deal with the public, Thomas Carlyle was able to be rather cavalier in dismissing the public as "an old woman"—his words, not this author's—who should be left alone to "maunder and mumble." Organizations in today's society can't afford Carlyle's suggested treatment, but instead they need to view their publics carefully. The nature of an organization usually dictates its publics, but there are distinctions that have to be made by each organization. Five major distinctions, applied to the nature of organizations and their publics, are as follows:

1. Organizations with similar goals and purposes usually have similar publics.
2. The unique nature of an organiation can often make its publics different from those of organizations that seem similar to it.
3. There's a pecking order among publics as well as among chickens.
4. Publics shift as organizations shift.
5. Latent publics have to be handled with special care.

Organizations with similar goals and purposes usually have similar publics. All colleges exist for the purpose of educating students, hence the student public is a basic college public. All appliance manufacturers exist by selling their products to consumers, hence the consumer public is a basic appliance manufacturer public. Every daily newspaper in the country exists by attracting readers and advertisers, hence the reading and advertising publics are basic publics for daily newspapers. However . . .

The unique nature of an organization can often make its publics different from those of organizations which seem similar to it. Yes, it's true that all colleges exist for the purpose of educating students, but some colleges only admit women, some only admit men, some admit both men and women, some draw students from their immediate area, and some draw students from the entire country. In each case, though all colleges exist for the purpose of educating students, the college in question may have a public vastly different from the others.

There's a pecking order among publics as well as among chickens. All men and women are created equal, but some publics are much more important than others. Pinpointing publics in order of importance is a crucial matter for the public relations practitioner and shouldn't be handled routinely. Consider, for example, a 100-year-old, private university which has an alumni body numbering more than 100,000 and compare it with a 10-year-old public college which has an alumni body numbering less than 5,000. Obviously, the importance of its alumni public is greater to the first institution than to the second.

Keep in mind that publics shift as organizations change. Because we live in a fast-changing world, organizations are in a state of flux. Today's small private college is liable to become a part of a state university tomorrow. Today's manufacturer of widgets is liable to become a part of some vast conglomerate tomorrow. Yesterday's March of Dimes to combat infantile paralysis is today devoted to combating birth defects, and who can tell what will need combating tomorrow? As organizations change in nature and purpose, so do their publics change; an outdated list of publics is about as worthless as last year's calendar.

Beware the latent public. Keeping track of such major publics as customers, employees, and the like is generally not a difficult task. But there are publics within publics and many of them are hidden from view and in a latent state. As issues arise which are important to them, these latent publics begin to stir, to write letters to editors, to become organized, and to surface and cause innumerable problems if their presence is not detected beforehand and steps taken to handle them. Exhibit 8.1 illustrates the point.
The lessons one can learn from the Wilbert State Hospital situation are found in the answers to the questions one can raise. How important was the time frame in which the

situation occurred? Could the opposition of the latent public have been anticipated? If yes, why? If no, why not? What, if anything, could the state mental health department have done? What other information do you need to answer the questions?

NO-MAN'S-LAND: THE GAP BETWEEN PUBLIC AND OPINION

Lying somewhere between "public" and "opinion" is a vast no-man's-land made up of mores, stereotypes, and attitudes. Virtually unexplored except by the social scientists, this land is an important link between public and opinion. Anyone who hopes to understand public opinion must first understand the mores, stereotypes, and attitudes which exist between and link public and opinion.

Mores (mo-rays) are *deep-rooted, customary ways of looking at and doing things in a society.* They are persistent, nonrational, deeply ingrained, and taken for granted as being the ground rules of daily existence within a society.

Mores, which have also been termed folkways, are compelling and rigid in nature, accepted as right, true, proper, and necessary for the proper functioning of the society in which they exist. Unfortunately for the public relations practitioner, mores and folkways are largely *unwritten and are endemic to the society in which they exist.*

Curtis D. MacDougall, professor emeritus of journalism at Northwestern University, points out that folkways are "instruments of social behavior" which became mores when given a higher degree of social sanction. Stating that mores are "folkways with a sanction," he reminds us that they compel some obedience upon threat of social ostracism. "Traditions, conventions, proper etiquette, rituals and ceremonies must be observed in customary fashion," he states. "*Social codes* compel obedience; *taboos* forbid disobedience."[2]

Noting that legal codes supplement religious, moral, and social codes as society becomes more complex, MacDougall states that even legal codes will not be enforced when they're inconsistent with the unwritten codes. As an example he cites the widespread disobedience during Prohibition.[3]

Here are a few examples of mores and folkways:

> Whistling in America is a means of indicating either contentment (e.g., while one works) or fear (e.g., while walking past a cemetery on a dark night). Whistling in Europe is a way of showing disapproval at a soccer match.

> Throwing rice at the newlyweds, kissing the bride, holding a wake, shaking hands, and blessing a sneeze by saying "Gesundheit" or "God bless you" are all contemporary customs and folkways whose ancient origins have long since been forgotten.[4]

> Before John F. Kennedy, an all-pervasive "rule" of American political life was that no Catholic could become President of the United States. That particular stricture became extinct with Kennedy's election to the highest office in the land.

The last example illustrates two important aspects of mores. One is that mores are persistent and deeply ingrained. The second is that mores are subject to change, though the change is as slow-moving as the advance of a glacier. Because mores are so persistent and nonrational, it is difficult to resist or try to change them. A person or organization runs grave risks when taking a stand or action which is contrary to public mores; hence the necessity to know when one is dealing with public mores or with public opinion.

The mores of Puritan America regarding sex were light-years removed from general American sexual mores of today. At the same time, however, in certain sections of the country views about sex are still not far removed from those of Puritan America, and it's imperative to understand how strongly and to what degree mores govern thought and action in rural and urban America, in Appalachia, in the Northeast, and throughout the entire country.

Stereotypes are conventional labels or preconceptions which are acquired from the culture. Psychologist William Albig reminds us that stereotypes may be counterfeits of reality, but they are also psychological realities.[5] Stereotypes, like mores, are generally unwritten ways of viewing things and people, but they can become embellished through the written word.

The concept of stereotypes was first enunciated by Walter Lippmann in his 1922 book, *Public Opinion,* in which he described the world of the 1920s as one that was "out of sight, out of mind." He meant that for most Americans of that period the world was that of Sinclair Lewis's Sauk Centre, Minnesota, or of Chicago, Illinois, but certainly not that of Germany, Russia, Japan, or China. Not only was the world far removed to the average American, said Lippmann, but the average American was too busy with his own life to pay much attention to what was going on thousands of miles away.[6]

Lippmann further noted that there were major factors that limited access to the facts about the wider world beyond America, and he cited them as follows:

1. Artificial censorship

2. The limitations of social contact

3. The limited amount of time available in each day for paying attention to public affairs

4. Distortions arising because events have to be compressed into very short messages

5. The difficulty of making a small vocabulary express a complicated world

6. The fear of facing those facts that would seem to threaten the established routine of people's lives

Despite these barriers to a true understanding of the wider world, Lippmann said, the American nonetheless made for himself "a trustworthy picture inside his head of the world beyond his reach," and all too often this picture was a stereotype, or what Albig referred to as a "counterfeit of reality."

Do we still stereotype our vision of the world when today television brings the world right into our living room? To a disquieting extent, the answer is yes. Some examples to prove the point:

> Many Americans still see the Russians as uneducated peasants (until we learn they've put as many satellites into the sky as we have). When it's convenient for him to do so, the President punctures our stereotyped impressions of the Russians by saying they're ahead of us in both missiles and nuclear warheads.

> Many American manufacturers believed there was nothing like Yankee manufacturing ingenuity (until the Japanese and German automakers entered the American market and made a huge dent in it).

> Many Americans considered American military might to be invincible (until we fought an undeclared war in Vietnam and 56,000 of us died).

One might logically conclude that the world of today is very much unlike that of the 1920s when Lippmann listed six major factors that limit access to the facts about the wider world beyond America. After all, we now have radio and television, more social contact and free time, and we are now better educated and supposedly have better vocabularies. But we still manage to hang on to our stereotyped impressions and ideas of the wider world beyond America and within America as well. A study conducted in the late 1970s by the Council on Interracial Books for Children proves this point all too well.

> Reviewing seventy-five widely available children's picture books, the Council reported that in these books American Indians are still depicted today as fierce, violent, toma-hawk-brandishing fancy dancers.

> Among the numerous misconceptions, said the Council, are beliefs that "Indians always wear feathers and headdresses, frequently brandish tomahawks, live in teepees, are fierce and violent, lurk behind trees, spend much time dancing on one leg and live in a mystical past."

> The Council concluded that the main perception that non-Indian children gather from their picture books dehumanizes the Indian people, degrades their culture, and distorts non-Indian children's perceptions of Native Americans.

> "In an effort to debunk the stereotypes," said the Associated Press in its story about the study, "the non-profit Council has produced a film strip and teachers' handbook for non-Indian elementary school children."

The lesson is all too clear: we have to understand the extent of stereotyped thinking that exists today, and we ought to do what we can to ensure that the pictures in people's heads conform to reality. As communicators, however, we also have to understand the difficulty in seeking to deal with such thinking. Producing a filmstrip and a teachers' handbook is one way of combating children's stereotyped views of the American Indian, but they're small slingshot stones to toss at the Goliath of stereotyping.

Attitudes are the *predispositions, thoughts, or feelings of people toward issues that have not yet materialized in a specific way.* Attitudes have been described as the sum-total of one's feelings, inclinations, notions, ideas, fears, and convictions about any specific topic or issue. As such, they represent a tendency to act in a particular manner. They form the raw material out of which public opinion develops, and hence understanding the nature of individual and group attitudes is critical to understanding the nature of public opinion.

Attitudes and opinion are so closely intertwined it's often impossible to ascertain any distinction between the two terms. It is generally agreed that, with certain exceptions, opinion is usually consistent with attitude. (One such exception, for example, would be the verbal response or opinion given by a bigoted person to a racial question; under social pressures, such a person may well state an opinion which is inconsistent with his or her attitude.) Because of the close connection between attitude and opinion a fuller discussion of the roots of attitude and opinion will be held in abeyance until later in this chapter.

OPINION

Opinion is to attitude what the hand is to the arm. One is an extension of the other.

Simply defined, an opinion is *an expression of attitude.* Some authorities contend that opinion is a *verbal* expression of attitude, and although verbal means are the most common way of demonstrating expression, a person can express opinion by nonverbal means. A grimace or a gesture may often express better than words the opinion held by a person. This nonverbal method of expression must, however, be capable of being readily translated into words.

One of history's most famous examples of a nonverbal expression of attitude which showed opinion is that of Winston Churchill's "V for Victory" expression of determination and faith in England's ability to defeat Hitler's Germany.

A less famous but nonetheless clear indication of a nonverbal expression of attitude which showed opinion was given by Governor Nelson Rockefeller (N.Y.) in mid-1970 when he was heckled by some young people in the midst of a speech he was giving. Rockefeller's response was to hold high his right middle finger. The picture made front pages all over the country, and there was no need for a caption to make clear Rockefeller's response to the heckling.

The hand serves in many ways to indicate nonverbal expression. The raised thumb indicates approval or victory; the thumb held down indicates disapproval. The forefinger held high indicates "We're Number One," the clenched fist indicates power to us, and the nose held between thumb and index finger means something is rotten in the state of Denmark (or wherever one happens to be).

Whether verbal or nonverbal, *an opinion is always the opinion of a person, not a group.* By expressing his or her opinion a person may *suggest* that he or she is speaking for a group, but it's misleading to think in terms of a "group mind," because public opinion always refers to a collection of individual opinions. This point will be explained in more detail after a brief analysis of the dimensions of an opinion.

The characteristics or dimensions most commonly used to describe an opinion are *direction, intensity, stability,* and *latency.* Each of these is discussed in the sections that follow.

DIRECTION

Describing an opinion in terms of its direction means to state whether a person approves or disapproves of something. In the pioneer days of opinion measurement this approval-disapproval was indicated via a pro-con dichotomy, but as techniques of measurement became refined the simple pro-con description has been complemented by finer distinctions of opinion.

Simple pro-con, for-against, yes-no measurements of direction all too often conceal wide gradations of opinion. Asking a woman whether she is for or against the death penalty could easily produce statistics which are misleading. A person may be for the death penalty in certain circumstances, but not under other circumstances. A simple for-against or pro-con expression of opinion would obviously provide an insufficient measurement of the direction of opinion about the death penalty.

Scaling, which means providing a choice ranging from one extreme to the opposite extreme, is used to set forth more accurately the direction of opinion. The opinion of an individual can be located at one of many points along a scale, and thus sets forth a better estimate of public opinion direction than was possible through the earlier pro-con method.

> V. O. Key cities the difference between the pro-con and the scaling methods of measuring direction in the following example: "A division of people who support and oppose government ownership of industry does not provide a useful indication of the nature of public opinion on the question of government policy toward economic activity. Views on economic policy may be arranged along a scale from the extreme left to the extreme right. The opinion of an individual may be located at any one of many points along such a scale. One person may favor governmental ownership of all the means of production; another may be satisfied with a large dose of governmental regulation; still another may prefer only the most limited control of the economy; and others may wish to abolish whatever controls exist."[7]

National opinion polls utilize both simple pro-con measurements of direction and scaling to provide gradations of direction. First, here's an example of a question asking for a single pro-con response:

> Regardless of the party you may favor, do you lean more toward the liberal side or the conservative side politically?
>
> *from ABC News, November 2, 1982*

Second, here's an example of a question providing for a scaled response:

> There's been a lot of discussion about the way morals and attitudes about sex are changing in this country. If a man and a woman have sex relations before marriage, do you think it is always wrong, almost always wrong, wrong only sometimes, or not wrong at all?
>
> *from National Opinion Research Center, General Social Surveys, 1977, 1978, and 1982*

Finally, here are two different ways—simple pro-con and scaled—of asking the public to assess the way the president of the United States is doing his job:

> Do you approve or disapprove of the way Ronald Reagan is handling his job as president?
>
> *from survey by CBS News/New York Times, November 2, 1982, and by ABC News, same date*

> How would you rate the job President Reagan is doing as president—excellent, pretty good, only fair, or poor?
>
> *from survey by Louis Harris and Associates, 1982*

INTENSITY

The intensity of opinion describes the *strength of feeling* existing in that opinion. Certain issues may induce strong feelings of opinion among people while other issues may be of little importance. In dealing with people's opinions the public relations practitioner would be wise to know which issues arouse or are likely to arouse opinions of high intensity and which arouse or are likely to arouse opinions of low intensity.

Political scientist Key suggests that we use common sense in seeking to distinguish between high and low intensity issues. This may well be too generalized a guideline for those who seek a more scientific way of prejudging the expected intensity of opinion about issues, but it makes sense to anyone who keeps abreast of social, economic, and political issues in the country.

> In 1983 issues which aroused a high intensity of opinion were the nuclear weapons freeze; inflation; and foreign policy as it applied to Central America. Issues which aroused a low intensity of opinion were civil rights; busing; and foreign policy as it applied to Southeast Asia and South America.

The same strictures apply to the measurement of intensity of opinion as apply to the measurement of the direction of opinion. Scaling, rather than the simple pro-con method of measurement, provides distinctions which ensure a more accurate assessment of opinion. Scaling indicates not merely the low and high of intensity of opinion on an issue but also gradations in between.

During the debate in the late 1970s over the Panama Canal treaty between the United States and Panama, the national opinion polls ran numerous questions at periodic intervals to measure various dimensions of opinion. One such dimension was intensity of feeling about the treaty, and the CBS News/New York *Times* poll in October 1977 used this question to measure the intensity of feeling of those who said they either approved or disapproved of the treaty:

> Do you feel strongly enough about the way your senators vote on the Panama Canal treaty to change your vote because of it when they run again?

Commenting on opinion about the treaty, Professor Everett C. Ladd stressed the importance of the intensity factor in this commentary: "The surveys . . . indicate that the more informed Americans are about the treaties, the more likely they are to favor them. But if better informed Americans are generally more supportive, the intensity factor is on the side of the opposition: many more foes than supporters say they feel so strongly about the issue that they would vote against a senator who joins the other side."

Some words of caution are in order. Polls only measure how people feel about an issue at the time they're polled. Whether people with strong feelings about an issue at one point in time will have the same feelings some years later is uncertain. Fortunately for senators, they come up for reelection only once every six years. Today's strong feelings may well be weak ones tomorrow, provided that by "tomorrow" we mean some years from now.

STABILITY

Whether an opinion has stability is of concern to the public relations practitioner because it indicates the degree of commitment to the issue in question. Opinions which have a high degree of stability are not easily changed. They demonstrate that the individual having that opinion has held to it for a long period of time, considers it important, and is not likely to alter it readily. Low stability or unstable opinions, on the other hand, are not important to those holding them and may readily be changed given the proper circumstances.

Public opinion polls taken over a long period of time that ask the same questions at varying intervals show that on certain issues there is a high degree of opinion stability. Over a period of many decades the majority of Americans have been consistently negative in their opinion about communism and consistently firm in their feeling that America should maintain a strong military establishment. Opinions about the job being done by the president, however, have been highly unstable, and it doesn't seem to matter who happens to be the president. According to the Gallup Poll, President Truman's approval rating during his first twenty months in office ranged from a high of 87 percent to a low of 32 percent, and similar sharp swings in approval were shown for succeeding presidents. The unstable nature of presidential popularity is shown in the chart below, which shows the highest and lowest approval ratings during the first twenty months in office of presidents from Truman through Reagan. The percentages represent approval responses to the question "Do you approve or disapprove of the way (name of the president) is handling his job as president?"

Highest/Lowest Approval Ratings During First 20 Months

	Highest	Lowest
Truman	87%	32%
Eisenhower	75%	59%
Kennedy	83%	66%
Johnson	80%	64%
Nixon	68%	53%
Ford	71%	37%
Carter	72%	39%
Reagan	68%	41%

Source: Surveys by American Institute of Public Opinion (Gallup), most recent in 1983. See *Public Opinion*, April/May 1983, p. 32.

Although there has been a high degree of instability of opinion regarding personalities, as a general rule there has been a high degree of stability of opinion concerning matters of basic concern to most people. Pollsters Charles Roll, Jr., and Albert H. Cantril report that the major concerns of the American people "continue to be good health, a better standard of living, peace, the achievement of aspirations for one's children, a good job, and a happy family life."[8] Political scientist Alan D. Monroe suggests the following reasons for the relative stability of public opinion on most substantive issues:[9]

1. People resist changing their minds, and social factors such as economic status, race, and religion reinforce this tendency.

2. Personal contact reinforces stabilization of opinion because people tend to talk to others who hold the same views.

3. The political system also works against change. Parties, political leaders, and loyal followers tend to hold to the same positions over the years.

4. Individual changes of opinion largely cancel each other out.

LATENCY

Latent opinion, according to V. O. Key, is "really about the only type of opinion that generates much anxiety" in the practice of politics and government. He suggests the following kinds of questions should be asked of latent opinions: "What opinion will develop about this prospective candidate? What opinions will be stirred by this legislative proposal? What opinions, anxieties and moods will be generated by this event or by that action?"

A Poll Watcher Sums Up the Stability Factor

In the fifth anniversary issue (April/May 1983) of *Public Opinion* magazine, Senior Editor Everett C. Ladd looked at five years of surveys and concluded that mass public opinion is remarkably stable. Stated Ladd:

> Over the five years that my colleagues and I have been closely monitoring opinion research for this magazine . . . we have had reason to remark upon the underlying stability of public opinion.
>
> Since the first issue of *Public Opinion* appeared in the spring of 1978, American politics has had its fair share of turbulence and change. Three national elections have intervened. . . . The economy has moved from high inflation to high unemployment; from a petroleum shortage with sharp price increases to an "oil glut" and price moderation. . . . We have read over the past five years of the rise and fall of "taxpayers' revolts," of a major "swing to the right" in public preferences followed by a "return to the center," of a "sweeping Reagan mandate." . . .
>
> Yet . . . we are struck by how little the nation's attitudes and values have shifted in the face of the kaleidoscopic changes in the political setting. The basic distribution of partisan preferences, as reflected by party identification, has been almost unaltered over the years from 1978 to 1983. So, too, has been the description Americans give to their ideological commitments—in liberal-conservative or left-right terms. The public's views of the country, its prospects, and its central institutions have changed hardly at all. Attitudes toward government, and taxing and spending, have shown great stability. So have a broad array of social and cultural values. . . .
>
> Stability, not sudden lurchings this way and that, is the norm. When shifts in underlying attitudes do occur, they do so gradually, in response to lasting transformations of social organizations and the reapplication of old values therein made necessary.[10]

Key's questions certainly apply to policies, statements, and actions of all, not merely political, organizations and institutions. The college mulling the size of a tuition increase should ask: "What opinions will develop about this prospective increase?" The trade association advocating a fair trade law should ask: "What opinions will be stirred by this legislative proposal?" The company trying to decide whether to close a plant and move it elsewhere should ask: "What opinions, anxieties, and moods will be generated by this event or that action?"[11]

Key suggests that in considering latent opinion we should distinguish between latent opinion of the "attentive public" and the "great inattentive public." As examples of the attentive public he cites the American Medical Association, the National Association of Manufacturers, and the AFL-CIO, and he says that over the short run the latent opinions of such groups can be anticipated because, as he puts it, "these attentive publics have their patterns of reaction that serve as bases for predictable response." The inattentive public, on the other hand, poses a much more difficult problem and situation. The problem, Key says, results from "uncertainties about whether mass attention will be mobilized or whether it will remain indifferent and uninformed."[12]

Handling latent opinion, then, becomes a matter of predicting and sensing when public response to an issue or event will be temporary or more than just of the moment. It would be wise to view latent opinion as one might view a sleeping German shepherd dog. Because it's dormant doesn't mean it's dead; because it's sleeping doesn't mean it can't be aroused; because it seems so peaceful doesn't mean it's not powerful once aroused.

Estimating latent opinion involves the estimation of three elements:

1. Those sectors of society—the various publics and subpublics—affected by the issue

2. The nature of the event or issue

3. The intensity of feeling one might expect from the aroused latent opinion

All three elements are interrelated, so the practitioner must use careful judgment in assessing and dealing with them. However, the nature of the issue or event seems to be the crucial factor in trying to assess its impact on latent opinion. Some issues and events are of such a universal nature that they're bound to command a wide audience and arouse strong feelings in that audience. Others will be perceived as being of minor significance and will impact only on a small number of people. Not to be overlooked is the fact that issues and events are in competition with themselves for public attention; an issue or event that might normally be expected to arouse strong feelings among many segments of society may pass unnoticed because it takes place at the same time as a far more profound issue or event.

Is there a guideline for attempting to assess the impact of an issue, event, or statement? Key makes the following suggestion:

> An action that clearly conflicts with a widely held attitude may be expected to stir up controversy if it comes to public attention; an action patently within the limits of the firmly held norms may pass unnoticed or arouse only mild approbation. Many governmental actions attract little attention because they raise questions within the permissive limits fixed by latent opinion. The excoriation of cancer, the idealization of the American mother, and the condemnation of sin never get a politician in trouble.[13]

PUBLIC OPINION

In attempting to define public opinion the social scientists have had as much trouble as the poets and philosophers have had in attempting to define beauty. To John Keats, "Beauty is truth," and if that doesn't help he proposes that "truth is beauty" and advises us that it is all we know on earth and all we need to know. Taking the safer approach, philosopher George Santayana tells us in one breath that beauty is indescribable and he then proceeds to describe it as "a pledge of the possible conformity between the soul and nature." Kahlil Gibran conceives of beauty as "eternity gazing at itself in a mirror." Those who seek to capture the essence of beauty by relying on the poets and philosophers have been given some fascinating choices; they can either find it in truth, the indescribable, or eternity.

Though they are considered to be a more practical lot than the poets and philosophers, the social scientists have been equally obtuse in trying to define public opinion. Their attempts to pin down the term range from the simple to the complex, from the tentative to the definitive, from being so all-inclusive as to be virtually unfathomable.

This conclusion is evident from Floyd H. Allport's article in the very first issue of the *Public Opinion Quarterly*, in which he described public opinion as follows:

> The term public opinion is given its meaning with reference to a multi-individual situation in which individuals are expressing themselves, or can be called upon to express themselves, as favoring (or else disfavoring or opposing) some definite condition, person, or proposal of widespread importance, in such a proportion of number, intensity, and constancy, as to give rise to the probability of affecting action, directly, or indirectly, toward the object concerned.[14]

If you're adventurous you might try playing Allport's definition on your flugelhorn, but it won't be of much help if you try to use it to deal with public opinion in a practical situation. Allport's definition is important, however, because it indicates his tortuous attempt to cope with the many contingencies which involve public opinion. All too often those defining public opinion do so from the vantage point of their special interest. Note, for example, the connection (in italics by the author) between the specialist and the definitions cited below:

> *Political scientist* V. O. Key defines public opinion as "those opinions held by private persons which *governments* find it prudent to heed."

> Lucien Warner, writing about *public opinion surveys,* describes public opinion as "people's reactions to *definitely worded statements and questions under interview conditions.*"

> James Bryce, one of the earliest writers on the *government process,* saw public opinion as "the power exerted by any such view, or set of views, when *held by an apparent majority of citizens.*"

> *Sociologist* G. A. Lundberg described public opinion as "that opinion though it be the opinion of a *single individual* in which the public in question finds itself for any reason constrained to acquiesce."

> *Social psychologist* L. L. Bernard considered public opinion to be "any fairly uniform collective expression of *mental or inner behavior reactions.*"

Harwood Childs felt it necessary and important to cut through the verbiage and to eliminate the specialist's approach. His simple definition, which this author believes sufficient for the purposes of this book, states that public opinion is *"simply any collection of individual opinions designated."* Though he admits his definition is a very broad one, he believes it's applicable to public relations because both "public opinion" and "public relations" are very broad in meaning and assume validity when they relate to particular publics. Noting that an opinion is always that of a person, Childs stresses that public opinion always refers to a collection of individual opinions and hence *if we want to ascertain a given state of public opinion we have to ascertain the opinions of individuals.*[15]

Childs is also critical of those who set forth certain principles of public opinion or who would narrow the meaning of the term to include only those collections of opinion which have a specific degree of uniformity. In his view *there are no public opinion principles which are applicable under all circumstances.*

"All principles," he notes, "hold true only under certain circumstances. Given the conditions, the principles will apply. But the conditions must be stated. This is what makes the study of public opinion and public relations so difficult. Conditions vary; publics differ; the relations between groups are always changing. Generalizations regarding human behavior and human relations are peculiarly hazardous to make."[16]

As for the alleged need for the existence of a degree of uniformity, Childs points out that this is a matter of investigation not an a priori condition of public opinion. As he puts it: "The degree of uniformity is a matter to be investigated, not something to be arbitrarily set up as a condition for the existence of public opinion."[17]

Summed up, then, public opinion is a general and inclusive term. It always refers to a collection of individual opinions. It can be studied with some degree of significance when related to a particular public and to specific opinions about definite subjects. The source for the opinions of individuals and an analysis of how opinions are formed will be examined in the section that follows.

THE FORMATION OF PUBLIC OPINION

Of crucial importance to the student of public relations is not merely understanding the nature of publics, opinion, and public opinion, but also understanding how public opinion is formed. Unfortunately for those who dote on pat answers that can be highlighted by multicolored markers, there are no pat answers to the process of opinion formation. So many factors are involved in the process of opinion formation that it is well-nigh impossible to state with certainty that this factor, that factor, or a set of factors causes opinion to develop in a certain way. At best, one can seek the answer to the quandary of opinion formation only in very broad, general terms. Stated in such terms, the two major elements in the process of opinion formation are the *person* and the *environment*.

THE PERSON

When we look at the individual we should recognize that the list of tangible and intangible attributes that can be used as factors to explain personality, attitude, and opinions is endless. Some authorities concentrate on such factors as perceptions, habits, complexes, frames of reference, and values. Others cite self-esteem, loyalties, moods, and drives. Still others cite traits such as introvert, extrovert, and inner- and outer-directed. The list of personal attributes of the individual is infinite and impossible to weigh and assess with any degree of certainty.

Though it may not be possible to weigh personal attributes accurately, their importance in the process of opinion formation cannot be denied. Our physiological, biological, and psychological traits and makeup undoubtedly play a role in the way we view issues, actions, and events. Thus they form an integral share of the mix that results in the formation of our opinions.

THE ENVIRONMENT

As with personality traits, there is no end of environmental factors affecting the process of opinion formation. Some are general and some specific; some are remote and some proximate; some are stable and some changeable; some are large and some small. The list includes economic, religious, and political institutions; physical, biological, and sociological factors; demographic, climatic, and topographical features; professional, peer, ethnic, and special-purpose groups; the government; and mass media of communication. Mind-boggling in its array and diversity, the list is of great importance because each element can play a vital role in the formation of public opinion.

> The dubious reader may cast a jaundiced eye on some of the previously mentioned environmental factors, but consider the answers to the following questions.
>
> *Re climate:* Would the cold climate of the frozen north cause an Eskimo to have an opinion on certain issues different from that of an Amazonian who lives in the torrid climate of the equator?
>
> *Re demography:* Would a woman aged 76 have a different opinion of Social Security than a young woman aged 21?
>
> *Re profession:* Would a doctor have a different view of malpractice insurance than a trial lawyer?
>
> *Re sociology:* Would an inner city mother have a different view of busing than a suburban mother?

The answer to all four questions is yes, chiefly because of environmental factors influencing the people concerned. Of course, the factors have been posed here within the context of situations to which they are directly related. In most cases, however, such a connection between environmental factors, situation, and opinion formation is much more tenuous. Those factors which are significant and those which are insignificant in the formation of opinion usually cannot be sorted out.

In the early formative years of most people three environmental factors—the family church/religion, and the school—are considered to be of paramount importance.

The **family** is the source of one's first impressions, early habits, likes, dislikes, prejudices, and goals. The family has a direct influence on the selection of childhood companions and on attitudes towards a wide variety of subjects. Because the family isolates the small child from other countervailing forces, it has a great influence on his character, motivation, personal habits, and ideals.

The **church and/or religion** begin to make their influence felt at a very early age and for many people continue throughout a lifetime. In addition to providing the basis for beliefs and opinions relative to God, life after death, salvation, and other tenets, the church and religion influence opinions about sin, sex, tolerance and intolerance, economic, social, and political matters.

The **school,** and especially the public school, commences the process of socialization which continues throughout a lifetime. Traditions, learning, and skills necessary to maintain a society are transmitted through the schools. The range of information about public policies increases in direct proportion to the amount of schooling an individual has. On economic and political matters, the school tends to reflect family and community attitudes. Observes V. O. Key: "In the largest sense the educational system is a great mechanism for *conserving* the values, the institutions, the practices of the political order, as it inculcates from the primary school even through college the memories, the unities, and the norms of the system."

As the child becomes the youth and the youth the adult, other key environmental factors come into play and either reinforce or subvert the early influences of family, church/religion, and the school. By the manner in which they funnel information, entertainment, and opinion the media provide the means whereby the individual ascertains facts, perceives and identifies issues and problems, and becomes aware of alternative solutions. Peer, professional, and interest groups exert a modifying influence on individual opinions, and in some cases profoundly shape such opinions. Even the issue itself—the time it takes place and its setting—becomes an environmental factor influencing opinion formation. All these factors play roles in the opinion formation process. Trying to ascertain the relative importance of each factor becomes a task worthy of a Solomon, and even he might not be up to handling it.

THE FORMULA APPROACH

In attempting to bring order out of the chaos of the many factors involved in the process of opinion formation, some authorities have evolved tidy formulae to describe the process. They usually imply or directly contend that opinion formulation is an orderly, rational procedure with debate pro and con followed by some form of agreement or consensus.

For example, here is how one book describes the process of opinion formation:

1. A number of people recognize a situation as being problematic and decide that something ought to be done about it. They explore possible solutions and do some fact-finding.

2. Alternative proposals for solving the problem emerge, and these are discussed back and forth.

3. A policy or solution is agreed upon as best meeting the situation recognized as problematic. Agreement and a decision to promote its acceptance lead to group consciousness.

4. A program of action is undertaken, and this is pressed until the requisite action is obtained or the group becomes weary of the battle and its members turn to other projects and other groups.

Another author has a shorter version of the opinion formation process: "A treatment of the dynamics of public opinion formation must concern itself with at least three major phases: (1) the rise of the issue; (2) the discussion about the issue and proposed solutions pro and con; and (3) the arrival at consensus."

The major problem with the above-mentioned formula approaches to the opinion formation process is that either they seem to be taking place in some sort of apolitical vacuum or else they're describing how organizations supposedly debate alternative solutions to problems. Properly labeled, they may well describe "How Insiders Debate An Issue and Decide On Action To Be Taken."

But *public* opinion, which is the subject being discussed, is not arrived at so tidily, nor is the public usually privy to the discussion and the pro and con that may well take place before some organization decides on a policy or action. Further, the public is not some sort of neat entity which by some means or other goes through a series of steps to reach a decision on an issue. To visualize opinion formation as a standard pattern is to engage in a set of generalizations which can lead only to the illusion of reality but which reality itself belies. The members of publics and subpublics may well form opinions about issues and events, but they are seldom in the position to have a direct influence or part in the actions taken by authorities and organizations. V. O. Key sums up the criticism of the tidy formula approach to the process of opinion formation in the following words:

> More is lost than is gained in understanding by the organismic view of the public. Occasionally, in relatively small communities, citizen concern and involvement over an issue may be widespread and community consideration may move in close articulation with the mechanism of authority to a decision that can realistically be said to be a decision by public opinion. At far rarer intervals great national populations may be swept by a common concern about a momentous issue with a similar result. Yet ordinarily a decision is made not by the public but by officials after greater or lesser consideration of the opinion of the public or parts of the public.[18]

In summation, the following can be said about the process of public opinion formulation:

1. The factors involved in the formation of public opinion relate to the *person* and the *environment* but they are so numerous it is impossible to state which are paramount and which secondary.

2. The influence on opinion of the family, church/religion, and the school are considered to be of paramount importance in the formative years. Thereafter, other key environmental influences begin to be felt.

3. There is no pat formula to describe the process of opinion formation. The process is too full of variables; untidy rather than tidy; often irrational rather than rational.

NEWSOM'S PUBLIC OPINION SIGNPOSTS

Seekers of truth, wandering among the public opinion thickets, will be helped along the way by four signposts erected by veteran counselor Earl Newsom.[19] Newsom notes that many carefully conceived and executed campaigns designed to "educate the public" subsequently fail because of myopia about the intended audience of these campaigns. All too often, says Newsom, the sponsor of an idea, point of view, or opinion fails to ask this simple question: "Does it clearly help toward the solution of a problem which worries those I am addressing?" If the answer is yes, the sponsor of the idea has correctly read Newsom's first signpost, which is cited below.

THE IDENTIFICATION SIGNPOST

"People will ignore (or won't support) an idea, an opinion, a point of view unless they see clearly that it affects (in a positive way) their personal fears or desires, hopes or aspirations."

Self-motivation—an expression of the id and the ego that possess all of us—is a powerful force. "What's-in-it-for-me?" asks the recipient of a message. In too many instances the sender is too busy composing his message to consider the recipient, and there are far too many cases where the sender is so inconsiderate he sends the message "to whom it may concern." Sending messages without careful consideration of a specific audience and of the desires, hopes, and ambitions of its members is like blowing dandelion seeds into the wind.

To reach people, to influence their opinions, a first necessity is to *appeal to their personal interests*, to show them clearly that your words or actions *identify in a positive manner with their present and pressing problems.*

This is often more easily said than accomplished. It *presumes* that the sender of an idea, opinion, or point of view has knowledge and understanding of the personal interests of the recipient. But if the sender and the recipient live in different social and economic worlds—as is most often the case—the gap between them serves as an effective barrier to knowledge and understanding. On a clear day one can easily see the South Bronx from a window high up on a Madison Avenue office building. On any weekday that same Madison Avenue public relations writer or advertising copywriter rides past block after block of crowded inner-city housing on his or her way to life in the "safe" suburbs. But sight and proximity do not equate to real knowledge and understanding, and that's one reason why many public relations messages and advertising commercials are either laughed at or ignored by their intended audience.

Being able to identify with your audience is even more difficult when the audience is not in sight nor close by. And yet, as you read this text, hundreds of public relations practitioners in New York, Chicago, Los Angeles, and other large cities are composing messages beamed at people living and working in the so-called hinterlands. At worst, practitioners blithely assume that messages exist in some sort of limbo land where life is uncomplicated and people are so unsophisticated that they don't know what is in their own self-interest. At best, practitioners should at least *recognize* the identification problem and attempt to solve it through observation, reading, research, and careful monitoring of audience mood, interests, and opinion.

THE ACTION SIGNPOST

> "*People do not buy ideas separated from action—either action taken or about to be taken by the sponsor of the idea, or action which people themselves can conveniently take to prove the merit of the idea.*"

We tend to reject words which are divorced from actions. An organization's words and its actions must be compatible if the words are to be believed. In forming their opinions about organizations, individuals base their judgments as much on what organizations *do* as on what they say. And if what they "do" is contrary to what they say, the public will generally base its opinions on the doing rather than the saying.

Modern-day life abounds with illustrations—usually in the negative—of the action guidepost. There's the corporation which touts the free enterprise system in its advertising but which engages in price-fixing and other anticompetitive activities. There's the legislator who promises to cut down on unnecessary government spending but then votes himself a hefty salary boost. There's the United States of America which is dedicated to democratic principles but which at times provides economic and military aid to totalitarian regimes.

Eliza Doolittle spoke for the cockney in all of us when she shouted "Show Me!" in response to a torrent of words, words, words about love. We seek to be shown by actions, not merely by words, and our opinions tend to be positive when we perceive that the actions of organizations are those which affirmatively affect our important personal interests.

Summed up, the action signpost warns that words are insufficient by themselves to engender favorable public opinion. Taken together, words and actions support themselves if they are compatible, honest, and appeal to people's self-interests.

THE FAMILIARITY AND TRUST SIGNPOST

"We the people buy ideas only from those we trust; we are influenced by, or adopt, only those opinions or points of view put forward by individuals or corporations or institutions in whom we have confidence."

Simple ideas sometimes have profound meanings, and this third Newsom signpost teaches an important lesson about the formation of public opinion in the twentieth century.

The world is too much with us yet, as William Wordsworth reminded us in the eighteenth century. Wordsworth was able to retreat from his world by turning to nature, but modern men and women retreat by turning off the world. Wise in the knowledge that the world is too complex and complicated to understand, the individual today must nonetheless have opinions and judgments. Wisely or not, the individual relies on the opinions and judgments of those he trusts.

Very often these "trustees" of opinion and judgment are newspaper columnists and editorial writers, radio and television commentators, political figures, teachers, doctors and priests, rabbis and ministers. Or, on a smaller scale, the trustees may be certain key people among the many groups to which we belong. To the leader who rises up to serve our needs, we entrust our opinions, our judgments, and our decisions.

"Our every act," says Newsom, "is the voicing of a preference. We 'vote' when we pick our grocery store, our gas station, our doctor, our college, the movie we go to, the radio program to which we listen, the charities to which we send our checks."

Is our vote based on intimate knowledge of the store, the gas station, the doctor, etc.? Scarcely, because we haven't the time to acquire this knowledge. We give them our vote because we've learned at some time or another to have confidence and trust in them; once we lose this trust and confidence we cast our vote elsewhere.

Wise practitioners recognize the importance of Newsom's third signpost. They know that the building of trust is not an overnight matter, but one that takes years to achieve. They also know the value of "trustee endorsement," and they therefore cultivate those people, groups, and institutions in whom people have a great deal of trust and confidence. A few words of endorsement from a trusted source are of far greater value than a torrent of words from a relatively unknown, distant, or untrusted source.

THE CLARITY SIGNPOST

"The situation must be clear to us, not confusing. The thing we observe, read, see, or hear, the thing which produces our impressions, must be clear, not subject to several interpretations."

The American landscape is unfortunately littered with statements which are obtuse, unclear, confusing, and open to varying interpretations. On the presidential level there's the press secretary's use of the word "inoperative" to explain away his own crossed signals. On the professional level in almost every field there's the use of jargon, circumlocution, and obfuscation in phrases which talk about:

maximization of profits
delimitation of debts
cancellations
factor analysis by means of chi
    square deviations

empirically derived taxonomies
normative sanction patterns of
    causative behavior
the limited channel capacity of the
    perceptual system

Reading the above, one wonders what's happened to the English language. Organizations can't expect others to understand them if they can't explain their actions clearly and without equivocation. The basic trouble seems to reside in the fact that the truth of an action or statement, simply and clearly stated, seems to be an insurmountable barrier among organizations which are afraid to trust the people with simple, unvarnished truths. But if we can't trust people with the truth, then we don't deserve their support.

Newsom's fourth signpost is predicated on the premise that the action point of view being clarified is one that reflects favorably on the organization or individual taking the action or advocating the point of view. There are two circumstances, however, where the action or point of view reflects unfavorably on the proponent and yet is illuminated with such blinding clarity as to remain indelibly fixed in the public mind.

The first of these two unfortunate circumstances most often occurs on impromptu occasions and usually results from off-the-cuff remarks or from hasty responses to press inquiries. The thoughtless statement which triggers unfavorable public reaction almost never occurs as a result of carefully designed and written statements because these are usually edited with care and foresight. Rather, it's the quick response that brings about the negative reaction, and it takes place in interviews; at question time following press conferences; on radio and television talk shows; and at impromptu sessions during political campaigns. There's little the public relations specialist can do about such situations except to brief his client or spokesman in advance or to batten down the hatches and try to repair the damages once the winds blow.

The second of the two unfortunate circumstances involving clarity occurs when remarks are stated clearly but subsequently are either wrongly reported or simply distorted. Public relations men and women are, of course, not responsible for the manner in which statements and remarks are handled by the media. However, it is their responsibility to monitor press treatment of statements and/or actions and to suggest appropriate and, hopefully, judicious response and reaction. The response, of course, may well be a decision not to respond. The decision whether to respond or not to respond becomes a matter of professional judgment, experience, and thoughtful assessment of expected public reaction.

Whether the fault lies in the one who makes the statement or in the media handling of the statement, Newsom's clarity signpost holds true and should be a steadfast guide: the situation must be clear . . . not confusing. The more clear the situation, explanation, or statement, the less likely it will be misinterpreted. Even though we identify with our publics, even though we have their trust, and even though our words and our actions are compatible, we don't gain public approval or understanding unless we explain ourselves clearly.

ENDNOTES

1. Richard W. Skinner and William L. Shankin, "The Changing Role of Public Relations in Business Firms," *Public Relations Review*, Summer 1978, p. 4.
2. Curtis D. MacDougall, *Understanding Public Opinion* (Dubuque, Iowa: Wm. C. Brown Co., 1966), p. 66.
3. Ibid., p. 67.
4. Ibid., p. 64.
5. William Albig, *Modern Public Opinion* (New York: McGraw-Hill, 1956), p. 83.
6. Walter Lippmann, *Public Opinion*, Macmillan Paperbacks edition (New York: Macmillan, 1960), pp. 29-32, 79-94.
7. V. O. Key, Jr., *Public Opinion and American Democracy* (New York: Alfred A. Knopf, 1961), p. 11.
8. Charles W. Roll, Jr., and Albert H. Cantril, *Polls* (New York: Basic Books, 1972), p. 122.
9. Alan D. Monroe, *Public Opinion in America* (New York: Dodd, Mead & Co., 1975), p. 241.
10. Everett C. Ladd, "Public Opinion: Questions at the Quinquennial," *Public Opinion*, April/May 1983, p. 20.

11. Key, p. 262.
12. Ibid., p. 265.
13. Ibid., p. 266.
14. Floyd H. Allport, "Toward a Science of Public Opinion," *Public Opinion Quarterly*, January 1937, pp. 7-23.
15. Harwood Childs, *An Introduction to Public Opinion* (New York: John Wiley & Sons, 1940), pp. 44-45.
16. Ibid., p. 46.
17. Ibid., p. 47.
18. Key, p. 9.
19. From a lecture by Earl Newsom at the New School for Social Research, New York City, April 12, 1950.

PROJECTS, ASSIGNMENTS, AND MINIS

1. THE PRESIDENT OF OTIS ELEVATOR DELIVERS A TALK: A MINI-CASE CLASSIC*

Not many weeks after the Alexander Smith Carpet Company moved its mills from Yonkers, New York, to a new location in the South, President Le Roy A. Petersen of the Otis Elevator Company delivered a talk to an invited audience of over two thousand Otis employees and Yonkers city officials. (The same talk was given to employees of Otis in Harrison, New Jersey.)

At the time (January, 1955) Otis had been part of the industrial base of Yonkers for 101 years, had a local yearly payroll of more than ten million dollars, and was one of the community's major taxpayers. The talk was given at 9 a.m. and the setting was the Brandt Theatre in Yonkers.

President Petersen began his talk by citing the loyalty of the two thousand Otis men and women who had received service pins the previous year for service records ranging from 25 to 55 years with the company. Stressing the fine reputation of the company in the design, manufacture, and installation of elevators and escalators, Petersen discussed the large number of competitors who had entered the field in the past decade.

"These statements," he said, "should not be interpreted as indicating that the Otis Elevator Company has ceased to be a profitable company or is on the verge of becoming an unprofitable one. On the contrary, it is anticipated that, since our income is derived from a variety of sources, including a substantial service business and extensive operations throughout the world, the annual report for 1954 will show an increase over the previous year in sales and earnings. In addition, it is believed that our backlog will assure a profitable level of operations in 1955.

"However, the Yonkers Works is primarily engaged in the manufacture of equipment for new elevators for domestic use and has relatively little to do with service or foreign operations and its performance must be judged solely by the quality and cost of the products it makes. . . .

"The Otis Elevator Company has prospered and has been a source of employment in Yonkers for more than a hundred years because it has continued to manufacture high quality product at a cost sufficiently low to permit it to be sold with a fair profit at a competitive price.

"Unless we can continue to do this, we will cease to be a prosperous company and will also cease to be a source of employment. It is, therefore, my duty and obligation as president of this company to take such steps as may be necessary to maintain Otis quality and still reduce costs to the point where we can continue to secure the necessary volume at a profitable price."

Stating that an extensive study had been conducted to ascertain how the needed reduction in cost could best be accomplished, Petersen said:

"Of particular interest to you, however, is the result of the study relating to manufacture, and this study indicated that an annual saving in manufacturing costs of several million dollars could be secured by building a single plant to replace the Yonkers and Harrison plants, and that this plant should be located in the Middle West near the geographical center of our elevator market. . . .

"A further careful study has, therefore, been made which indicates that about half of the savings that are attributable to a new midwestern plant could be accomplished in our present plants, provided we secure the enthusiastic and understanding cooperation of our employees and of the city authorities.

---

*Although this case took place in the mid-fifties, it has continued to serve as the focal point of valuable pro-con discussion and is therefore carried over into the third edition of this book.

"With the purpose of preserving as many as possible of your jobs with Otis in Yonkers and a local payroll amounting to about ten million dollars per year, we are willing and anxious to make every effort to continue the operation of the Yonkers plant provided we are able to accomplish, with a minimum delay, the reduction in cost which we believe is reasonably obtainable in this location.

"A definite decision to take such steps as are necessary to reduce costs substantially has already been made, and the only question remaining is which of the known methods will be chosen. If we are unable to bring about these reductions in cost in our present plants, we will have no choice but to transfer our manufacturing, as soon as possible, to a new midwestern plant—and will not hesitate to do so if it becomes clearly necessary. . . .

"Kindly note that our plans for reduced costs are not based upon any change in our past policy of paying all who work for Otis at least as much as is paid by other reputable and comparable companies for similar jobs, both in the form of wages and salaries and in supplementary benefits. It is still our desire to keep the Yonkers Plant not only a place in which to work, but a *good* place in which to work.

"Rather, our ability to secure reduced costs here and now is dependent upon our receiving your active cooperation in eliminating avoidable and unjustifiable expense and in reducing lost time and motion, in increasing the efficient use of existing equipment, and in utilizing to the utmost the production capacity of such new equipment as may be warranted in installing. We will welcome your suggestions.

"In seeking to accomplish our objectives, we propose, of course, to work with and through the unions which you have selected as your bargaining agents and to solicit the active cooperation of their officials. . . .

"I trust that you will clearly understand that this is not an attempt to persuade you to do anything that you do not want to do or which you do not recognize as being clearly in your own interest.

"It should be apparent that the Yonkers Works has, in effect, become a community enterprise. The Company, because of its earnest desire to retain its present organization and to continue to provide good jobs for its loyal employees, has indicated its willingness to forego some of the larger savings obtainable by other methods and to continue to operate the Yonkers Plant as long as it can afford to do so. It cannot afford to continue to operate it under present conditions—but is offering you an opportunity to create the conditions under which we could afford to continue its operation.

"We could, of course, have decided to go ahead imediately with the building of a new central plant, basing our decision solely upon the outcome of the study which clearly showed savings sufficient to justify the investment, the cost of transfer and the loss on existing plants.

"We could, and some may say that we should, have done this without prior discussion with you. I trust that you feel, as I do, that in fairness to you and to the City of Yonkers, this prior general discussion is desirable.

"I also trust that you realize that we are trying to help you retain your jobs with Otis and that we hope that, together, we will be successful in doing so.

"Next week, we will present to your union officials concrete proposals outlining the conditions which we consider reasonable and essential for continued future operations in Yonkers.

"We sincerely hope that these proposals will be recognized as consistent with the interest and welfare of our Yonkers employees and that agreement will be reached for their early adoption.

"We are prepared to make substantial additional investment in the Yonkers Plant, if such investment appears to be clearly justified. We will do our best to further improve our methods. We will look to the city authorities for fair treatment on taxes and for a disposition to help in all other ways consistent with the welfare of the city as a whole.

"The rest is up to you, and we hope that you will give the problem careful consideration."

The day following Mr. Petersen's talk, the New York *Times* reported it in a front-page story with the headline:

OTIS ULTIMATUM
GIVEN IN YONKERS

City Officials and Employees
Told Costs Must Be Cut or
Elevator Company Moves

The lead paragraph stated that "The Otis Elevator Company issued an ultimatum today to 2,000 employees and city officials. It said: 'Cooperate to cut costs or the company will move to a new plant in the Midwest.' "

After reporting the essence of Petersen's talk, the story continued: "Members of the audience sat throughout the talk quietly. There was scattered applause when the company president walked from the wings to a mid-stage lectern. There was no interruption of his speech and no visible reaction at its conclusion. His listeners filed quickly and silently from the big theatre."

The story quoted the union representing the Yonkers plant employees as calling attention to the following points:

> The Otis Elevator Company has averaged over $9,400,000 net profit for the last eighty years. This represents a return of 18 percent of net worth. Most companies regard 8 percent as a high return. A few short months ago Mr. Petersen in reporting to the stockholders of this corporation stated that the outlook for the future was for increased business. He also reported a record for bookings.

"The existing contract between Otis and the union," the story continued, "does not expire until next June. In 1947 the company closed its Buffalo plant, employing 1,000, and transferred operations to the Yonkers and Harrison works. The move was attributed to 'changes in the elevator industry and the plant's obsolete equipment.'

"Last month Mr. Petersen announced an extra common stock dividend of 50 cents a share. At the same time a regular quarterly dividend of 62½ cents was declared. Dividend declarations for 1954 came to $3 a share, or 25 cents a share more than in the previous year. The net income for the first nine months of 1954 was $6,689,057. For the same period in 1953 the net wa $6,179,807.

"Charles Curran, Yonkers City Manager, when asked for comment on Mr. Petersen's appeal for 'fair treatment on taxes and for a disposition to help in all other ways consistent with the welfare of the city as a whole,' declared:

" 'We certainly don't want to lose Otis. We'll give them all the cooperation we can.' "

Questions for Discussion

1. What's your judgment of Mr. Petersen's talk—its contents, circumstances of delivery, and reported audience reaction—as it relates to the four signposts of Earl Newsom? That is, evaluate the speech in terms of Newsom's signposts for achieving favorable public opinion.

2. Assume that you are public relations counsel to the Otis Elevator Company. You have been shown a draft of the speech prior to its delivery and have been told when, where, how, and to whom it will be given. You are asked to provide your professional advice about the speech and its projected delivery. Please do so, and justify your conclusions.

3. What questions would you ask and what kind of information about the Otis situation would you want to know which has not been given in the case description?

4. Comment on the following release, which was sent out by public relations counsel to the company:

FOR: OTIS ELEVATOR COMPANY
FROM: (Name, address, and phone
        number of PR counsel)

NOT FOR RELEASE BEFORE 12:00 NOON
SATURDAY, JANUARY 15, 1955

(*Note:* Copy which follows
    was double-spaced)

At a meeting held today at the Brandt Theatre in Yonkers, New York, L. A. Petersen, President of Otis Elevator Company, told over 2,000 employees of the Otis Yonkers Works and a group of city officials that sales and earnings in 1954 were expected to exceed those of 1953 and that satisfactory operations were anticipated in 1955.

He pointed out, however, that the number of competitors had more than doubled during the last eight years to a present total of 262 and that substantial reductions in cost were necessary to retain the company's competitive position.

Mr. Petersen stated that an extensive study had indicated that a saving of several million dollars could be secured by establishing a single midwestern plant to replace the present plants at Yonkers, New York, and Harrison, New Jersey, but that, in consideration of the hardship that would be imposed upon present employees, every effort would be made to secure a sufficient reduction in costs in the present plants to avoid the necessity for moving to a new central plant.

Mr. Petersen emphasized that the plans for reducing cost were not based upon any change in the past policy of paying all who work for Otis at least as much as is paid by other reputable and comparable companies for similar jobs, both in the form of wages and salaries and in supplementary benefits, but that such plans were based upon the efficient use of new and existing equipment.

He expressed the opinion that the success of these efforts would depend upon the cooperation received from employees and union officials.

A similar meeting was held later on today at the Otis plant in Harrison, N.J.
—30—

5. In response to a request by the author, the account executive of Otis's public relations counsel sent the above news release and a copy of Mr. Petersen's remarks. He closed by stating: "I am sure you will understand how delicate a matter this is and that it requires the utmost fairness and tact. Mr. Petersen approached the problem and the employees in this spirit."

What is your reaction to his statement?

2. DOCUMENTING A PUBLIC OPINION CASE: A RESEARCH PAPER

You are required in this assignment to select a situation occurring within the past month or two months and involving the manner in which a ꞏꞏꞏ ꞏꞏꞏ ꞏꞏꞏ ꞏd/or organization dealt with public opinion.

In meeting the requirements of this assignment you should prepare a paper which explains the following:

1. The nature of the situation and its relationship to the person and/or organization involved.

2. The dimensions of public opinion expressed about the situation and the person and/or organization involved.

3. The manner in which the person and/or organization attempted to deal with the expressed public opinion.

4. Your evaluation of the judgment and public relations skills demonstrated by the person and/or organization in dealing with the situation and the expressed public opinion.

Documentation for this paper should stem from articles and stories in newspapers or magazines. Use appropriate footnote references where necessary. Append photocopies of source material when such material is available.

3. REPORTING/EVALUATING A PUBLIC OPINION ARTICLE: A MINI-ASSIGNMENT

Select an article about public opinion appearing within the past year in one of the following publications: *Public Opinion Quarterly; Public Relations Review; Public Relations Journal; Public Relations Quarterly; Communication World.*

In a memorandum to your instructor write a report **summarizing the main points** of the article and setting forth **your evaluation of the article.** Do have a point of view about the article and seek to justify this point of view with reasons and references to specific aspects of the article.

9

RESEARCH (1): FACT-FINDING; PUBLIC RELATIONS, COMMUNICATIONS, AND SOCIETAL AUDITS

Virtually every introductory public relations textbook stresses the importance of research in the public relations process. The texts do so because their authors recognize that research is, and should be, the foundation upon which the process is built.

But research, like public relations itself, encompasses so many facets it's difficult to pin down. There's academic, theoretically-oriented public relations research and there's commercial, problem-oriented public relations research. There's survey research, focus group research, trend analysis, issue tracking, and quick-tab survey research. What's more, even though most practitioners acknowledge the value and importance of research, a large number of them make little use of it. Peter Finn, chairman of Research & Forecasts, reported in 1982 that a survey of 400 senior communication executives of *Fortune 1,000* companies showed that 48 percent were users and 52 percent were nonusers of public relations research.[1] Their companies, of course, were among the largest and most affluent in the country and hence were most likely to have the money and resources needed to carry out public relations research. Yet the major reasons given for not using public relations research were budgetary difficulties; management doubts about the value of research; lack of time to carry out research; and admitted insufficient understanding of research and research techniques on the part of the public relations executives. Despite the reservations concerning research, 82 percent of those surveyed said that the use of communications research in the corporate sector will increase in the next five years.[2]

Both public relations teachers and practitioners echo the refrain that not enough research is being done but more is needed and to be expected in the near future.[3] To assist the reader in being prepared to meet this need and expectation, this chapter and the following one aim to strip the mystique from public relations research and show how its usage aids and abets public relations practice.

RESEARCH AND THE PUBLIC RELATIONS PROCESS: MEANING AND BENEFITS

Professor Edward J. Robinson provides a simple definition of research when he describes it as "methods used to obtain reliable knowledge." He further points out that everyone uses reliable knowledge merely to function as human beings and that the major difference between the scientist and the nonscientist is how this reliable knowledge is achieved.[4]

The nonscientist, says Professor Robinson, depends on his own judgment, intuition, hunches, and previous experience in attempting to solve problems. The extent of his use of reliable knowledge is personal and nontransferable. The scientist, on the other hand, makes his decisions on the basis of knowledge gained from scientific research and according to a set of rules or steps. There is no agreement about the number and kind of rules involved, but Professor Robinson cites nine steps in the scientific research process: (1) statement of the problem, (2) narrowing the problem to manageable size, (3) establishing definitions, (4) searching the literature, (5) developing hypotheses, (6) setting the study design, (7) securing data, (8) analyzing the data, and (9) interpreting and drawing conclusions about the results and reporting them.[5]

Professor John Marston conceives of public relations research as *"planned, carefully organized, sophisticated fact finding and listening to the opinion of others."*[6] The connection between the Marston and Robinson descriptions of public relations research is apparent. Both stress the collection of data—one terming it "sophisticated fact finding" and the other "reliable knowledge"—and both stress the need to apply the scientific approach.

No matter how one approaches the public relations process, the need for research is paramount.

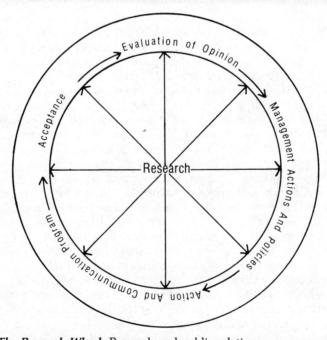

FIGURE 9.1 *The Research Wheel.* Research and public relations seen as a continuous process with research as the core with spokes to the major elements of the process.

In Chapter 1 we described the public relations process as involving the evaluation of public attitudes and opinions; counseling management on policies and actions to ensure they're socially responsible and in the public interest; and executing an action and communication program to secure public understanding and acceptance. In an ensuing chapter programming will be described as a series of steps ranging from a preliminary study to communication and evaluation. As a continuous process—no matter how it's viewed—public relations in action is circular in motion. If we were to compare the public relations process to a wheel, research is the center core with spokes to the outer rim at all key points (see Figure 9.1).

There are six major benefits derived from research support of the public relations "wheel":

1. Research provides input about public attitudes and opinion.

2. Research provides factual input for programming.

3. Research serves as an "early warning" system.

4. Research serves to secure internal support for the public relations function.

5. Research increases the effectiveness of communication.

6. Research lubricates the public relations machinery.

RESEARCH PROVIDES INPUT ABOUT PUBLIC ATTITUDES AND OPINION

Research, primarily opinion-survey research, is the means whereby the practitioner is able to use the scientific method to ascertain public attitudes and opinions. Surveys of attitudes and opinions may be initiated at the onset of a program, while a program is in process, or after a program has been carried out. They may be used to spot trends or for short-range, more immediate purposes. They may be self-produced by the practitioner or assigned to professional organizations which specialize in such research.

RESEARCH PROVIDES FACTUAL INPUT FOR PROGRAMMING

Ascertaining public attitudes and opinions enables the practitioner to pinpoint with some degree of accuracy the relative standing of his organization vis-a-vis its important publics and sub-publics. Given this raw material, the practitioner is then able to fashion a program designed to solidify or improve that standing.

Research also serves the valuable purpose of providing *data* useful in subsequent programming. Through library sources and electronic retrieval systems the practitioner is able to secure basic information which is so vital in public relations planning and programming.

RESEARCH SERVES AS AN "EARLY WARNING" SYSTEM

Countless hours of time, effort, and talent are wasted handling public relations problems after they arise. Research, which can serve to spot problems *before* they arise, enables the practitioner to use his time, effort, and talents to purposes more productive than solving problems that could have been prevented.

Using research to keep abreast of those developments in our society that have consequences for organizations served by public relations is crucial to effective handling of the function. Gathering information and data about such developments is similar to the role intelligence-gathering serves with the military. Such research helps spot long-range trends in society and short-range trouble spots which can develop into festering sores.

RESEARCH SERVES TO SECURE INTERNAL SUPPORT FOR THE PUBLIC RELATIONS FUNCTION

As a relative newcomer to the management of organizations, public relations often finds itself at a disadvantage when matched against legal, financial, and marketing departments. When a problem arises in which there are differences of opinion among these departments and the public relations department, the others often win out because they rely on factual data and evidence to support their point of view.

Research provides the means whereby the public relations practitioner gains support for his/her point of view by evidence secured through scientific methods. Research replaces hunch with facts and data and thereby strengthens and supports the counsel and advice put forth by the practitioner. Research is thus not merely of value because of its substantive aid, but also because of the manner in which it builds and sustains status.

RESEARCH INCREASES THE EFFECTIVENESS OF COMMUNICATION

Studies which explore the communication process provide important lessons for those practitioners who seek scientific evidence about the effectiveness of the various forms and means of communication. Such studies are reported in articles and books and are readily available to those practitioners who seek to mine this valuable resource.

Research aimed at measuring the effectiveness of communication can also be used by the practitioner himself as part of an ongoing program. A limited number of practitioners have used before-and-after studies to measure the effect communication has had on various audiences, while others utilize communication research on a regular basis as part of the total public relations program.

EXHIBIT 9.1

Bethlehem's Three Studies

The use of survey research by the Bethlehem Steel Corporation in conjunction with its corporate advocacy (public relations) advertising campaign in the late seventies illustrates some of the multi-benefits stemming from such research.

At the time Bethlehem's advocacy advertising in thirteen magazines concentrated on three issues considered important to the company. To determine the impact of such advertising and "to provide a new road map for copy and media plans," the company carried out three surveys. One was an attitude survey of subscribers of the magazines. A second was a benchmark reader awareness study of Bethlehem's corporate advertising. The third was a follow-up study to measure the impact of the company's advocacy advertising.

Of interest is to note how many of the benefits of research are exemplified in the following conclusions drawn by William A. Latshaw, Bethlehem's manager of advertising:

> The benchmark study and follow-up established two points of interest to us: 1) awareness level of Bethlehem Steel; and 2) awareness of our efforts and agreement or disagreement with our views.
>
> The benchmark gave us a base from which to build. The follow-up, conducted after our . . . advocacy campaign, showed a positive result. And the attitude survey told us where our audiences lay, while providing a tool to buy media for our corporate ad campaign more intelligently, selectively, and efficiently.
>
> With this background and reinforcement, our management agreed to our corporate advertising proposals . . . and approved a budget increase of 50 percent to enable us to carry out their programs.[7]

RESEARCH LUBRICATES THE PUBLIC RELATIONS MACHINERY

All machines, including the public relations machine, need periodic lubrication. Research is often the lubricant needed to oil all parts of public relations programming: at the commencement of a program; at various intervals during the program; and after the program has come to a halt.

When there is uncertainty about public attitudes and opinions, research can be applied to find out what motivates the public. When there are doubts about steps to be taken in programming, research can be applied to resolve these doubts. When there are concerns about the effects of program activities, research can be applied to ascertain effects (see Exhibit 9.1).

MAJOR WAYS RESEARCH IS USED

A convenient way to deal with research and the public relations process is to consider the major ways in which research is used. They range from the simple screening of the local daily newspaper and electronic media to the carefully designed public issues screen procedures developed by some of America's largest corporations. Some cover the entire spectrum of the public relations process, while others are involved only with the listening phase. No matter what its scope or degree of sophistication, public relations research usage has one major goal: it is designed to obtain reliable knowledge and thus to facilitate the public relations function.

In this and the following chapter the discussion of major ways in which research is used will center on the following:

1. **Record keeping and fact-finding,** including database retrieval systems. To be covered in this chapter.

2. **Public relations and communications audits.** To be covered in this chapter.

3. **Environmental and social audits, including emerging public issues.** To be covered in this chapter.

4. **Public opinion surveying.** To be covered in the next chapter.

5. **Evaluating program effectiveness.** To be covered in a later chapter.

RECORD KEEPING AND FACT-FINDING

Maintaining records about the organization for which the practitioner works and about its public relations activities is an important and basic part of the public relations process. So is the ability to find facts and information in a hurry. In the past these research activities have been a manual operation, but within the last five years electronic database retrieval systems have added the new dimension of *speed* to the research process of fact-finding and record keeping.

The Basic Fact File

As depicted in far too many movies and novels the typical public relations practitioner solves organizational problems by dashing off a fast press release. In reality, the work done by the responsible practitioner is the result of long hours of careful research and fact-finding, just as the case presented in court by the trial lawyer is the result of similar long hours of research and preparation. Both the public relations practitioner and the trial lawyer may *seem* only to have a glib command of language, thought, and expression, but this is merely the surface appearance of the hard preparation which preceded the public presentation.

There are sound reasons for this preparatory fact-finding on the part of the practitioner. First, the public relations department should be the natural source of information about the organization. Unless the organization has a library and information department of its own—and only the largest organizations have such libraries and information departments—queries directed to the organization by the public, media, and by others in the organization will normally be referred to the public relations department. Such queries can best be answered when files of reliable material are available.

Second, no respectable and responsible public relations practitioner would dare practice his profession without recourse to authoritative facts and data. Because the practitioner's work deals with every aspect of the organization, it is the practitioner—more than anyone else—who has to be an authority about the organization. He has to know its history; key personnel; objectives; operations; products and/or services; and its role and place in the field and in society. In his dealings with publics and sub-publics, the practitioner will find daily need to call upon the resources of his fact-file of information and data. Compiling, maintaining, and keeping this fact-file up to date becomes one of the prerequisites of sound public relations practice.

Though there are many ways one can compile, maintain, and keep a fact-file current, there are two essential elements to the process. One is to establish a library of basic reference books, and the other is to establish a basic system of compiling and maintaining data.

The public relations department's *basic library* cannot, of course, be expected to rival that of the average public or university library and will obviously be limited by available space, money, and the special needs of the organization. At a minimum, the following basic library is recommended:

Britannica Book of the Year. Encyclopaedia Britannica, Chicago, Illinois (Annual update of the *Encyclopaedia Britannica*)

Census of Population, U.S. Government Printing Office, Washington, D.C.

Columbia Encyclopedia. Columbia University Press, Columbia University, New York, N.Y. (Latest edition)

Facts on File. Facts on File, Inc., New York, N.Y. (Weekly)

New York Times Index, New York *Times,* New York, N.Y. (Biweekly)

Official Congressional Directory. U.S. Government Printing Office, Washington, D.C. (Annual)

Statistical Abstract of the United States. U.S. Government Printing Office, Washington, D.C. (Annual)

U.S. Government Manual. U.S. Government Printing Office, Washington, D.C. (Latest edition)

Vital Statistics of the United States. U.S. Government Printing Office, Washington, D.C. (Annual)

Who's Who in America. Marquis Co., Chicago, Illinois (Latest edition)

World Almanac and Book of Facts. Newspaper Enterprise Association, New York, N.Y. (Annual)

Webster's Third New International Dictionary of the English Language, Unabridged. C & C Merriam Co., Springfield, Mass.

Whether one uses an alphabetical file or simply places material into compartments, there must be a *basic system of compiling and maintaining data.* The following alphabetical classification system should suffice to cover public relations source material for fact-file purposes:

Background material on the organization, including historical, statistical, and legal material

Biographies of key personnel in the organization

Competitor and opposition literature and data

Government agencies, committees and hearings related to the organization

Legislation: pertinent bills, laws and regulations

Organizational communications: public relations ads, press releases, feature stories, speeches, and the like

Press clippings from newspapers, magazines, and trade publications

Public opinion studies relevant to the organization

Reference materials dealing with the organization's special field

Trade association literature

Setting up the above system is a relatively simple task; much more difficult is maintaining and keeping it current. Such files tend to get out of hand quickly, but as public relations departments learn to use computers, data banks, and terminals, more sophisticated retrieval systems are put to use. When background material and data are needed in a hurry—as they usually are—there's no reason why they can't be conjured up by the push of a button. By 1984, that's just what was being done in public relations offices through database retrieval systems.

Database Retrieval Systems

Accurate, timely, and comprehensive information is a core necessity for public relations practitioners. Until very recently the library search was the means whereby such information was secured and compiled, but the coming of age of electronic databases in the early 1980s brought a virtual revolution in database retrieval.

Simply stated, electronic databases are repositories of all kinds of information. They are obtained and compiled from print media, then put into computer memories, and made available through on-line computer terminals for random access and retrieval and subsequent print-out. At present, thousands of public, academic, and corporate libraries provide or utilize electronic database retrieval systems, most of them made available to public relations practitioners by database vendors.[8] Two such services are **Nexis,** a service of Mead Data Central, and **Dialog** Information Services, a subsidiary of Lockhead Corporation.

Nexis, which describes itself as the world's largest full-text database of business information and news, is a computerized electronic library containing the full text of stories and articles carried in major newspapers; wire services; magazines; specialized newsletters, publications, and services; the *Federal Register;* and the *Encyclopaedia Britannica.* Included among its wire service base in 1983 were AP, UPI, Reuters, and the PR Newswire. Newspapers within its database were the Washington *Post, Christian Science Monitor,* and the New York *Times.* Key news and business magazines were *Business Week, Newsweek,* the *Economist,* and *U.S. News and World Report.* The base also included scores of specialized and industry-oriented publications.

Nexis added considerably to its databases in 1983 when the New York *Times* and Mead Corporation reached agreement to grant Mead Data Central exclusive rights to distribute databases produced by New York Times Information Services to **Nexis** users. Thus, by 1984 **Nexis** was able to offer its subscribers a search and retrieval of the full text or abstracts of more than 160 major national and international newspapers, magazines, newsletters, and wire services.

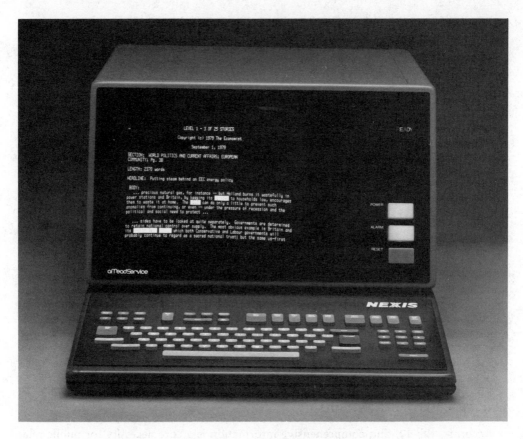

FIGURE 9.2 *Nexis terminal with keyboard and VDT screen.*

Source: Copyright © 1980 Mead Data Central. Reprinted with permission.

One **Nexis** subscriber described his use of the service in the following words:

> The user virtually converses with the computer, refining the search for information on the basis of *any* words or phrases that the user thinks will lead to the desired information. It is a heuristic process: The user learns while searching, with no researcher or abstract writer blocking the way to the information. One push of the button establishes contact with the computer, and a typical search, browse and printout of useful information takes only a few minutes.

> One recent search, for example, was conducted by a partner preparing a speech for a large corporation's chief executive officer. In discussing corporate tax policy, the CEO wanted to cite the "underground economy," based on tax-avoidance devices, that has grown up in reaction to high tax rates. One touch of a button displayed the number of articles on the underground economy in the database, and the places where they had appeared (in this case the Washington *Post, Newsweek,* the *Congressional Quarterly,* and the *Economist*). Another touch displayed highlights of the most recent story. Another displayed the full story. And another caused the full text of the story to be printed out for use. . . .

> In another instance, a foreign client, an agency of the Australian government, telexed a query for background on 15 theme parks in Texas. The Australians were considering doing something similar at the government's historic estate park. Within minutes, we had detailed information on the parks, the leisure-time facility consultants who designed them, the rate and pattern of tourist traffic, and the local and national press coverage on the parks. . . .

Each of these searches saved many hours of laborious research by phone or personal interviews. Against that consideration, the costs are modest: a $50 per month subscription fee, plus an average of $1.25 to $1.50 per minute (1981 costs) for searches that averaged only a few minutes, thanks to the nearly instantaneous computer response.[9]

Dialog, which was started with a single database in 1969, dealt chiefly with scientific, technical, and bibliographic information in its early days, but it has since branched out and now includes more than 150 databases. **Dialog** describes itself as "the largest system of its kind in the world," containing more than 55 million records which provide references to technical reports, conference papers, newspapers, journal and magazine articles, patents, and statistical data. Its initial focus on education and science has been expanded to include databases in the arts, current affairs, business and finance, social sciences, law, medicine, and the humanities. More than 60,000 journals, written in more than forty languages, are referenced and cited within the **Dialog** system. The service offers full records including abstracts printed online right at the user's terminal or offline at the **Dialog** facility and mailed to the user at a lower cost.

FIGURE 9.3 *Information.* Some of the more than two hundred disk drives in the **Dialog** computer room.

Source: Copyright © Dialog Information Services, Inc., 1982. Reprinted with permission.

In its Database Catalogue, the service lists the individual databases under file numbers. File 47 contains close to 600,000 citations from 370 general-interest magazines. File 75 has more than 90,000 citations relating to current information on a variety of business- and management-related topics. File 211 is a daily index of more than 2,000 news stories, information articles, and book reviews from more than 1,400 newspapers, magazines, and periodicals. File 78 provides records of all 21,800 U.S. foundations which award grants.

Exhibit 9.2 illustrates how **Dialog** would be used to search the sources of recent articles on the effect of stress on executives.

EXHIBIT 9.2

A Typical Dialog Search

Shown below is a suggestion of the kind of a conversation you might have with DIALOG during a typical search. On the facing page is a replica of the actual printout that would be generated at your computer terminal during the search.

From start to finish the search took less than five minutes. During that time more than 20,000 documents were examined and eighty pertinent ones were identified.

PURPOSE OF THE SEARCH: You want to find the sources of recent articles on *the effect of stress on executives.*

WHICH DATABASE TO SEARCH? DIALINDEX, the online subject index, shows you that File 15 ABI/INFORM contains information about articles on business and management.

Here, in effect, is what takes place at your computer terminal.

What you say to Dialog	How Dialog responds
1 I'd like to search File 15, please.	What would you like me to find for you?
2 Do you have any articles that include the word *stress* or the word *tension*?	Yes, I have 1564 that refer to *stress* and 395 that include a reference to *tension* for a total of 1840 documents that mention either or both terms.
3 How many articles do you have that mention *executives* or *managers* or *administrators*?	I have the following references: *executives*—7072; *managers*—14,435; *administrators*—997; for a total of 20,707.
4 How many of those articles or documents contain the terms *stress* or *tension* AND ALSO the terms *executives* or *managers* or *administrators*?	460.
5 I'm interested only in *recent* articles. How many of those 460 were published during 1981?	80.
6 I'd like the following information about the first of those 80 documents: record number, title, journal title, date, pages, and an abstract on the article if available.	Title of the article is "Executive Stress: Pressure in a Grey Flannel Suit." It's by Roger H. Lourie and appeared in Direct Marketing Magazine, volume 44, number 8 on pages 46 to 49 of the December 1981 issue. An abstract of the article follows: (For complete text of the abstract please refer to the sample printout on the facing page.)
7 For the next 9 articles please give me only the basic information, no abstracts.	(For detailed response, see printout at right.)
8 Thank you, I'm finished. Please log me out and give me a record of this search and its cost.	This search was made on February 19, 1982 and completed at 11:54:10 A.M. The user's identification number is 3468. Cost for computer time was $5.91. Time required to conduct the search was 0.081 hours. The search was made in File 15. Six descriptive terms were used to make the search. Communications cost (TELENET) was $.49 and the total estimated cost was $6.40.

Source: "Worldwide Information on Command," brochure, © Dialog Information Services, Inc., 1982. Search done on the DIALOG Information System, offered by DIALOG Information Services, Inc.

EXHIBIT 9.2 (cont.)

If you had wished to do so you could have requested that the references be printed offline and mailed to you, typically more cost effective if many references are desired.

Most databases contain abstracts or summaries of the original document such as that shown in our sample search. Often these abstracts provide enough information to answer your question. Should you decide that you want to order the full text of the article abstracted, you can do this easily while still connected to the DIALOG computer through Dial-Order, DIALOG's online ordering system. You simply type .ORDER and just the record number from the upper left of each reference.

This search is an example of how simple yet powerful a DIALOG search can be. As you grow in familiarity with DIALOG you'll find yourself taking advantage of the many additional search capabilities that can improve the speed, increase precision, or lower costs.

1
? BEGIN 15
File15:ABI/INFORM – 71–82/JAN
(Copr. Data Courier Inc.)
| Set | Items | Description. |

> STATEMENTS UNDERLINED ARE ACTUAL COMMANDS TO DIALOG

2
? SELECT STRESS OR TENSION
	1564	STRESS
	395	TENSION
1	1840	STRESS OR TENSION

3
? SELECT EXECUTIVES OR MANAGERS OR ADMINISTRATORS
	7072	EXECUTIVES
	14435	MANAGERS
	997	ADMINISTRATORS
2	20707	EXECUTIVES OR MANAGERS OR ADMINISTRATORS

4
? COMBINE 1 AND 2
| 3 | 460 | 1 AND 2 |

5
? SELECT S3 AND PY = 1981
| | 26623 | PY = 1981 |
| 4 | 80 | S3 AND PY = 1981 |

6
? TYPE 4/7/1
4/7/1
82001738
Executive Stress: Pressure in a Grey Flannel Suit
Lourie, Roger H.
Direct Marketing   V44N8   46–49   Dec 1981

  Chronic stress in business executives is usually found more in middle management than in top management. It is characterized by a continuous sense of time urgency and an incessant need to accomplish too much. Such changes in work pattern as concentrating on only the important items, taking frequent "day dreaming" breaks, and staying an extra half hour to avoid rush hour traffic can help relieve stress. Transcendental meditation, biofeedback, encounter groups, and yoga are also useful in understanding and relieving tensions and stress. However, more important than any artificial technique is an individual's self-realization that he is exhibiting outward symptoms of stress and inner tension and that he must personally take action to reduce this pressure-building situation. The current emphasis on stress-relieving techniques helps make the public aware of the dangers of stress.

7
? TYPE 4/3/2-10
4/3/2
82001706
Preventing Environmental Stress in the Open Office
Rader, Martha; Gilsdorf, Jeanette
Jrnl of Systems Mgmt   v32n12   25–27   Dec 1981

4/3/3
82000967
Managing Stress for Increased Productivity
Huber, Vandra L.
Supervisory Mgmt   v26n12   2–12   Dec 1981

4/3/10
81027568
Does Your Head Hurt?
Cohen, Irving J.
Inc.   v3n12   117,119   Dec 1981

8
? LOGOFF
19feb82 11:54:10 User3468
$5.91   0.081 Hrs File15 6 Descriptors
$0.49   Telenet
$6.40   Estimated Total Cost

PUBLIC RELATIONS AND COMMUNICATIONS AUDITS

The public relations audit and the communications audit are being discussed under a common heading because they have so much in common that the terms have been used interchangeably. Although terminology in regard to audits isn't of substantive importance, clarity is best achieved when the two are recognized for what they are. The basic difference between the two audits is found in the scope and breadth of each.

Public Relations Audit

The public relations audit has been described as a "broad-scale, loosely structured research study exploring a company's public relations both internally and externally."[10] Carl Byoir & Associates describes the public relations audit as follows:

> The Public Relations Audit . . . involves a comprehensive study of the public relations position of an organization; how it stands in the opinion of its various publics—stockholders, employees, customers, suppliers, investment community, thought leaders and the public at large.
>
> It points out public relations strengths and weaknesses . . . public relations assets and liabilities. It analyzes specific problems, sharpens objectives and evaluates the adequacy of the methods used to gain goodwill and patronage.[11]

In short, the public relations audit is a research tool used specifically to describe, measure, and assess an organization's public relations activities, and to provide guidelines for future public relations programming. The methods used in carrying out an audit vary widely, but they usually include comprehensive interviews with knowledgeable people both within and outside of the organization; various forms of public opinion surveys; a careful analysis of the organization's current public relations practices, procedures, and personnel; and recommendations for future programming.

As a general rule, the key elements of a public relations audit include:

- a careful analysis of the publics—both internal and external—considered to be of key importance to the organization being audited
- surveys of these publics to ascertain their attitudes, opinions, and knowledge of the organization
- survey and analysis of current and past public relations programming and communications
- recommendations for future public relations programming and communications

Public relations audits have been carried out for all kinds of organizations, profit and nonprofit. As a general rule they have been assigned to public relations counseling firms, and they can be executed at various stages of a client relationship. Generally they are done most often in the early stages. As Professor Lerbinger points out: "The whole purpose of the public relations audit is to study the public relations position of an organization so that communications plans can be drawn."[12] That purpose is achieved when skilled researchers provide the client with an honest assessment and a plan for future public relations programming based on research findings. (The use of research through the public relations audit is explored further in discussion of the preliminary study stage of program planning in Chapter 11.)

Communications Audit

A communications audit concerns itself mainly with the internal and external communication means and methods utilized by an organization. It has been described in a variety of ways:

[A communications audit] is a complete analysis of an organization's communications—internal and/or external—designed to "take a picture" of communication needs, policies, practices, and capabilities, and to uncover necessary data to allow top management to make informed, economical decisions about future objectives of the organization's communication. An audit should also lead to a series of recommendations.[13]

[The communications audit] is comprehensive research that evaluates the communications function, the messages that are getting through to the client's audiences, analyzing the effectiveness of the techniques used for communications, the timing and response that they elicit from the client's target publics.

With this kind of input, the public relations consultant is in a position to make detailed meaningful recommendations for improving client communications, identifying problem areas that may need further research and counsel, and elicit the client's authorization to move into new service areas.[14]

Thus, the communications audit provides management with:

- **meaningful information** about an organization's communications media, policies, practices, and programs;
- **important data** for developing and/or restructuring an organization's communications media, policies, practices, and programs;
- **recommendations** for action in regard to the above, based on analysis of data and information.

Subjects to be covered in a communications audit, according to Kopec, are as follows:[15]

- *Communication philosophy*—formal written policies (if any), standing, and relationship to other functions.
- *Objectives and goals*—long-range objectives, short-range goals.
- *Organization, staffing, compensation*—organizational structure, duties, and salaries.
- *Current communication programs*—description and analysis of present communications techniques, methods, media, and vehicles used to reach internal and external publics. Includes print and electronic materials, media, and means.
- *Personal communications*—description and analysis of interpersonal communications, internally between management and employees and externally between organizational representatives and such outside publics as media, legislators, and financial analysts.
- *Meetings* as they relate to communications with internal and external publics.
- *Attitudes towards existing communications*—how internal and external publics view present communications from the organization.

Methods and means used to carry out a communications audit are many and diverse. A comprehensive audit might include all of the following, whereas an audit limited to certain aspects of an organization's communications might include one or a few of the following:

Attitude and opinion surveys. These are carefully designed surveys utilizing the same techniques used by such national polling organizations as Roper, Harris, and Gallup. They are described in detail in the next chapter.

Readership studies. Carried out periodically to ascertain patterns of readership of print media published by the organization. Can serve as a guide for communications editors.

Depth interviews. Usually held with a limited number of key people considered important to an organization's communications program. Could include media personnel who are recipients of communications from the organization, as well as those within the organization who are responsible for communications.

Content analysis. Study of both internal and external publications to ascertain the type, kind, quantity, and quality of articles, stories, editorials. Can be informal or formal, simple or complex. Utilized to measure, codify, analyze, and/or evaluate external print and electronic coverage of an organization, its people, and its activities. Technique has been used most often to monitor the press, but it's also useful for measuring the content of books, speeches, TV and radio programs, and letters. Exhibit 9.3 describes and illustrates an example of content analysis.

Before-and-after surveys. Used to test the effectiveness of a planned communications program. Survey is taken of the target audience before communication is put into effect, and then another survey is taken after the audience has been exposed to the communication.

Focus group interviews. Involves informal, give-and-take sessions in a controlled setting with a small group of people—usually eight to twelve—led by a trained moderator. Has been used mostly to test advertising, but can be utilized to test various forms of communication, the clarity of copy or films, or to reveal elements of strength and weakness. Its proponents contend that well-led focus-group discussion can provide the opinion researcher with insights, spontaneous thoughts, and language unlikely to emerge from other interviewing techniques.[16] Ina S. Hillebrandt explains focus-group uses in these words:

> Though our work is often proprietary, I can relate that we are very involved in futures work. My clients and I believe that it is not enough to have trends identified; it is critical to understand the attitudes underlying the trends. Thus, we are exploring behavior related to vast changes going on in America today, particularly those changing values and habits that relate to clients' products and services.
>
> Focus groups also have been used as a means of interpreting or mediating between communities and government officials and politicians, and community programs and arts sponsors. Data from group discussions can provide highly effective guidance for structure and modification of programs and publicity to members of the community.
>
> We also have used the technique with great success in employee relations work, where, as outsiders, we can speak with employees at different levels, and assess highlights and pitfalls of ongoing programs. We then work with management to modify these programs and strengthen internal relations, thus maximizing employee output and reducing turnover.[17]

Because of the small number of people involved, focus groups should be valued for the quality rather than the quantity of their responses and reactions. In many cases they are useful as a first step in the development of a large-scale attitude and opinion survey. Their chief value remains that of "discovering underlying reasons for purchases or behavior . . . and determining latent motivations and psychological meanings."[18] Clearly, handling focus group interviews is not for amateurs.

EXHIBIT 9.3

Content Analysis Described and Illustrated

In explaining how content analysis works, Walter K. Lindenmann, president of Group Attitudes Corporation, states that the element to focus on is the *unit* of analysis. For example, a corporation interested in knowing how it is described whenever it is mentioned in the media would consider adjectives that modify the company name as the "unit" of analysis. A check would then be made to ascertain how often a negative, positive, or neutral adjective is used when the company is mentioned. The researcher would then work out a system for codifying key words or phrases and checking them in a representative sample of news stories.

"In public relations," states Lindenmann, "content analysis usually involves four steps: sampling, data collection, data coding, and analysis. For a typical publicity monitoring and evaluation program, for instance, this would involve continuous sampling of the print and broadcast media on a national or regional basis, collection of all articles and news items in the sampled media that refer to an organization or to any of the various public policy issues or product categories of importance to that organization, coding of article themes, and statistical analysis of the material."

As an example, Lindenmann cites a sophisticated content analysis of the print media's stance on an extensively covered, very sensitive public policy issue. The analysis was based on a collection of one thousand news clippings a month for a year and it included interpretation of content in terms of fifteen different variables. Among them were news item source, item length, potential audience reach, subject matter, general attitudes towards the client, etc. The chart below shows the content analysis tracking over a one-year period of unfavorable, favorable, and neutral press coverage.

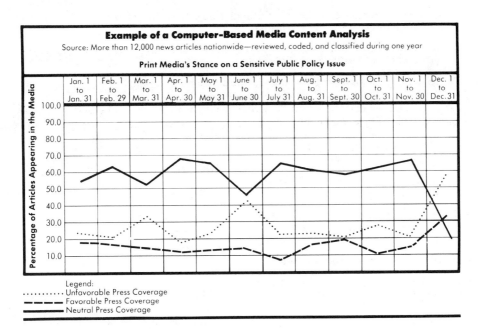

Source: Walter K. Lindenmann, "Content Analysis," *Public Relations Journal*, July 1983, pp. 24-25. Reprinted with permission.

Semantic differential. This is a scaled method of measuring meanings. Devised by Charles Osgood, the scale used in the semantic differential schema consists of several bipolar or opposite adjectives with seven points in between. Usually the respondents are provided with a concept and then asked to check that point on each bipolar scale which best describes their view of the object being examined.[19]

Osgood holds that there are three dimensions used by people to describe concepts. One is *evaluative.* Bipolar adjectives operating in this factor would be good-bad, beautiful-ugly, positive-negative, valuable-worthless, etc. The second factor relates to *potency,* and typical bipolar adjectives here would be large-small, strong-weak, heavy-light, and thick-thin. The third factor is an *activity* variable and the bipolar adjectives would be fast-slow, active-passive, hot-cold, and such.[20]

In using the semantic differential in a communications audit respondents could be asked to check points on a bipolar scale which would indicate the respondents' view of the truthfulness of articles or editorials in an internal publication. From the ratings of the respondents a profile of the truthfulness concept can be made showing how the publication measures up in terms of that concept.

Carrying out the communications audit is a process involving any or all of the methods and means previously cited. A college, for example, may be interested this year in auditing all communications with alumni, hence only such communications would be subject to an audit. A hospital may want to do an audit of communications with patients, and thus only such communications would be the focus of an audit. A large corporation may have its public relations agency do a complete audit of all of its communications, and this could entail use of all the methods cited in this chapter. Counselor Joseph Kopec says there's very little mystery to the actual implementation of an audit, and he describes the usual pattern as follows:[21]

1. A planning meeting to determine the audit's objectives, identify question areas, plan an approach, and develop a schedule.

2. Interviews with top management to determine management's attitudes about communications and probe for problems in functional areas.

3. Collection and analysis of communications materials currently being used.

(At this point the audit splits into one part dealing with internal publics and the other part dealing with external publics.)

Internal Audiences	External Audiences
4. Focus-group interviews followed by face-to-face interviews with a cross section of employees	4. Content analysis of media usage of communications material by means of Dialog or Nexis services
5. Preparation, administration of survey of attitudes, opinions, knowledge concerning internal communications	5. Identification of key publics and media contacts
6. Tabulation, summarization results	6. Focus-group and depth interviews with reps of external publics, media contacts
7. Communication of results to employees	7. Preparation, administration of public opinion survey; tabulation and summarization of results

8. Preparation and presentation of audit report to management; includes summary of findings, detailed findings, recommendations

Exhibit 9.4 shows the process as outlined by Kopec in chart form.

EXHIBIT 9.4

Kopec's Chart of Communications Audit Process

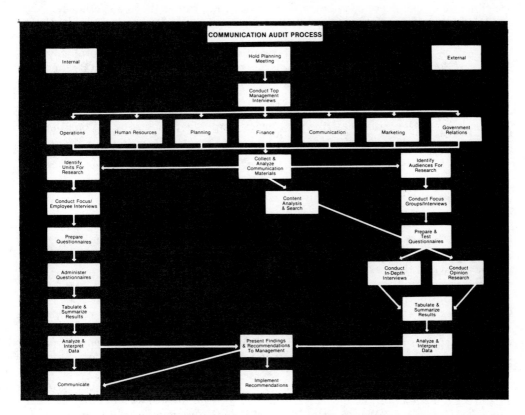

Source: Joseph A. Kopec, "The Communications Audit," *Public Relations Journal*, May 1982, p. 24. Reprinted with permission.

ENVIRONMENTAL AND SOCIAL AUDIT: EMERGING PUBLIC ISSUES

Commencing as a small blip on public relations radars in the late 1960s, a new activity of interest and concern grew so fast that by the late 1970s it was called "the fastest growing area of public relations research." In fact, it grew so fast that practitioners were even uncertain about what to call it. Some termed the activity *environmental monitoring.* Others labeled it *social auditing.* Many preferred to term it *emerging public issues management.* Not wanting to slight any of the three, we've put them under one heading.

In actuality, the new activity that engaged the close attention of practitioners had its genesis when Bernays and Childs first emphasized the need for practitioners to be concerned about vital societal trends and issues. Four decades later the concept of emerging public issues management became a "hot" topical item in professional public relations circles. How to deal with emerging public issues has been on the public relations "agenda" at national public relations conferences and regional seminars and has been written about fairly extensively in public relations publications. Spurred on by the work of W. Howard Chase, a past president of the PRSA who is generally regarded as the one who popularized the term "issue management," scores of issues specialists have been active in promoting the concept. Executives responsible for public policy issues formed the Issue Management Association in 1982, electing Chase as chairman and Ray Ewing of Allstate Insurance Companies as president. Some of the country's largest corporations have established public policy issues departments, but ambiguity remains about the exact nature of public policy issues, about the exact location in the managerial hierarchy for handling such issues, and even whether the entire matter of handling public policy issues is simply a new title for an old activity.

In dealing with the problem of emerging public issues management it is probably wise to start at the beginning and come to some agreement about what we mean by the term. As already noted, such agreement is hard to achieve. Societal issues have been referred to in terms of being "emerging issues," "strategic issues," "public policy issues," "emerging public policy issues," and the like. Robert H. Moore, public affairs executive with Alexander and Alexander, described an "emerging public policy issue" as one that:

1. has arisen/rearisen, or recombined with other issues, but definition and interest positions are still evolving; and

2. is a matter on which affected private institutions can and should participate in the public policy process concerned; and

3. is or is likely to be an active subject within a rolling three-year time frame.[22]

The term "emerging issue," Moore observes, is often elusive. What might be an emerging issue for one organization could well be a well-established problem for another. He also suggests that there's a need to distinguish between strategic and public policy issues. **Strategic issues** are those environmental trends or forces which determine how a company does business, and as such they affect the company's survival and success. **Public policy issues** are usually those problems in the public domain on which managements believe they should take a stand, even though the issues do not seem to be crucial to the company's success or survival. Finally, some issues have both strategic and public policy aspects for an organization, and what may be a public policy issue for one company may be a strategic issue for another.[23]

Howard Chase and his associate, Barry L. Jones, conceptualized "issue management" as a process made up of definite steps, and they incorporated these into what they call the "Chase/Jones Issue Management Process Model."[24] A simplified illustration of their model is shown in Figure 9.4.

As noted and illustrated, the Chase/Jones model shown in Figure 9.4 is a simplified version. The complete model uses four sets of concentric rings, and within each there is a series of interlocking circles representing phases of the particular module. Other models divide the issue management process into two or three parts, but the general view favors a four-step approach. Research is involved in all steps, but as it is especially important in the first two steps—issue identification and issue analysis or ranking—these two will be described in the sections that follow.

Identification of issues may sound like a simple matter, but it's more complex than it seems on the surface. Chase/Jones state that this part of the process forces the user to find out *what* issues confront the organization and in *what* number. This module, like the other three, begins at its center with the continuous interaction of three interlocking circles representing citizens, business, and government. The next ring of the module represents key social, economic, and political trends. This leads to a third circle wherein the trends are related to basic corporate goals, providing a preliminary opportunity to determine the relevancy of the trends to such objectives and goals.[25]

Moore emphasizes that there is *no one right way* to run an issue identification system and cites the following seven steps, which emerged from research by The Conference Board:[26]

1. The chief executive officer designates the issues.

2. Senior executives, through informal discussions, management workshops, or annual management retreats, develop a list of issues.

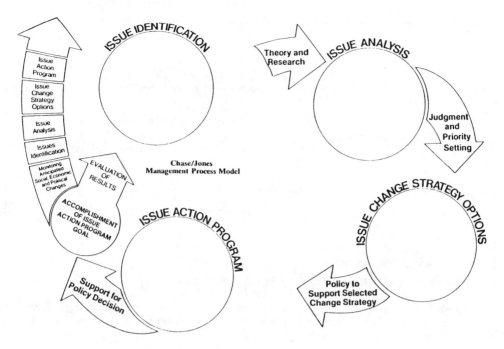

FIGURE 9.4 *Chase/Jones Issue Management Process Model.*

Source: Copyright © by W. Howard Chase and Barrie L. Jones, 1977. Reprinted with permission.

3. Through structure polling, senior executives establish a list.

4. A staff unit is charged with the specific responsibility of developing an issues list for senior management's collective consideration and refinement.

5. Issues are first set forth by division or profit centers.

6. A formal "exploratory planning process" is established to develop a list that goes well beyond the typical three to five years' limit of "the strategic plan" that many companies employ.

7. Issues are identified by a cadre of volunteers who scan a wide variety of publications and use specialized scanning services.

A Master Scanner

In his 1982 blockbuster bestseller, *Megatrends,* John Naisbitt presents ten major transformations which he contends are reshaping America and our lives. Where did he learn about these ten megatrends? From the bottom up.

It's Naisbitt's contention that America is a "bottom-up" society, that new trends and ideas begin in local communities and cities, not in New York City or Washington, D.C. So, in order to understand what's happening in America, Naisbitt and his colleagues monitor the country. The staff of Naisbitt's *Trend Report* monitor 6,000 local newspapers each month. From this daily exposure to local action in cities and towns across the country the staff traces, analyzes, and evaluates important issues and trends.

Thus, the findings in *Megatrends* are based on an analysis of more than two million local articles over a 12-year period and from Naisbitt's own reading and scanning of thousands of other newspaper, magazine, and journal articles.[27]

EXHIBIT 9.5

Identifying and Ranking Issues at John Hancock

In 1978, John Hancock's Advertising and Public Relations Department became Corporate Communications, with Advertising, Public Relations and Public Issues as co-equal divisions. The purpose of this move was to assist senior management to deal with issues in a coordinated fashion, proactively rather than reactively, with the Massachusetts tax issue as a prototype. Our aim was to integrate more fully social and political considerations into the management process by:

1. Dealing more effectively with the priority issues.

2. Arriving at coordinated company positions.

3. Participating more effectively in the process of formulating laws, regulations and public policy.

At John Hancock we define public issues as those external events or trends that could have an impact on the company, to which we should respond in organized fashion and over which we might reasonably expect to exercise some influence. Through our issue identification process we achieved an initial ranking of 30 issues on a scale of one to five. Here's how they fell into place:

High priority: Inflation. Federal agencies. Health care costs. Taxes, federal and state. Consumerism. Massachusetts fiscal, revenue, government. EEO. National health.

Middle priority. Boston fiscal, revenue, government. Social Security. Public pensions. Public opinion. Massachusetts property tax. Labor unions. Mandatory retirement. Crime. Privacy. Corporate accountability. Role of directors. Education. Energy.

Low priority: Population changes. Changing lifestyles. Transportation. Media. Unemployment. Elderly. Environment/pollution. Postal service. Savings Bank Life Insurance.

As part of the Public Issues Division's development, we used two priority issues as prototypes for application of our process:

• Federal regulation, with emphasis on Federal regulation of the insurance industry.

• Massachusetts/Boston fiscal and revenue problems.

We established steering committees on both, with initial investigation and studies carried out by working committees. Reports were completed and our recommendations presented to the Executive Committee, which endorsed the recommendations and work of these groups, and this approach to issues generally. In the case of the Massachusetts/Boston group, its work also resulted in a special senior officers' forum.

Source: Frank T. LeBart, "Campaigning on the Issues," *Public Relations Journal*, November 1982, p. 30. Copyright ©1982, *Public Relations Journal.* Reprinted with permission.

Analyzing and ranking issues calls for a winnowing process. Issues comes in all sizes, shapes, and forms. So do organizations, and that's why Issue A may be of vital importance to Organization X but of little importance to Organization Y. Furthermore, issues do not exist in laboratory isolation, but are deeply related to the social, political, and economic environment in which they arise and flower or wither and die. What may have been a low-priority issue yesterday could well be today's high-priority issue. Here are some approaches that have been taken:

- **Establish a time frame.** This is one way to bring down to manageable size the usually large number of issues that make up an original list. Clearly, some issues will be immediate, others intermediate, and still others long-range.

> Tamper-proof packaging for over-the-counter analgesics was not an immediate public policy issue of great importance in August 1982, but it certainly became a crucial one one month later when several people died as a result of ingesting cyanide in Tylenol capsules.

- **Decide which issues are of direct and which of indirect importance** to your organization. This point relates to Moore's observations about strategic public policy issues. Equal rights and facilities for women athletes has marginal importance for a public utility but distinct importance for colleges and universities. Furthermore, it has more importance for a large coeducational university than for a small all-women's college.

- **Group issues according to relative overall significance.** In the overall scheme of things, the issue of nuclear weapons is more significant than the issue of sex education in kindergarten. What about the issue of nuclear power for nonmilitary purposes compared to the issue of sex education in kindergarten? What about nuclear power for nonmilitary purposes compared to sex education in junior high school? Clearly, judgment calls have to be made, and they can be very difficult to make. It's little wonder that identifying and ranking issues is most often left to a group rather than a single individual.

In the excerpt shown in Exhibit 9.5, Frank T. LeBart of the Public Issues Division, John Hancock Mutual Life Insurance Company, explains how one company established a public issues mechanism and set priorities.

By 1984 it was clear that virtually no one in public relations practice undervalued the importance of researching and tracking societal trends as they affected or might affect organizations. It was also clearly recognized that dealing with emerging public policy issues—that is, the core concept of issue management—was an important function of management. What was not so clear was the function's place in the management hierarchy; its role in public relations practice; and whether issue management was mainly terminology or was managerial and scientific. The enthusiastic and the less-than-enthusiastic views are represented in the comments below.

The Enthusiastic View

> Two major predictions about managing the "new social climate of the 80s" seem justified.
>
> 1. Senior managers will devote more time, talent, and budget to the public policy decision-making process. They will find a way, or ways, to satisfy social goals, and at the same time make enough profit to survive. They literally have no other choice.
>
> 2. The role of executive or senior vice president in charge of public policy will be as important as that of executive vice president of marketing, finance or production. The goals of this new executive breed will be to achieve effective corporate participation in the public policy arena. The means to the end will be the scientific process of issue management, starting with issue identification, proceeding with issue analysis, issue priority setting, and finally with issue-action programming.
>
> The management of the 80s—at least those that survive—will expect and demand the same scientific process-management from their "issue managers" that they now expect from their profit-center officers.[28]
>
> —W. Howard Chase

We're putting more emphasis on research and analysis, on priority setting and development, on formal positions and strategy, on being more proactive and interactive. . . . In my judgment, a public issues orientation is the wave of the future for both internal and external corporate communications.[29]

—Frank T. LeBart

The Less-Than-Enthusiastic View

It is clear that public issues are corporate concerns. . . . However, recent surveys, editorials, and business press articles on how corporations manage issues lead to a number of discouraging observations. I have identified only 60 corporations whose issues programs are cited regularly, although I find references to 200 corporations that are "interested" in issues. . . . Only a handful of companies formally tie these programs to their corporate planning systems or include issues management in their performance appraisal systems.[30]

—Steven E. Goodman, issues management consultant

What emerged (from a survey of 120 PRSA members) was a picture that showed that the overwhelming majority of respondents did not consider "issue management" anything new; rather they merely viewed "issue management" as being a new term for an everyday type of activity that has been going on for a long time. Moreover, the methods to be used in "issue identification" were viewed as informal, simplistic ones which barely rose much above reading the New York *Times* and several business publications. Finally, few regarded "issue management" as "exclusively a public relations tool," while the majority (85 percent) were emphatic that "issue management" was a managerial process in which anyone in the organization could engage or that it was the kind of management that was engaged in primarily by top-line executives (excluding public relations practitioners).[31]

—William P. Ehling and Michael B. Hesse

ENDNOTES

1. Peter Finn, "Demystifying Public Relations," *Public Relations Journal*, May 1982, p. 12.
2. Ibid., p. 17.
3. Albert Walker, "End-of-Decade Survey Shows Academic Growth in Public Relations," *Public Relations Review*, Summer 1982, p. 57; T. Harrell Allen, "Public Relations Education in the Decade Ahead," paper presented to the Association for Education in Journalism, Boston, August 1980; Frank B. Kalupa and T. Harrell Allen, "Future Directions in Public Relations Education," *Public Relations Review*, Summer 1982, pp. 31-45.
4. Edward J. Robinson, *Public Relations and Survey Research* (New York: Appleton-Century-Crofts, 1969), p. 9.
5. Ibid., p. 10.
6. John Marston, *Modern Public Relations* (New York: McGraw-Hill, 1979), p. 207.
7. William A. Latshaw, "Target Group Research: New Tool for Advocacy Advertising," *Public Relations Journal*, November 1977, p. 28.
8. George L. Beiswinger, "Database Update," *Public Relations Journal*, March 1982, p. 37.
9. A. E. Jeffcoat, "A Touch of Amazement," *Public Relations Journal*, May 1981, p. 34.
10. Joyce F. Jones, "Audit: A New Tool for Public Relations," *Public Relations Journal*, July 1975, p. 6.
11. Otto Lerbinger, "Corporate Use of Research in Public Relations," *Public Relations Review*, Winter 1977, p 16.
12. Ibid.
13. Joseph A. Kopec, "The Communications Audit," *Public Relations Journal*, May 1982, p. 24.
14. James B. Strenski, "The Future of the Consultancy," *Public Relations Quarterly*, Spring 1983, p. 20.
15. Kopec, p. 25.
16. Ina S. Hillebrandt, "Focus-Group Research: Behind the One-Way Mirror," *Public Relations Journal*, February 1979, p. 17.

17. Ibid., p. 33.
18. Remarks by Eleanor Holtzman at a meeting of the American Marketing Association Qualitative Conference, New York City, quoted in column by Philip H. Dougherty, *New York Times*, Dec. 8, 1982, p. D-19.
19. Alexis S. Tan, *Mass Communication Theories and Research* (Columbus, Ohio: Grid Publishing Co., 1981), pp. 48-49.
20. Charles E. Osgood, George Suci, and Percy Tannenbaum, *The Measurement of Meaning* (Urbana, Illinois: University of Illinois Press, 1957), pp. 36-37.
21. Kopec, pp. 25-26.
22. From a talk given by Robert H. Moore at a 1978 conference sponsored by the PRSA's National Capital Chapter.
23. Robert H. Moore, "Planning for Emerging Issues," *Public Relations Journal*, November 1979, p. 43.
24. From *Guide to the Chase-Jones Issue Management Process Model*, ©1979 by Geyer-McAllister Publications, New York City, p. 4.
25. Ibid., p. 5.
26. Moore, p. 44.
27. From the Introduction to John Naisbitt's *Megatrends* (New York: Warner Books, Inc., 1982), pp. 1-9.
28. W. Howard Chase, "Adjusting to a Different Business/Social Climate," *Public Relations Quarterly*, Spring 1980, p. 24.
29. Frank T. LeBart, "Campaigning on the Issues," *Public Relations Journal*, November 1982, p. 33.
30. Steven E. Goodman, "Why Few Corporations Monitor Social Issues," *Public Relations Journal*, April 1983, p. 20.
31. William P. Ehling and Michael B. Hesse, "Use of 'Issue Management' in Public Relations," *Public Relations Review*, Summer 1983, p. 29.

PROJECTS, ASSIGNMENTS, AND MINIS

1. MONITORING COVERAGE OF YOUR SCHOOL: A RESEARCH PROJECT

In this content analysis assignment members of the class—acting either individually or as members of teams named by your instructor—are to research the coverage of your institution by the daily or weekly newspaper closest to your school. (You are referred to Exhibit 9.3 for a description of the elements and manner whereby a typical content analysis is carried out.)

Your instructor will decide the time period to be covered by your research, but it should extend a minimum of one month and a maximum of three months. Your analysis research should deal with all news and feature articles, editorials, and columns about your school appearing in the designated paper.

Your report should include not only the data resulting from your content analysis, but also your interpretation of that data.

2. RESPONSE ANALYSIS FOCUS GROUPS: A READING FOR DISCUSSION

Response Analysis of Princeton, New Jersey, conducts survey research utilizing a wide range of research techniques, and included among these techniques are focus group interviews. The firm explained its usage of focus groups in the following statement, which is set forth here for class analysis and discussion.

Focus Groups

Group interviews fall into the family of research methodologies referred to as developmental or qualitative research. Often developmental studies are followed by quantitative studies to "put numbers" on the hypotheses that are generated in group interviews. However, group interviews can stand alone as a research methodology when the researcher's primary concern is to gain insight into consumer attitudes and behavior. The developmental approach has aided many clients in understanding overall consumer reactions to new product and service concepts and in defining which topics need to be studied in a quantitative survey. Group interviews can help identify "winners" and "losers."

The Response Analysis group interview is usually a two-hour tape-recorded session. Eight to ten respondents, prescreened for desired characteristics, meet with a professional moderator trained in group techniques and with a background in social or behavioral sciences. The Response Analysis moderator works from a topic guide that covers the main issue areas, but the moderator has complete freedom to depart from the plan and explore new leads.

Special techniques are frequently used to provide additional information that may not be obtainable through normal discussion. A few of the more common techniques used by Response Analysis are:

- **Deprivation**—This is a technique whereby respondents are asked to give up something related to the discussion (e.g., not using the mail to pay bills or not being able to conduct transactions using cash). We begin by seeing how many participants would be willing to be "deprived" without monetary compensation and then gradually up the ante to see at what point money compensates for loss. This is useful as a positioning tool for determining respondent dependence on the object of deprivation.

- **Brainstorming**—Brainstorming is a situation in which participants are encouraged to suggest as many ideas about a particular topic as they can, without thought as to the practicality of the suggestion. The group members act as stimuli to one another. No criticisms are allowed. We use brainstorming primarily as a way of understanding what is important to the respondents, although occasionally clients have become interested in a suggestion for its own sake. The openness and spontaneity of brainstorming sessions have inspired many new products, product names, etc.

- **Card Sorting**—In this technique we generally begin by asking respondents to physically sort cards with statements on them into piles based on concepts we define—such as "convenient/inconvenient." After the cards have been sorted into specified categories several times, we then ask respondents to sort the statements and to define their sorting methods to us. As the more obvious concepts are used up, underlying concepts that often have significant value are those the respondent uses for this task. For instance, we could determine which transactions or dealings are satisfying, why they are satisfying, and why others are not.

- **Design Teams**—During the group interview we divide the participants into smaller groups or teams, assign each a specific task to be completed over a 10-20 minute period of time, and then reconvene the entire group so that design teams can report to each other. Sometimes teams are asked to debate a particular side of a topical controversy.

- **Role Playing**—Often we ask group participants to role play in order to better understand someone else's thinking, attitudes, experiences, and preferences. Role playing is frequently done in groups that contain more than one kind of participant (e.g., husbands and wives, purchasers and non-purchasers, executives and secretaries, etc.).

Response Analysis encourages its clients to observe the group interview and to interact with the group participants at the end of the session. This is a valuable opportunity for clients to gain immediate feedback on the material being discussed. Frequently, personal contact with respondents sparks a client's own thought process.

After the group interview has been completed, the Response Analysis moderator discusses the results of the group session with the client. A report on the group interview is then prepared. The format of this report varies with the needs of the client. It can be a memorandum that summarizes the moderator's impressions of what transpired during the group session, or, if time allows, it can be a more formal report that incorporates the moderator's free associations and verbatim comments taken from a transcript of the group interview.

Response Analysis maintains its own conference-type focus group facility in Princeton; we also have direct experience in conducting focus groups at more than 25 similar group facilities all over the United States and Canada. Both our own facility in Princeton and those located elsewhere offer video and audio recording of group comments. We always insist that this be done only with the prior knowledge and approval of participants.

(Reprinted with permission.)

Questions for Discussion

1. What would you consider to be the major difference between quantitative and qualitative survey research?

2. What do you think is the meaning of the statement that "group interviews can help identify 'winners' and 'losers' "?

3. In what specific ways can each of the focus group techniques cited by Response Analysis—deprivation, brainstorming, card sorting, design teams, and role playing—be used for public relations purposes and in the public relations process? In answering, try to cite some examples in each instance.

An Assignment

As an outside assignment your instructor would like you to read a recent article on focus groups and to write a report summarizing the article's major points, evaluating the total article and explaining in what ways the article may be of help to public relations practitioners.

3. ROBERT MOORE'S LITTLE LIST: A MINI-CASE

When Moore addressed the Washington Chapter of the PRSA in May 1978, he was asked to provide the group with a list of some emerging issues for the 1980s. He told the group that it's "not possible to satisfy the request in any sensible way because one company's emerging issue may be another's chronic problem." However, an obliging guest, Moore proceeded anyway to offer a list of a dozen issues that he felt might well affect many in the audience in the years ahead. Following are the first ten of the twelve issues as described by Moore.

1. Consider the issue of demographics. The trend toward smaller families means more disposable family income and, for an airline for instance, this means more pleasure air trips. Thus, demographic projections will be built into airlines' demand forecast.

2. The changing ramifications of EEO programs. Today it is women and blacks who are at the forefront of attention. Tomorrow it may be the Vietnam veterans, the aging, and the handicapped. Some believe there have been more changes in the last five to eight years in employment practices than in the previous century and the changes are by no means all at the federal level.

3. The declining ability of high school students to read, write, and compute properly.

4. The growing unwillingness of junior and middle-aged executives to relocate. This reflects a sharply growing concern in American society with the quality of life, and in the long run such trends could have a severe impact on the personnel policies of corporations.

5. The increasingly politicized nature of American society. Thus, if one's basic premise is that public attitudes are sooner or later sure to be translated into legislation, then the resulting issue identification system will be highly sensitive to political concerns.

6. For the diehard futurist, I offer volcanic eruptions which are apparently creating problems in some agricultural areas due to the ensuing blockage of sunlight. This in turn affecting matters such as planned reclamation, fertilizer applications and runoff problems, as well as the need to develop other growing areas.

7. Consider that the post-World War II economic and political stability of Europe may be severely tested in the next decade by a juxtaposition of events that would separate U.S. interests from those of Western Europe. These may include an energy shortage, at least partially successful efforts of European Communist parties to achieve power, and a U.S.-U.S.S.R. confrontation under conditions of nuclear parity when, this time, we may "blink" first because we have less at stake in Central Europe than does the U.S.S.R.

8. Migration to the "sunbelt" states will continue. Population problems will increase in the southeast and southwest while declining population in the northern states will cause political and economic problems.

9. We may reach a crisis in water quality. Only now are we beginning to discover some of the exotic chemicals contained in surface water, rivers, and streams, and their health effects are not clearly defined.

10. The long-term impact of the deferred cost of retirement programs including Social Security, state, local and Federal Civil Service and military retirement programs. Private pension programs are also a problem in some instances but the biggest risk centers around the many government programs.

(Reprinted with permission of Robert Moore.)

Assignments

1. You are to assume that you are considering Moore's list as of the time you are reading this text. Decide which five items on his list are, in your opinion, of *lesser* importance

than the other five. Then draw up a new list of five issues you feel should replace those you've eliminated, and briefly explain why you've selected each of the items on your substitute list.

2. You are to assume that you are a public relations counselor who has three major clients: General Electric, Stauffer Chemicals, and Burger King. You are to consider each item on Moore's list as of the time you are reading this text and to rate the items in terms of what you believe to be their comparative importance to **each** of your three clients. A suggested rating system for each item and each client: very important, important, not very important. Briefly justify each of your ratings for each item and each client.

10

RESEARCH (2): PUBLIC OPINION SURVEYS AND POLLS

S urvey research in the form of public opinion surveys and polls is the most scientific and prevalent form of research used by public relations practitioners. Its techniques—particularly those developed by such national polling organizations as the Harris organization, the American Institute of Public Opinion (Gallup), Opinion Research Corporation, the Yankelovich organization, the Roper organization, Response Analysis, and others —have been refined and honed to the point where they are universally accepted as scientifically proven ways of measuring public opinion. National organizations with large public relations departments use their own resources to carry out public opinion polls, but the more common practice is for public relations departments and counseling firms to contract for surveys with professional polling organizations.

Public opinion polls and surveys consist of a series of steps or procedures, the number and complexity depending on the degree of refinement desired. At a minimum these include the following: (1) *defining the purpose;* (2) *identifying the population;* (3) *selecting the research method;* (4) *selecting the sample;* (5) *constructing the questionnaire;* (6) *interviewing and processing data;* and (7) *analyzing, interpreting and reporting the data.*

DEFINING THE PURPOSE

Defining the purpose is as important and crucial a step in public opinion surveying as defining the problem is in public relations planning and programming. Taking a survey without a clear understanding of the reasons for the survey can lead to no end of trouble and can be a sheer waste of time, money, and talent.

On the surface, there seems to be no problem involved in defining the purpose of a survey. After all, isn't a survey conducted to ascertain public opinion? The answer is "yes, but" with public relations becoming the "butt" when results turn out to be negative instead of positive.

All too often when managements approve the commissioning of a survey of public opinion they do so on the assumption that said opinion will be favorable. Unduly sensitive managements tend to consider negative public opinion to be a personal affront to their competence—which it sometimes is—and although they may seem to approve an impartial survey they really expect the mirror on the public opinion wall to show them to be the fairest of them all. When it doesn't, public relations is blamed for the bad image the mirror reflects.

Thus, one of the first steps to take when surveying public opinion is to find out if management really and honestly wants to ascertain public opinion or wants to go through

---

EXHIBIT 10.1

The Board That Didn't Listen

The board of directors of a young women's social/health agency in a city of 82,000 retained a local public relations counseling firm one summer to ascertain whether the agency would be successful in raising $350,000 for some long-needed capital improvements. The board explained that it had been waiting for five years for permission to hold a fund drive and that it had finally received permission from the United Way, to which it belonged, to run a capital fund drive in February. The agency asked the counseling firm to find out community knowledge and opinions about the organization and how the drive would be viewed by those community leaders experienced in raising funds for similar organizations. The counseling firm proposed two surveys: a mail public opinion survey of the community at large and a series of depth interviews with twenty-five community leaders who were veterans of similar fund drives.

Given the go-ahead by the board, the counseling firm conducted the two surveys and subsequently presented its findings in a written report and oral presentation to the board at a noon luncheon meeting on September 20. The major findings were that the agency was well respected in the community, but there were many gaps of knowledge about the agency and its programs. The fund-raising experts were almost unanimous in concluding that the times were not propitious for a capital fund drive and that if one were held the agency should not expect to raise more than $140,000. Only a few among the twenty-five said they would be available and willing to work on the drive.

Following the presentation the board expressed its high degree of satisfaction with the work of the counseling firm, thanked the firm's principals for their recommendations (which stated that the drive be postponed for a year and a public education campaign begun instead), and then excused the principals to complete the board's business.

To the total surprise of the counseling firm's principals, the next day's daily newspaper reported that the board of directors of the social/health agency had decided at its noon luncheon the previous day to conduct a capital fund drive in February seeking to raise $350,000 for needed capital improvements, which were outlined in the story. No mention was made of the counseling firm's two surveys, but the story did state that the board had signed a contract September 15 with a nationally-known fund-raising organization and that a representative of that organization would start initial work within a week.

To this day, the head of the counseling firm that did the two surveys has no idea why his firm was retained and why the board spent much-needed funds for the surveys. He does know, however, that the fund drive was held, as scheduled, in February. It raised $36,000 in direct contributions and $100,000 in pledges.

---

the motions of a survey but really doesn't want to face up to any negative findings. Securing the answer to this question is no simple matter, but the practitioner must settle the problem of purpose—whether directly or by circumlocution—before the survey has been taken.

John Pollock, president of Research & Forecasts, emphasizes this point in the following reminder:

> A flag of caution should be raised. Even the best research will be useless unless there is a genuine commitment to treat the results seriously. This means a willingness to face findings that may contradict favorite hunches.
>
> Commitment is easier to gain if superiors and colleagues are involved with the research throughout; at the beginning, to instill excitement; during the project, to reinforce enthusiasm, and at the end, to generate support for action on the results. The ground rule is clear: Effective research begins with effective in-house support.[1]

Assuming that management does seek honest answers, the practitioner must decide just what he wants to know. Does he seek to find out what people *know* about his organization? Does he seek to find out what people *think* about his organization? Is he seeking public reaction to *specific organizational actions, policies, and/or plans?* Does he want to measure and assess the *impact and effectiveness of the organization's public relations program* or specific aspects of said program? Is he attempting to *assess trends* in public attitudes and opinion? Is he seeking to *assess probable public reaction to projected organizational and public relations actions and programs?* Is he seeking, through the survey, to give the organization *more visibility?* Each of these purposes is a valid target and goal of survey research, but each calls for a specific set of questions. Such questions cannot be devised properly unless the purpose or purposes have been clearly established in advance. It's usually Trouble City when there's ambiguity or unclarity about purpose, as shown in the Exhibit 10.1 illustration.

IDENTIFYING THE POPULATION

People, not inanimate objects, form the audience for public opinion surveys, but that's about the easiest distinction that can be made. *Who* forms the population becomes a matter of setting parameters and eliminating the noninvolved.

Assume your firm has been asked to conduct a survey to ascertain who will be elected alderman in Ward 10 of a city of 80,000 population. First, forget about the entire city and concentrate on Ward 10. Second, eliminate all those under 18 years of age. Third, eliminate those of voting age but not eligible to vote. Fourth, try to screen out those most likely to stay away from the polls. Those remaining form the true population for your survey.

Another example. The Calcium Chloride Institute has budgeted for a survey of attitudes and opinions about the use of calcium chloride to keep down dust on Iowa roads in the summer and to clear ice off roads during the winter. Accepting the assignment, you have an initial interview with the CCI and learn that county highway engineers and county supervisors have responsibility for highway maintenance and the purchase of appropriate highway clearance agents. Your population is not the adult population of Iowa but the county highway engineers and county supervisors.

These are two examples of problems connected with the determination of the population to be surveyed in public opinion polling. Similar problems arise in all surveys, whether you are surveying *employees* (all employees, hourly employees only, division employees, field employees only?); the *college* community (all students, full-time students only, dormitory residents, faculty, administration?); the *community* (adults only, everyone 16 years and older, opinion leaders, everyone except those in nursing homes and hospitals?); and similar general groupings of people. In each case a clear distinction must be made of the exact population to be surveyed.

SELECTING THE RESEARCH METHOD

There are a variety of ways to describe and discuss the major survey research methods available to public relations practitioners, but the simplest is to consider them as *unstructured* or *structured*.

UNSTRUCTURED

The **depth interview** is the most common and widely used form of the unstructured survey and is best described as informal in nature and lasting from a half hour to an hour. The interviewer usually compiles in advance a series of "probe points," but these are not set up in the form of carefully designed and worded questions but rather as general areas to be explored with the interviewee. The basic idea of the depth interview is to explore in depth the respondent's ideas, attitudes, opinions, knowledge, and expertise on a series of subjects.

The depth interview has plus and negative factors. On the plus side is the fact that such an interview provides a more intensive reading of the respondent's mind and thinking than is possible from a structured questionnaire interview. The relatively free-wheeling atmosphere of the depth interview often brings out information, ideas, and opinions not anticipated by the researcher. Because the interviewee is not restricted by the confines of specific and carefully worded questions, the interviewee is able to express his or her intrinsic and honest thoughts, attitudes, opinions, and feelings.

On the other hand, few interviewers have the talents required for depth interviewing and such interviews are costly because of the time and talent involved. Furthermore, tabulating, codifying, assembling, analyzing, and reporting the results are extremely difficult tasks. Because such interviews are free-wheeling, long, and involved, the answers to "probe questions" are also free-wheeling, long, and involved. Yet for purposes of reporting the results, answers have to be compressed, analyzed, and put into final report form, and this inevitably leads to editorial tinkering and interpretation. Finally, because of the time, talent, and cost factors already cited, depth interviews cannot economically be used for large samples or where respondents are widely dispersed. Because of these limiting factors, depth interview surveys are seldom representative of total populations but represent the views of a limited number considered to be unusually well-informed about the areas being surveyed.

Exhibit 10.2 describes the methodology of an in-depth interview study carried out by Group Attitudes Corporation, wholly-owned research subsidiary of Hill & Knowlton, Inc.

STRUCTURED

The most common form of the structured public opinion survey utilizes a questionnaire as its basic tool. Such surveys are carried out in three major ways: by personal interviewing, by mail, and by telephone. The best method to use is dependent on a variety of factors: the subject of the survey, the population to be surveyed, the geographic location of the population, the length and complexity of the questionnaire, and the time needed for and the cost of the study.

Personal interviewing was once the most prevalent of the three forms, but increasingly it is sharing popularity with telephone interviewing. A major advantage of the personal interview is that it permits flexibility in regard to the type and kind of questions that can be asked. Researchers consider that complex questionnaires are best administered by personal interviewing. Scaling can be used to permit respondents to indicate the dimensions of their responses. Questions can be placed on cards, and respondents can be given the chance to read the question and choose their responses from a list. Complex questions can be read out and repeated, and interviewers can probe and secure explanations when desired.

National polling organizations have refined their sampling techniques to the point where they're assured of a true representative sample in national surveys with totals of between 1,500 and 2,000 respondents. By using callbacks they're usually able to obtain completion rates from 90 percent of the designated sample, and their record of accuracy in predictions measured against final results in voting surveys has been generally excellent.

In recent years, however, personal interviewing has encountered serious difficulties for a number of reasons. Because of the national concern with crime, many people refuse to open their doors to strangers. Because of the increasing number of women entering the job market, the problem of "not-at-homes" has intensified. In many urban areas personal interviewing has become almost impossible to carry out.

In Exhibit 10.3 Herbert Abelson, president and chairman of Response Analysis Corporation, explains how his organization handles the problem of interviewing respondents in controlled-access locations.

There are other reasons for the declining use of personal interviewing by national polling organizations. Personal interviewing is the most costly of the three methods and also the most time-consuming (other than small studies carried out in one or a few locations). Other drawbacks of personal interviewing relate to the kinds of questions that can be asked and to the interviewers. Because of the face-to-face nature of personal interviewing, interviewers claim that questions of a personal nature cannot easily be asked. It is also claimed that an interviewer can bias results by the manner in which he or she handles the interview and the questions.

Mail surveys are far less costly and time-consuming than are personal interviews, and they have a special advantage when the population to be surveyed is widely dispersed or

EXHIBIT 10.3

Herbert Abelson
on
CONTROLLED ACCESS
LOCATIONS

Maintaining satisfactory data quality and response rates for probability sample designs has required all kinds of new tactics over the past 15 years or so. Many circumstances, both societal and personal, have increased the difficulty of reaching respondents in order to complete an interview or questionnaire by any means: face-to-face, telephone, or mail.

Because nearly all Response Analysis' studies specify a probability sample design and because so many of these studies require face-to-face interviews in households for data collection, the company has tried to identify the main sources of nonresponse and to work out suitable remedies to increase response rates. In this activity, Response Analysis is not alone. Other companies and organizations, as well as our professional societies, have been working to diagnose the problem in order to improve the completed interview rate.

I thought you might be interested in one remedy that works: the Response Analysis procedures for reaching respondents who live in controlled access locations—wherever there are a group of households protected from uninvited visitors by a security system.

As you might imagine, increasing numbers of apartment buildings and housing developments have guarded entrances and require proof that a visitor is welcome. Interviewers typically make first visits without prior notice, often because our sampling department may supply addresses, but rarely the names of occupants.

Over the last several Response Analysis' nationwide studies, something like 7 percent to 9 percent of designated households had protected access, which means that interviewers could not get past the doorman or guard. Response Analysis permits no substitutions of locations or households. Substitutions give interviewers unwarranted control over the selection of respondents, a practice which introduces unknowable elements into a probability design. When a contract calls for a 75 percent or higher response rate, which many do, you can appreciate the premium that we place on successful access to protected developments and apartment buildings.

One controlled access location can depress response rates for several surveys. For example, if several sample locations all happen to be included within one large controlled access development and interviewers find it impossible to have access to residents for sampling and listing (and ultimately interviewing) purposes, then we have to write off that location not just once but for as many surveys as it takes to "use up" the units in the sample.

As it has worked out, access to controlled locations is not that hard. In one recent nationwide study using the system described below, every protected location—including an Indian reservation—was eventually made available for interviewing. In the case of the reservation, it took two months to obtain a letter from the chairman of the Navajo nation, which permitted us to get on with the work. If only the chairman of every condominium could deal from such authority.

The two keys to the system are:

(1) One person on our Princeton staff is the only person allowed to work on controlled access locations for a particular study; and

(2) Interviewers are trained to stop as soon as they identify a protected location, and are instructed not to try to get in.

That's it. There is no goodwill wasted because our interviewer has not tried to talk his or her way in. The interviewer reports the situation. The "access" person gets together any past history and a current description of the location and then uses one of several strategies to get interviewing permission.

Before starting negotiations with a manager or rental agent, the "access" person makes sure that a member of the local police department is familiar with both the survey and the names of interviewers and is also available as a reference.

Source: Herbert Abelson, "Controlled Access Locations," *The Sampler*, Spring 1981. Response Analysis Corporation, Princeton, N.J. Reprinted with permission.

is situated in hard-to-reach rural or inner-city areas. Interviewer bias is eliminated because there are no interviewers. The questionnaire can be answered at the convenience of the respondent, not at the convenience of the interviewer. Because mail surveys are handled from a central office, there is no problem with controls and checks. Because the respondent has the questionnaire in hand, there is less problem with complex questions than there is in personal or telephone surveys.

Mail surveys have certain drawbacks inherent in their basic nature. Such surveys have to be drawn from lists, and in certain circumstances there simply isn't an available list. For example, there is no readily available mailing list for a probability sample of the national population. In some cases lists do not represent a true sample of the universe to be surveyed, and in other cases the list is incomplete, old, or unreliable.

Another drawback of the mail survey is in regard to the length and nature of the questionnaire. In very few instances are respondents willing to complete a questionnaire of more than four to six pages. If the questionnaire is not carefully designed—so that easy-to-answer and noncomplex questions come first—the survey document won't be returned. Because no interviewer is involved, the questionnaire and its covering letter must stand on their own without chance for amplification, explanation, or motivation by a third party.

The final drawback of mail surveys concerns both the response rate and the representative nature of the response. Because almost all surveys involve sampling from a list representing the universe to be polled, an estimation must be made in advance as to the expected response rate. Paul Erdos, authority on mail surveys, says that "no mail survey can be considered reliable unless it has a minimum of 50 percent response, or unless it demonstrates with some form of verification that the nonrespondents are similar to the respondents."[2] Another authority—John Pollock of Research & Forecasts—states that "for most mail surveys, most research professionals consider something in the range of 30 percent acceptable."[3]

Although there are differences of opinion regarding an acceptable response rate, all professional researchers seek to maximize response rates. When time permits, a second mailing and sometimes a third is sent out. Pollock suggests the following as steps that can be taken to increase response rates in mail surveys: (1) personalizing both letters and envelopes; (2) using stamps instead of standard business return or prefranked envelopes; (3) signing letters with broad, felt-tip pens using blue ink; and (4) whenever possible preparing a cover letter from the head of the sponsoring organization.[4]

One way to prove that the respondents are representative of the universe being probed is to include demographic questions in the questionnaire and then compare the demographic answers with the known demographics of the total universe probed.

Telephone surveys, although not as versatile as personal surveys, have become the most often-used type of public opinion survey because of several factors. With the introduction of Wide Area Telecommunications Service (WATS) it is now possible to conduct a national survey from a central location at far less cost and with far more speed than it is possible to conduct a personal interview survey. The fixed line rental makes it possible to conduct a large survey in a short period of time. The fact that 95 percent of American homes now have telephones has also been a major reason for the use of surveys by telephone. Refinement of techniques, such as drawing the sample by means of random digit dialing (RDD), is a further reason why the major polling organizations have turned to telephone interviewing. Random digit dialing, in effect, is a means of compensating for the fact that unlisted telephones have been on the increase and hence would not normally be included if a telephone survey were to be based on a sample drawn from telephone directories. Klecka and Tuchfarber describe the RDD system as follows:

> This method requires the identification of all working telephone exchanges in the target geograhical area. A potential telephone number is created by selecting an exchange and then appending a random number between 0001 and 9999. Subsequent numbers are created by repeating these two steps. Nonworking numbers, nonresidential telephones,

and households outside of the geographical area are excluded during the interviewing process. Households with more than one telephone number are downweighted accordingly.[5]

There are many advantages to telephone surveys. As already noted, two main advantages are speed and lower cost. If properly planned, a national survey of public opinion can be conducted immediately after an event, and the results can be reported shortly thereafter by the use of computers. Because the interviewing process can be controlled and monitored from a central location, the quality of information obtained tends to be better than that achieved from personal interviewing. Although telephone surveys encounter the same not-at-home and refusal problems as do personal interviews, repeated callbacks can be more easily made by telephone, so a higher response rate can be achieved. The problem of hard-to-reach respondents, encountered increasingly in personal interviewing, is minimized by telephone surveys because telephones are so widely in use today.

Blankenship, in his authoritative book about telephone surveys, says that one of the characteristics of such surveys is that frankness of response is facilitated because the respondent does not see the interviewer or the interviewer's reactions. He reports that controversial topics can be covered best by telephone for the same reason, and he notes there is less interviewer bias and cheating.[6]

Telephone interviewing has its disadvantages, and a major one is the fact that a telephone survey cannot be too long. Replies also tend to be shorter, it is more difficult to

FIGURE 10.1 *Response Analysis Telephone Center.* Making telephone calls is a serious business for the more than one hundred telephone interviewers who staff the Telephone Center at the Response Analysis Corporation in Princeton, N.J. The RAC Telephone Center has the line capacity to handle quickly any size survey and utilizes a state-of-the-art Computer Assisted Telephone Interviewing (CATI) system. The majority of the telephone interviewers are college-educated and skilled in both executive and consumer telephone studies.

Source: Photo courtesy of Response Analysis Corp.

probe, and there is a tendency to give neutral replies. Open-ended questions are usually limited because respondents become impatient while waiting, on a seemingly dead line, for the interviewer to write down the responses.

Despite its drawbacks, telephone surveys have become the major means of measuring after-event public opinion. An example of telephone survey use was a survey carried out for the New York *Times* and CBS News in mid-1983 to ascertain public knowledge and opinion concerning Central America. Here is how the *Times* described the survey procedure:

> The latest New York *Times*/CBS News Poll is based on telephone interviews conducted June 20 through June 26 with 1,365 adults around the United States, excluding Alaska and Hawaii.

> The numbers called were selected by computer from a list of all telephone exchanges in the country and were chosen to insure that each region of the country was represented in proportion to its population. For each exchange, the telephone numbers were formed by random digits, thus permitting access to both listed and unlisted residential numbers.

> The results have been weighted to take account of household size and to adjust for variations in the sample relating to region, race, sex, age, and education.

> In theory, in 19 cases out of 20 the results based on the entire sample will differ by no more than 3 percentage points in either direction from what would have been obtained by interviewing all adult Americans. The error for smaller subgroups is larger. For example, the margin of sampling error for those who know that the United States supports the Government of El Salvador is plus or minus 6 percentage points.

> In addition, the practical difficulties of conducting any survey of public opinion may have resulted in other errors in the poll.[7]

Of major interest is the speed with which the survey was taken and reported. The national poll was conducted June 20 through June 26 and a story citing the results appeared on page 1 of the *Times* on July 1. The national polling organizations which measure public opinion in national elections do their polling through the last weekend and report the results on the day before the elections.

SELECTING THE SAMPLE

Polling a sample of the population or universe rather than the entire population or universe is a basic feature of virtually all public opinion polls today, yet the concept of sampling seems to be least understood by the lay person. In their national pre-election polling and predictions the polling organizations work with samples ranging between 1500 and 2500 adults of voting age, and these numbers inevitably cause doubters to question how such minute samplings—when compared to the total number of persons of voting age—can be considered representative of the entire universe of voters. The answer is found in an explanation of sampling theory, practice, and procedures.

The first important point to understand about sampling is that *the size of the sample is far less important than representativeness.* The key to proper and effective sampling is to use a system of sample selection which gives each individual in the universe an equal opportunity to be selected in the sample polled. If improperly drawn, a sample of one million cannot be considered a true indicator of the universe it supposedly represents. Properly drawn, a sample of 1500 can be considered a true indicator of the opinion of millions.

RANDOM OR PROBABILITY SAMPLING

To make sure that the sample polled is representative of the universe, the major polling organizations draw a random or probability sample. This type of sample is selected in such a manner that *each element* in the universe has an equal or known chance of being in the chosen sample. The term "random" should not be taken to mean that selection has been obtained willy-nilly, but rather that the sample has been obtained without bias and by a carefully designed process. Further, probability sampling enables the pollster to specify the degree by which the sample is representative of the universe. Here is an explanation by the Gallup Organization of the manner in which it designed the sample for a national survey:

> The design of the sample is that of a replicated probability sample down to the block level in the case of urban areas and to segments of townships in the case of rural areas.
>
> After stratifying the nation geographically and by size of community in order to insure conformity of the sample with the latest available estimates by the Census Bureau of the distribution of the adult population, about 320 different sampling locations or areas were selected on a strictly random basis. The interviewers had no choice whatsoever concerning the part of the city or county in which they conducted their interviews.
>
> Approximately five interviews were conducted in each such randomly selected sample point. Interviewers were given maps of the area to which they were assigned, with a starting point indicated, and required to follow a specified direction. At each occupied dwelling unit, interviewers were instructed to select respondents by following a prescribed systematic method and by a male-female assignment. This procedure was followed until the assigned number of interviews was completed.
>
> Since this sampling procedure is designed to produce a sample which approximates the adult civilian population (18 and older) living in private households in the U.S. (that is, excluding those in prisons and hospitals, hotels, religious and educational institutions, and on military reservations), the survey results can be applied to the population for the purpose of projecting percentages into number of people. The manner in which the sample is drawn also produces a sample which approximates the population of private households in the United States. Therefore, survey results can also be projected in terms of number of households when appropriate.

Selecting a random probability sample by means of a list is another way of ensuring representativeness in the sample. It is important, however, that the list include everyone in the universe under consideration and that the list be up to date. Let's assume we want to survey student opinion in a college with 10,000 students. If we determine to use a sample of 200, then we would first divide 200 into 10,000 and thus arrive at intervals of 50. By random selection we would choose a starting point within the first 50 on the list. If the choice falls on the 25th person, then that person would be the first to be interviewed and the next person would be the 75th on the list. The resulting 200 interviews would comprise a probability sample reflective of the key characteristics of all 10,000 students.

The list procedure can also be used in drawing a probability sample of a town or city, though in such a case we would want to deal with addresses rather than individuals. Using an up-to-date city directory we would first number every single household address, including apartments, in the city. (We do this because people move, but houses and apartments don't.) If the last numbered address turns out to be 30,000 and our designated sample is 300, we would divide 300 into 30,000 to arrive at an interval of 100. Again, by random choice we would select a starting number within the first 100 addresses and then interview at intervals of 100.

Instead of using intervals and drawing every nth name from a designated list, another way to select a sample is to utilize a table of random digits. Such tables are sometimes found in the appendix of a statistics textbook; a valuable source is The Rand Corporation, *A Million Random Digits with 100,000 Normal Deviates*, The Free Press, 1955. Each page of such published tables of random digits contains a large number of random digits divided into blocks of five for the sake of convenience. The digits can be read in groups of two, three, or more to produce multiple-digit numbers. The starting point is selected haphazardly. Following is an excerpt from a table of 10,000 random digits:

Line No.	1-5	6-10	11-15	16-20	21-25	26-30	31-35
0	10097	32533	76520	13586	34673	54876	80959
1	37542	04805	64894	74296	24805	24037	20636
2	08422	68953	19645	09303	23209	02560	15953
3	99019	02529	09376	70715	38311	31165	88676
4	12807	99970	80157	36147	64032	36653	98951
5	66065	74717	34072	76850	36697	36170	65813
6	31060	10805	45571	82406	35303	42614	86799
7	85269	77602	02051	65692	68665	74818	73053
8	63573	32135	05325	47048	90553	57548	28468
9	73796	45753	03529	64778	35808	34282	60935

To use the above table the first necessity is to number every name (or address) on the list representing our universe. The next step is to decide on the size of the sample, and then to draw the sample from the table of random digits. As an example, assume the last number on our universe list is 2,530 and we want to draw a random probability sample of 200. We have chosen as our starting point line 2, column 3. Reading four digits across and then down, our first eight four-digit numbers are 4226, 0190, 8079, 0657, 0601, 2697, 5733, 7964. Because they're under 2530, the first numbers to be included in our sample would be 0190 (190), 0657 (657), and 0601 (601). Continuing to draw from the table, our next numbers would be 2533, 4805, 8953, 2529, 9970, and so on running down columns six, seven, eight and nine. Of the five numbers, only 2529 would be included in the sample selection because it's the only four-digit number that is lower than our 2530 limit. We would continue our selection of four-digit numbers ranging under 2530 until we had reached a total of 200, the size of our sample.

Thus, in choosing a sample from lists we can either use a procedure of selecting every nth number or make our selection by means of a table of random digits. The remaining questions about sampling concern the way in which we can calculate the chances that our sample is representative of the universe, and this is done through the statistical concept known as "sampling error."

SAMPLING SIZE AND ERROR

Samples are used in polling public opinion because it is usually impossible to poll the entire population, and even if it were possible, the cost would be prohibitive.

The same points enter into the consideration of how large a sample must be to secure a truly representative reading of public opinion. Deciding on the size of the sample is a matter of achieving a balance between the cost of the survey and the degree of precision needed. The end goal is to use a sample that will produce results within *acceptable margins of error*, and it is important to understand that in dealing with probability sampling reasonably accurate findings can be achieved with surprisingly small samples.

Professional polling organizations operate on what is known as a 95-confidence level, and this means in effect that in an infinite number of similarly designed and executed surveys the percentage results would fall within a given margin of error in 95 percent of these surveys. Thus, as shown in Exhibit 10.4, the Gallup Poll's estimated margin of error at the 95-confidence level is three percentage points for a sample of 1,500; four percentage points for a sample of 1,000; five percentage points for a sample of 600; and six percentage points for a sample of 400. If a Gallup Poll survey of 1,500 interviews shows the president having the support of 50 percent of the population he might actually be supported by as few as 47 percent or as many as 53 percent. If the sample consisted of 400 interviews that 50 percent support could be as high as 56 percent or as low as 44 percent.

EXHIBIT 10.4

Table of Suggested Tolerances for the Gallup Poll

The table below provides the suggested sampling tolerances for the Gallup Poll's standard sampling unit on the basis of procedures presently in use. The figures take into account the effect of the sample design upon sampling error. They show the range, plus or minus, within which results can be expected to vary with repeated samplings under exactly similar conditions.

In Percentage Points (at 95 in 100 confidence level)*							
Sample Size							
	1500	1000	750	600	400	200	100
Percentages near 10	2	2	3	3	4	5	7
Percentages near 20	2	3	4	4	5	7	9
Percentages near 30	3	4	4	4	6	8	10
Percentages near 40	3	4	4	5	6	8	11
Percentages near 50	3	4	4	5	6	8	11
Percentages near 60	3	4	4	5	6	8	11
Percentages near 70	3	4	4	4	6	8	10
Percentages near 80	2	3	4	4	5	7	9
Percentages near 90	2	2	3	3	4	5	7

*The chances are 95 in 100 that the sampling error is not larger than the figures shown.

To use the table above, these directions should be followed. Suppose a reported percentage is 33 for a group that embraces 1500 respondents. Since 33 is nearest 30 in the table, look in row 30 under the column headed 1500. The number in the table is 3, which means that the 33 percent figure obtained in the survey is subject to a sampling error of plus or minus 3 percentage points. Another way of saying this is that very probably (95 times in 100) repeated samplings of this size would yield figures ranging between 30 and 36, with the most likely figure being the 33 percent obtained.

It should be noted that the table deals with the normal sample unit now employed by the Gallup Poll. Many surveys of this organization embrace a far greater number of persons, usually multiples of 1500 unit.

Reprinted by permission of The Gallup Poll.

Roll and Cantril raise an important question that relates to the suggested tolerance of error shown in the preceding table. They ask: "Would it be worth nearly doubling the cost of a survey by increasing the sample size from 750 to 1,500 in order to reduce the expected sampling error from plus or minus four percentage points to plus or minus three percentage points?"[8]

The answer would be "no" when considering most surveys carried out for public relations purposes. If our survey reveals that 60 percent of those surveyed think poorly or highly of our organization's policies and actions, it really doesn't make that much difference if the percentage is 56 percent or 64 percent. The important consideration for the practitioner is to make sure that the sample is a carefully drawn random-probability sample which is broadly representative of the universe and which has given every individual an equal opportunity of being selected. One can then contend that the results of the survey are reasonable approximations of opinion and behavior. Ladd and Ferree state the case as follows:

> Survey research as an instrument of social inquiry has attained widespread usage not because it is capable of ascertaining public opinion or political behavior with complete precision, but rather because it *yields approximations of opinion and behavior that are the most systematic and complete and unbiased that it is possible to derive in many areas without prohibitive costs.* Polling is a science to the extent that it provides for the systematic collection of information that sustains the best possible *approximation* of often-complicated social events and processes.[9]

CONSTRUCTING THE QUESTIONNAIRE

The major tool used in structured random-probability survey research is the questionnaire. Designing the questions to be asked and arranging them in proper order requires the most careful attention on the part of the researcher. There is a definite knack to question design, as Stanley Payne implies by the title of his book (*The Art of Asking Questions*, Princeton University Press), and this art will be discussed in respect to the placement, form, and wording of questions.

PLACEMENT

Unless one is willing to have the interviewing terminated early in the interview, difficult or challenging questions should not be among the first questions asked. The initial questions should be the kind that are easy for the respondent to answer. They should not challenge the respondent's intelligence or knowledge, but should be of such a nature as to put the respondent at ease. Preferred as opening questions are those which can be answered with a simple yes or no, will give the respondent confidence in himself, and are not of a sensitive or embarrassing nature.

There should be a logical arrangement of the questions, and this is best achieved by grouping them so that the conversation leads logically from one question to another. Thus, questions relating to a specific area of concern should follow one another and not be spread throughout the questionnaire. When posing general and specific questions, ask the general ones before asking the specific questions. If this is not done, the respondent is likely to answer the general questions in terms of the specific ones asked earlier. Avoid grouping sensitive questions, but rather intersperse them with neutral ones. If a question poses some long or involved alternatives, put these on cards which can be handed to the respondent. The interviewer then reads out the question and asks the respondent to make his choice from the card.

> The Gallup organization utilized an unusual "card" type of question in pre-election polling in the 1980 elections. It went like this:
>
> "Suppose you were voting TODAY for president and vice president of the United States. Here is a Gallup Poll Secret Ballot listing the candidates for these offices. Will you please MARK that secret ballot for the candidates you favor today—and then drop the folded ballot into the box."[10]

FORM

There are three basic forms of questions with many varieties of each form. Only the basic forms will be described here.

Dichotomous questions are those which provide two options. Examples of dichotomous questions are those which pose a choice between yes and no, approve and disapprove, good and bad. Proper procedure is to provide also for a third response, such as don't know, no opinion, or neither. If the third possibility is not provided, then the question may force respondents to make a choice that they really do not want to make.

On the positive side, dichotomous questions are simple, easy to pose, understandable to the respondent, and easy to tabulate.

On the negative side, such questions may force respondents to make a choice they do not want to make. Opinions about many subjects do not fall readily into a simple yes-no choice, but may fall in between the two extremes.

Multiple-choice questions in a variety of styles provide alternatives not available in dichotomous questions. Such questions are most often phrased to provide three-, four-, and five-point rating scales. Examples of three-point scales: above average, average, below average; higher, the same, lower. A four-point scale would be excellent, good, fair, poor. Some five-point scales: much greater, somewhat greater, equal, somewhat less, not at all; strongly approve, approve, undecided, disapprove, strongly disapprove.

A refinement of the verbal multiple-choice rating scale is the graphic rating scale in which the respondent is asked to show strength of opinion on a line of numbers. Highest approval might be a plus five, middle would be zero, and lowest would be a minus five.

The virtue of multiple-choice, rating-scale questions is that they allow degrees of opinion to be expressed. On the negative side is the fact that such questions tend to be long and place a heavy burden on the respondent's remembrance of the choices. When the question itself is long, the burden is especially heavy, as shown in this question from a survey by ABC News/Washington *Post*:

> **Question:** Some people say it doesn't make any difference which candidates win the election for the U.S. Congress because regardless of who wins, nothing much changes. Others say which candidates win elections makes a big difference. How much difference do you personally think it makes: a great deal, a fair amount, only some, or just about no difference at all?[11]

Open-end questions make up the third major form of questions. Instead of providing preconceived response choices they permit the respondent to answer the question freely and allow wide latitude for answers. Their major virtue is that they pick up the full flavor of a response and often reflect unanticipated opinions. Their major problem is that they are hard to categorize and often have to be forced into a mold for tabulation purposes.

WORDING

Though the wording of questions seems to be a simple matter, it actually requires a great deal of care and skill. The following major guidelines are suggested:

1. Use simple rather than complex words. Aim questions so they're understood by those with a tenth-grade level of education.

2. Be precise and absolutely clear. Payne suggests the following six-point test of a proposed question:[12]

a. Does it mean what we intend?

b. Does it have any other meanings?

c. If so, does the context make the intended meaning clear?

d. Does the word have more than one pronunciation?

e. Is there any word or similar pronunciation that might be confused?

f. Is a simpler word or phrase suggested?

3. Cover only one point at a time, not two or more in one question. Asking "Do you like the taste of wine and cheese?" assumes that everyone considers the two in combination with each other when judging their taste. It's possible for someone to like the taste of wine and dislike the taste of cheese, but the question does not permit such an answer.

4. Avoid leading questions. Any question that is likely to produce a biased answer can be considered to be a leading question. Leading questions lead to misleading answers. Unless the surveyor is deliberately trying to secure predetermined answers, he should avoid phrasing the question to bring about desired answers.

5. Make sure the question will elicit the exact information sought. Questions which are not explicit enough will often produce answers that can't be combined for data reporting. For example, asking employees to estimate how much profit their company makes can bring answers in dollar figures, percentages, and gradations ranging from "a lot" to "not much." If you want the figure to be in dollars, specify dollars in the question. Further, does the question mean "net profit" or "gross profit"? If the surveyor is not sure what he means then he can't expect the respondent to be sure.

6. Frame alternatives carefully and honestly. Provide the same number of alternatives for each side of a question. Recognize that the more alternatives, the less likely respondents will favor the extremes. Try to phrase alternatives realistically, the way people think and feel about problems and issues. Do not combine issues and partisan arguments. Balance the wording of alternatives so as to avoid biasing the results.

INTERVIEWING AND PROCESSING DATA

Good interviewers are basically good listeners rather than good talkers. Interviewing requires the ability to be at ease in social situations and to be able to adapt easily to one's surroundings. Above all, interviewers must be reliable, honest, and able to work on their own. Although interviewers have to go through a preliminary training session, thereafter they work independently and hence must be trustworthy.

Mullen and Bishop consider the field-work aspect of public opinion polling to be an area of real concern. They cite laziness and dishonesty as two human failings with which all organizations must do constant battle. "When just a little of either creeps into an interviewing organization," they state, "accuracy in survey research is no longer possible. Given large doses of either or both, the value of a survey is totally destroyed."[13]

Guarding against bias or inaccuracy resulting from interviewing failures is a constant problem for polling organizations. The national ones rely on checking and supervision to weed out undesirable interviewers, but checking is difficult when interviewers are widely dispersed and work independently, as all interviewers do. Finding good supervisors is even more difficult.

Handling survey data is done chiefly through machine processing and has reached a stage that cannot be described in detail in a textbook of this nature. The major polling organizations use skilled punch-card and data-processing operators and machines for sorting, compiling, and storing the survey data, and this calls for a preliminary coding of responses. In small surveys this work can be done manually, but the task is a tedious one that calls for the utmost care and attention to detail in handling data and percentages.

Robinson describes the steps in preparing data for analysis:

> Translation of raw data into analyzable form requires a number of steps, some comparatively simple and others much more complex. Easiest is the straightforward tabulation of the various direct questions (age, income, and so forth) that were precoded beforehand and which require only a checkmark or a circle on the part of the interviewer. The open-ended questions and the various indirect data collection techniques require more elaborate rate procedures. Generally these questions elicit answers that range from a few

words to hundreds of words, depending upon the question and the purpose of the survey. In order to make sense out of these thousands of words, they must be analyzed and put into response categories that *reflect* the content of the answer in manageable form. This process is known as *content analysis.* Essentially, it is a technique which permits a systematic, objective, and exhaustive analysis and classification of the responses or "thought units" obtained from all of the interviewees in a given survey into response categories that sum up their replies to a certain question or series of questions. . . .

After the raw data have been prepared for analysis (by simple tabulation or content analysis), they are generally expressed in terms of tables, which pull together all of the replies to a given question and enable the researcher to make his interpretations.[14]

ANALYZING, INTERPRETING, AND REPORTING DATA

If wrapping up the results of survey research were only a matter of presenting the data in tabular form, life would be relatively uncomplicated. The facts could speak for themselves. However, as Robinson warns, there is no such thing as a fact standing by itself. Raw data have to be reassembled into some form of logical order and interpreted to those for whom the survey is designed. One way to achieve such meaning is to *apply percentages* to the findings. A second is to *describe* the findings by means of adjectives and adverbs, and a third is to apply some interpretation to the findings.

Percentages are important because they widen the narrow focus of the sample figures and make them applicable to the universe. Let us say we used a sample of 100 respondents and the universe is 2,000 people. A response to a question shows that 75 out of the 100 are "very much" in favor of a particular action. Widening this finding we can say that 75 percent of the universe are "very much" in favor of the action.

Stating this same finding in descriptive words we can say that "a high proportion" or "three-quarters" or "more than seven out of ten" people favor the particular action.

Thus, by the use of percentages and descriptive words we're able to express the findings in a variety of ways and at the same time to place them in perspective. Relatively dull figures take on life through such techniques, but description and interpretation should honestly reflect the figures on which they are based. Unfortunately, managements often either expect interpretation to gloss over deficiencies or else don't want to face up to negative findings. The positive ones are always easy to handle; the negative ones can be the moment of truth for the public relations practitioner.

RESEARCH, ONLY THE BEGINNING

In concluding this chapter on reseach it's appropriate to cite this reminder by Professor Robinson: "A research study, survey or otherwise, seldom tells the practitioner what to do."[15] Through the use of fact-finding, trend study, and public opinion survey research, the practitioner gains valuable information for subsequent public relations programs and activities. Ways of making the most intelligent use of research findings will be explored in the chapters that follow.

ENDNOTES

1. John Crothers Pollock, "Getting the Most from Your Research," *Public Relations Journal*, July 1983, p. 17.
2. Paul L. Erdos, *Professional Mail Surveys* (New York: McGraw-Hill, 1970), p. 144.
3. Pollock, p. 17.
4. Ibid.
5. William R. Klecka and Alfred J. Tuchfarber, "Random Digit Dialing: A Comparison to Personal Surveys," *Public Opinion Quarterly*, Spring 1978.

6. A. B. Blankenship, *Professional Telephone Surveys* (New York: McGraw-Hill, 1977), p. 44.
7. New York *Times*, July 1, 1983, p. A-2.
8. Charles W. Roll, Jr., and Albert H. Cantril, *Polls, Their Use and Misuse in Politics* (New York: Basic Books, 1972), p. 73.
9. Everett C. Ladd and G. Donald Ferree, "Were the Pollsters Really Wrong?" *Public Opinion*, January 1981, p. 13.
10. Ibid., p. 19.
11. *Public Opinion*, December/January 1983, p. 21.
12. Stanley Payne, *The Art of Asking Questions* (Princeton, N.J.: Princeton University Press, 1951).
13. James Mullen and Michael Bishop, "Clinical Interviewing in Public Relations Research," *Public Relations Quarterly*, Spring 1975, p. 24.
14. Edward J. Robinson, *Public Relations and Survey Research* (New York: Appleton-Century-Crofts, 1969), p. 97.
15. Ibid., p. 99.

PROJECTS, ASSIGNMENTS, AND MINIS

1. THE PROFESSOR DESIGNS A QUESTIONNAIRE: A MINI-CASE

An economics professor decided to measure student opinion at his college about the local daily newspaper. He therefore designed a questionnaire for students to complete. The newspaper was an afternoon daily whose average issue ran to twenty-eight pages. The editorial page of this daily usually contained several editorials, three national columns, and letters to the editor. The front page always contained only national and international news from the Associated Press; local and area news ran on inside pages. The college had a student enrollment of 2,300. The economics professor taught three courses, each containing twenty-five students, and the questionnaire was completed by these students in class on a Friday. The questionnaire follows:

Questionnaire

1. Do you read the Gazette?   Daily _____ Frequently _____
   Seldom _____ Never _____

2. Do you read any other newspapers?   Yes _____ No _____ Which
   ones? (1) _____ (2) _____ How often?   Daily _____
   Occasionally _____ Sundays only _____

3. What part of the newspaper do you usually read first?
   Comics _____   Front page stories _____
   Sports _____   Advertisements _____
   Editorials _____   Obituaries _____
   Local news _____   Other _____
   Favorite columnist _____

   What do you read next? _____

4. Do you read the editorials?   Daily _____ Frequently _____
   Seldom _____ Never _____

5. Are there some parts of the paper you never read?   Yes _____
   No _____ Which parts?   (1) _____ (2) _____ (3) _____

6. Which candidate in the current presidential campaign does your newspaper support?
   (Check one)
   Reagan _____   Carter _____

7. Do you feel that your newspaper is giving fair news coverage to both major candidates?
   Yes _____ No _____ Don't know _____ If not, who is more
   favored? _____

8. Do you think the editorials deal fairly with both candidates?
   Yes _____ No _____ Don't know _____

9. Do you think the columnists deal fairly with both candidates?
   Yes _____ No _____ Don't know _____

10. Do you think both the Republican and Democratic viewpoints are presented by the
    editorials and columnists in your newspaper?
    Yes _____ No _____ Don't know _____
    Do you approve of this? _____
    Why? _____

Questions for Discussion

1. In your opinion, which questions need rewording? Specifically, what is wrong with the questions that you think need to be reworded?

2. What's your opinion of the sample selected to answer the questionnaire?

Assignment

Rewrite the questions which the class found unacceptable.

2. CLINICAL INTERVIEWING: A MINI-EXAMPLE FOR DISCUSSION

As an alternative to large-scale quantitative research utilizing structured question-naires and scores of interviewers, two authors suggest that a useful substitute in public relations cases is the in-depth, unstructured interview with a sharply limited sample of respondents. Their method, which is a form of depth interviewing, is called "clinical interviewing," and they cite the following as an example of how it works:

One study concerned the use of bank credit cards. The organization behind the card had a number of unanswered questions concerning the acceptance, use, and nonuse of its card. Among the questions were these: (a) Who is a good prospect for a bank credit card? (b) Why do some people keep a bank card but fail to use it? (c) Is there a difference in per-ception of bank card credit vs. other types of credit among users? (d) Why do some people use these cards only for "big ticket" items while others use them for anything *but* such items? (e) How have various bank public communications (personal contact, letters, media advertising) been received by users and prospective users?

Such "why" and "how" questions as these have represented a prime source of difficulty for those using regular survey research. One can't be certain about what constitutes the universe when dealing with such a diversity of questions. (To include everyone who should be involved in *one* part of the study would mean that large numbers of people could be included who should *not* be involved in *other* parts.) Using the clinical method, any person interviewed would contribute only to those sections of the study where his contribution is relevant.

In order to obtain answers to these questions using quantitative survey methods, it may have been necessary to draw three or four separate samples and prepare a specific ques-tionnaire for each. Instead, the authors were able to obtain useful results with just one small sample and no questionnaire. They conducted all 75 interviews themselves (in three states, in communities of varying size, with old and young, rich and poor, black and white). They were able to stop with 75 interviews as they found they were getting little new information and were largely confirming what they had already learned.

The project cost much less than would have a series of quantitative studies, and all parties concerned were convinced that the results (while not projectable) were reliable and therefore useful. Three years after the study was completed, its conclusions are still being employed as a basis for guiding successful corporate communications.*

Questions for Discussion

1. What's your opinion of the study and the authors' conclusions about its effectiveness?

2. Do you agree or disagree with the authors' contention that finding answers to the questions would have required three to four samples and surveys using quantitative survey methods?

3. What criticism, if any, do you have about the composition of the 75 interviews?

4. What questions do you have about the selection of the sample of 75?

---

*Source: James J. Mullen and Michael E. Bishop, "Clinical Interviewing in Public Relations Research," *Public Relations Quarterly,* Spring 1975, p. 23.

3. A CITY COMMUNICATIONS AUDIT: A MINI-CASE

In order to assess the effectiveness of its communications department and to provide guidelines for its future work, a major United States city retained the services of a public relations counseling firm and asked it to conduct a communications audit. At the time the city's population was close to 400,000 and the city was known nationally and internationally both as a tourist and convention center and as a center for investment, business, and finance.

The stated major objective of the communications audit was to ascertain the present standing of the city in regard to tourism, conventions, investment, business, and finance and to evaluate its future public relations needs. In seeking to meet this major objective, the counseling firm aimed to determine how the city was perceived by its residents and by the outside world; how the city wanted to be perceived; how effective were its communications activities; and what kind of communications organization would be needed to best meet its communications objectives.

Three different public opinion surveys were carried out by the counseling firm in handling its assignment. The three were as follows:

1. **Telephone interviews** with top executives at the vice-presidential level or above at ten multinational corporations on the *Fortune 500* list. A total of thirty-three such corporations were contacted and there were twenty-three refusals or nonreplies.

   Those responding answered five questions asking them to rate the city with three others of comparable stature as regional centers of national and international trade, investment, transportation, distribution, tourism, recreation, conventions, and banking. Respondents were also asked to judge which of the four cities was most likely to emerge in the future as preeminent in these areas.

2. A **national mail survey** of tourism, business, financial, and travel editors and columnists and of some private business and tourism representatives. A total of 600 questionnaires were mailed and 54 replies were received. The questions on the mail survey were essentially the same as those asked in the telephone interviews, although a bit longer.

3. A **local mail survey** among a randomly distributed sample of community leaders and city residents. A total of 700 questionnaires were mailed and 106 replies were received. Respondents were asked a total of eight questions—some divided into subcategories—relating to city services, taxes, communications, and goals for the years ahead.

A *Communications Audit Report*, submitted by the counseling firm and containing the results of the three surveys, recommendations, and appended tables, ran to more than seventy pages. The report also contained representative comments from individuals among the groups surveyed.

Questions for Discussion

1. What's your opinion of the—

   a) composition of the three groups surveyed;

   b) survey methods employed by the counseling firm;

   c) total number of persons sampled in each method and the total number of respondents in each method?

2. If your answers to any of the above are affirmative, explain the reasons for your conclusions. If your answers to any of the above are critical or negative, explain the reasons for your conclusions and set forth alternatives.

3. If you were the counseling firm, how would you go about deciding what to charge the city for your surveys and report? Try to be specific, not general. What do you consider would be a reasonable fee?

Assignment

You are to assume that you handle research assignments for the counseling firm cited in the case fact pattern. Prepare five questions which could be included in the mail survey of a randomly distributed sample of community leaders and city residents.

11

PLANNING AND PROGRAMMING

*A*fter two decades of experience preparing programs for clients and would-be clients, counselor Jack R. Nowling emphasizes the importance of planning and programming in these words:

> Program writing tests our intelligence, our experience, and our creativity in a special way, almost a unique way. It forces us to survey our mission in its totality. It compels us to rationalize our goals, to establish our priorities, to organize our activities—and then, as the ultimate booby-trap, it demands that we project the results.[1]

As an experienced practitioner Nowling recognizes that public relations planning and programming involves a disciplined approach to organizational problems and objectives plus the need for creative freedom in solving such problems and meeting objectives. In seeking to develop a viable program the public relations practitioner can draw up the most detailed plan, but often improvisation takes over simply because so many ingredients necessary for successful completion of the planned program are *out of the control of the planner.* Most public relations projects involve a combination of events, people, and media, and though the practitioner has control over his own events and his own people, he certainly has no control over other events which affect his project; no control over most of the people affected by his project; and certainly no control over the mass media. Therefore, through long experience the seasoned practitioner develops a program which starts with a plan but which recognizes the inevitability of the unplanned taking place.

David Finn of Ruder & Finn notes there are two schools of thought about public relations programming:

1. *The inspirational school,* which operates on the assumption that sound programming is at best a matter of keen intuition and that the practitioner is most effective when he is alert to problems that arise from day to day.

2. *The planned school,* which operates on the assumption that working on the basis of a carefully charted program is the only way to be businesslike and to enable management to know clearly what the practitioner is doing at all times.

Recognizing there is merit to both approaches, Finn feels the solution is found in a *balanced* program.

"The key to balanced service," he says, "may be program development not as a schedule of activity to be followed but rather as a thoughtful document setting forth the major direction which public relations effort should take."[2]

Finn is undoubtedly correct when he contends that programming involves part planning and part inspiration. The experienced chef follows a set routine in preparing a souffle but uses instinct and judgment in deciding the exact moment to take it out of the oven. The experienced practitioner follows certain routines in carrying out public relations activities but also uses instinct and judgment in deciding when the activities are half-baked or well done and in dealing with day-to-day problems that require creative thinking. Whether baking a souffle or carrying out public relations activities, one is advised to start with a plan.

Three of the major advantages of public relations planning are as follows:

1. The thinking that goes into planning helps clarify the problems(s).

As has been emphasized several times in this book, public relations practitioners are problem-solvers, but the problems they deal with generally do not come in convenient, prepackaged shapes. Public relations problems are most often untidy and amorphous and must be clarified long before the attempt is made to solve them. The thinking that goes into planning helps induce such clarification.

2. The plan provides a blueprint and a working schedule.

Public relations problems are more often complex rather than simple. The more complex the problem, the greater the need for an operational blueprint to enable activities to proceed in an orderly and predetermined fashion. Plans will often be subjected to sudden changes, but the blueprint and working schedule serve to provide *direction* and guidance.

3. The creation and approval of a plan prevents misunderstandings.

Public relations is such a relatively new field and management tool that there is need to ensure understanding of its essential nature and thrust. In almost all but the very smallest organizations, most plans involve rather large groups and require the cooperation and understanding of other departments. As a "support" function, public relations itself needs internal support. Further, when approved, the plan provides the practitioner with needed authority and serves as a "document of record."

Counterbalancing the advantages of planning are some common pitfalls, and Finn cites the following three:

1. Overprogramming

Public relations people, like advertising men, often are guilty of "running it up the flagpole," which is a euphemistic way of suggesting as many ideas and projects as one can conceive to see if they'll be "saluted." The trouble with saluting is that it can turn into a mindless exercise, and the trouble with overprogramming is that the plan will contain too many projects to be carried out successfully. Having projects which do not meet basic objectives is as mindless and unproductive as oversaluting.

Overprogramming can be especially dangerous when a department is undermanned. Inevitably in such circumstances there will be counterpressures on staff members, and as a result one or more programs will suffer. In recognizing this dilemma, a Byoir staffer offers this tip:

> Even Robinson Crusoe couldn't get everything done by Friday. Set achievable time-tables, and if slippage occurs, be sure the client knows it early—not when you have to show up at deadline with empty hands. When the workload surges and you find yourself over-extended, get help. Don't try to do everything yourself, which is a classic public relations syndrome. Be sure the client knows the situation and accepts it. Most management people are reasonable and will accept legitimate explanations for unexpected delays or derailments.

2. Undue program rigidity

The Byoir staffer's warning about unexpected delays or derailments applies particularly to the common pitfall known as undue program rigidity. In two circumstances of the unexpected—one labeled *opportunity* and the other *crisis*—program rigidity can lead to program rigor mortis. When unexpected opportunities or crises arise, the practitioner must be prepared to deal with them, even though this might well mean temporarily abandoning a planned program or project.

Such situations are akin to following a road map while on a trip. When taking a long trip it's helpful to have a detailed road map, but when you come to a detour that is not on the map, it's better to obey the dictates of the detour rather than the map. When the unexpected happens—as often occurs in public relations activity—it's wise to discard the plan and take care of the unexpected.

3. Losing faith in the approved plan

The fact that detours do show up from time to time does not mean that all road maps are obsolete. Following a planned public relations program is often as difficult as driving a car with three backseat drivers shouting, "Turn right!" "Turn left!" "Go back to that last crossroad!" There are many backseat public relations "experts" in every organization, and the practitioner has to have sufficient faith in his or her own ability and judgment to disregard well-intentioned, but unwise, advice from the backseat drivers.

However, having faith in one's ability and judgment is only part of the problem in dealing with managements. The other part, equally as important, is securing management's faith in the practitioner's ability and judgment. As another Byoir staffer explains the problem:

> Today, many professional managers are running companies and this trend can be expected to become the rule in the future. They are a different breed than the old entrepreneurs who had great seat-of-the-pants instincts. The new CEOs want to apply computer analysis and zero based budgeting to public relations as they do to any other company function. They listen to counsel, but are likely to pull in several opinions. They like consensus and are much harder to reach with warning flags. The public relations counselor of the future, in my opinion, will have to win the confidence and support of the entire management team to have his ideas listened to at the very top.

There are many kinds of public relations plans, programs, and actions, but they can be divided into two broad groups. One consists of daily, ongoing activities carried on from year to year, and the other consists of special, planned projects, events, and activities meshed into a blueprint for action. The former will be discussed briefly in the section that follows. The major part of the remainder of this chapter will be devoted to the latter type.

DAILY, ONGOING ACTIVITIES

In many organizations the public relations function has become so routinized it seems to exist like the gyroscope spinning in its own orbit impervious to outside forces. This is particularly evident in those organizations where public relations is handled by one or two professionals who provide public relations advice (when asked) and also produce public relations "hardware." The latter could take the form of news releases, feature stories, some internal publications, and brochures. As the organization grows in size, or as new public relations activities are called for, additions are made to the public relations staff to handle them and in time these new activities become routinized and are carried on from year to year.

There seems to be little planning and programming in the above situation, but this does not mean the public relations function is being handled poorly. So long as the staff's activities are geared to meet specific public relations objectives and goals, the fact that formal planning and programming hasn't taken place does not automatically imply a failure on the part of the public relations staff.

Furthermore, even in large organizations where there is formal planning and programming there are always certain public relations tasks and activities which are so obviously necessary there is no need to plan for them. At some point in time someone responsible for the function had to make a decision to carry out the activity and that decision became part of the regular program of the department.

The important point about programming in this type of arrangement is that it consists chiefly of daily, ongoing activities carried on from year to year, and these involve both counseling and public relations "hardware" such as releases, internal publications, etc.

SPECIAL PLANNED PROJECTS, EVENTS, AND ACTIVITIES MESHED INTO A BLUEPRINT FOR ACTION

This second type of public relations programming is that referred to by David Finn when he speaks of "balanced service," and it is the kind of programming most often developed and followed by counseling firms when they take on a new client. Internal public relations departments also follow the same general procedure, although not as frequently as counseling firms because there is usually not the same need for internal departments to develop broad new programs. However, when a counseling firm takes on a new account, there's an imperative need to present the client with a plan and a program, and in essence to provide a blueprint for action.

Such programming involves a series of steps or procedures. The pattern provides a logical means of handling public relations problems via the following steps:

1. Making a preliminary study

2. Defining the problems (or setting forth the situation)

3. Establishing objectives and goals

4. Defining the audience

5. Establishing a theme

6. Initiating action and activities: projects, tactics, and timing

7. Communicating and evaluating

Each of the above steps will be discussed in detail in the following sections, but it's important to understand that not all of them are followed each time a program is planned. Some situations are such that a preliminary study is not needed. Some situations present problems that are so clear and self-evident there's no need to "define the problem." In some situations a basic theme is not needed.

In short, one might well skip one or two of the above steps in setting up a plan, program, and activities, but such a decision will be based on the specific situation. The important point to remember is that the seven-point blueprint establishes a time-tested means for handling public relations situations and problems.

MAKING A PRELIMINARY STUDY

Folklore has it that the public relations practitioner is a magic medicine person with secret potions to cure organizational ills. Actual practice is far removed from this stereotyped impression. The experienced practitioner knows that it's impossible to carry out an effective public relations program without having intimate knowledge of the organization he or she represents.

When a counseling firm is retained, almost inevitably the *first action taken does not involve public relations per se* but research concerning the organization and its environment, policies, people, publics, problems, and reputation. How does the counselor go about conducting such research? Very much like a veteran reporter assigned to cover an involved story. Interviews are held with key personnel within the organization and with outsiders who are most likely to have knowledge about the organization. If the client is a business or industry, then important sources of information are editors of business, trade, and financial publications; key suppliers, dealers, and customers; trade association executives; and any others who are most likely to be knowledgeable about the client. Valuable sources of print material—such as annual reports, brochures, publicity files, etc.—are also consulted. Like the investigative reporter, the counselor probes to find weaknesses and strengths, to become intimately aware of almost every conceivable facet of the client organization. The end result of the investigative reporter's probing will be an article or series of articles; the end result of the counseling firm's probing will be a written report which forms the foundation for subsequent public relations activities.

Reading the above paragraph has probably taken about a minute or two, but compiling data for a preliminary study and writing a background report can take a month to six weeks. It takes time and skill to interview key personnel and editors, conduct library research, gather facts and data about an organization's history, facilities, products, people, etc. Into the preliminary study goes much hard, unglamorous but extremely valuable work which, as one practitioner declares, serves three functions: (1) *it provides a logical foundation for the program;* (2) *it enables the account executive to secure a solid grounding in the client organization;* and (3) *it demonstrates to the client that the counseling firm has the proper background and experience to interpret the client to its publics.* From a substantive point of view the first function served by the preliminary study—that is, providing a logical foundation for the program—is most important. Without a logical foundation based on data and facts about the organization, a public relations program would be like a house built on hot air—supportable for a limited amount of time only.

Thus, if the preliminary study or background report is to be solid enough to support the superstructure of the public relations program, it has to be built with this superstructure constantly in mind. No two studies will, or should, be exactly alike, but at the minimum they should encompass the following elements:

1. *Facts and data about the organization* as they relate to the organization's public relationships. For example, if the organization is a business, what are its products; gross sales and net profits; employee force; customers; rank and place in its industry; dealers; suppliers; past history; future possibilities?

2. *Reputation and standing.* What do others—especially those in a position to know—think about the organization? Is it held in generally good or ill repute and why?

3. *Personnel.* What kind of management does the organization have? Who are the key people? What do they think about public relations and what is their level of sophistication about the public relations function? What's the relationship between management and its employee force?

4. *Past and present public relations practices.* What has the organization done in the past about public relations and what is it now doing? What changes ought to be made, and what seems to be the climate for acceptance of proposed changes? What should be retained and/or modified?

5. *Weaknesses.* What, if any, activities or policies of the organization are causing unfavorable opinions about the organization? Will the organization be receptive to suggested changes or modifications of these activities and policies?

6. *Strengths.* What, if any, activities or policies of the organization are causing favorable opinions about the organization, and has the organization sufficiently capitalized on these? Are there any unique or unusual activities or policies which can be emphasized in future public relations programming?

7. *Opportunities.* Is there anything about the present climate or the situation of the organization which provides opportunities for creative use of public relations?

8. *Obstacles.* Is there anything about the present climate or situation of the organization—including personnel and "politics"—which would cause obstacles to public relations programming?

9. *Conclusions and judgments.* Is the background report factually correct, will it sustain careful scrutiny and criticism, and does it convey the proper analytical and professional tone?

Each of the above elements is amplified by questions for a specific reason: no public relations textbook can provide instant answers to public relations problems. However, in going through the process of asking proper questions of a situation the practitioner finds that complex problems narrow down. The answers to the right kind of questions suggest a focus for future public relations programming, but before any programming can begin the questions have to be posed and answered.

DEFINING THE PROBLEMS (OR SETTING FORTH THE SITUATION)

Practically every organization of size has public relations problems, and these range in scope and intensity from those which can be safely ignored to those which demand immediate attention lest they get out of control. The preliminary study, like a medical checkup, will uncover many problems. Many of them can either be cured by simple treatment or be dismissed as being relatively inconsequential. Others will need action taken to check their development, and finally a number of them will be so deep-seated and dangerous as to call for surgery.

It should be obvious that immediate, pressing problems are the least difficult to define because they seem to shout for attention and resolution. Though such problems may not be the most important to an organization, time dictates their immediate solution.

If, for example, a small college finds in May that its fall semester entering class is 30 percent short of expectation, the public relations department will probably be asked to drop everything and put its energies, resources, and skills into attracting more entering students. The immediate problem of declining enrollment may well be due to a variety of basic factors that should have been remedied years ago, but there's time to work at these factors after college commences in the fall. Thus, although the immediate problem may not be the most important to the organization, time dictates an immediate solution.

The small college public relations staffer is undoubtedly fortunate because he will probably be cognizant of the enrollment problem. In large organizations he or she may not have this advantage. As one counselor points out:

> Given adequate notice, and full input from the client, we can anticipate problems and, at times, turn a potential negative into a positive. But, if given last-minute notice and sketchy details, the public relations practitioner's performance is hampered.

> The public relations professional is like the navigator in a plane. He can tell you where you are, where you're going and when you'll get there; but not if he's blindfolded.

The skilled practitioner, like the skilled internist and navigator, is able to make *distinctions* about problems. Public relations problems come in all sizes and shapes. Some are internal and some are external; some are temporary and some are permanent; some are on the surface and some are deep-rooted. Recognizing, dissecting, and handling them calls for skills born out of years of experience.

"One of the greatest shortcomings of public relations programs, and of the planners who write them, is *failure* to understand the problem," states H. Zane Robbins, director of communications, Arthur Andersen & Co. "Most public relations men and women can tell you in 25 words or less: 'The company's basic problem is . . .' But that doesn't mean they really understand the broad implications of that problem. There's a wide gap between enunciating a problem and comprehending it."

The gap that Robbins cites can be bridged by applying a fourfold approach to problems: (a) ask the right questions, (b) recognize that problem identification is largely a result of assumptions, (c) get rid of nonessentials, and (d) establish an order of priorities.

Ask the Right Questions

As in the preliminary study stage of programming, it is essential to ask the right questions about a situation. Asking the right questions doesn't necessarily mean that the right answers will be immediately forthcoming, but start with questions to come up with answers. Fools rush in with answers; wise men ask questions. Note the emphasis which the late Earl Newsom put on questions in a talk he gave at the New School for Social Research:

> [There] is an implication that we are the white-haired boys who have easy answers to everything and are responsible for all the good deeds of our clients. That isn't true, of course. The facts are much less dramatic and, I am afraid, not nearly so complimentary. This kind of thing is much nearer the truth: somebody in some department of management finds himself with a problem—or a potential problem—that cuts across the interests of large groups of people. He calls us up and says, "We would like to talk to you about this." He might also quite properly bring in the head of the company's public relations department or the officers of other departments that might also be involved. So we sit down and consider the situation. It might be, for example, a threatened strike. Primarily, of course, this is a problem of industrial relations. But it becomes a problem of public relations because not only are the employees an important part of the company's public, but in moments of tension of this kind the whole situation is apt to become a public matter.

> I hope you don't get the notion that we hurry into such a meeting and say, "Well, what you should do is this." Such problems are complicated and many things have to be considered besides what the public will think. How will actions that the company might take affect the industry as a whole? How do they relate to national policies as set in Washington? What do polls show about trends of public thought? What do economists have to say about the future? What is the wise thing to do about this? In those discussions our voice is no louder than our judgment, or the opinion of our client on how good we are in matters we are supposed to be good about. . . .

> Or another kind of thing. Somebody in Washington on the floor of the House may get up and say something that is untrue or misleading about a client corporation. A first ques-

tion is, "How important is this?" Who made the statement? Why did he make it? Should we do something about it? So we're apt to get together and talk about it and present our ideas. Perhaps the president of the corporation should telephone or telegraph the Congress and ask to be heard. If so, facts have to be gotten together and help given in assembling them.

Those are problems that are apt to come up. You can't do business without stepping on the toes of people and the problem is to deal with it as best you can.[3]

Newsom's questions, it should be noted, aim to broaden one's view to extend beyond the seemingly narrow scope of the problem. Perceptive questions expose the ramifications which exist within most public relations problems and enable the practitioner to get to the real crux of a situation. Asking the right questions, in short, is where one starts to define the problem(s).

Recognize That Problem Identification Is Largely a Result of Assumptions

In developing a conceptual framework to analyze the public relations function, Professor Edward J. Robinson stated that one of the key factors in isolating or identifying problems is the assumptions that the practitioner brings to the problem-solving situation. He points out that in dealing with a problem all of us make certain assumptions, even though we may not be consciously aware of doing so. These may be true or untrue, but the important thing is that *assumptions influence the way we look at the problem and then attempt to solve it.* If our assumptions are correct this can help clarify the problem, but if they are incorrect they can lead us down many a wrong path. Robinson therefore suggests that the practitioner ask himself continually:

What are my assumptions?

What have I assumed to be true (or false) in this particular situation?

What implicit assumptions have I made about the *human* element—i.e., what convenient generalizations have I made about human behavior?[4]

The relationship that assumptions have to problem viewing is similar to the relationship that a cataract has to sight. We see because light rays move freely through the lens of the eye to reach the retina:

Light rays →lens →retina = clear vision

However, when the normally transparent lens of the human eye becomes clouded by a cataract, clarity of vision is lost because the rays are blocked from moving through the lens to the retina:

Light rays →cataract = diminished vision

Substitute "assumptions" for the lens of the eye. If one's assumptions are correct, then the light rays thrown on the problem will move freely through the lens of correct assumptions to the retina of clear perceptions of the problem:

Light rays →lens of correct assumptions →retina
= clear perceptions of the problem

However, if one's assumptions are incorrect, then the light rays thrown on the problem will be blocked by the lens of incorrect assumptions and will result in opaque perceptions of the problem:

Light rays → lens of incorrect assumptions
= cloudy perceptions of the problem

If we are to view problems with clear vision we must be vigilant about the assumptions we bring to problem-solving situations. In today's fast-moving world, it is particularly important that our assumptions about people and society are in tune with the times; in trying to cope with problems, attempts based on outdated and false assumptions are almost certain to flounder.

Counselor George Hammond provides an excellent illustration of the relationship between assumptions and programming in the following remarks:

> When The Road Information Program hired us, their first instructions were for us to develop a nationwide publicity program in support of a second system of interstate highways. That's what they wanted. It would mean lots of business for the roadbuilders.

> But we asked for time and used that time to conduct a survey of attitudes among the press and the public. What we found out was that the public didn't want a second interstate system. What they wanted was an easier commute, lower operating expenses for their cars, safer transportations to school for their kids, lower food and fuel costs, and so forth.

> So we went back to the organization's board of directors—a tough-minded group of 20 highway builders—and told them we'd have to do it differently, that people wouldn't buy new highways but that our surveys showed that the best appeal we could make was to the values that people already embraced about prices and the ease of living, and that new values such as new highway systems were almost impossible to sell.

> Now we're deeply involved in a program that translates road improvement into the values most people already hold dear, and the roadbuilders support it vigorously. In fact, we've been able to win millions of dollars in government funds for the kinds of projects we have proposed. It's a striking example of how a public relations agency can change the direction of an entire industry by demonstrating, through a trusting relationship with its client, a new and profitable pathway to growth.[5]

Hammond's example is also an excellent illustration of how assumptions can cloud one's vision and how research can be used to check the validity of assumptions and at the same time to point out directions for future programming. That same research, it should be noted, also provided the means for meshing an organization's private interests with public interests, resulting in clear benefits for all concerned.

Eliminate Nonessentials

Problems, like grapes, tend to come in clusters, and one of the difficult tasks of the practitioner is to eliminate from the cluster of problems what the late Verne Burnett called "nonessentials." In his view handling public relations problems calls for a process of elimination.

> For instance, a trade group asked a public relations firm to get the general public conscious of twelve facts about an industry. All of these facts seemed important to the trade group. There was an ancient law suit, but the public would have no interest in that. There had been some involved labor negotiations several years ago. Again the public wouldn't bother to learn the details. One by one the twelve points were whittled down until there were three to which the public might pay attention. Finally the three, which were closely related, were condensed into one. Thus it was possible for the public relations worker to concentrate all efforts on explaining a single idea, with considerable success.[6]

Burnett's advice to whittle down problems is echoed by most veteran public relations practitioners. They realize that the public finds it difficult, or doesn't have the interest, to grasp a mass of information very extensive or complex. Given a set of problems, the practitioner strips away the relatively unimportant ones and by a process of elimination tries to focus on those that are primary and essential. The process is simple when the major problem is obvious, but requires sound, objective judgment when the major problem is obscured by a host of other problems. Since almost every public relations problem situation is unique, the process of defining the key factor by stripping away nonessentials is always a challenge, but one that must be met before further action is taken.

Establish an Order of Priorities

The act of defining the problem will culminate, whether by design or accidentally, in establishing an order of problem priorities, which will lead in turn to a similar order of solution priorities.

The usual way of establishing priorities is to decide which problems are immediate and which are long-range. Put another way, which problems should be handled today and which can be taken care of over a period of months or years? Another method is to rank problems in order of importance, though the end result is usually the same because of the general assumption that immediate problems must be most important because they must be taken care of at once while long-range problems aren't as important because their handling can be delayed.

Such an assumption—as with many assumptions examined superficially—has to be scrutinized carefully. While it is true that practitioners tend to concentrate on immediate problems—chiefly because practitioners can't very well ignore their existence—these are not necessarily the most important problems facing an organization. In fact, one of the fatal flaws of many public relations programs is that they tend to be "fire-fighting" efforts aimed at dousing the flames caused by immediate problems. Because the practitioner is so busy trying to solve immediate problems, long-range problems are ignored even though they may be more important.

The sensible way of insuring that proper attention will be given to all problems is to establish a realistic order of problem priorities and put it in writing. If it's possible to rank problems, then the ranking ought to be in terms of most important, next most important, and so on down the line to those considered least important. If an immediate problem turns out to be the most important problem then the practitioner has a perfect match. However, if an immediate problem is not the most important one but still has to be handled immediately, the practitioner must remember that the most important problem still exists and must be treated at some time. The practitioner may still handle the immediate problem at the moment it faces him, but he shouldn't put the most important problem on the back burner indefinitely.

ESTABLISHING OBJECTIVES AND GOALS

The act of establishing public relations objectives and goals is a logical follow-up to the problem-definition stage of programming because of the close affinity between problems and objectives. If, for example, it has been decided that an immediate major problem facing a publicly financed organization is virtual ignorance about the organization among financial analysts, then an obvious immediate public relations objective and goal would be to inform these analysts so they will recommend its stock as a good buy.

The example is illustrative of several important criteria of sound public relations objectives and goals: (a) they should be directly related to the basic objectives of the organization, (b) they should be specific rather than general, and (c) they should be set forth in order of importance and time.

Public Relations Objectives Should Be Related to the Basic Objectives of the Organization

There is no utility value to public relations objectives with little relationship to the basic objectives of the organization they supposedly serve. It is, at times, very tempting to set forth a public relations goal that can be achieved through some dramatic and imaginative program, activity, or event, but if that goal has little relationship to the basic goals of the organization the result will be a meaningless waste of time, money, and manpower. There's little point in trying to increase applications to a prestigious law school when that school already has so many applications it can accept only 10 percent of those who apply. It makes little sense to aim your public relations efforts at establishing among citizens in Plant Community A that your firm's plant there is a strong, stable one if management has already decided to close the plant a year from now. If a public relations program is to keep in step with reality, the objectives of that program and the objectives of the organization must march to the same tune.

The previous paragraph seems to imply that it's the responsibility of public relations to keep in step with the organization of which it's a part. There are times, however, when the preliminary study and setting forth of problems show that the policies and actions of an organization, not public relations, are clearly out of step with public opinion, the public interest, and commonly accepted standards of behavior. Knowing this to be so, does the practitioner continue to march along with his plans and programs or does he come to a parade rest?

Those who have read the earlier chapters in this book ought to know the answer to that last question. **If an organization's basic policies and actions are clearly counter to the public interest and to commonly accepted standards of behavior, it's the responsibility of the practitioner to use his influence to modify or seek changes in policies and actions.** In the short run it is conceivable—and it has happened—that clever use of techniques might camouflage shoddy organizational policies and practices, but in the long run they will be shown up for what they are. The time to align organizational and public relations policies, actions, and objectives with the public interest and in accordance with commonly acceptable bounds of behavior is before, not after, programming has begun.

Public Relations Objectives Should Be as Specific as Possible

Though public relations, as a general concept, aims to bring about the end result of "goodwill, understanding, and acceptance," programming objectives must be stated in more specific terms if they are to be meaningful and acceptable to management. Particularly in business and industry, but also in other areas of human endeavor and activity, managements expect, demand, and receive specific inputs and goals from the various main functional areas of organizations. These are then measured against end results. The sales department doesn't project a general increase in sales, but rather a 2 percent or 5 percent or 10 percent increase. The production department doesn't project a general increase in production, but rather a 2 percent or 5 percent or 10 percent increase. The admissions director of a college doesn't project a general increase in the freshman class, but a 2 percent, 5 percent, or 10 percent increase. In each instance the responsible executive is held to account if end results fail to measure up to forecasts. Public relations, though involved with factors more difficult to measure than the production and sale of products and the admissions of students, should expect to be held to thorough measurements and management expectations.

Unfortunately, many public relations objectives and goals are fuzzy in conception and much too general in nature. Note, for example, the following "seven objectives of a representative gas utility," and decide which are specific and which are general:

1. To establish the company as a valuable citizen

2. To make all personnel more PR-minded

3. To offset competition

4. To cultivate and maintain goodwill of customers, editors, and key citizens

5. To devise new ways of interpreting modern gas service to the public

6. To strengthen private management of utilities

7. To educate the public on need for adequate utility earnings

In setting forth a public relations program to support a chemical company's marketing efforts, a public relations counseling firm emphasized a two-pronged set of objectives. It first cited the primary objective of the program and then specified objectives in relation to specific markets. There were two products involved in this 1982 program—chlorinated solvents and magnesium—and the 54-page proposal set forth the objectives for the first product as shown in Exhibit 11.1.

EXHIBIT 11.1

Objectives of a Public Relations/Marketing Proposal

Analysis of the current situation and major marketing goals dictates the following objectives:

CHLORINATED SOLVENTS

Primary objective of this program is:
To effectively educate industrial management decision makers on the use of chlorinated solvents in diverse applications while simultaneously dispelling preconceived misconceptions of the product in areas of toxicity, flammability, and air pollution.

More specifically, the program has the following market objectives:

For electronics: To position the company as a preferred supplier of solvents and to promote the benefits of chlorinated solvents for high-volume board houses.

For coatings: To convince the coatings industry that "compliance solvents" are a long-term alternative; to increase awareness of chlorinated solvents for achieving air quality; and to dispel concerns over toxicity.

For adhesives: To expand the use of 1-1-1 trichloroethane by stressing the safety of nonflammable contact adhesives.

For metal cleaning: To communicate the reliability and proven performance of chlorinated solvents vs aqueous systems.

For aerosols and urethane foam blowing: To create awareness of the benefits of the company's patented formulation in foams and to aggressively promote the concept of methylene chloride in personal care products.

For drycleaning: To create a stronger company identification in the marketplace through promotional tools.

Those who feel that public relations objectives should be set forth in specific, measurable terms would undoubtedly approve of the public relations objectives established by the Silverman and Mower firm of Syracuse, New York, in its proposed program for the New York Racing Association. To reverse declining attendance at the association's three thoroughbred racing tracks at Belmont Park, Aqueduct, and Saratoga, the agency proposed a "Newcomer's Program" to attract new customers through special group and individual sales activities. Here's how Silverman and Mower phrased the program's objectives:

> Obviously the general objective for a Newcomer's Program is to increase attendance at the track. This is both a short-term goal for next year and a long-term goal for years to come.
>
> However, more specific objectives are proposed:
> 1. Increase overall track racing attendance.
> 2. Attract 1,000 newcomers per week to the track.
> 3. Increase group sales activity to a documented 10 percent of total attendance during first full year of implementation.
> 4. Document a 20 percent return of newcomers and group members on their own within one month.
>
> In addition, two other factors should be kept in mind:
> 1. There must be a quantifiable way of measuring the Newcomer's Program after one year of implementation; and
> 2. The first year is a developing year, a building year, in which the program is honed and sharpened but not quite ready for full capacity.[7]

For a variety of reasons, most practitioners do not "lay it on the line" as directly as do Silverman and Mower, but few would argue the wisdom of being specific rather than general. The value of specificity applies particularly to the matter of relative importance of objectives and the time frame in which they are set.

Public Relations Objectives Should Be Set Forth in Order of Importance and Time

As with problems, public relations objectives and goals should be set forth in order of their importance and the time period within which they are expected to be reached. In effect, this means setting priorities for objectives and goals.

Some objectives are so clearly important and immediate there is no question about the need to meet them at once. Others, while important, can await their solution over a longer period of time. When Whitaker and Baxter, for example, took on the assignment of handling the American Medical Association account more than three decades ago, they defined their objectives in this manner:

> The first objective was an uncompromising immediacy: to stop the Compulsory Health Insurance legislation then pending (in Congress).
>
> The second objective, longer-range and more constructive, was to establish firm proof with the majority of the people that the American medical system not only is the finest in the world's history, but that it can meet the medical needs of the people by voluntary means and without Government control.[8]

Depending on one's views, one might argue the merits of the issue, but no one can argue about the specific nature of the campaign's objectives. They were direct, to the point, and included both short- and long-range goals. In effect, they provided the client (or management) with a timetable and a way to judge whether the program was proceeding according to schedule.

Management by objectives (MBO) is a technique that has been adopted by public relations departments to meet managerial demands for accountability and measurement. Time and space preclude a full discussion of MBO, but the basic elements can be explained briefly.

MBO calls for the establishment of organizational and departmental goals; the development of objectives to meet these goals; the establishment of deadlines and target dates; and a means of evaluation and revision. **Goals under MBO are general guides for**

---

action, while objectives—set both for the department and for individuals within it—are measurable targets set within a time frame. For measurement purposes, terms should be set qualitatively and quantitatively.

Anita H. Thies of Pennsylvania State University explains goals and objectives as follows:

> By definition and purpose, an objective is a statement that is specific, single-purpose, measurable, set in a time frame, and achievable.
>
> Objectives grow from goals and help determine progress toward the accomplishment of ideas set forth in goals. Goals are broad, general statements, usually neither quantifiable nor set in a time frame, and usually not attainable as stated.[9]

As an example of the above, Thies notes that one of Penn State's public relations goals is to achieve more recognition for the university. In targeting staff objectives to meet this goal, she explains, one objective is to have each news bureau writer produce two or three "statewide" stories per week; another is to have the Speakers Bureau arrange an average of one speaking engagement per day; and a third is to have each staffer ask faculty members to write monthly opinion pieces for the editorial pages of target newspapers.

In warning about the dangers of overquantifying when writing objectives, Thies puts her finger on the major reason why MBO is not used more extensively by public relations practitioners. She points out that overquantifying may misdirect staffers to play a numbers game, and it also takes up a considerable amount of staff time in following intricate measurement systems. Finally, she notes, the real measurement of performance in public relations involves a judgment of quality that cannot be quantified. As she puts it: "While we try to quantify wherever possible, we also know that a story's importance to an institution isn't necessarily measured by its length or newsplay."

One might well add this reminder about timetables: too rigid a timetable can be dangerous because public relations practice calls for flexibility. Unless one provides for flexibility in setting objectives and programs, there will be too many instances of missed opportunities and of programs outdated by unforeseen events. By all means be specific and work according to a timetable, but don't be inflexible.

DEFINING THE AUDIENCE

All public relations programs are aimed at some group or groups in our society, and therefore the audience should be precisely defined and delineated *before* a program is charted and put into effect. Usually this process is a matter of simple, logical deduction. As the practitioner goes through the process of defining an organization's essential public relations problems and objectives, the audience for the ensuing public relations programming should come into focus. Problems arise because of relationships with *people*; objectives deal with goals concerning *people*; to meet these objectives one must first zero in on the *people* to be reached.

Charting the audience can be achieved in a variety of ways. Audiences can be defined as *primary*, *secondary*, and *tertiary*, and obviously such a delineating implies that the main effort of the program will be directed first at the primary audience and later at the secondary and tertiary audiences. Or, the audience can be divided into *internal* and *external* groups with specific programming aimed at each or both. Audiences are often divided into *local*, *regional*, and *national* groupings and again subsequent programming can be charted for each group.

As a simple example, let us assume that the Boy Scouts of America are having difficulty attracting inner-city youngsters to scouting. The problem results from the fact that inner-city youngsters of scouting age feel that scouting has little relationship to their lives. The objective of the public relations program is to demonstrate that modern-day scouting bears a close and direct relationship to the lives of inner-city youngsters. Logical deduction tells us that a public relations program designed to attract inner-city youngsters to scouting ought to be directed specifically at inner-city youngsters and not at youngsters living on farms.

However, research reveals that inner-city youngsters have such a deep-seated suspicion of the so-called Establishment they reject the usual type of appeals stemming from the Scouting Establishment. Further research reveals that well-known professional athletes are looked at with awe and respect by inner-city youngsters of scouting age. These athletes might become the primary audience and the conduit for a public relations program aimed at attracting inner-city youngsters to scouting. Thus, though audience-projection is often a matter of simple logical deduction, circumstances may indicate that a straight line is not the most effective way of moving from Point A to Point B.

No matter what system is used in focusing on the audience(s), certain questions have to be posed:

- Who are we trying to reach?
- Which publics are most important?
- Where are they?
- Who are their opinion leaders?
- What do they read, listen to, and view? In short, *how* do we reach them? (To be discussed under action plans and programs.)

In Exhibit 11.2 we find examples of how different organizations and a Congresswoman targeted audiences for public relations programming. Establishing a target list is not particularly difficult, but what is difficult is **reaching** the audiences on the list. In some cases groups can be reached directly, but in other instances indirect means have to be utilized. Thus, depending on the particular situation and the audience to be reached, the public relations practitioner may in one instance depend heavily on mailings of print material, in another instance on the mass media, and in a third instance on both direct mailings and the mass media.

EXHIBIT 11.2

Targeting Audiences: Some Examples

- **Matson College,** which had traditionally drawn its student body from a 40-mile radius, decided to expand its student search. The public relations department proposed a program aimed at high school juniors, seniors, and guidance counselors; parents of high school students; and the general public in three states contiguous to that of the college.

- **Extruded Metals,** whose products were sold throughout the country, concentrated its public relations efforts on a product publicity campaign aimed at industrial customers and prospects, field sellers and distributors, and the national trade press.

- **Women United for Peace,** concerned about nuclear weapons, targeted its efforts at the national Administration, Congress, and the general public.

- **The State of Alaska,** seeking to correct misperceptions about Alaska among people in the lower forty-eight states, established a public relations program aimed at these same people.

- **Congresswoman Joan Wrigman,** up for reelection in November, concentrated her public relations efforts on those in her district eligible to vote. Because exit polls in the last election had shown her to be weak among young voters, she decided to make a special effort to reach such voters.

ESTABLISHING A THEME

Public relations programs which involve a variety of projects—as most successful programs do—achieve a unity of purpose through the use of a basic theme or set of themes. In the continuum of public relations planning and programming a theme bears close relationship to musical and literary themes. In both music and literature a theme is the underlying tie that runs through an entire work and binds it together. In similar fashion, a theme is the underlying tie that runs through the various facets or projects in a public relations program and makes for a unified, consistent approach to public relations problems.

A theme is to public relations programming as thread is to the tailor. With thread the tailor fashions a suit; without it he's got so many swatches of cloth. With a theme the public relations practitioner fashions a campaign; without it he's got so many isolated projects. When Whitaker and Baxter were handling political campaigns in California, themes formed the core of all their campaigns. Before starting a campaign the husband-and-wife counseling team would work out a theme and a plan, and then with equal care they would work out another theme and plan. Both themes and plans were then matched against each other and a decision made as to which would be used in the forthcoming campaign. Every subsequent speech, poster, brochure, television and radio spot would then emphasize and develop the campaign's basic theme.

A theme can be set forth in a variety of ways. It may be expressed in the form of a summary statement or of a slogan, but its basic purpose remains that of providing unity to programming. Whatever its form, a theme should—

1. make its point clearly;

2. be capable of being retained by those at whom it is directed;

3. be relevant and honest.

The last point bears close analysis because of the too often glib way in which some themes are put into effect.

David Finn makes the case for relevancy and honesty in the following words:

> It is not the slick job that does the trick, but the job that most genuinely reflects the way management feels about itself. Dapper Frank Floyd Wright did not have a better public image than tousled Albert Einstein. Both won public respect and affection because they looked like what they were: people could feel that both of them were being honest with themselves. Above all, the way they looked was consistent with what they stood for, and this is the key to good graphic public relations.[10]

Because catchy themes have eye and ear appeal there is often the temptation to employ themes whether they honestly reflect the organization that uses them or not. But on ethical, moral, and practical grounds irrelevant, dishonest, and meaningless themes should be avoided. Such themes may gain immediate approbation for the practitioner who creates them, but in the long run they serve no useful purpose, do little intrinsic good, and eventually backfire.

Today's public is too wise, jaded, and jaundiced to be taken in by superficial slogans and themes, and this conclusion is particularly true in relation to those organizations whose products and services are sold to and used by the general public. If the product purchased by the average consumer proves to be shoddy or if the service rendered proves to be abysmal, no catch theme or slogan is going to convince him to "put his trust" in that company's products or services. As Finn puts it: "A theme makes sense only when it is deeply felt by the people running the business. All of the company's publics then recognize that the idea or theme is genuine and not an artificial concoction of clever promoters."

INITIATING AN ACTION AND ACTIVITY PLAN OF STRATEGY: PROJECTS, TACTICS, AND TIMING

At the core of most successful public relations programs is an action and activity plan of strategy involving three major elements: projects, tactics, and timing. *Projects* provide the vehicle whereby public relations objectives and goals are reached; *tactics* involve the mechanics of carrying out planned projects; and *timing* is often the crucial difference between success and failure.

Projects

Projects come in all shapes and forms and are limited only by the imagination and ingenuity of the practitioners who plan, create, and carry them through to completion. One veteran public relations man sees projects as "the only convenient way in which an otherwise nebulous undertaking can be analyzed, organized, and controlled," and in his opinion the more projects clustered around a theme the better.

Some projects are of such a magnitude that a single project may comprise the entire public relations program. Into such a project would go all the talent, manpower, and resources that public relations can provide. Most often, however, programs are built around a variety of projects that overlap each other and act as a series of waves cresting towards a common shoreline goal. The analogy to waves is deliberate: at times practitioners initiate and carry through projects that demonstrate activity is taking place, but unless projects build towards a common public relations objective and goal, the practitioner is merely going through the process of making waves that go nowhere.

A project may be as simple as a normal press conference announcing a new product or may be as complex as a twenty-city teleconference involving two-way audio and video. A project may be just local in nature, such as an Open House initiated to have residents in a plant community learn firsthand about an industrial organization, or it may be national and involve a sixteen-city tour by a well-known personality to demonstrate to a wide geographical audience the virtues of a product. A program may consist of a major, one-day event—such as a Walk-a-Thon for a disease-fighting agency—or it may entail several major events and some minor ones spread out over a months-long campaign.

Projects and public relations program activities are not easily categorized because they exist in a wide variety of guises, and new ones are constantly being initiated by imaginative and creative practitioners. However, some projects and activities have gained such widespread acceptance their utilization by practitioners justifies their listing as major types. By no means should one consider that the following project and activity categories represent the only effective ones to be used in programming. The listing is chiefly a means of setting forth some major ways in which projects and activities have been used in public relations programming.

Projects or activities that support, display, and/or dramatize an existing event, facility, or situation. Virtually every organization, at one time or another, carries out activities or events that need public relations support, and in many instances the facilities of organizations are also the focal point of public relations activity. Some facilities, events and situations utilize public relations support on a regular, recurring basis, others as the need arises.

For example, every local United Way organization in the country conducts a yearly fund-raising campaign aimed at raising sufficient funds to support the agencies belonging to the United Way. Usually of a month's duration, these campaigns inevitably commence with a kick-off dinner or event, are followed by periodic report meetings and luncheons, and culminate in a final victory dinner or event. Throughout the entire campaign period the UW's public relations department serves a key role in devising ways and means of supporting, dramatizing, and communicating the activities and events taking place during the campaign. Some typical projects include an opening day parade; a lighted thermometer placed on top of a large building to indicate fund-raising progress; a fireworks display to demonstrate the campaign has gone over the top; a costume ball to increase attendance on the final report night.

The United Way campaign as an existing event requiring public relations support is duplicated in many ways. Colleges and universities hold convocations, commencements, Parents' Days, and Alumni Days. Cities and department stores sponsor and run the Tournament of Roses Parade, the Thanksgiving Day Parade, the Peanut Queen Festival, and the Kutztown annual Pennsylvania Dutch Folk Festival. There's the annual Westinghouse Science Talent Search, the Sealy Golf Classic, and the American Legion Boys' State and Boys' Nation. Rockefeller Center has its outdoor skating rink, major resorts have outdoor ski slopes, and a number of large cities have a variety of gaslight, take-me-back-to-the-good-old-days areas. Each of these existing events, facilities, and situations is supported and dramatized by public relations projects and activities.

Even factories and plants—not usually considered prime areas for public relations programming—have been utilized to good public relations advantage because someone with imagination figured out that wineries and breweries could attract millions of visitors if tours of their facilities were spiked with sampling of the product at the end of the tour. Designing, establishing, managing, and promoting many of these tours has become partly or wholly a function of public relations departments. In some instances the facility tour has become so succcessful a drawing card that the sponsoring company has split it off from the brewery operation, broadened the scope of the attraction, and run the activity as a profit center. An example is the Busch Gardens operation of Anheuser-Busch, Inc., in Tampa, Florida. For another example see Exhibit 11.3.

EXHIBIT 11.3

Alaska's National Communication Program

The Alaska National Communication Program, May 1981-May 1982,[11] illustrates the use of projects and activities by a state agency to "support, display and dramatize an existing facility or situation." In this instance, the "facility" was the State of Alaska, and the situation was the misperceptions people in the lower forty-eight states had of Alaska. Here, in summary form, are key elements of the program:

1. **Alaska Information Center.** Recognizing that Alaska is inaccessible for reporters on limited budgets, the program planners established an information office in New York City to maintain contact with media representatives; monitor local, regional, and national press coverage; provide timely and accurate information to the news media; work with writers and editors to develop news and feature stories about the state; and coordinate special events concerning the state.

2. **National Television Documentary.** This was a three-phased effort involving the writing and production of a one-hour news documentary about Alaska. The film was researched and shot on locations throughout the state over a six-month period. Narrator was Hal Holbrook. A second element was the establishment of an ad hoc network of sixty-six television stations representing approximately 70 percent of the national television markets. The third element consisted of publicity and advertising to promote the program to local TV audiences.

3. **Editorial Visits to Target Cities.** As part of the communication program the sponsors arranged to have Governor Jay S. Hammond meet informally with media representatives during two trips to the lower forty-eight. He talked candidly to editorial staff members and fielded questions from top executives at *Time, Newsweek,* and the Boston *Globe,* and he was also interviewed by wire service writers who subsequently wrote articles about the state.

Projects or activities that support and/or dramatize communication events or actions.
There is a narrow but significant difference between existing organizational events and communication events supported and/or dramatized by public relations projects and activities. By *communication events* are meant those designed as part of public relations programming rather than those that exist as part of an organization's activities. For the most part communication events are "one-shot" affairs, although they can prove so successful and integral to an organization that they become recurring affairs and thus an integral part of an organization's activities.

Criticism has been leveled against communication events for being "manufactured" and "pseudo," and the criticism has a good deal of validity. However, if the communication event serves purposes other than merely being reported by the media, the argument that it is manufactured loses a good deal of its weight and substance. Practitioners can create event after event, but unless they interest the public they will inevitably fail to bring about media coverage. **The test, therefore, is not in the event but in the substance of the event.**

There are innumerable ways in which communication events are meshed with public relations programs, projects, and activities. Some of the more common ones are seminars, forums, competitions, special awards, surveys, educational campaigns, conferences, and convocations. The best of them—

1. **meet and dovetail with fundamental objectives and goals of the organization;**

2. **provide a public or publics with information, knowledge, or ideas that are in the public interest;**

3. **merit and secure media attention and coverage.**

This threefold test is difficult to meet. Only those created communication events that are the most thoughtful and imaginative pass with high marks. A variety of such created communication events are cited in the examples that follow, and it should be instructive to discuss, rate, and judge each event's public relations effectiveness by applying the threefold test previously listed.

A Communications Conference

At their first meeting in October members of the Blank College chapter of the Public Relations Student Society of America decide that their major chapter project of the year will be the staging in March of the First Southwest Collegiate Communications Conference. Planning takes up the chapter's attention for the entire academic year. Two mailings are sent out to all PRSSA chapters and to journalism and public relations schools, departments, and teachers in the southwest. Speakers and panelists at the March event include two nationally known public relations practitioners and journalists from the southwest. Attendance at the two-day conference consists chiefly of public relations students of Blank College—many of them to handle classroom assignments based on conference activities—and fourteen students from four other southwest colleges and universities. Good media coverage of conference activities is given by media in the Blank College area, and brief mention of the conference is also carried in national public relations newsletters, the *Public Relations Journal,* and the PRSSA's *Forum.* The Blank College *Weekly Record,* student newspaper, runs many pre-conference stories and a long story with pictures the week after the conference.

An Automobile Competition

By arrangement with local and state automobile clubs, an international oil company which markets its products throughout the United States conducts a cross-country automobile competition. Entries are restricted to one-owner automobiles which are at least twenty years old. Local, state, and regional elimination competitions are held, and the final race consists of twenty automobiles in a race from Paramus, New Jersey, to San Francisco. All entrants have to use gasoline and oil produced by the sponsoring oil company. The winner is feted at a dinner in Detroit addressed by the president of one of the major automobile manufacturers, and the automobile which won the race is put on permanent display in a new National Automobile Museum erected on the outskirts of Detroit. The winner is awarded the top of the line in a new-model car of the winner's choice. Media coverage is excellent on all levels: local, state, regional, and national. The oil company "merchandises" the races and final winner in newspaper, magazine, radio, and television advertisements and commercials and by point-of-sales displays at its gas stations throughout the country.

The annual **Harveys Bristol Cream Tribute to the Black Designer** serves as a good example of an activity which started out as a communications event and proved to be so successful it has since become an annual affair sponsored by the Harveys unit at parent company Heublein, Inc. The Harveys Bristol Cream Tribute to the Black Designer '83 was held on March 23, 1983, at Avery Fisher Hall, Lincoln Center for the Performing Arts, and was the fifth to honor outstanding black fashion designers. The gala evening included a fashion show featuring creations by the honored designers; performances by three black groups who were beneficiaries of a $50-per-ticket reception; and an exhibit of historic garments selected from the Black Fashion Museum. In attendance at this fifth annual tribute were one hundred press representatives and more than two thousand guests, who included the leaders of the New York City black community.

Among the photos and captions included in the press kit given to the media reps and also mailed to media nationwide were those shown in Figures 11.1 and 11.2.

Projects or activities that support and/or dramatize products, sales, and services. Public relations projects and activities conceived and carried out to support an organization's products, sales, and services are so common they're often handled on a regular basis by staffers specifically assigned to this purpose. Such projects and activities are also the ones most enthusiastically supported by other functions and divisions of organizations because of the direct help they provide to these functions and divisions.

Product, sales, and service promotion comes in many forms. It can consist chiefly of press releases and feature stories sent to trade and consumer publications, newspapers, syndicates, radio, and television outlets. Sometimes it takes the form of making the product available to moviemakers and television producers and subsequently to millions of viewers when the film is released for distribution. Though this is a form of subliminal impact which is hard to measure, there is no doubt that some members of the movie and the television audience will be influenced by seeing the product.

Introducing a new product to the market is primarily a function of the sales department, but public relations assistance is often provided in the form of press releases, press conferences, advance showings, press showings, packaged presentations for use on morning and afternoon television shows, and a host of other devices and methods.

A common form of product promotion is to tie it up in a promotional package and take it on a tour of leading cities and markets by a personality accompanied by a public relations representative who schedules bookings and appearances and works with the media in the cities visited. Another common form is the tie-in promotion, wherein the product is put to use and shown in action at some facility that draws millions of visitors. Power boats and outboard motors are an integral part of the daily shows at Cypress Gardens in Winter Haven, Florida; they may as well be X powerboats and Y outboard motors as anyone else's.

For public relations projects or activities tied to products or sales, no matter how developed and executed, the key word to keep in mind is *support*. Robert K. Marker, manager of press services in the Advertising and Marketing Services Department of the Armstrong Cork Company, emphasizes the point in these words: "If you're a marketing-support function, as we are, it's imperative to get yourself plugged into the marketing communications planning process, and actively participate in it." He further amplifies the point as follows:

> There are seven operating divisions in our company, and each division is responsible for forecasting its own sales and profit levels for the next five years. There's a general mar-

FIGURE 11.1 *Cool designs for spring shown at black designer tribute.* Expecting a hot spring, designers honored in the Harveys Bristol Cream Tribute to the Black Designer '83, held March 23 in Avery Fisher Hall, New York, had cool-looking clothing on display. Indianapolis designer Alpha Blackburn showed a kimono-inspired white silk jacquard wrapped dress (upper left) with a hip-hugging belt of white satin and black ultra-suede. Malaysian hand-painted batik designs are the mark of Lepenski of New York and Washington, D.C. At the upper right is his long cotton skirt in gray, white, and smoke topped off with a white linen blend jacket that features cap sleeves and shawl collar. At the lower right is his black-and-white sleeveless dress with ruffled collar. There is a cross-grain ribbon at the waist to accent the design. A hot pink cotton blouse with a circle-veil collar is matched with a hot pink mini, two-pocket shirt by Lester Hayatt.

Source: Courtesy of Heublein/Spirits Group. Photography by Dennis Williford.

FIGURE 11.2 *Evening wear shown at Harveys Bristol Cream tribute.* Dramatic evening wear for spring was among the highlights of the Harveys Bristol Cream Tribute to the Black Designer '83 held March 23 in Avery Fisher Hall, New York. A cast-in-bronze appearance is created by the metallic satin two-piece dress (upper left) designed by Jon Haggins of New York. The top has a cowl back; godet skirt with godets on the sides. The fabric was cut on the bias. A black pebble crepe dress (upper right) with bateau neckline and mushroom pleated ruffled organza sleeves is among the offerings of Mark Anthony Pennywell of Pittsburgh. Classic evening wear designed by Myra Everett of Chicago includes this blue print chiffon dress with gold thread (lower left). It has a deep armhole sleeve; the skirt is sheared with front and back pleat; gold thread highlights are accentuated by blue and gold hip-yoke belt. From the Harold Stone collection comes a black lamb-skin suede, wrap camisole with peplum that gradually gets longer in the back and radiates tucks from the waistline (lower right). The silk taffeta wrap skirt is lined in silk chiffon with a graduating hemline that forms geometric detail at the front. The necklace, of inlaid mother-of-pearl onto horn, is designed for Stone exclusively.

Source: Courtesy of Heublein/Spirits Group. Photography by Dennis Williford.

keting plan developed which explains how the division expects to achieve its long-range goal; and there's a very specific plan drawn up which charts the division's course in the coming year.

After these programs are reviewed and approved in the President's Office, each division sits down with Advertising and Marketing Services and lays out its plans and objectives for the ensuing year. These meetings take place in late summer, and that's our cue to start thinking about our own program for the next year.

The first step is to carefully review the divisional marketing objectives, and develop from them a list of *communications objectives*—that is, a statement of what it is we want to try to accomplish through communications next year to help the divisions reach their goals. The communications objectives are written out, discussed with the marketing divisions, fine-tuned if necessary, and then ordered in terms of priority.

Our next step is to develop written *strategies*—how we propose to accomplish the communications goals that we and the marketing people have agreed are important in the coming year. Who do we want to reach, and how often? What's the best way to reach them? What should we say to them? There's more discussion and fine-tuning, and at this point, the operating budget for our department begins to take shape.[12]

Supporting products and sales by means of public relations projects and activities is easier to achieve than supporting services, chiefly because the former lend themselves more readily to dramatization.

An effective way of dramatizing services is to substitute things or people for services, and to utilize these in subsequent dramatization and promotion. The United Way of America did this very effectively with public service cameos on pro football television broadcasts, utilizing a brief statement by a pro football star, showing him in action, then switching to someone who has benefited by the services of a United Way agency, and finally combining both the star and the United Way client in a wrap-up sequence.

In a similar manner, Smokey Bear was used for many years to personalize messages about the dangers of forest fires, while Reddy Kilowat was used as the symbol for services performed by an electric utility. To show the services they render to their communities, high schools and colleges often allow their athletic fields, pools, and auditoriums to be used by community groups. In times of disasters many companies have donated supplies and manpower to help those whose homes have been devastated by floods, tornadoes, and fires. Project Hope was a service project on an international scale supported by funds, manpower, and supplies provided by American companies and industries. The white hospital ship which brought medical supplies, teachers, and treatment to other countries is a fine example of a project that serves others and at the same time brings goodwill to the sponsors.

Projects or activities built around special occasions. One day may be just like another to the average person, but not to the alert public relations practitioner who builds projects around the days that are special in American life.

Holidays are special days, and many a public relations project has been tied in to Columbus Day, Independence Day, Labor Day, Ground Hog Day, and all the other days spelled with a capital D. The key to a tie-in is that the project be intrinsic and not foreign to the day to which it is allied. You've got to be a near genius to carry out a public relations project that connects Grandma Brown's Beans to Columbus Day, but it just takes a little forethought and planning to tie Franco-American spaghetti to that same day. Ground Hog Day is a natural for an organization that is concerned with the weather, but not to a lumber company. The latter might better try to do something with Paul Bunyan Day.

Most of us check the calendar to see how many days are left until the weekend comes, but alert practitioners check their calendars to see what important years may be in the offing. In public relations offices throughout the land plans and projects were being fashioned in 1974 and 1975 for the all-important year 1976 when the country would be celebrating its bicentennial. If you're going to produce a special movie, book, series of publications, or other means of connecting your organization with the nation's 200th birthday, you don't start it on January 1, 1976, but a year or two earlier.

To those two certitudes—death and taxes—one can add a third meant particularly for public relations people: special days and occasions lend themselves neatly to public relations projects, but the competition is fierce because this knowledge is widely shared. To capitalize on these days and occasions the practitioner has to plan wisely in advance and be more imaginative than the competition.

Two reminders are in order in summing up the subject of projects in public relations programming. First, projects should be closely related to organizational and public relations objectives and goals and should not be undertaken unless this relationship is clear.

Second, projects should provide a blueprint for public relations action and indicate clearly to management the strategy of a program; the manpower and resources needed to carry out the program; and the budget and funds needed to support the activities set forth in the program's blueprint. By setting forth a series of projects the practitioner offers management a choice of options, and thus if management decides—usually for financial reasons—not to authorize the entire package, there should still be sufficient projects remaining to make up a viable program.

> The proposed Newcomer's Program—devised for the New York Racing Association and previously mentioned in connection with objectives and audience—ran to fifty-six typewritten pages and therefore can be but briefly capsulized here. However, it clearly centered on a basic theme and approach and was so organized as to permit flexibility.
>
> To attract newcomers—the target audience—the Silverman and Mower agency devised a packaged "Day at the Races" which could be implemented any day, regardless of weather, and which included details about transportation, convenience, and ease of execution. The major elements were: (1) a Continental breakfast; (2) a multitheatre experience; (3) a track tour; (4) a wagering seminar; (5) lunch; and (6) between-races activities.
>
> To tell the track story and close group sales, the program included a Newcomer's Bureau that would identify groups, set up speaking engagements, and utilize scripts, a slide-sound or film presentation, brochures, displays, and bounce-back coupons.
>
> Stressing the flexibility of the program, the proposal noted that it could probably not be implemented all at once, but would have to evolve over a period of time.
>
> "The first step in implementing this proposal is deciding on a timetable," stated the agency. "Two elements that must be considered are: (1) What are the most important aspects of the proposal? and (2) What can be economically and physically accomplished within a given time?
>
> "Many elements are relatively easy and inexpensive to implement, and should be gotten up and running immediately. Some others may have to wait. The important thing is that we start going out and closing the sale by telling the exciting story of thoroughbred racing and offering a unique package at the track."[13]

As the above example illustrates, it's to the advantage of the practitioner to offer management a choice of options. Though "A Day at the Races" was a single, unified concept, it offered management the option of accepting all elements or of selecting certain ones and phasing in the others as time and finances allowed.

Tactics

In setting forth a program composed of a series of projects the practitioner should also indicate a clear order of priorities based on a descending degree of importance. Project A, for example, should head the list because the practitioner, as the expert in public relations, considers it most important in terms of reaching objectives and goals. Last on the list should be the project considered least important.

In setting up an order and description of planned projects, more than one list may be needed. For example, a campaign may well involve actions to be taken on a national and local level, and if so there would be an order of priorities within each list of projects.

The program blueprint should also indicate the funds, talent, and mechanics necessary to carry through various projects. In dealing with the latter great care should be taken to distinguish between those which are within the control of the practitioner and those which are not. Project D, for example, may involve a sixteen-city tour by a national personality, and it is tactically within the practitioner's control to arrange contracting with the personality and setting up all the minute details of the tour. Guaranteeing that specific media will cover the event in each city and print stories about it is *not* within the control of the practitioner and hence is tactically unwise; such a guarantee is also ethically wrong and indefensible.

One of the virtues of initial research is that it often provides clues to strategy and tactics. As has been mentioned several times in this book, public relations practitioners are problem-solvers, and research often uncovers clues, tips, and leads to solutions.

In the long run, however, experience, creativity, and organizational ability and follow-through are the things that lead to success in carrying out public relations programs. Experience tells the practitioner that establishing grassroots committees will be effective in certain instances, but not in others. Creativity is the flair that distinguishes the ordinary from the unusual and that enables the practitioner to make the most of opportunities. But the most successful practitioner is the one who combines experience and creativity with the organizational ability to pursue carefully designed tactics. At times this practitioner will pursue local-level tactics, and in other instances he or she will work on both the local and national levels. In some cases, it will be tactically wise to operate independently, but in other cases it will be best to join forces with others. It may even be found wisest to join with one's critics rather than to fight them, as the example below testifies.

In the early seventies, the salt industry faced serious opposition to the use of its product for melting ice on winter roads. Critics claimed the salt damaged cars, pavement, and vegetation and endangered water supplies and wildlife. Though every public works agency in the thirty-three snow-belt states used salt to keep winter roads safe and traffic moving, the industry recognized that salt had been improperly stored or spread inefficiently in some localities, thus causing environmental problems.

Retained by The Salt Institute, the Byoir organization began its study of the problem by visiting editors and news directors in 115 key communities in eleven snow-belt states. The field research was supplemented by a mail poll of all snow-belt public works directors concerning their salting practices. The results showed that (1) salt was often misused; (2) the industry itself was guilty of poor storage practices; (3) newsmen wanted specific information about local conditions and solutions; and (4) issues varied from one community to another depending on local factors.

Byoir's approach to the problems was to establish a "Sensible Salting" program of citizen action to help communities make their own decisions about salt use. As the agency explained it, here's how the program worked:

"To augment its small staff, the Institute conducted a week-long seminar to train two dozen representatives of member companies as field men who worked in assigned territories. To correct salt misuse by public works agencies, 24 environmental seminars were conducted to teach some 1,875 snowfighters modern and efficient salt-use procedures.

"To monitor use throughout the snow belt, the Institute launched an industry-wide policing program to bring poor storage practices at industry depots to the attention of top management. To obtain prompt reports of citizen protest of salt misuse, the Institute established an alert system with quick-action forms sent to all salt company field employees. To provide accurate and useful information, a fact-filled Sensible Salting Kit was produced and distributed to 1,600 citizens and officials.

"Simultaneously, Byoir initiated a broad publicity program to counter inaccurate news accounts about salt effects and to explain ways of preventing salt pollution."[14]

What was so unusual about the Sensible Salt program was the tactical decision to join rather than to fight the critics. According to Byoir's George Hammond, the client had asked the agency to mount one of its high-impact publicity campaigns that would over-power the environmentalists who were against salt. However, Hammond noted, "the environmentalists were right with the times . . . and they kept coming up with studies that showed salt ruined roadside vegetation, rusted cars and damaged drinking water supplies." So the plan emerged to have the salt people and the environmentalists join in a program to "use salt smarter." That it worked was shown by the fact that three states and more than one hundred communities reversed legislation that would have banned salt.

A postscript is in order at this point. The tactic used by the Byoir people worked because they had the ear of top management. "We sat, fortunately, among the highest councils of the salt industry," says Hammond. "We were able to sell this program because we were in a position to recruit the trust and excite the interest of the people who were paying for our service. . . . The program worked because the client relationship worked and enabled us to embark on an uncharted path to win this almost unwinnable battle."

Timing

Experienced practitioners know that poor timing is the fatal flaw that can upset even the most carefully designed program and project. Many aspects of timing can be antici-pated in advance, and from long experience the practitioner takes these into consid-eration in planning. For example, it's a well-known fact that Saturday morning and afternoon newspapers are the thinnest of the week. The news "hole" for such papers is meager, and therefore events scheduled for Friday evening may never be covered in the next day's newspapers. Because the early evening network news shows need sufficient lead time to process film and to match sound with film, events scheduled for late after-noon have little chance of being covered. Most of the material in Sunday newspapers has to be set in type Thursday or Friday; hence a feature submitted on Saturday stands little chance of being published in Sunday issues.

These anticipated aspects of timing deal essentially with technical aspects of the mass media, but there are others which are more directly within the purview of the practi-tioner. Most of these deal with the *spacing* of events, activities, announcements, and similar aspects of programming. It's generally not wise, for example, to schedule two major activities on the same day because they will inevitably compete with each other for public and media attention. Scheduling an event on election day is like committing public relations hari-kari; major disasters may be able to vie at such a time with the political news, but certainly not a press conference announcing the selection of a firm's new chief executive. Taking their cue from political campaign managers, astute public relations practitioners are aware of the danger of "peaking" too soon when spacing a project over a period of time, but they are also aware of the need to be on top of a situa-tion and to take advantage of unexpected breaks.

Unfortunately for the novice, there are no hard-and-fast timing ground rules, but there is the need to be sensitive to the ebb and flow of the tides of public interest in issues and events. An organization's private project may have solid, substantive value and interest, but has little chance of gaining public attention if promoted at a time when pub-lic and media receptivity is low. How does one know when public interest is high or low? Chiefly through a great deal of reading of daily newspapers and weekly news magazines, viewing network television news shows, keeping abreast of what's going on in national, state, and local community affairs, and being sensitive to the things that are of interest to those publics which are most important to an organization.

COMMUNICATING AND EVALUATING

Lumped together as the final elements of planned programming are two areas of professional endeavor in which the average practitioner is both the most and the least adept.

Communication, particularly the use of the written word and knowledge of media to reach various publics, is the one skill common to most practitioners. The average practitioner may not know much about communication theories, but he is generally skilled in writing and communicating, and he uses these skills to inform, influence, and gain public understanding and acceptance.

On the other hand, evaluation of plans, programs, and public relations activities is often more noticeable by its absence than by its presence. Two of the reasons for this absence are the fact that a good many public relations activities and programs do not lend themselves to accurate evaluative measurement, and the fact that evaluation can be a proposition whose costs managements are unwilling to assume.

Because both communication and evaluation are such key factors in programming, they will be discussed in full detail in chapters to come. For the moment, they stand as the final steps in the orderly consideration of planning and programming.

SUMMATION

Planning and programming is at the core of successful public relations practice, whether we're considering the internal practitioner or the counselor. Though this chapter has explored the facets of plans and programs at some length, it has admittedly merely scratched the surface. In the continuum of the practice of public relations there is a wide gap between the beginner and the experienced practitioner, and this gap is bridged chiefly by the degree of sophistication possessed by the two extremes.

Given the assignment of promoting reflectorized highway signs the beginner sends out releases and art publicizing the signs; the veteran organizes seminars and develops features dealing with highway hypnosis, well aware of the fact that reflectorized signs help alleviate this danger to highway safety. Given the assignment of changing the stereotype of a metropolitan Chamber of Commerce, the beginner produces self-serving advertisements extolling the virtues of the chamber; the veteran creates a Business Advisory Bank, manned by chamber members who provide assistance in eight problem areas to more than four hundred small businessmen in one year. Where the beginner is most likely to program along a line that promotes the private interests of company or client, the veteran programs to reach that point where the line of self-interest intersects the line of public interest, and when there is no intersecting point he follows another line that will intersect.

In summation, the programs developed by veteran practitioners—

1. mesh organizational objectives and interests with public objectives and interests;

2. have continuity, are not overtly commercial, and lead to predetermined and determinable results;

3. consist of units which have individuality but which join well with each other and can be packaged and "merchandised" to maximize audience exposure and diverse organizational interests.

ENDNOTES

1. Jack R. Nowling, "How to Write the PR Program," *Public Relations Journal*, July 1976, p. 12.
2. David Finn, *Public Relations Management* (New York: Reinhardt Publishing Co., 1960), p. 55.

3. Earl Newsom, "Some Considerations in Dealing with Public Opinion," talk at the New School for Social Research, New York City, April 12, 1950.
4. Edward J. Robinson, *Communication and Public Relations* (Columbus, Ohio: Charles E. Merrill, 1966), p. 132.
5. George Hammond, "Meeting Client Expectations," remarks made at seminar, East Central District, PRSA, Detroit, May 16, 1978.
6. From a talk by Verne Burnett at the New School for Social Research, New York City.
7. From a proposal document submitted by Silverman and Mower, Syracuse, N.Y.
8. From a Whitaker and Baxter brochure describing the campaign the firm carried out for the American Medical Association.
9. Anita H. Thies, "Practicing Public Relations by Objectives," *Case Currents*, January 1978.
10. Finn, p. 14.
11. *Alaska National Communication Program, May 1981-May 1982*, a case study (Boston, Massachusetts: Boston University School of Public Communication, 1982).
12. Robert K. Marker, "The Armstrong Public Relations Data Measurement System," *Public Relations Review*, Winter 1977, p. 53.
13. From a proposal document submitted by Silverman and Mower.
14. From George Hammond seminar remarks. (See 5 above.)

PROJECTS, ASSIGNMENTS, AND MINIS

1. TWO HIGHER EDUCATION CASE STUDIES: MINI-CASES FOR DISCUSSION*

Associations representing higher education in Washington, D.C., began two ambitious public relations efforts in 1981. The associations involved did not have histories of working together on national public relations programs. It is notable that two such efforts were mounted the same year.

The programs are interesting because they involved cooperation among organizations that represented different interests in higher education; the programs were national in scope; they enlisted major support; and they were successful.

The objectives of the two programs were different but complementary. One sought to counteract the Reagan administration's proposals for further cuts in student financial aid programs by arousing public awareness of the effects of the reductions. The other set out to galvanize public support for higher education in general through messages emphasizing the important contributions it has made in the past and must make in the future.

Different patterns of cooperation were involved. One program was a cooperative effort by 20 associations with leadership and coordination provided by an "umbrella" council. The other effort was conducted by one specialized association on behalf of, and with encouragement and support from, the others. The "specialized" association, not surprisingly, is made up of college public affairs professionals.

Action Committee for Higher Education

Late in 1981, governmental affairs officers of the American Council on Education (ACE) became convinced that the Reagan administration was preparing additional large reductions in federal student aid programs for fiscal 1983. The higher education community had accepted, with little resistance, sizable budget cuts for fiscal 1982 as its "fair share" of a national effort to reduce federal spending. However, the 1983 cuts, when added to those for 1982, seemed unnecessarily severe, approaching a 50 percent reduction from 1981 levels. More important, the reductions constituted a renunciation of the federal government's 25-year policy of trying to achieve universal opportunities in higher education.

In 1980, the new Reagan administration, still flushed with victory and with a mandate to cut spending, recommended across-the-board reductions of 12 percent for fiscal 1982. In the drawn-out budget process, student financial aid programs were slashed three times: once in the original Reagan budget proposal, again in the budget reconciliation act, and yet again in the fiscal 1982 appropriations. Student aid emerged from this process with reductions amounting to nearly 12 percent, although other social service programs took cuts amounting to approximately 4 percent.

When leaks began to indicate the size of the student aid budget planned by the administration for 1983, the leadership of the American Council on Education felt it was time for higher education to resist. The colleges and students had taken more than their fair share of reductions the previous year.

The American Council on Education is the umbrella organization for all higher education in the United States. It is both an association of colleges of all types—two- and four-year, public and private—and a council of associations. The Council serves to con-

---

*These two cases appeared in "Higher Education: Two Public Relations Case Studies," by Roger Yarrington, *Public Relations Review*, Fall 1983, p. 40, which is reprinted here with permission. Professor Yarrington was associate dean of the College of Journalism, University of Maryland, at the time he wrote these case studies.

---

vene and coordinate when associations representing specific types of colleges and functions need to work together.

Coordination has been most consistent among the governmental affairs officers who represent the associations' interests on Capitol Hill, although such coordination has been somewhat limited at times because the interest of colleges of different sizes, types, and sponsorship are sometimes split on specific legislative issues. Coordination of the broader public relations efforts, aimed at the general public and the mass media, was attempted several times in recent years but was less consistent.

Charles Saunders, a veteran advocate for higher education and former HEW official, is ACE vice president for governmental relations. He and his colleagues learned from contacts inside the administration what the Reagan 1983 budget proposals for student aid were likely to be several weeks before the information was officially released. Bob Aaron, director of public affairs for ACE, alerted his counterparts, the public relations officers of the other associations, and they began drafting a national program to tell the public what the effects of the proposed cuts would be.

A strategy meeting was convened in December 1981, by J.W. Peltason, president of ACE. The presidents of the other higher education associations indicated they were prepared to cooperate in an unprecedented national public information campaign aimed at students, parents, the media, and ultimately, the Congress.

Each association was asked to contribute funds and some time from its public relations office. Five associations contributed $10,000 or more, several others contributed slightly less, and others contributed what they could from their budgets, most of which had not anticipated any such expenses. A fund of just under $95,000 was put together. Office space was contributed by the American Association of Community and Junior Colleges at One Dupont Circle, Washington, D.C., where most of the educational associations are located. An Action Committee staff was created, primarily Aaron, Nancy Raley from the Council for the Advancement and Support of Education, and other public relations officers from associations representing private colleges, land-grant colleges, independent colleges, Catholic colleges, graduate schools, and associations representing trustees, professors, business officers, minorities and others.

In January the Action committee informed the higher education community—including student groups and colleges across the country—that it was in business. It prepared its first press kit, set up a toll-free hot line, and scheduled a press conference for February 2, a week before President Reagan was to announce his budget recommendations. Aaron refers to that press conference as a "pre-emptive first strike." The higher education community was in a unique position—it was prepared to counter the administration's proposals with data on the effects of budget cuts before the proposed reductions were announced.

Garven Hudgins, public information officer for the National Association of State Universities and Land Grant Colleges, and a former foreign correspondent for the Associated Press, alerted public affairs officers of NASULGC institutions by mailgram that there would be a major press conference affecting them on February 2. He suggested that they alert local and state media and have them request coverage by AP. "It is an old device," he said. "The papers that are members of AP request coverage. The AP covers the event. And when the story comes back over the wire, the papers go back to area colleges for information on local ramifications."

The January kit was sent to colleges across the country. It contained a five-page press release explaining the complicated student aid programs and budget process. The lead was:

> The Reagan administration will send to Congress next month a new federal budget severely slashing five U.S. programs aimed at helping students pay for college and university educations.

The release identified the five student aid programs:

- Pell grants, formerly called basic educational opportunity grants (BEOG), which would be cut 45 percent from 1981 levels;
- College work-study funding, which would be reduced 27 percent;
- Supplemental educational opportunity grants (SEOG), state student incentive grants (SSIG), and national direct student loans (NDSL), all of which would be eliminated.

Guaranteed student loans (GSL) would have increased fees and interest rates and would eliminate graduate student participation. Social security benefits going to students were already scheduled to be phased out by 1985, so they would be cut in 1983 as well.

The release said the proposed cuts in the Pell grants alone would remove 1 million students from the program. Another 1.3 million students would lose awards from the other program cuts proposed. The committee used quotes from each of the recent Presidents, from Eisenhower to Carter, to illustrate the national commitment to achieve educational opportunity for all citizens.

In addition to the news release, which could be adapted by colleges for local use, there were draft op ed pieces and editorials, color-coded fact sheets on each of the student aid programs and on the congressional budget process, a directory of association media contacts, and suggestions on how to set up a campus action committee.

The press release in the second media kit, prepared for the February 2 press conference on Capitol Hill, had this lead:

> President Reagan's fiscal 1983 budget—halving student aid programs for the 1983-84 school year, by which time college costs are expected to climb another 15-20 percent—"would put college beyond the reach of several hundred thousand young Americans," J.W. Peltason, president of the American Council on Education, charged today.

When the administration presented its budget, the Action Committee's forecasts of the proposed cuts and the materials it had provided the press were on target. "The media and the public had a better understanding of student financial aid programs and the effects of the proposed cuts because of the Action Committee's work," Charles Saunders said. "It took the initiative away from the Administration."

During February and March the clipping service commissioned by the Action Committee produced 2,000 newspaper clippings and radio and TV transcripts that resulted from information provided by the committee. The committee embarked on a huge photocopying project. Clippings were grouped by congressional districts, copied, and sent to members of Congress to be sure they had not been overlooked—and that the impressive totals were made apparent.

The media attention generated increased letters, phone calls, and visits by students and parents to congressmen. Some colleges organized schedules for calling that kept their congressmen's lines busy for days.

A third media kit was produced in March. Copies were sent to the associations' combined press lists as well as to the colleges. It contained additional releases and fact sheets. It pointed out the effects the proposed budget cuts would have at a time when college costs are going up and noted that such a move was at odds with public opinion as measured by a February *Newsweek* poll and a March *Washington Post*-ABC poll. The fact sheets explained further who received student aid and in what amounts. The losses to be suffered by states and by colleges were presented in data displays. Further, the contributions of higher education to the U.S. and local economies were detailed using data from federal sources.

By the end of March, the Action Committee was receiving letters from congressmen "clarifying" their positions on student aid. Virtually all of them, including prominent conservative legislators in the forefront of the "supply-side" and "Reaganomics" supporters, said, "I am with you."

Network radio and television coverage began to snowball. Association officials familiar with the intricacies of student aid and the budget process found themselves in demand for interviews and talk shows. The CBS Evening News did a five-minute segment on a Saturday and Charles Saunders debated Secretary of Education Terrell Bell on a CBS Morning News program.

A fourth press kit was produced for a May 12 press conference. Media and congressional responses to the proposed cuts were distributed as were the higher education community's responses to some Senate budget committee proposals that would have put a freeze on student grant programs for three years and eliminated GSL interest subsidies. More fact sheets and policy statements by the associations were distributed. All three networks, plus the Mutual radio network, covered the news conference.

This effort, along with the Action Committee's day-to-day work on the hot line responding to questions from colleges and reporters, produced an additional 4,000 clippings by July. Of the editorials clipped, 95 percent were favorable to the Action Committee. Many of the clippings were generated by colleges using the committee's materials in local interviews and in commencement addresses.

A June 3 article by Bryce Nelson for the *Los Angeles Times*, reprinted in other papers, was one of the Action Committee's favorites because it illustrated in specific human terms the effects of the national data being provided by the committee from Washington. Nelson told of a 37-year-old mother in Kentucky, wife of a disabled miner, who got up at 4:30 a.m. each day to get four children off to school and then drove 30 miles to Pikeville College. She was dependent on student aid to better herself and her family and said, "I'm on pins and needles about whether these cutbacks they're talking about in Washington will stop me from finishing college. If things were cut so much I couldn't go to school, I'd rather have a knife in my back."

Bob Aaron displays file drawers full of such newspaper stories from all over the country. The clippings are from small local papers and others such as the *New York Times, Washington Post, Chicago Tribune, St. Louis Post-Dispatch, Detroit Free Press, San Francisco Chronicle, Miami Herald, Christian Science Monitor* and *Wall Street Journal*, as well as magazine pieces from *Money, Congressional Quarterly, Ladies Home Journal*, and others. "The *LHJ* piece produced a lot of mail and calls to us," Aaron said. "Their readers really responded."

A second effort to send photocopies of recent clippings to congressmen from papers in their districts was begun in August in preparation for a mailing right after Labor Day.

John Mallan, vice president for governmental relations at the American Association of State Colleges and Universities, said he and the legislative advocates of the other associations had been skeptical about the association public relations officers becoming involved in a substantive way. But the lobbyists changed their minds when they saw the hometown letters and newspaper articles being read by congressmen and their staffs. "We received many compliments from Hill staffers on the work the associations were doing," he said. "The congressional opponents of the Reagan budget cuts thought we had not done enough to fight the cuts the previous year."

"Congressional staffers were in awe of the support higher education associations were able to muster," said Saunders. "They told us, 'You guys have really done a job.' They felt like they had heard from higher education. They had a new respect for the interests of our constituency," he said. He was impressed that the complaints from home about the cuts prompted a group of first-term conservative congressmen to issue a joint statement that they did not support further reductions in student aid. Even conservative Senator Orrin Hatch of Utah issued a release after the House and Senate conference on the budget resolution, claiming credit for stopping any further cuts in GSL. Other conservative members of Congress issued press releases for home consumption, distancing themselves from the Administration on reductions in student aid.

Congress utilized a continuing resolution to keep funds flowing. In the end, the 1983 budget for student aid had essentially the same levels of spending as the previous year. Higher education did not gain large new funds from the work of the Action Committee.

But it held its own and that was regarded as a victory. The work of the Action Committee clearly had an effect. The President's proposals to cut student aid did not gain the support they had the previous year. His recommendations never captured the initiative. That belonged to the Action Committee from the beginning.

"What we saw," said Saunders, "was a complete rejection by Congress of the President's proposals to further reduce student aid."

William Blakey, counsel to the House subcommittee on postsecondary education, verified the effectiveness of the Action Committee campaign—so far. He said it was "the first time the higher education community acted cohesively in its own self-interest. A successful effort was mounted." But, he cautioned, "the Administration will be back each year and the Action Committee will need to be there, too." . . .

Bob Aaron and others involved agree with the assessment of Blakey that the committee is going to be needed again and again. But, Aaron confesses, "Success has bred some apathy. Many of the colleges feel the heat is off. It may be difficult to move them to act as promptly and as well in the future."

The Mindpower Campaign

The Mindpower Campaign, conducted by the Council for Advancement and Support of Education (CASE) with cooperation and support from 30 national associations and endorsements from 80 state associations, began in the summer of 1981. . . .

CASE is an association involving higher education "advancement" professionals: persons with assignments in development, public relations, and alumni work. It was formed through a merger of two associations—the American College Public Relations Association and the American Alumni Council.

When James Fisher came to CASE as president in 1978, the council conducted a survey to determine the services the members wanted most. One item clearly identified was more national media attention. CASE responded with the Mindpower Campaign.

Charles Helmken, vice president and special assistant to the president of CASE, proposed the idea of the Mindpower Campaign in the fall of 1979. The concept was approved by the CASE board in the summer of 1980. No budget was allocated. The staff was told it would have to raise the necessary funds. In the months that followed, more than $250,000 was raised. The Exxon Education Foundation contributed $100,000. The rest came from other foundations and corporations and from CASE members and other colleges and associations. Magazines have given space for public service ads valued at $3 million. PSAs on radio and TV have used air time valued at $7 million.

The campaign slogan is "America's Energy Is Mindpower." Helmken said he wanted a fresh contemporary image to illustrate the slogan. He remembered a sculpture for Bloomingdale's by Nick Aristovulos which looked like a light bulb, except the bulb was the shape of a human head and the filament was the shape of a heart. He contacted John Jay, art director for Bloomingdale's, and found that the sculpture still existed and could be adapted. The filament heart was made to resemble a human brain. A photograph was made by Shig Ikeda. Helmken's concept and Ikeda's photo were translated by Jay into a dramatic poster with the caption: "America's Energy Is Mindpower: Make Higher Education Your Priority." The light bulb figure is known as CASEy Kilowatt and is used in all of the campaign's print materials.

The art and text used on the poster were used to develop a series of public service ads in a variety of formats. They have been used in 20 national magazines—such as *Newsweek, Time, U.S. News, People, Ladies Home Journal, Reader's Digest, New York, Penthouse,* and *Money*—as well as in newspapers and many magazines published by the associations and colleges.

Helmken credits George Simpson, director of corporate affairs at *Newsweek*, for helping to get the first public service ads. Simpson hosted a luncheon for some of his counterparts in New York and got the ball rolling. "Once *Newsweek* and *Time* agreed to use the ads," Helmken said, "other magazines joined in." He noted that five of the seven Time, Inc. magazines have used the PSAs.

Joel Weiner, vice president for marketing at Seagram's, also was helpful in getting the ads placed. He sent personal letters to 30 key people at periodicals CASE wanted to reach.

Television PSAs were developed with assistance from Bob Fisler, former vice president for promotion at Time, Inc. (now retired). He enlisted Young and Rubicam agency personnel to brainstorm ad ideas. Time donated its film footage on "American Renewal" which was developed by Y&R. A new script and sound track were produced to create a 30-second PSA which was distributed to more than 400 television stations and was used by all three networks. Eight radio PSAs also were created and sent to 700 stations.

The National Collegiate Athletic Association created another 16 PSAs utilizing the Mindpower theme and ran them during televised football and basketball games in 1981 and 1982. Thirteen additional PSAs were developed and used in the 1982-83 seasons.

The CASE Communications Network was created to distribute the PSAs and other media kits. Over 1,000 press kits were distributed by the network. CASE estimates that 21 million people were reached through the magazine ads. Public Service Management is assisting with analysis of TV coverage. The CASE estimate for households reached with TV messages is now over 50 million.

The nation's colleges were provided with Mindpower materials. There was an ad repro package, a logo package, and a messages package—a series of brief phrases that built on the central theme. Also, there were draft op ed pieces and news releases. An observance manual was available to help colleges tie into the National Support Higher Education Day, July 16, 1981, when the campaign was given its kick-off at a "gala" in Washington, D.C.

Two features of the gala were presentation of the first Jefferson Medal by CASE to John Gardner for his contributions to education and the naming of Mary Eleanor Clark, professor of biological sciences at San Diego State University, as the first national "Professor of the Year." The latter award provided additional TV coverage for Mindpower through an appearance by Professor Clark on the NBC "Today" show.

An 80-page program booklet was printed for the gala. It included a 24-page, four-color photo essay on higher education with text drawn from an address at the University of Sheffield in 1946 by John Masefield, poet laureate of England. The photo essay was made available to institutions as a separate publication and as a slide presentation.

Materials produced by CASE were used by 1,200 colleges to develop their own "mindpower" events. CASE added to its annual awards competition a special category to recognize outstanding efforts by colleges in support of the Mindpower Campaign. The awards program was sponsored by *Newsweek*. A wide variety of colleges won awards. The grand award was won by the University of Vermont. The CASE booklet of 101 program ideas for "mindpower" events describes 26 of the college programs in some detail and lists another 25 programs to stimulate the imaginations of campus coordinators.

In the fall of 1982, CASE prepared a new Mindpower focus on business and education cooperation. The slogan "Mindpower: Ignite It with Your Match" was used to stimulate additional interest in the matching gifts programs of companies which match the contributions their employees make to colleges. The 1982 campaign reached 70 million persons, according to CASE estimates. The goal for the 1983 campaign is 100 million.

An October 9 program at the Jefferson Memorial in Washington, D.C., was used to launch the new focus. It was called a "national convocation" celebrating National Higher Education Week, October 2-9. CASE got all 50 governors to proclaim the week in their states. Local colleges obtained similar proclamations from mayors of the 20 largest cities. "Local and state proclamations produce more media attention than a national one," Helmken said.

The October 9 convocation included education, government, and business representatives from every state in academic regalia and presentation of the Jefferson Medal to the

Reverend Theodore M. Hesburgh, president of Notre Dame University—with the Jefferson Memorial as the setting. A new Professor of the Year was announced: Anthony F. Aveni, professor of astronomy and anthropology at Colgate University. . . .

So far, the Mindpower Campaign has won awards from the American Society of Association Executives; Education Press Association; University and College Designers Association; Printing Industries of America; the Art Directors Club of Washington, D.C.; *Print* magazine; and the Direct Marketing Association. These are nice, Helmken says, but he has been convinced by his advertising and public relations advisors that the Mindpower Campaign must sustain itself for at least three years with essentially the same logo and message if it is going to have a major impact nationally.

Questions for Discussion

1. What's your opinion of **each** of the two higher education programs? In evaluating, measure each of them in terms of the planning and programming elements cited in the chapter.

2. What do you consider to be the major strengths and weaknesses of each of the two programs?

3. Which one of the two programs do you consider to be the superior one? Why?

4. If you had the opportunity, what changes—if any—would you have recommended for each of the two programs?

5. What lessons have you learned from these programs?

2. SETTING FORTH SOME THEMES: THREE MINI-PROBLEMS

1. Assume you have been given the assignment of setting forth two major themes which can be used as the basis for public relations programming for your college or university for the coming academic year.

    In a memorandum to your vice-president for public relations explain the essence of the two themes you would propose for your institution. Do *not* use a slogan format, but explain the nature of your proposed themes in a paragraph for each.

    As a supplement to your memorandum, explain *why* you have proposed each theme. In short, justify your themes.

2. Themes can be discerned in most major advertising campaigns of national concerns and organizations. Some are astute, relevant, and honest, and some are not.

    Select and analyze one such major, current advertising campaign of a national concern or organization, and in a memorandum to your instructor explain the nature of the theme or themes you discern in the campaign; provide illustrative material from the campaign to demonstrate how these themes are used; and critique the use of said themes in terms of their effectiveness, relevancy, and honesty.

3. Select any organization with which you are familiar—it can be local, regional, or national; profit or nonprofit—and set forth two major themes which can be used as the basis for a projected public relations campaign for the coming year.

    In a memorandum to your instructor explain the essence of the two themes you would propose for the organization. Do *not* use a slogan format, but explain the nature of your proposed themes in a paragraph for each.

    As a supplement to your memorandum, explain *why* you have proposed each theme. In short, justify your themes.

3. PSAs FOR THE PUBLIC RELATIONS SOCIETY OF AMERICA: A MINI-ASSIGNMENT

You are to assume that the National Football League has agreed to allocate to the Public Relations Society of America ten 30-second public service announcements which will be put on the air during games next season.

The Board of Directors of the PRSA has raised the funds needed to cover production costs for the ten cameos and has tentatively assigned you total responsibility for the project. The board's major stipulation is that there be a basic or central theme to the cameos and that each of them should follow the same format but differ in regard to the personalities involved. Before giving you final approval for the project the board requests that you prepare and send it a position paper covering the following:

a) A concise statement explaining why you perceive the NFL cameo opportunity meets the basic goals and objectives of the PRSA.

b) An explanation of the specific central theme which you propose be exemplified in each of the ten 30-second spots.

c) A brief explanation of the proposed format of the ten cameos.

d) A rough video-voice script for two of the cameos.

12

COMMUNICATION (1): PURPOSE, FORM, PROCESS, THEORIES, AND BASIC MODEL

*I*n handling the five major elements of public relations in action—assessing public opinion, researching, planning and programming, communicating, and evaluating results—public relations practitioners consider that communicating presents the fewest problems. This is not because the art of communication is quickly and easily mastered, but because it is most closely allied to the practitioner's prior professional life experience. Starting with the pioneers who commenced the practice of public relations early in this century, practitioners traditionally have begun their professional life as journalists. The basic tool of the journalist has been the word—written in the case of the print journalist and verbal in the case of the electronic journalist—and he has used it to communicate effectively with readers, listeners, and viewers. When practitioners moved from journalism into public relations they took along their skill in communicating through the word.

Newcomers to the field of public relations discover quickly that effective communication is still the core element of successful public relations practice. A few practitioners may carry out successful practice by assessing public opinion, conducting research, planning, and programming, but the biggest game in town is still communication. Practitioners must understand the nature of public opinion and must be able to counsel and plan programs, but unless they can communicate they don't last long in the field.

And so the practitioners communicate, often successfully and effectively. But don't ask too many of them to provide a rational, thoughtful description of the communication process, to discuss how communication works, or to explain *why* some communication will effect opinion change, some behavior change, and some neither. This chapter will provide some of the answers about the nature and process of communication, and at the same time will raise some questions for which there are no ready and simple answers. The following chapter will dissect the four major elements of the basic communication model.

THREE BASIC CONSIDERATIONS

The primary approach to communication in this chapter will be by means of a communications model, but first some observations are in order about the *purpose, form,* and *process* of communication.

PURPOSE

Idle conversation—a form of daily communication engaged in by most people—serves the purpose of passing away the time of the day, but this is not the main reason why public relations practitioners engage in communication. There's purpose behind all successful communication, and this elementary fact has to be recognized and purpose clarified *before* communication is set in motion.

The mass media, the major means of communication utilized by public relations practitioners, serve three main purposes: to *inform, influence,* and *entertain.* Harold Lasswell, who pioneered in the study of communication, placed these in a social context when he postulated that the three major social functions of communications are: (1) surveillance of the environment; (2) correlation of the different parts of society in responding to environment; and (3) transmission of the social heritage from one generation to the other.[1] Thus, providing information serves as a means of surveilling the environment; editorials, columns, and commentaries serve to correlate the different parts of society in responding to the environment; and it is through the various means of entertainment that the mass media help to transmit the social heritage.

Valuable as the threefold division of purpose may be, it is neither distinctive nor purposeful enough for the kind of professional communication tasks assigned to or undertaken by public relations practitioners. David K. Berlo suggests a more definitive role for communication when he proposes that the nature of the *response* to be sought from communication be its paramount purpose.

"All communication behavior," says Berlo, "has as its purpose, its goal, the production of a response. When we learn to phrase our purposes in terms of specific responses from those attending to our messages, we have taken the first step toward efficient and effective communication."[2]

Berlo's suggestion that communicators concentrate on the response to be sought is highly relevant to public relations practitioners, and at the same time it is not necessarily antithetical to the threefold-purpose model. If one wants mainly to provide information, that's fine, but at least recognize this purpose and the response to be sought. If one wants mainly to entertain, that's fine also so long as the communicator recognizes what response is to be achieved from entertainment.

In Berlo's opinion, the main purpose of communication is to influence or, as he puts it, "to affect with intent." In the following criticism that Berlo makes of numerous communication efforts is a valuable lesson for public relations practitioners:

> Too often, writers think that their job is to *write* technical reports rather than to *affect the behavior* of their reader. Television producers and theatrical directors forget that their original purpose was to affect an audience—they get too busy "putting on plays" or "filling time with programs." Teachers forget about the influence they wanted to exert on students and concentrate on "covering the material" or "filling fifty minutes a week." Presidents of civic and professional organizations forget they are trying to influence or affect their members—they are too busy "having meetings" or "completing programs." Agricultural extension workers forget they are trying to affect farmers and homemakers—they get too busy "giving out information" or "reporting research."[3]

Berlo could well have added that public relations practitioners often are so busy writing and mailing out hundreds of press releases they forget that the first purpose of a release is to be accepted and used by the mass media and the second is to be read; so busy creating stunts and activities they fail to relate them to the objectives and goals of the organization; so busy "doing" they forget that behind the doing there has to be the purpose of achieving a predetermined response.

FORM

The form that communication takes is divisible in many different ways. One can consider communication as being personal or impersonal, oral or written, private or public, visual or nonvisual, internal or external, tactile or nontactile, face-to-face or interposed, indoor or outdoor, and even hot or cold. The form that a particular communication takes may be dictated by the circumstances surrounding it or may be at the control of the communicator; it may be influenced by the social controls of the society in which it takes place; and it may be dependent on technological circumstances.

Form is more than just an idle exercise in semantics or academic gamesmanship, particularly when the communicator has to make a choice. If you're an Indian chief whose tribe is being surrounded by an overwhelming army force, do you send up smoke signals to bring help or do you send a warrior on a fast pony? If you're Samuel Adams, do you send a letter protesting the stamp tax or do you stage an event and dump tea into Boston harbor?

Neither of the above examples illustrates conventional forms of communication, but they make the point that communication can take all sorts of forms, many of them unconventional, in an attempt to "get the message through" and to persuade others. Symbols are a form of communication, as witness the use of the American flag at rallies of both the far right and the far left. Anyone who has gone past a stinking, burning garbage dump on the outskirts of a large city will recognize that both sight and smell are powerful means of communication. Sound is a form of communication, as anyone who has ever attended a rock festival will clearly testify.

These varieties of form are a reminder that there's more to communication form than a speech, feature story, press release, or television appearance. Given the choice, the practitioner uses that form most appropriate to the situation and most likely to bring about the desired response.

PROCESS

Communication involves process. Communication does not take place in a vacuum or void, and is not singular but pluralistic. Do not expect communication to ensue if you lock a person for weeks in an airtight, totally dark, escape-proof, soundproof, perfectly bare dungeon with walls three feet thick; that person will not only be unable to communicate, but will undoubtedly die. Put two people in the same dungeon and they may also die, but they will communicate.

How they will communicate depends on a wide number of variables—their ages, education, nationality, ingenuity, state of mental and physical health, dexterity, and so forth. What if one of the two is ten years old and the other forty? What if one has a sixth-grade education and the other a Ph.D. degree? What if one is American and the other Hungarian? The human spirit being what it is, the two will overcome all barriers to communication. The barriers themselves are cited to illustrate that communication does not take place in a vacuum or void but in a situational context that affects it. The dual nature of those in the situation is a reminder that communication takes place only when there is more than one person involved.

A BRIEF SYNOPSIS OF SOME COMMUNICATION
THEORIES/MODELS/PROCESSES

One of the reasons that public relations practitioners have had difficulty dealing with communication as a field of study is that its disciples are found in so many different fields: psychology, journalism, sociology, speech, anthropology, and engineering. Communication models and theories have often reflected the specialized academic orientation of the model makers and theorists. General principles have been hard to come by, and even more difficult for the practitioner has been the task of making theory applicable to everyday practice. However, as Schramm reminds us, "a good theory gives the researcher an intellectual handle for taking hold of the problem of analysis. The fact that it may eventually be demonstrated to be incomplete, or even incorrect, and its importance in the field diminished does not take away its importance as a starting place. Communication study is in debt to several such theories."[4]

The "hypodermic needle" theory of communication serves as one of the theory starting places to which Schramm refers. A simplistic approach to the communication process, this theory postulated that the communicator sends his message through the mass media to bring about certain behavior on the part of the audience. News stories, radio and television programs were likened to a hypodermic needle which took the messages sent by the communicator, stuck them in the minds of the audience, and produced desired effects. Rogers notes that the theory was much too mechanistic, simple, and gross to provide an accurate accounting of the effects of mass media.[5]

A refinement of this theory was the "two-step flow" hypothesis, which theorized that ideas flow from the media to opinion leaders and then from them to the less active elements of the population. The key study which led to this theory was conducted in Erie County, Ohio, in the 1940 presidential election by Paul Lazarsfeld and colleagues at the Bureau of Applied Social Research of Columbia University. Using the panel research technique, the researchers concluded that very few people reported being influenced by the media about voting but rather by personal contacts and face-to-face persuasion by opinion leaders.[6] Another study, conducted among women in Decatur, Illinois, concluded that there are different levels and degrees of opinion leadership, that some women are opinion-forming influentials when it comes to movie-going, others when it comes to fashion, etc.[7]

The fault with both theories is that they fail to recognize that communication is a process in which key elements are constantly interacting with each other. As Schramm puts it: "The idea that something 'flows,' untransformed, from sender to receiver in human communication is a bit of intellectual baggage that is well forgotten. It is better to think of a message as a catalytic agent with little force of its own except as it can trigger forces in the person who receives it."[8]

A third communication model/theory/process—the **diffusion of innovations**—began to take root in the 1950s and came to general public attention with the publication in 1962 of Everett Rogers' *Diffusion of Innovations*. The third edition of his book, published in 1983, cites more than 3,000 diffusion publications and 2,300 empirical diffusion research reports. Clearly, Rogers was justified in claiming a coming-of-age for a "more unified and cross-discipline viewpoint in diffusion research."[9]

Just what is diffusion? Simply **the process whereby an innovation**—a new way of doing things, for example—**is communicated over a period of time and through certain kinds of channels among members of a social system.** One well-known example is the way in which farmers in Iowa adopted the use of hybrid corn. Those researching the diffusion process carry out empirical studies dealing with the spread of messages that are new ideas. These studies show who are the early adopters of a new idea or concept, who are the ones to follow, etc. Rogers and his fellow researchers consider that there are five **adopter categories** among members of a social system: (1) innovators, (2) early adopters, (3) early majority, (4) late majority, and (5) laggards. As to the innovation-decision process, Rogers cites five steps: (1) knowledge, (2) persuasion, (3) decision, (4) implementation, and (5) confirmation. The diffusionists find that the mass media play a crucial role in creating **knowledge** about innovations, but interpersonal channels are the most effective when it comes to forming and changing attitudes toward the new idea and thereby playing a key role in the decision to adopt or reject an innovation.[10]

The diffusion process has many variables to it, hence is much more complicated than the truncated explanation cited above. It also should be of much interest to public relations practitioners for several reasons. There have been, as already noted, a great many studies of the process in action. There's a cumulative tradition of research studies which have built on each other, and they provide excellent case studies of how new ideas and concepts have been diffused through a variety of social systems. The studies also cut across many disciplines and involve a wide variety of situations. None of the studies deals with or has been done for public relations purposes, but they certainly provide valuable nuggets for the public relations practitioner who wants to sift through the findings for lessons in communication. Exhibit 12.1 summarizes two diffusion studies cited by Rogers.

EXHIBIT 12.1

Brief Summary of Two Diffusion Studies

When modern math was adopted by the public schools in Allegheny County, Pennsylvania, it was first brought in by one school superintendent in 1958. Rogers reports he was a "sociometric isolate" in the local network who traveled widely outside the area. All thirty-eight superintendents in the system had adopted the modern math by the end of 1963. The cosmopolite innovator, notes Rogers, was too innovative to serve as an appropriate role model for his superintendent peers. They took their cues from a six-member clique who were the opinion leaders of the group.[11]

Analyzing the diffusion of a new antibiotic drug, Columbia sociologists found that the doctors under study had plenty of information about the drug from reading articles about it and learning about it from "detailmen," but their main reason for adopting the drug was recommendations from other doctors. Not just any other doctors. The main reasons for following the lead of the innovators were such factors as religion, age, and professional affiliations.[12]

A fourth theory or model of the communication process receiving much attention in recent years is the **transactional model.** As its name implies, this model explores influences from both the communicator and the audience. One researcher, W. P. Davison, cites this view of the audience:

> The communicator's audience is not a passive occupant—it cannot be regarded as a lump of clay to be molded by the master propagandist. Rather, the audience is made up of individuals who demand something from the communications to which they are exposed, and who select those that are useful to them. In other words, they must get something from the manipulator if he is to get something from them.

Leonard J. Snyder, writing in the late seventies, emphasized this new direction of the transactional model when he reviewed what has been called "the **uses and gratification**" approach to communication research. Rather than take the communicator as the starting point, this approach considers the media consumer as the starting point. The view of the audience is one where its members actively utilize media content to meet their own individual needs and wants. "It is increasingly evident," stated Snyder, ". . . that patterns of media use are shaped by audience needs, wants, and expectations, and that these are important determinants of media effects."[13]

This stress on the audience's "needs, wants, and expectations"—another way of emphasizing "uses and gratifications"—will be explored further in the next chapter during discussion of the message stage of a simple communications model. Readers of this text may also recall that one of Newsom's guideposts to public opinion—the identification guidepost—puts the same stress on the need to identify with the needs, hopes, aspirations, and desires of the intended audience.

A CAUTIONARY NOTE

The public relations practitioner is well advised to view communication much as he or she views public relations. Both are dynamic, and neither process has a beginning, a middle, and an ending. Both public relations and communication in action are continuous, always in a state of flux, with their basic elements constantly interacting with and upon each other. Life for the practitioner would be simple if it were possible to freeze the communication process and set it off in time and space, but communication cannot be frozen.

What do we mean when we say that communication is not frozen in time and space? Simply that all communication takes place in a setting, and the setting is an important factor in determining whether communication will be effective and in trying to predict audience reaction.

Though the setting for communication is a vital factor in the whole process of communication, it was not given much consideration by the "hypodermic needle" and "two-step flow" researchers, and unfortunately most experimenters in communication continue to err in drawing conclusions from their experiments as though they had been conducted in a milieu frozen in time and space. Because people differ and because the situations in which people find themselves differ, it is not wise to draw sweeping conclusions about human communication on the basis of what tends to be a controlled environment.

This does not, however, justify the equally sweeping conclusion that human communication experiments serve no valuable purpose at all. On the contrary, they help to underscore the important fact that communication is a process and that certain key elements are involved. Therefore, in order to understand the process and to learn lessons from it, these key elements need to be identified, analyzed, and discussed. To achieve these purposes, communication scholars have developed relatively simple—perhaps deceptively simple—communication models, and it is through such a model that the process of communication will be explained in the section that follows.

A COMMUNICATION MODEL: INTRODUCTION

A basic, simple communication model has been selected for discussion because it contains the four major elements present in virtually all forms of human communications: the **sender** or source; the **message**; the **channel**; and the **receiver** or recipient. Harold D. Lasswell, media theorist, capsulized a similar convenient way of describing an act of communication by saying it should answer the following questions:

> Who
> Says What
> In Which Channel
> To Whom
> With What Effect?[14]

If we were to project the first four elements in Lasswell's question set to explain the communication process in linear form, our model would work out as follows:

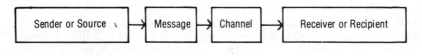

FIGURE 12.1

In its simplest form communication involves a source or sender whose purpose is to send a message through a channel in order to reach a receiver or recipient. Three other sub-elements, however, are usually present in the communication act, and these involve **encoding, decoding,** and **feedback.**

Encoding is essentially a matter of translating the ideas of the source and giving them meaning. Usually this is performed by the motor skills possessed by the sender, who uses his vocal mechanisms to produce oral words or his muscle system to produce written words or gestures. In simple communication situations the source and encoder are the same person, but the two are generally separate entities in complex communication situations in which an organization is involved. As an example, the organization may want to communicate with its union public but entrusts the encoding of the message to its public relations department.

Decoding represents the reverse of encoding and means a retranslation of a message into a form that the receiver can use. In face-to-face communication the encoder is the set of motor skills used by the source, while the set of sensory skills used by the receiver is the decoder. The source encodes by using speech or writing; the receiver decodes by using hearing or reading. In a more complex situation the functions of encoding and decoding are separable from the source and receiver functions.

Berlo reminds us that the concepts of source, encoder, decoder, and receiver should not be interpreted as being separate things, entities, or people, but as the names of behavior performed when communication takes place. Thus, one person may be both a source and a receiver and encode and decode messages. In complex communication patterns these functions would be carried out by different people. As an example to describe the communication behavior of a complex organization, Berlo cites the operation of a large-city newspaper.

> The operation of the newspaper involves a complex network of communication. The newspaper hires people whose prime job is decoding—reporters who observe one or more kinds of events in the world and relay them to the "central nervous system" of the paper, the "desk" or "slot" or central control office.
>
> When these messages are received, some decision is reached by the editorial staff. As a result of these decisions, orders are given from the control desk to produce or not produce a given message in the paper. Again, the encoding function becomes specialized. The paper employs rewrite men, proofreaders, . . . pressmen, delivery boys. They are all responsible for one or another part of the encoding and channeling functions, getting the message out of the control office on to the pages of the newspaper, and thence to a different set of receivers, the reading public.[15]

In the example cited above there is no direct line from source to message to channel to receiver, but rather a set of activities interrelated to each other, almost indivisible, and constantly in motion. Communication within this organization is also affected by the perceptions, attitudes, and beliefs of those involved in the process; by the standards and codes of the paper; and by the situation existing at the time the communication process takes place.

Among the factors involved in the dynamics of the communication process is the concept known as **feedback.** It operates at all levels, but is of particular importance at the source level. *Feedback is essentially a return flow from the message as it is received from the recipient.* Its impact and effect can be instantaneous and powerful—as in face-to-face. communication—or delayed and weak—as in mass communication. When a skillful speaker addresses an audience he is constantly making use of audience feedback to judge the impact he is making. Because this feedback is instantaneous and immediate he is able to change his delivery, tone, and even the talk itself in order to adjust to the feedback he receives from the audience. Contrast this with communication by means of television, where the audience is remote, removed, and out of sight. Here feedback is delayed, weak, and almost nonexistent. It's for this reason, among some others, that television shows are performed before specially assembled, live audiences, even though the real audience is somewhere out there in the remote land of the home receiver set. Feedback is what actors mean when they say there's a dynamic quality in the air when performing in the theatre as compared to the static quality when performing before the movie camera.

Feedback is highly important to public relations practitioners because it enables them to adjust, modify, or change messages in accordance with the dictates of the feedback. Practitioners can use all the skills at their command when sending a message through mass media channels, but without feedback they have no way of knowing the immediate impact these messages have on the intended recipient.

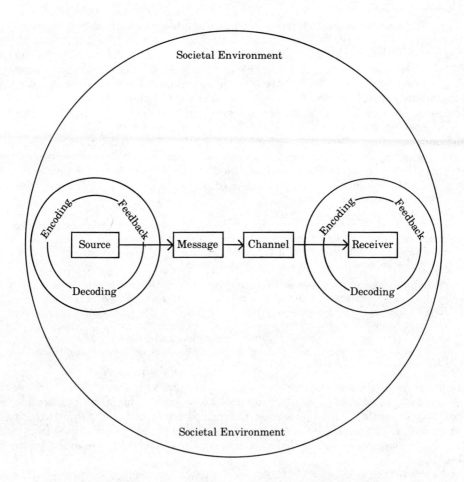

FIGURE 12.2 *The dynamics of the communications model.*

THE MODEL SUMMED UP

In very brief form we have examined the elements that must be present if communication is to take place. There has to be a *source*—one person, two people, or an organization—with some reason for engaging in communication. This source *encodes* to translate his or her ideas, information, or thoughts, and at the same time can be *decoding* and receiving *feedback*. He or she then *assigns meaning* to the ideas, information, or thoughts and puts them in the form of a *message*. The message is sent through a carrier or *medium* and is thereby channeled to a *receiver*. The receiver may be one person, two people, or an organization, and the receiver *decodes* the message to give it meaning. At the same time he or she may be encoding and receiving feedback.

The entire communication act, operating within a societal environment, is a matter of a process in which the key elements overlap, interact, and feed back upon each other. Thus, as seen in Figure 12.2, the process is both linear and circular. It is not static, but is dynamic, and it takes place in the context of a societal environment whose elements affect the communication act.

ENDNOTES

1. Harold D. Lasswell, "The Structure and Function of Communication in Society," in Lyman Bryson, ed., *The Communication of Ideas* (New York: Harper and Brothers, 1948), p. 38.
2. David K. Berlo, *The Process of Communication* (New York: Holt, Rinehart and Winston, 1960), p. 12.
3. Ibid., p. 13.
4. Wilbur Schramm and William E. Porter, *Men, Women, Messages and Media* (New York: Harper & Row, 1982), p. 110.
5. Everett Rogers, *Diffusion of Innovations*, 3rd ed. (New York: The Free Press, 1983), p. 272.
6. Paul F. Lazarsfeld, Bernard Berelson, and Helen Gaudet, *The People's Choice* (New York: Duell, Sloan and Pearce, 1944).
7. Elihu Katz and Paul Lazarsfeld, *Personal Influence* (New York: The Free Press, 1964).
8. Schramm and Porter, p. 50.
9. Rogers, p. 39.
10. Ibid., pp. 1-38.
11. Ibid., p. 64. Study cited is that of Dr. Richard O. Carlson, *Adoption of Educational Innovations* (Eugene, Oregon: University of Oregon, 1965).
12. Ibid., p. 68. Study cited is that of James Coleman, *Medical Innovations: A Diffusion Study* (New York: Bobbs-Merrill, 1966).
13. Leonard Snyder, "Uses and Gratifications to Implement a Public Relations Program," *Public Relations Review*, Summer 1978, p. 34.
14. Lasswell, p. 37.
15. Berlo, p. 35.

PROJECTS, ASSIGNMENTS, AND MINIS

1. APPLYING THE COMMUNICATIONS MODEL TO A PROGRAM PROPOSAL: A MINI-CASE

Spotless Laundries, a hitherto privately owned commercial laundry in Wilmington, Delaware, whose chief customers are restaurants, colleges, and hospitals in the state of Delaware, was sold one year ago to a three-member group in their early thirties.

Determined to extend the operations of the firm, the new owners went "public" in order to raise more capital and for the past six months the stock has been traded on the American Stock Exchange. With the modest amount of new capital which has accrued, the new owners built a new plant in Bethesda, Maryland, and the two plants in Wilmington and Bethesda now service customers in the two states and in the District of Columbia.

Traditionally, the commercial laundry field has consisted mainly of firms very similar to Spotless in that their business is mostly local, and in some cases regional, and serves customers within one day's driving range of the firm's trucks. To break this pattern and with the eventual goal of becoming a truly national firm, the new owners of Spotless have aimed their efforts at capturing an increasingly larger and larger share of the lucrative college and hospital linen fields. The former is served chiefly by local commercial laundries and the latter by local commercial laundries and by laundries owned and operated by the hospitals themselves.

The new owners have set up two wholly-owned subsidiaries of Spotless—College Linens of America, Inc., and Hospital Linens of America, Inc.—and are now planning to extend their operations. As the necessary finances become available, the owners hope first to build new plants anywhere in the Northeast where there is a reasonable certitude that colleges and hospitals will make use of their services, and then to move out into other geographic areas of the country. The major selling tool of both subsidiaries is a "total systems approach" which CLA and HLA have developed and which is demonstrably able to provide interested colleges and hospitals with faster, more dependable and cheaper service than they can secure from either their own facilities or from local commercial laundries.

At this stage in their planning, the owners of Spotless contacted a public relations counseling firm, provided the firm with the previously cited information, and asked the firm to present a plans/program proposal. In summary form, the proposal consisted of the following ten major projects:

1. **Case History Program:** CHLA's satisfied clients are its best press agents. We would ask you to open doors for us. Then we would go in, interview some of your customers, prepare their comments in article form, and place them for publication. Among other things, this is a very valuable way for CHLA to improve its client relations.

2. **Byliner Program:** The top executive of CHLA ought to receive a certain amount of exposure in important publications via bylined articles. These could deal with the total CHLA service, but more likely possibilities would deal with particular aspects of the service, how it solves specific problems, etc.

3. **A Standard Logo:** Ready identification can be established for CHLA by the development of a new, distinctive, and impressive logo which can be used on everything from calling cards to signs on delivery trucks.

4. **Sales Slide Presentation:** Our graphics and multi-media departments will prepare an exciting slide presentation which can be used to sell CHLA to prospective customers. We would schedule this presentation for important college and hospital industry meetings, trade shows, and similar gatherings.

5. **Survey and Report:** We can put this technique to use in several ways valuable to CHLA. We would design a telephone or personal interview survey to spotlight the views of specific audiences, and then we would report the results of the survey through appropriate media. The technique lets you know what your prospects are thinking and it provides a means for spot publicity. Subject matter can range all the way from how business leaders view their community hospital problems—or college financial problems—to the way hospital purchasing agents view their linen problems. The material developed through surveys would also have many secondary uses: in subsequent articles, speeches, booklets, and sales manuals.

6. **Sales Brochures:** We would develop two of these to be used for a local and national program. They would stress the systems aspects of the service and show how it differs from the ordinary linen supply operation.

7. **Monographs:** We would contract with leading authorities to write a series of informative monographs dealing with various aspects of college and hospital management, and these would be given wide distribution throughout both fields to college and hospital executives. The monographs would be noncommercial in nature and the only reference to CHLA would be on the cover page.

8. **Seminars:** Here is another noncommercial way of establishing CHLA as the leader in its field. We would contract with leading authorities to take part in these seminars—to be held throughout the country—and to discuss important college and hospital problem areas. The seminars would generate local publicity in print and electronic media, while national exposure would be gained by selective mailing of seminar summary remarks to a key list of important community and professional leaders.

9. **Speaking Dates:** Another useful way of gaining valuable exposure for CHLA is to have some of your executives speak before local and regional business and professional organizations. The talks would have to be broad in nature, rather than commercial, and would help sell CHLA as the authority in the hospital and college fields.

10. **Reprints:** This is Standard Operating Procedure, but it's an excellent means of keeping your name before important individuals and groups.

(Names and locations have been disguised.)

Questions for Discussion

1. What's your overall opinion of the program devised by the counseling firm? Justify your answer.

2. Which of the ten projects do you consider to have the most merit? Why?

3. Which do you consider to have the least merit? Why?

4. If you were to rearrange the order of the projects, how would you rearrange them?

Written Assignment

In a memorandum to your instructor explain how each project fits into the simple communications model described in the chapter.

In handling this assignment you may find it advisable to set up a table, list the four communications model elements at the top of the table, and then summarize how each project fits into each of the four elements of the model.

2. EXEMPLIFYING THE COMMUNICATIONS MODEL: TWO ASSIGNMENTS

a) In a memorandum addressed to your instructor, **describe** and **evaluate** five relatively recent examples which demonstrate the simple communications model discussed in the chapter. The communication in each instance can be one that took place immediately or over a period of time. Do *not* duplicate personalities or organizations, but rather deal with a different one in each example. Your examples should involve communications that have taken place within the last two months. Append appropriate material (clippings, etc.) where such will help in explaining the example cited in the body of your memo.

b) In a memorandum addressed to your instructor, **describe** and **evaluate** five relatively recent examples demonstrating the process of feedback in a communications situation. The feedback in each instance can be one that took place immediately or over a period of time. Do *not* duplicate personalities or organizations, but rather deal with a different one in each example. Your examples should involve feedback that has taken place within the last two months. Append appropriate material (clippings, etc.) where such will help in explaining the example cited in the body of your memo.

13

COMMUNICATION (2):
THE MODEL DISSECTED

The purpose of this chapter is to examine each of the four major elements of our communication model from the viewpoint of possible maximum effectiveness. As hi-fi enthusiasts know, the quality of sound produced by the system is at its maximum level when there is no interference anywhere within the system. Similarly, the quality of communication produced by a communication system is at its maximum level when there is no interference anywhere within the system. To produce maximum-efficiency-level communication, therefore, one must dissect the communication model and explore the *factors within the four major elements that lead to maximum communication effectiveness.*

SOURCE-SENDER

The most common role played by the public relations practitioner within the communication act or system is as the source or sender of messages. As discussed earlier in this book the practitioner is also a listener and an assessor of public opinion, but his success or failure is most often based on the way in which he communicates. A score of factors are involved in this aspect of public relations practice, but four major ones concern the communicator's degree of **empathy, credibility, situational acuity,** and **communication skills.**

EMPATHY

According to the dictionary, **empathy** is the "imaginative projection of one's own consciousness into another being," and in the communication act the other being is the intended receiver. Naive communicators send their messages "to whom it may concern" and hope they will reach someone. When the owner of a pleasure boat finds his boat is sinking he sends out a "Mayday" call, hoping to reach someone.

In contrast, the skilled communicator composes messages with a specific audience in mind, and when sent out these messages are directed to the specified audience. Wireless operators on large ocean vessels keep in constant touch with other ships, and if trouble occurs they know exactly where these ships are.

The wise communicator, therefore, develops a keen sense of empathy regarding his intended receiver or audience. He recognizes that everyone exists within a variety of systems, among which are the system of self or personality; the cultural system of ideas, beliefs, values, and symbols; and the social system of human relationships and social structures and organizations. Each of these has an important influence on the receiver's view of the world, his role and the role of others in the communication process, his reaction to messages, his use or nonuse of various channels, and so forth.

Some communicators are very good at developing empathy, others very poor. The best ones, in effect, try to step out of their own skins and into those of the audience they're trying to reach. They view communication situations not from their point of view, but from that of the audience. They are as much concerned about how a message will be perceived and received as how it is worded, written, and sent. The poor ones are either uncaring, insensitive, or oblivious to the audience they're trying to reach. They write from their point of view—or that of the organizations they represent—and are more concerned with the form of their words than they are with their impact.

CREDIBILITY

Source **credibility**, like empathy, is a key factor in establishing effective communication because of its connection with the receiver or recipient. By source credibility we mean the degree of faith and trust that the receiver has in the sender of a message, and the effect that this trust has on the receiver.

Psychological studies of opinion change conducted by Hovland, Janis, and Kelley of Yale University drew the following basic conclusions about source credibility:

1. When a person is perceived to have definite intentions to persuade others, it is likely he will be viewed as having something to gain and therefore less likely to be trusted.

2. The very same presentation tends to be judged more favorably when made by a communicator of high credibility than one of low credibility.

3. When dealing with issues and problems of a highly technical nature, an individual will be especially susceptible to influence by persons who are perceived to be experts.[1]

The above broad conclusions about source credibility were drawn chiefly from experimental studies with small groups of people under controlled conditions. In addition, they leave unanswered many questions about variations in source credibility as a factor in communication effectiveness—for example, how about an expert who does not inspire trust?—but they do underscore the fact that source credibility is an important factor in persuasive communication.

The implications for public relations practitioners are manifold because the research indicates that *cues about a communicator's intentions, expertness, and trustworthiness significantly affect the way in which communication will be received.* There is great practical value in knowing that **people are likely to distrust communication when they perceive it stems from a source that has much to gain from the communication.** There is similar practical value in knowing that a communication from a high-credibility source is more effective than one from a low-credibility source, and that it is wise to use an expert when dealing with communication technical in nature.

It's not surprising that the scientific research of communication sources has documented the effectiveness of high-credibility and expert sources and the ineffectiveness of communication from sources perceived as having an axe to grind. In the early days of the republic, when life was relatively simple but communication difficult, people learned to accept communication from sources they considered reliable. Even though the level of education has risen, there has been such an explosion of knowledge and information, so many complex issues and activities taking place and being disseminated by so many different means and methods, that people have found it impossible to deal with them personally. In trying to cope with the flood of messages, people turn to sources they can trust: a favorite columnist; commentators; political leaders who seem honest and forthright; the local bartender, mailman, and friends who have proven to be sagacious and wise.

Some Examples

The use of source credibility to enhance the effectiveness of communication has long been recognized in advertising, politics, and public relations practice—though not always wisely utilized. Television commercials feature nationally and internationally acclaimed personalities to promote products. When Congressmen of the same political party as the president are up for reelection, they find it useful to have him make a fast stopover during the campaign, or they send out photos showing them in serious conversation in the Oval Office. Grandma Brown seems to give her personal blessing to every can of baked beans; Mickey Mouse and his friends are stamped on almost every product sold at two vast family entertainment centers in Florida and California. The communication message is clearly the same: you can put your trust in our products because they're endorsed by Grandma Brown and Mickey Mouse. The fact that the products are the end result of vast, highly organized commercial organizations recedes conveniently into the background.

There is more to source credibility, however, than simply centering communication messages on personalities who inspire trust and confidence. What is sometimes forgotten is that there has to be some relevancy between the source and the product or institution being extolled. Many people will readily identify the famous baseball player seen in a supermarket scene selling the virtues of a coffee maker, but just as many will wonder about the connection between pounding a baseball and making coffee. Having a famous sports announcer appear in auto commercials during big league baseball telecasts is a neat juxtaposition of commercial and sports, but one wonders what makes him an expert on automobiles. The credible becomes incredible when relevancy is missing.

Public relations practitioners seeking to maintain source credibility in large organizations operate on levels far above those of television commercials. There's the inner-managerial level within their own organizations where the practitioners seek to establish responsible officials as reliable and trustworthy sources of information. There's the outer-media level where in their relationships with the mass media the practitioners seek to establish themselves as reliable and trustworthy sources of information. Between these two levels, however, there is a level not often discussed openly that causes no end of problems.

For want of a better word, let's call this level the *buffer-zone, the no-man's-land in which public relations practitioners so often find themselves in trying to establish and maintain source credibility.* Managements make mistakes, but don't like to admit them. Managements have to close plants and lay off employees, but don't like to admit it. But reporters learn about these things, and they inquire. Such inquiries are directed at the public relations practitioner or they come in to management which in turn directs them at the practitioner. That's when the public relations person lands in the buffer zone.

Even children no longer believe the old chestnut about George Washington and the cherry tree, so it comes as no surprise that people lie from time to time. However, if public relations practitioners find themselves lying, obfuscating, and being disingenuous as a matter of routine, they'd better forget about establishing source credibility.

Source credibility, in summation, is so valuable a factor in the process of communication it requires careful cultivation and deserves the hard fight practitioners must put up in the buffer zone between their managements and the media and the public.

SITUATIONAL ACUITY

Although not a term commonly used in public relations circles, **situational acuity** plays an important role in determining the effectiveness of practitioners as a communication source. Given a communication situation, Practitioner A will suggest action along a certain set of lines, Practitioner B along another set of lines, and Practitioner C no action at all. It's hardly likely that all three proposals will result in the same degree of effectiveness, and hence the practitioner whose keenness of judgment about the situation—situational acuity—is greatest will be the one whose proposed action or inaction will bring about the most effective communication results.

The need for situational acuity arises in all instances where people interact with each other, but it has particular relevance in the communication process. *How* the source sizes up a communication situation will determine in large degree what he or she does about it and the results. It could be an internal communication matter involving employees; an external one involving a community public; a media matter involving an inquiry from a newspaper reporter; or any matter in which communication is involved and which forms such an important aspect of daily public relations practice.

One might well raise these questions: Why stress the need for public relations practitioners to have situational acuity? Do not other management personnel need the same sense of keenness about situations? The answer is that the need is greater for the public relations practitioner because his activities and communications involve the entire organization and affect all of its publics. As the source for most of the communication emanating from an organization to its many publics, the practitioner has the heavy responsibility of ensuring most effective communication. *Sizing up the situation—the milieu—within which communication takes place* thus becomes a matter of real concern and great importance.

Unfortunately, there are no simple ground rules—no ten easy steps—for achieving situational acuity. Public relations situations involving communication seldom duplicate themselves, and people, organizations, and times change. The men and women who run today's large businesses, colleges and universities, and the armed forces are a different breed from those who ran them thirty and forty years ago. The men and women who work on assembly lines or punch buttons in plants, who attend colleges and universities, and who serve in the armed forces are a different breed also. Today's factory and plant are a far cry from factories and plants of thirty and forty years ago, as are colleges, universities, and military installations. The situation, in short, has changed and the communicator has to be keenly aware of the change and its implications.

The source has to be aware also that changes in communication situations occur not only on large but also on small scales, yet there is still the same need to be keenly tuned in to situational nuances. When your candidate for senator promises during the campaign he will conduct himself with total candor if elected, does he mean the same thing one year later when an enterprising reporter calls and says he has information about illegal contributions made to the now-elected senator? When your firm's earnings have declined appreciably and there's a dispute between you and the finance vice-president about the degree of candor in reporting it in the annual report, what does the president mean and what do you do when he suggests the two of you "work it out" so no one will look too bad?

Can one develop situational acuity to make for a more effective communication source? Experience, of course, is an answer, but one doesn't have to drown in order to handle a drowning situation. The wiser course is to learn from near-drowning experiences.

COMMUNICATION SKILLS

Communication skills are the string that wraps up the package of the three other factors—empathy, credibility, and situational acuity—which produce source effectiveness. Even though the source is empathetic and credible and has keen judgment in sizing up situations, he will be ineffective if unable to communicate thoughts, ideas, and information with a high degree of competence and skill.

The skills of the communicator are those of speaking and writing, and they're put to use every working day of the communicator's professional life. Surveys of public relations practitioners repeatedly demonstrate that their most common activities involve some form of speaking or writing: writing speeches or giving talks; writing releases and feature stories; composing memoranda, reports, and statements; conferring with management and editors. Such skills are chiefly encoding skills, but in carrying out the communication process the source also decodes, and here the practitioner puts to use the skills of listening and reading.

Entire books have been devoted to exploring the four communication skills of speaking, writing, listening, and reading, and their importance to the source is self-evident. As sources of information, public relations practitioners stake their professional careers on mastering each and all of the skills needed to make communication effective.

Within the communications model the skills associated with communication from the source deal chiefly with messages and media, and these will be discussed in detail in the sections that follow. Media or channels are so all-important, however, that they call for further amplification—hence the decision to include in this third edition a full chapter on media relations and publicity techniques. That chapter follows this one.

MESSAGES

One way to deal with the message stage of a communication model is to treat it from the standpoint of the semanticist, anthropologist, or social scientist. In doing so we would consider factors such as learning, abstraction, extensional and intensional meanings, social reinforcement, referents, language acquisition, and a score of other epistemological features, all of which might well make for confusion rather than elucidation on the part of the readers of this book. The English language translation of that last sentence is that it's the author's opinion there are some simple, key points about message effectiveness which can be presented without resorting to complicated language. This is not to gainsay the value of the semanticist's approach to the study of language—on the contrary, such an approach can have a high degree of significance for the public relations practitioner—but simply to point out that it's not within the purview of this book.

Further, there's need to stress that there are no immutable laws about messages, and it must be emphasized that messages do not have a life of their own. They exist within the context of the communication process, and the process itself can change the meaning and effect of a message.

KEY CONSIDERATIONS FOR ACHIEVING MESSAGE EFFECTIVENESS

Given these cautionary observations, there are certain key aspects to messages as they apply to public relations communication situations. Both research studies and practical experience have shown that if certain key considerations are kept in mind, practitioners will increase the possibility of communication effectiveness by obeying the dictates of these message considerations. Their presentation will be listed and discussed in no particular order of importance but in terms of their relevance to public relations situations.

To Be Effective, a Message Must Reach Its Intended Audience

Three astute observers of the public relations scene—Earl Newsom, Edward Robinson, and Gerhard Wiebe—arrive at the same conclusion about the need for "message reach," though each phrases his ideas in a different way.

In setting forth his four public opinion signposts—described in the chapter on public opinion—Newsom prefaced his conclusions with the observation that people don't stand still to be educated. The average person, he reminds us, is preoccupied with everyday problems and personal matters which take up most of that person's waking hours and many of the hours when he or she should be sleeping. Trying to catch the attention of this average person are thousands of individuals and organizations who want to "educate" him or her about their particular area of interest. Newsom concludes that it's little wonder, therefore, that the average person, preoccupied with personal problems, not only won't stand still to be "educated" but in sheer self-preservation because of the countless educational messages beamed at him will tune himself or herself out.

Wiebe, former dean at Boston University's School of Public Communication, postulates the "gyroscopic phenomenon" to explain the public's reluctance to be educated. Like the gyroscope, says Wiebe, people spin within their own orbits and resist outside forces. He makes his point in the following perceptive paragraph:

> If you accept this image of the public, you will necessarily reject an image that has been around too long and that dies hard—the image of the public as a bunch of nice, leisurely, receptive people who will absorb your message if you just use short simple sentences and good pictures. It isn't that simple. It is more the rule than the exception that a public relations message must be so contrived that it penetrates a field of resistance, a resistance generally characterized by a massive disinterest in your company's concerns, and an avid preoccupation with what we have called the sustaining of people's own systems of dynamic equilibrium.[2]

Robinson adds another dimension to the problem of catching audience attention, and he phrases it in terms of **nonmotivation** on the part of the audience to messages beamed at them. He describes the problem of audience nonmotivation by asking the following questions:

> Who cares if the company our . . . public relations practitioner represents has been a good corporate citizen and has done its share in trying to solve a particular community problem?

> Who cares if such-and-such nonprofit health group is making progress in finding a cure for some disease that very few persons know anything about in the first place?

> Who cares if some small liberal arts college has drastically revised its educational standards and is providing good solid liberal arts education for a certain number of students, but is now in critical financial straits?[3]

Is there an answer to the problem of audience preoccupation, disinterest, and nonmotivation? Robinson suggests you must make sure your message is available to the audience—that is, select a medium that reaches the intended audience—and you must anticipate and counteract the numerous competing factors that may intervene between source and recipient. Of course, having done this still doesn't solve the problem of audience preoccupation, disinterest, and nonmotivation, but recognizing the problem is the important first step: it forces the communicator into the realization that the audience is not breathlessly waiting for those words of wisdom which will "educate" it to his or her point of view.

The Impact of a Message Depends on How It Identifies with the Interests of the Intended Audience

Two common faults made by communicators are associated with the concept of interest-identification. One fault is to misunderstand or fail to understand the interests of the intended audience, and the other is to confuse the communicator's interests with those of the intended audience. Both failures lessen the impact of messages, and in many instances make them totally ineffective.

Identifying with the interests of the intended audience can best be achieved through *empathy, observation,* and *perception.* Fortunately for the astute communicator, these are not inherited traits but traits which can be learned, developed, and refined. In many cases the matter of interest-identification is mainly one of being careful not to operate under assumptions which are not warranted by reality.

Being careful not to confuse the communicator's interests with those of the intended audience is most often a case of being honest with one's assessment of a communication situation. It's all too easy, for example, to conclude that the audience will be interested in what we have to communicate simply because we want them to be; so we engage in a little game of self-deception in hopes our interests will somehow coincide when we honestly know they don't.

Professor Robinson provides a valid reminder about audience-interests when he notes that reactions to messages are interwoven with the drives and needs of their recipients. "A message," he points out, "must arouse certain needs in a potential recipient and indicate how these needs can be satisfied." It's also his opinion that **public relations communicators tend to rely too strongly on delivering information and not strongly enough on satisfying personal needs and motivations.**[4]

Messages Should Relate to Common Experience and Meaning

This precept, like the first two already cited, stresses the vital need to tie the source to the receiver of messages and emphasizes that *common experience serves as a unifying force between sender and receiver.* When this common experience is expressed in words and terms shared and understood by the source there's even more reason to expect that communication will be well received.

There are, of course, problems concerned with the common experience precept. Very often there are no common experiences that have been shared by source and receiver, and there are many times when messages are expressed in words and terms that have lost meaning or are irrelevant to the receiver. Some communicators, however, seem to go out of their way to avoid common experience by beaming messages that are either cute or far-fetched and which might relieve life's daily tedium but do little to bring about desired communication effects.

The world of the television commercial continues to serve up intriguing examples of messages which violate sound communication precepts. They bring us white knights who ride through our kitchen waving magic cleansing potions; charming ladies who discuss their intimate underarm and "feminine hygiene" problems in the middle of cocktail gatherings; smiling gasoline attendants who not only gas up our cars but are willing to spend precious minutes discussing shock absorbers, mileage tips, oil treatment cues, and tire rotation principles.

There's one small problem with all these scenes; they have little relationship to reality. White knights don't ride through kitchens, and even if they did they'd seem very much out of place in the kitchens of the millions of blacks who have the same cleaning problems as the rest of us. The last thing in the world that charming ladies discuss at cocktail parties is deodorants. Gasoline station attendants not only do not smile very much, but if we are to judge from the growing number of self-service pumps, they haven't even the time to gas up our autos, much less discuss all those other problems the commercials indicate they're so willing to talk about.

Thus, one of the first lessons for the communicator is to avoid stressing and creating uncommon experiences in fashioning messages. The second is to seek out, stress, and communicate common experiences in words and terms that have meaning and relevance to the recipient. And the third is to find ways to uncover common experiences when they don't seem to exist.

The last point requires some careful thought and a dash of creativity. When polling organizations conduct surveys in Watts or Harlem they make sure their pollsters are blacks and not whites. When colleges send representatives to College Days, they don't send the oldest members of the admission staff but those who have most recently been graduated. Although relatively small sums are collected from house-to-house canvassing, local social and health organizations continue to utilize such neighborhood canvassing because they know it brings better understanding of their activities, since the canvasser and those canvassed share common experiences and talk the same language.

These examples all show the use of selectivity by large organizations in choosing the sources to put across their messages, and the common denominator in such selectivity is common experience with the recipients. The precept operates on all levels. If you want to reach the scientific community, you utilize by-lined articles by scientists within your organization because they share the same experience and use the same language as the readers of the publications in which their articles appear. If you want to have a new journalism textbook adopted for classroom use, you seek endorsements from leading journalism professors. The wise communicator, in short, selects those representatives who have most in common with and talk the same language as the intended audience.

Messages Should Be Tailor-Made for the Situation, Time, Place, and Audience

Elsewhere in this text it has been pointed out that tailor-made suits have a distinct advantage over mass-produced suits because they fit better. They also cost more because of the time and skills involved, and of course this has to be taken into consideration, particularly if you're operating on a limited budget.

There is no doubt, however, that given the time, talent, and money necessary to cover their cost and other production aspects, tailor-made messages have a distinct advantage over other messages. Because they're crafted with care they indicate to the receiver that "this message is meant for you."

Innumerable examples can be cited to illustrate the principle of the tailor-made message. One doesn't address a street gang as one would a gathering of bank officials. Yelling "fire" in the middle of a noisy city street won't have the same effect as yelling "fire" in a crowded and hushed theater. When a father is concerned about an impending layoff he doesn't react kindly to a request for a new car, though he might listen if you hit him up just after his ten-dollar bet paid off at 30 to 1 in the fourth race.

If you care to go back that far—and who does?—you might recall the kind of messages you sent out when you were between the ages of five and eight and wanted an ice cream bar on a hot summer day.

At the age of five you simply asked for an ice cream bar and if you got it, fine; if not, a few tears. At the age of six you didn't just ask for an ice cream bar but demanded it, and as this became a test of wills you more than likely didn't get it. At the age of seven you not only demanded an ice cream bar but you pointed out quite clearly that you were the only kid on the street who wasn't allowed to have an ice cream bar. At the age of eight you began playing off your father against your mother, and if that didn't work you went out and bought the bar yourself with money from your piggy bank.

What you were doing was applying the tailor-made principle by changing your message to fit the situation, time, and audience and at the same time using feedback and peer group pressures as a wedge. The only variable remaining constant was the place, though of course that could have been a factor had you been at home one year, on vacation the next, etc.

The same principle applies in the adult world. At one period or another, a message might be tailored to fit a situation with the other three variables remaining constant. Or, it might be tailored to fit both a situation and an audience, with the other two variables remaining constant. Here are some examples:

It is August 1 and you have announced you will be a candidate for reelection in the November mayoralty election and will run on your record of having maintained full employment in your city. On August 30 the largest plant in the city announces it is closing down effective next week. The time, place, and the audience have remained constant, but the situation now calls for a new message to be beamed at the electorate.

It is August 30, same city. You are director of public relations for the firm which owns the plant that will be closed down next week. This is but one of thirty such plants in the country and it is obsolete, and hence the decision to move its operations to a more modern installation. The firm's profits are at an all-time high and the firm is in excellent shape in all respects. The story announcing the closing will be shaped one way as released locally; another way as released in the city to which the operation will be moved; and another way as released to national trade and business publications. Thus, the situation and time remain constant, but the place and audience differ and thus will require different message treatments.

Tailoring a message should not be construed as telling one story to one audience and an entirely different story to another, for this would be akin to selling one piece of goods to one customer and a cheaper piece of goods to another and charging both the same price. You can alter the fit, but you should be sure that the basic material of the message is the same.

CHANNELS

In the communication process a channel is a *passageway, pathway,* or *means* by which a message passes from source to receiver. Used in this way, it's clear that a communication channel can be a smoke signal; the voice in face-to-face situations; radio, television, newspapers, magazines, and books in communication by means of the mass media. It is also possible to categorize channels in terms of whether they are **interpersonal or mediated** (face-to-face versus a telephone conference call); **personal or impersonal** (a meeting of 10 people versus an outdoor gathering of 50,000 addressed by means of loud speakers); **assembled** or **nonassembled** (the same outdoor gathering versus a television audience of millions watching and listening to a political speech in their homes). Although in each instance the forms set forth above seem to be in contrast to each other, they should not be thought of as being opposed to each other or mutually exclusive. As Schramm points out, "Distinctions and boundaries are much less clear than that. Most campaigns aimed at teaching or persuading try to combine media and personal channels so that one will reinforce and supplement the other. Political campaigners use all the media but still arrange door-to-door visits and public meetings. Family planning, agricultural, and health campaigns maintain field staffs but support them with all the media they can afford."[5]

The majority of communication situations involving public relations practitioners call for channels or message vehicles that are impersonal and/or mediated. This does not mean that they are more effective than other forms of channels—on the contrary, they are often less effective—but simply that the communication situation makes it impossible to use other channels. *Modern society is structured to make it an impossibility to deal with receivers or recipients of messages on a face-to-face, personal, direct basis in most situations.* For this reason the professional communicator has to rely on channels that are impersonal, indirect, and usually nonassembled.

This means in turn that there will be some intervening mediating mechanism, force, or organization occupying the channel between source and receiver. Even when the group to whom we are addressing our messages is assembled in one place, the group may be so large that the intervening, mediating mechanism has to be some method of voice amplification. When the group is out of sight the intervening, mediating mechanism or force could be in the control of the public relations practitioner—such as in the case of an internal publication, annual report, or annual meeting—or it could be out of the practitioner's control.

The channels to be considered in the discussion that follows are those that are out of the control of the practitioner but are nonetheless of the most importance and significance in the process of reaching mass audiences. These channels are the four mass media: *newspapers, radio, television,* and *magazines.* These mass media channels will be analyzed in terms of the following five questions raised by Berlo:[6]

1. What is available?

2. Which channels are received by the most people?

3. Which channels have the greatest impact?

4. Which channels are most adaptable to the source's purpose?

5. Which channels are most adaptable to the content of the message?

After analysis of the five questions raised by Berlo, we will sum up our discussion of channels by relating them to a relatively new concept called "agenda-setting."

KEY CONSIDERATIONS ABOUT CHANNELS

In taking up these five questions we will deal mainly with newspapers, radio, television, and magazines because they are the mass media that reach people on a systematic, regular basis and are most often used by public relations practitioners as message channels. Books and films—especially the sponsored film—are important and valuable channels for public relations messages, but they are not used as frequently as the four media on a regular basis by practitioners, and in addition the sponsored book and film are within the control of the practitioner and hence outside the parameters of this analysis.

What Is Available?

For the most part when communication scholars analyze the communication process and discuss the mass media they do not dwell at length on the subject of availability. Presumably this is a nonacademic matter, but for the public relations practitioner the subject of availability is highly relevant. To what avail—other than that of making the practitioner wiser—is knowledge and understanding of the mass media channels if these media are unavailable? Obviously, availability embodies very practical considerations for the public relations practitioner.

A quick, knee-jerk reaction to the question of mass media availability might be, why of course they're available, accessible, ready for use. But are they really, and to what degree? Even the beginner knows that if you want to promote Product X or Idea Y you can't just wave a magic wand and find your story on the AP or UPI wire, the front page of the Chicago *Tribune*, or a prime-time television show. Something stands between the wish and the fulfillment, and that something is most easily described by the term known as "the gatekeeper."

The mass media gatekeeper has been described in a variety of ways. The fact that the mass media are highly organized and complex means that the organization itself serves as a gatekeeper and therefore the practitioner has to understand how the media operate if he or she is to get past the gatekeeper.

The term *gatekeeper* means a person involved in guarding the mass media gates against intrusion by outsiders, and this person is found at numerous stages in the process of transmitting information, ideas, opinions, and entertainment by means of the mass media. Some typical gatekeepers are the person who selects the guests that appear on popular late-evening TV shows; the section editor of a business publication and the editor of a trade publication; the disc jockey on local radio shows; wire service editors on state and national levels; assignment editors on network news organizations and on daily newspapers; the copy desk editor on all dailies.

Each of these goes through a process of *selection* and *elimination* in choosing from the "glut of occurrences" those items which, in the opinion of the gatekeeper, deserve to win out in the competition for attention. In the final analysis, therefore, it's comforting to know that the mass media are available to the public relations practitioner, but it's more important to know that at the same time the gatekeeper is constantly on guard to permit entry only to those messages which deserve to reach the mass audience. What the practitioner wants and desires is important, but **more important is to understand the professional wants, desires, and interests of the gatekeepers, because they open the gates only when these are met.** Gatekeepers make their selection on the basis of maximum appeal to the audience served by their medium, and thus the most important factor in eventual use of material is the gatekeepers' perception of what will most interest their audience.

Which Channels Are Received by the Most People?

In order to understand the nature of the mass media audience, it's important to understand the complexities of the mass media system. To an increasing extent, this audience in 1984 was a much more fragmented one than existed in the 1970s. A major reason for this fragmentation was the fact that cable television by 1984 was able to reach more than 40 percent of the national television audience. Another was the slippage in the audience figures for the three major television networks. A third was the advent of teletext and videotext into the television market. Thus, by 1984 the total audience pie had to be cut into more slices than in the 1970s, hence the fragmentation of the total media audience.

The mass media system is much more complicated than seems evident on a surface reading of its figures. For example, there were in 1983 over 700 more daily newspapers (1,730) than television stations (1,000 commercial and public stations), and five times as many weekly newspapers (between 8,000 and 10,000) and radio stations (9,800) as daily newspapers. However, the number of television households reached the 83 million figure in 1983, while the total circulation for all daily newspapers was 62.2 million.

Another way to look at the mass media audience is to note the audience for single units within each medium. For example, the combined circulation of all *Reader's Digest* editions is more than 28 million and the audience for a prime-time television show numbers about 21 million. The first installment of the miniseries "The Thorn Birds" attracted 80 million viewers when it was aired in March, 1983. In that same month Gannett's new national newspaper, *USA Today*, reached the 1.1 million mark and the circulation of *Time* magazine stood at 4.5 million.

A final way of looking at the mass media audience is to recognize that it's an overlapping one. Though there are millions of people who only look at television and do not read a daily newspaper or magazine, there are more millions who not only view television but also listen to radio and read a daily newspaper and magazine.

Thus, the public relations practitioner must not only know data relating to the number of radio and television sets in American homes, stations, and networks; the number of daily and weekly newspapers and magazines; the nature of affiliations; and the audience for each medium; but he must also analyze the **specifics about the data as they relate to the organization he represents.** The data, in summation, have meaning only insofar as they are carefully applied to the practitioner's public relations needs and problems.

Which Channels Have the Greatest Impact?

Study after study has demonstrated the pervasive role of the mass media in American life. They show the following:

> Eight out of ten adults read one or more daily newspapers on the average weekday and spend an average of 35 minutes a day on them.

> On any weekday evening, 100 million Americans are likely to be watching television. The average home set is in use more than 6 hours a day and individual viewing is now more than 3 hours a day.

> The approximately 40 percent of Americans who read magazines regularly spend an average of 33 minutes a day on them.

> The one-third of Americans who read books regularly spend an average of 47 minutes a day on them.

> The audience for radio is far greater than that for any other single medium of mass communication.[7]

There is no doubt about the profound impact that mass media make on public information, knowledge, culture, and patterns of living. There is considerable speculation, however, about the extent of *specific effects* resulting *from exposure to specific media.* On occasion, it has been possible to prove the spectacular effect that exposure to a specific medium has had on people, but these instances are few and far between.

> The evening of October 30, 1938, Orson Welles and his CBS radio theatre group dramatized an imaginary invasion from Mars. The hour-long drama was prefaced by the announcement that the show was a dramatization of a novel by H. G. Wells. The show itself consisted of extremely realistic bulletins and newscasts, interspersed with music, flashes from the "scene," interviews with "experts," the police, and eye-witnesses.

> The reaction was panic on the part of thousands of listeners and others who were contacted by listeners. Thousands of people called the police and agencies of the federal government; other thousands warned their friends; and still other thousands took direct action by packing up their family and belongings and driving away from the Eastern seaboard where the invasion from Mars was supposedly taking place.

Few of the effects of the mass media are as direct and sharp as those resulting from the "Invasion from Mars" radio broadcast. For the most part, the effects of the mass media are cumulative, long-term, and hard to isolate. There is more or less general agreement that the mass media:

1. **Do not ordinarily have a direct effect on audiences but rather operate through a variety of mediating factors and influences.**

2. **Basically reinforce rather than convert.** Thus, most studies show that exposure to mass media campaigns solidifies the attitudes and opinions of their audience but does not generally change attitudes and opinions.

3. **Serve to confer status.** The mass media focus attention on people and organizations,

and they also tend to "feed on" each other. Hitherto relatively unknown people and organizations suddenly become known throughout the country because they catch the attention of the mass media and are featured in newspaper stories, on talk shows, and in magazine articles.

4. **Provide the source with credibility.** Because they're considered to be impartial and nonpartisan, mass media messages are deemed to be more credible than those stemming directly from a public relations source.

Answering the question as to which of the mass media has the greatest impact is difficult if not impossible because of public exposure to the message by multi-media. We do know radio provides the **swiftest** means of information dissemination; that television provides the **most dramatic** coverage of events; that newspapers and magazines provide the most **in-depth** dissemination of news and information; and that all of them combined provide our basic view of the American scene and Lippmann's world which is "out of sight, out of mind."

Which Channels Are Most Adaptable to the Source's Purpose and to the Content of the Message?

The two questions relating to channels are so closely related they are being taken up as a unit rather than individually. The key word is "adaptable" and it correctly implies that each medium has certain characteristics that make it more suitable than the others for specific purposes. All too often practitioners utilize a particular channel—most of the time it's the newspaper—because they're more at home in that channel's milieu. But the newspaper may not be the best medium for the source's purpose or for the content of the message; hence the question reminds us that there's a need for purposeful rather than random communication.

Marshall McLuhan, the Canadian sage who was much in vogue in the sixties, cryptically maintained that "the medium is the message." If he is taken literally he means that the nature of the medium itself, irrespective of the contents of the message, is what makes the difference in the communication process. Another way of stating McLuhan's thesis is that form is more important than substance.

Though McLuhan presents us with an intriguing view of the media and though there is validity to his contention about the unique importance of the nature of the media, his thesis is too all-embracing and sweeping to be accepted at face value. The nature of the medium does affect communication, but so do the nature of the source, message, channel, and receiver. A more fruitful line of inquiry in regard to the question about the media and their adaptability to the source's purpose and the content of the message is to consider the question in terms of the three essential roles of media: to inform, influence, and entertain.

If the purpose of the source is to **inform,** one has to rate print media as being more adaptable than the electronic media for the transmission of *detailed* information. It is true that radio and television may be the first to inform us of events, actions, and activities, but the information they provide is admittedly sketchy and superficial. As a nationally known, highly respected television commentator has observed, the entire contents of a half-hour network news show would take up only one part of the front page of the New York *Times.* Furthermore, as to content of the message, the more complex and specialized the information, the more adaptable it is to newspapers and magazines.

Thus, if the source wants to get across information quickly and is not dealing with detailed and involved material, the electronic media would best suit the source's purpose. However, if the source is dealing with information not easily digested at a glance or a first hearing, newspapers and magazines would be more suitable both for the source's purpose and for the contents of the message.

If the purpose of the source and the message contents are meant to **influence,** we are faced with a situation where no one medium has a singular advantage over all the others. Radio and television have the advantage of *immediacy* in terms of influencing people, but there is no evidence to support the view that this influence has long-range, carry-over effects. Television's unique ability to take its audience right into the middle of an event or activity with both sight and sound provides that medium with vivid impact value, but again there is no evidence to support the view that this influence has long-range, carry-over effects. Highly respected print media—particularly columnists with large followings and publications that influence others through their editorials and investigative reporting—have immediate and also carry-over impact when their ideas and thoughts are picked up by others. But again, there is no conclusive proof of their long-range effects.

Equally important in the context of the relationship among source purpose, message content, and adaptability is the problem of *entry* and *control.* The three network evening news shows reach an audience of between forty and forty-five million homes, but getting past the gatekeepers on these shows is a very difficult task. Getting past newspaper and magazine gatekeepers is also difficult, but not as difficult as with television because the total "news hole" is larger on print media. Of course, control of the material is always in the hands of the media except in the case of paid advertising.

Because it is paid for and its composition is in the hands of the practitioner, public relations advertising surmounts both the entry and control problem and has been used often by practitioners by way of the print media. Such advertisements can be targeted to specific publics and later "merchandised" to other audiences for maximum exposure. There have been instances where they've had considerable impact—two that come to mind are the Byoir advertisements in behalf of the A&P and the Whitaker & Baxter advertisements in behalf of the AMA—but there has been no proof about the effects of the vast bulk of such public relations advertising.

If the purpose of the source and the message contents is to **entertain,** there is no doubt that television is the prime medium. People receive a good deal of their information about the world and are influenced in many respects by what they view on television, but the major strength of the medium is in its ability to entertain. Further, if we consider entertainment in the broadest sense we find that television also has the ability to meet Lasswell's concept of the media as transmitters of culture and the social fabric. Through its combination of sound and picture, television brings us the world of dance, music, drama, manners, dress, living patterns, and the many other aspects of our national life. Print media entertain and transmit culture through features, comics, essays, columns, and long articles, but they come in a poor second to television—and one might say, even a second to radio in terms of popular music—when it comes to entertainment.

Summing up, in considering adaptability of the various media to the source's purpose and message content, the practitioner has to understand and recognize the major assets and deficits created by the nature of the individual medium. In most instances, this will result in the use of all media by the practitioner, but with careful attention to the specific reasons for communication by the source. Some advantages and disadvantages of four mass media are set forth in Table 13.1.

Channels as Agenda-Setters

The *agenda-setting* function of the mass media is of major interest to the practitioner who uses research as a tool in the public relations process. By agenda-setting we mean *the ability of the media to influence the public's perception of the important topics and issues of the day.*

The concept of agenda-setting can be traced back to Walter Lippmann, when he noted more than half a century ago that the press is a major factor in forming "the pictures in our head" of the unseen world around us. Neither Lippmann nor Bernard Cohen, who

TABLE 13.1

Advantages and Disadvantages of Four Mass Media

Television

Advantages	*Disadvantages*
1. Combines sight, sound and motion attributes	1. Message limited by restricted time segments
2. Permits physical demonstration of product	2. No possibility for consumer referral to message
3. Believability due to immediacy of message	3. Availabilities sometimes difficult to arrange
4. High impact of message	4. High time costs
5. Huge audiences	5. Waste coverage
6. Good product identification	6. High production costs
7. Popular medium	7. Poor color transmission

Radio

Advantages	*Disadvantages*
1. Selectivity of geographical markets	1. Message limited by restricted time segments
2. Good saturation of local markets	2. No possibility for consumer referral to message
3. Ease of changing advertising copy	3. No visual appeal
4. Relatively low cost	4. Waste coverage

Magazines

Advantages	*Disadvantages*
1. Selectivity of audience	1. Often duplicate circulation
2. Reaches more affluent consumers	2. Usually cannot dominate in a local market
3. Offers prestige to an advertiser	3. Long closing dates
4. Pass-along readership	4. No immediacy of message
5. Good color reproduction	5. Sometimes high production costs

Newspapers

Advantages	*Disadvantages*
1. Selectivity of geographical markets	1. High cost for national coverage
2. Ease of changing advertising copy	2. Shortness of message life
3. Reaches all income groups	3. Waste circulation
4. Ease of scheduling advertisements	4. Differences of sizes and formats
5. Relatively low cost	5. Rate differentials between local and national advertisements
6. Good medium for manufacturer/dealer advertising	6. Poor color reproduction

Source: Leon Quera, *Advertising Campaigns: Formulation and Tactics* (Columbus, Ohio: Grid Publishing Co., 1973), pp. 71-74. Reprinted with permission.

analyzed the role of the press in shaping foreign policy in the sixties, called the concept "agenda-setting," but they perceived it as such nonetheless.

It was in the seventies that Maxwell McCombs, Donald Shaw, and their fellow mass communication researchers started to carry out the first formal empirical tests of the agenda-setting hypothesis. Through their many field studies these researchers explored the different ways in which the mass media as channels tell us *what to think about.* These studies, which are continuing at time of this publication, concern themselves with the manifold ways in which the media "set the agenda" for public knowledge, attitudes, and opinions. As McCombs puts it:

> Through its patterns of selection and play of the daily news, the press presents the public a continuous stream of cues about the relative importance of various topics and events. Newspapers clearly communicate salience through page placement, headline size, and the amount of space accorded an item. Television news formats also provide cues about the relative salience of news events.
>
> . . . Agenda setting is a relational concept specifying a positive relationship between the emphases of the news media and the perceived importance of these topics to the mass audience.
>
> . . . Effective public relations requires lead time, and opportunities to communicate before an issue is approaching its zenith.[8]

The agenda-setting role of the mass media in the communication and public relations process is a vital one. By carefully watching the media and by keeping up with communication research studies, the practitioner can track issues and events as they become part of the "public agenda." In so doing he or she should be able to deal with issues when they first appear rather than after they've reached their apex.

RECEIVER-RECIPIENT

Just as Banquo's ghost hovered in the background to haunt Shakespeare's Macbeth, so does the receiver-recipient hover in the background of the communication process to haunt the source. As has been noted, the receiver is all-important, although all too often he is neglected or given insufficient thought by the source-sender when messages are conceived and transmitted.

> Most big-league pitchers don't simply throw baseballs to big-league batters and hope their good old fast ball will smack in the strike zone. They study the line-up before the game, picking out the weak and the strong hitters and planning their general pitching strategy. When they face the batter they take note of the particular situation existing when the batter comes to plate; study his stance; try to figure out what the batter knows about the pitcher's delivery and whether he's a sucker for a fast ball, curve, or change-up. Then, after an exchange of signals with the catcher and some tugging at his cap, the pitcher slams one over.

Public relations practitioners would do well to emulate successful big-league pitchers. This calls for a careful study of the receiver from many different angles and perspectives, the most important of which are the *receiver's knowledge, communication skills, predispositions and group membership,* what Schramm has termed the *"fraction of selection,"* and *opinion leaders.*

THE RECEIVER'S KNOWLEDGE

In considering the receiver's knowledge we are thinking of two forms of knowledge: general knowledge and knowledge about the source.

General knowledge provides a clue about the receiver's ability to absorb information or ideas transmitted by the source. For the most part, communicators err when they operate on the assumption that the average person is well informed simply because he's bombarded on all sides with information from a wide variety of sources. Despite the advanced stage of media in the United States, the widespread ownership of radio and television sets, the millions who read newspapers and magazines, the fact remains that only a fraction of information and ideas gets through the invisible net that people seem to cast about themselves.

Study after study has proven that people are ignorant about such elementary facts as the name of their congressman and senators, vice-presidential candidates, the secretary of state, etc. Little wonder, therefore, that even after repeated exposure to mass media identification messages millions of people don't know whether it's Goodrich or Goodyear that sponsors those blimps; whether it's Westinghouse or General Electric in whom you can put your trust; and whether it's Vantage or True that has the lowest nicotine and tar content. If there's so little knowledge about high officials and oft-repeated slogans—and there is—then a wise course is to **assume that most people have less knowledge about your organization than you think they have.** Better yet, rather than draw assumptions, conduct a study to ascertain for certain the degree of knowledge held by the publics you're trying to reach. Readership studies provide tangible evidence of reader knowledge as well as opinions about employee publications, and public opinion surveys provide similar input about public knowledge and opinions about organizations.

THE RECEIVER'S COMMUNICATION SKILLS

Communication skills are important factors for the source, but they are equally important for the receiver although they involve a different set of skills. When dealing with the receiver's communication skills we are concerned mainly with the skills of reading, listening, and viewing (and tangentially with the skills of writing and speaking as they relate to feedback). When we're writing for an employee public we need to know the *decoding skill levels* existing within that public, and we should be cognizant of the probability that a management audience will be more highly educated than an hourly employee audience and hence can understand and absorb a higher level of language, expression, and thought.

Similarly, in dealing with the television audience we should recognize that the decoding level of the audience at 7:30 p.m. will differ from that of the audience at 11:30 p.m., not merely in terms of educational levels but in terms of sophistication and insight.

In short, there's need to understand there are different decoding communication skill levels that operate within, as well as between and among, media audiences. With some exceptions, one shouldn't expect to find the same decoding communication skills among readers of the median-sized daily newspaper of 18,000 circulation and among the readers of the New York *Times;* among the vast radio audience and the readers of *Scientific American;* among readers of the *Reader's Digest* and readers of the *Atlantic.* Preparing communications for these disparate audiences entails recognizing the varying decoding communication skill levels existing within each audience and then tailoring messages to match these levels.

> Although hourly employees do not generally have as high a level of language, expression, and education as management personnel, they should not be treated and viewed condescendingly.

> A major flaw of much employee communication is the tendency of the source to "talk down" to the receiver. The average hourly employee may not have the skills needed to decode messages about the international balance of payments, but he certainly has the skills needed to decode messages relating to *his* job, *his* paycheck, and *his* union. In matters affecting him closely and personally, he can decode company propaganda and "snow jobs" better than a cryptographer can decipher enemy messages.

AUDIENCE PREDISPOSITIONS AND GROUP MEMBERSHIP

Within every audience there exist certain *predispositions* that govern the way in which members of the audience will react to messages. In part these predispositions are individual in nature and tied to an individual's basic personality, early upbringing, and education. To a great extent—as noted by the Yale psychologists Hovland, Janis and Kelley—these predispositions result from conformity tendencies induced by group membership. They are based on the individual's perception of the behavior expected of him by the group to which he belongs and often govern the manner in which he will react to messages from the source. Hovland states the point this way:

> An analysis of the influence of groups upon the attitudes of their members is of obvious importance to the general problem of changing opinions through communications. Communicators often use these social incentives to facilitate acceptance of the opinion they advocate. For instance, community leaders frequently assert that group approval will follow upon the adoption of their recommendation or that disapproval will be the consequence of failure to accept it. On the other hand, a specific recommendation may encounter resistance because a group provides strong incentives for holding original opinions. Certain methods of persuasion entail lowering the importance of the incentives delivered by the group . . . or increasing the incentive value of competing groups.[9]

The concept of group membership affecting reception of messages is a reaffirmation of the point made earlier in this chapter about the modification of the old "hypodermic needle" theory. That theory, as may be recalled, postulated that each individual is directly needled by the message sent through the media. However, everyone is part of a network of family, occupational, and social groupings, and these influence an individual's opinions and reactions to messages. **How an individual is affected by messages transmitted by the source is shaped in large part by the groups to which the individual is attached.**

Thus, when the statement is made that public relations practitioners should be applied social scientists, this means that practitioners have to understand and be sensitive both to individual predispositions and to group membership because of the important role they play in the reception to messages. Members of the mass audience may be anonymous to the communicator but they are not inert. Rather, they are part of an active social environment, and it's the wise communicator who acknowledges, understands, and keeps that environment in mind when he fashions and transmits messages.

> One of the differences between journalists and public relations practitioners is that journalists take data and facts and fashion them into a story without too much concern for other factors. In dealing with facts and data practitioners must be constantly aware that both they and their intended receivers are members of their group environments with all the pressures that such environments may exert. The message that passes from source to receiver is inevitably affected by the groups to which *both* are linked—hence the need for the practitioners to recognize not merely their own group allegiance, but also that of the source.

SCHRAMM'S "FRACTION OF SELECTION" HYPOTHESIS

As a rule-of-thumb way of explaining the chance of an individual selecting any given communication, Wilbur Schramm devised an interesting formula which he calls the "fraction of selection" hypothesis. His formula is stated as follows:

$$\frac{\text{Promise of reward}}{\text{Effort required}} = \text{Probability of selection}$$

The promise of reward, as Schramm sees it, refers chiefly to the content of messages and the likelihood that they will satisfy needs as felt at any given time. The effort required refers to the availability of media and the ease of using a particular medium.

According to Schramm, the probability of a particular communication being selected can be raised *either* by decreasing the lower term (the expected difficulty) or by increasing the upper term (the expected reward).

Thus, notes Schramm, people select an easily available television show rather than entertainment which they have to go out of their homes to see or hear. In short, there is little effort required of the recipient in choosing television entertainment over other forms. At the same time, perhaps from past experience from viewing a particular show, the recipient seeks out those shows which have rewarded him in the past.

"Over the years," says Schramm, "a person tends to seek the kinds of communication that have rewarded him in the past—his favorite television programs, a built-in expectation of reward developed from looking in certain places. Beyond that, he tends, other things being equal, to select the cues of information which are close at hand and easy to find in the glut of communication."

Schramm is well aware that his fraction of selection approach is a generalized one because he warns that at some time and in some situations, some information is so important a person will go to almost any effort to secure it. As an example, he notes that we may be willing to spend years studying to get a Ph.D. even though the easier path is to be satisfied with an undergraduate degree.[10]

OPINION LEADERS

The role that opinion leaders play in the communication process has been studied chiefly by sociologists and political scientists and has resulted in field studies carried out in both small towns and cities. These studies have assayed the manner in which political decisions are made and influenced by opinion leaders; the manner in which decisions on selected issues have filtered down from small groups of influentials to the mass public; the manner in which influentials use the mass and specialized media to influence their information-input patterns and in turn influence selected publics; and similar patterns of selectivity, leadership, and influence by key persons. From the many studies which have focused on selected field situations have come some generalized concepts of opinion leadership as they apply to the communication process. These are summarized briefly below:

Opinion leaders and the people they influence are often very much alike and typically belong to the same primary groups.

What this concept means is that we not only find so-called elite opinion leaders, but we find opinion leaders operating within groups and sub-groups. There is seldom a group of leaders who influence everyone in all groups on all issues, but rather leaders who influence—to name some examples—union members, political clubs, social organizations, ethnic groups, educational bodies, and so forth. The problem for the practitioner is in ascertaining who are the opinion leaders in each group considered important to the communicator. If this can be done, then the communicator can key messages to these leaders in the expectation that the leaders in turn will transmit them to a wider sub-public.

Opinion leaders are more exposed than others to contact with the outside world by means of the mass media.

A study relating to the use of hybrid seed corn showed that it took fourteen years to gain widespread adoption of the new seed corn by farmers. The study showed there were five stages to adoption: awareness, interest, evaluation, trial, and adoption. The leaders in adoption—those who first demonstrated awareness—were the most widely read. However, one should not automatically assume there is a simple two-step flow from media to opinion leaders to followers. Opinion leaders rely on *many* sources for their information and ideas, and they are also influenced by others whom they consider to be leaders.

Opinion leaders utilize a variety of media and means in relating their groups to relevant parts of society.

A study carried out in Decatur, Illinois, showed that large-city newspapers served to relate fashions to the fashion leaders. A study of doctors showed that out-of-town meetings were important sources of information about new medical ideas. The hybrid seed corn study showed that contact with the city and with farm bureaus of agricultural colleges were important for the farm innovators. Thus, general media, meetings, colleges, specialized media, and a wide variety of sources are used by opinion leaders in gaining information and ideas.[11]

In summation, opinion leaders are important as they relate to the receiver in the communication process, but once again we must remember that we are talking about a process in which an almost limitless number of factors are involved. Being aware of these factors and their roles in the process is only the first step in achieving real understanding of the complex nature of communication between and among people.

ENDNOTES

1. Carl Hovland, Irving Janis, and Harold Kelley, *Communication and Persuasion* (New Haven: Yale University Press, 1953), p. 269.
2. From a talk by Gerhard Wiebe, reprinted in Raymond Simon's *Perspectives in Public Relations* (Norman, Oklahoma: University of Oklahoma Press, 1966), p. 138.
3. Edward J. Robinson, *Communication and Public Relations* (Columbus, Ohio: Charles E. Merrill, 1966), p. 212.
4. Ibid., p. 225.
5. Wilbur Schramm and William E. Porter, *Men, Women, Messages and Media* (New York: Harper and Row, 1982), p. 109.
6. David K. Berlo, *The Process of Communication* (New York: Holt, Rinehart, and Winston, 1960), p. 65.
7. Schramm and Porter, p. 139.
8. Maxwell McCombs, "The Agenda-Setting Function of the Mass Media," *Public Relations Review*, Winter 1977, p. 90.
9. Hovland, Janis, and Kelley, p. 134.
10. Schramm and Porter, pp. 96-98.
11. Elihu Katz and Paul Lazarsfeld, *Personal Influence* (New York: The Free Press, 1964).

PROJECTS, ASSIGNMENTS, AND MINIS

1. A LESSON IN INTELLIGENCE OPERATIONS: A MINI-CASE

In his book *The Man Who Never Was*, Ewen Montague tells how British Intelligence used a dead man to pull off an intelligence coup in World War II prior to the invasion of Italy. They took an unknown dead man; provided him with a complete life history and identity as a major in the Royal Marines; packed him in ice; shipped him off on a submarine after planting a letter and some documents on him; and dumped him into the sea in the dead of night near Huelva on the southwest coast of Spain. These elaborate procedures were followed to give the impression that the "officer" had gone down in a plane crash and washed up on shore in an area where the British knew a German intelligence person was operating. The hope was that the Germans would be fooled into believing that the Allies did not intend to invade Sicily (which they did) and would draw away their troops and vessels. In describing the "vital document" which was the means by which he hoped to fool the Germans, Montague cited the problem as follows:

> If the German General Staff was to be persuaded, in face of all probabilities, to bank on our next target being somewhere other than Sicily, it would have to have before it a document which was passing between officers who *must* know what our real plans were, who could not possibly be mistaken and who could not themselves be the victims of a cover plan. If the operation was to be worthwhile, I had to have a document written by someone, and to someone, whom the Germans knew—and whom they knew to be "right in the know."

> So I put up the proposal that General Sir Archibald Nye, the Vice-Chief of the Imperial General Staff, should write the letter and that he should write it to General Alexander (who commanded an army in Tunisia, under General Eisenhower) at 18th Army Group Headquarters. . . . The letter should be what we junior officers called "the old boy type" . . . and the sort of friendly letter which can give information and explanations that can't be put into an official communication. That sort of letter, and that sort of letter only, could convey convincingly to the Germans the indication that our next target was not Sicily, and yet could be found in the possession of an officer and not in a bag full of the usual documents going from home to our army abroad.

> I was aiming high, and I had to. I expected something of an explosion, and I got it. For many of even the most able and efficient people failed to appreciate what was wanted for this sort of job; for to realize that needed a particular sort of approach and a peculiar sort of mind that could look at the same puzzle from several different angles at the same time.

> You are a British Intelligence Officer; you have an opposite number in the enemy Intelligence, say in Berlin; and above him is the German Operational Command. What you, a Briton with a British background, think can be deduced from a document does not matter. It is what *your opposite number*, with his German knowledge and background, will think that matters—what construction *he* will put on the document. Therefore, if you want *him* to think such-and-such a thing, you must give him something which will make *him* (and not *you*) think it. But he may be suspicious and want confirmation; you must think what inquiries will *he* make (not what inquiries *you* would make) and give him the answers to those inquiries so as to satisfy him. In other words, you must remember that a German does not think and react as an Englishman does, and you must put yourself into his mind. . . .*

Questions for Discussion

1. In what specific respect do the above case and excerpt illustrate and exemplify some of the major key points made about communication in this chapter?

---

*Ewen Montague, *The Man Who Never Was* (Lippincott, 1954), p. 43.

---

2. What lessons does the case teach you about the communication process?

3. Can you cite any personal communication experiences or observations of your own to illustrate the same points?

2. A TEST OF SITUATIONAL ACUITY: A MINI-CASE

You are 27 years old and the coordinator of external publicity of a profitable division of a large industrial corporation. The division sells information services rather than a hard product, and its customers are other business firms.

Head of the communication department to which you belong is a director whose background has been chiefly in advertising. Reporting to him are two managers, one of whom is your immediate superior.

Your division has recently had a change of presidents, switching from an outgoing, affable, publicity-conscious chief executive to a more reserved president whose background is technical and who is very wary of the press. One of the new president's first moves is to schedule a meeting with the director and the two managers of the communication department, but due to an unavoidable conflict in his schedule the manager to whom you report is unable to make the meeting. He is to be gone a week, and the director agrees that you can substitute for him at the briefing which is scheduled a week from today.

Before leaving, your superior calls you into his office to warn you that the new president does not believe in interviews with the press "particularly because investigative reporting has even filtered down into the ranks of the business and trade press." He further says: "In no circumstances say that interviews with him are necessary or desirable because his philosophy is that he won't grant interviews."

These remarks disturb you because your job is to get favorable publicity for the division. Both of you are aware that you were given a relatively free hand to arrange interviews with the previous president and the record shows that the ones you scheduled resulted in excellent coverage by the trade and business press. However, because your superior is obviously in a rush to take off on his trip you don't press the point.

A half hour before the scheduled morning briefing with the president—and as a result of a good deal of spadework on your part over the previous weeks—your contact on a leading national business publication calls to inform you that he has been assigned to handle a cover story the two of you had been discussing. The story will deal in depth with the information service field, and as your division is a leader in the field the writer would like to interview your new president. You tell him you will see what you can do, and it is agreed you will call back that afternoon.

Because the call came in just prior to the meeting you have no time to discuss it with the director of the communication department. You are well aware, though, that he reports directly to the president and has remarked more than once that whoever signs his paycheck is entitled to deal with the press in any manner he chooses.

When your turn comes to make your presentation you do a very good job, and you know it's good because the new president nods warmly at its conclusions and says something like "very impressive" to the director of the communication department. The president then turns to you and says: "What do you think of my policy against personal interviews?"

Questions for Discussion

1. What would you say in response to the president's question? Do not generalize, but state exactly what you would say. (The instructor may want to set up a role-playing situation here.)

2. Explain *why* you would respond in the manner you have answered the president. In

short, how do you see the situation as it relates to you; to you and your immediate superior; to you and the department director; to you and the president?

3. What questions might you want to raise about the situation which may, in your opinion, have a bearing on your response? Given the answers to these questions, in what way might they change the nature of your response to the president's question?

3. A TEST OF SOURCE CREDIBILITY: A MINI-CASE

For several years, at an appropriate time and without indicating he was testing a hypothesis, the author has submitted the following quotation to groups of people and then asked the members to indicate their opinion of the statement in a space below it provided for remarks:

> . . . But all agree, and there can be no question whatever, that some remedy must be found, and quickly found, for the misery and wretchedness which press so heavily at this moment on the large majority of the very poor.

> . . . By degrees it has come to pass that working men have been given over, isolated and defenseless, to the callousness of employers and the greed of unrestrained competition.

> . . . And to this must be added the custom of working by contract and the concentration of so many branches of trade in the hands of a few individuals, so that a small number of the very rich men have been able to lay upon the masses of the poor a yoke little better than slavery itself.

Each time the above statement was distributed and opinions asked of it, the group surveyed—unknown to its members—was divided in half. At the top of the statement given to half the members was the notation: "The following statement was printed recently as an editorial in the official publication of the Socialist Workers Party of America." At the top of the statement given to the rest of the members was the notation: "The following statements are taken from an encyclical by Pope Leo XIII in 1891."

In short, the statement remained the same; the only difference was the attribution to sources.

Questions for Discussion

1. What effect, if any, do you think the two differing notations as to the source of the statement would have on receiver reaction to it?

2. What connection do you think might exist between the statement, source credibility, and probable receiver reaction when we consider the receiver's religion? Economic status? Social status? Job or profession? Educational level?

3. What conclusions do you draw from this example about source credibility?

4. First, for those who are curious, the statement is from the encyclicals of Pope Leo XIII in 1891. Second, you might care to try the experiment on a group of colleagues not in this class. Simply duplicate the statement and on half the copies use the notation from the Pope and on the other half the notation from the SWPA.

4. ILLUSTRATING SCHRAMM'S "FRACTION OF SELECTION" HYPOTHESIS: A PROJECT

In a report to your instructor cite and explain five to ten examples to illustrate Wilbur Schramm's "fraction of selection" formula/hypothesis in action. The examples can be personal ones or can be taken from situations which you have either observed or discerned from your reading of mass media.

14

COMMUNICATION (3): MEDIA RELATIONS AND PUBLICITY

*I*n the two previous chapters various communications theories and the concept of communication as a process were examined. We also explored a communications model involving four elements: the sender, the channel, the message, and the recipient. In an earlier chapter concerned with public opinion, we dealt at length with the recipient in analyzing the public, attitudes, opinions, and the nature of public opinion and opinion formation.

This chapter is concerned chiefly with so-called downward communication, communication that comes from the communicator and moves through the media which serve as channels for messages. As with all elements of the public relations process, the downward communications stage deals with relationships—in this instance the relationships between the practitioner and the media. At no time static, these relationships are constantly changing and in motion. They can mean the difference between communications success and failure.

But the state of practitioner-media relations is but one part of the process. A second part of the process relates to the degree of skill with which the practitioner fashions messages and sends them through media channels—hence the chapter's concern with publicity techniques.

MEDIA RELATIONS

UNDERSTANDING THE MEDIA'S ROLE

In the so-called "good old days" when life often depended on a king's whim, being a messenger to the king was a hazardous calling. The messenger who brought good news was rewarded for his efforts; the messenger unfortunate enough to be the bearer of bad news lost his head.

We're more civilized today. We don't behead messengers, but we often excoriate them. Modern managers tend to vent their wrath on the messengers—the mass media who carry the news of the day—rather than deal with the contents of the messages the media carry. Any issue of a daily newspaper or weekly news magazine provides numerous illustrations to prove the point.

When the wire services carry stories reporting government inefficiency, the reaction of government officials is to charge that they're the victims of a media vendetta. When prestigious daily newspapers carry reports of price collusion or the distribution of bribes by representatives of American companies in overseas markets, the reaction of the concerned businesses is to charge that the media are responsible for the public's low opinion of business. Not enough of the executives who manage our organizations seem to recognize that they should be more concerned with the content of the messages than with the messengers who report them.

The source of the problem lies in the fact that too few executives understand the role of the mass media in American society. In a free society such as ours, the mass media are independent entities whose main functions are to report the news of the day, provide entertainment, reflect cultural changes, and, in the proper place, comment and editorialize. In carrying out these basic functions, the media are supposed to be responsible, but responsibility is difficult to measure, is open to interpretation, and is often uncontrollable. Thus, we find differences of opinion about the media's role and about the media's degree of responsibility.

> A daily newspaper runs a front-page story reporting that the city's largest employer has laid off one-third of its work force (previously unannounced) and is scheduled next week to lay off another one-third. The story is factually correct, but the paper is accused of being irresponsible.

> Another daily newspaper in another city carries a similar story about a reduction in force by the city's largest employer. The story is accurate, brief, and is run on an inside page of the second section of the paper. The executives of the company, though not happy to have the news reported in the paper, are pleased that the paper has shown responsibility.

To what degree have the above-mentioned newspapers been responsible, and to whom should they be responsible? It's obvious that there are serious economic and other consequences when a city's major employer lays off a sizable share of its work force. Reporting and printing such news also brings consequences, and although some media critics may doubt it, most editors are keenly aware of these consequences when they make decisions about news coverage and placement. It's therefore wise to recognize that although few managers like to read, hear about, or view negative news about their organizations, the primary responsibility of the mass media is to *report* the news—whether the news is good, bad, or indifferent.

In dealing with the mass media one must understand this primary responsibility of the mass media. A few simple precepts should help to clarify such understanding:

1. We live in a society whose members are more inclined to be interested in conflict than in harmony. It is not newsworthy when a company concludes ten years without labor strife. It is news when a strike is called and the labor force walks out.

2. Most people and most organizations pursue their destinies in a decent, lawful fashion. That's not newsworthy. But when someone robs a bank; when an executive is found guilty of misappropriation of funds; when a company is adjudged to have carried out unlawful acts—that's news, and the media will report it.

3. The all-important wire services—AP and UPI—which supply the bulk of the state, national, and international news appearing in our daily media, try to present a bal-

anced report of news events, and this is especially true when the event concerns differences between two or more sides or groups.

However, media can't provide balance when one side makes itself unavailable for comment, and this happens all too frequently when large organizations find themselves in trouble. In such cases hitherto available executives play a game of musical chairs in an effort to be seated when the music stops. He who is left standing becomes the goat.

What should one do when a major internecine dispute erupts between the top executives of an organization? There are no simple answers. Silence may well be golden. Certainly, you can't put your foot into your mouth if you keep your mouth shut. But if you can't be reached for comment when it's obvious that press inquiries will be forthcoming, you're sure to confirm a media precept about public relations people: they're the media's best friend when the going is easy, but they're seldom around when the going is tough. Whether the precept be fact or fancy depends on the special kind of relationship existing between the practitioner and the media. That multifaceted relationship is discussed in the next section.

IT'S A MARRIAGE, FOR BETTER OR WORSE

Some marriages seem made in heaven and some in hell, but most exist in between these two extremes. In the latter category one could well place the forced marriage between public relations practitioners and the media.

As has been noted earlier in this book, public relations is often referred to pejoratively by the media. Whereas journalism is considered to be a noble calling protected by the First Amendment to the Constitution, public relations is considered to be a less than noble activity protected only by the wits of those who practice its alleged black arts. Journalists see themselves as independent writers who present only the truth and who are beholden to no one. They perceive public relations practitioners to be hired hands who bend the truth for unseen clients and companies who employ them to deceive the public.[1]

As with most perceptions, reality is clouded by the dark glasses through which perceptions are filtered. Remove the glasses, and this picture comes into focus:

1. There are very few truly independent journalists today who are totally free to write as they please. However, journalists are certainly more free and impartial than are public relations practitioners, because the latter are advocates and journalists are not. This sense of unfettered writing freedom—though illusionary at times—enables the journalist to sneer at his public relations cousin. The sneer may be small comfort to the journalist, whose monetary rewards are so much lower than those of the practitioner, but it's a comfort nonetheless.

2. Though the journalist doesn't like to acknowledge or admit it, the newspaper, radio, or television station for which he works is a business entity. As such, it is guided by unwritten ground rules that affect what is written and what is left unwritten. The smaller the entity—and the *average* newspaper, radio, or television station is a small business—the more likely the unwritten ground rules apply. So, although journalists are more pure than public relations practitioners, they are certainly not so pure as they profess or imagine themselves to be. However, no one likes to face up to the truth when it mirrors a reality less comforting than illusion. Therefore, if the journalist is pleased to consider himself pure and the public relations practitioner impure, allow him that small luxury.

3. Reality dictates that the journalist and the practitioner cohabit despite their differences. If one were to take the average daily newspaper and the newscasts of the average radio and television station and eliminate from them all the stories that stemmed in some

fashion from public relations sources, the end product would be an emaciated version of the original. It could be done, of course, but at a cost that the owners of these media are unwilling or unable to bear. It would mean larger staffs, bigger payrolls, and smaller or few profits.

So the media grudgingly, not too happily, use the material, ideas, and help offered by the public relations practitioner. Some media use a great deal of the material, help, and ideas, and often use the material without editorial changes. Some media use some of the material, help, and ideas, and often change the material in the process. Some media use public relations material some of the time, use little material at other times, and always make considerable editorial changes in what they eventually use. Virtually no media use no public relations material at all.

4. In the game of wits between the media and the practitioner, some ground rules are set by the media and some by the practitioner, but unfortunately there is no universal rule book and no referees to resolve disputes. Perhaps that's what makes the media-practitioner game so interesting, and perhaps that's why it requires skill, imagination, and a certain amount of luck to play it. A few examples:

- Newspapers don't take kindly to seeing the same story in two different parts of the paper. Ground rule: **don't send the same story to two different section editors.**

- Editors know full well who is advertising in their papers, and they don't take kindly to reminders of this from practitioners seeking to have their news releases printed. Ground rule: **by all means advertise, but don't use your ads as a bludgeon.**

- Practitioners who want to give all media an even news break embargo releases for use at a specific future time. But editors often feel free to ignore embargoes, and some will print stories ahead of the specified release time. Ground rule: **embargo if you must, but do so sparingly.**

- Practitioners will often favor large-circulation papers with their best news releases in order to secure maximum exposure. To assuage the anger of the smaller papers, they'll throw an occasional release sop their way. Ground rule: **dole out your goodies, but share them.**

As the game of wits is played between the media and the practitioner, the hardened, experienced practitioner recognizes that he will win some and he'll lose some. He learns quickly that to promise that a story will surely be carried in a particular medium is to gamble with the fickle finger of fate. Every editor knows that although he and the practitioner are bound together for better or for worse, in reality the practitioner is but a guest in the house. Fortunately for the practitioner, he recognizes that if matters really get too bad he can always move to another house—to another medium—where he will be more welcome.

SOME ELEMENTARY GROUND RULES

"I spent two days working on this talk. It was very important that we warn our employees that if they don't improve productivity their jobs are in jeopardy. It cost the company a lot of money to stop work for an hour so I could talk to all of them, on our time, and impress on them the gravity of the situation. I praised them for their hard work, gave them the facts of foreign competition, said we all have to work harder. What did I get for my troubles? The lead story in the lousy newspaper said I threatened the work force. That's what I got for all the trouble I went to."

—Comment from the chief operating
officer of a national company after giving
a talk to the work force of a local plant
of the company

"More than 500 people put countless hours of time and effort into this year's campaign. We raised more money than we've ever raised before, and we almost reached our goal but just couldn't put it over the top. I can't understand why a newspaper which depends on the support of the community would use a headline stating that the 'UNITED WAY FAILS TO REACH ITS GOAL.' "

—Comment from the campaign chairman
of a local United Way drive

"When we had this important announcement about a new product we went to great trouble to accommodate the two local television stations. Instead of making the announcement at company headquarters in Chicago we set up a press conference at our plant here, and we timed it to give TV plenty of leeway to develop their film for the evening news. What did we get? Nothing, absolutely nothing. They said something about two fires and some lousy auto accident in which a family of six were killed."

—Comment from the vice-president of
marketing of a national company

Three separate comments from three separate sources, all harping on the same theme: the media can't be trusted to tell their stories the way they ought to be told. This sound and fury from disgruntled executives is heard daily throughout the land. What it really signifies is a failure to understand the rules of the media game. Finn emphasizes that the public relations practitioner plays a crucial role in how he or she interprets the media to the chief executive officer and to the corporation:

Most public relations professionals . . . see their role as that of minimizing misunderstandings between business and the media. Public relations professionals may also help the corporate world face their problems honestly, no matter how painful the problem may be. Executives often rationalize the negative aspects of a particular story or event. When a harshly critical news account appears they are convinced that the reporter was "out to get them" with a sensational story. While it is true that news media want to publish or broadcast stories that will be interesting or exciting to their readers, listeners, or viewers (a marketing point of view that should be acceptable to executives), we believe that most reporters make a determined effort to present an honest, objective portrayal of what they consider to be the facts.[2]

As has been noted, there is no universal rule book, and some of the problems stem from this fact. However, veteran public relations practitioners have learned to play by the rules without benefit of a rule book. This section aims to set forth some of the ground rules that need to be mastered if one wants to succeed at the media game.

Space Is Limited, Time Inexorable

Only the New York *Times* would dare to claim it runs all the news that's fit to print, and even the *Times* knows that it can't possibly measure up to an impossible standard. Getting out a daily newspaper and a weekly news magazine; producing a half-hour newscast; publishing a monthly magazine; airing a five-minute radio news broadcast—each of these involves a drastic process of *elimination* and telescoping of information. Finished diamonds aren't plucked raw from the bowels of the earth, but are the end result of a sifting out process involving tons of raw material. The news stories we read in our daily newspaper and hear and view on radio and television are the end result of a similar sifting out process.

This sifting out process takes place in all media. Whether they're local, regional, or national, all media receive and process far more news than they use. The so-called "glut of occurrences" is a flood of news and information that inundates the newsrooms of the nation.

It has always been so with news in America, but today space demands are more severe than ever before. Chiefly for reasons of cost and economy, the news hole on the average daily newspaper is limited. It is even more limited on radio and television. Only about twenty news stories make up the half-hour network nightly news program, and the longest of these runs less than three minutes. Stories are cut to the bone, and a journalistic version of the Darwinian theory of the survival of the fittest rules the selection of news.

Darwin theorized that only the most fit and sturdy of a species will survive. The journalistic version of this theory adds a time dimension to the survival process. It simply means that Story A may be less newsworthy than Story B, but if Story A arrives first in the newsroom it may well be dummied into the paper early and survive the winnowing process because Story B arrived too late for inclusion.

Thus we must add time to space demands when dealing with the media. An entire newspaper becomes a finished product in the short period of several hours. Deadlines for print and electronic media are inflexible. Both the journalist and the practitioner must meet these deadlines in order to survive.

Editors Determine What Is News

Beginning journalism textbooks define news in many different ways, but in reality each editor determines what is news and what isn't news. Richard M. Detwiler, public relations consultant, explains it this way:

> Importance in news is important only to the extent that the editor thinks it is important, and what the editor thinks is important is not necessarily important.[3]

Detwiler's explanation may sound like something out of *Alice In Wonderland*, but it makes sense to every editor and should make sense to every practitioner. Editors determine newsworthiness on the basis of long years of experience in sizing up what will interest their readers. Most of them have a very keen understanding of what will interest readers, listeners, and viewers, and there is a surprising amount of agreement among editors on this score. One of the major reasons why former newsmen are good at handling the media is that they've been part of the media and understand how editors view potential news items.

However, there are many variables affecting the actual coverage and eventual publication of news. It is therefore dangerous to try to predict how a potential news item will be treated by individual editors. Consider, for example, some of these questions:

- *What day of the week is it?* The same news item will get one kind of coverage on a light news day and another on a heavy news day.

- *What time of the day is it?* If you run a press conference at 10:30 a.m. you'll have a better chance of making the evening news than if you run the conference at 4:30 p.m.

- *What news are you competing against?* You can have a perfectly good news item considered newsworthy on almost every score, but if several other major news stories break at the same time, you may well find your item either not carried or else relegated to an inside page.

- *Does your news item fit the standards of the medium?* If your news release is single-spaced and takes up four pages, don't be surprised to find that it's been cut to three paragraphs. If your story involves abstract, nonvisual material, don't be surprised to find that television is not interested in it.

- *How much will it cost the media to cover your event?* Travel takes time and is costly, so don't expect coverage if your news site is miles from town.

Each of the above deals with the mechanics of covering and handling potential news. Mastering the mechanics is essential to success. Once you know the mechanics you are at least assured of having editors pay attention to your story. Whether they'll print it or put it on the air is another matter, but you'll have a fighting chance rather than no chance at all.

Media Need Cultivation

If it's true that each editor determines what is and what isn't news, then it makes good sense to know each editor with whom you have to deal. The same principle applies to key reporters and to those who make assignments for print and electronic media.

If you're in the habit of sending out mass mailings to hundreds—sometimes thousands—of media, it's impossible to be personally acquainted with all those who handle your news. As a general rule, however, every practitioner finds that there are a limited number of media and media personnel who are of special importance to him. Determining who these are is not a particularly difficult task:

Step 1: Decide which public or publics are most important to your organization.

Step 2: Ascertain which media are important to this public or to these publics.

Step 3: Determine which reporters, editors, and others working for these media are important to you.

Step 4: Get to know and work with these reporters, editors, and others.

Applying the above four-step process becomes an individual matter for each practitioner. The process is applicable whether one works in the internal public relations department of an organization or is a counselor serving clients.

Example 1

The practitioner is a counselor. The client is listed on the New York Stock Exchange and is headquartered in Des Moines, Iowa, where it has a manufacturing plant that produces aluminum castings. Its three major publics are the Des Moines community; the financial and business community; and firms that use aluminum castings. The important media for this practitioner are the Des Moines newspapers, radio and television stations; financial and business publications; and the trade press in the aluminum field and in those fields that utilize aluminum castings in their manufacturing processes. Editors, news directors, and reporters of these media are the ones who should be cultivated by the practitioner.

Example 2

The practitioner is director of public relations for a hospital in Atlanta, Georgia. Its major public is the Atlanta community and various sub-publics within that community. The important media for this practitioner are the Atlanta newspapers, radio and television stations. Editors, news directors, and reporters of these media are the ones who should be cultivated by the practitioner.

How does one "cultivate" media personnel? As a first step, if this is a new relationship, the practitioner should visit each important medium and get acquainted with its key personnel. A second step is to hand-deliver important stories when the occasion warrants such delivery, though this may be impossible or very difficult in large cities. A third is to avoid taking up a newsperson's time when he or she is near a deadline. A fourth is to be available when called. A fifth is to provide news tips and ideas for features that are keyed to the needs and interests of particular media. A sixth is to gain respect by knowing one's business, knowing the special needs of each medium, and by being a reliable source of news and information about the organization one represents.[4]

The perceptive reader will note that the relationship described above seems to indicate a state of affairs in which the practitioner gives and the journalist takes. In most instances, this is what happens. But there will be certain important, crucial days when the "taker" gives. Such a day arrives when a reporter calls the practitioner first to get his side of a negative story; when an editor decides to run a negative story on an inside page or to downplay it on a newscast; and when a trade publication producing a major roundup story seeks out the practitioner in order to cite him as one of the reliable and authoritative sources in the field.

Credibility Isn't Gained by Chance

Handling media inquiries that put the practitioner on the spot is one of the most difficult tasks of the public relations practitioner. Such inquiries don't occur daily, but they happen often enough to be a source of concern. They're especially important if the practitioner hopes to maintain a respected relationship with the media. Credibility and reliability are the practitioner's stock in trade. He has little or no stock left if he loses one or both of these attributes. Consider these suggestions about the kind of response to give media or the kind of action to take when the telephone rings and the journalist poses some tough questions:

Don't react too hastily or without careful thought. A hasty, ill-conceived response can get you into trouble. You gain time for thought and for a response by asking for the journalist's deadline and by promising to get back to her before that deadline. This is a perfectly sound reaction on your part, and especially so when the inquiry concerns a matter about which you have little or no knowledge. Even if the inquiry concerns a matter about which you do have knowledge, time provides you with the opportunity to come up with a reasonable response.

When possible, try to anticipate inquiries. If you've ever worked as a newsperson—or if you can think like a newsperson even though you haven't any news experience—you should be able to know or sense when an inquiry will be forthcoming about certain kinds of situations. If you can anticipate the inquiry, you should be able to figure out an appropriate response *before* it is made, not when that telephone rings.

> You're director of public relations for a college. Today is Wednesday, and you get word that the weekly student newspaper, due out on Friday, will carry a front page editorial demanding that the president of the college resign. Will the media be calling? You may just as well ask if Friday will follow Thursday, and you had better anticipate inquiries and the response you will make (or be allowed to make).

Visualize your response in print or on the air. As many a practitioner has learned to his dismay, skilled journalists can have a field day with some of the dodges used to avoid answers to questions. The English language at the command of some practitioners— most often those who practice their art in the political or business world—is sometimes used like a foil in a fencing match. The answers, ranging from the simple to the complex, all end up as a nonresponse to the question. There's the simple "No comment," and then there's the more complex "I can neither confirm nor deny that." Another variation of the nonresponse is the delaying ploy: "We are investigating that." A fourth variation takes the form of the disappearing practitioner: "So-and-so could not be reached for comment," or "So-and-so was unavailable for comment," or "So-and-so was out of town." At times so many practitioners are so often "out of town" in tight situations one wonders if there exists a permanent convention of unavailable practitioners who meet regularly so as to be out of town when they should be answering media inquiries.

But journalists are used to such nonresponse dodges, and they can utilize them in such a way as to make the practitioner rue the use of a nonresponse when he sees it in print or hears it on the air. Just one nonresponse in print or on the air raises the public's suspicion that the practitioner is trying to hide something. The practitioner may have a short-run gain, but in the long run the practitioner who gets the reputation for dodging questions loses credibility and invites a rapidly deteriorating relationship with the media.

Keep Up with the Times

The successful public relations practitioner who professes to be an expert when it comes to dealing with the media must keep up with the times, and this means more than just the New York *Times*. Reading, listening, and viewing are essential tools for the practitioner. One learns best about media needs, wants, and interests by keeping abreast of the media. You gain firsthand knowledge about the *Times, Time, Newsweek,* and about general, business, and trade publications by reading them. Similar firsthand knowledge about radio and television news, talk, and entertainment programs comes from listening and viewing.

However, because there simply isn't enough time in the work day or evening hours to monitor all media or even a fraction of them, the practitioner must rely on professional publications devoted to news about the media and about the public relations field. Richard Weiner, veteran public relations counselor, has compiled a list of newsletters and of weekly, monthly, and quarterly periodicals of particular importance to public relations practitioners. An updated version of the list, cited in Exhibit 14.1, testifies to the wide variety of publications of value to all practitioners.

Sending Up the Trial Balloon

Can a balloon serve as a public relations tool? Not if it's your ordinary blue, green, yellow, red, you-name-the-color balloon, and not when it's in the hands of your average public relations practitioner. But when it's the balloon known as the trial balloon and it's held by a skilled political public relations pro, then it's a public relations tool for sure.

The trial balloon is very similar to that other political public relations tool: the leaked story. Just about every officeholder from the county highway superintendent to the President of the United States plays the trial-balloon game. In olden days when a government official wanted to find out which way the political wind was blowing he would wet a finger and hold it up in the air. Today he sends a trial balloon up into the air.

A trial balloon is a leaked story, attributed usually to either "an unnamed administration source" or to a "high administration official," which reveals some action planned to be taken by the source. If the story—the trial balloon—is well received by commentators, columnists, editorial writers, and the general public, the source knows there will probably be little opposition to the planned action and it will then be announced officially. If the trial balloon is punctured and shot down, that's indication there will be opposition and it's then second-thought time.

The political public relations specialist and the cooperating journalist seem to be as satisfied with their trial balloon as a kid is with his toy balloon. The rules of the trial-balloon game are not written ones, but neither are the rules of the games that kids play. All participants seem to know the unwritten rules, and if they don't obey them they don't get to play the trial-balloon game. Figure 14.1 shows the trial-balloon ploy as played by a mouse.

PUBLICITY TECHNIQUES

THE PUBLICITY RELEASE

The publicity release is to the publicist what the wrench is to the plumber and the drill to the dentist. Sometimes called a *handout*, the publicity release is a special tool used to convey information, news, and feature material from the publicist to the media. Professionals who handle it skillfully find that it gains them entry to print and broadcast out-

EXHIBIT 14.1

A Periodical List for All Seasons

The following list of newsletters, weekly, monthly, and quarterly periodicals of particular value to public relations practitioners was originally compiled, with brief notations, by Richard Weiner, veteran public relations counselor. The list has been updated by the author.

Advertising Age, 740 N. Rush St., Chicago, IL 60601. Weekly devoted chiefly to advertising but valuable for its articles dealing with the mass media. Includes columns and a special magazine section.

AIM Report, Accuracy In Media, Inc., 777 14th St., N.W., Washington, DC 20005. Accuracy In Media, a nonprofit organization, monitors publications and programs for fairness and accuracy. Orientation is decidedly conservative. . . .

Business Wire Newsletter, 235 Montgomery St., San Francisco, CA 94104. Free. . . . Four-page monthly newsletter includes promotional material, but it is one of the most up-to-date, comprehensive regional media publications in the country. . . .

Columbia Journalism Review, 700 Journalism Bldg., Columbia University, NY 10027. Articles have broad popular appeal. . . .

Communication World, 870 Market St., Suite 940, San Francisco, CA. Monthly publication of the International Association of Business Communicators. Articles researched and written by notable authors in the communication, public relations, and business management fields. Also contains columns and book reviews. First issue (November 1983) combined two previous IABC publications, *Journal of Communication Management* and the old *Communication World*.

Communique, Box 2226, Hollywood, FL 33022. Coverage includes marketing, advertising, media and public relations in the Carolinas, Georgia, Alabama, Louisiana and Texas. . . . Focus is the advertising industry. . . .

Editor & Publisher, 850 Third Ave., NY 10022. Weekly bible of the daily newspaper field. Features data about new publications, syndicates, supplements and other print media, editorial personnel changes and other news about the fourth estate. . . .

editor's newsletter, Box 243, NY 10021. Four-page, monthly compilation of news and comments about trends and techniques of business communications. Of greatest use to house organ editors. . . .

The Gallagher Report, 230 Park Ave., NY 10017. Confidential letter to marketing, sales, advertising and media executives. Covers public relations only peripherally, but is extremely valuable for its data and comments about media and advertisers. . . .

in black and white, Associated Editorial Consultants, Box 2107, La Jolla, CA 92038. Four- to eight-page, biweekly newsletter "for those who write, report and edit for publications." . . .

Jack O'Dwyer's Newsletter, 271 Madison Ave., NY 10016. Competes with *pr reporter* and *Public Relations News* by taking a totally different approach. Independent, entertaining, easy to read. . . . Also publishes two directories on public relations agencies and public relations departments.

Journal of Communication, Annenberg School of Communication, U. of Penn., Philadelphia, PA 19103. Quarterly journal with scholarly articles on theory, research, policy and practice of communication.

Media Industry Newsletter, 75 E. 55th St., Suite 201, NY 10022. News, features, research, reports, predictions and candid opinions about publishers and broadcasters crisply reported in eight-page weekly newsletter. Primarily of interest to advertising, marketing and media people, and not specifically oriented to public relations.

EXHIBIT 14.1 (cont.)

pr reporter, PR Publishing Co., Inc., Box 600, Exeter, NH 03833. Weekly, four-page newsletter with . . . comments on broad aspects of public affairs and communications. Supplements include one-sheet, bimonthly summary of articles in social science and other journals. . . . Company also publishes two directories, *Who's Who in Public Relations* and the *PR Blue Book.*

Practical Public Relations, Box 3861, Rochester, NY 14610. . . . Often contains publicity tips and practical advice rarely found in most of the newsletters. Easy-to-read, attractive format justifies its slogan, "the practical newsletter for professional Communicators."

Public Opinion, 1150 17th St., N.W., Washington, DC 20036. Published bimonthly by the American Enterprise Institute for Public Policy Research. Contains in each issue a score of contributed articles about public opinion and also an Opinion Roundup section citing survey data from the major public opinion survey organizations.

Public Relations Journal, Public Relations Society of America, 845 Third Ave., NY 10022. Monthly publication of the Public Relations Society of America. Each issue focuses on a single topic of interest to public relations practitioners. Six to eight major articles in average issue. Has the largest circulation (12,500) of any public relations publication. . . . One of the most useful features is collection of monthly columns on relevant topics.

Public Relations News, 127 E. 80 St., NY 10021. Four-page newsletter with largest circulation of any newsletter in the public relations field. First half of each issue is devoted to news and comments about public relations events, accounts and people. Second section consists of a case study, with details about materials and results of

recent campaigns, projects and special events.

Public Relations Quarterly, P.O. Box 311, Rhinebeck, NY 12572. . . . PRQ often publishes in-depth articles with detailed advice and comments, and is a useful component of the public relations library. . . .

Public Relations Review, College of Journalism, University of Maryland, College Park, MD 20742. The Foundation for Public Relations Research and Education, Inc. started this quarterly journal to build a bridge between public relations and social and behavioral sciences. Articles, generally by social scientists, often report or comment on research. . . .

Publishers Weekly, 1180 Ave. of the Americas, NY 10036. Bible of the book publishing industry. Includes section of media, with information of value to all publicists. . . .

The Quill, 35 E. Wacker Drive, Chicago, IL 60601. Published since 1912 by Sigma Delta Chi (The Society of Professional Journalists). Popular (circulation 30,000) monthly magazine with news about members and chapters, as well as articles about print media. . . .

The Ragan Report, Lawrence Ragan Communications, Inc., 407 S. Dearborn St., Chicago, IL 60605. Four-page weekly newsletter, with each issue supplemented by a two- to four-page commentary by outside contributor. Potpourri of news and views, mostly about employee magazines and other special-interest publications. . . .

Writer's Digest, 9933 Alliance Road, Cincinnati, OH 45242. Primarily for beginning and professional free-lance writers. Most articles not likely to be of value to publicists. However, descriptions of new and offbeat media often include material not found elsewhere. . . .

Source: Richard Weiner, "A Periodical List for All Seasons," *Public Relations Journal,* August 1977 p. 12. Portions reprinted with permission of Richard Weiner and the *Public Relations Journal.*

FIGURE 14.1 Mouse sends up some trial balloons to fool the cat.

lets. Amateurs who mishandle the publicity release find that it ends up in the circular file.

Format

There are many varieties of release form, but the basic publicity release follows these simple rules:

- It should be typed on plain white paper, 8½ × 11 inches. Fashion publicists sometimes use colored stock, but this is not considered advisable for the average release.

- Identity of the sender should be carried in a block of copy single-spaced in the upper left-hand corner of the page. Identification should include the name and address of the organization; the name of the publicist; the office telephone number; and a number to call after 5 p.m.

  Counseling firms also list the client's name by noting the release has been prepared for such-and-such a client. A counselor-client identification block would look like this:

John Peters and Associates
4654 Lawrence Avenue
Pittsburgh, PA 15222
Contact: Steve Charming
(412) 263-1102
After 5 p.m. 263-1506

For: The Pyramid Company
      Gateway Center
      Pittsburgh, PA 15222

- Release date information should be about an inch below the identification block, but on the right-hand side of the paper. This information is usually underlined.

  If the material is to be used when received, it will contain notation to this effect. Common forms used are "For Immediate Release" and "For Release on Receipt."

  If the material is to be used at or after a specific time, it should specify day of the week, the month, and the date. Do not include the year (since the year is obvious). Some common examples include: "For Release Thursday, October 21, or Thereafter"; "For Release PMs, Thursday, October 21, or Thereafter"; and "For Release 12 Noon, Thursday, October 21, or Thereafter."

  If the release is directed to one publication, this information should be indicated in a line double-spaced directly under the release time line. An example:

For Release On Receipt

Exclusive To The Pittsburgh Post

The above notation means that the release has been sent only to the *Pittsburgh Post.* A variation of such notification is to indicate that the release is *"Exclusive In Your Circulation Area."* A third is to state that the release is being sent *"Special To The Pittsburgh Post,"* and the implicit understanding is that the release is not exclusively or only for the *Post* but that other papers in its circulation territory have not received the same release.

- The release proper should start about one-third down from the top of the page. It is advisable to try to leave about one-and-a-half to two inches between the release date information and the start of the release. This permits room for editorial notations or for small headlines that can be machine-set.

- The release itself should be double-spaced. Single spacing makes it difficult for the editor to make corrections or changes in copy.

- The word "more" should be placed in brackets at the bottom of the page if the release is to run more than a page.

- At the top of the second page, on the left, put an identifying slug-line followed by several dashes and the number 2.

- At the end of the release put a "30," centered immediately after the last sentence of the release.

- For filing purposes, a file number and the date the release is sent out should be carried at the bottom of the last page of the release. This date should include the month, day, and year and should run flush left.

Headlines?

The use of headlines on releases is a matter of debate. Some organizations always run a headline with their releases, placing it in the white space between the release date information and the release proper. Those who use headlines argue that they provide editors with a quick summary of the most important aspects of the release. Further, they note, there's always the possibility that an editor may use the suggested headline and if this is done the publicist can score twice—both through the headline and through the release itself.

Others argue that there are so many different sizes and families of headline type it is impossible to come up with a headline that will fit the space specifications of all media to whom the release is sent. Editors will therefore have to edit out the headline, so why use it in the first place? Further, the nonusers contend, editors resent the use of headlines because they feel it's an unwarranted intrusion on editorial prerogatives.

If decision is made to use a headline, make it an all-cap, two-line head, both lines justified left and right.

Datelines and Time

Because an editor may not have the time or the inclination to check a possible time ambiguity in a release, it's important that the publicist be absolutely clear when he uses "today," "tomorrow," or "yesterday." For example, when a story states that it is "For Release On Receipt" and the lead mentions "today," what day is today?

One way to clear up the ambiguity is to put the date in brackets immediately after "today." This may not be the proper form usually utilized by the medium, but it is expected that editing will take care of form. Here's an example:

For Immediate Release

The Worthington Company revealed today [October 21] that it will build a new $12 million plant on a site ten miles outside Excelsior, Ohio.

Another way to clear up ambiguity is to use a dateline to lead off the first paragraph. An example of this form would read as follows:

For Immediate Release

Excelsior, Ohio, October 21—The Worthington Company revealed today that it will build a new $12 million plant on a site ten miles outside of this city.

Recognizing that the media place much store in timely news, publicists often use the fact of an announcement as the peg for timeliness. They do this by citing the news in the lead clause and having the announcement with its "today" appendage as the end of the lead sentence. The same item would then read as follows:

For Immediate Release

The Worthington Company will build a new $12 million plant on a site ten miles outside of Excelsior, Ohio, it was announced today [October 21] by President Jonas Worthington.

GETTING MAXIMUM COVERAGE

Thousands of press releases are sent out daily to the media in this country, but only a small percentage of them get into print or on the air. Securing maximum coverage for your organization calls for careful attention to details and attention to the special needs of the various media that make up the mass communications mix. Key elements of this communication mix as it relates to maximizing publicity efforts are brought into focus under the following heads:

- The Media Distribution System
- The Public Relations Wire Services
- Don't Take the "A" Train, Take the Local
- Orchestrate When Possible
- The Press Conference
- Case Histories: Valuable Product Publicity Tool
- Comes the Technological Revolution

The Media Distribution System

The media distribution system in the United States, which was discussed in the previous chapter in the section on channels, has an important bearing on the effectiveness of publicity output and efforts. Consider the following aspects of this system:

- The bulk of international, national, regional, and state news and feature material appearing in daily newspapers and on radio and television broadcasts is supplied by two major sources: the Associated Press and the United Press International. Additional sources are various syndicated services.

- News and features transmitted over the wires generally emanate from state bureaus, move on to regional distribution points, and finally to the national A wires. Editing occurs at each point in the distribution system, but for the most part the starting point for publicists is the state bureau(s).

- If you can make the A wire with your story or feature, you've reached virtually every daily newspaper, radio and television station in the country. One six-inch AP story, for example, might appear in more than 1,000 daily newspapers and be read by more than 40 million people.

- A few media have an importance far beyond their readership, listenership, and viewership. It was the Washington *Post*, for example, that first broke the Watergate story, and it was the New York *Times* that first ran the Pentagon Papers. Both papers are important because they're read by other editors and because they're also read by so-called opinion leaders and organizational executives. Although each of the three network evening news shows carries only twenty-two minutes of news and features, each relatively brief in nature, they're seen and heard by millions of Americans.

- News and feature assignment editors are often imitators rather than innovators. *Times* editors read the Washington *Post,* and vice versa. *Time* editors read *Newsweek* and vice versa. The AP runs a story on a new teenage craze, and suddenly dailies all over the country discover the same craze in their own communities. As noted earlier in this chapter, editors determine what is important, and this determination often occurs because some other editors have deemed a story important.

- In every field, business, profession, and organization there exist specialized publications that may not be known to the general public but that are vitally important to those who read these publications. One story in such a publication may be worth hundreds of stories in the nontrade press.

It is mainly through experience that the publicist learns to work within the media distribution system of the country. The system seems simple, but it's complex because of the multiplicity of media and the media networks within which news and features are transmitted. These networks are both national and regional in scope, and on the very large individual media highly specialized functions exist. Thus, for example, one finds numerous departments and department heads on publications such as *Time* and *Newsweek;* on wire services such as the AP and UPI; on newspapers such as the New York *Times,* Chicago *Tribune,* and Los Angeles *Times;* on business magazines such as *Business Week;* and on the three network television news shows. Contacts become vital, but equally vital is knowledge about how the media operate. Today's contact becomes tomorrow's retiree, but knowledge about how the media operate transcends contact with personnel.

The Public Relations Wire Services

Complementing the media distribution system in the United States are the press relations wire services. These services—which should not be confused with the Associated Press and the United Press International—transmit press release information over their own private line circuits directly into the newsrooms of the nation's major print and broadcast media. Cost of the service is borne by the clients of the service, who usually pay a membership fee plus a charge for each release transmitted. The services act essentially as middlemen between the sponsors of releases and the media to whom they are sent. Their basic value to the practitioner is that they transmit releases swiftly, simultaneously, and directly to the media after editing for news style, attribution, and accuracy.

The original public relations wire service is PR Newswire (PRN), now a wholly-owned subsidiary of United Newspapers, which went operational in 1954. Other public relations wire services, mostly local or regional in nature and coverage, are the Business Wire, San Francisco; PR News Service, Chicago; Newswire Central, Minneapolis; Southeastern Press Relations Wire, Atlanta; Southwestern Press Relations Newswire, Dallas; and services in Detroit, Washington, and Philadelphia. Because it provides national and international coverage and is the major such service in the country, PR Newswire will be discussed in detail in this section.

In marking its twenty-fifth year of operation, PRN in 1979 initiated its "second generation" wire service and put into full operation a computer-based system geared to complete compatibility with the automated editorial newsrooms of America's print, broadcast, and wire service media. PRN's sophisticated computer system enables it to deliver copy at speeds up to 1,200 words per minute in upper- and lower-case using joint AP/UP copy style. This copy is transmitted directly to PRN's high-speed terminals at the media or into the media's own computers, which are linked to the media's automatic typesetting equipment. Just as do the AP and UPI, PR Newswire flashes news simultaneously to all (or any) points served by its system; generates copy indexes or "abstracts" for immediate retrieval and review by editors on teleprinters or VDTs at their desks; and

FIGURE 14.2 *The center.* The editorial and transmission center of PR Newswire's New York headquarters closely resembles the newsrooms of computerized newspaper and wire service bureaus in staff, equipment, and activity.

Source: Photo courtesy of PR Newswire.

stores, retrieves, changes, transmits, or repeats in seconds any copy issued over its system (see Figure 14.2).

PR Newswire serves more than 350 news points in about 150 cities on its various national and regional News-Lines. A total of 65 of the news points are in the New York metropolitan area and in 30 of the largest newspapers in the country. An average of 125 releases are transmitted each day, and on some days the number reaches 300.

David Steinberg, president of PR Newswire, reported in 1983 that PRN was transmitting releases for about 7,500 news sources. Major corporations and public relations firms are frequent users of the service, releasing financial information, press conference notices, personnel change announcements, photo tips, obituaries, memos to editors, feature stories, and general news information to print and broadcast media, the wire services, and financial institutions. Seventy-five percent of the volume carried by PRN consists of business news, and the remainder is entertainment, travel, and other news and features.

"Immediate Release" financial news transmitted over PRN's *Basic News Line* is automatically issued 15 minutes later over the system's *Investors Research Wire*. In this way PRN carries financial news not only to the media—thus helping clients meet Security and Exchange Commission requirements—but also to the brokerage and investment community and to leading stock exchanges. Among nonpress points served by PR Newswire are the New York, American, and Pacific Stock Exchanges; banks; insurance companies; mutual, trust, and pension funds; brokers; and underwriters. Headquartered at 150 East 58th Street, New York, New York 10155, PR Newswire has offices in Boston, Los Angeles, and Miami.

Don't Take the "A" Train, Take the Local

The "A" Train, immortalized in song by Duke Ellington, is an express that runs between 57th Street and 125th Street in Manhattan without an intermediate stop. It's a very fast subway ride, bypassing in a quick blur the many local stops between the two points on the line.

Taking the express is a very efficient way to get from 57th Street to 125th Street. It's an inefficient way to move publicity material from publicist to daily newspapers. Therefore, if you want to reach and interest editors of daily newspapers, don't take the "A" Train—take the local.

A crucial fact about media in America is that they are local rather than national. Most countries have national newspapers that circulate throughout the entire nation. The closest we have to a national paper is the *Wall Street Journal*, but its focus is on business and financial news. (As a side point, this is one reason why business and financial organizations are pleased when their news is carried by the *Journal*. Because the *Journal* is printed and distributed throughout the country, it reaches a national business and financial public.) As of 1984, the New York *Times* was publishing a **mailed** national edition, and Gannett's new *USA Today* was on its way to becoming a nationally-distributed daily newspaper. The dominant daily newspaper pattern, however, remained the daily which was printed and circulated locally.

The average daily newspaper in America carries four kinds of news: national, international, regional/state, and local. As already noted, this paper secures the first three kinds of stories from one or both of the wire services and from syndicates. Its local news comes from its own staff and from public relations and publicity sources. This same newspaper will generally carry as much local news as the other three kinds of news combined, and very often it will carry *more* local news than the other three combined.

The same situation exists among broadcast media. The average radio or television station receives its national, international, and regional/state news from the two wire services. Either station personnel read this news or else the station puts it on the air as broadcast by the networks or the audio services of the wire services. The local news results from the efforts of the station's own staff or comes in from public relations and publicity sources.

Local news means exactly what it says. It is local in nature and is considered of interest to readers or listeners because it concerns what's happened in their town, city, or area. It's usually the kind of news that would have little interest elsewhere because it is so local in nature, but it's one of the main reasons why people buy the local newspaper and read and listen to the local broadcast media.

That sounds simple, doesn't it? **Yet thousands of press releases are mailed from public relations sources every day to the country's dailies and broadcast stations, and the great bulk of them are quickly discarded for one major reason: they have no local interest.** An occasional release will slip by because of its intrinsic human interest, and sometimes a release will be printed and put on the air because it fits an open slot and nothing else is available at the moment. For the most part, however, these nonlocalized releases are a waste of time, money, and talent.

Therefore, whenever possible, think local when you're dealing with the raw material of release matter. Ask this simple question: **Is there anything about this material that would have local appeal to a particular medium?** Ask another question: **Is there any way I can shape the material so that it will have local appeal to a particular medium?** Ask a third question: **Is there any way I can underscore local appeal to certain media in a release that is otherwise general in nature?** The answers, surprisingly enough, aren't difficult to come by.

Example 1

A national concern with many distribution centers throughout the country makes an announcement concerning one of its products. It sends a release from its headquarters in Chicago to all 1,730 dailies in the country. Very few get printed.

Another national concern with many distribution centers throughout the country makes an announcement concerning one of its products. It tailors a release so that attribution of the story is applied to the local manager at each distribution center. Most of the stories get printed in dailies serving the localities of the distribution centers.

Example 2

After an intensive national competition, a major educational foundation selects fifty high school seniors as winners of four-year college scholarships. It sends out a national release to all United States dailies summarizing the total amount of scholarship money granted and listing the names of the winners at the end of the release. Pickup by the newspapers is minimal.

The next year, following another competition and selection of winners, the foundation sends out another release. Instead of simply listing the names of the winners at the end of the release, the foundation appends a listing of winners arranged by states and localities and citing winners by name, age, and local address. A note to editors advises them of the appended list, and, where applicable, each name is circled whenever the winner's town or city matches a local newspaper. Pickup is excellent.

It's obvious that not all releases can be localized. It's just as obvious that many which aren't localized have the possibility of localization. The lesson is clear: think local, and you'll find your story used more often than you thought possible.

Orchestrate When Possible

Having your story carried by one medium is an achievement, but it's a more effective achievement if the story is carried by many media. Bringing about this desired result calls for careful orchestration of your basic release.

The key to orchestration is to recognize that different media have different deadlines and to work within these deadlines when transmitting your release. As an example, assume that your release is meant for use in a community that has an afternoon daily newspaper; a weekly newspaper that goes to press on Wednesday and is distributed on Friday; several radio stations; and a television station. If you want to give all media an even break, then you should peg your release for use on Friday, seeing that it gets to the weekly by Wednesday, the daily newspaper by Friday morning, and the radio and television stations before noon on Friday. Although the weekly will receive the story two days before the stated release time, the weekly won't use it until publication day (Friday). The afternoon daily will have to have the release Friday morning if it wants to get it into print that afternoon. The radio and television stations will be able to air the news by noon, but it is generally considered fair to give the broadcast media a few hours lead time over print media. (If a story is meant to be used by a morning newspaper, then it is considered fair to release it to broadcast media the evening before, either for their early or for their late evening newscasts.)

Orchestrating a release in the above manner should be attempted only when the release time is within the control of the publicist. It should not be attempted when you're dealing with a spot news event, because the event itself will determine release time. Thus, if you're handling an activity that takes place on a Tuesday, you can't very well set your release time for Friday simply because you're trying to get maximum coverage. An activity taking place on Tuesday should be released on Tuesday.

However, if you have the option of setting release time—such as occurs when you are making an announcement—you may as well make the announcement on a Friday as on a Tuesday if a Friday suits your orchestration plans. Or, as often happens, you can schedule the activity for Friday if you have the option of so doing.

The Press Conference

Every college professor has had to face that moment of truth when, in the midst of what he considers to be the lecture of the academic year, he looks closely at a student in the back row and sees sheer glaze. Professors teaching a course in public relations have learned to recognize the glaze as the Walter Mitty Look. It's the look that indicates clearly that the student is dreaming he's a public relations Walter Mitty orchestrating a stupendous press conference attended by hundreds of media representatives busily taking down every word of the student's client, the president of one of the country's largest companies.

Who can blame the student for dreaming about his moment of professional glory? A press conference is a much more exciting affair than is a classroom lecture. There's real satisfaction in bringing off a successful press conference after long hours of careful preparation and hard work, and the payoff in resultant media coverage can be eloquent tribute to the competence of the initiator. But for every successful press conference there's one that didn't quite succeed, and there's also the ultimate horror: the press conference that bombed. The difference between the successful and the unsuccessful press conference is usually found in one or more of the elements discussed below.

What's the Subject? Long before you hold a press conference, you have to decide whether you have a subject worthy of a conference. Your decision will be based on the answers to several crucial questions, and the most important of these is whether the media will be interested enough in your subject to attend the conference. For certain kinds of press conferences there's no problem judging probable media interest: a presidential press conference is a sure media draw. If the chairman of the board of a major corporation fires the chief operating officer and calls a press conference to announce and discuss it, that's another sure media draw. If your company plans to build a multi-million-dollar plant and calls a press conference to announce details, that's another sure media draw.

Those are easy. Assume, though, that your company is in Chicago and it calls a press conference to announce details about the promotion of ten middle-management people. Or assume that you're in charge of sports publicity for a small college and you call a press conference to announce the hiring of a new varsity swim team coach. Or assume you're director of publications of a small midwestern tool company and you've brought your new president to New York City to introduce him to the media at a press conference. Will the media show up in sufficient force at these conferences? Will it rain two weeks from Tuesday? What team will end the season in your conference with a .500 season average? No one can really supply the answers to these questions, and that's what makes long-range weather predictions, conference standing predictions, and press conference media coverage predictions a gambler's choice.

Your reputation as a practitioner requires that you be right more often than wrong when calling a press conference. Although you can never predict accurately the kind of media turnout for a conference, you can be more often right if you call a conference only when you're reasonably sure of success. Use the conference route sparingly—make reasonably certain that you've got a subject that will interest media reps.

Choose Your Site and Time Carefully. Selection of a press conference site is dependent on many variables, but the most important consideration is convenience. The site should be one that is most convenient to the bulk of invitees. In a large city, this usually means a downtown location. This could be a well-known dining establishment (which is usually glad to have its facilities used in the morning hours), a club, or a large hotel. In every large city, each of these establishments usually has the facilities and the experience in handling press conferences. If, on the other hand, you decide to hold the press conference at your own location, then you have to take care of transportation of the media to and from the conference site. When possible, bring the conference to the media, a technique that saves media time, trouble, and expense.

The exact time for holding the press conference is the time that's most convenient to the media. Generally this means a midmorning, midweek conference. Some press conferences are tied to the lunch hour and therefore include lunch as part of the program. The midmorning conferences generally include light refreshments.

Take Care of Details. Veteran press conference sponsors often work from checklists of things-to-do, checklists that contain scores of items. Among the many details that have to be covered are the following:

- *Invitations* are usually sent out anywhere from one to two weeks before the conference. They should be brief, incite interest, be clear about details, and include a return card or envelope.

- A *telephone check* of invitees is usually made a day or two before the conference to serve as a reminder to those who have indicated attendance and to elicit attendance from those who have not responded.

- The *conference program* should be carefully designed so that the conference runs smoothly according to plan. Decision has to be made in advance regarding the person who will be running the conference; the people who will speak; what they will talk about; how long they will talk; and how questions will be handled.

  Provision has to be made in advance for the special needs of the various media. Television, in particular, has specific equipment needs, but at the same time television equipment proves bothersome to print media. One way to handle this problem is to provide for prearranged television interviewing in an adjoining room before the conference begins.

- *Press kits* should be prepared in advance, should include the kinds and amount of material most likely needed by the media covering the conference, and should be distributed to those who attend.

  At a minimum, the press kit should contain a basic press release summarizing the subject of the conference; some sidebar releases about ancillary features of the subject; photographs relating to the subject; and a basic data sheet relating to the subject if it is scientific or complex in nature.

  Exhibit 14.2 reprints two pages of the basic three-page release which was included in the press kit prepared for the Harveys Bristol Cream Tribute to the Black Designer '83. Photos from the press kit were reprinted in Chapter 11.

  Figure 14.3 shows two photos with captions distributed by IBM's Research Center to demonstrate discovery by IBM scientists of a new phenomenon called ablative photodecomposition.

  Careful tab should be kept of those who do *not* attend the conference. When the conference ends, press kits should be transmitted to those who did not attend, and sometimes this calls for immediate delivery by messenger service. Kits should be mailed to others who don't need immediate service, but who may be likely to use the material.

- *Tabulating media pickup* calls for arrangements to be made in advance to record the amount and kind of coverage given by television, radio, and print media. There are organizations that monitor and report electronic coverage, and clipping services do the same for print media. A post-conference report should include a summary of media coverage and should include examples of coverage by television, radio, and the print media.

- A *post-mortem report* to yourself should provide details about what went right and what went wrong. Score one for your side if you had far more "rights" than "wrongs," and make sure you right the wrongs the next time you set up a press conference.

Case Histories: Valuable Product Publicity Tool

A valuable product publicity tool to use is the one known as the "case history." Usually directed at trade publications, the case history is a full-length article, generally accompanied by photos, which demonstrates and documents the use of a product or system application by a customer. The best case history reads as though it were written by a

EXHIBIT 14.2

From: Robert M. Weintraub
      Paladin Public Relations, Inc.   For Immediate Release
      1412 Broadway
      New York, N.Y. 10018
      212/840-7812; 516/798-4974

For: Harveys Bristol Cream

HARVEYS BRISTOL CREAM TRIBUTE TO THE BLACK DESIGNER '83 SALUTES SPRING FASHIONS FROM 12 DESIGNERS' STUDIOS

NEW YORK, N.Y., March 23—In a dazzling display of color, line and fabrication, a dozen Black fashionmakers saluted the beginning of spring before 2,000 people at the Harveys Bristol Cream Tribute to the Black Designer '83 in Avery Fisher Hall, Lincoln Center for the Performing Arts, here tonight.

Styling included men's and women's wear in shops and boutiques this spring. The quick tempoed beat of the evening was punctuated with performances by three of the beneficiaries of Tribute '83: The United Negro College Fund Choir, the Negro Ensemble Company and the Dance Foundation of Harlem.

At a glittering $50-per-ticket black-tie reception preceding the show, the leaders of the New York Black community gathered with more than 100 press representatives and guests to meet the honored designers. Placed around the Avery Fisher Hall promenade were historic garments selected from the Black Fashion Museum which, along with the Harlem Institute of Fashion, was also a beneficiary of the event. In addition, a grant for two scholarships was given to the Fashion Institute of Technology.

MORE

staff writer of the publication to which it is sent; provides information and application ideas which can be of value to the readers of the trade or industrial publication; and does not give the impression that it is self-serving or overly promotional in tone.

A good case history, says Ketchum Public Relations, should serve the reader by—

EXHIBIT 14.2 (cont.)

Tribute '83

Page 2

The fifth Harveys Bristol Cream Tribute to the Black Designer, hosted by Debbie Allen, star of "Fame," selected its designers through a national screening process involving fashion editors of newspapers across the country who nominated twenty-eight designers. A critics panel then selected nine women's wear designers to be honored, based on creativity and professional success. Among them were:

Alpha C. Blackburn of Indianapolis, Myra Everett of New Orleans and Chicago, Jon Haggins and Lester Hayatt of New York, Rudolph Lepenski Jones, recently moved from Washington D.C. to New York, Tina King of Philadelphia, Mark Anthony Pennywell of Pittsburgh and Harold Stone of New York.

In addition, special presentations in the gala event were made to Jeffrey Banks, the New York men's wear designer who was named the Outstanding Designer of 1982 in the Coty Fashion Critics Awards, the design team of Kevin Thompson and Robert Miller for their avant garde, style-setting men's wear fashions in leathers and suede, New York milliner Frederick Jones and to Arthur McGee, "dean" of Black fashion designers in New York.

The Critics Panel that selected the final complement of designers was comprised of Susan Taylor, editor of Essence Magazine, Bernadine Morris, fashion editor of the New York Times, and Joan O'Sullivan, lifestyles editor of King Features.

MORE

1. describing a solution to a problem;
2. documenting a payback or cost-savings;
3. focusing on a timely subject; or
4. featuring a unique or unusual application.

Preparing a case history involves a series of steps. The first step is to analyze your organization's products (or services) and decide which of these you intend to make the

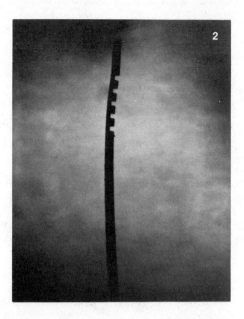

FIGURE 14.3 *IBM scientists discover new phenomenon.* The new discovery is known as ablative photodecomposition, in which a far-ultraviolet laser beam can etch biological and polymeric materials without heating effects. In 1, the chemiluminescent glow shown in the photograph occurs when energetically excited molecules are emitted from the fingernail as a result of irradiation with a single laser pulse lasting only 12 billionths of a second. No physical sensation was experienced by the owner of the finger, even though a loud "pop" accompanies this miniexplosion. A single laser pulse can remove material down to a depth of several ten-thousandths of a millimeter over an area defined by the shape of the laser beam. In 2, the single human hair shown in the photograph demonstrates that the technique can produce exceptionally clean etching cuts, without evidence of charring. Those cuts were each produced by approximately 120 repeated laser pulses in less than 10 seconds. Their shape was determined solely by the shape of the laser beam, which was aimed at the hair from the right.

Source: Photos courtesy of Dr. R. Srinivasaan and the IBM T. J. Watson Research Center, Yorktown Heights, N.Y.

subject of your case history. From the line people in your organization you then secure information about the product and the customers who buy it. Select from these customers one (or several) whose use of the product would be of interest to others in that customer's field. Contact and then subsequently visit the customer's facilities to secure information, interesting comments, and aspects of the customer's usage of the product. Meanwhile, contact a selected trade or industry publication to ascertain if the editor would be interested in your proposed case history article. If the answer is affirmative, send the editor your completed article with art. If the answer is negative, query the editor of another trade or industry publication.

Crucial to success in a case history placement is the editor to whom the article is sent. A Ketchum survey in mid-1983 of a representative sample of trade publication editors in twenty-three industries concluded with the observation that case histories are subject to increasing editorial scrutiny and therefore must be written in an objective fashion. Stated Ketchum: "There is too much competition for space coming from magazine staff writers, other suppliers and users, to risk losing a placement due to an improperly prepared or overly promotional article. Once published, however, the case history shines with an aura of credibility. It also can be a potential door opener for your company's sales personnel."[5]

Some of the findings of the Ketchum survey are cited in Exhibit 14.3.

EXHIBIT 14.3

Trade Magazine Editors' Views of Case Histories

Following are some data from the summary report of a survey of trade and technical publication editors conducted by Ketchum Public Relations in mid-1983.[5] The 118 responding editors represented publications in 23 industries, ranging in circulation from 1,600 to 170,000.

- More than six out of ten (64 percent) editors of trade and technical publications said they publish industrial case histories.

- Only 38 percent of the editors who publish case histories rely primarily on their own staffs to produce the majority of these articles, and only a few refuse outside submissions altogether.

- Two-thirds of the responding editors said they have tightened up their editorial standards in the past five years.

- Slightly more than half of the editors (51 percent) said they prefer a telephone call first to discuss a story idea, and another 26 percent said that submitting an outline or written summary of the story idea is the best first step.

- A common complaint from the editors is that case histories submitted by outside sources are often written with an overly promotional tone.

- When it comes to determining what editors want in a case history, the answer is: know the publication, know its readers, know its writing style, and avoid being too commercial.

Courtesy of Ketchum Public Relations.

Comes the Technological Revolution

The advent of the 1980s brought important technological changes affecting the processing of communication and the mass media. These changes, in turn, have affected the practice of public relations. They are so far-reaching that they will be discussed and analyzed in a forthcoming separate chapter within the last section of this text.

ENDNOTES

1. For an affirmation of the journalist's view of public relations, see David Finn's *The Business-Media Relationship*, a research study conducted by Research & Forecasts, Inc., in cooperation with the American Management Associations (New York: AMACOM, 1981).
2. Ibid., p. 15.
3. Richard Detwiler, "The CEO and the Practitioner," *Across the Board*, May 1977. New York: The Conference Board.
4. In its April 19, 1982, issue (p. 90), *Newsweek* carried an insightful article detailing what it terms the "media handlers," prominent people across the country who have special talents in dealing with the press directly. Their ways of handling the media provide a virtual primer on how to achieve excellent media coverage and relations.
5. "What Trade Magazine Editors Look for in Case Histories," brochure summarizing a survey of top U.S. industrial trade publications (New York: Ketchum Public Relations, May 1983).

PROJECTS, ASSIGNMENTS, AND MINIS

1. THE OWENS-CORNING FIBERGLAS CORPORATION'S ENERGY CONSERVATION AWARDS PROGRAM: A MINI-CASE

In 1982, for the eleventh consecutive year, the Owens-Corning Fiberglas Corporation sponsored an Energy Conservation Awards competition open to all registered architects and engineers in the country.[*]

Refined and executed by Burson-Marsteller for its client, the Owens-Corning Fiberglas Corporation, the awards program was instituted in 1972 and subsequently endorsed by the White House, the U.S. Department of Energy, the American Institute of Architects, and the American Society of Heating, Refrigeration, and Air-Conditioning Engineers. The competition was designed to recognize architects, engineers, and building owners who have made significant contributions to energy conservation and the environment through design and construction techniques.

The program had two major public relations objectives: (1) to create a favorable business environment for Owens-Corning and its product line among the nation's leading architects and engineers, and (2) to create greater awareness among architects and engineers of the need to design energy-efficient buildings.

The Owens-Corning program entailed a nationwide search for building projects, completed or on the boards, that demonstrate a harmonious blending of function, form, and energy-efficient operation. Eligible to enter the eleventh annual competition were registered architects and professional engineers practicing in the United States. Deadline for entries was set for the end of August; judging took place in September; and announcement of the winners was made at a press conference held in mid-November at the Sheraton St. Regis in New York City.

The four winners and their categories were:

Einhorn Yaffee Prescott Krouner, P.C., architectural firm of Albany, New York, winner in the **Governmental-Built** category for the firm's design of the New Passenger Terminal at the Albany County Airport in Colonie, New York. The 57,000-sq.-ft. structure, an addition to the terminal built in 1960, employs a skylit "solar court" that provides 40 percent of the building's lighting needs and 20 percent of its heating requirements.

BRW Architects of Minneapolis, Minnesota, was named winner in the **Institutional-Design** category for its design of the Civil/Mineral Engineering Building at the University of Minnesota. Designed under a state mandate as an earth-sheltered, energy demonstration building, the $12.9 million structure was expected to achieve an estimated 50 percent reduction in heating and cooling costs, primarily through location of 95 percent of the total building area underground.

Cannon Design Inc., Grand Island, New York, a member of the Cannon Group, was selected winner in the **Commercial-Design** category for its design of the $15 million Norstar Building, headquarters for the Liberty National Bank, in Buffalo, New York. The building's exceptional energy performance was achieved without sacrificing other important client goals: that the building be an example of well-executed urban design; establish a clear identity for the bank; and provide attractive, cost-competitive rental space.

TAC (The Architects Collaborative Inc.) of Cambridge, Massachusetts, was named winner in the **Governmental-Design** category for its contribution in the design of the 1.35-million-sq.-ft. Governmental Service Insurance System Headquarters in Manila, Philippines. TAC collaborated with architects Jorge Y. Ramos & Associates, Manila, on the project. The facility, which accommodates 4,000 employees and 3,000 daily visitors, provided for a "front line" banking hall, 760,000 sq. ft. of flexible open-plan office

---

[*]Case material courtesy of Owens-Corning Fiberglas Corporation and Burson-Marsteller.

space, three dining facilities, retail shops, art gallery, computer center, training center, library, auditorium, gymnasium, outdoor athletic facilities, and enclosed parking for 600 cars.

Guy O. Mabry, senior vice-president at Owens-Corning, told the press conference attendees that the four winners represent a merger between the traditional and the new. "These buildings manifest a return to good design basics concerning site and building orientation, coupled with advanced technologies," Mabry said. "The result is unequivocally one of design excellence and efficiency."

Each press representative at the conference received a thick press kit containing remarks by Owens-Corning officials; a list of the winners, giving award, project, and entrant; individual stories about each of the firms and their projects; and photographs of their entries. The kits and separate stories were later distributed to key trade publications in the architectural, construction, and engineering fields and to newspapers, consumer magazines, and electronic media.

Following a practice set the previous year, those responsible for execution of the program held separate local awards luncheons for each of the four winners in the eleventh annual Energy Conservation program. These luncheons took place in January, 1983, in Albany and Buffalo, New York; Minneapolis, Minnesota; and Boston, Massachusetts. Two awards were given at each luncheon to representatives of the winning firm. One was a commendation from the U.S. Department of Consumer Affairs for the firm's contribution to energy-conscious building design, and the other from Owens-Corning Fiberglas Corporation for the winning entry in one of the four competition categories.

Questions for Discussion

1. What's your opinion of the Energy Conservation Awards program as a public relations project? Justify your answer.

2. In what respects does the combination of elements or aspects of the Energy Conservation Awards program make it one that seems to meet the interests of the sponsor, the entrants, and the public?

3. What changes, if any, would you suggest be made in the Energy Conservation Awards program? Why?

4. If you were asked to do so, how would you go about justifying the cost of the program? Try to be as specific as possible.

Projects and Assignments

1. As a member of the account team at Burson-Marsteller, you have been assigned the task of compiling a list of trade and professional publications to which releases can be sent following announcement of the awards. Compile and present your list in a memorandum to your instructor.

2. Each winner in one of the earlier energy conservation awards competitions received a Steuben crystal trophy entitled *Triangles*. This Steuben crystal was described as a "floating sculpture that captures and reflects light from multiple triangular planes."

    It has been suggested that a different kind of award or trophy be given to each winner. In a memorandum to your instructor, cite and describe or explain *two* other kinds of awards or trophies that could be given to the winners. You can assume a total budget of $30,000 for the awards or trophies.

3. You are to assume that you have been given the responsibility of handling media coverage for each of the luncheons held in January. Your instructor will tell you which of the following assignments will be handled by you and which by others:

a) Prepare a complete list of the local print and electronic media to be invited to each of the four luncheons to be held in January.

b) Write a "pitch" letter to be sent to local print and electronic media inviting them to the luncheon.

c) Write a "pitch" letter to be sent to local radio and television talk shows asking if they would be interested in interviewing a member or members of the winning firm. Include in the letter five to seven suggested questions.

d) Write the first four paragraphs of each of the local releases to be included in material to be given to press representatives attending the local luncheons.

(Note: Your instructor may decide to assign you to deal with "a" through "d" after you have read and discussed the material in Chapter 14.)

2. PROMOTING THE CABBAGE PATCH KIDS: A MINI-CASE

There was no doubt about *the* toy story of 1983: the Cabbage Patch Kids were the undeniable hit of the Christmas shopping season. Setting the scene for its December 12 cover story about the $25 doll, *Newsweek* led off with this introductory paragraph:

> The first tramplings of the season traditionally take place in the third week of December, but this year they struck early and hard: in Wilkes-Barre, in Des Moines; in Greenville, S.C. It was as if an army had been turned loose on the nation's shopping malls, ravaging the *Ficus* trees, sloshing through the foundations, searching for the legendary stockrooms said to be filled with thousands of the dough-faced, chinless, engagingly homely dolls that have become the Holy Grail of the 1983 Christmas shopping season: the Cabbage Patch Kids. Clerks were helpless before the onslaught. When the Hillandale store in Silver Springs, Md., got a shipment of Cabbage Patch dolls recently, the manager stacked them right inside the doors, so that the crowd would spare the rest of the store as they stampeded for them. Other stores parcelled out their stock, one doll at a time, to people who had waited in line for as long as 14 hours—and who then were afraid to leave the stores and brave the ravening mobs in the parking lots.

Clearly, the Cabbage Patch Kids sound like a public relations practitioner's dream product. So they were. The reality behind the dream is told in the following article from *Jack O'Dwyer's Newsletter:* *

CABBAGE PATCH PR BUDGET: UNDER $500,000

The runaway blaze of demand in the "Cabbage Patch" was fanned to life by a PR budget that is "under $500,000," according to Robert S. Wiener, executive VP of Richard Weiner, Inc. (and no relation to president Dick Weiner).

Initial [1983] PR budget . . . was under $100,000. It went up as the concept of the new type of doll caught on but it will still total less than $500,000 for 1983, Wiener added.

Advertising appears to have played only a small role in touching off the public mania for the soft dolls, which . . . far outstripped supply.

There have been no print ads and only some TV commercials on Saturday morning and in the early evening "fringe" hours.

Richard Schwarzchild, president of Richard & Edward's, Coleco's ad agency, would not tell TV spending but the TV Bureau/Broadcast Advertisers Reports showed that only $598,000 was spent in spot TV through Oct. 31. . . . Only $94,000 was spent on network TV through Sept. 30.

Asked to assess the roles of PR and advertising in touching off the craze, Schwarzchild said: "All elements had to come together for a success like this but I have unbounded regard for the Weiner agency. They did an outstanding job."

Jack O'Dwyer's Newsletter, December 14, 1983, p. 3. Reprinted with permission.

Great PR Success Story

The Cabbage Patch moppet mania of 1983 that swept the stores (injuring some of the shoppers) can be traced back largely to PR efforts—although credit must also be given to a product that is unusually attractive to consumers.

The PR placements that started to mushroom in November were the result of months of PR spadework, according to Wiener.

PR planning began early in February with the PR firm assisting in the development of CP dolls as "real people" with adoption papers, names, unique appearance for each doll, etc. Ravelle Brickman, VP assisting Wiener on the account, . . . wrote the "Parenting Guide" which accompanies each doll. The firm hired two psychologists to attest to the appeal of the soft dolls with the goofy "I-need-someone-to-love-me" look. Columnist Joyce Brothers took up the theme, writing she thought the popularity of the CP dolls was "wonderful."

Kickoff in New York

Some 200 reporters attended the national kick-off lunch June 9 at the Manhattan Laboratory Museum.

Groundwork was laid for stories that would break in almost all the major women's magazines in September and October boosting the CP Kids as a fine Christmas gift idea.

About 14 Weiner agency staffers became involved in pitching the TV networks, mailing press kits to the major dailies and setting up media tours for Coleco spokeswomen Kathy McGowan and Karen Gershman.

Letters and calls went to producers for the network morning TV shows. A doll was even sent to NBC-TV Today Show host Jane Pauley, . . . at home awaiting childbirth.

Such efforts led to a 5.5 minute segment on "Today" Nov. 18. This blast seemed to uncap a geyser of media attention.

A 3.5 minute segment was originally booked on Nov. 10. Weiner staffers worked closely with "Today" writer Doreen Jagoda and producer Marty Ryan. Host Connie Chung would interview Kathy McGowan.

"Million Calls"

Brickman recalls "making a million calls" to put together a realistic Cabbage Patch set plus 24 dolls and a variety of licensed products like strollers and layettes. Two Weiner staffers worked "through the night" of the 17th to perfect the set.

Sensing a bigger story, "Today" producers expanded the segment by two minutes and rescheduled it from 8:30 a.m. (when most people would have left for work) to 7:37—"prime morning time." The two other TV nets soon had similar segments and stations across the nation followed suit. *Newsweek* put "The Kids" on the [December 12] cover. . . .

However, by late November, stories of consumers fighting over the dolls caused concern at Coleco. "People were getting hurt physically and emotionally," said Brickman. Wiener, Brickman and other staffers went to a meeting at Coleco in Hartford Nov. 28 at which it was decided that all advertising should be halted. The company had not foreseen that many people would buy more than one of the dolls.

Internal PR Helps Agency

Wiener said credit should be given to Coleco PR manager Barbara Wruck and others "who made sure we got what we needed."

Although some analysts are saying the craze will add only $50-$60 million to the company's [1983] sales . . . Wiener feels sales of the dolls and related products will top $1 billion [in 1984].

Brickman feels the dolls are popular because other dolls got too sophisticated—talking, wetting, etc. "Kids don't need all those problems. They just want something to love," she said.

Questions for Discussion

1. What specific categories of media persons would you invite to the kick-off luncheon June 9? What's your opinion of the early June date for the lunch? Of the media turnout?

2. What's your opinion of the promotional activities carried out by the Richard Weiner public relations agency? In answering, deal with specifics rather than generalities.

3. As noted in the case fact pattern, Coleco spokeswomen went on media tours to promote the dolls. If you were asked to set up such tours, what media would you have them visit and what would you have them do on such visits? Be specific rather than general.

4. What lessons have you learned from this case?

Assignments

1. You are to assume you're responsible for arranging to have the Coleco spokeswomen appear on TV talk shows in fifteen major cities in the United States. Write the "pitch" letter which can be sent to these stations.

2. It is February 1984 and you are a member of the agency account group handling the Cabbage Patch Kids account. It has been decided that the group will be divided into two-member teams and that each team will bring to the next group meeting a proposed public relations program for the coming year. Your program can include elements from the previous year, but it should concentrate mainly on new projects and elements. Be prepared to make an oral presentation to the group. Your instructor will give you a deadline date.

15

EVALUATION, MEASUREMENT, AND REPORTING

In considering the communications model, feedback was described as a key factor in the source and receiver stages. Feedback as discussed in this chapter is the factor that closes the public relations process circle that began with public opinion and progressed through research, planning/programming, and communication. Composed of three parts—evaluation, measurement, and reporting—feedback has three major functions:

1. It tells management *what* has been achieved through public relations activities and actions.

2. It provides management with a quantitative means of *measuring* public relations achievements.

3. It provides management with a means of judging the *quality* of public relations achievements and activities.

As a general rule, most human and organizational activities and performance are subject to reporting, measurement, and evaluation. Salesmen send back weekly sales reports to the home office. Corporations mail quarterly and annual reports to their stockholders and hold annual meetings where reports are given. The president of the United States delivers an annual State of the Union message in which he reports to the Congress and to the entire country.

Competitive athletes and teams are measured by their ratio of wins to losses. Students are measured and evaluated by grades; professors by student evaluations; deans by presidents; and presidents by boards of trustees. Beginning in kindergarten and lasting throughout his or her entire working life, the individual is the subject of reporting, measurement, and evaluation via a wide variety of forms. Some are rigidly organized, some informal; some are quantitative, some qualitative; some are intuitive and personal; some are precise and impersonal.

The public relations field bears witness to the plethora and variety of forms used for reports, measurements, and evaluations, and this chapter will deal with them in orderly fashion. Because reporting is more prevalent than the other two, it will be discussed first.

REPORTING

Reports are the means whereby the practitioner details public relations activities, actions, and results achieved over a specified period of time. The report is another way of stating: this is what we have accomplished. It can be a series of brief statements; it can be pegged to previously stated goals and objectives (in which case it provides a form of measurement); and it can include work that remains to be done.

The report is an excellent way of stating accomplishment in quantitative terms. It can state, for example, how many releases were prepared and mailed out; sum up the column inches of copy resulting from use of the releases by the print media and the minutes of air time resulting from use of the releases by the electronic media; cite the circulation and audience of the media where the material appeared.

The report enables management to keep tabs on the public relations function and the people responsible for carrying out that function. It provides valuable input and serves to provide the intelligence data needed for managerial decisions relating to public relations activities. When presented regularly and in accordance with predetermined patterns, it enables comparisons to be made over a period of time.

On the other hand, the report is generally a poor way of stating accomplishment in qualitative terms. Reports seldom deal with the *quality* of the work accomplished or with the *results* of such accomplishment. To mention, for example, that a specific release was carried by the Associated Press or by the United Press International is one thing. To sum up the number of newspapers that actually printed the story is a more difficult matter, and to draw definite conclusions about the *impact* of such coverage is an almost impossible task.

For example, consider the following extracts from a monthly public relations report:

1. Gave two talks to Rotary and Kiwanis in Burlington.
2. Release on taurine eliminate carried by the *Post Gazette,* the *Brollin Observer,* and the *Mead Daily Press.*
3. Taurine eliminate brochure delivered by the printer and mailed to our A-B-C lists.

It's possible to add up the number of people who heard the talks, the circulation of the three papers which carried the taurine eliminate story, and the number of people who received the brochure. What *effect* the talks, news stories, and the brochures had is open to conjecture.

Reporting of public relations results is done both informally and formally.

INFORMAL REPORTING

A good share of the reporting of public relations activities is done through informal means, at irregular intervals, and as part of the normal operations of an organization. One should not assume, however, that informal reporting has little or no value. On the contrary, such reporting can be of more value than the formal type of reporting since it is carried out without much advance warning.

Large counseling firms with a sizable number of account executives operating under the supervision of a small number of executive vice presidents are frequent users of informal reporting. The author spent an entire working day sitting in the office of an executive of such a firm noting what transpired. A good share of that executive's day was spent going over the status of various accounts with the account executives responsible for activities on behalf of the clients. In effect, what the executive was doing was to touch base with the account men under his jurisdiction, asking questions about what had been done, what was being done, and what was planned for the future.

Similar informal reporting is also carried out in the public relations departments of organizations. Where the department is actually a single public relations person, he or she keeps in touch informally with the executive to whom he or she is responsible. Where the department is of some size, the head of the department follows the same procedure used by the counseling firm executive by touching base informally with those in the department who are responsible for various public relations activities.

Time—or the lack of time—is one of the main reasons executives rely on informal reporting as a means of checking on the work of those under them. Formal systems of reporting which require meetings and conferences take up sizable chunks of valuable time, both on the part of the executive and those reporting to him. An informal accounting takes no more time than is required for a short interoffice call or visit. The following comment made to the author by the head of a large public relations department emphasizes the problem of time:

> One reason for abandoning it (a formal audit) was that I have been too busy. . . . Now, as best I can, I follow what each staff member is doing, note areas of improvement, and from time to time broaden a discussion on a specific phase of work into a general review, with my criticisms and suggestions. A less formal approach, but more successful too.

FORMAL REPORTING

There are four major ways in which public relations results are formally reported: *memoranda and reports* provided at regular intervals; *plans board, group, and committee meetings; briefings and presentations;* and *year-end and annual reports.*

Memoranda and Reports

Probably the most common form of reporting by formal means is through the use of memoranda and reports submitted at periodic intervals, and these can range from the simple to the elaborate. Depending on the circumstances, such memoranda and reports are provided weekly, semimonthly, or monthly and portray a picture of account activity as described *by the person responsible for the activity.* (For this reason, one seldom finds failure writ large in said reports.)

The most common form of such reports is a simple listing of activities in the period covered by the report. No attempt is made to cite activities in order of importance, nor does the report state the degree of difficulty and time involved in carrying out the activity. A stark recital of factual reporting, the memorandum or report simply sets forth work accomplished, partly accomplished, and/or still to be put into motion. In most cases the report or memorandum is a single copy sent to a superior; where circumstances warrant it, copies are sent to others.

In counseling firms account executives often send a monthly activity report to the client with a copy to the executive vice-president supervising the account executive. In addition, counseling firms often require that account executives, particularly those handling several accounts, send reports to their superiors in the firm summarizing activity on all the accounts being handled.

An example of a bimonthly report delineating the activities of a one-person public relations office is that prepared by the director of community relations for the Psychi-

EXHIBIT 15.1

MEMORANDUM

To: Allan Weissburg   **Date:** May 22
From: Benay Leff
Subject: Activity Report of the Community Relations Office for March and April

- Completed all production work on new PI nursing recruitment brochure—blue line received May 21; brochure will be ready approximately June 1.
- Arranged the following speaking engagements, radio and TV appearances:
- Jeanne Mitchler-Fiks spoke at Catholic University;
- National Town Meeting—WETA/FM radio—3 PI staff members;
- Dr. Fram on WRC-TV (Channel 4) news feature;
- Clare Foundraine on "Everywoman."
- Coordinated publicity and tours for Black Nurse Recruitment Day, Tuesday, March 4.
- Prepared and distributed letters notifying students' parents of Developmental School change to foundation status.
- Served as member of Afro-American Day Planning Committee; coordinated publicity and arranged for hostesses; wrote memoranda of appreciation to kitchen staff and hostesses.
- Served as member of the D.C. Mental Health Association Planning Committee for May 15 Annual Meeting Day; attended approximately six meetings; designed, prepared, and arranged for printing of advance promotional flyer and program and did other publicity work.
- Met with Tineke Haase, *Montgomery County Journal* reporter, to discuss PI programs and services for article to appear in the *Journal.*
- Met with Rev. Duke Lundeen to discuss Augustana Mental Health Center PR efforts and relationship to other PI services.
- Made initial contact with Dr. Elizabeth Schoenberg for appearance at April's Combined Clinical Conference.
- Met with the Park Manager of Glen Echo Park to discuss their programs for children and adults; explored potential relationships with PI's Personal Resource Center.
- Initiated new monthly coffee social in March; assumed responsibility for coordinating on regular basis.
- Met with Helen Burr, PI Gerontology Consultant, to plan and design Gerontological Consultation Service brochure.
- Met with Bart Kraff, Allan Weissburg, and Kaja Brent to discuss PR impact of PI admission policies.
- Designed and arranged for printing of the Admissions Office "Aftercare Planning Form."
- Met with representatives of Mailtech to compare costs and services with current bulk mailing fees incurred by PI.
- Arranged for reprinting of Children's Unit family information guide and for the printing of five PI staff members' business cards.

In addition to the aforementioned activities, the Community Relations staff maintained its publication of the BULLETIN, completed several questionnaires, responded to innumerable inquiries regarding PI's programs, attended regular staff meetings, and answered routine correspondence.

Reprinted with permission.

atric Institute of Washington, D.C. The report, in the form of a memorandum, is shown in Exhibit 15.1.

It should be noted that the institute report is a straightforward listing of activities and work accomplished by the director of community relations. The report does not group activities and work under appropriate headings, nor does it attempt to distinguish such work and activities by degree of relative importance and value. It does, however, demonstrate a wide-ranging scope of work and accomplishments, and it clearly shows that the director of community relations hasn't been sitting on her hands during the two-month period.

A variation of the report which contains a straight listing of activities is one which lists accomplishments under appropriate headings. In this way the report details work done with media, for example, or with community groups, executives, and the like. Another breakdown commonly used groups activities under the title of projects. Another method is to cite predetermined objectives and match results to the objectives. (Such a method provides the means for a comparison between objectives and results and thus sets forth the raw materials for evaluation.)

Plans Board, Group, and Committee Meetings

Operating on the premise that several heads are better than one, many counseling firms and public relations departments—especially the larger ones—utilize plans board, group, and committee meetings for the purpose of reporting public relations activities. Such meetings serve other purposes—they are particularly valuable for exchanging ideas for programming—but one of their major purposes and the one discussed here is to bring all concerned up to date on what is happening.

In the majority of cases those attending report meetings will have a common interest or central administrative tie that binds them together. In attendance at any such meeting might be the operating heads of the various units that make up the central public relations department of a company, or the account executives who report to an executive vice-president in a counseling firm, or all professional staff members of a public relations departmental unit or of a service unit in a counseling firm.

Achieving full attendance at report meetings poses more problems for counseling firms than for internal public relations departments. Client demands take precedence over report meetings of counseling firms, and such demands often mean that the counseling staffer cannot attend a scheduled meeting because duty calls for him to be elsewhere. Obviously, serving the client is more important than reporting about the client.

Briefings and Presentations

Where there seems to be a felt need for formal reporting of public relations activities, counseling firms and internal departments rely on briefings and presentations. The chief public relations officer of Client X may request that the counseling firm make a presentation as part of an annual meeting or conference of the chief executives of the client organization. Where no counseling firm is involved, the public relations department may be called upon to brief the firm's chief executives or make a presentation about public relations activities.

Annual sessions of this kind are tightly organized affairs which deal with the most important facets of corporate and organizational life. Public relations is just one small part of the corporate entity and is usually given a proportionately small amount of the available time. Because they will be in the spotlight for a brief amount of time, public relations executives wisely prepare their presentations with great care. Knowing that an oral presentation may be quickly forgotten they use such devices as slides, large charts and graphs, transparencies, and film. In some instances a presentation has been made in the form of a specially commissioned film, although it's wise to keep in mind that there's such a thing as overkill; money-conscious corporate executives may question whether a film showing the results of public relations activity is worth the expenditure of corporate monies for what is generally a one-shot showing. One way of forestalling or countering this criticism is to be prepared with a plan to use the film not only at the annual meeting or conference but subsequently at other suitable and appropriate affairs. Thus, in effect, the filmed presentation can be likened to a "premiere" with other showings scheduled later.

Year-end and Annual Reports

The annual report, which is often the responsibility of the public relations department, is basically the means by which the corporation sums up its financial affairs. Prepared in coordination with the financial department, the annual report consists of financial tables, charts, and descriptive material. In recent years the report has been expanded to include four-color printing and art work as well as brief reports about all activities of a company. Public relations, as an important staff function, sometimes reports its activities in the annual report along with those of other functional areas of the company.

Some public relations departments prepare and print their own individual annual report to sum up the year's activity. This is particularly true where the department is a large one engaged in a wide variety of tasks and assignments. As with the use of a specially-commissioned film presentation, one has to use judgment in deciding how much money to spend on a report showing the results of spending money for public relations activities.

INFORMAL AND FORMAL REPORTING SUMMED UP

As this section has demonstrated, there are numerous ways of reporting public relations activities, and all of them serve the useful purpose of informing management what public relations personnel are doing. Compiling reports takes time, and it can be argued that time might be more usefully spent carrying out rather than reporting activities. However, the management that is ignorant of the activities of its public relations people and department may have little respect for the function. Reporting thus not merely serves to keep management informed but builds support for the function and the activities carried out by the practitioner responsible for the function.

MEASUREMENT AND EVALUATION

Methods used to demonstrate and/or prove the *effectiveness* of public relations personnel and activities are what is meant by measurement and evaluation. The difference between *reporting* public relations activities and results and *measuring* and *evaluating* public relations activities and results is qualitative rather than quantitative. One measures and evaluates to assess the quality and value of public relations counsel, actions, and activities, and this inevitably means that some *standards* are being used in the process of measurement and evaluation. These standards may be implied or they may be stated in explicit terms. They may be set forth to stand on their own or they may be compared with others. Standards are yardsticks, and whether implied or explicit they form the means of judging effectiveness.

Having accepted the public relations function as a legitimate and valuable one, the managements of both profit and nonprofit organizations want to know the *value* accruing from public relations. Increasingly, public relations practitioners are being pressed by their managements to account in a meaningful way for the worth of their activities. This value-oriented view is emphasized in observations made by four communications veterans: James F. Tirone of the American Telephone and Telegraph Company;

Robert K. Marker of Armstrong Cork; Paul H. Alvarez of Ketchum Public Relations; and Burns W. Roper of the Roper research organization.

Tirone contends that public relations managers are ill-advised to claim that public relations is "different" and therefore can't be judged the same way other functions are judged.

"The corporation," says Tirone, "is better served, and I think so is our profession, when public relations deliberately attempts to fit itself into the standard procedures of the corporation by meeting the same tests of performance as other functions and other managers."

For this reason, Tirone adds, the Bell companies implemented various measurement systems in 1978.

"The Bell companies," he reports, "have started down the road of measurement, and the results already seem productive. We are not likely to turn back."[1]

In telling the following story about his experience with management, **Marker** of Armstrong shows that other companies share the same view as the Bell companies:

> I was asked by a marketing executive at Armstrong to inform him, as succinctly as possible, just what he was *getting* for what he was *spending* on PR. . . . I came prepared with a considerable volume of newspaper clippings, magazine features and case histories that we had produced in support of his product line that year.
>
> I laid all this out in front of him, along with an impressive circulation summary, and watched intently as he scanned the headlines, photos and copy. . . . I could see he was impressed.
>
> "I had no idea you fellows were generating all this press coverage for us," he said, looking appreciative. I leaned back in my chair, feeling confident that the day was won. And then it came, the question no one had ever asked before: "But what's all this *worth* to us?"
>
> I stammered for a moment and said something to the effect that I thought the material spoke for itself. After all, this was highly coveted editorial space we were talking about, chock full of credibility and dripping with third-party endorsement. I said it would be difficult to attach a specific value to it.
>
> He smiled. "My boy," he said, "I have to attach a value to *everything* in this operation, or else I'm not doing my job. Why don't you go back and write me a memo outlining clearly what this function does for us, and then we'll talk about your operating budget for next year."[2]

Marker says he had a difficult time writing the requested memo because the public relations people felt they knew what they were doing but weren't taking the time to analyze it, to spell it out, and to report back to the people who were providing operating funds. The conversation, he reports, eventually led to the formalized system the Armstrong press department has been using for the past decade to set communication objectives, monitor activities, and measure and interpret results.

Alvarez, chairman and chief executive officer of Ketchum Public Relations, also sees **accountability** as the key to a new era for public relations:

> The core concept behind successful public relations businesses in the 1980s is accountability—being accountable to clients in terms of results measured against agreed-upon goals. . . . Today's professional has to adjust creative skills to a very businesslike environment. Knowing how to get results within established cost parameters has become as essential as good writing skills. . . . We must know how to create the right message for the right market and how to get it there. And we will not do anything right without a clear understanding of the client's business and objectives.[3]

Roper, the fourth member of our quartet of communications veterans who recognize the need to prove the value of public relations activities, explains management's views as follows:

> There is a degree of skepticism on the part of managements who are users of public relations—even managements that employ large public relations departments of their own and outside public relations counsel as well. As a concept, modern management is aware of the value of public relations—or at least they are not sure enough that it is valueless to ignore public relations activities. At the same time, doubts are frequently voiced as to whether or not a particular public relations campaign is really working, as to whether or not the sponsoring organization is getting results.

> This skepticism is natural, because public relations operates in the field of ideas, attitudes and men's minds. There are no laboratory tests that will measure whether a public relations campaign works or does not work. You can't put a campaign in a test tube. But management nevertheless wants concrete proof of the value of public relations, just as it wants concrete proof of its other activites.[4]

How does management secure concrete proof of the value of activities other than public relations? In some cases, very easily; in other cases, the task is difficult. Almost all *line* areas of organizations—that is, those which are engaged in producing the product or service—are measured and evaluated against a set of standards. If the organization is one that manufactures and sells automobiles, the manufacturing department is measured and evaluated on the basis of the number, cost, and quality of the cars produced in a given period; in similar fashion, the sales department is measured and evaluated on the basis of the number of cars sold in a given period. Obviously, measuring the number and cost of cars produced is easier than measuring the quality of cars, but nonetheless number, cost, and quality are all measured and evaluated. If the number, cost, and quality do not measure up to predetermined quotas and standards, management takes action to bring about desired results. Processes and procedures may be changed; personnel may be shifted around, demoted, or moved out.

On the other hand, a good number of veteran practitioners point out that they serve a staff function in which they counsel, advise, recommend, and initiate actions and activities designed to assist their managements and their line people. These practitioners argue that much of the work they do—especially in the area of counsel and advice on public relations matters—cannot adequately be measured and evaluated, and certainly not by the conventional statistical means of measurement. They ask such questions as these: "Who measures what I've said in a policy meeting? It could have profound impact on the corporation. Who measures the impact of what I don't say or write? Who measures corporate policy action (not stories) and their impact?" The Emhart Corporation's **John F. Budd, Jr.,** who raises these questions, agrees that there are instances where some degree of measurement serves a valid purpose, but not when one is talking about public relations in the broadest, management sense. States Budd:

> I can assure you that it is **relevance** not statistics that will make you an integral part of the management function. Much of what passes for public relations measurement is **not** relevant to management. It is not relevant because it doesn't have credibility . . . because it often diminishes rather than enlarges public relations' role . . . and because it is served up in convoluted jargon that creates suspicion not support.

> It seems to me that even when—and if—we develop a realistic system to gain some input from the operational end of public relations activities, it still is only addressing the implementation phase. Left uncovered is the real "meat," the policymaking, the judgmental areas. How do you "measure" a meeting of corporate officers where action based on public relations considerations is taken? It may never result in hard copy or tangible activity. In fact, it may actually table such activity. To me, this is the cutting edge—and all media analysis and other so-called qualitative evaluation systems are totally missing the essence of the profession.[5]

Budd's arguments are difficult to refute. As Roper points out, public relations operates along lines that are extremely difficult to measure and evaluate, and in addition public relations campaigns are not like laboratory experiments. One might very easily design and carry out two public relations campaigns along identical lines, but with dissimilar results because of circumstances beyond the control of the practitioner. It's with good reason that Roper, whose professional life has been devoted to survey research, concludes that "measuring public relations effectiveness with research techniques is only slightly easier than measuring a gaseous body with a rubber band."[6]

Measurement and evaluation are as difficult as Roper states, but practitioners are utilizing a variety of techniques to achieve measurement and evaluative ends. Such tools and methods are discussed, described, and analyzed in the sections that follow.

TOOLS AND METHODS OF MEASUREMENT AND EVALUATION

The tools and methods used in measuring and evaluating public relations counsel, actions, and activities range from the primitive to the sophisticated with various way stations in between these two extremes. In all cases where public relations is being evaluated certain value judgments are made, and these are made by people. Thus, the fact that a value judgment is based on a relatively primitive method—for example, a judgment made through personal observation rather than by means of a computer printout—does not imply that the evaluation or judgment is faulty. In the end, evaluation depends as much on the perception and wisdom of the judge as it does on the tools and methods available to him and used by him in forming judgments. For this reason, the tools and methods described and discussed below are presented in no particular order of intrinsic value and importance.

PERSONAL OBSERVATION AND REACTION

Judgment of public relations performance based on personal *observation* and reaction by a superior is one of the most common methods used in evaluating public relations effectiveness. At all levels in all types of organizations public relations personnel and their performance are judged and evaluated by those to whom they report.

Counselor Kal Druck describes one level of evaluation as being *intuitive judgment*, and if we follow the dictionary definition of intuitive he means judgment made without the conscious use of reasoning. Thus, the public relations practitioner proposes an activity and management's intuitive response is "this is a good thing to do," or the practitioner takes actions and carries out an activity and management's response is "that was well done." Pinning one's professional hopes on such intuitive judgments entails a good deal of reliance on faith and charity, and where these cease to be forthcoming management's reaction could very well be "this is not a good thing to do," or "that was not well done."

Faith, hope, and charity being practiced more in the breach than in the observance these days, practitioners wisely provide their managements with tangible evidence of their performance and, as has already been noted, such evidence most often takes the form of reporting practices that have previously been discussed. Management, of course, can form its judgment by personally observing and reacting to *discernible* activity or results ensuing from public relations programming. Thus, if one aspect of the public relations program of an internationally known department store is the staging of an imaginative parade on Thanksgiving Day, the executives of that store need only observe that parade in progress to form some judgment about its effectiveness.

MATCHING OBJECTIVES AND RESULTS

As has been noted in the chapter dealing with planning and programming, public relations activity without a clearly designed purpose is not uncommon. Clearly, however, setting objectives is vital to successful programming. Even a generalized set of objectives is better than none at all, though objectives presented in *specific* terms are the most meaningful because they provide direction and also lend themselves to accurate measurement and evaluation.

When the specific terms set forth by objectives relate to actions, activities, or media coverage there is little problem in measuring and evaluating results. Thus, if a program's stated objective is to set up one thousand "coffee houses" in order to increase the use and consumption of coffee by young people, it's not difficult to count the number of such houses established over a period of time and even to measure coffee consumption by those frequenting such establishments. If a program's stated objective is to write and place a series of feature stories about such coffee houses in at least one thousand daily newspapers, reaching x number of people, it's not difficult to count and measure newspaper pick-up and circulation.

Computers have been put to good use by practitioners to provide the data for the reporting of public relations results, chiefly where a large amount of publicity is being generated. A common practice in the past, and one which is still relied upon today, is to take clippings as they come in from the clip services, paste them neatly in bound books or reproduce them in a variety of fancy print, and send them along to management. At annual meetings of trade associations or large organizations there are often several large standing panels on which are pasted large numbers of press clippings. The obvious conclusion is that the public relations department or counseling firm has been busy and productive, the releases have resulted in loads of press clippings, and somewhere "out there" people have been influenced.

The computer has modernized this "bushel basket" method of measuring results, has channelized and systematized the reporting, and has made it possible to draw comparisons between periods and years. A good example of how this is done is shown by the way the computer is used by Armstrong Cork Company.

Product publicity output at the Armstrong Cork Company—described in the chapter on planning and programming—is closely aligned with marketing and communication objectives. Insofar as it is possible, product publicity disseminated by the company's Press Services Department contains specific "messages" aimed at target audiences to achieve agreed-upon communication objectives.

To keep track of Armstrong's press results, the department uses the services of PR Data Systems of Rowayton, Connecticut, which utilizes a computerized system of media reporting and analysis. Armstrong's Robert K. Marker describes the system as follows:

> The computers are programmed at the beginning of each year with our complete message list, organized by division, and then by the applicable communications objective. In other words, we tell the computer what we want to do that year, and it analyzes each piece of publicity that comes in from our clipping services to determine how well it met the objective for which it was intended.

> This analysis is done four times a year, always from published material which appeared during the previous quarter. . . . Shortly thereafter we receive an analysis which gives us an up-to-date reading on two things: Quantitative, we know from quarter to quarter just how we stand in relation to the previous year on total number of stories in print or on the airways; total column inches of print space or minutes of broadcast time logged to date; dollar value of the space or time if purchased as advertising; and the number of photographs published. We get this information for each division of the company, and the figures are totaled during the quarter to give us a picture of how the company's overall program is doing in relation to the comparable period a year ago.

> Secondly, the PR Data reports tell us qualitatively how we're doing with respect to message delivery—in other words, what information is actually getting across to our target audience. Each clipping is analyzed to see what message it contains, and this tells us how

well, and how thoroughly, we're pursuing the objectives we establish at the beginning of the year.[7]

The information received from PR Data is used by Armstrong's Press Services Department to monitor the department's activities and also for internal reporting. The latter is done twice a year by means of summary reports prepared for each of the marketing divisions and for the office of the company president.

Paul Alvarez of Ketchum Public Relations is another practitioner who has put the computer to good use meeting the demands for accountability in public relations work. By mid-1983 his firm had three years of experience with a computer-based measurement system designed specifically to evaluate publicity programs. The system, termed the Ketchum Publicity Tracking Model, is described by Alvarez in Exhibit 15.2.

The systems in use at Armstrong and Ketchum do demonstrate that the computer can be used effectively to measure certain kinds of publicity results with stated publicity objectives. It is much more difficult, however, to set forth objectives in terms of specific attitudes and opinions to be changed or modified as a result of public relations programming and then to measure and evaluate how well such objectives have been met. When we are dealing with this kind of programming we are not dealing with actions or activities that are tangible things or objects. Rather, we're dealing with intangibles relating to points of view, frames of reference, mind-sets, and other aspects of attitude and opinion. Little wonder, then, that objectives relating to men's minds are not often couched in specific terms and not too often measured and evaluated when a program has ended and results are in.

If it's any consolation to public relations practitioners, their advertising brethren do not fare much better. Steuart Henderson Britt, nationally known professor of marketing and advertising, analyzed "proofs of success" for 135 campaigns by 40 advertising agencies and he concluded that almost none of the agencies really knew, or even could know, whether or not their campaigns were successful. Britt reported that 99 percent of the agencies did not state campaign objectives in quantifiable terms; most of the agencies did not prove or demonstrate the success of the campaigns that they themselves had publicly stated were successes. Concluded Britt:

> Advertising of a product or service must prove its success as advertising by *setting specific objectives*. Such general statements of objectives as "introduce the product to the market," "raise sales," and "maintain brand share" are not objectives for advertising. Instead, they are the objectives of the entire marketing program. And even when considered as marketing goals, such statements still are too general and broad to be used to determine the extent of a plan's success or failure.
>
> Advertising goals should indicate (1) what basic message is to be delivered, (2) to what audience, (3) with what intended effect, and (4) what specific criteria are going to be used to measure the success of the campaign.
>
> When the advertising campaign is over, the advertiser can best judge the results by comparing them with the intended results, as expressed in the campaign objective. Only when he knows what he is intending to do can he know when and if he has accomplished it.[8]

If we are dealing with a public relations campaign, we can justifiably substitute public relations for advertising in Britt's above-mentioned conclusion. And if we do we will find that items one and two relating to goals—indication of the message and audience—will usually be covered in public relations programming, but items three and four, relating to *intended effect* and *criteria to be measured*, will most often be noticeably absent.

The Team Approach

Communications researcher Harold Mendelsohn suggests that one way to achieve attitude and behavior modification through public information campaigns is to involve the evaluators (communications researchers) in the campaign. Mendelsohn rightly points out that public relations practitioners and the communications researchers live in different worlds. As an alternative, he proposes that teams of practitioners and researchers work together in the development of information campaigns that utilize research principles rather than work separately. Further, he advises, the teams can then evaluate the campaigns' effectiveness in terms of actual rather than assumed intent and effect. If this is done, says Mendelsohn, such public information campaigns will have a high potential for success provided—

1. the campaigns are based on the recognition that most of the target audience will either be only mildly or not at all interested in what is communicated;

EXHIBIT 15.2 (cont.)

Sample Tracking Report

Placement Type	DMA Target Audience (in thousands)	Average Size/ Length	Average Media Units	Publicity Exposure Units (in thousands)	Average Impact Factor	Publicity Value Units (in thousands)
Newspapers	4,552	1/9 page	0.93	4,233	1.26	5,334
Magazines	268	1/2 page	1.66	455	1.47	656
Television (network)	95	5:10 min	1.93	183	0.81	149
Television (local)	504	6:05 min	2.13	1,073	1.81	1,946
Radio (local)	200	10:00 min	2.60	520	1.40	728
Totals	5,619		1.15	6,454	1.37	8,813

Publicity Exposure Norm = 5,960,000
Publicity Exposure Index (6,454/5,960) = 1.08
Publicity Value Index (8,813/5,960) = 1.48

Notes:

The Publicity Exposure Norm is established by estimating the target audiences (adults 18-49, weighted 60 percent male, 40 percent female) and exposure of a "good" hypothetical placement schedule.

The Publicity Exposure Index suggests that the campaign's exposure was 1.08, as good as expected on a normal (= 1.00) basis.

The Publicity Value Index suggests that the impact value of the campaign was 1.48 times as good as expected on a normal (= 1.00) basis.

The columns for average impact factor and publicity value units indicate the degree to which key 'selling' points in the copy were mentioned in the exposures. Note that the average impact factor for network television is low (0.81). The reason is that although the subject of the campaign (a special event) was mentioned fairly often (1.93 average media units), mention of specific dates and other key copy points did not meet expectations.

The tracking model also demonstrates in advance what a publicity program will do. Thus it is a tool for deciding whether or not a program is worth carrying out. If the decision is 'go,' it then reports how well objectives were met. Instead of guesswork, we now have a method for placing accountability to the client on a factual basis.

Source: Reprinted with permission from the July 1983 issue of *Public Relations Journal.* Copyright 1983.

2. the campaigns seek to achieve carefully delimited goals;
3. specific target audiences are delineated according to their lifestyles, value and belief systems, and personal and psychological attributes.

Mendelsohn cites as one example of his thesis a television safety program devised by the National Safety Council, the Communication Arts Center of the University of Denver, and the Columbia Broadcasting System. The target audience were so-called "bad drivers," and the aim was to reach three middle-range objectives: (1) to overcome public indifference to traffic hazards caused by bad driving; (2) to make bad drivers aware of their faults; and (3) to call attention to community social mechanisms designed to correct bad driving.

To implement the objectives a team of communications researchers, traffic safety experts, and television production personnel devised "The CBS National Driver's Test." A massive promotional campaign was instituted to attract a vast national audience to the program, which was subsequently aired just prior to a Memorial Day weekend. Both during the airing of the program and afterwards, evaluation research was carried out to determine the success of the program in meeting the specific objectives it had set up for itself.

Results? Approximately 30 million people watched the program. CBS received mail responses from 1.5 million viewers. Nearly 40 percent of the licensed drivers who participated in the broadcast test failed it, and 35,000 drivers enrolled in driver improvement programs nationwide following the telecast. States Mendelsohn:

> The lessons learned from this exercise suggest that innovative information-giving formats, abetted by strong prior promotion, can overcome preexisting so-called public apathy to a great degree. Second, it is clear that reasonable middle-range goals, narrowly defined and explicitly stated, are amenable to successful accomplishments.[9]

Management by Objectives

Mendelsohn's formula of practitioner-researcher team efforts is one way to achieve successful campaign results and to evaluate their effectiveness. Another is through the technique of *management by objectives*, which was discussed when we considered public relations planning and programming. The process is basically a method whereby an executive and each major subordinate manager under the executive work out together the identification of common goals, clearly define the subordinate's major area of responsibility in terms of expected results, and then use these measures as guides for operating the unit and evaluating the work of the subordinate and the unit.

The important elements of the process include joint agreement between superior and subordinate about goals that are agreed upon in advance. At the end of a time period the subordinate's performance and that of his unit are reviewed and evaluated, usually by joint participation of superior and subordinate in the review and evaluation process. If necessary, during the specified time period adjustments are made and inappropriate goals are discarded. If there are gaps between goals and performance or results when the final mutual review is made, then steps are taken to ascertain what might be done to overcome the problems.

The major advantage of the management by objectives process is that it involves mutual commitment to goals and objectives, a clear charting of objectives, and mutual review of results and evaluation. In effect, the process provides a map or chart to be followed in setting forth objectives, an order of priorities, and a method of review and evaluation. It can be used very effectively where objectives and activities to achieve them lend themselves to measurement and evaluation; it's difficult—as it is under almost all other systems—to use the management by objectives chart process as a means of measuring and evaluating programs and activities expected to lead to changes in attitudes and opinions.

The system used at Howard Community College (HCC) in Columbia, Maryland, provides a good example of a Management by Objectives program. At HCC goals are established for the entire college staff, and objectives for the college are set forth in terms of one-year and five-year objectives. Each unit in the college—and this includes the Office of Community Information—is then required to compile an annual "MBO Performance Plan." This plan is reviewed by each unit's appropriate supervisor and, as approved, it provides a tangible means of evaluating and measuring the activities of the unit for the academic year.

Exhibit 15.3 lists seven of twenty-six specific activities advanced by the Director of Community Information for approval by the unit's supervisor in one academic year. As

EXHIBIT 15.3

MBO Performance Plan: Office of Public Information
Howard Community College, Columbia, Maryland

Specific Statement of Outcome	Type of Objective*	Plan of Attack (What actions will you take to get the planned results?)	How Will Achievement Be Measured or Judged?	Measures of Achievement (Criteria can include quality, quantity, cost, time, completeness, accuracy, currency) Minimum	Average	Maximum	Priority E—Essential I—Important D—Desirable
Prepare and release news and feature articles to appropriate media to maintain a constant flow of information about HCC to the public.	R	A. Circulate "Newsfinder" forms monthly to encourage staff and faculty to identify news possibilities. B. Meet with faculty, staff and students to develop publicity for special programs. C. Write and distribute 3-4 releases per week. D. Suggest story ideas to editors and reporters. E. Arrange for photo coverage of significant college events.	The Community Information Office will maintain a clipping file and tabulate year-end results.	150 releases 500 published articles	175 releases 550 published articles	200 releases 600 published articles	E
Revise, update and maintain adequate supply of all brochures for instructional programs.	R	A. Meet with division chairmen to assess existing and new publication needs. B. Rewrite and/or edit content where needed. C. Supervise graphic design and production.	Publication of revised brochures by established deadlines; ratings of publications in student services and staff evaluations conducted by Office of Institutional Research.	Jan. 1980 revision date 2.5 rating	Dec. 1979 revision date 3.0 rating	Nov. 1979 revision date 3.5 rating	E

EXHIBIT 15.3 (cont.)

Specific Statement of Outcome	Type of Objective*	Plan of Attack (What actions will you take to get the planned results?)	How Will Achievement Be Measured or Judged?	Measures of Achievement (Criteria can include quality, quantity, cost, time, completeness, accuracy, currency)			Priority E—Essential I—Important D—Desirable
				Minimum	Average	Maximum	
Publish college catalog to meet all legal requirements for document and to provide necessary information to students and accrediting institutions.	R	A. Develop schedule for production to be distributed to college deans for submission of revisions. B. Obtain bids and select printer. C. Create improved format.	Publication by specified date. Judged by student and staff Services Evaluation.	June 1 2.5 rating	May 1 3.0 rating	April 1 3.5 rating	E
Update Speakers Bureau brochure and coordinate and promote usage by the community.	R	A. Develop form for staff to indicate interest in participating in Speakers Bureau. B. Publish revised brochure by April 1. C. Develop mailing list and distribute to community groups.	Publication by specified deadline for usage by community.	5 engagements annually	10 engagements annually	15 engagements annually	I
Serve as advisor to the student newspaper.	PS	A. Provide professional guidance to students on content, design and journalistic ideals. B. Assist editorial staff in dealing with management and fiscal issues. C. Attend regular meetings of college newspaper staff.	Attendance at meetings. Publication of predetermined number of issues.	70 percent attendance 11 issues annually	80 percent attendance 12 issues annually	90 percent attendance 13 issues annually	D

EXHIBIT 15.3 (cont.)

Specific Statement of Outcome	Type of Objective*	Plan of Attack (What actions will you take to get the planned results?)	How Will Achievement Be Measured or Judged?	Measures of Achievement (Criteria can include quality, quantity, cost, time, completeness, accuracy, currency)			Priority E—Essential I—Important D—Desirable
				Minimum	Average	Maximum	
Develop program of sports information to increase coverage of HCC intercollegiate athletics.	PS	A. Will meet with athletic director to define needs for program literature and press coverage. B. Will produce brochure on athletic program. C. Will distribute stories on sports events and athletes.	Production of articles on athletic programs and HCC's "Sports Stars".	60 percent coverage of inter-collegiate events 3 features	70 percent coverage of inter-collegiate events 5 features	80 percent coverage of inter-collegiate events 8 features	I
Recruit and supervise intern for community information.	PS-I	A. Contact area schools with journalism and/or public relations programs. B. Supervise intern.	Recruitment of intern.		One intern per year	Two interns per year	D

*R—Routine
P/S—Problem Solving
I—Innovative
P/G—Professional Growth

Reprinted with permission.

noted, the chart sets forth each activity, type of objective, plan of attack, means of measuring or judging achievement, criteria for measuring achievement, and degree of priority. Not included in the plan are such routine objectives and activities as serving on committees and attending public meetings.

PUBLIC OPINION SURVEYS AND PANELS

Survey research in the form of public opinion surveys and survey panels is a major method used in gathering empirical evidence to measure and evaluate public relations performance.

Public opinion surveys are utilized in two ways: either by means of a single survey taken at the end of a campaign or after a specified period of time, or by means of a before-and-after set of surveys. In both instances use is made of the survey techniques described in the chapter on research techniques: objectives of the survey and the universe are set forth; a random probability sample is drawn; a questionnaire is designed and administered; data are collected; and a report is written and delivered to management. The major objective of public opinion surveys as used in evaluation is to ascertain measurable results stemming from public relations performance and/or programs in regard to people's knowledge, attitudes, and opinions. The single survey makes no attempt to measure attitudes, opinions, and knowledge in advance of programming, but does so after the program has been carried out for a period of time.

> Company Y, a leading manufacturer of chemicals, has scores of plants throughout the country. One such plant, the Zulch Plant, is located on the banks of a heavily polluted river in the Midwest. In the late 1970s pollution of this river became so bad that citizens formed an antipollution committee that campaigned for cleanup of the river. Media supported the drive with numerous editorial campaigns, and one of the chief targets was the Zulch Plant.
>
> Called in by the plant management to give counsel and advice and to propose action was the central public relations department of Company Y. An independent outside agency was retained to conduct a study of the river's pollution, and its results showed that the Zulch Plant was but a minor contributor to the pollution. By means of meetings with concerned citizens and opinion leaders, a press conference announcing the results of the study of the river's sources of pollution, and other measures the public relations department told the story which exculpated the Zulch Plant.
>
> A public opinion survey conducted shortly thereafter showed that 88 percent of those surveyed considered the river to be dangerously polluted; 58 percent knew who were the main polluters; and 63 percent felt that the Zulch Plant went to much trouble and expense to avoid polluting the river. In almost all respects, the Zulch Plant was given high marks and considered in favorable terms by the respondents.

Thus, by the use of public opinion surveys the public relations department of Company Y was able to cite favorable survey results to measure the effectiveness of its campaign. Instead of merely reporting counsel given and action taken and then concluding that the program had been a success, the public relations department went directly to the public concerned, measured its knowledge and opinions, and cited results of the survey to prove effectiveness.

There is one single but important flaw to the above illustration. Because no survey of public knowledge and opinion had been taken *before* the program was instituted it was impossible to show that the program had changed lack of knowledge to knowledge and/or had changed unfavorable attitudes and opinions to favorable ones.

Before-and-After Survey

The *before-and-after survey* technique is a means of correcting the flaw cited in the above-mentioned case. As its name implies, this technique consists of two public opinion surveys, one taken *before* a campaign or program has been instituted and one taken *after* it has run for a period of time or has been concluded. The technique thus enables the practitioner to show numerical and percentage changes in public knowledge, attitude, and opinion taking place before and after public relations action and activities had been instituted, thereby enabling the practitioner to cite more reliable effectiveness proof than could be cited by means of the single public opinion survey.

The before-and-after survey technique is not often used in actual practice for several reasons. For one thing, it is expensive. Most managements are unwilling to incur expensive obligations for the sake of measuring effectiveness, but would rather put their money into actual programming. Another reason is that public opinion surveying requires a special expertise not generally found in public relations departments or counseling firms. A third reason is that the circumstances about many public relations programs do not lend themselves to precise before-and-after measurement and evaluation because there are too many variables involved. A fourth reason is that when dealing with a large universe, those surveyed before and after will inevitably be different samples of the universe; and even though these will be probability samples they are really different groups of people. A fifth and final reason is that before-and-after surveys could be the "moment of truth" for the practitioner by revealing that his carefully prepared and executed campaign produced either no change in public opinion or a change along negative lines, and certainly no one relishes that prospect.

The Alaska National Communication Program, cited in Chapter 11 (see Exhibit 11.3), provided for before-and-after surveys as a means of first identifying public attitudes and knowledge about Alaska and then later measuring the educational impact of the one-hour TV documentary about Alaska narrated by Hal Holbrook. The "before" survey was carried out in the spring of 1981 by the Dittman Research Corporation and its subcontractor, Burke Research. The "after" survey was conducted in the spring of 1982 by the Boston University School of Public Communication. Details of the Alaska National Communication Program and of the surveys are to be found in *Alaska National Communication Program, May 1981-May 1982,* a case study prepared and published by the Boston University School of Public Communication in 1982. The Boston University paperback deserves a careful reading because it illustrates some of the problems that arise in carrying out an educational program and evaluating it by means of before-and-after surveys.

The Survey Panel

The *survey panel* is used in measuring public relations effectiveness because it doesn't have the disadvantages of the single public opinion survey or the large cross-section samples used in before-and-after surveys. The panel is a sample of the same people interviewed more than once over a period of time. It is usually much smaller than the samples used in general cross-section public opinion surveys. Care is taken to ensure that the panel remains constant when the group is used to measure knowledge, attitudes, and opinions before and after a campaign has been instituted. Because the panel is small, its use as a measuring device is far less expensive than the larger cross-section sample. When the panel remains relatively constant it's possible to secure realistic measurement of campaign results as they affect the same group of people.

On the other hand, the survey panel poses another set of problems. When the panel is small—and most are small when compared to the larger samples used in normal cross-section surveys—any diminution in the number of panel members changes the basic nature of the sample used before the campaign and the sample surveyed after the campaign. When the survey sample is as large as that used in normal cross-section samples there is an inevitable mortality that occurs in any population over even a brief period of time. Second, the smaller the survey panel the more likely it will not be truly representative of the universe. Finally, because most panelists become aware that they are being used for measurement purposes, they become unduly conscious of their role and thus cannot be considered typical of the universe from which they were drawn. Despite these drawbacks, the survey panel offers the practitioner a relatively inexpensive, reliable, and simple means of measuring program effectiveness when used properly and with awareness of its methodological pitfalls.

INTERNAL AND EXTERNAL AUDITS

The process of auditing, which is most commonly identified with the field of accounting, has been used increasingly in recent years in public relations. The accounting audit entails an examination of records and accounts to check their accuracy. The public relations audit is most often used not so much to check accuracy as to check and improve the effectiveness of programs.

The Internal Audit

The *internal audit* takes the form of evaluation by one's peers and/or superiors within a public relations department or within a public relations counseling firm. The focus is usually on three areas summed up by three questions: what have you been doing and with what results; what are your problems; and what do you plan to do?

Sometimes the internal audit is a one-on-one evaluation of a staffer by his or her superior, but most often it's an evaluation by a "team" or committee selected for the sole purpose of conducting the evaluation. When the evaluation is completed, the team or committee is disbanded. Departmental audit teams are generally made up of the public relations department head and two or three middle-level or section heads. An audit of the account executive within a counseling firm is generally handled by a team composed of an executive vice-president who does not directly supervise the account executive and two or three other account executives.

When a staffer or account executive is being audited, he or she is inevitably given advance notice and, in many cases, is requested to prepare an advance-audit memorandum summarizing account or program activity, problems, and future plans. This enables the audit team to focus on specifics and has the added advantage of pushing the auditee into self-analysis. The audit itself is most often informal in nature, provides the auditee with valuable inputs from colleagues and superiors, and gives the auditors insights into account activities and programs they knew little about prior to the audit.

There are certain practical and psychological negative aspects to internal audits. An audit takes time, and time is precious in departments and counseling firms. Within departments public relations staffers have their own functional problems and committee meetings to attend, and the same applies to counseling firm account executives and supervisors. Those whose perceptions and judgments are excellent for audit team purposes are usually using these perceptions and judgments to handle accounts and important departmental tasks, and hence they cannot be called upon too often for an audit. Obviously, this problem can be taken care of by spreading auditing assignments, but not in small departments or in small counseling firms.

The psychological barrier can be a serious one because relatively few creative people react with equanimity to criticism, and there is a tendency for an auditee to be defensive. Thus, the audit team must use a good deal of tact as well as judgment when an audit is being conducted.

The practical and psychological problems involved in internal public relations audits are summed up succinctly in the following excerpt of a letter sent to the author by the head of a large public relations department:

> There are two reasons why we abandoned the audit: I have been too busy, and the method was not successful—psychologically.
>
> Had I time, we could probably remedy the latter defect and resume the audit. The method was to sit down regularly with each section head and one of his staff peers for a

discussion of his work. Objectives were re-examined, progress was discussed, and suggestions made for improvement. The difficulty with this procedure was that the co-auditor frequently did not have sufficient background for his task, and some section heads were defensive in their reaction. . . .

The author had the opportunity to spend several weeks one summer at Hill & Knowlton, where account audits are conducted regularly within the firm. At H & K audit teams are called into being from within the organization, each team usually being unique and existing for the purpose of one audit. After the team has been selected, the account executive whose account is being audited prepares a memorandum describing the main aspects, objectives, plans, and programs of the account. Distribution of the memorandum is made to the team, following which the account executive and members of his staff (where there is a staff) meet with the team to discuss the items in the memorandum and to be critiqued by the auditors.

The author's interviews with various H & K people indicate that the audit brings out new ideas that can be put to valuable use. At the same time, those on the audit team gain from the process because they get insights about accounts unfamiliar to them. The chief executives of the firm do not sit in on audits, but they receive all audit correspondence, and thus the system not only brings about an evaluation of program effectiveness but also provides better all-agency service to clients. A more or less typical H & K pre-audit memorandum is reprinted in the case at the end of the chapter.

The External Audit

The *external audit* differs from the internal audit in one obvious, major way: it is conducted by those outside of the organization being audited. In some cases the organization may contract with an outside expert or a panel to come in and conduct a one- or three-day audit of practices, procedures, and programs, and to make recommendations for improving effectiveness. More common, however, is the comprehensive audit service now being offered by an increasing number of public relations counseling firms.

In many respects the external audit is similar to the preliminary study undertaken by counseling firms when they first take on a new account. Through research, interviews, and analysis a thorough study is made of the organization's goals, publics, products and services, public relations objectives, short- and long-range plans, etc. The major difference between the preliminary study and the external audit is that in the former case the counseling firm usually carries out its analysis prior to establishing and carrying out a public relations program; in the latter case the analysis is usually made of an existing public relations program and is therefore an analysis and measure of the public relations effectiveness of the program. Most external audits go beyond measuring effectiveness and provide suggestions and/or a blueprint for future public relations activity. The audit is considered here chiefly as a tool for measuring public relations effectiveness.

The axiom that "you get what you pay for" applies to the external audit as well as to the purchase of most products and services. An audit may be completed in five or six weeks or it may take six months; it can deal with only one aspect of a public relations program or it can encompass the entire program; it can be carried out entirely by the counseling firm's own staff or the firm may call in national research organizations. Properly handled, the external audit is an effective means of practical research that provides management with another tool to measure public relations efforts.

ENDNOTES

1. James F. Tirone, "Measuring the Bell System's Public Relations," *Public Relations Review*, Winter 1977, p. 21.
2. Robert K. Marker, "The Armstrong/PR Data Measurement System," *Public Relations Review*, Winter 1977, p. 51.

3. Paul H. Alvarez, "And Now Comes Chapter III," *Public Relations Journal*, July 1983, p. 27.
4. Burns W. Roper, "Can We Measure Public Relations Results?" *Public Relations Journal*, April 1958, p. 3.
5. From a presentation by John F. Budd at an American Management Associations program, New York City, July 10, 1980, and from a letter to the author from Mr. Budd, July 29, 1980.
6. Roper, p. 3.
7. Marker, p. 56.
8. Steuart H. Britt, "Are So-Called Successful Advertising Campaigns Really Successful?" *Journal of Advertising Research*, vol. 9, no. 2.
9. Harold Mendelsohn, "Some Reasons Why Information Campaigns Can Succeed," *Public Opinion Quarterly*, Spring 1973, p. 55.

PROJECTS, ASSIGNMENTS, AND MINIS

1. SETTING GOALS AND OBJECTIVES FOR YOUR SCHOOL'S PUBLIC RELATIONS DEPARTMENT: AN ASSIGNMENT

In setting goals and objectives, a western college established a system whereby each department in the college was required to set forth broad departmental goals and then to follow each goal with one or more five-year objectives and, in some cases, with one or more one-year objectives. One example of a goal and objectives for the public relations department read as follows:

> **Goal:** The public relations department will assist in fostering positive attitudes among students towards themselves and the college.
>
> **Five-Year Objective:** The department will biennially assess the attitudes of the students and report the results to the president.
>
> **One-Year Objective:** The department will implement, on a pilot basis, the instrument to assess the attitudes of the students.

You are to assume that your school has decided to establish a goals-and-objectives system similar to the one cited above. You have been given the responsibility of establishing **five** major goals for the public relations department, five-year objectives, and, in some cases, one-year objectives for each goal. Prepare a memorandum to your instructor carrying out this assignment, and be prepared to present an oral report to the class detailing your ideas. The class, in effect, will be role-playing the leading officials of the school.

2. THE CINCINNATI UNITED NATIONS CAMPAIGN: A MINI-CASE CLASSIC

In a world of swift-moving change, what happened just yesterday seems to be medieval history. Therefore, the educational campaign conducted in Cincinnati in 1947 must seem like ancient history. Yet that campaign and the surveys associated with it remain a classic case of before-and-after measurement and evaluation. The case is classic chiefly because it has seldom been duplicated in the years since; therefore, it deserves our attention.

What was involved here was an information campaign designed to make Cincinnati residents better informed about the United Nations and world affairs. What makes the case of interest and importance to public relations students and practitioners is that sufficient funds were provided through a grant to carry out independent before-and-after surveys to determine the effectiveness of the six-month campaign. The "before" survey consisted of interviews in September with a random/probability sample of 745 persons; the "after" survey consisted of interviews in March with a random/probability sample of 758 persons, 592 of whom had been interviewed in September. (The last 20 percent of the original sample either refused to be interviewed a second time or could not be located.)

Between the two surveys a massive educational campaign was conducted in Cincinnati to make its residents more intelligently informed about world affairs and about the United Nations. A total of 14,000 children in the Weekday Church Schools held a World Community Day program; training courses were given to 150 leaders in the Cincinnati Council of Church Women; close to 13,000 people were reached through programs on world understanding put on by the Parent-Teachers Association; UN literature was given to every school child; radio stations and newspapers aired and printed UN news and information during the entire six-month period. A total of 60,000 pieces of literature were distributed, 2,800 clubs reached by speakers, and hundreds of documentary film presentations made. The slogan "Peace Begins with the United Nations, the United Nations Begins with You" was shown everywhere and repeated in every conceivable manner.

The effectiveness of this massive informational campaign was measured by the results obtained by the two surveys, and they showed relatively few changes in public knowledge and attitude. A total of 65 percent in September and 66 percent in March were of the opinion the United States should take an active part in world affairs rather than keep out of them; 76 percent in September and 73 percent in March were of the opinion that the United States should join with other nations to establish an international police force to maintain world peace. In September 30 percent could not tell the main purpose of the United Nations, and by March the number had dropped to 28 percent. In September 55 percent knew that one job of the UN was to see that all people get equal rights and 50 percent knew another UN job was to improve health conditions everywhere; by March the comparable figures were 60 percent and 55 percent respectively. In March people blamed or praised the UN for the very things they had blamed or praised it for earlier and by virtually unchanged percentages.

Questions for Discussion

1. What is your opinion of the before-and-after design of the surveys as a means of measuring the campaign's effectiveness?

2. What is your reaction to the survey results? Can you cite reasons why there was so little change in public knowledge and opinion after such an extensive educational campaign?

3. After consulting appropriate sources to ascertain the nature of international and UN relationships between September and March of 1947, explain the connection you see between these relationships and the survey results.

4. What lessons do we learn from this case?

3. AN INTERNAL AUDIT MEMORANDUM: A MINI-EXAMPLE

Preparatory to an internal audit at Hill & Knowlton, the account executive responsible for Account X wrote and disseminated the following pre-audit review memorandum* which was sent to those on the audit team:

Background
The client manufactures a wide variety of products which are sold through independent wholesalers. The account was relatively dormant until a new president was installed and the client switched from a fee-plus-staff time basis to a monthly minimum that provides a specific service for every dollar spent.

PR Objectives
H & K's main efforts are focused on getting maximum exposure in all media for those products and brand names of the client listed under Item A on the attached list. The company's internal p.r. staff also is helped to service routine financial news. The management and its public relations department were advised on strategy to fight off possible tender offers a few years ago. . . .

Problems
The overriding concern is to give the client satisfactory performance and results without pricing ourselves out of the market. Staff charges for creative talent are expensive com-

---

*Reprinted with permission of Hill & Knowlton.

pared to the salaries paid the internal publicity department which is located in a non-metropolitan area. Another complication is that H & K's system of hourly charges does not make it practical to assign a writer permanently to develop ideas and news outlets for the client's products. We do not specialize in the area represented by these products and the publicity department would need to gear up to placing articles in trade magazines important to the account.

A serious situation within the company is the lack of liaison between public relations and advertising and sales promotion. This impedes sales promotion from capitalizing on later publicity placements to dealer organizations.

The new president of the company has been avoiding interviews with financial and business publications until he has established, as he says, a track record, an obstacle which may be surmounted as he gains confidence in his position.

Recommendations
Since the client's internal public relations staff is fairly competent, H & K charges can be kept within reasonable bounds by feeding his people ideas which they can proceed to develop. Such suggestions can be given more impact by uncovering new outlets for product publicity unexplored by the client. We can also bring the client to the attention of influential groups and audiences he is not now reaching.

A fertile, untapped field for the client is the real estate section in local newspapers. The product publicity managers are greatly impressed by circulation figures tabulated and analyzed by PR Data. These figures, in turn, are presented enthusiastically to the Division managers who underwrite the public relations program. Anything that can be done to boost the circulation totals will fortify our position.

This suggestion can be expedited by getting two or three other H & K clients with related interests to participate in a monthly clip sheet directed to special editors and sections of newspapers. Done properly, the project would go far beyond a mat sheet beamed only to weeklies and small dailies.

The client's conservative approach to publicity must be changed by generating stories with popular appeal. Pollution is a subject that is in the news, and as the client's products effectively reduce pollution this can be brought to the public's attention in a variety of ways. Service features can be developed pointing up areas where use of the client's products can be most advantageous, and publicity can also be developed to demonstrate unusual product applications. TV can be exploited profitably by developing a traveling show for interview programs, with a company representative demonstrating the various ways in which client products are useful to the consumer.

Questions for Discussion

1. What is your opinion of the tone, format, and contents of the above pre-audit memorandum?

2. What questions would you ask about the problems cited in the memo? At this point, without knowing the answers, what advice—if any—would you give to help solve the problems?

3. What is your opinion of the recommendations cited in the memorandum?

4. If you were on the audit team, what points in the memorandum would you want to explore further?

5. If you were the H & K executive to whom the writer of the memorandum reports, in what ways would the memorandum influence your evaluation of the writer?

4. STUDIES OF SEAT BELT USE: A MINI-CASE

In April and May, 1977, Motorists Information, Inc., an organization formed by the four domestic automobile manufacturing companies to promote the use of seat belts, conducted a media campaign in Grand Rapids, Michigan, to increase use of seat belts. The campaign theme, "Somebody Needs You," was used in television, radio, newspaper, and outdoor advertising. In June, on the basis of telephone interviews of a random sample of licensed drivers, Motorists Information reported that the number who said they used seat belts "always" or "most of the time" rose from 29 per cent to 41 percent during the campaign.

Using Milwaukee, Wisconsin, as a control city in seeking to compare the results of the Grand Rapids interviews to interviews in another city not exposed to the campaign, Motorists Information also questioned drivers in Milwaukee. The random sample of drivers in that city claimed a level of seat belt use "always" and "most of the time" at 48 percent.

To measure actual belt use after the campaign, Leon S. Robertson of the Insurance Institute for Highway Safety conducted a study* in which belt use was directly observed in the two cities in which Motorists Information conducted its telephone surveys. (The IIHS describes itself as "an independent, nonprofit, scientific and educational organization . . . dedicated to reducing the losses resulting from crashes on the nation's highways. The Institute is supported by the American Insurance Highway Safety Association, the American Insurers Highway Safety Alliance, the National Association of Independent Insurers Safety Association, and several individual insurance companies.")

Ten sites on major thoroughfares in each of the two cities were chosen for observation by Robertson. Lap and shoulder belt use of drivers and shoulder belt use of passengers in the right-front seat were observed and recorded. More than one thousand drivers were observed in each city.

Results of the IIHS direct observance study showed that 87 percent of the drivers and 95 percent of the passengers in Grand Rapids and 88 percent of the drivers and 97 percent of the passengers in Milwaukee were *not* using belts. Shoulder belt use was only 7 percent among drivers in each city and even less among passengers—5 percent in Grand Rapids and 3 percent in Milwaukee. Concluded Robertson: "The claim by Motorists Information, Inc., and others that more than 40 percent of drivers are using belts is a myth based on claimed use rather than actually observed use."

Questions for Discussion

1. If you were to judge the Motorists Information campaign in Grand Rapids on the basis of the results of its survey of licensed drivers, would you consider it a reasonably successful campaign? Why or why not?

2. What information, other than that cited in the case fact pattern, would you want to know about the Motorists Information campaign and study? The IIHS study?

3. What reasons can you think of for the IIHS to conduct its own study of actual seat belt usage and subsequently report its findings as compared with those of Motorists Information?

4. What lessons about reporting, measurement, and effectiveness have you learned from this case?

---

*Leon S. Robertson, "Auto Industry Belt Use Campaign Fails," Insurance Institute for Highway Safety, Washington, D.C., August 1977, pp. 1-4.

Part

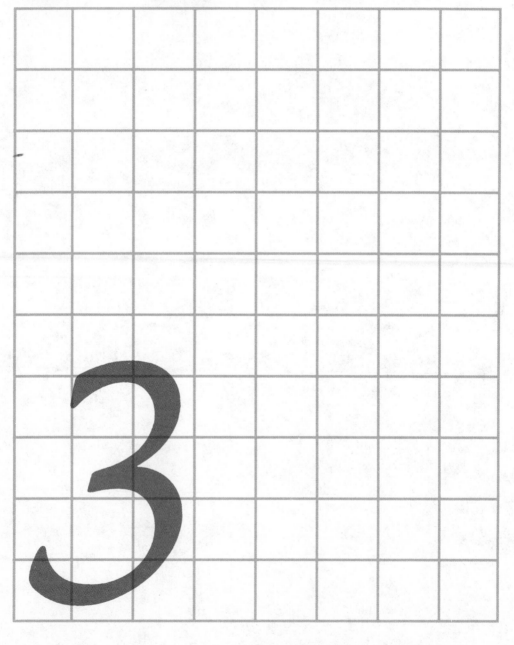

3

PART 3
CONTEMPORARY
CONCERNS

C ontemporary concerns, the focus of the remaining chapters of this book, requires a preliminary explanation to clarify the meaning of contemporary. As applied to public relations practice, such concerns are defined herein as those which reflect special interest for the decade of the eighties. Some of them are carryover concerns from the previous decade and may well prove to be of concern into the nineties. Others are so new and changing so swiftly it's difficult to predict their ultimate role within the public relations field, but their relevancy makes it important that they be discussed and analyzed.

Professional people in all fields are justifiably sensitive to the relationship of the law to their calling, and public relations practitioners share this sensitivity with those in other fields. Chapter 16 seeks to deal with certain legal elements—libel, copyright, and privacy, to name just a few—which seem to be most important for those who practice public relations. The chapter should provide a foundation upon which can be installed legal building blocks developed from contemporary cases.

Among the legal cases having had an effect on public relations are those involving corporate political expression, and these form the core of Chapter 17. One case dealing with banks and the other two with public utilities are explored in depth, and these are followed by an in-depth look at advocacy advertising as seen by its proponents and critics.

Chapter 18, dealing as it does with the technological revolution and public relations practice, was deliberately placed at the end of this book. Technological changes, mostly in the area of communication via the electronic media, have come about in such swift profusion as to make conclusions about them a difficult task. However, the attempt must be made to understand these technological changes because of their connection to public relations practice, and this is what the chapter attempts to do.

The final chapter in this book should have special relevance to students because it deals with those personal concerns which students have shared with the author over several decades. These concerns are ethical, practical, educational, and professional. They're left to last because they should be fresh in students' minds. They deserve to be aired because the airing leads to sharing, and that in turn should help those who have had the fortitude and the interest to last the course.

16

LEGAL ASPECTS OF PUBLIC RELATIONS PRACTICE

roof that today's so-called litigious society has affected public relations practice is found in a comparison of public relations textbooks over a ten-year period. In the early seventies such subjects as libel and privacy were noticeable by their absence in public relations texts. Virtually all of the texts published in the early eighties deal in a substantial way with the legal aspects of public relations practice.

The reason is simple. Whether we consider public relations to be a business, field, or profession, those who practice in it sometimes find themselves up to their eyeteeth in legal actions. The practitioner who writes and sends out a press release which defames a private person may well find himself or herself as defendant in a libel suit. The financial public relations specialist who is not conversant with modifications in Securities and Exchange rules and regulations can find himself the subject of an SEC action aimed at him and his firm. The public relations director of a large hospital may well find herself and the hospital charged with a violation of her state's Freedom of Information Act as a result of topics discussed at a closed meeting of the hospital's board of trustees. The activist organization which brought the matter to the attention of the proper state authorities may have been advised to do so by its director of public relations.

Thus, whether on the plaintiff or defendant side of a legal action or situation, it behooves the practitioner to be well versed in those aspects of the law which impact on public relations practice. The aspects are far too numerous for all of them to be covered thoroughly in this basic public relations textbook, but certain major ones will be discussed in the pages that follow. These include libel and privacy; access to information, meetings, and the media; copyright regulations; and financial regulations. Those interested in more specifics about financial regulations are referred to the official interpretation of the PRSA code as it applies to financial public relations, in Appendix A, and to Robert W. Taft's 1982 table of Corporate Reporting Requirements, reprinted as Appendix B.

TORT LAW: LIBEL AND PRIVACY

Libel and privacy are two areas of tort law which have definite ramifications for public relations practice and practitioners. Defamatory statements made in organizational publications, news releases, press conferences, and such can bring on suits for libel. Conversely, practitioners or the organizations they represent can sue others for defamation. Clearly, it's to the advantage of the practitioner to understand the elements, nature, and scope of both libel and privacy.

LIBEL

Both libel and slander are forms of defamation. Slander is oral communication and libel is written. For the sake of convenience, in the discussion to follow the term libel will be used to cover both forms.

Defamation, which comprises the twin torts of libel and slander, has been described as follows:

> Defamation is . . . that which tends to injure 'reputation' in the popular sense; to diminish the esteem, respect, goodwill or confidence in which the plaintiff is held, or to excite adverse, derogatory or unpleasant feelings or opinions against him.[1]

There are other, more comprehensive descriptions of defamation, but inherent in almost all of them is the requirement that the plaintiff's **reputation** must be affected adversely.[2] A libel is a communication which damages the reputation of a person. "The defamatory communication," states Pember, "must be capable of lowering a person's reputation in the eyes of a significant number of people, and unless unusual circumstances exist, these people must reflect fairly representative views."[3] In elaborating, Pember notes that persons can be injured through libel in a variety of ways. The statement may simply hurt their reputation. It may, by lowering their reputation, diminish their social contacts or their ability to hold a job or make a living. If a plaintiff can show actual harm in any of these ways, he has a good chance of recovering damages.[4]

It's obvious that a wide variety of words and expressions are potentially libelous, but Gillmor and Barron suggest that empathy is the best guide to use in estimating libelous words. They ask: "What words, allegations, charges would you consider a hurtful attack on your reputation and personality? Make your own list and think of it as comprising words which form the boundaries of a legal mine field."[5] Another authority, Marc Franklin, says that words and expressions that are potentially libelous are those that contend that a person is inept in his profession, field, or trade; committed a crime; or is a member of a group of a political party that is in disrepute in the community. "It is enough that the published statement be of the sort that would lead a segment of the community to think less of the plaintiff."[6] The segment of the community that Franklin speaks of need not be large. If, for example, a person is an expert in some field and the libelous words reach a small group of other experts in his field, that small group could well think less of the plaintiff and he would have a good case for libel.

One cannot be too careful when it comes to communications which have the potential to be considered libelous. Nelson and Teeter cite a case in which a publication lost a libel suit because it made editing changes in a press release. Details are given in Exhibit 16.1.

What about corporations? Although a corporation does not have a reputation in a personal sense, it does have standing and prestige in the field in which it operates. There-

EXHIBIT 16.1

Pat Montandon, author of *How to Be a Party Girl,* was to discuss her book on the Pat Michaels "Discussion" show. *TV Guide* received the show producer's advance release, which said that Montandon and a masked, anonymous prostitute would discuss "From Party-Girl to Call Girl?" and "How far can the 'party-girl' go until she becomes 'call-girl'." *TV Guide* ineptly edited the release, deleting reference to the prostitute and publishing this: "10:30 Pat Michaels—*Discussion* 'From Party Girl to Call Girl.' Scheduled guest: TV Personality Pat Montandon and author of 'How to Be a Party Girl'." Montandon sued for libel and won $150,000 in damages. On appeal, the court noted that *TV Guide* editors had testified that they did not believe the average reader would interpret the program note in the magazine as relating Montandon to a call girl or labelling her as a call girl. The appeals court said the testimony "flies in the face of reason" and upheld the libel judgment.[7]

fore, states Prosser, statements which "cast an aspersion upon its honesty, credit, efficiency or other business characteristics may be actionable. The same is true of a partnership or an unincorporated association."[8] As for nonprofit organizations, they may depend on donations and therefore they may be defamed by attacks which would tend to decrease contributions.

The Elements of Libel

When a libel suit is brought it's up to the plaintiff to prove several elements even before the defendant is required to establish a defense. The plaintiff must prove that the communication was published; that the plaintiff is the person referred to in the libel; that the statement made is defamatory; and that negligence on the part of the publisher was involved.[9]

Publication in a libel action is not the same as that normally associated with the word. Publication in the legal sense takes place when just one person, in addition to the writer and the person defamed, sees or hears the material. In the case of *Ostrowe* v. *Lee*, a man dictated a letter to his secretary in which he accused the addressee of grand larceny. The letter was subsequently typed and mailed. The accused brought a libel suit and the court held that the publication took place when the stenographic notes were read and transcribed.[10] An Illinois circuit court jury granted a $9.2 million libel judgment against the *Alton Telegraph* for words that the newspaper never published. The words were in a memorandum that two of the paper's reporters sent to a Justice Department task force on crime, alleging connections of Alton citizens to organized crime.[11]

The lesson for public relations practitioners should be clear: "publication" in a libel situation exists even when only three people are involved: the communicator, another person, and the person who claims he has been libeled.

There is another important aspect to the publication element, and that's republication. Every republication of a libel creates a new libel. Thus, as Pember notes, if the *Sentinel* is being sued for libel because it called Smith a Communist and the *Gazette* in reporting the story notes that the *Sentinel* called Smith a Communist, the *Gazette* has republished the libel.[12] Further, republication means that everyone in the chain of publication—that is, the reporter, rewrite, the editor, the copyperson, etc.—is liable in a lawsuit.

Identification, the second libel element, means that the plaintiff must demonstrate that he was identified in the alleged libel. In most cases, the plaintiff is clearly and accurately named and so there's no problem regarding identification. However, a careless error—such as wrong initials, a typographical error, an incorrect address—can link an innocent person with a crime, immorality, unethical business practices, or another activity that is the basis for a libel suit.[13] A major reason why it's sound journalism practice to provide complete identification of people is to avoid instances of mistaken identity in potentially libelous situations. Double-checking names should become a habit, not an afterthought that is sometimes forgotten.

What about situations where a group is libeled and a member of the group sues for libel? Although the answer is not entirely clear, if the group is especially large—say, for example, most lawyers—there can be no suit by an individual lawyer. However, if the group is small, then each member can bring suit. How small is "small"? Three, four, or five is small, and some authorities consider that twenty-five is small.

Defamatory words, as already mentioned in this section's initial remarks about libel, are those which injure reputation. In bringing suit, a plaintiff will claim that certain words or expressions have defamed him; the judge or jury will decide the merit of his claim. In so doing they are supposed to consider words in their ordinary meaning. Many are clearly libelous on their face. Stating that someone has done something illegal is libelous. Stating that someone is dishonest is libelous. Comments about business ethics can be defamatory. Although the law does not consider that business or professional people are perfect, it's dangerous to impute incompetence to doctors, teachers, businessmen, lawyers, and such. Pember suggests this litmus test when evaluating whether something is defamatory: "Will the people in the community think less of this person after I publish this story than they do before I publish it? If the answer is yes, then the statement, remark, or comment is probably defamatory."[14] A reminder is in order at this point: it's still defamatory even when you attribute it to someone else.

Negligence, the fourth libel element, is what is known as "fault" on the part of the person who publishes the alleged libel. In the landmark 1974 case of *Gertz* v. *Welch* (418 U.S. 323, 94 S. Ct. 2997) the United States Supreme Court ruled that in order to succeed in a libel suit purely private or nonpublic persons must show negligence on the part of the defendant. Negligence can be shown in many ways: a story was erroneously published; the writer was negligent in evaluating the defamatory nature of the words; someone failed to catch a typographical error; there was mistaken identity. In its *Gertz* decision the Court did not set forth the standard of conduct to be used as the yardstick in judging negligence, but left it up to the individual states to establish such standards. State legislatures have taken different routes in so doing, hence the need to know state laws on this matter.

Some years before *Gertz* the Supreme Court established a new "fault" standard for public officials and public figures. In the landmark 1964 *New York Times* v. *Sullivan* case (376 U.S. 254, 84 S.Ct. 710) the Court ruled that in order to succeed in a libel case involving a public official it must be shown that the fault of the news medium amounted to *actual malice.* That means the plaintiff has to prove that the defendant publisher either knew that the communication was false or else recklessly disregarded its truth or falsehood. In subsequent cases the Court extended the *Times* rule to cover public figures.[15]

Libel Suit Defenses

Assuming that the plaintiff has established he has a cause for libel action, what defenses are open to the defendant? There are the common-law defenses of truth, privilege, and fair comment, and there is the constitutional defense of the First Amendment. In addition there is the statute of limitations. In most states if a libel action is not brought within one to five years after publication of the alleged libel, no libel action is possible.

Truth as a Defense

Truth is recognized in most states as a complete defense in a libel action.[16] Pember notes that the words may be defamatory and they may well harm the reputation of the plaintiff, but the injured party will lose his suit for libel if the statement is true and if the defendant can convince the jury that what he has published is the truth.[17] In short, it's up to the defendant to prove the truth of what he has published, and that's not often easy to do. Sanford emphasizes this point when he states:

> Therefore, the best safeguard against a libel suit is to make certain before publication that any potentially libelous statement is true and, even more important, can be proven true.[18]

A point of caution is in order at this point. One does not demonstrate the truth of a charge simply by showing that one has correctly quoted or accurately reported what someone else said. Truth can be sustained only by proving the substance of a libelous charge.[19]

Privilege as a Defense

Newspapers or broadcasters who report fairly and accurately libelous statements made in official proceedings of legislatures, the courts, and governmental meetings are protected in a libel action by the doctrine of conditional or qualified privilege. (Absolute privilege attaches to those who are serving in an official capacity in legislatures, courts, and government. So long as the potentially libelous statements are made in pursuance of their official duties, such utterances have absolute privilege.)

Pember points out that certain conditions have to be met if conditional or qualified privilege is to apply, and he cites them as follows:

- The privilege applies only to reports of certain kinds of meetings, generally meetings of governmental bodies, public meetings on issues of public importance, and other public proceedings.

- The privilege applies only to reports which are a fair and accurate or truthful summary of what occurred at the meeting.

- Publication of a report cannot be motivated by malice such as ill will.[20]

Utterances that are protected by the privilege defense lose that protection when made outside of official proceedings. What an attorney or a judge tells a reporter in the hallway after a trial is not privileged. Even a United States Senator can lose his absolute privilege by issuing a press release. Stated the Supreme Court in ruling against Senator Proxmire in a 1979 case: "A speech by Proxmire in the Senate would be wholly immune and would be available to other Members of Congress and the public in the Congressional Record. But neither the newsletters nor the press release was 'essential to the deliberations of the Senate' and neither was part of the deliberative process."[21]

Fair Comment as a Defense

The fair comment defense protects the media for expressing opinion about public performances of those who voluntarily place themselves before the public: sports figures, politicians, entertainers. In many states the defense has been extended to cover caustic social commentary, political rhetoric, and criticism of the arts, so long as the comment is clearly an expression of opinion.[22]

Sanford says that a good rule to follow when expressing an opinion is to cite the facts on which you base your views and then state your opinion. He also says that the fair comment defense will generally apply when it meets these criteria:

- The comment or criticism is based on a matter of public interest.

- The comment or criticism is based on certain stated facts which are believed to be true and are fully stated.

- The comment or criticism is not an allegation of fact and is purely comment or criticism.

- Malice has not been involved in the comment or criticism.[23]

The First Amendment as a Defense

As has already been mentioned in the section on negligence, in the landmark *New York Times* v. *Sullivan* case the Supreme Court ruled that a public official cannot recover damages for a defamatory falsehood relating to his official conduct unless he proves that a statement was made with 'actual malice'—that is, with knowledge that it was false or with reckless disregard of whether it was false or not.[24]

In subsequent cases the Court extended the *Times* rule to "public figures" and in the *Gertz* case defined them as persons "who occupy positions of such persuasive power and influence that they are deemed public figures for all purposes" or who are otherwise private individuals but have voluntarily thrust themselves or been drawn into the vortex of a significant public controversy in order to influence the resolution of the issues involved.[25]

Among the reasons why *Gertz* is important is that Gertz was a prominent Chicago lawyer, but the Court ruled he was not a public figure because he had not thrust himself into a significant public controversy. Therefore, he didn't have to prove actual malice in bringing his suit but as a private person needed only prove a level of fault short of actual malice.

To those involved in a libel suit it clearly makes a big difference whether the private or public figure designation applies, because it is more difficult to prove actual malice than to prove negligence. Both executives and corporations should consider not only the legal but also the public relations ramifications when considering bringing a libel suit against critics they feel have defamed them.[26] Suits by prominent figures against major media for large sums of money inevitably result in considerable media coverage. This may be fine when the plaintiff wins, but it's not so fine when he loses.

RIGHT OF PRIVACY

Public relations practitioners find themselves involved with the right of privacy both as plaintiffs and defendants. Communications deals with names, photographs, news, publicity, and all of these are tied to the concept known as the right of privacy.

It is a right not easily described. Prosser states that it is not one tort, but a complex of four: "To date the law of privacy comprises four distinct kinds of invasion of four different interests of the plaintiff, which are tied together by the common name, but otherwise have almost nothing in common except that each represents an interference with the right of the plaintiff 'to be let alone'."[27]

The four privacy elements that Prosser speaks of are **appropriation; intrusion; private information publication;** and **publication of false facts.**

Appropriation is an invasion of privacy in which a person's name, picture, photograph, or likeness is taken and used without his permission for commercial gain.[28] Appropriation usually is connected with the use of a person's name or likeness for advertising or trade purposes without written consent. However, most states have held that the news media may use the name or picture of a person without his consent when said usage is part of the coverage of a news event. Pember cites the rule this way: "Use of a person's name or likeness to inform as opposed to sell is protected."[29]

Applying this rule to certain kinds of public relations communications raises questions. "Presumably," says Simon, "routine use thereof [of an employee's name or picture] in connection with some 'news item' of interest to his fellow employees should not be a privacy violation, assuming that it does not go beyond the limits of normal reporting and interest and is in good taste. However, any such use in an external house organ, distributed widely outside the 'corporate family'—among a public which normally has no interest in an employee—might raise serious questions."[30]

One sound answer to questions about appropriation is found in this advice: when in doubt, don't punt; get written consent.

Securing a *consent release* provides a sound defense against an invasion of privacy charge. Consent can be implied or written, and in most cases written consent is the safer route for the practitioner to follow.

Because courts recognize a consent release as a form of contract, *consideration* or value must be exchanged in order for the contract to be binding on the part of the parties to it. If a person signs a consent release but no consideration is involved, the practitioner can find himself in trouble later because the consenter can revoke his consent at any time.

The "something of value" that the courts require will usually not be questioned by a court in terms of its magnitude. Many consent releases involve the exchange of only $1 between the parties, and sometimes the free publicity that may result is considered to be sufficient consideration.

Duration is another element important in a consent release, and this refers to the length of time the consent is to be in force. There is no typical or required duration period, but it's safe to say that a period of five to ten years would be considered reasonable. Most courts will not recognize a consent release written so as to be in force forever.

Practitioners should make sure that the consent release applies to all situations in which a person's likeness or name is likely to be used.

Intrusion has been described as "an intrusion into [the victims'] 'physical solitude or seclusion' or into their 'private affairs'."[31] Some common examples of intrusion are the wrongful use of tape recorders, cameras, microphones, etc., to record someone's private activities. It's intrusion when a reporter misrepresents himself to gain access to a place or person or else trespasses upon private property.[32]

Private information publication is considered one of the most controversial and difficult of privacy rights to pin down. Sanford describes as examples of this type of invasion of privacy sensational disclosures about a person's health, sexual activity, social or economic affairs, and other private matters. However, a story or photograph of an event that takes place in public is not actionable, no matter how sensational or embarrassing it may be.[33] If the story or photo is about a public official or public figure, has public interest, or comes from the public record, the defense is in a good position to win a suit even though the plaintiff can show embarrassment. The cases the media have lost have mostly been those which generally involved involuntary public figures, that is, private people who were thrust unwillingly into the limelight, and where the stories had little public value.[34]

Publication of false facts is very similar to libel because it involves an element of falsity, in this case placing a person before the public in a false light. It most commonly occurs when the media seek to condense or fictionalize so as to come up with a dramatic news or feature story. When an otherwise true story is embellished with a few falsehoods, that's fictionalization. False light takes place when the writer gives readers a false impression by publishing facts which are not true about a person.[35]

The incidental, nondefamatory use of the name of an actual person in a fictionalized account is generally not considered actionable. However, wholesale creation of a fictionalized character who closely resembles a real person can lead to liability.[36]

ACCESS TO INFORMATION, MEETINGS, AND THE MEDIA

Access, the ability and/or right to gain entry, has particular importance to public relations practitioners in three areas: to secure information; to be able to attend meetings of governmental bodies; and to have their communications appear in print or over the air. Access is important to the practitioner no matter whether he represents an organization which is seeking access or whether he represents an organization denying access. The practitioner who represents an agency of the federal government, for example, would view access in one way and the practitioner who represents an organization seeking information from that same agency would tend to view access in another way. Clearly, knowing the dimensions and boundaries of access has a bearing on the way the practitioner functions, and will be explored in this section.

ACCESS TO GOVERNMENT INFORMATION

Of special importance to those practitioners working for government agencies or for other organizations seeking information in the files of such agencies is the Freedom of Information Act, passed by Congress in 1966 and amended in 1974. It was felt that the FOI Act would be used mainly by journalists, and although they are among the major users of the act's provisions, the main users have been businesses that needed government information.[37]

What the FOI Act does is to give all persons access to the records of all federal agencies, and these include executive and military departments, government corporations and government controlled corporations, other executive agencies, and the independent regulatory agencies. The act does not cover Congress or the courts. Specifically exempt from the act's provisions are the nine categories of records cited in Exhibit 16.2.

EXHIBIT 16.2

Records Not Covered by the Freedom of Information Act

The nine categories of records which are not covered by the FOI Act of 1966 as amended in 1974 are:

1. Documents that have been properly classified as confidential or secret to protect national security or foreign policy.

2. Documents that relate solely to the internal personnel rules and practices of an agency.

3. Matters that are specifically exempted by statute from public disclosure.

4. Trade secrets and certain other financial and commercial information gathered by government agencies.

5. Inter-agency or intra-agency memoranda or letters which would not be available by law to a party other than an agency in litigation with the agency.

6. Personnel and medical files and similar files the disclosure of which would constitute a clearly unwarranted invasion of privacy.

7. Investigatory files compiled for law enforcement purposes, but only when such files must be kept secret to prevent interference with law enforcement, to protect someone's right to a fair trial, to avoid invading someone's personal privacy, to avoid disclosing investigative techniques, and to protect the safety of law enforcement personnel.

8. Reports used by agencies regulating banks and other financial institutions.

9. Oil and gas exploration data, including maps.

At least two letters and a payment of fees set forth in a published schedule are required for those making formal requests for information in the files of federal agencies. In the first letter those requesting information are expected to state exactly what records are sought under the FOI Act. The agency is expected to reply within ten days by either supplying the information or else denying it and explaining the reasons for the denial. If the request is denied, a second letter of appeal can be made through the agency's appeal procedures. The next step is the federal courts. Federal judges have the right to review the requested documents in private and then rule on the agency's decision.

Given the nature of the nine exceptions cited in Exhibit 16.2, it is not surprising that thousands of requests have been denied and that thousands of lawsuits have been filed in federal courts. The act certainly has not opened wide all the doors of all federal agencies, but it has made available a great deal of government information which ordinarily would not have seen the light of day.

Those intending to use the FOI Act can secure a valuable booklet from the Reporters Committee on Freedom of the Press, 1125 15th St. N.W., Room 403, Washington D.C. 20005. The booklet, "How to Use the Federal FOI Act," contains government agency FOI directories and fee schedules; general instructions and samples of request letters; appeals letters; fee waiver requests; and the legal documents needed to file a lawsuit.[38]

ACCESS TO MEETINGS

Access to meetings on the federal level is covered under a 1977 act of Congress and on the state level by open-meeting laws.

The 1977 Government-in-the-Sunshine Act (5 U.S.C. 552b) requires that **fifty federal agencies** hold their meetings in public. Any meeting, whether formal, regular, or simple quorum, in which business is discussed is to be open to the public. Notice of such meetings must be given at least a week in advance. The act set forth ten conditions of exemptions for closed meetings, and nine of these are the same exemptions as apply in the FOI Act.[39] The tenth subject that may be discussed in a closed meeting is pending litigation. When a meeting is closed the agency must keep accurate and complete records of what transpired and of any votes taken at the meeting. Although any person may bring a lawsuit against an agency that seems to be violating the provisions of the act, the act itself contains no civil or criminal penalties for government officials who violate its provisions.[40]

Among the agencies that are subject to the act are the Commodity Credit Corporation, Consumer Product Safety Commission, Equal Employment Opportunity Commission, Federal Communications Commission, Federal Power Commission, Federal Reserve Board, Federal Trade Commission, National Labor Relations Board, Occupational Safety and Health Review Commission, and Securities and Exchange Commission.

All states by 1979 had open-meeting laws or constitutional provisions guaranteeing some degree of access to meetings. These laws vary so widely it's impossible to summarize them in detail in a book of this nature, but they do have certain features in common. Most of them apply to agencies of both state and local government and they usually require that school boards, state boards and commissions, city councils, and county governing boards hold open meetings at regularly announced places and times. Almost all states provide for closed or "executive" sessions and they spell out the circumstances under which these sessions can be closed to the public.[41]

Some common reasons for allowing closed sessions under state open-meeting laws are those in which discussion will be held on personnel matters, litigation, and labor negotiations. A number of state open-meeting laws in recent years set forth specific legal remedies for violations and permit any person to sue the offending body for an injunction to halt further illegal closed meetings. Furthermore, in a number of states the laws authorize the courts to invalidate actions taken at an unlawful closed meeting, and in some states it's a misdemeanor for government officials to take part in a closed meeting if they know beforehand the subject on the agenda should be discussed only at an open meeting.[42]

ACCESS TO PRINT AND ELECTRONIC MEDIA

Do practitioners have a "right" of access to the mass media? The answer is a definite no in regard to the print media and a qualified no in regard to the electronic media.

Print Media

In the past two decades a strong case for creating a right of access to newspapers has been made by those who argue that there is inequality in the power to communicate ideas. These advocates of a right of access contend there is no longer a "free marketplace of ideas" because virtually all but a handful of daily newspaper cities are one-newspaper cities. Professor Jerome Barron, perhaps the foremost advocate of a right to access, argues the access need in the following words:

> The changing nature of the communications process has made it imperative that the law show concern for the public interest in effective utilization of media for the expression of diverse points of view. Confrontation of ideas, a topic of eloquent affection in contemporary decisions, demands some recognition of a right to be heard as a constitutional principle. It is the writer's position that it is open to the courts to fashion a remedy for a right of access, at least in the most arbitrary cases, independent of legislation. If such an innovation is judicially resisted, I suggest that our constitutional law authorizes a carefully framed right of access statute which would forbid an arbitrary denial of space, hence securing an effective forum for the expression of divergent opinions.[43]

Barron's eloquent arguments for a right to access failed to convince the Supreme Court of their merits when he represented a political candidate seven years later in a right to access case. The case was *Miami Herald Pub. Co.* v. *Tornillo*, and it was unanimously decided in 1974 in favor of the newspaper.[44]

The issue in the case was "whether a state statute granting a political candidate a right to equal space to reply to criticism and attacks on his record by a newspaper violates the guarantees of a free press."[45] Pat Tornillo, a candidate for a seat in the Florida House of Representatives, was editorially criticized by the *Herald*. Tornillo, relying on an untested 1913 Florida statute giving candidates for public office the right to reply if a newspaper assails his personal character or official record, asked the Miami *Herald* to print his reply verbatim. The paper refused to give him space and Tornillo filed suit. The trial court held in favor of the newspaper's First Amendment defense, but the Florida supreme court reversed the lower court ruling by a six-to-one decision. In finding for Tornillo, the state's highest court said:

> The statute here under consideration is designed to add to the flow of information and ideas and does not constitute an incursion upon First Amendment rights or a prior restraint, since no specified newspaper content is excluded. . . . Freedom of expression was retained by the people through the First Amendment for all the people and not merely for a select few. The First Amendment did not create a privileged class which through a monopoly of instruments of the newspaper industry would be able to deny to the people the freedom of expression which the First Amendment guarantees.[46]

In his opinion for a unanimous Supreme Court reversing the Florida supreme court in favor of the newspaper, Chief Justice Warren Burger agreed there is a need for a right of access to the media by citizens, but forcing the press to provide such access brings direct confrontation with the First Amendment. Said Burger:

> . . . the Florida statute fails to clear the barriers of the First Amendment because of its intrusion into the function of editors. A newspaper is more than a passive receptacle or

conduit for news, comment, and advertising. The choice of material to go into a news-paper, and the decisions made as to limitations on the size of the paper, and content, and treatment of public issues and public officials—whether fair or unfair—constitutes the exercise of editorial control and judgement. It has yet to be demonstrated how govern-ment regulation of this crucial process can be exercised consistent with First Amendment guarantees of a free press as they have evolved to this time.[47]

A careful reading of the *Tornillo* decision indicates that the Court affirmed the right of a publisher to control the entire contents of his publication, not merely the news sec-tions. Until another ruling comes about, *Tornillo* holds there is no right of access to print media.

The Electronic Media

Although radio and television are granted the same First Amendment rights as news-papers and magazines, these rights are not as clear-cut when applied to the electronic media. The reason is found in the nature of the medium itself and in two applications called the Fairness Doctrine and the Equal Time Rule.

Radio, television, and newspapers are clearly mass media, but the first two are limited in their operations by the fact that only a limited number of air frequencies are available. Congress quickly realized when radio and then later television came into being that some form of regulation was needed to allocate fairly the limited number of frequencies in the radio/television spectrum and to make sure that there was some form of control over these frequencies in the future. The Congressional answer was found in the establish-ment of the Federal Radio Commission in 1927 and then the seven-member Federal Com-munications Commission in 1934. Under the terms of the Federal Communications Act of 1934, the FCC was established to set up rules and regulations and to see that broad-casters operate their stations in "the public interest, convenience and necessity." In carrying out its Congressional mandate, the FCC not only licenses stations but also promulgates certain rules and doctrines, and among the latter is the Fairness Doctrine.

The doctrine was set forth by the FCC in 1949 and is not a part of the act which estab-lished the agency. (Congress, however, amended sections of the original act in 1959 and its language in so doing has led some to conclude that Congress approved the Fairness Doctrine. This remains a matter of dispute and interpretation.)

Broadly speaking, the Fairness Doctrine is concerned with the airing of controversial issues and public affairs programming. It requires broadcasters to devote a "reasonable" percentage of their air time to public issues and states that in so doing they must be "fair" in the sense that contrasting points of view are given the opportunity to be presented on "controversial" issues. The doctrine does not require that the broadcaster present both sides of an issue within the same program, but is expected to make provision for oppos-ing views in his overall programming. Further, stated the FCC in 1974, "there is no requirement that any precisely equal balance of views be achieved, and all matters con-cerning the particular opposing views to be presented and the appropriate spokesmen and format for their presentation are left to the licensee's discretion subject only to a standard of reasonableness and good faith."[48]

Of some interest to public relations practitioners is that the Fairness Doctrine has been applied not merely to programming but also to advertising that specifically addresses controversial issues. It does not apply to product advertising, even though the claims made in such ads may be controversial. A federal appeals court in 1978 upheld an FCC ruling that eight television stations had violated the doctrine by carrying pro-nuclear power commercials but did not present the anti-nuclear power point of view.[49] Practi-tioners should recognize that broadcasters may still reject idea and advocacy ads if they wish to do so, but if they air an advertisement which takes a stand on a public issue then they must present the other side under the Fairness Doctrine. To avoid this problem many broadcasters, and especially the three major networks, simply refuse to carry such advertisements.

The case that upheld the constitutionality of the Fairness Doctrine was the *Red Lion* case. At issue here was the "personal attack" rule of the doctrine, a rule which requires that when an attack is made on a person or group during the presentation of views on a controversial issue of public importance, the broadcaster must within a week's time provide the person attacked with an opportunity to respond over the licensee's facilities. The Red Lion station aired such an attack on the integrity of author Fred Cook, but refused to allow him equal time. When the station challenged the FCC on the ruling, a federal appeals court and then the U.S. Supreme Court in a unanimous ruling upheld the personal attack rule. "It is the right of the public to receive suitable access to social, political, esthetic, moral and other ideas and experiences, which is crucial here," stated Justice White in the Court's opinion. "That right may not constitutionally be abridged either by the Congress or by the FCC."[50]

Thus, the Court upheld the constitutionality of the personal attack rule and of the Fairness Doctrine. Application of the doctrine has come down to us on a case-by-case basis as court cases clarified various aspects of a doctrine that has to be followed carefully to understand all its ramifications. Understanding the doctrine and its application is of special importance to the practitioner who is required to deal with a personal attack situation or with a situation wherein his organization or client is involved with a controversial issue of public importance.

Access to cable television was required of the larger systems under FCC rules until 1979. These rules required that new cable systems had to allocate four of their channels to public, educational, local government and leased access. However, in 1979 the Supreme Court ruled[51] that the FCC has no authority to require cable companies to carry public access channels, and thus there are currently (in 1984) no uniform federal standards governing public access to cable channels.

Despite the fact that there are no federal rules calling for access, there's a good deal of access in the larger wired cities as a result of franchise agreements made when franchises are allocated to cable systems. Designed for noncommercial community use, these access channels provide a great many opportunities for those practitioners who represent nonprofit and community organizations. In mid-1983 there was a growing movement by both community groups and such multiple-systems operators as Cox Cable Communica-

---

EXHIBIT 16.3

Some Access Ventures as of June, 1983

- In New Orleans the Cox cable system had a total of eighteen access channels, and made available to users five access studios, five vans complete with portable video equipment, and a staff to assist those using the channels.

- The National Federation of Local Cable Programmers and the Center for New Television were sponsoring educational programs to teach how-to skills.

- Chicago, which was yet unwired in 1983, asked bidding cable companies to contribute a portion of their revenues toward a public access facility. A total of twenty-four access channels were planned and the city had established a fifty-member governing board to administer the city's public access facilities.

- In Cranston, Rhode Island, the Cox cable system had a public access studio which was open to children producers five afternoons a week. Cranston's local origination channel also featured a morning exercise show, Italian language programs, and Rhode Island's "first and only" live comedy show, "Club Genius."

---

tions, Cable Systems, Group W Cable, Rogers Cable, and Warner Amex to upgrade and also to experiment with public access programming. Exhibit 16.3 cites some of the access ventures as of June, 1983.[52]

COPYRIGHT REGULATIONS

Public relations practitioners are affected by copyright law in two ways: (1) as a right to control or profit from a literary, artistic, or intellectual production, and (2) as a defense for making fair use of material which has been copyrighted by others. Setting the rules for copyright are the common law, statutes passed by Congress, and court cases.

Practitioners often utilize material copyrighted by others; hence the need to know and understand the rights of those who have created the material. By statute, Congress established these rights in the Copyright Act of 1909 and then made the first major change in the rules when it revised the act in 1976.

Nelson and Teeter describe copyright as "an exclusive, legally recognizable claim to literary or pictorial property . . ., a right, extended by federal statute, to entitle originators to ownership of the literary or artistic products of their minds."[53] They emphasize that (1) facts or ideas cannot be copyrighted because copyright applies only to the literary style of books, articles, and other literary productions and not to the ideas, themes, or facts contained in the material; (2) copyright both protects and restricts communication media.[54] One cannot copyright the news, but one can copyright a description of a news event. One cannot copyright historical and scientific information, but one can copyright a specific description of the facts.[55]

Obtaining copyright protection for a creative work is not difficult. A copyright notice—the usual form is "Copyright©1984 by Joe Author"—should be placed in a prominent spot on the material. The proper registration form (which can be secured from the U.S. Copyright Office, Library of Congress, Washington, D.C. 20559) should be completed and forwarded with the $10 registration fee and two copies of the work sent for deposit in the Library of Congress.

The "works for hire" provision of the Copyright Act gives to the employer copyright on works for hire. Thus, if you as a practitioner write a press release or a book or booklet for your firm and the firm decides to copyright the material, the copyright belongs to the firm, not to you. The same principle applies to journalists who work for newspapers, magazines, or broadcasting stations.

One of the major changes in the 1976 revision of the federal copyright statute relates to the duration of the copyright. The old law granted copyright for twenty-eight years, subject to a renewal for another twenty-eight years. The new law provides copyright protection for the life of the author plus another fifty years. Materials created for hire or anonymously are protected for seventy-five years from publication date.

To what extent can a practitioner use or cite from material that is under copyright by another? The answer is found in the "fair use" provisions of the copyright statute and also in court decisions. The idea of fair use is to permit a certain amount of copying from copyrighted works, but establishing what is and what is not fair use can be an exercise in frustration because of the uncertainty surrounding fair usage.

Under the Copyright Act of 1976 the following four factors must be considered in determining whether the use made of a copyrighted work is fair use:

1. the purpose and character of the use, including whether such use is of a commercial nature or is for nonprofit educational purposes

2. the nature of the copyrighted work

3. the percentage of the total work that is used, that is, the amount and substantiality of the portion used in relation to the copyrighted work as a whole

4. the effect the use will have on the value or profit-making potential of the original work

---

Unfortunately for those who seek more concrete ground rules, there is no simple answer or formula for determining what is infringement and what is fair use. The courts, in effect, determine the boundaries of the fair use provisions of the federal statute by their decisions on a case-to-case basis. A conclusion that has been drawn from these cases is that the courts have generally been lenient with quotations used in critical reviews or scholarly works but not so lenient when it's a matter of the use of copyrighted material for commercial purposes or in works which are in competition with the original copyrighted material.[56]

FINANCIAL REGULATIONS

More so than any other single specialized area of public relations practice, investor or financial relations is governed in much of its operations by specific legal requirements. This results from the fact that publicly held companies are bound by regulations of the Securities and Exchange Commission and the various stock exchanges.

One of the basic purposes of the Securities Act of 1933, the Securities Exchange Act of 1934, and the Investment Company Act of 1940 is to insure that publicly held companies provide timely and adequate disclosure of corporate information affecting investment decisions. Failure to do so can lead and has led to lawsuits brought by the Securities and Exchange Commission, and in a number of these suits public relations practitioners have been held responsible for violations of SEC rules and statutes concerned with investments.

One should not conclude that the SEC prohibits financial publicity. On the contrary, it encourages financial publicity. In its *Special Study of the Securities Market*, published in 1963, the SEC devoted an entire section to corporate publicity and public relations. It prefaced the section with this comment:

> Informal corporate publicity is an important supplement to disclosures required by the securities acts. In order to keep shareholders, the investment community, and the general public continuously informed of corporate developments, it is desirable for issuers to disseminate publicity through the channel of news distribution as well as by other means. This fact has been recognized by the Commission, which has encouraged publicly held corporations to employ publicity and public relations for this purpose.[57]

THE NEED TO DISCLOSE

The responsibility for publicly held companies to disclose corporate information is imposed by the SEC, the New York Stock Exchange, and the American Stock Exchange. **This disclosure responsibility requires that a company publicly report any corporate development, whether it be favorable or unfavorable, that might affect the market of its securities or influence investment decisions.** Rule 10b-5 of the SEC makes it "unlawful for any person . . . (1) to employ any device, scheme, or artifice to defraud; (2) to make an untrue statement of a material fact or to omit to state a material fact necessary in order to make the statements made, in the light of the circumstances under which they were made, not misleading; or (3) to engage in any act, practice, or course of business which operates or would operate as a fraud or deceit upon any person, in connection with the purchase or sale of any security."

Materiality is one of the crucial elements in disclosure. It is clear that the rules of the SEC and the exchanges regarding disclosure call for the release of **material** information which might affect the market for a company's securities or influence investment decisions. But what do we mean by material information? The American Stock Exchange

Company Guide lists the following as among those which would require prompt release:[59]

- A joint venture, merger or acquisition
- Declaration or omission of dividends or the determination of earnings
- A stock split or stock dividend
- Acquisition or loss of a significant contract
- A significant new product or discovery
- A change in control or a significant change in management
- A call of securities for redemption
- The borrowing of a significant amount of funds
- A tender offer for another company's securities

- The public or private sale of a significant amount of additional securities
- Significant litigation
- Purchase or sale of a significant asset
- A significant change in capital investment plans
- A significant labor dispute or disputes with subcontractors or suppliers
- An event requiring the filing of a current report under the Securities and Exchange Act
- Establishment of a program to make purchases of the company's own shares

There may well be additional kinds of information which would fall under the disclosure blanket, but in general information should be considered material when it is essential to an investor's informed decision-making process. Further, the information that is released should not be misleading or false, and it should not omit important and significant facts.

In the *Texas Gulf Sulphur* case, the SEC charged the company with violating provisions of Rule 10b-5, and in its 1968 decision a federal court of appeals found the company guilty of "insider" trading and of issuing a false and misleading press release which played down a significant ore discovery. The U.S. Supreme Court subsequently refused review of the case. Among the general points established by the case were the following:[60]

- Corporate insiders—and these include public relations practitioners—violate the law when they engage in securities dealings on the basis of material corporate information which has not been made public.

- Unless there is a legitimate corporate reason for withholding announcement, material corporate information should be disclosed to the investing public.

- It is a violation of the securities law to issue a press release which either omits important facts or presents misleading or false information that would operate to defraud in connection with the purchase or sale of a security.

One way to test whether materiality applies is to ask yourself if the information is of such a nature that it's what a prudent investor would want to know in deciding whether to buy, hold, or sell the company's securities. If such information were disclosed it would also reasonably be expected to affect the price of the company's securities.[61]

WHEN TO DISCLOSE

According to the authoritative Hill and Knowlton report on financial reporting, the SEC requires companies to make full and prompt disclosure, but it has left the regulation of timing to the stock exchanges. The New York Stock Exchange recognizes that at times there may be a valid business reason for delaying disclosure, but in general it requires that companies "release quickly any information which might reasonably be expected to materially affect the market for securities." Similarly, the American Stock Exchange calls for "immediate public disclosure."[62]

Both exchanges mean by "quickly" and "immediate public disclosure" that news must be released by the fastest means possible. A release sent through the mail is not considered satisfactory, nor is one that has an embargoed "Hold For Release" date. Companies are required to release immediately to at least two of the major financial wire services (Dow Jones and Reuters' Economic Services) and in addition are encouraged to release to the Associated Press and United Press International. The Amex also requires and the NYSE encourages releases to the New York *Times, Wall Street Journal, Moody's Investors Service* and *Standard & Poor's* Corporation. Use is also encouraged of PR Newswire.[63]

INSIDER TRADING AND THE PRACTITIONER

As has already been noted briefly, the public relations practitioner is considered by the SEC and the stock exchanges to be an insider when he is involved in financial information disclosure. This means that when a practitioner learns about material information not yet disclosed to the public, it is unlawful for him to pass on this information selectively (that is, to give tips to others about the information) or to use the information as the basis for trading in the company's securities. To avoid impropriety, corporate officials and public relations practitioners should wait until after the release of important developments has appeared in the press before making a purchase or sale. The American Stock Exchange recommends a 24-hour waiting period following publication.[64]

In policing the financial markets to ensure that individuals and companies act in compliance with provisions of the exchange acts, the SEC can bring and has brought suit against those considered to be in violation of the acts. As corporate "insiders" financial relations directors have been brought to court by the SEC, usually as subjects of civil injunctive actions. Exhibit 16.4, Litigation Release No. 10084 of the SEC, describes the Commission's charges against a financial relations director and his subsequent consent to the entry of a Final Judgment of Permanent Injunction.

THE SEC'S INTEGRATED DISCLOSURE SYSTEM

Effective May 24, 1982, the Securities and Exchange Commission adopted a new "Integrated Disclosure System" whose core Regulation S-K compresses the many other documents previously required for disclosure and other filing with the SEC. Details of the SEC's action were carried in the agency's release 33/6383, which ran for ninety-five pages in the March 16, 1982, Federal Register.[65]

Those who are interested in or involved with financial public relations are referred to Appendix A of this book, which includes the official interpretation of the PRSA code as it applies to financial public relations, and also to Appendix B, Robert W. Taft's table of **Corporate Reporting Requirements,** including the SEC's integrated disclosure system, effective May 24, 1982.

ENDNOTES

1. William L. Prosser, *Law of Torts*, 4th ed. (St. Paul, Minn.: West Publishing Co., 1971), p. 739.
2. Morton J. Simon, *Public Relations Law* (New York: Appleton-Century-Crofts, 1969), p. 213.
3. Don R. Pember, *Mass Communication Law* (Dubuque, Iowa: Wm. C. Brown, 1977), p. 100.
4. Ibid., p. 101.

5. Donald M. Gillmor and Jerome A. Barron, *Mass Communication Law*, 3rd ed. (St. Paul, Minn.: West Publishing Co., 1979), p. 197.
6. Marc A. Franklin, *The First Amendment and the Fourth Estate*, 2nd ed. (Mineola, N.Y.: The Foundation Press, 1981), p. 75.
7. Harold L. Nelson and Dwight L. Teeter, Jr., *Law of Mass Communication*, 4th ed. (Mineola, N.Y.: The Foundation Press, 1982), p. 64. The case cited is *Montandon* v. *Triangle Publishing, Inc.* 45 Cal App. 3d 938, 120 Cal Rptr. 186 (1975).
8. Prosser, p. 745.
9. Pember, p. 102.
10. Nelson and Teeter, p. 88. See 256 N.Y. 36, 175 N.E. 505 (1931) for details of the case.
11. Ibid., p. 93.
12. Pember, p. 104.
13. Nelson and Teeter, p. 89.
14. Pember, p. 111.
15. Nelson and Teeter, p. 91.
16. Franklin, p. 87.

17. Pember, p. 123.
18. Bruce W. Sanford, *Synopsis of the Law of Libel and Right of Privacy*, revised paperback ed. (New York: World Almanac Publishing, 1981), p. 16.
19. Pember, p. 125.
20. Ibid., p. 127.
21. From the majority opinion by Chief Justice Burger in *Hutchinson* v. *Proxmire*, 443 U.S. 111 (1979).
22. Wayne Overbeck and Rick D. Pullen, *Major Principles of Media Law* (New York: Holt, Rinehart and Winston, 1982), p. 87.
23. Sanford, pp. 19-20.
24. 376 U.S. 254, 84 S. Ct. 710 (1964).
25. 418 U.S. 323, 94 S. Ct. 2997 (1974).
26. Scott M. Cutlip and Allen H. Center, *Effective Public Relations*, revised 5th ed. (New York: Prentice-Hall, 1982), p. 283.
27. Prosser, p. 804.
28. Pember, p. 169.
29. Ibid., p. 174.
30. Simon, p. 254.
31. Overbeck and Pullen, p. 113.
32. Sanford, p. 30.
33. Ibid.
34. Pember, p. 194.
35. Ibid., p. 200.
36. Sanford, p. 31.
37. Overbeck and Pullen, p. 198.
38. Ibid., p. 200.
39. Gillmor and Barron, p. 460.
40. Overbeck and Pullen, p. 208.
41. Ibid., p. 210.
42. Ibid.
43. Jerome A. Barron, "Access to the Press—A New First Amendment Right," 80 *Harvard Law Review* 1641 (1967).
44. *Miami Herald Publishing Co.* v. *Tornillo*, 418 U.S. 241, 94 S. Ct. 2831 (1974).
45. Ibid.
46. 287 So. 2d 78, 82-83.
47. See note 44.
48. Federal Communications Commission, *Fairness Report*, 48 F.C.C. 2d 1, 30 R.R. 2d 1261 (1974).
49. *Public Media Center* v. *F.C.C.*, 587 F 2d 1322.
50. *Red Lion Broadcasting Co. Inc.* v. *Federal Communications Commission*, 395 U.S. 367, 89 S. Ct. 1794 (1969).
51. *F.C.C.* v. *Midwest Video Corp.*, 440 U.S. 689 (1979).
52. Suzanne Riordan, "New Outlets Attract Home Grown Talent," *Advertising Age*, June 13, 1978, p. M-20.
53. Nelson and Teeter, p. 295.
54. Ibid., p. 256.
55. Overbeck and Pullen, p. 133.
56. Nelson and Teeter, p. 278.
57. Securities and Exchange Commission, *Special Study of the Securities Market* (Washington, D.C.: Government Printing Office, 1963).
58. 17 C.F.R. 240 10b-5, as noted by Simon, p. 748 note.
59. Cited in Hill and Knowlton's *The SEC, The Securities Market and Your Financial Communication*, 5th ed. (New York: Hill and Knowlton, 1979), p. 15.
60. *Securities and Exchange Commission* v. *Texas Gulf Sulphur Co.*, 401 F. 2d 833 (2d Cir. 1968). For full account of this case see Kenneth Patrick, *Perpetual Jeopardy* (New York: Macmillan, 1972).
61. Richard S. Seltzer, "The SEC Strikes Again," *Public Relations Journal*, April 1972, p. 22.
62. Hill and Knowlton's SEC report, 1979.
63. Ibid.
64. Ibid.
65. Robert W. Taft, "Order Out of Chaos," *Public Relations Journal*, April 1982, p. 25.

PROJECTS, ASSIGNMENTS, AND MINIS

1. LIBEL POTENTIALITIES IN YOUR COLLEGE NEWSPAPER: A RESEARCH ASSIGNMENT

In a report to your instructor cite illustrations of potentially libelous articles, editorials, columns, and letters to the editor appearing in your school newspaper in the past few months.

Each example should summarize the nature of the item being discussed; those aspects of the item which you consider to be potentially libelous; and the reasons why you consider the material to be libelous.

Where possible, append photocopies of the items cited in your report.

2. ASSESSING YOUR STATE'S OPEN-MEETING LAW: A RESEARCH ASSIGNMENT

As noted in this chapter, by 1979 all states had open-meeting laws or constitutional guarantees providing for some degree of access right to meetings. You are to write a report detailing the important provisions of your state's open-meeting law or of your state's constitutional provisions guaranteeing the right of access to meetings.

In the concluding sections of your report explain the connection between public relations practice and open-meeting laws and constitutional guarantees in your state. Try to be specific rather than general.

3. THE BOARD OF EDUCATION AND OPEN-MEETING GUARANTEES: AN ASSIGNMENT

You are to assume that you are director of public relations for the board of education in the largest city in your state. The board holds twice-monthly regular meetings every second Tuesday and these meetings are open to the public and the press. Recently, however, the board has gone into "executive session" at various times during the regular meetings, and at such times the press and the public have been excluded from these sessions. During these executive sessions the board has discussed a variety of subjects, including personnel matters, building projects, and pay raises for teachers and administrators.

In letters to the editor of the local newspaper citizens have complained about the practice of the board to go into executive session. The letter writers have contended that this practice is in violation of the state's open-meeting law or of the state constitution's guarantee of open meetings. In two editorials the local newspaper has taken the same stand as the letter writers and has been highly critical of the executive session practice.

The superintendent of schools has asked you to research the matter of executive sessions and to write him a memorandum summarizing the important provisions of the law as they relate to open meetings and executive sessions. He has also asked you to include in your report your professional opinion concerning executive sessions as they relate to the school system's public relations.

4. UTILIZING CABLE ACCESS CHANNELS: A POSITION PAPER

As noted in this chapter, by mid-1983 there was a growing movement by community groups and by multiple-systems cable TV operators to facilitate and make use of public access programming.

You are to assume that there is a cable TV system servicing the community in which your college is located. The general manager has written to you, director of public relations for your college, and has advised you that two months from now one channel of the system will be open to programming by community groups and organizations. His letter concludes as follows:

> We believe that your school would be interested in taking advantage of this opportunity to present television programs of interest to subscribers of our system. One of our fully-equipped studios has been set aside for programming by local organizations such as your school, and there will be no charge for use of the equipment, the studio, and the technicians manning the equipment.
>
> We envision a weekly program which would run a half-hour in prime time, but we would expect that you will provide the programming and the participants. We would therefore appreciate it very much if you would let us know if you are interested in accepting this invitation. If the answer is affirmative, please provide us with a summary of **five** program suggestions which you feel would be viable and of interest to our viewers. I would suggest that there be a theme and format to each of the five program suggestions and that the programs be of such a nature that they could be aired weekly throughout the academic year.

Your president has enthusiastically endorsed your recommendation that the school accept the cable system's invitation. Prepare a letter to the system's general manager summarizing the five program suggestions he has requested.

5. ALLEGHENY DECIDES TO COPYRIGHT: A MINI-SITUATION

According to the July, 1982, issue of San Jose State University's *Trends and Topics*, the *Wall Street Journal* of May 14, 1982, reported that Allegheny International Inc. of Pittsburgh decided to copyright its annual report and proxy statements to insure that the press would not use company information without permission. A company spokesperson was cited as saying that "this just might give us some comfort that the information wasn't being improperly used."

In commenting on this step by Allegheny, *Trends and Topics* stated that "the effect of Allegheny's copyright announcement is minimal. In fact, it may even be detrimental in the respect that some reporters—scared off by such pompous announcements—will strive to use their own words (and possible distortions) about a company instead of quoting the carefully worded material in the proxy statement or annual report."

In a memorandum to your instructor, explain the legal need (or non-need) to copyright annual reports and proxy statements. Comment also on the public/media relations aspects of the Allegheny action, and on the reaction to it by *Trends and Topics*.

17

TAKING A STAND: CORPORATE POLITICAL EXPRESSION AND ADVOCACY ADVERTISING

Although the First Amendment has been a part of our Constitution since 1791, it wasn't until 1978 that the Supreme Court clarified the status of corporations as to their rights to political expression. At issue was a corporation's right under the First Amendment to purchase and sponsor advertising to oppose a state referendum allowing establishment of a graduated personal income tax. The state of Massachusetts said the corporation had no such right because the referendum was not materially related to its business. The corporation argued otherwise, and the issue was joined in the case known as *First National Bank of Boston et al. v. Bellotti.*[1]

THREE CORPORATE FREE SPEECH CASES

The Bellotti case was one of three important corporate political expression cases to reach the Supreme Court in 1978 and 1980. Bellotti concerned a banking institution and the other two involved public utilities. All three cases are important for public relations practitioners because they dealt with corporate free speech rights and set forth certain guidelines for practitioners to follow in handling such rights. Each case will be considered separately in this section. The remainder of the chapter deals with institutional/image and advocacy advertising.

THE BELLOTTI DECISION

A Massachusetts criminal statute prohibited business corporations from making contributions or expenditures "for the purpose of . . . influencing or affecting the vote on any question submitted to the voters, other than one materially affecting any of the property, business, or assets of the corporation." The First National Bank of Boston and several other companies sought to publicize their views on a proposed state constitutional amendment that was to be submitted to the voters as a ballot question in the coming general election. Frank Bellotti, the Attorney General of Massachusetts, informed First National that he intended to enforce the state's statute prohibiting their proposed action, and the bank thereupon brought suit against Bellotti seeking to have the state law declared unconstitutional. The state's highest court upheld the Massachusetts law, but upon appeal the United States Supreme Court, by a vote of 5-4, invalidated the Massachusetts statute as being an unconstitutional infringement of free speech.

In reaching this decision, the majority opinion of Justice Lewis Powell did not establish a corporate First Amendment right of free speech equivalent to that of the press or individuals. But he did say that the political argument which the bank wanted to set forth is protected by the First Amendment.

At several points in his opinion Justice Powell took the trouble to stress that the Court was not establishing a corporate right of free speech equal to that of natural persons, stating that the Court "need not survey the outer boundaries of the Amendment's protection of corporate speech, or address the abstract question whether corporations have the full measure of rights that individuals enjoy under the First Amendment."

The proper question, in Powell's opinion, was whether the corporate identity of a speaker deprives his proposed speech of the First Amendment protection to which it would normally be entitled. The Court held that the speech proposed by the bank "is at the heart of the First Amendment protection" because the referendum issue was a matter of public concern. "If the speakers here were not corporations," wrote Powell, "no one would suggest that the State could silence their proposed speech. It is the type of speech indispensable to decision-making in a democracy, and this is no less true because the speech comes from a corporation rather than an individual. The inherent worth of the speech in terms of its capacity for informing the public does not depend upon the identity of its source, whether corporation, association, union, or individual."

The meaning of the *Bellotti* decision is clear in one respect for corporate public relations practitioners, but unclear in another. Certainly, so far as referenda on public issues are concerned, a corporation can spend money to express its views. *Bellotti* tells the practitioner that the corporation has the same right as individuals when it comes to First Amendment protection from state action in matters put to voters at election time. What *Bellotti* does not tell the practitioner is whether the corporate right to political expression is an all-inclusive one. As with other First Amendment interpretations, the Court seems to have left that decision to another time and to other cases.

Two years later the Court dealt with two such cases: *Consolidated Edison Co.* v. *Public Service Commission of New York*[2] and *Central Hudson Gas & Electric Corp.* v. *Public Service Commission of New York.*[3] As can be noted, both cases involved public utilities and the state body which regulates them. In each case the Supreme Court found for the corporations, by a 7-2 vote in the case of Con Ed and by an 8-1 vote in the case of Central Hudson. Justice Powell, as he did in *Bellotti*, wrote the majority opinion in the two utility cases and Justice William Rehnquist was the dissenter in both cases. The two decisions were handed down on the same day, June 20, 1980.

THE CONSOLIDATED EDISON DECISION

In *Con Ed* the utility sought review of a Public Service Commission order which prohibited public utilities from putting into monthly customer bills inserts discussing controversial issues of public policy. The insert in this instance, placed in Con Ed bills of

January, 1976, stated the utility's views on the benefits of nuclear power, saying that they "far outweigh any potential risk" and that nuclear power plants are safe, economical, and clean. In its prohibition order, the Commission concluded that Con Ed's customers who receive bills containing inserts are a captive audience of diverse opinions who should not be subjected to the utility's views on controversial issues of public policy. The Commission also argued that ratepayers (customers) should not be made to subsidize the cost of bill inserts. The Commission did not in its order bar the utility from sending bill inserts which discuss subjects that are not "controversial issues of public policy."[4]

In upholding the utility, the Supreme Court ruled that the Commission's prohibition of discussion of controversial issues "strikes at the heart of the freedom to speak"[5] and "directly infringes the freedom of speech protected by the First and Fourteenth Amendments."[6] In reaching its decision the Court noted that customers were not forced to read the insert, but could simply toss it into the wastebasket.[7] Justice Powell also stated that "there is no basis on this record to assume that the Commission could not exclude the cost of these bill inserts from the utility's rate base."[8]

Having disposed of the Commission's arguments and upheld the utility's right to free expression, the Court noted that in certain circumstances a prohibition of speech may be permissible.[9] It cited the following three constitutional bases permitting a limitation on speech:

1. A "reasonable time, place, or manner" regulation that serves a significant governmental interest and leaves ample alternative channels for communication.

2. A permissible regulation of the subject matter of communication.

3. A narrowly-tailored restriction aimed at serving a compelling state interest.

The Court indicated that any one of the above circumstances could permit a state action limiting speech, but it concluded that the Commission's ruling against inserts was "neither a valid time, place or manner restriction, nor a permissible subject-matter regulation, nor a narrowly-drawn prohibition justified by a compelling state interest."[10]

THE CENTRAL HUDSON DECISION

Unlike *Con Ed*, the *Central Hudson* case concerned commercial speech, which was defined by Justice Powell as "expression related solely to the economic interests of the speaker and its audience."[11] At issue was a 1973 order of the New York State Public Service Commission requiring that electric utilities in New York cease all advertising that "promotes the use of electricity." In supporting the order, the Commission said it was based on its findings that there were insufficient fuel stocks to meet customer demands. Three years later, when the Commission extended the prohibition, it declared that all promotional advertising was contrary to the national policy of conserving energy.[12]

In upholding Central Hudson's appeal against the Commission's order, Justice Powell first noted that the Constitution accords a lesser protection to commercial speech than to other constitutionally guaranteed expressions. However, said the Court, the government's power to prohibit such speech is circumscribed when the communication is neither misleading nor related to unlawful activity. "The State," wrote Powell, "must assert a substantial interest to be achieved by restrictions on commercial speech."[13]

In evaluating the regulation of commercial speech, the Court in *Central Hudson* said the following four-part analysis would apply:

(1) At the outset, determination must be made whether the expression is protected by the First Amendment.

(2) For commercial speech to come within the protection of the First Amendment, it must concern lawful activity and not be misleading.

(3) There should be a substantial governmental interest calling for the regulation of the communication.

(4) The regulation should directly advance the asserted governmental interest and should not be more extensive than is necessary to serve that interest.[14]

In applying the above four-step analysis of commercial speech to the Commission's arguments in support of its ban on promotional advertising, the Court ruled that the restriction set by the Commission was more extensive than necessary to further the State's interest in energy conservation. Thus, the critical issue for the Supreme Court concerned the total ban on promotional advertising. Because the ban was all-encompassing, the Court ruled that "to the extent that the Commission's order suppresses speech that in no way impairs the State's interest in energy conservation, the Commission's order violates the First and Fourteenth Amendments and must be invalidated."[15]

What's the meaning of *Con Ed* and *Central Hudson* for corporate public relations practitioners? Though once again the Supreme Court did not go so far as to declare an unlimited First Amendment freedom of speech right for corporations, it certainly extended the reach of *Bellotti*. In *Con Ed* the Court reiterated the right of a corporation to express itself on controversial issues of public policy. *Bellotti* established the right of a corporation to express its opinion about a referendum issue, even though the issue of the referendum has no direct connection with the business of the corporation. *Con Ed* says that a public utility, even though a monopoly, has the right to use inserts in customer billings to express the corporation's views on controversial issues of public policy. The practitioner can assume that the right to use inserts would extend to the right to use such channels as employee pay envelopes, internal company publications, or reports to stockholders.[16]

Central Hudson recognizes that commercial speech has slightly less Constitutional protection than idea-oriented, noncommercial speech, but it has protection so long as it concerns lawful activity and is accurate and not misleading. Restrictions on commercial speech must meet the fourfold test set down by Justice Powell, and it's clear that distinctions between commercial and noncommercial speech have been narrowed.

In summation, *Bellotti* and the two utility cases extended the First Amendment rights of corporations and of their public relations practitioners responsible for corporate communications bearing on public policy issues. Two commentators view the rulings as having broad ramifications for all corporations even though the three cases concerned only banks and utilities. In drawing conclusions about the cases, they state: "It seems apparent that when the court granted additional free speech rights to these highly regulated industries, such rights must automatically extend, perhaps with even greater force, to ordinary business corporations."[17] Whether this interpretation holds true depends on future cases coming before the nation's highest court. For the moment, corporate practitioners have greater First Amendment rights than existed prior to 1978 and 1980 when *Bellotti*, *Con Ed*, and *Central Hudson* were decided.[18]

INSTITUTIONAL/IMAGE AND ADVOCACY ADVERTISING

INSTITUTIONAL/IMAGE ADVERTISING

Corporate use of advertising as a communication tool has been commonplace for several decades, and, as with most forms of communication, it has gone through distinct phases. For our purposes, it should be made clear that such advertising differs significantly from the usual product or service advertising. Instead of promoting or selling products and services, advertising used for public relations purposes aims to "sell" a corporation or a point of view. As with product advertising, this form of advertising can be soft-sell, hard-sell, or neutral in tone and scope.

Such public relations advertising has been called by various names, and the names tend to indicate the phases in which they occurred. Most of the early public relations advertising was called *institutional* or *corporate image* advertising, and its aim was to build up the public image of the corporation, creating for it the image of a good citizen and institution in our society. By no means extinct, institutional advertising is still used as a means of communicating to the public the activities, growth, and strength of the corporation and to serve as a bridge between the corporation and its publics. Corporate image or institutional advertising is generally noncontroversial and nonargumentative. Some critics consider it a waste. As described by a scholarly observer, S. Prakash Sethi of the University of Texas, "institutional advertising is expensively and beautifully produced; is generally dull, bland, and self-serving; and is seldom taken seriously by anyone."[19]

Perhaps a major reason institutional/corporate image advertising is not taken seriously is that its effects are so difficult to measure. Particularly difficult to measure have been the various attempts to "sell" the free enterprise system and the virtues of American business and industry. At various times in our recent past American business-men have launched campaigns to promote our economic system through institutional advertising. It has been felt that by proclaiming the virtues of the system, business can "educate" the American public to appreciate and better understand the system. Billions of dollars have been spent on such advertising, but there is little evidence that it has had much of an effect or that it has been needed. Commenting in the early fifties about the attempt to sell the free enterprise system through advertising, William H. Whyte, Jr., came to this conclusion: "The free enterprise campaign is psychologically unsound, it is abstract, it is defensive, and it is negative. Most important, in a great many of its aspects it represents a shocking lack of faith in the American people, and in some cases down-right contempt." Of interest is the fact that Whyte's comments were made in an article in *Fortune*, a magazine sympathetic to business and to the American enterprise system.

Despite the criticisms leveled against it, institutional or corporate image advertising is still considered of value as a communication tool. Among major users are the large con-glomerates who feel it's important to establish in the public mind some understanding of what they represent. Under headings such as "Who We Are," these companies describe themselves and explain some of the diverse companies and subsidiaries that come under their corporate wing. A very large, diversified corporation could with justification believe it is important to run a series of corporate image advertisements, each carrying several paragraphs describing the parent corporation and the remaining paragraphs describing an individual offspring company. Properly packaged, an entire campaign can be reprinted and "merchandised" in numerous ways to specific publics.

Thomas Garbett of Doyle Dane Bernbach explained the rationale of institutional/image advertising in these words:

> The objective of most corporate advertising today is neither to change society nor secure changes in government regulations or laws. Companies simply want to be better under-stood among those publics that they think are important to them in the hope that they will be more supportive of the company. . . .

> The objectives may vary greatly from company to company and the advertising of course takes the form best calculated to meet the company's objectives. Companies are finding that this image advertising is important as a cohesive force to pull together the large, increasingly diverse corporations.[20]

United Technologies, a conglomerate which has utilized a variety of advertising styles and formats in its corporate advertising, struck a responsive readership chord with its institutional/image campaign in the early eighties tied to simple truths and verities. Each ad in the series ran as a full page in the *Wall Street Journal* without logo or any identifi-

EXHIBIT 17.1

Some Typical United Technologies Ads

Decisions, Decisions

Sometimes
the decision
to do
nothing
is wise.
But you can't
make a career
of doing
nothing.
Freddie Fulcrum
weighed everything
too carefully.
He would say, "On
the one hand . . .
but then, on the
other," and his
arguments
weighed out so
evenly
he never did
anything.
When Freddie died,
they carved
a big zero
on his tombstone.
If you decide
to fish—fine.
Or, if you decide
to cut bait—fine.
But if you decide
to do
nothing,
you're not going
to have fish
for dinner.

Anything You Can Do They Can Do, Too

While you flex
your muscles in
front of your
morning mirror
and congratulate
yourself on your
nimble brain,
consider this:
The light over your
mirror was perfected
by a deaf man.
While your morning
radio plays, remember
the hunchback who
helped invent it.
If you listen to
contemporary music,
you may hear
an artist who is
blind.
If you prefer
classical, you may
enjoy a symphony
written by a composer
who couldn't hear.
The President who set
an unbeatable American
political record
could hardly walk.
A woman born
unable to
see, speak or hear
stands as a great
achiever in
American history.
The handicapped can
enrich our lives.
Let's enrich
theirs.

Little Things

Most of us
miss out
on life's
big prizes.
The Pulitzer.
The Nobel.
Oscars.
Tonys.
Emmys.
But we're
all eligible
for life's
small pleasures.
A pat
on the back.
A kiss
behind the ear.
A four-pound bass.
A full moon.
An empty
parking space.
A crackling fire.
A great meal.
A glorious sunset.
Hot soup.
Cold beer.
Don't fret
about
copping life's
grand awards.
Enjoy its
tiny delights.
There are plenty
for all of us.

Will You Commit Larceny Today?

You may be
committing larceny
and not even
know it.
You could
be stealing
from someone
important to you.
Two of the most
important equities
you have
are money and time.
If you steal money
and get caught,
you suffer.
If you steal time,
someone else suffers.
When you have a date
at 9 o'clock,
be there at 9,
not 9:15.
Otherwise,
you have stolen
15 minutes.
Your theft
can push
everybody back.
The person
scheduled for
5 o'clock may
be bumped and
have a tough time
getting rescheduled.
Put yourself •
in his position
and perhaps
you won't
be late.
If *you're* the
person being
robbed, hand
this page
to the thief.

cation except for this invitation in small type: "How we perform as individuals will determine how we perform as a nation. Free: If you would like an 8½ × 11 reprint of this message write to Harry J. Gray, Chairman and Chief Executive Officer, United Technologies, Box 360, Hartford, CT 06141." The first fifty ads in the campaign produced 520,260 letters asking for 2,448,000 reprints.

Exhibit 17.1 reproduces four of the ads in the United Technologies series. The headlines, subjects, and copy typify the other ads that appeared in the series.

ADVOCACY ADVERTISING

Although it is often considered synonymous with institutional advertising, *advocacy advertising* is significantly different from the older form of advertising and can be viewed as a separate means of corporate communication. Unlike most institutional or image advertising, advocacy advertising is usually argumentative, deals with controversial subjects, and is directed at either specific or general targets and opponents.

Advocacy advertising, says Sethi, presents facts and arguments that "project the sponsor in the most positive light and opponents' arguments in the worst." John E. O'Toole sees two major forces—the system and the adversary culture—involved in an increasing number of issues. Advocacy advertising, he says, is a legitimate and appropriate way for the system—industries, businesses, and financial institutions—to counter the adversary culture, which he describes as "those in intellectual and academic pursuits, some political activists, and 'consumer interest' groups who seek basic changes in the system."[21]

In brief, advocacy advertising is directed at an opponent—at times a specific opponent and at times an unspecified one—which is considered to be "the enemy." The target can be political activists, the media, competitors, consumer groups, or government agencies. As used by its sponsors, advocacy advertising has been utilized to "set the record straight"; to gain adherents; to counteract public disapproval of business; to stress the value of the free enterprise system; and to provide "facts" that counteract alleged bias in news reports or in the opposition's advocacy advertising.

One of the earliest examples of advocacy advertising was the campaign devised and carried out several decades ago by the Byoir organization on behalf of the Great Atlantic and Pacific Tea Company when that company was faced with threatened antitrust action by the government. More recent users of advocacy advertising have been Mobil Oil, American Telephone and Telegraph, Exxon, General Motors, Allied Chemical, Union Carbide, the American Petroleum Institute, American Electric Power Company, Texaco, Edison Electric Institute, Atlantic Richfield, U.S. Steel, Gulf Oil, and AMOCO Chemicals.

Illustrative of more recent advocacy advertising campaigns was the one mounted in the seventies by the American Electric Power Company against environmental groups, against the Environmental Protection Agency, and against other private and government groups. Another energy-centered example was Mobil's advocacy advertisement campaign, which was critical of the Federal Energy Administration, environmental groups, and other government agencies. Mobil has also taken on the media for alleged bias in newspaper and broadcast coverage of energy matters. Herbert Schmertz, Mobil vice-president responsible for the company's aggressive advocacy advertisement campaign, believes there's a good deal of unfair coverage of corporate activities and news by both print and broadcast media. Under his direction, the company has not been hesitant to tackle the media when it feels the media deserve it.

Although the preponderance of advocacy advertising campaigns aim their attacks at groups outside the corporate world, take-over and merger situations sometimes produce internecine advocacy advertisement warfare between two opposing corporate bodies. One such print battle was waged by United Technologies and the Carrier Corporation of Syracuse, New York, when the former made a tender offer to purchase the latter's stock and merge Carrier into UTC. Exhibit 17.2 is a reproduction of one of the full-page ads

EXHIBIT 17.2

The Proposed Merger:

Everyone Will Benefit

Ever since we proposed a merger of Carrier Corporation and United Technologies, concern has been expressed about the potential effects of such a merger on the Syracuse community.

Scare talk has been rampant. Fears have been raised about a drying up of jobs . . . about a loss of small businesses in Central New York dependent on Carrier . . . about a lessening of Carrier's role in the economic, civic, and cultural life of this community.

These fears are all groundless. There's no valid reason for concern. There is no justification for anxiety. United Technologies is a responsible, sensitive, sensible corporation. We will not act irresponsibly. We will not hurt Carrier, or its employees and their families, or the community.

We know how much Carrier means to this community. We want to contribute. We respect Carrier. We want to help strengthen it as a business enterprise, as an employer, as a supplier, and as a productive corporate citizen of Syracuse.

We've been operating in New York State since 1853. That's when our wholly owned subsidiary, Otis Elevator Company, was founded. Our newest affiliate, Ambac Industries, which joined us in July, is also headquartered in this state.

We already contribute to the economy of New York State. We'd like to play a larger part. We have about 2,500 employees in the state now. This year, we'll pay them more than $50 million in wages and salaries. We'll spend more than $1 million in New York state and local taxes. We'll buy more than $250 million worth of goods and services from New York businesses.

A merger with Carrier would be yet another step in the continuing expansion of our business operations in New York State. We believe a Carrier-United Technologies affiliation would be good for the state and its people, particularly in the Syracuse area. We believe a merger would benefit Carrier employees and their families.

We sincerely believe we can help bolster Carrier's business. This would bring expansion of Carrier's operations, increased job opportunities in its plants, and greater job security for its people. We reaffirm what we have already told Carrier's management in our invitation to negotiate a merger: We will protect the pension and other employee-benefit plans of its people.

Carrier is a superb company, with competent management. We want to keep its organization intact.

In a merged organization, we intend to have Carrier continue to operate under its present management at its present locations. Carrier headquarters would remain in Syracuse. And Carrier would continue to draw on this community for its employees. We will continue our historic emphasis on local management of our facilities . . . and our long-standing policy of hiring within the communities where our plants are located.

We're sorry about the unwarranted anxieties aroused a few days ago by a published prediction of the loss of some small companies in Central New York through what was alleged to be a planned shift of Carrier purchases to Connecticut under a so-called "centralized purchasing system."

We don't have a centralized purchasing system at United Technologies, and we have no plans to establish one. We're not going to disturb Carrier's existing supplier relationships. Each of our operating units makes its own purchasing decisions. That's how each subsidiary can really control its own profits. Each chooses its own suppliers. Carrier would do the same when merged with us. It would continue to buy from the same companies, large and small, with which it now does business.

Carrier is an exemplary corporate citizen of Syracuse. The company and its people contribute generously to the quality of life here.

Like Carrier in Central New York, United Technologies and its people in Connecticut take part in a broad range of community and civic activities. If the two companies are merged, we'll encourage Carrier to build on its fine record of corporate citizenship. So there is absolutely no justification for concern that there would be any weakening of Carrier's involvement and participation in community life as a result of the merger we have proposed.

Our philosophy at United Technologies is that the responsibilities of business go beyond the balance sheet; that a successful company must apply its resources, both human and financial, to community needs.

That's a philosophy we practice in our home state of Connecticut, where we give about $1.5 million a year in support of health, education, social welfare, recreation, and the arts. It's a philosophy that Carrier carries out so well in Syracuse.

We hope that we'll be allowed, through a merger, to expand our contributions to the economy of New York State and to participate, with Carrier, in the life of Syracuse. Everyone will benefit.

UNITED TECHNOLOGIES

Pratt & Whitney Aircraft Group • Otis Group • Essex Group • Sikorsky Aircraft • Hamilton Standard
Power Systems Division • Norden Systems • Chemical Systems Division • United Technologies Research Center
United Technologies Corporation, Hartford, CT 06101.

This advertisement appeared in the Syracuse, New York POST-STANDARD and HERALD-JOURNAL on October 5 and 6, 1978, and the HERALD-AMERICAN-POST-STANDARD on October 8, 1978.

Reprinted with permission.

UTC ran in the Syracuse and other papers to present its case to the general public and to Carrier's stockholders.

Exhibit 17.3 is a reprint of the ad which Mobil ran in 1983 to sum up its twelve years of experience with advocacy advertising and to set forth its reasons for running advocacy ads.

Advantages

Proponents of advocacy advertising contend that it has the following major advantages over other forms of communication:

1. Control of the message is in the hands of the sponsor.
2. Complex issues can best be handled within the context of an advertisement.
3. Messages can be directed to specific audiences.
4. An entire campaign can best be mounted through a series of advertisements.

Such arguments have a good deal of validity to them. Once a press release is distributed, for example, the sponsor loses control of its contents and its final appearance in print media or on the air. There is no way of knowing how much of the release will be used, when it will be used, and how it will be used. Because it is paid for, however, an advertisement appears as it is written. It can be scheduled for a specific time, and there is even the opportunity to schedule the place of its appearance. Mobil Oil, for example, contracted for placement of advocacy ads on the Op-Ed page of the New York *Times*, and that's where they've appeared every week because the company has been willing to pay for this preferred space. As of 1983, Mobil advocacy ads were also running weekly in the Washington *Post*, Denver *Post*, Dallas *News*, Houston *Post*, Boston *Globe*, Los Angeles *Times*, and Chicago *Tribune*.

There is also no doubt that complex issues can best be handled within the context of an advertisement, that messages can be directed to specific audiences by means of advertising, and that an entire campaign can best be mounted through a series of advertisements. Thus, although advocacy advertising is costly, it certainly has built-in advantages for those willing to bear the cost.

Disadvantages

On the other hand, there are also disadvantages to advocacy advertising. When a press release, for example, is processed through the media machinery, it tends to lose sponsor identification and is seen by the recipients as news rather than as a special pleading. Advocacy advertising, however, bears the sponsor's identification and is recognized as representing the point of view of the sponsor. Very often it is looked upon as corporation propaganda, and thus it bears the stigma associated with the term *propaganda*.

Advocacy advertising can also incur a backlash unless handled with extreme care. When the courtroom advocate presents his or her case, no one expects him or her to be *fair*, but rather to make the best possible presentation for the client. However, when the corporation presents its case through advocacy advertising, the reader expects a fair presentation; unfortunately, the reader does not always get one. If readers perceive that they are being lied to or if they perceive that the corporation is dissembling, then that corporation loses the very credibility that is needed to make advertising effective.

When the target of advocacy advertising is one or more of the media, there is special need for the sponsoring corporation to be on solid ground in presenting its case. Responsible publications, for example, do not react lightly to charges that they are biased in their presentation of news. The corporation that charges the media with bias—as some

EXHIBIT 17.3

Why do we run those op-ed messages?

For more than 12 years now, we've been addressing Americans with weekly messages in principal print media. We've argued, cajoled, thundered, pleaded, reasoned and poked fun. In return, we've been reviled, revered, held up as a model and put down as a sorry example.

Why does Mobil choose to expose itself to these weekly judgments in the court of public opinion? Why do we keep it up now that the energy crisis and the urgent need to address energy issues have eased, at least for the present? When our problems are with cost-cutting and increasing productivity, not with voters, politicians and customers?

Our answer is that business needs voices in the media, the same way labor unions, consumers, and other groups in our society do. Our nation functions best when economic and other concerns of the people are subjected to rigorous debate. When our messages add to the spectrum of facts and opinion available to the public, even if the decisions are contrary to our preferences, then the effort and cost are worthwhile.

Think back to some of the issues in which we have contributed to the debate.

• Excessive government regulation—it's now widely recognized that Washington meddling, however well intentioned, carries a price tag that the consumer pays.

• The folly of price controls—so clear now that prices of gasoline and other fuels are coming down, now that the marketplace has been relieved of most of its artificial restraints.

• The need for balance between maintaining jobs and production and maintaining a pristine environment—a non-issue, we argued, if there's common sense and compromise on both sides, a view that's now increasingly recognized in Washington.

Over the years, we've won some and lost some, and battled to a draw on other issues we've championed, such as building more nuclear power plants and improving public transportation. We've supported presidents we thought were right in their policies and questioned Democrats and Republicans alike when we thought their policies were counterproductive.

In the process we've had excitement, been congratulated and castigated, made mistakes, and won and lost some battles. But we've enjoyed it. While a large company may seem terribly impersonal to the average person, it's made up of people with feelings, people who care like everybody else. So even when we plug a quality TV program we sponsor on public television, we feel right about spending the company's money to build audience for the show, just as we feel good as citizens to throw the support of our messages to causes we believe in, like the Mobil Grand Prix, in which young athletes prepare for the 1984 Olympics. Or recognition for the positive role retired people continue to play in our society.

We still continue to speak on a wide array of topics, even though there's no immediate energy crisis to kick around anymore. Because we don't want to be like the mother-in-law who comes to visit only when she has problems and matters to complain about. We think a continuous presence in this space makes sense for us. And we hope, on your part, you find us informative occasionally, or entertaining, or at least infuriating. But never boring. After all, you did read this far, didn't you?

Mobil®

corporations have done—should be able to document its charges and should certainly not be guilty in its presentation of the very kind of tampering with facts it attributes to the media it is attacking. News personnel have long memories and many ways of retaliating. Those who challenge the media through unfair advocacy advertising may well find they win some battles, but end up losing the war.

Dangers

Though Sethi and Schmertz have often disagreed on aspects of advocacy advertising, they both recognize—as did the Supreme Court in the Bellotti ruling—inherent dangers in such advertising. A major danger relates to the point that corporations, because of their economic power and wealth, may dominate public debate on crucial societal issues.

"Through constant repetition," states Sethi, "a corporation is able to shape the minds of its publics regardless of the inherent accuracy or objectivity of the message. Advocacy advertising campaigns, therefore, when pursued over a period of time, can overwhelm the information mix received by the public."[22]

Though not as concerned as Sethi about the ability of corporations to "overwhelm the information mix," Schmertz understands that "rights carry responsibilities, and the American legal tradition has never been very tolerant of those who use economic bulldozers to get their way." He warns against excesses in the following statement:

> All rights carry with them heavy responsibilities, and corporations should not take them lightly. The dividing line between First Amendment rights and potential violation of corrupt practices acts can be razor thin. And while the letter of the law applies equally to obscure individuals and prominent corporations when such violations occur, such transgressions will cause far greater embarrassment to companies with a high profile.[23]

Inherent in Schmertz's remarks is the recognition that there is both a political and an economic base to advocacy advertising. An advocacy advertisement is a corporate statement to the world. As such, it is bound to be subject to careful scrutiny and to criticism. Though it advocates a point of view, it must be fair in fact and reasoning. Because it is often aimed at a hostile or indifferent audience, its message must be credible. Because it forms only a small part of the total impressions the public has of its sponsors, it must be compatible with company actions and policies. Sethi sums up these imperatives about advocacy advertising in the following statement:

"Unless corporate activities are congruent with the public image it wishes to promote," he says, "there will be a spate of other images about the corporation, carried through alternative communication forms, that will be incongruent with the image the corporation intended to develop through its institutional advertising program. Advocacy advertising can play a healthy role only if a company is making other efforts to bring its performance in line with public expectations."[24]

Summed up, advocacy advertising—as with public relations—can be effective only if words and actions are compatible.

ENDNOTES

1. 435 U.S. 765, 98 S.Ct. 1407 (1978).
2. *Consolidated Edison Co. of New York* v. *Public Service Commission of New York,* 447 U.S. 530, 100 S.Ct. 2326 (1980).
3. *Central Hudson Gas and Electric Co.* v. *Public Service Commission of New York,* 447 U.S. 557, 100 S.Ct. 2343 (1980).
4. 100 S.Ct. 2326, p. 2330.
5. Ibid., p. 2332.
6. Ibid., p. 2337.

7. Ibid., p. 2336.
8. Ibid.
9. David N. Bateman and R. Stanley Tyler, "Court Cases Further Loosen the Gag on Corporate Communication," *Journal of Organization Communication*, Vol. 10, Number 2, 1981, p. 18. See also 100 S.Ct. 2326, p. 2332.
10. 100 S.Ct. 2326, p. 2337.
11. 100 S.Ct. 2343, p. 2349.
12. Ibid., p. 2347.
13. Ibid., p. 2350.
14. Ibid., p. 2351.
15. Ibid., p. 2353.
16. Bateman and Tyler, p. 20.
17. Ibid.
18. For a critical view of the decisions in *Bellotti, Con Ed*, and *Central Hudson*, see Charles Rember, "For Sale: Freedom of Speech," *The Atlantic*, March 1981, p. 25.
19. S. Prakash Sethi, *Advocacy Advertising and Large Corporations* (Lexington, Mass.: D. C. Heath, 1977), p. 8.
20. Tom Garbett, "What Companies Project to Public," *Advertising Age*, July 6, 1981, p. S-1.
21. John F. O'Toole, "Advocacy Advertising Shows the Flag," *Public Relations Journal*, November 1975.
22. S. Prakash Sethi, "Alternative Viewpoints: Should Business Aid the Opposition?" *Public Relations Journal*, November 1978, p. 19.
23. Herbert Schmertz, *Corporations and the First Amendment* (New York: American Management Association, 1978).
24. Sethi, *Advocacy Advertising and Large Corporations*, p. 328.

PROJECTS, ASSIGNMENTS, AND MINIS

1. BYOIR AND THE A&P: A MINI-CLASSIC

When the Great Atlantic and Pacific Tea Company (the A&P) was threatened by national legislation aimed at breaking up and divorcing the company's retail outlets from its manufacturing and distribution operations, the company turned to Carl Byoir & Associates, its public relations counsel, for assistance in meeting the governmental challenge. A wide variety of approaches were available to meet the threat to the company, but the Byoir organization decided to rely chiefly on advocacy advertising.

The Byoir people prepared a series of full-page advertisements, each one aimed directly at the vast American public. The messages stated that government bureaucrats were trying to destroy "your" A&P, cited the A&P's long service to the buying public, and suggested that readers support the A&P by rallying to its support because to do so was in the public's interest. Cost of the advertising campaign, which ran to hundreds of thousands of dollars, was covered by replacing the usual A&P full-page product advertisements with the advocacy advertisements every second week for a period of weeks. The end results were a series of endorsements of the A&P's position by a wide variety of national organizations, an outpouring of favorable letters from the general public, and the dropping of the threat to break up the company's manufacturing, distributing, and selling operations.

Whereas advertising and public relations practitioners at times find themselves in an internal organizational conflict, in the A&P antitrust case the division of responsibility was clearly established to avoid such conflict. The Byoir people, considered to be skilled in communicating institutional messages, were given responsibility for conceiving and writing the advertisements. Preparation of the graphics and placement of the advertisements in the media became the responsibility of the advertising men.

Reproduced here in its entirety is the first full-page advertisement prepared by the Byoir organization for the A&P (Exhibit 17.4). The ad was carried in more than one thousand daily newspapers across the United States in place of the usual full-page A&P product advertisement.

Questions for Discussion

1. What's your opinion of the basic theme, tone, writing style, and content of the advertisement?

2. What do you think would be the probable reader reaction to the advertisement?

3. What's your opinion of the overall public relations effectiveness of the ad?

Assignment

In a memorandum to your instructor evaluate the advertisement in terms of *each* of Earl Newsom's four guideposts to achieving favorable public opinion. (The four were discussed on pages 129–132.)

2. MOBIL OIL TAKES ON THE NEW YORK *TIMES:* A MINI-CASE

This mini-case concerns a New York *Times* article and the reaction to it three weeks later in an advertisement by the Mobil Oil Corporation on the Op-Ed page of the *Times.*

EXHIBIT 17.4

Do You Want Your A&P Put Out Of Business?

Last Thursday in New York, the anti-trust lawyers from Washington filed a suit to put A&P out of business.

They asked the court to order us to get rid of most of our stores and also the manufacturing facilities which supply you with A&P coffee, Ann Page products, Jane Parker baked goods, and other quality items we produce.

This would mean higher food prices for you. It would mean less food on every dinner table and fewer dollars in every pay envelope.

It would mean the end of A&P as you know it.

This poses a basic question for the American people: Do they want to continue to enjoy lower prices and better living? Or do they want to break up A&P and pay higher prices, and have lower living standards?

What do *you* want?

Why Destroy A&P?

This suit was brought under the anti-trust laws. These are good laws. They were passed about fifty years ago to prevent any company, or any group of companies, from getting a monopoly in a field and then raising prices to the public.

A&P has never done any of these things.

> Nobody has ever shown that we have anything even approaching a monopoly of the food business anywhere. As every housewife knows, the retail grocery business is the most competitive in the country and we do only a small part of it.

> Nobody has ever said we charged too high prices — just the opposite. This whole attack rises out of the fact that we sell good food too cheap. We would not have had any of this trouble if, instead of lowering prices, we had raised them and pocketed the difference.

> Nobody has ever said that our profit rate was too high. During the past five years our net profit, after taxes, has averaged about 1½¢ on every dollar of sales, which is less than almost any other business you can think of.

The American people have shown that they like our low-price policy by coming to our stores to do their shopping. If A&P is big, it is because the American people, by their patronage, have made it big.

Obviously, it is the theory of the anti-trust lawyers that the people have no right to patronize a company, if their patronage will make that company grow; and that any big business must be destroyed simply because it is big, and even if the public gets hurt in the process.

Do You Want Higher Prices?

There is much more involved in this case than the future of A&P. The entire American system of efficient, low-cost, low-profit distribution which we pioneered, will face destruction and the public will suffer.

A&P was the first chain store in this country. For more than ninety years we have tried to build a sound business on the simple formula the founder gave us: "Give the people the most good food you can for their money." Year after year we have tried to do a better job, make our business more efficient, and pass the savings on to the consumer in the form of lower prices.

Our efforts along these lines have led other grocers to keep their costs and profits down.

In the old days before A&P, food that cost the grocer 50¢, often sold as high as $1.00 at retail.

Today, food that costs the grocer 50¢ generally sells to the public at less than 60¢.

The methods we pioneered have been adopted not only by other grocers, but by merchants in other lines. There are today literally hundreds of chain stores, voluntary groups and individual merchants operating with the same methods and in the same pattern here under attack.

If the anti-trust lawyers succeed in destroying A&P, the way will be clear for the destruction of every other efficient large-scale distributor.

Who Will Be Hurt?

There has never been any question in our mind that it is good business and good citizenship to sell good food as cheaply as possible. As Fortune Magazine said about A&P some time ago, "It is firmly attached to the one great principle — the selling of more for less — that has made the desert bloom and the nation wax great."

> We sincerely believe that we have helped the American people eat better and live better.

> We believe that the hundreds of thousands of farmers and manufacturers who have voluntarily sought our business have profited by our fast, low-cost distribution of their products.

> We know that our 110,000 loyal employees enjoy today, as they always have, the highest wages, shortest hours and best working conditions generally prevailing in the retail food industry; and that these men and women have found in A&P good opportunities for security and progress.

> We know that thousands of businessmen — the landlords who rent us our stores, the haulers who operate our trucks, the people who supply us with goods and services — have a big stake in our operations.

Obviously, all these people will suffer if this company is put out of business.

What Shall We Do?

We admit that the interests of the owners of A&P are of little importance.

Frankly, they could make an enormous amount of money by breaking up A&P, as the anti-trust lawyers wish, and selling off the parts.

But is this what the American people want? Do they agree with the anti-trust lawyers that our food prices are too low, and that we should be put out of the picture so other grocers can charge more?

Frankly, if this were the case, we would not want to continue in business.

But we seriously doubt that this is the case. Twelve years ago, an effort was made to tax this company and other chain stores out of business. The public rallied to our support. They said they liked our quality foods and our low prices. As a result of their opposition, the tax was defeated.

Now we are faced with this new attack through the courts. We are faced with the heavy costs and all the trouble that lawsuits involve.

But we believe this attack is a threat to millions of consumers who rely on us for quality foods at low prices; to farmers who rely on us for fast, low-cost distribution of their products; and to our loyal employees.

We feel that it is our responsibility to all these people to defend, by every legitimate means, this company and the low-price policy on which it was built.

THE GREAT ATLANTIC & A&P PACIFIC TEA COMPANY

Reprinted with permission.

(The *Times* story is summarized below; students may prefer to check their library for the complete story.)

On Thursday, August 7, 1975, the New York *Times* carried a 23-paragraph story, with a Washington, August 6, dateline, written by David Burnham. The story was 26 column inches in length and ran on an inside page under a three-column headline which read:

2,300 Scientists Petition U.S. To Cut
Construction of Nuclear Power Plants

"In a petition presented to the White House and Congress," the *Times* lead stated, "more than 2,300 scientists warned today that the dangers of nuclear power were so grave that the United States should make a 'drastic reduction' in the construction of new reactors.

"Calling for a major program of research on reactor safety, plutonium safeguards and nuclear waste disposal, the scientists said that 'the country must recognize that it now appears imprudent to move forward with a rapidly expanding nuclear power plant construction program.' "

Noting that the country has 55 operating reactors which generate about 7 to 5 percent of the nation's electricity, the story said that government planners hope there will be 830 reactors producing more than 50 percent of the country's electricity within 25 years. It pointed out that the petition was presented to the President and Congressional leaders on the 30th anniversary of the dropping of the atomic bomb on Hiroshima.

"The petition," stated the fifth paragraph of the article, "was presented by the Union of Concerned Scientists in the debate over the potential dangers of nuclear reactors as an electric power plant engineering concern—Ebasco Services, Inc.—made public a national poll it had sponsored indicating that about two-thirds of those interviewed favored the building of more reactors."

The article quoted Dr. Henry Kendall, physics professor at M.I.T. and a founder of the Union of Concerned Scientists, as declaring the petition was significant because it destroyed the industry argument 'that no reputable scientists had doubts about the safety of reactors.'

"Among the 2,300 biologists, chemists, engineers, physicists and other scientists who signed the petition," the article noted, "were James Bryant Conant, the retired president of Harvard University; George D. Kistiakowsky, professor of chemistry, emeritus; and Victor Weisskopf, former chairman of the M.I.T. physics department, all of whom were intimately involved in the World War II effort to develop the nuclear bomb.

"Another signer was George Wald, professor of biology at Harvard and one of the nine Nobel laureates who endorsed the petition. . . .

"To gain the signatures for its petition, the Union of Concerned Scientists sent the statement last June to 16,000 persons, most of whose names were drawn from the mailing lists of the Federation of American Scientists and the Bulletin of Atomic Scientists.

"Dr. Kendall said that the 2,300 scientists who responded represented about 20 percent of the 12,000 scientists and engineers on the two mailing lists. The physicist said this was a far better response than the 1 to 2 percent reply rate that he said mailing experts had told him to expect. The union itself has less than 100 members."

Burnham then reported that the petition said there are three major problems connected with the widespread use of nuclear power. The article went into detail about each of these three problems as set forth in the petition. It then said that the scientists call for a "greatly enlarged national effort to conserve the use of energy, and to develop techniques for using coal without polluting the atmosphere and for harnessing the energy of the sun, the wind, the tides and the heat of the earth's crust."

Paragraph 16 of Burnham's story stated that "a public opinion survey taken last spring showed that 63 percent of those interviewed favored the building of more nuclear power plants and 19 percent were opposed, according to Ebasco Services, Inc., an electric power-plant engineering concern for which Louis Harris and Associates, Inc., conducted

EXHIBIT 17.5

The people speak.
But the message gets lost.

From time to time we have criticized Congress for its tardiness in enacting sound national energy policy. But how can our elected representatives know the facts needed for sound legislation when the energy information they see in the press gives a misleading impression of how Americans feel on this issue?

Consider, for example, *The New York Times* article on August 7 headlined, "2,300 Scientists Petition U.S. to Reduce Construction of Nuclear Power Plants."

The hasty reader gained the impression that a survey of the scientific community showed scientists solidly opposed to the new plants. No such thing. In reality, the 2,300 were those who indicated by mail their support of a position of the Union of Concerned Scientists. And they represented only about 20 percent of the 12,000 professionals polled.

Was this an impressive response, even so? Far from it, says Hugh Hoffman, who heads three opinion research organizations and is a recognized expert in the field. "If the petition's viewpoint were strongly held in the scientific community, a 60 percent return wouldn't have been surprising, given the fact that these were articulate, concerned individuals."

The Times did, in the same article, report a public opinion survey showing that 63 percent of the people favor building new atomic plants, while only 19 percent are opposed and 18 percent undecided. Among those living near existing nuclear plants, the same majority—63 percent—favor new A-plant construction.

But that survey, unfortunately, wasn't mentioned until the fifth paragraph and supporting detail was relegated to the last part of the 23-paragraph story. *The Times* had "balanced" the news. But had it, really? Many readers, we suspect, never got that far down in the article.

We were sorry, too, that *The Times* did not cite—as the *Washington Post* did in its story on the petition—another petition of scientists which strongly supported A-plants. (Signers included 11 Nobel Prize laureates, six of them in physics, the science most associated with nuclear development.) In the *Post* article, a Nobel Prize laureate was quoted as comparing opposition to nuclear power to earlier-day opposition to the advent of airplanes and railroads.

We were disappointed, too, that *The Times* chose to overlook another recent poll, by Opinion Research Corporation, which found that 56 percent of a cross section of American engineers believe nuclear power should receive immediate priority. Sixty-three percent of this group felt present atomic-safety regulations are basically adequate.

Why is an oil company worried about nuclear power? Obviously, because the atom can lift a great deal of the burden from oil and gas. But also because this case clearly tells why Congress and other officials aren't getting their constituents' thinking about energy. Why the message isn't getting through.

Isn't it time both sides of energy issues were presented more objectively? So that everybody can understand what's really happening, and how people really feel? So that the country can get the facts needed to formulate a sound energy program? We think so.

Mobil

Reprinted with permission.

the poll." The article reported that a total of 1,537 persons were interviewed in person nationwide between March 21 and April 3 and were asked: "In general, do you favor or oppose the building of more nuclear power plants in the United States?"

The remaining six paragraphs of Burnham's story cited data from the Harris survey showing more people in favor of than opposed to speeding up construction of the Alaska oil pipeline; increasing efforts to produce oil shale in Western states; starting off-shore drilling for oil off the Atlantic, Pacific, and Gulf coasts; and allowing more strip mining of coal.

Questions for Discussion

The Mobil Oil advertisement (Exhibit 17.5) appeared on the Op-Ed page of the New York *Times* on August 28, 1975. After reading it, answer and discuss the following questions:

1. Do you feel the criticisms of the *Times* story cited in the Mobil advertisement are justified? In expressing your conclusions, cite specifics to prove your point of view.

2. What do you perceive to be Mobil's public relations objectives in writing and running the ad in the *Times*? What's your opinion of these objectives? Do you think the advertisement will achieve these objectives?

3. What's your personal opinion of the ad? Your professional opinion?

Assignment

Assume that you are public relations counsel to Mobil. A draft of the advertisement has been sent to you on August 14 with this notation: "Following is a draft of an advertisement we are thinking of running in the *Times* on August 28 in our regularly-scheduled spot on the Op-Ed page. We would appreciate your professional opinion of the advertisement and our intention to run it."

Write a memorandum to the vice-president of public relations of Mobil, giving your reaction to the proposed advertisement and Mobil's intention to run it on the Op-Ed page on August 28.

3. EDISON ELECTRIC INSTITUTE'S THIRD-PARTY ADVERTISEMENTS: A MINI-CASE

Advocacy advertisements featuring third-party spokespersons were a key element of a communications program developed and executed in 1982 for the Edison Electric Institute (EEI) by its public relations counsel, Harshe-Rotman & Druck.

Targets of the program, which was termed by EEI as its "financial viability" campaign, were the state utility commissions. These state agencies regulated the 200 investor-owned utilities that comprised EEI, the trade association headquartered in Washington, D.C., and representing 77 percent of all U.S. utility companies. According to the Edison Electric Institute, "the erosion of utilities' financial viability is for the most part a direct result of a short-sighted adversary approach to power company regulation by a majority of state utility commissions. The key to the future of the nation's electrical energy delivery system—and the businesses, industries and individual citizens who rely on it—is in the hands of these same regulators."*

---

*This quote and those in the remainder of this case are from *Communication Update*, November 1981, six-page newsletter published primarily for its members by the Edison Electric Institute. The quotes and the advertisement (Exhibit 17.6) are reprinted with permission of EEI.

Primary goal of the 1982 campaign was to stimulate action to "create a more reasonable regulatory and rate climate," and bring about "realistic rates of return; expeditious rate proceedings; automatic rate adjustments to compensate for inflation, capital costs and other factors beyond utility management's control; and recovery of construction costs as work progresses."

To tell its story to regulators, legislators, the financial community, and the "influentials" the Edison Electric Institute program utilized advocacy advertising, press briefings, articles, consumer columns, syndicated columnists, op-ed pieces, personal appearances, audiovisuals, and letters to the editor. The advertising which formed an integral part of the communication campaign consisted of a series of full-page ads carried in publications read by "the 15 million men and women that research shows to be the activists—the people whose record of accomplishments shows not only that they are interested in vital public issues, but that they will do something about their convictions: they write elected officials or news organizations to express their views; they address public meetings and hold office in community-wide organizations; they're active in political parties or hold government positions." Included among the publications were *Nation's Business, Newsweek E* (executives), *Psychology Today, Smithsonian, Time B* (business), *U.S. News & World Report* "Blue Chip," New York *Times, Wall Street Journal*, and Washington *Post*. Some ads appeared in other publications as circumstances warranted.

Each ad in the series featured a bylined message from a third-party spokesperson who did not have a direct connection with the utilities forming the EEI, but who had an interest in utilities. A heavy, bold-face headline topped each ad, followed by a picture and brief bio of the spokesperson, the message/copy which formed the body of the ad, and a note at the end from the Edison Electric Institute explaining the role of the spokesperson.

The spokespersons featured in the first six ads were as follows: **Charles J. Cicchetti**, former chairman, Wisconsin Public Service Commission, and professor of economics, University of Wisconsin-Madison; **Alvin L. Alm**, former White House energy advisor and director, Energy Security Program, Kennedy School of Government, Harvard University; **Eugene M. Lerner**, professor of finance, Graduate School of Management, Northwestern University; **Claire V. Hansen**, president and chief executive officer, Duff and Phelps, Inc.; **Clarence M. Mitchell III**, Maryland state senator and president, National Black Caucus of State Legislators; and **Sanford I. Weill**, chairman, Shearson-American Express, Inc.

Reproduced as Exhibit 17.6 is the advertisement featuring the message by Claire V. Hansen.

Questions for Discussion

1. What's your opinion of the use of third-party spokespersons in the EEI advocacy advertisements?

2. What's your opinion of the six people used as spokespersons in the series? Suggest some alternates as substitutes.

3. What's your opinion of the Hansen ad which is reprinted in this case? Discuss format, layout, headline, copy, and the end statement from EEI.

4. An article in *Advertising Age* (March 14, 1983) cited James W. Plumb, president of Ruder Finn & Rotman's Washington office, as stating that "the advertising was hard-hitting but risky." In what respects do you consider the EEI advertising to be "risky"? (Ruder Finn & Rotman was the successor agency to Harshe-Rotman & Druck.)

5. To measure effectiveness of the ads, EEI commissioned Cambridge Reports to conduct a national opinion leader survey in three waves. One of the findings showed that of the state public utility commissioners surveyed, more than three-fourths said they had seen advertising about the electric utility industry's problems. Regarding believ-

EXHIBIT 17.6

A message from one of the nation's leading authorities on utility securities ...

ADVERSE REGULATION HINDERS UTILITIES IN CAPITAL MARKETS

By Claire V. Hansen, C.F.A.

President and Chief Executive Officer, Duff and Phelps, Inc.

Claire V. Hansen, president of Duff and Phelps, Inc., is a recognized authority on valuation and a chartered financial analyst.
For more than 50 years, Duff and Phelps has provided investment research and financial analysis to institutions and corporations. The firm has long been a leader in utility investment research, tracking more than 200 utility companies across the country. In addition, Duff and Phelps issues credit ratings on fixed income securities and commercial paper.

Electric utilities are the nation's most capital intensive businesses. They constantly face vigorous competition for the investment dollars required to maintain a healthy and reliable energy delivery system.

To compete effectively for capital, utilities must be able to earn rates of return that compensate for the additional risks of an inflationary environment. In many states, restrictive and erratic regulation has increased investor risk while holding returns below those offered by such investments as money market funds, savings certificates and some government securities.

In evaluating utility securities, a major consideration is whether the governing regulatory commission permits the company to earn a sufficient return on equity to:
1) **provide adequate funds to meet rising debt service requirements;**
2) **sustain dividends at levels that at least keep pace with inflation;**
3) **accumulate internal cash to reinvest in the system.**

For the average electric utility company we track, the ratio of pre-tax earnings to debt interest payments has dropped by more than one-third since 1970. In the same period, while average reported dividends have increased 60%, dividends after adjustments for inflation actually decreased by 30%.

Consequently, credit ratings have deteriorated, and most utilities must pay premium interest rates on bonds to compensate for increased investor risk. To raise equity capital, companies often must sell stock at prices below book value. As a result, the ownership of those who have already invested in the company is diluted.

The impact of regulation on utility creditworthiness becomes evident when bond ratings are correlated with regulatory environment. Of the 13 companies that have our highest ratings (D&P #1 or #2), all have operations in states we consider to have reasonable regulation (see "How D&P Rates the Regulators").

Utilities in states where reasonable rates are permitted have higher credit ratings. Therefore, they can raise funds at lower cost to the consumer for plant and equipment modernization, conversion to lower cost fuels, new technology development, transmission grid maintenance, and meeting basic local growth requirements. Denial of reasonable earnings will inevitably result in degradation of service — including possible power rationing and brownouts — and even greater escalation of costs to consumers over the long term.

When establishing allowable rates of return, regulators must balance their efforts to keep down immediate consumer costs against the even more important responsibility to assure adequate power supplies for the future.

Claire V. Hansen

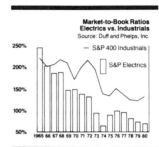

Market-to-Book Ratios
Electrics vs. Industrials
Source: Duff and Phelps, Inc.

— S&P 400 Industrials

S&P Electrics

How D&P Rates the Regulators

In addition to rating utility company securities, Duff and Phelps rates state regulatory commissions. It looks for:
1) **decisions based on realistic projections of sales, expenses and investments, rather than on out-of-date historical data;**
2) **permissible rates of return on equity that are competitive in financial markets;**
3) **prompt rate decisions.**

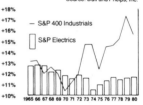

Return on Common Equity
Electrics vs. Industrials
Source: Duff and Phelps, Inc.

— S&P 400 Industrials

S&P Electrics

This is one of a series of messages sponsored by the Edison Electric Institute, representing the investor-owned utilities that deliver 77% of the nation's electricity.

Participating independent authorities are not paid for these messages, but present them because they believe the issue is of critical national significance. EEI welcomes your comments.

Edison Electric Institute
The association of electric companies
1111 19th Street, N.W., Room 716, Washington, D.C. 20036

Nations Business — 2/1/82
Time "B"   — 3/1/82
U.S. News & World Report "Blue Chip" — 3/1/82
Newsweek "Executive" — 2/22/82

Smithsonian — 3/1/82
Psychology Today — 3/1/82
Survey of Wall St. Research — 1/82 - 2/82
The Wall Street Journal — 1/14/82

The New York Times — 1/17/82
The Washington Post — 1/17/82
The Arizona Republic/
    The Phoenix Gazette — 1/14/82

ability, 12 percent of the commissioners said they found the ads "very" believable, 63 percent found them "somewhat" believable, 24 percent "less than" believable, and 1 percent had "no opinion." Of those commissioners who were aware of the advertising, 35 percent identified EEI as the sponsor. Another 15 percent specified a particular local utility, and 21 percent didn't know the sponsor. The rest of the answers were scattered over a half dozen other categories.

What's your opinion of these findings? How would you view them if you were the EEI?

Assignments

1. As each ad was introduced into the program, a news release on each spokesperson's message was prepared and distributed nationally.

   Write the release to be sent out in connection with the Hansen ad.

2. A basic premise of the EEI advocacy ads was that a majority of state regulatory commissioners had an "adversary approach to power company regulation." Research the validity of this claim and in a report to your instructor explain whether it was or was not justified.

3. In 1983 the Edison Electric Institute changed the focus of its spokesperson advertising. Though continuing to feature third-party spokespersons, the campaign shifted its focus to the benefits of a healthy utility industry, with a greater emphasis on factors beyond price-related regulation. Among the 1983 spokespersons were **John M. Albertine,** president, American Business Conference; **David Packard,** chairman of the board, Hewlett-Packard Company; and **Warren M. Anderson,** chairman of the board, Union Carbide Corporation.

   Among the publications in which the Albertine ad appeared were the *Wall Street Journal* (Feb. 17), New York *Times* (Feb. 20), Washington *Post* (Feb. 20), *USA Today* (Feb. 24), and *Nation's Business* (April 1). Read the ad and in a report to your instructor evaluate it in comparison with the Hansen ad.

18

COMMUNICATIONS TECHNOLOGY AND PUBLIC RELATIONS

Every decade seems to bring a new challenge to public relations practice, and the challenge of the eighties is the communications technology revolution. Almost all revolutions bring changes in the society in which they occur. This one is no exception. The changes and the challenges which the communications technology revolution pose for public relations practitioners are evident in the following statements by John Budd, Chester Burger, and T. Michael Forney:

Corporate video today is not simply a new generation of visual aids, a souped-up method of corporate film-making. Video, especially non-broadcast private video, represents a new and dynamic medium of communications. Cable TV's emergence has redefined video's role in communications. Whether we achieve that communications millennium or simply squander a unique opportunity for really effective communications will depend in large measure on the sensitivity of corporate professionals to the profound implications of today's video—especially cable TV—in all its flexibility, and on their ability to creatively harness the medium.[1]

All the technology is here, granted, not in one integrated system. But sooner than you can imagine, your corporate communications job will change. At first, it will appear only in the form of individual pieces of technology. Only later will you begin to realize that the communications revolution has reached you. And life will not be the same for any of us. It is a challenge we should relish and welcome, and be grateful that we should be a part of the time in history when it occurs.[2]

361

Enhanced two-way communication systems using cable, satellite, computer and video-disc technologies will revolutionize the information transmission and receiving process. As a result, audiences will become much more segmented and specialized, forcing public relations professionals to discard many of the traditional methods used to reach and influence their publics. . . . The Information Age will bring forth profound societal change in the next decade. Consequently, public relations professionals are faced with an upheaval no less dramatic than that experienced by the calligraphers in Gutenberg's era. The task will be to anticipate the future and prepare to use it, or perish.[3]

Budd, Burger, and Forney were wise enough not to place date marks on their look into the electronic future. By 1984, however, many of the communications developments they predicted had already been born. Some were still in the womb stage, and some had been aborted. Clearly, the time has come, as Lewis Carroll's Walrus said, to step through the looking glass and talk of the wondrous things wrought by technology for use by communicators. The first group of technological "things" to be discussed are those which directly affect the way in which public relations people carry out their functions. The second group are mainly those which directly affect the way the mass media operate and thus indirectly impact on the work done by public relations practitioners.

TECHNOLOGICAL DEVELOPMENTS
AFFECTING PRACTICE

The use of **word processors** and the use of **video for organizational communications purposes** constitute the two main ways in which technological developments directly affect public relations practice. They will be discussed in turn in this section.

WORD PROCESSORS

A simple way of describing a word processor is to state that it's a typewriter with a memory. Another way is to say it is simply a microcomputer. A third is to say it involves a keyboard, a display terminal, and a printer.

Any of the above three would suffice because a word processor fits all three descriptions. Perhaps a more useful explanation is to say that a word processor enables its user to correct errors in copy, move whole paragraphs around at will, and even eliminate grammatical mistakes by means of the proper software.

A word processor can be a standalone unit or part of a multistation system. The typical standalone unit has one keyboard, a video display holding about a half-page of text, one or more diskette units for storing text, and a letter-quality printer. The multistation systems simply link more than one keyboard and display to a storage unit and one or more printers.

In visualizing a word processor in action, view it as a typewriter without paper. When you strike keys on the keyboard, the characters appear on the display screen instead of on paper. Single characters or entire lines can be changed at any time, insertions and deletions made, paragraphs moved around. When you're satisfied with your display of text, you press a key and release it to storage. It can be called back from storage at any time, or it can be wiped out when no longer needed.

Modem Expands Use

Through the use of a modem—a device which converts the text of your word processor into a form for transmission over telephones lines, and vice versa—one can expand greatly the use of the average word processor. In effect, a word processor in one office can communicate and interface with one in another office anywhere in the country. A word processor equipped with a modem can tap into data banks; transmit releases to PR wire services for subsequent distribution to the media; send texts to clients for clearance; and transmit texts and graphics to typesetters.

Chester Burger, who foresaw the new communications technology's importance long before most of his colleagues in the public relations field, tells a story that illustrates the use of a word processor with modem for research purposes. Because he was pressed for time, one of Burger's associates hadn't been able to compile data preliminary to a meeting. As Burger then explained:

> We have in our office a standard word processor, no different from anyone else's. We have turned it into a research tool through a Bell System modem (which is a little black box of electronics) that connects our word processor to a telephone line. Our secretary simply sat down at the word processor and dialed the Dow Jones Data Bank. In about 15 seconds, she had access through the word processor to its entire memory. She typed in some code words, and out came page after page of information, printed out at the rate of 20 seconds a page. A summary of every single item that's been published in the newspaper about this company in the last few years, their current financial statement, a list of all litigation pending against the company, all officers of the company, the names of the board of directors . . .[4]

In summation, the simplest type of word processing unit facilitates and improves the writing and editing process, saves costly rewrite time, and increases productivity in the public relations department. The more complex units interact with other units anywhere in the country, produce not merely text material but also headlines and graphic layout designs, and have the ability to interface directly with typesetting units. As to the future, one authority predicted in 1982 that one could then "envision an internal communication system based almost solely on desktop video display terminals linked to centralized data banks and full-scale management information systems."[5] Exhibit 18.1 cites examples of actual 1982 usage of word processors/desktop computers by various public relations practitioners.

EXHIBIT 18.1

Some 1982 Users of Word Processors/Desktop Computers

- **The Strayton Corporation,** public relations counseling firm of Wellesley, Mass., used four machines in three cities with a total of twenty-nine keystations. By using telephone lines the firm exchanged text material between the three cities and with six clients and affiliates in London and Frankfort who had compatible equipment. The firm used its word processor to localize press releases; type presentations and reports for clients; insert standard paragraphs into releases and letters; produce internal bookeeping reports; and personalize press conference invitations.

- **Newsome & Company,** Boston-based public relations firm, made use of a word processor with three keystations and one printer for writing and editing copy, addressing and mailing purposes, and all of the firm's billing and accounting. The unit also automatically recorded the amount of time spent on the unit for each project, cued orders for printouts, and kept track of time spent on clients by employees.

- **Doremus & Company's** New York City headquarters installed its word processing units in 1978 and by 1982 was using them to type presentations for clients and prospects and by tie-in with a teletypewriter system to send financial and other releases simultaneously to the Dow-Jones, Reuters, AP, UPI wire services and to PR Newswire and Business Wire. The tie-in was achieved by using the word processing unit to punch out copy automatically on paper tape and feeding it to the teletypewriter without rekeying.[6]

VIDEO FOR ORGANIZATIONAL COMMUNICATIONS PURPOSES

Television—in short, video—is truly ubiquitous and seems to have been around for ages. Actually, it's in the teen stage when compared to the older media: newspapers, magazines, and radio. Little wonder, therefore, that it wasn't until the late seventies and early eighties that some bright, adventurous practitioners began to use video for corporate communications purposes. Not television as we know it in the commercial world of the networks and local affiliates, but rather **video used as a corporate communications tool.**

What these practitioners did was to take the hardware elements that make television work—the camera, audio, a means of transmission, and the receiving set—and put them to use in reaching various publics. That it hadn't been done before was due to the high cost of connecting the communicator with the audience. Stationary electronic birds high in the sky did the trick. With the advent of communications satellites in fixed orbit 22,300 miles above the equator, video for organizational communications purposes became a viable reality. The average small concern or organization couldn't afford the cost—a major reason why nonprofit organizations haven't made much use of video—but large and even medium-sized corporate entities could. The result is corporate video used to televise analyst presentations, annual meetings, annual reports, multipoint conferences, and press conferences.

Analyst presentations are normally routinized to the extent of being sleep-inducing, but they're even more important than sleep to corporations seeking to impress security analysts. In fact, it's probably because of their importance that few corporations have dared to be different in making presentations to the analysts.

The Emhart Corporation of Hartford, Connecticut, is a company that took a chance on being different, and it did so through the use of videotapes. Emhart machines are involved in the production of glass, hardware, glue, shoes, locks, and similar other practical but less-than-fascinating items. Camera crews went into the field and filmed some fast-paced tapes of Emhart machinery being produced or being used in customer plants. This footage was cut down to videotaped color clips, each running from one to one and a half minutes and then integrated into the oral, live presentation made to security analysts by company executives.[7] States John Budd, Emhart's vice-president for external relations: "In effect, what was offered was videotaped plant tours, abbreviated to be sure, but more sharply focused on the interesting aspects without the time lost in travel or the shoe leather spent in tramping miles of plant floor."[8] (See Figure 18.1.)

The **annual meeting,** a major form of communication between a corporation and its shareholders, is usually a half-day affair which follows a set pattern, attracts a minuscule fraction of a large corporation's shareholders, and seeks to avoid dissent from the floor. In attempting to enlarge the annual meeting audience, many companies have taken the annual meeting "on the road" by presenting it at various sites around the country. The audience, however, has remained a small fraction of the total number of shareholders.

Video offers at least two solutions to this problem of audience. One is to videotape the entire proceedings, edit them down to a viewable length, and offer videocassettes on a loan basis to shareholders. Another is to use satellite transmission and feed the entire meeting live to shareholders at viewing sites in selected locations. Both methods are now being used by corporations tuned in to the use of video for financial reporting.

Annual reports, those slick, four-color publications sent out every year to millions of stockholders, analysts, brokers, libraries, and others, have taken on a new look via video. Here, again, Emhart was ahead of almost the entire field when, in 1980, it produced and telecast a 22-minute highlight videotape of the company's annual report. By linking satellite transmission with cable TV the company made its video version available to shareholders in eight states nationwide via a one-time network of twenty-two cable operators in 100 communities. Other major companies that have followed

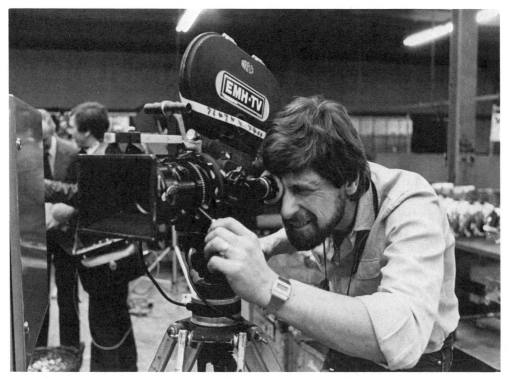

FIGURE 18.1 A cameraman zooms in during typical videotaping at an Emhart plant. His shot of Emhart machinery in action will form part of the videotape presentation made to security analysts by Emhart.

Emhart's lead with their video annual reports are the International Paper Company, CIBA-GEIGY, Royal Trust, and TransCanada Pipeline.

Budd provides this warning to the many companies that have expressed an interest in producing a video annual report: "Never forget that the video report is designed to complement, not substitute for, the printed report. It goes without saying that its distribution must follow, not precede, the distribution of the printed version."[9]

Starting one's own **business news network via satellite** became an actuality in August, 1982, when BY/MEDIA, INC., a wholly-owned subsidiary of the Carl Byoir & Associates counseling agency, put into operation Corporate Headline News as part of its BY/MEDIA Satellite Network.

Initial plans called for 30-minute transmissions every Wednesday sent via the Westar V satellite to more than 300 commercial TV stations and hundreds of cable systems throughout the country. The material to be sent via the network was chiefly 15-second bulletins dealing primarily with financial reports, acquisitions, new products and services, plant openings, technological breakthroughs, personnel changes, and other business news. In addition the network scheduled 30- and 60-second PSAs and features.

Made available to any public relations agency or organization desiring to distribute brief business news items, the service was described by president Michael McCurdy of BY/MEDIA as making possible substantial savings when compared with the traditional method of producing individual tapes and shipping them to television stations. The service was offered at no charge to the stations.[10]

Teleconferencing, also known as **videoconferencing,** began to come of age as we moved into the mid-eighties. Here's how Barbara Kaye Greenleaf, director of commu-

nications for VideoStar Connections, Inc., a satellite networking company, summed up
the state of the teleconferencing art in late 1983:

> People who try it by and large like it. They stage more and more events in their own
> dedicated networks. Indeed, a few companies such as Hewlett-Packard and Chrysler are
> already doing just that. All of which leads me to believe that videoconferencing has
> arrived.[11]

There are several distinct reasons why videoconferencing has arrived on the American
scene. Travel costs have made distant conferences expensive affairs. Travel to such conferences has always been time-consuming; it doesn't take a math wizard to figure out
that it takes less time to attend a two-hour teleconference than to attend a two-day meeting 900 miles or 2,000 miles away from one's home base. Such travel time cuts down on
productivity, hence the videoconference route makes for greater efficiency. Finally, the
early bugs that bedeviled initial teleconferencing have been greatly reduced. The new
technology has made teleconferencing a communications instrument that has great
appeal and practical value to a good many organizations and groups.

In simplest terms, three elements combine in a videoconference: (1) the uplink or
ground source which transmits the originating signal to (2) the satellite or space station
orbiting the earth, which relays the signal back to (3) the downlink or earth station
receiving the transmission.

Of crucial importance is the ability to access each of the three elements. Special production equipment and expertise are needed to transmit television and radio signals from
uplink to satellite. Space on the satellite is at a premium, hence the need to have access to
a transponder, the specific receiver on the satellite that transmits the signal back to
earth. Finally, more special equipment and expertise are needed at the downlink element
of the videoconference troika.

Prior to 1980 the lack of uplink and downlink stations inhibited the growth of teleconferencing, but that situation improved in the next few years. Two major hotel
chains—Hilton and Holiday Inns—established teleconference installations and capabilities at several hundred of their units, thus providing users with a networking system. In
coordination with the Robert Wold Company the Hilton Hotel Corporation launched
its nationwide satellite videoconference service in late 1981, offering "a single-source
turnkey package, including program design, production, satellite transmission and
reception, large screen projection, and conference accommodations."[12] Similarly, in
coordination with another telecommunication organization, Holiday Inns offered the
same range of videoconference services and a networking capability through their
nationwide hotel system.

Among developments advancing teleconferencing in the early eighties were the following:

- Not merely hotel chains, but also a wide variety of telecommunication service organizations entered the field and offered full teleconferencing services for both profit
  and nonprofit organizations.

- Public Broadcasting System stations made themselves available for uplink and downlink telecasting, thus forming an integral element for one-time networking.

- Teleconferencing consultants became a familiar part of the national electronic communications scene.

- Western Electric announced the introduction of Picturephone® Meeting Service (registered trademark of AT&T), offering two-way television that can also handle graphics
  and slides, facsimile transmission, and an electronic blackboard for handwritten use
  during conferences. The service, available either in public rooms provided by the Bell
  System or in private rooms at customers' premises, was in operation in fifteen cities in
  1982 and projected to increase to forty-two cities by the end of 1983.[13]

- Western Union Corporation moved into teleconferencing in August, 1982, by announcing the formation of Western Union VideoConferencing, Inc. Joining Western Union under a two-year "contractual association" were Netcom International of San Francisco, handling the transmission network and the facilities at the remote sites, and Momentum Enterprises of New York, handling video production and providing large-screen projection television systems for the remote sites. Western Union made available a pool of seven of their Westar system transponders for videoconferencing throughout the day.[14]

- Corporations large enough to afford and have need for telecommunications between and among installations and headquarters established their own in-house videoconferencing capabilities.

By 1984 public relations practitioners were applying videoconferencing in a variety of ways. (See Exhibit 18.2.) It has been utilized to—

- announce the results of important national studies;

- introduce new products and models to dealers, the press, and the general public;

- coordinate communications activities within large corporations and between public relations counseling firms and their clients; and

- hold electronic press conferences where the subject and the need have been important enough to warrant dissemination of information in all parts of the nation simultaneously.

Videoconferencing, however, is not the answer to all public relations problems. It should not be considered a substitute for all meetings and occasions. In many situations personal contact is a vital ingredient for effective communication. Nor should one forget that videoconferencing is live television, open to mis-cues and mistakes that can't be recalled. It demands expertise that few internal public relations departments have, thus the need for outside telecommunication organizations to carry out production, transmission, and distribution tasks. Videoconferencing is flashy, but costly; it should be used with discretion, not with wild abandonment.

TECHNOLOGICAL DEVELOPMENTS AFFECTING MASS MEDIA

Technological communications developments in the early eighties brought changes affecting not only the way in which public relations people carry out their functions. They also changed the way in which the mass media operate. Because of the role the mass media play in public relations practice, changes affecting the mass media have important public relations ramifications. This section will therefore examine some of the key mass media changes brought on by technological developments in the early eighties and then seek to relate them to public relations practice.

CABLE TELEVISION

Cable television has been evolving at such a rapid rate it's very difficult to assess where it stands at any given moment. To determine cable's place in the media sun we can rely on certain factual information, but unfortunately the information leads to good news/bad news conclusions. Judge this for yourself as you read the following cable news notes:

EXHIBIT 18.2

Some Examples of Teleconferencing

- When **Johnson & Johnson** was ready to bring Tylenol back on the market in late 1982 with its triple safety-sealed, tamper-resistant package, it did so by means of a national press briefing involving a thirty-city video press conference via satellite. Originating in New York, the 90-minute telecast was carried live by satellite-TV transmission to more than 500 media representatives in thirty cities. After remarks by Johnson & Johnson chairman James E. Burke, reporters in New York, Philadelphia, Washington, Chicago, and Los Angeles asked questions that were telecast throughout the closed-circuit system. Arrangements for the video press conference were made by the Burson-Marsteller counseling firm and overseen by Lawrence G. Foster, J&J's corporate vice-president, public relations.

- Within a six-month period **President Ronald Reagan** in 1982-83 held three video teleconferences, all broadcast from a U.S. Chamber of Commerce studio in Washington and transmitted via satellite to thirty-seven cities throughout the country. The first two teleconferences were political fundraisers sponsored by the Republican National Committee and the third teleconference was aired to publicize the Jobs Training Partnership Act.

- When the **International Association of Business Communicators** sponsored a 1982 conference on "The New Technology," it did so appropriately via teleconferencing. The conference originated in Dallas and was broadcast live by satellite to more than 1,200 communicators in twenty-one other U.S. and Canadian cities. Divided into two two-hour segments, the teleconference featured speakers who discussed various aspects of the new communication technology. A 90-minute break between sessions allowed local AIBC chapters to present live programs related to the conference theme.

- To achieve wide dissemination of its fourth biennial study of the American family, **General Mills** and its public relations counsel, Padilla and Speer, arranged in 1981 a hook-up of nineteen Public Broadcasting System stations. Findings of a national survey of American families by the Louis Harris organization were seen by a live New York audience in WNET-TV and by reporters watching in eighteen cities at PBS stations linked by satellite. Following the presentation of findings, two-way audio was used to answer questions from the live audience and from the reporters in the other cities. After a lunch break 250 community leaders in the nineteen teleconference cities convened for panel discussions to react to the study findings.

- To introduce its new model EXP in 1981 the **Ford Division of the Ford Motor Company** held three separate video conferences in one day, each one live via satellite. The first, held the morning of February 26, involved Ford Division executives gathered at the Public Broadcasting System studios outside Detroit. They "met" with more than 6,000 dealership owners in thirty-eight cities. After lunch the executives communicated via satellite with more than 15,000 dealer sales personnel, and in the evening they engaged in a press conference with the press in fifteen cities. Video was one-way and audio two-way in all three transmissions.

- By 1984, there were close to 6,000 cable system operators serving 34 million subscribers. Cable TV thus had the potential of reaching 40 percent of the country's 83 million homes. The growth of cable had outpaced expectations and predictions.[15]

- By 1983, via satellite transmission to cable operators, Ted Turner's superstation WTBS was reaching 26 million subscribers—31 percent of all TV households and 81 percent of all cable households. WTBS had not yet moved into the black, but it was expected to do so by the end of that year. At the same time Turner's Cable Network News was reaching 20 million subscribers, representing 24 percent of all TV households and 63 percent of all cable households.[16]

- In mid-October, 1983, after a bitter cable news war, ABC and Group W gave up their battle against the Turner cable news organization and sold out their Satellite News Channel to Turner for an estimated $24 million. At the time of the sale SNC was reaching close to 8 million homes and most of them would be added to the Turner cable news base. It was estimated that SNC lost between $40 and $60 million in the 16 months it was in operation. An ABC Video Enterprises executive was quoted as saying: "There just wasn't enough advertising to support all of that news programming on broadcast and cable. We were killing Turner and he was killing us. It made no sense to continue that way."[18]

- In 1983, WSM, Inc., of Nashville (owner of the Grand Ole Opry) and Group W Satellite Communications debuted The Nashville Network, beaming the country music channel into 7 million homes via 725 cable operators. The debut was described as "the largest subscriber launch in the history of cable television."[18]

- After a brief five-month existence, *Time* in September, 1983, closed down *TV-Cable Week*, *Time*'s ambitious television-listings venture. At the time of the closing, circulation, advertising, and distribution figures were well below expectations.[19]

- After a brief nine-month existence, The Entertainment Channel, RCA's 24-hour-pay-cable network that sought to offer quality entertainment, closed down in March, 1983. At the time of closing, the channel was reaching 50,000 subscribers via 84 cable systems. Estimated loss: more than $34 million before taxes. The previous November CBS terminated CBS Cable, a much-praised cultural service available to five million cable subscribers, with losses of more than $30 million.[20]

These news notes from the land of cable television should be of special interest to public relations practitioners. They show, for example, that this relatively new medium of communications has grown at a much swifter rate than anticipated and has a very sizable potential total audience. At the same time, they also show that the cable field in 1984 was still going through its shakedown/shakeout phase. Some of the country's most experienced and well-financed companies have had their financial fingers burned trying to grab hold of cable television's brass ring. Cable television should certainly figure in organizational public relations plans, but just how it fits in must be carefully examined. Such an examination is explored in the subsections that follow.

Narrowcasting

A simple description of narrowcasting is that it is the opposite of broadcasting.[21] An organization gets involved in broadcasting for public relations purposes because it wants to reach a broad, mass audience. That same organization gets involved in narrowcasting in order to reach a limited, narrow audience with specialized interests. Public relations people call this shooting with a rifle instead of a shotgun.

The problem is in lining up one's target. If you can be sure that your audience will be tuned in to a network aimed at a specialized group comprising your audience, then that network is your target. Cable television provides such networks. For example, to name two such networks, consider the Entertainment and Sports Programming Network (ESPN) and the USA network, both of which are primarily devoted to sports and available through cable. ESPN, advertiser-supported and offered free to cable households, had 28.5 million subscribers in 1984, and by anybody's reckoning that's a lot of sports enthusiasts. At least they had better be because sports are what the network offered its subscribers 22 hours a day, ranging from coverage of National Collegiate Athletic Association and United States Football League games through billiards and karate. Of considerable interest to business and industrial organizations is the fact that ESPN also offered two hours of business coverage.

The old saying hawked by those selling sports programs still holds true: you can't tell the players without a program. If you intend to get into narrowcasting, you need to know the nature of the specialized programming reaching a share of the 40 percent of all television homes. When a network such as ESPN transmits 22 hours of sports a day, surely there have to be some opportunities for public relations practitioners whose firms or clients are involved in some way with sports. They might not easily break into the coverage of a major sports event, but ESPN in 1984 was broadcasting several times a day an hour-long sports report, and such a report feeds on sports news and information. In securing franchises in major cities many cable operators promise to offer up to 70 channels, and that means a huge programming maw which must be fed regularly. To do so the operators have opened their channels to specialized groups and audiences, and that means a virtual invitation to the public relations practitioner astute enough to take advantage of it.

Public Access Cable

Mack the Knife, Kurt Weill's anti-hero, claims that if you look a gift shark in the mouth you'll probably find a row of pretty teeth. Be that as it may, one gift shark that cable has opened to local organizations—especially in large cities with many cable channels—is the public access channels that accompany the granting of a franchise. Although federal law does not require cable companies to make channels available to community groups, the fact is that cities granting franchises have demanded and been given such channels by the cable company awarded the right to wire an entire city or part of a city.

Public access channels are especially designed for noncommercial groups, and they offer a unique opportunity for such nonprofit organizations as social and health agencies, hospitals, colleges, and cultural entities. The opportunity is found in the fact that in large cities especially the number of public access channels can amount to a total of eighteen, as they do in New Orleans where Cox Cable Communications supports public access as a matter of public policy. That support has included providing five access studios, five vans complete with portable video equipment, and a staff to aid those using the access channels.[22]

In Chicago four different franchises were awarded when wiring of the city was started, and the inclusion of twenty-four access channels in the wiring plans meant that these channels would provide more airtime than all of Chicago's network stations put together. In cities with access channels most multiple-system operators conduct free technical workshops, and in addition Cox and Group W Cable also sponsor internship programs aimed at giving local college students hands-on experience.

Given the opportunity for programming on public access channels, it's puzzling to note that in some cities the opportunity is ignored. Cable operators say that in some cities there's a waiting line for public access channels while in others the operators have to go out and speak to groups in an effort to entice them into using the channels. Education on a national level may help to increase usage. According to one report, some members of the New Orleans cultural arts coalition formed a National Cable Arts Council in 1983 and that body functions as a consulting service for similar groups across the country. Educational programs where the public can learn "how-to" skills needed for access have also been started by the National Federation of Local Cable Programmers and the Center for New Television in Chicago.[23]

Videotex and Teletext

Four years of experimentation and trial ended in late 1983 when Viewtron, the videotex system developed by Knight-Ridder Newspapers and the American Telephone & Telegraph Company, was launched in southern Florida. Goal of the Viewdata Corporation of America, Knight-Ridder's subsidiary which designed the system's software and maintains its central database and computers, was to have Viewtron in 5,000 upscale households by the end of 1984.[24]

Whether Viewtron succeeds is a question upon which millions of dollars and high expectations are riding. If it does, then videotex and its cousin teletext are important considerations for public relations practitioners because they represent new ways in which people secure news and other information and do their banking and shopping.

As perceptive readers will have noted, videotex does not end with a *t*, but teletext does. The reason is one of the mysteries of the modern world of communications, but the other difference between the two systems is not mysterious.

Videotex is interactive, which means that those who use it in their homes can communicate with the system. It is two-way, whereas **teletext is one-way.**

What both systems do is to transmit data and information through the home television set. Access to Viewtron's 75,000 "pages" of information and data is by means of the Sceptre terminal provided to subscribers by AT&T at a 1983 cost of $600. By typing instructions subscribers are able to summon data and news from the central computer, order merchandise from retail stores, play computer games, bank at home, read sports schedules and movie reviews, send messages, and do a host of other interactive things. In addition to the cost for the Sceptre terminal, users of Viewtron pay a monthly fee to access the computer and a fee to the telephone company for use of its lines. Considering these costs, it's understandable why Viewtron was aimed initially in 1983 at customers who are from the upper income bracket of the economy.[25]

If one is to consider videotex as a two-way system similar to the telephone, then teletext should be considered as a one-way system similar to broadcast television.[26] Access to teletext is by means of a decoder plugged into the home TV set, and the system provides a narrower choice of information than videotex. In the initial trials of teletext in the early eighties subscribers were offered some 200 rotating "pages" of information from which they selected the one wanted. As with conventional television, the sole economic support for teletext was planned to be advertising.[27]

As of 1984, it was difficult to predict acceptance of videotex and teletext by the American consumer. Videotex had finally become a commercial reality with Viewtron, but it remained to be seen whether there would be enough subscribers in southern Florida to sustain its operation. Conventional wisdom among those who had been watching the two systems go through their trials was that teletext had a better chance of being accepted once in operation commercially. However, in late November, 1983, Time Inc., a pioneer in the teletext market, announced that it was discontinuing its two-year experiment with the technology and would not offer a commercial teletext service. Sources were quoted as saying that Time had spent $20 million to $30 million in its trials with teletext conducted on Time-owned cable TV systems in Orlando, Florida, and in San Diego, California. A spokesperson was quoted as stating: "For Time Inc., at the present time and with the present economics, we did not feel that this was a business for us in the near future."[28]

A number of newspapers seem to feel that it's better to be safe than to be sorry, and therefore at least 69 of them continued to make arrangements to provide character-generated text and video services over local cable systems.[29] Knight-Ridder's Miami *Herald* was the basic news source for Viewtron when it went on-line, and the company planned to use its newspapers in Philadelphia, Detroit, San Jose, Charlotte, and St. Paul if and when the company initiated Viewtron in those cities. Preliminary joint-publishing agreements were signed with publishers in Boston, Fort Worth, Kansas City, Baltimore, and Seattle, contingent upon Knight-Ridder's opening Viewtron in those cities. Finally, the Times Mirror Company, through its Videotex American subsidiary, announced that it was making its system available in suburban Los Angeles in early 1984.[30]

Thus, if videotex and teletext take hold, a revolutionary means of information delivery will be available in the 83 million American homes with television. We may or may not be "reading our newspaper" on the television screen, but those who have an interest in delivering news and information—and you can certainly number public relations practitioners in this group—would be wise to keep track of this intriguing new development in information processing.

DIRECT BROADCAST SATELLITE TELEVISION

In the space age technological developments in communications seem to take place as swiftly as communication itself. Cable television had just about become an established part of the national communications picture when a new competitor entered. It's called DBS, or direct broadcast satellite television, and it received Federal Communications approval in mid-1982. Within the year eight companies, including two television networks and a new subsidiary of the Communications Satellite Corporation, had lined up to start the new service.[31]

Direct broadcast satellite television simply bypasses conventional and cable television by beaming its signal from three or four powerful satellites placed into synchronous orbit facing the United States. DBS's high frequency transmissions reaching rooftop antennas are then converted by other equipment to the frequencies handled by the householder's television set. Those subscribing to a DBS system can either purchase or lease one of the three-foot diameter earth receiver dishes needed to pick up signals beamed from the satellites, and in addition are asked to pay a monthly subscription fee. The main users of DBS are expected to be the millions of people who live in those parts of the country that can receive no over-the-air TV signals and/or who are not wired by cable.[32]

Although there were predictions that the market for DBS would not develop until the late 1980s, United Satellite Communications, Inc., of New York began satellite-to-home broadcasting in October, 1983, to homes in twenty-six states, most of them in the Northeast. Initial offering consisted of two channels of movies, a news channel, a sports channel, and one broadcasting special children's and cultural events programs. Subscribers had to lease or buy the rooftop antenna dishes (at about $500 a dish) and pay between $30 and $40 a month for programming. To prevent pirating, the DBS signals were scrambled.[33]

The opportunity for public relations practitioners in DBS is chiefly in regard to the news programs and those aspects of other programming which would be open to information and features from outside sources. As with the other forms of broadcasting discussed in this section, DBS can provide many opportunities for practitioners if the service and the system catch on.

TECHNOLOGY AND NEWSPAPERS

Although technological communications developments were not as extensive in newspapers as in television, they played an important role in the newspaper field as the eighties unfolded. Continuing a trend that began in the 1970s, newspapers in the 1980s increased their use of computers for writing, editing, and production tasks, became more heavily involved in cable, and found satellite transmission the answer to national distribution.

Computers proved to be the key to the breakthrough that led to the electronic newsroom of the seventies. By 1980 typewriters had begun to disappear from the newsrooms of the nation's daily newspapers as reporters and editors turned to electronic keyboards and VDT screens and then subsequently to microcomputers, floppy disks, and mainframe computers.

By 1984 several papers around the country began to lead the way to **pagination**—the electronic composition and layout of pages on a video computer screen—and to the use of **lasers** for platemaking. Composing rooms disappeared as reporters and editors took over most of the tasks formerly carried out by composing room personnel. Portable computers linked to the home newsroom by telephone modems became more common and enabled beat reporters and those covering in person fast-breaking stories to shorten story transmission time. The end result of these technological developments was the assumption of control by the newsroom of the composing and printing tasks and a speeding up of the entire newspaper process.

Public relations practioners responsible for dealing with daily newspapers recognize that these changes affect public relations practice. Releases, for example, have to be more tightly written. Deadline changes have to be noted. Compressed time means quicker thinking when emergencies occur. Thus, as newspapers and the people who produce them become more efficient at their tasks, there's little room for inefficiency on the part of those who deal with them.

Cable and satellites, as noted earlier in this chapter, were integral to the advent of videotex and teletext. Playing a role in the introduction of these new technologies were newspapers throughout the country. Their role was one of supplying the major share of the text material that made up the news transmitted in both systems. In addition, database retrieval systems instituted by the larger newspapers and the wire services provided much of the data available through videotex and teletext.

Among the newspapers and groups involved with the trials of the two systems in 1982 and 1983 were the following:[34]

- The Los Angeles *Times* tested videotex over both phone lines and two-way cable systems in Palos Verdes and Mission Viejo, California.

- The Chicago *Sun-Times* supplied news and features in a test of teletext in Chicago. Central to the test was transmission by Field Electronic Publishing, parent organization of the *Sun-Times*, of a teletext magazine built around such local information as news, sports, weather, theatre and TV listings, traffic reports, and so forth.

- The Louisville *Courier Journal* and Louisville *Times* used leased channels on area cable systems to carry out a test of both cabletext and teletext in the Louisville market.

It should be noted that all of the above were tests of videotex and teletext systems. It was too early to tell whether consumers would be willing to pay for the new services, though some newspapers wanted to get in on the ground floor if the tests proved successful. As has already been noted, Viewtron was the first on-line service and it had only gotten started in 1984.

Exhibit 18.3 demonstrates that cable and the newspaper can make for an interesting marriage of skills and technologies.

Satellites have continued to be an important part of the national news and feature distribution plans of the major press wire services and of the three major newspapers seeking to be national in scope.

Both the **Associated Press** and **United Press International** pushed forward with the replacement of telephone line connections by satellites for distribution of news, features, and photos. In February 1983 UPI announced it had signed an agreement with Equatorial Communications Company to provide 1,000 communications satellite two-foot dish antenna earth stations for use by UPI customers.[36] The AP was installing their small dish antenna earth stations at AP newspapers and other customer installations at about the same rate.

USA Today, the *Wall Street Journal*, and the New York *Times* continued on the road to being national newspapers. Launched on September 14, 1982, in Washington, D.C., *USA Today* was being sold in seventeen markets nationally one year later and had a circulation just over one million. Composition was done at one location, sent up to a satellite, and then transmitted to downlinks where much of the printing was done at Gannett newspapers.[37]

By the start of 1983 the *Wall Street Journal* completed a two-year construction program which increased its production plants from twelve to seventeen. The *Journal* at that time was printing 2.2 million copies in two editions for distribution each business

EXHIBIT 18.3

A Marriage Between Newspaper and Cable

Cable and *Newsday*, Long Island's dominant newspaper outside of New York City, made an interesting couple as the 526,000-daily-circulation paper started a test of a 24-hour video and text cable channel in mid-June 1983.

Backed by the full resources of the paper and its parent Times Mirror Company, the Newsday Channel began its nineteen hours of text information and five hours of video programming on May 1, carried on the Cablevision system.

An interesting feature of the newspaper channel is "Inside Newsday," an hour-long newscast aired every weeknight at 10 p.m. and repeated the following day. Taped earlier in the evening, the news show uses the paper's newsroom as a backdrop and mostly features Long Island-based stories. Staff writers for the program prepare most of their stories by interviewing the newspaper's reporters about their assignments and preparing a television version. Bob Greene, assistant managing editor of *Newsday*, is executive editor of the hour-long newscast and co-anchor with Karen Hasby, formerly with UHF Channel 21 on Long Island.

In addition to "Inside Newsday," the newspaper-cable channel offers several video shows hosted by members of *Newsday*'s staff: "Cable News Conference," featuring *Newsday* reporters questioning a guest; "Newsday Magazine," a twice-weekly, taped show covering a variety of subjects; "The Critics," dealing with movies, theatre, and music; and "Street Signs," bringing news and features about Wall Street.

Of interest to public relations practitioners seeking to reach Long Island residents is that the Newsday Channel planned to carry "infomercials," a term indicating they would be along the line of the video version of Op-Ed page institutional and image advertising. It should be obvious that the 24-hour channel also offered other opportunities for public relations output by practitioners astute enough to keep track of the channel's programming needs.[35]

day throughout the country. Editorial material was entered into computers linking the *Journal*'s New York office with its Chicopee, Massachusetts, composition and production plant. It was then sent by microwave to the paper's plant in New Jersey and from there transmitted via Westar V satellite to the seventeen printing plants.[38]

Aiming chiefly for the top 1 percent of potential readership, the New York *Times* in early 1983 was printing a national edition consisting of two sections and reaching 100,000 subscribers daily. One section contained all of the paper's national and international news, editorial and op-ed pages, and selected regional and cultural news. The second section was devoted entirely to business news and was essentially Section D of the paper's regular four-section daily edition. Microwave was used to transmit the pages of the national edition from the paper's New York headquarters to its New Jersey printing plant. The pages went from there via satellite to a printing plant in Chicago and to printing plants in Florida and southern California, and then were delivered to customers throughout the country from those plants.[39]

ENDNOTES

1. John F. Budd, Jr., *Corporate Video in Focus* (Englewood Cliffs, N.J.: Prentice-Hall, 1983), preface.
2. From a talk by Chester Burger at meeting of the New York chapter, Public Relations Society of America, April 2, 1981.
3. T. Michael Forney, "The New Communication Technology," *Public Relations Journal*, March 1982, p. 23.
4. Chester Burger, "Telecommunications in the Public Relations Workday," *Public Communication Review*, Spring 1982, p. 37.
5. Forney, p. 23.

6. "Using Word Processing in Public Relations," *Publicist*, March/April 1982, pp. 6-7 of **Publicity Craft** section.
7. John F. Budd, Jr., and Bruce Pennington, "Financial Reporting by Television," *Public Relations Journal*, April 1982, p. 39.
8. Budd, *Corporate Video in Focus*, p. 102.
9. Ibid., pp. 103-108.
10. "PR Spots to Move via Satellite," *Advertising Age*, July 18, 1982, p. 46.
11. Barbara Kaye Greenleaf, "Monday Memo," *Broadcasting*, October 17, 1983, p. 19.
12. From press release, Hilton Hotels Corporation, November 12, 1981.
13. From press release, Western Electric, 1982.
14. "Western Union into Teleconferencing," *Broadcasting*, August 16, 1982.
15. New York *Times*, December 1, 1983, p. 1.
16. Ibid., August 14, 1983, p. 1.
17. Ibid., October 13, 1983, p. D-1, and *Time*, October 24, 1983, p. 70.
18. *Time*, March 21, 1983.
19. New York *Times*, September 16, 1983, p. D-1.
20. Ibid., February 23, 1983, p. 1.
21. Budd, *Corporate Video in Focus*, p. 32.
22. Suzanne Riordan, "New Outlets Attract Home-Grown Talent," *Advertising Age*, June 13, 1983, p. 20.
23. Ibid.
24. *Editor & Publisher*, October 29, 1983, p. 16.
25. Ibid.
26. Lawrence Zuckerman, "Hi-Tech News: the State of the Art," *Columbia Journalism Review*, March/April 1983, p. 42.
27. Special Report, *Broadcasting*, June 28, 1982, p. 38.
28. *Advertising Age*, November 28, 1983, p. 12.
29. Special Report, *Editor & Publisher*, June 26, 1983, p. 42.
30. *Advertising Age*, May 16, 1983, p. 53.
31. New York *Times*, June 24, 1982, p. 1.
32. Ibid.
33. *Newsweek*, June 6, 1983, p. 75.
34. Special Report, *Editor & Publisher*, June 26, 1982, pp. 41-47.
35. *Editor & Publisher*, June 11, 1983, p. 44.
36. Ibid., February 12, 1983, p. 31.
37. Ibid., September 24, 1983, p. 14.
38. Ibid., December 18, 1982, p. 20.
39. Ibid., February 19, 1983.

PROJECTS, ASSIGNMENTS, AND MINIS

1. THREE PROJECTS DEALING WITH COMMUNICATIONS TECHNOLOGICAL DEVELOPMENTS

a) Select any **one** of the subtopics in the chapter—teleconferencing, videotex and tele-text, or public access cable, as examples—and prepare a paper updating the material in the text about the subtopic. Your update should cover the period from the last citations in the text to the time when you are taking the course. Include a bibliography.

Be prepared to give an oral report to the class about your findings.

b) A communications technological development which is *not* covered in the chapter is that of low-power television. In a memorandum to your instructor examine developments of the past year in low-power television and explain how these may have an impact on public relations practice and the public relations function. Include a bibliography.

c) Carry out a week-long study of any **one** of the communications technological developments cited in the chapter. This should be a first-hand study in which you examine the development each day and report on it. For example, if you decide to study *USA Today*, you should read it for one week and then in a memorandum to your instructor discuss the publication in terms of its content, coverage, production, and other aspects which you believe would be important to know about the publication. In a concluding section of your memorandum you should express your opinion about the publication.

19

PERSONAL, PROFESSIONAL, AND EDUCATIONAL CONSIDERATIONS

I n practicing a new craft, most practitioners are so busy establishing themselves and their field that they have little time for such seemingly philosophical matters as ethics, right and wrong, and professionalism. As a relatively new field of professional activity, public relations has followed the pattern of older, more established fields.

The concerns of public relations practitioners in the decades between World War I and the end of the Vietnam War were mostly of a practical nature. Their actions and activities were governed chiefly by concern about what was permissible, legal, possible, and accepted by the public. As they entered the eighties, a number of public relations practitioners and their professional associations and societies showed increasing concern about the ethical aspects of their actions and their calling.

In so doing, the practitioners reflect a similar concern on the part of young people who are studying public relations in our colleges and universities and who hope to enter the field upon graduation. It is appropriate, therefore, to first examine in this last chapter the kinds of ethical and moral concerns that face the veteran practitioners today and are likely to face the neophyte tomorrow. Having done so, we will then turn our attention to topics considered of special interest to students: public relations education, the first job, and daily work routines.

PERSONAL ETHICS AND STANDARDS

Writing the final chapter of this book has not been an easy task. The subject of ethics is a very personal one, and the last thing in the world the author wants to do is to impose his standards on others. However, the author knows from three decades of teaching public relations that many students have serious reservations about the public relations field because of ethical questions, and these questions deserve a full airing and should be faced squarely and honestly. It's the author's hope that the approach he has taken to the subject will allow for a free and open discussion.

To be meaningful, any discussion of ethics requires an understanding of the term itself. When we talk about ethics, we don't mean only acting within the requirements of the law. To obey the dictates of the law is necessary, but not sufficient, because ethical behavior and actions *transcend* the law. Furthermore, the law is impersonal and clear—or at least, relatively clear—whereas ethics is unclear, generally murky, and usually highly personal. This should be quickly evident as we come to grips with the term.

The dictionary definition serves as a reasonable guide when it describes professional ethics as *"conforming to professional standards of conduct."* Thus, when we talk about ethical behavior in public relations we mean responsible professional behavior as applied to both group standards and individual morals.

Frank Wylie, a past president of the Public Relations Society of America, adds another dimension to the professional standards concept when he says that ethics includes a *concern for others.* "The ethical person," he declares, "acts and communicates in ways which express a concern for others. Acting in a concerned manner is the first part of the job. The second part is communicating that action."[1]

Admittedly, ethics by the dictionary definition seems to allow one's imagination almost full rein in galloping down the road towards a public relations Valhalla guided only by "professional standards of conduct" and a "concern for others." However, there *are* certain standards of conduct followed by public relations professionals, and it shouldn't be difficult to know when one's actions show a concern for others and when they are strictly hedonistic. One might, of course, deal with ethics by setting forth a detailed set of rules of acceptable behavior, but such an impossible task would be foredoomed to failure. Therefore, although the boundaries of ethics set forth by the concepts of conformity to professional standards of conduct and concern for others are admittedly broad, hopefully they are sufficient to serve as a guide for meaningful dialogue within the areas that follow.

ETHICAL PROBLEMS EXIST IN ALL FIELDS

For a variety of reasons public relations students seem to need assurance that ethical dilemmas are not the unique province of public relations practitioners, and perhaps this is the place to provide such assurance.

In no field or profession is there a magical Land of Oz somewhere over the rainbow where its practitioners live the ethical pure life undisturbed by questions of right and wrong. Doctors, lawyers, Indian chiefs, dentists, jurists, and outright thieves, all face ethical dilemmas in which their personal ideas of right and wrong may clash with the practical demands of their working lives. In some fields and professions this clash is weak and in others strong, but it is nonetheless all-embracing, occurring wherever men and women practice their craft, profession, and calling.

To explore ways in which lay people could analyze the ethical problems they meet in their occupations, the Department of the Church and Economic Life of the National Council of Churches sponsored a project in which people in six different fields met over a period of time to discuss ethical decision-making in their areas. Here are some conclusions cited by observers who attended the meetings of four of the groups:

Bankers

After a year of monthly meetings it can be affirmed that bankers are profoundly concerned over the conflict between their business role and their personal ethical standards as derived from their roots in church and family training. Not a session of the group was without reference to this dilemma and in some of the sessions it received attention exceeding even the practical aspects of banking.

Building Contractors

There seemed to be a consensus that for them the responsible position was somewhere in between complete cynicism and ideal or absolute integrity. There was a frank recognition that so long as we continue to live in a world that is involved in corruption and sin it is not possible entirely to avoid participation in evil; if one intends to stay in the construction business then one must on occasion do things that violate one's own standard of ethics. At all costs the tension must be maintained between what one's standard of honesty and integrity demand and what is possible and necessary in a particular given situation.

Personnel Professionals

There is a strong tendency within economic organizations to "translate" questions of ethics into questions of expediency. This tendency was apparent throughout the discussions. . . . It should be emphasized that there is nothing wrong in itself with expediency. Every organization with a certain purpose (even a religious one) will have to think of what is expedient for this purpose and what is not. But expediency is not ethics. It should also be stressed that ethics need not always be in conflict with expediency. Reasonable men will always hope for a modus vivendi between the two. . . .

Public Relations Practitioners

Ethical issues are no less complex in the public relations field than elsewhere. It is easy to speak in absolute terms about truth, for example, but there is no simple "rule of thumb" canon which will be universally helpful to a counselor involved in the day-to-day practice of his craft.

Thus bankers, building contractors, personnel men and women, and public relations practitioners face ethical problems of varying degrees of magnitude and frequency. If, as Spinoza notes, it is a comfort to the unhappy to have companions in misery, then the ethical purist might take comfort in knowing there are countless like him in fields other than public relations. The realist seeks ways in which he can best come to terms with the kinds of situations that may face him in life. This can best be achieved by first considering ethics from a personal point of view.

PERSONAL STANDARDS

The son of a merchant discovered how personal ethics is when he told his father one day that the teacher had been discussing ethics and the son asked his father to explain the term. "That's easy," said the merchant. "A customer comes in and he buys something and gives me a $10 bill. I go to put it in the cash register and I find it is two $10 bills stuck together. Now, ethics means . . . should I tell my partner?"

Codes of ethics probably won't supply the merchant with an answer, but they do set forth certain standards that members of groups are expected to follow in their professional lives. Yet ethical behavior still remains personal in the sense that every individual—whether consciously or unconsciously—is responsible for his own actions. John C. Merrill, a journalism professor, sums up the personal nature of ethics in the following words:

Ethics is truly a personal matter, personal in the sense that it arises from a personal *concern* for one's conduct. It is also personal in the sense that one's conduct is self-directed and self-enforced; the person voluntarily follows a code of conduct because he feels it is the thing to do. . . . It might be said that a person's ethics is: (1) personal, (2) directive or predictive, and (3) rational. It is personal in the sense discussed above; it is predictive in that it serves as a guide for conduct and indicates pretty well what one can be expected to do in a certain situation, and it is rational in that *reason* dictates its acceptance.[2]

The idea of a personal ethical threshold has been advanced by various writers concerned about ethics, and the concept is worth serious consideration. David Finn applies the threshold concept to companies when he says that "each company has its own threshold of what it is comfortable in doing from an ethical standpoint." He further notes that each of us also has—or should have—our own individual threshold. As he puts it: "Each of us has a breaking point beyond which we would not go because it would make us too uncomfortable, too conscience stricken. And this is our point of no compromise."[3]

Finn also suggests that public relations when functioning well acts as "the anvil against which management's moral problems can be hammered." However, this assumption presumes that: (1) public relations personnel have a set of ethical standards, (2) they are willing to put them to the test when circumstances call for it, and (3) managements are receptive to ethical testing by their public relations subordinates.

There is certainly no unanimity among practitioners about Finn's moral anvil concept. John Cook, a Phoenix, Arizona, counselor, contends that the corporate conscience role is both pretentious and illogical. In terming such a role a myth, Cook declares:

> There is no more in the makeup, background, training or experience of the average PR practitioner to qualify him to establish or monitor morality than there is in the makeup, background, training or experience of, for example, the engineering or sales vice president or the corporate legal counsel. Corporate social and moral responsibility is an expression of management policies and actions: PR isn't the corporate conscience, but the conveyor, interpreter and advocate of whatever conscience the corporation has. . . .[4]

Students may properly point out that they are not at the point of life when an ethical threshold has practical professional relevance, and certainly they are not now in a position to act as any kind of an anvil or conscience for hammering out management's moral problems. However, the best time to develop an awareness of and sensitivity to ethical and moral dilemmas is when one has the option of open discussion without the need to worry about the hard realities of decision and actions. Thus, the student may start this process by debating this proposition: With whose thesis—Finn's or Cook's—do you agree, and why?

The broad question of the practitioner's role in regard to ethical and moral dilemmas can be narrowed by consideration of two specific areas of personal concern: (1) advocacy and (2) truth and credibility.

ADVOCACY

The question of advocacy is a question of role, and it's succinctly phrased in these terms: To whom is the public relations practitioner responsible? There is virtually unanimous practitioner agreement that the primary responsibility of the practitioner is to employer or client. Admittedly, public relations practitioners are advocates.

However, just what is the extent of advocacy? To what degree is advocacy justified when the course of action that practitioners are supposed to advocate is contrary to personal convictions? And what should practitioners do when the course of action they are advocating is *not* in the public interest?

The dilemma that advocacy poses became apparent in the previously mentioned discussion among public relations practitioners in the sessions sponsored by the National Council of Churches. Exhibit 19.1 cites some of the comments revealing the range of opinion about advocacy and personal convictions. It should be helpful to ascertain class opinion about the statements in Exhibit 19.1.

The comments in Exhibit 19.1 relate primarily to the conflict that results when advocacy clashes with personal beliefs. But advocacy, as already noted, can also clash with

1. "The professional public relations man's job is to serve as a mouthpiece for the client, regardless of his personal views."

2. "One should decline jobs that run counter to one's personal views."

3. "Ethical considerations are usually not so sharply drawn that a clean choice of staying vs. quitting is posed."

4. "I can work with clients holding opinions at variance with my own *as long* as these don't affect my particular task with the client. If they do it becomes an ethical issue."

5. "If you have done everything possible in an effort to change the client's opinion on a certain issue and you have been unsuccessful, there may come a point at which you *have* to get out."

public interest. The problem here is more complicated. Everyone knows, or should know, what his or her personal beliefs are, but there is widespread disagreement about what constitutes the public interest (as noted in Chapter 3). There are very few instances where an action or activity will clearly be contrary to the interests of *all* people. The more common circumstance is one where the action or activity will be contrary to the interests of one group of people, but in the interests of another group of people. The practitioner, it is claimed, likens his role to that of the lawyer, and like the lawyer is an admitted special pleader for one side and not for both defense and plaintiff. However, actual situations turn this seemingly simple proposition into difficult questions, as noted below:

> What should the practitioner do when it is clear that the cause, action, or activity he is supposed to advocate is absolutely contrary to the interests of the broad spectrum of the people and only in the interests of the narrow group he represents?

> Is the "court of public opinion" the same as the "court of law" in that everyone and every organization is entitled to representation by an advocate?

> What should the practitioner do when the cause, action, or organization he represents starts out to be in the public interest but then changes in ways that are not in the public interest?

Those who argue that public relations practitioners are similar to lawyers do so on the ground that everyone deserves to be represented in the "court of public opinion" just as everyone deserves to be represented in the "court of law." Thus, the contention is made that the public relations practitioner should have no ethical compunction about representing somewhat reprehensible persons, corporations, or corporate actions and activities. However, in the opinion of Max Lerner, respected authority on American society, the public relations practitioner-lawyer analogy is specious and unwarranted. Here's how he views the comparison:

> Which is PR closer to? Is it closer to medicine which looks objectively as scientists on the human body, and so on, or to the lawyer who has to serve his client and make out a case for him and perhaps conceal something?

I hope that it will not be like law, and I will tell you why, and I am not saying anything basically against law now. But law operates by the adversary process . . . which means that you have got two adversaries. It is like a combat. Each of them is using weapons against the other, and presumably it is the constitutional right of each person that the best case should be made out that can be made out. . . . It is very important that the best things be said that can be said for him in this adversary process.

But notice also in this process law operates under the strict supervision of a judge who is watching all the time and of codes that we call rules of evidence, codes of the rights of the witness, and so on.

If public relations had that kind of encasement of a code, if it were encased within a social code, if it had judges watching all the time and trying to decide how the stuff was being presented, I would say, "It is all right to operate as lawyers." But if you haven't got it, this means you cannot use the kind of distortion the lawyers use and the kind of omissions the lawyers use.[5]

Two previously cited practitioners—Cook and Wylie—summarize the different views of advocacy in the following words, quoted here for your analysis and reaction:

Cook: "PR should provide its specialized input as to how various publics are likely to respond to a potential policy, statement or action. *But the PR man has as much to do with morality as a lawyer does with justice; counsel's role is to represent and advocate.* And just as the responsibility for seeing that justice is done resides in the judge and jury, responsibility for corporate morality resides in the board of directors, top management, and, ultimately, the law of the land."[6]

Wylie: "In public relations you serve as an advocate. If you are good at it, you are a dual-advocate: representing the public to your management, and the management to your public. I suggest . . . insist . . . that you should be extremely careful in your choice of clients and of the concepts which you advocate."[7]

TRUTH AND CREDIBILITY

It is most common for moralists and theologians to deal with truth in absolute terms—thou shalt not lie; thou shalt not steal—and it is not difficult to agree with these admonitions about moral and ethical conduct and behavior. Virtually no one, in any field or profession, would disagree with such standards, and this includes public relations practitioners. However, the problems connected with the dissemination of truth—or falsehoods—do not generally concern outright lies and falsehoods, but rather with *degrees* of truths, the *setting or circumstance* in which communication exists, and the factor known as *credibility.*

Telling outright untruths, issuing false statements, and lying can be quickly taken care of by concluding that such actions are unethical, immoral, and unwise. Watergate and its subsequent massive cover-up is a perfect example of the precept that lies and falsehoods lead to jail sentences in courts of law and to universal public condemnation in the court of public opinion. Ironically, Watergate was attributed in part to the machinations of public relations personnel and practices when in reality the leading figures in the Watergate cover-up were lawyers, former advertising executives, and government leaders. Watergate is also a prime example proving a basic premise cited throughout this book: actions speak louder than words, and when actions are taken to insure private interests at the clear expense of the broader public interest, they will eventually backfire and be seen for what they are.

Thus, from both an ethical and practical point of view, it's unwise and wrong to lie, to communicate untruths and falsehoods. If your college's year-end budget shows a deficit, you don't report a surplus. If your social agency falls short of its fund-raising goal, you don't report the goal was reached. If your company recalls thousands of one of this year's models, you don't say no recall has been made.

But you are still an advocate and, as Wylie indicates, you may be a dual advocate. Often, within your own organization, you will find yourself arguing for dissemination of information when others will be arguing for silence. You will find yourself urging a course of action and frank communication that others may not want to take. You may win some of these internal arguments and you may lose some, but ultimately you will be the person who presents your organization's face to the outside world of publics.

By serving as the "corporate conscience," the argument is made, you become more effective as a public relations person:

> Public relations persons who double as corporate consciences will be more effective because their credibility among all groups will be considerably higher than will the credibility of those who are merely advocates (in the narrowest sense) of management policies. By pointing out the pitfalls of some policies that are not in the public interest, they will save management considerable embarrassment and perhaps major losses later on; and they are in stronger positions to support management policies because they help formulate those policies.[8]

No one really expects an advocate to tell only the whole truth and nothing but the whole truth because so very few people do this except under oath in a court of law. Even journalists, who look with jaundiced eye on public relations pronouncements and who are presumably dedicated to telling the whole truth, seldom, if ever, get at or reveal the whole truth. Although public relations practitioners should not tell outright lies and untruths, they do try to put their best foot forward. While reporting that your college has had a deficit, you may want to point out that it represents only one-tenth of one percent of the total budget and is the first deficit in the 100-year history of the institution. While reporting your agency fell short of its goal by $100,000, you may want to point out that your area has had the highest unemployment rate of the past ten years and that the total sum raised this year exceeded last year's sum by $50,000. While reporting that your company has recalled one of this year's models, you may want to point out that the full cost of such a recall is being borne by the company.

At all times, you should keep in mind that credibility is your stock in trade, takes years to build, can be lost in a moment, and once lost is hard to regain. You want to put your best foot forward, but there are times and circumstances when nothing positive can be said. You are not a miracle worker who can turn red into bright blue, a deficit into a surplus, and a Watergate cover-up into some minor burglary. As Wylie puts it: "The foundation of communication is credibility. If we wish to be heard, we must first be believable. We gain such public credibility by our actions, and secondly by our words."

SUMMATION

A summation of the various major ethical and moral considerations discussed in this section leads to the following conclusions:

1. Those who practice their craft in all fields and professions are faced at one time or another with ethical and moral dilemmas involving their personal convictions and beliefs.

2. In order to deal effectively and rationally with such dilemmas it seems wise for individuals to be aware of and sensitive to such conflicts and to determine their own ethical thresholds.

3. Public relations practitioners have to be especially attuned to the need for ethical thresholds because they are advocates and are most often called upon to represent the face their organizations present to the outside world.

4. For most of their professional lives public relations practitioners will be dealing with activities and actions in which there may be little concern or connection with ethical and moral values.

5. There are, however, certain "gray areas," as David Finn terms them, "in which one person feels comfortable about telling certain kinds of untruths or engaging in certain kinds of moderately deceitful practices, while another person feels entirely different about it. . . ."

6. Therefore, to deal with these gray areas, it seems wise to be clear in our own minds about that point beyond which we are unwilling or unable to go and where we will not compromise.

7. Finally, keep constantly in mind that credibility underscores all effective communication. It is difficult to attain, more difficult to sustain, and once lost hard to regain.

PROFESSIONAL ETHICS AND CODES

The two-sided coin that passes for legal tender in the land of ethical standards bears the likeness of self on one side and represents the personal, self-imposed code of ethical behavior governing the individual. The other side of the same coin carries the imprimatur of the craft, field, or profession within which the individual operates and represents the impersonal, written, and unwritten codes governing those working in the craft, field, or profession. We have already examined the personal side of the ethical coin; it's time now to examine the back side of the same coin.

AN OVERVIEW

There has been considerable discussion over the years as to whether public relations is a profession, craft, calling, or trade. In the generally accepted sense of the term it's difficult to sustain the argument that public relations is a profession because it fails to meet all of the standards by which recognized professions—such as law and medicine—are judged. Both law and medicine, for example, require licensing preceded by specified education, examination, and experience, whereas anyone can enter the practice of public relations without meeting such prescribed standards.

On the other hand, public relations practitioners meet many of the other standards by which one judges whether a field is a profession. Education for public relations is now widespread; practitioners engage in a constant exchange of information by means of their journals, newsletters, institutes, and professional organizations; those in the field restrain their use of self-promotion; practitioners provide a good deal of service in the public welfare; and there is a serious concern with ethics and standards.

On balance, therefore, in weighing the pros and cons relative to the generally recognized hallmarks of professions, one would have to conclude that public relations is not a profession but that many of its practitioners are professional and that most of them follow and adhere to many of the benchmarks by which a profession is recognized by the public.

THE PRSA CODE

One of the benchmarks that denote a profession or professionalism is a written code of professional standards governing those within the field. The American Bar Association "Code of Professional Responsibility and Canons of Judicial Ethics" contains nine canons covering a lawyer's responsibilities and actions. A lawyer found guilty of misconduct can be dropped from ABA membership, and in addition a state appellate court can exercise final disciplinary authority by suspending a lawyer from the practice of law for a length of time and can even disbar him or her.

Public relations practitioners are not licensed nor are their activities and practices under state control. As of 1984, only 11,500 of the approximately 87,000 to 100,000 public relations practitioners were members of the Public Relations Society of America—the largest organization of public relations professionals—but the PRSA has a strong code of professional standards and rules of procedure for professional grievances very similar to the ABA.

The document that embodies ethical standards of behavior for PRSA members is the fourteen-point Code of Professional Standards for the Practice of Public Relations. The Society's first Code was adopted in 1954 and revised in 1959, 1963, and 1977. (The Code and official interpretations of various points in it are reprinted in their entirety in Appendix A.)

In revising the Code in 1977, the Society amended one provision and deleted another that had been questioned by the Federal Trade Commission on the grounds that they regulated prices (fees) and were in restraint of competition. The two provisions, applying mainly to counselor members of the Society, barred contingency fees and encroachment by one counselor on another's clients. They were worded as follows:

13. A member shall not propose to a prospective client or employer that the amount of his fee or other compensation be contingent on or measured by the achievement of specified results; nor shall he enter into any fee agreement to the same effect.

14. A member shall not encroach upon the professional employment of another member. Where there are two engagements, both must be assured that there is no conflict between them.

In its 1977 revision, the Society replaced the above-cited Article 13 with a new one that reads: "A member shall not guarantee the achievement of specified results beyond the member's direct control." The old Article 14, also cited above, was deleted entirely.

As with many codes, the fourteen-point PRSA Code contains some clauses that embody pious generalizations. Its basic strength is found in clauses that prohibit undisclosed or "false" fronts, the intentional dissemination of false or misleading information, practices that tend to corrupt the integrity of channels of communication or the processes of government, and the guarantee of the achievement of specified results beyond a member's direct control.

Point 6 of the Code, which prohibits a member from engaging in any practice that tends to corrupt the integrity of the channels of public communication or the processes of government, is particularly important. Its importance is found in the fact that it covers a key area of public relations practice in which there is a good deal of ambiguity. To clarify this ambiguity the Society provided the previously mentioned "official interpretation," spelling out in more detail the kind of practices, involving the mass media and government, that are prohibited. These include payment to secure preferential or guaranteed news or editorial coverage, undisclosed retainers to media employees to serve the private purposes of a member, vacation trips provided to media representatives where no news assignments are involved, and similar dubious arrangements between journalists and practitioners.

The fact that such specific prohibitions have been spelled out in some detail indicates that there have been instances of arrangements between media representatives and practitioners that involve unethical behavior, and also indicates that it takes two partners to dance the unethical tango. Thus, in every instance where a member might provide a vacation trip where no news assignment is involved there's a journalist willing to take that trip. The Society, of course, can control only the unethical behavior of its members, but journalists who criticize public relations practitioners might well consider that where there's a giver there's also a taker.

Enforcement machinery for the PRSA code is in the hands of nine district judicial panels with power to hear complaints relative to violations of the code. In 1962 the

Society established a Grievance Board with responsibility for investigating instances where no individual complaint is made but where there are indications that the code may have been violated.

Donald B. McCammond, chairman of the Grievance Board in 1983, explains the enforcement system in these words:

> The nine-member Grievance Board is part of the Society's judicial structure, which also includes a six-member Judicial Panel in each of PRSA's nine national districts. All proceedings before the Board and Panels are confidential.
>
> Grievance Board action is investigative, somewhat similar to that of a grand jury. The Board may act upon a complaint, or take action on its own where there is indication of Code Violation. Anyone, member or nonmember, may file a complaint with the Board or with the Judicial Panel in the complainant's area.
>
> The Board reviews evidence of the validity of an alleged violation from both sides, the application of the Code to the charge, the apparent intent of the individual involved—and sometimes the intent of the person filing the charge—and the attitude and degree of cooperation of the member involved. . . .
>
> Grievance Board decisions fall into a variety of categories: referral of the complaint to a district Judicial panel for hearing and judgment (final review and decision rest with the Society's Board of Directors); dismissal of the complaint as without basis following determination that the grievance is not covered by the Code, or that the condition has been corrected promptly after being brought to the member's attention; suspension of the complaint pending the outcome of a civil or criminal court proceeding already under way; or withdrawal of the complaint. . . .[9]

When a case is brought before one of the Society's nine Judicial Panels, the Grievance Board and its attorney conduct the prosecution and the panel sits in judgment in the role of a court. Following the close of the hearing the panel submits a report to the Board of Directors, as noted by McCammond, and recommends to the Board disciplinary action or exoneration. The forms of discipline are: warning, admonishment, reprimand, censure, suspension, or expulsion.[10]

Membership in the Society is on an individual basis. Only the practitioner, not his firm or organization, can be a member of the Society, and thus the code relates only to the conduct of the individual member and not to the firm or organization with which he or she is affiliated. Furthermore, though the ultimate form of discipline is expulsion from the Society, this has no bearing on the practitioner's ability to continue to practice.

LICENSING AND AN ALTERNATIVE

As has been noted already, public relations practitioners are not licensed, but the idea of licensing—or some alternative close to it—has been a live issue of debate among the professionals as far back as 1953 when Edward L. Bernays proposed that practitioners be licensed. Various study commissions and members of the PRSA have presented reports and white papers on licensing, but as of 1984 (when this chapter was written), the Society itself had never taken an official stand on the matter of licensing.

Surveys of practitioners and teachers demonstrate, however, that those against licensing are in the majority. In its annual survey of practitioners, the *pr reporter* noted in 1978 that almost two-thirds of those surveyed by the newsletter favor either a system of "open practice" (25 percent) or "voluntary accreditation by professional societies" (39 percent). Only one out of ten said they favor licensing, either by the state (6.8 percent) or by the federal government (3.6 percent).

In the early 1980s when the twenty-member prestigious Task Force on the Stature and Role of Public Relations—a group representing the PRSA and ten other national public relations groups and headed by Philip Lesly—issued its 23-page report, it came out firmly against licensing. As noted in Exhibit 19.2 the section on licensing, with two dis-

sents, rejected licensing of public relations practitioners chiefly because of a concern
about potential government intrusion.[11]

    Public relations teachers have also indicated that they do not favor licensing. Results
of a survey carried out by Professor Frank Tennant of California State Polytechnic University showed that the teachers are against government licensing by a 2.5 to 1 ratio.
However, close to 80 percent of those opposed to licensing believe that public relations
practices should be monitored to achieve professionalism.[12]

    As might be expected in considering such an important step, there are as many argu-
ments against licensing as there are in favor of licensing. Readers can make up their own
minds by considering the pros and cons cited below.

Arguments for Licensing

    Those who favor licensing of public relations practitioners usually cite the following
arguments to support their views:

1. Licensing is a key and indispensable ingredient of a profession.

2. Licensing would safeguard the public and the competent practitioners against the
   charlatans and incompetents.

3. A grandfather clause would protect those now practicing in the field.

---

4. If those now in the field do not regulate themselves, then outside agencies—usually the government—will take on this task.

5. Licensing will ensure that only qualified people will be permitted to practice and will thereby raise the entire level of the field and the view held of it by the public.

6. The PRSA is able to control and police only its own membership, whereas licensing would enable society to police all who claim to be public relations professionals.

Arguments against Licensing

Those who are against the licensing of public relations practitioners usually cite the following arguments to support their views:

1. Because of the difficulty in defining public relations it would be difficult to fashion a meaningful law.

2. Licensing poses serious constitutional questions relating to freedom of speech and press and would probably be in violation of the First Amendment.

3. Licensing does not automatically guarantee that the public will view the activity licensed as a profession, and one finds charlatans and incompetents in fields that are now licensed.

4. If, as is most likely, licensing would be by states, then what about reciprocity and differing state laws?

5. Licensing will inevitably mean control by outside agencies, and no one knows where that can lead.

6. Malpractice can be controlled by such existing laws as those relating to libel, fraud, dishonesty, misrepresentation, and breach of contract.

Alternatives to licensing have been proposed from time to time, but have not received much support from public relations practitioners. Jack O'Dwyer, publisher of the newsletter bearing his name, suggested in the mid-seventies a grievance panel to hear complaints involving practitioners. He suggested that the panel should be composed of practitioners and representatives of the public. At about the same time Neil A. Lavick called for the establishment of a national public relations council similar in nature, scope, and function to the press councils of Great Britain and Sweden. Neither suggestion received sufficient support or aroused sufficient interest to last beyond its initial appearance.

A FEW FINAL WORDS

Whether or not licensing or a grievance panel becomes a reality, the fact remains that the actions and activities of all those who practice public relations—and this includes non-PRSA as well as PRSA members—ultimately decide the kind of reputation the field will have in the mind of the public. For this reason, as they come to the end of this text, students seeking a career in public relations should recognize that the public view of the public relations field will depend on their personal role and conduct as future professionals. How they handle this role and how they conduct themselves pose a personal challenge to all individuals who practice public relations. This challenge was clearly set forth by an executive who was named to *Time* magazine's list of 200 emerging leaders in America. Here, in an article he wrote for the *Public Relations Journal*, is the way Luther Hodges, Jr., chairman of the board of the North Carolina National Bank of Charlotte, N.C., delineated the nature of the role-and-conduct choice for the practitioner and the future of his and her calling:

Let's consider the qualities I look for in a public relations executive. And I must note for the females that my use of the masculine line simply refers to all.

I'll begin by describing what the public relations professional is not. He is not a yes man.

If the boss says newspapers are no damn good, the yes man agrees. If the boss says to tell the reporter "no comment," he does so without question or argument. If the boss says let's stonewall it, he does just so. . . .

Nor does the good professional take the other extreme of disagreeing with everything and everybody all the time. The type of person who does this is the one who forgets that his salary is being paid by the company he works for—and not the local newspaper or television station. He forgets that he is hired, after all, as an advocate for a given business, industry, government agency or whatever. . . .

The really good professional stands somewhere between these extremes. He realizes that his function is not to run the company, but to provide input to those who do run the company, so that they can base policy decisions on public relations factors in addition to all other factors. In this role he often must play the devil's advocate—and he should.

He has the ability and the knowledge to tell management in advance what the predicted public relations reaction to a given action or policy decision will be. He has the ability and knowledge to make positive suggestions about how to change these actions or decisions, if necessary; and above all he has the self-confidence to argue convincingly for his beliefs.

At the same time, this public relations professional is pragmatic enough to realize that management decisions are based on many inputs—not just his own—and that his total wishes may not always be reflected in the final decision. He then has the duty of supporting that decision—and helping implement it, or, in fact, of resigning from the company if the decision is one that seriously violates his professional ethics and standards of conduct.[13]

PREPARING FOR A PUBLIC RELATIONS CAREER

As noted in the preface, this book's major purpose is to provide an effective teaching tool in the introductory course in public relations. The purpose therefore indicates the author's belief that a college education including course work in public relations is an effective and sound way in which young people can prepare themselves for a career in the field of public relations. This is not meant to contend that such a college education is *the* only way in which to prepare for a public relations career, and studies have shown that the vast number of practitioners now in the field did not study public relations while in college. This is not surprising inasmuch as public relations curricula and degree programs are relatively new phenomena on the American educational scene; although one or two courses in public relations were first taught in colleges in the early twenties, it's only been in the last two decades that the proliferation of courses and degree programs has taken place. Thus, the public relations veterans of today are mainly college-educated, but their college work did not include public relations courses. Most of these veterans entered the public relations field through either journalism, advertising, marketing, or that catch-all called "happenstance."

For the past two decades, as graduates of public relations degree programs have sought their first public relations jobs, they've run into the same road blocks that faced journalism school graduates trying to enter the newspaper field a few decades ago. Managing editors who had entered the newspaper field as copy boys and who had never themselves gone to college couldn't understand how a college education could possibly prepare one for a journalism career. The idea that such an education would also include work in journalism was considered even more outlandish, but this tunnel-vision view gradually gave way to a broader understanding as the world became more complex and the need for college-educated newspapermen and women became more obvious. In similar fashion, now that public relations degree programs have become more established and graduates of such programs have proved their value and become established in the field, there is growing recognition of the worth, value, and capability of these public relations graduates.

EDUCATION FOR PUBLIC RELATIONS

Students using this book will probably be taking a public relations course that either is required in a public relations degree program, is required or an elective in a public relations or other sequence within a journalism degree program, or is an elective within some other degree program or sequence. According to a 1980 survey carried out by Dr. Albert Walker of Northern Illinois University under a grant from the Foundation for Public Relations Research and Education, the predominant home college for public relations education is liberal arts and sciences; the predominant home department is journalism; and the basic curriculum is multimedia communications.

Dr. Walker's survey identified an initial "universe" of 256 colleges and universities offering some form of public relations education. Two mailings resulted in responses from 132 institutions, or a 51 percent response rate. The 132 institutions reported 14,284 undergraduate and 3,884 graduate students enrolled in public relations courses and programs. In summarizing the results of his study, Dr. Walker stated that "the 1980 survey of public relations education finds: (1) growth in full-time undergraduate and graduate study, and part-time study primarily on the graduate level; (2) academic programs designed to develop strong writing and editing, and media production skills; social and behavioral science knowledge, and a healthy balance between print and non-print communication; (3) opportunities for the application of skills and knowledge on campus and in the local community; (4) close partnership between public relations education and practitioners; (5) involvement of practitioners in part-time teaching and full-time teachers in consulting; and (6) public relations education highlighted by a strong applied approach."[14]

Public relations and journalism educators hold similar views when considering the relationship of required public relations and journalism courses to the total number of courses and hours needed for graduation. With few exceptions, schools offering public relations degrees or sequences require from 20 to 30 percent of total course work in public relations and/or journalism and the remainder in electives in other disciplines. The problem facing students is in deciding what courses will round out their college education.

Suggested Electives

There is no end to the number and kind of elective courses that well-intentioned practitioners suggest students take to prepare for a career in public relations. These range anywhere from the generalized statement "get a liberal arts education" to lists of courses that add up to as many as 201 credit hours. The usual practice in giving advice is to recommend courses which the practitioner has found useful in his or her own career, but the problem for the student is that no two careers will ever really duplicate each other. The wiser approach, it seems, is to consider as electives those courses that will most likely be of value no matter what special area of public relations is pursued, plus courses that may prove valuable for special purposes.

First, as to general courses, there seems to be agreement that courses in the social sciences—sociology, psychology, anthropology, political science, history, and economics—are sound fundamental courses to be taken. Courses in literature, the humanities, speech, and some of the fundamental areas of business administration—such as accounting, finance, organization, management, and marketing—are also considered wise educational investments. Students should take as many writing courses as possible.

Second, if the student knows in advance the area of public relations in which he or she hopes to pursue a career, it's advisable to take courses most closely related to the designated specialty. Thus, if you intend to handle public relations work in the social or health agency areas, take courses in the social work and health disciplines in your institution. If you hope to make your public relations career in education, take some education courses as electives. If you intend to seek public relations work in business or industry, the obvious choice of electives would be in the business area.

Third, be flexible enough to recognize that today's interest may be temporary and that you may start your career in one area of public relations and then move into another. For this reason it's wise to become as broadly educated as possible within the boundaries of your college's curriculum requirements.

Summed up, a sensible college education "package" for those intending to pursue a public relations career would include 20 to 30 percent of course work in public relations and journalism, and the remainder in electives in a broad range of disciplines and in a limited concentration within one discipline. The graduate of such a program should have knowledge of basic public relations principles and practices; a modicum of public relations and journalism skills; and a liberalizing, mind-broadening education.

A Recommended Curriculum

In a report issued in the mid-seventies, the Commission on Public Relations Education (group composed of three PRSA members and four educators from the Public Relations Division of the Association for Education in Journalism) recommended an undergraduate public relations curriculum of three major groups of courses. The report pictured the curriculum as made up of a series of three concentric circles: "The smallest, central circle would enclose those subjects specifically concerned with public relations practice. The second circle, somewhat larger, would encompass related subjects in the general field of communications. The third and largest circle would represent the general liberal arts and humanities background expected of all students. Additionally, one might envision a satellite or 'moon,' outside the largest circle, representing a secondary area of concentration for the student (a 'minor,' so to speak) representative of some special area of public relations practice. Thus, the 'minor' might be in the field of business administration for the student who plans to enter corporate public relations; or it might be in the field of public administration for the student who plans to enter government public relations, etc. . . ."[15]

1. General Education Courses

The report recommended there be at least four semesters of *English* (writing and literature); introductory courses in the *social sciences;* a "sprinkling" of courses in the *humanities;* one or two introductory courses in the *natural sciences;* at least one *foreign language* or *area studies* course; a course in *statistics;* and a course in *organizational structure and behavior.*

2. Communication Studies

This part of the program would encompass the following areas: *theory and process of communication; news reporting and writing; copyediting;* and *graphics of communication.*

Suggested are one or more of the following types of courses: *advertising principles and practice; media law and ethics; feature writing; introduction to survey research;* and *communication media analysis.*

3. Public Relations Core Courses

Recommended as an absolute minimum: *introduction to public relations; publicity media and campaigns; public relations case problems; internship or practicum.*

4. Electives

One or more of the following electives: *management communications; propaganda and public opinion;* and *magazine editing.*

5. "Satellite" Studies

Students interested in a "minor" or secondary area of emphasis should take at least two courses in a field related to their special area of public relations interest.

In its Gold Paper No. 4, issued in January, 1982, the Education and Research Committee of the International Public Relations Association concluded with seventeen recommendations. Three of them are pertinent to this section and they are cited below as set forth by the IPRA group:

1. Ideally, public relations full-time education should be offered in universities at second degree (master's) level. It must be accepted, however, that for the time being most education will continue to be given to young undergraduates taking first degrees (bachelor's degrees).

2. Public relations should by preference be taught as a social science with both academic and professional emphasis.

3. It is neither desirable nor necessary that public relations education should be uniform throughout the world. Rather is it essential that curricula should take into account local and national cultures, religions, and indigenous conditions.[16]

Suggested Extracurricular Activities

There are several reasons for suggesting that the undergraduate's four years of course work be accompanied by a reasonable degree of involvement in extracurricular activities. Properly selected, such activities provide the closest approximation to "on-the-job" training and experience available in a college setting. They enable the graduate to present to prospective employers a record of not merely academic but also practical experience. Finally, they're a testing ground for ascertaining personal abilities, weaknesses, and strengths.

The college newspaper, whether a daily or weekly, is highly recommended as the best extracurricular activity for the kind of experience most closely allied to public relations work. Students who work on a college newspaper will not only improve their reporting and writing skills, but will also gain valuable experience working with and managing others. The college newspaper also enables students to compile a sampling of stories and features that can be useful in demonstrating their competence when seeking a first position in the field.

Other valuable extracurricular activities include work at the campus radio or television station, participation in student government, and—if available on campus—a role in the local unit of the Public Relations Student Society of America. The last-named group, first organized in 1968, by 1983 had more than 4,000 members in chapters on 123 campuses and sponsors both regional meetings and a national conference usually held in conjunction with the annual conference of the parent Public Relations Society of America. The special pre-associate membership category of the PRSA, available at a greatly reduced membership fee for graduates who have been PRSSA members, is a quick and simple entry into the parent body.

In following the dictates of an academic program or sequence in public relations and the extracurricular options open at the average college or university, the student should keep in mind the kind of skills generally considered important for success in the field. The PRSA sums up these needed skills and attributes in the following terms:

Because public relations involves many kinds of tasks, many different qualifications are needed. Probably the "ideal," or at least popularly conceived, public relations man or woman is the highly articulate and imaginative individual with more than a little salesmanship in his or her make-up.

On the other hand, many public relations executives stress judgment as the most important single qualification that the worker must possess. Public relations practitioners are "counselors," and their services are often sought out when an organization is in trouble. Hence skill in practical action, based on reflective analysis, is an important part of the equipment of the able public relations worker. In addition he (and she) should have:

- Imagination, which is an important attribute for coping with new problems and commanding the attention of others.

- Verbalizing skills, which underlie competence in writing and speaking—combined with training in these arts.

- Extroverted traits, sufficient to make possible successful frequent face-to-face contacts with other individuals and groups.

- Sensitivity to other people. To profess a liking for people will not help a candidate get a job. However, both diplomacy and a more than ordinary ability to place oneself in the shoes of another are important in public relations work.

- Organizing and planning skill, leadership and administrative ability. As with many other occupations, managerial skills are invaluable assets for successfully climbing the public relations career ladder.[17]

GETTING THE FIRST JOB

By 1984 public relations had become one of the most popular majors or sequences in colleges and universities offering programs in mass communications subjects. It had become increasingly evident to young people interested in a communications career that salaries were higher and opportunities for advancement greater than in the more traditional fields taught in communications programs. Inevitably this meant that more seniors would be seeking the all-important first job in public relations come graduation day. Thus, competition for entry-level positions intensified. Graduates seeking an entry position in the public relations field therefore need more than just a degree: they need patience, diligence, and a carefully designed search plan in order to uncover that first all-important job.

The reason why graduates need to follow a carefully designed *search* plan is that, with some few exceptions, college placement offices are not regular stops for recruiters with public relations job offers. In this respect, the public relations and the journalism graduate have had to face the same problem of going out after the first job rather than finding the first job coming to campus. Entry positions are out there and at salary ranges equivalent to those offered in such fields as accounting and similar high-demand areas, but they tend to be awarded to those who are best prepared and who seek them out. Although there are many roads leading to success in securing the first job in public relations, the following route has proven to be a sound one to travel:

1. **Prepare a portfolio** that can be easily scanned and that will provide evidence of your work and abilities. Include in it news and feature stories you've written; brochures and flyers you've produced; research and other assignments you've completed in various courses. The portfolio need not be fancy but should be well organized, easy to carry to interviews, and self-explanatory.

2. **Prepare and have printed a resume,** one page long, which will include personal, educational, extracurricular, and work experience data. This material should be organized under the four appropriate headings. If there's room on the page, include the names and addresses of two or three references. Otherwise state that references will be supplied upon request.

    There is no single "right" form for the resume, but the resume shown in Exhibit 19.3 indicates the basic form to use and should suffice as an example. Note particularly that the resume does not use complete sentences and avoids the use of the first person singular.

    A final note: This is the resume of a recent graduate. Once a job record has been achieved, work experience will move to the fore on the resume and education will move into the background. After several years of work and professional experience, the applicant's major strength will be his or her previous positions and responsibilities.

EXHIBIT 19.3

A Sample Resume

ROBERTA VINCENT

Address until May, 1984
Box 154, South
Utica College
Utica, N.Y. 13502
(315) 792-3047

Address after May
23 Wills Drive
Uniondale, N.Y. 11553
(516) 354-6787

Personal Data
Date of birth: 4/1/62
Single
Will relocate anywhere

Education
Utica College of Syracuse University, Utica, New York 13502
Degree: Bachelor of Arts, May 1984; dual major in Journalism and Public Relations
Overall Grade Point Average: 3.2 of 4.0; average in major: 3.4 of 4.0
Courses Taken in Major: Newswriting, Reporting, Introduction to Mass Communications, Introduction to Public Relations, Reporting on Public Affairs, Graphics, Editing, Writing and Announcing for Radio/Television, Publicity, Magazine Article Writing, Cases and Problems in Public Relations. Remainder of college courses in liberal arts.

Honors
Tau Mu Epsilon, National Honorary Public Relations Society; Student Speaker, First Utica College Convocation; Regents Scholarship
Interviewer, Telephone Conference Call Program with Reuven Frank, former president of NBC NEWS; Jack O'Dwyer of O'DWYER'S NEWSLETTER; Skip Weiner, editor of WRITER'S DIGEST; and Babette Ashby, articles editor of FAMILY CIRCLE

Activities
Utica College Press Club; Public Relations Student Society of America; Utica College Student Newspaper, TANGERINE; DORMWEEK, Utica College Weekly Dormitory Newspaper, Founder and Editor

Employment (All part-time while attending college)

1/84 to 5/84	Utica College of Syracuse University, Utica, New York 13502 Resident Living Advisor, in charge of the 300 students in South Dormitory
1/84 to 5/84	Journalism Fieldwork: Course includes moderating four public service radio shows for WRUN in Utica and free-lancing to the local daily and weekly newspapers Supervisor: John Behrens, Professor of Journalism, Utica College
5/83 to 12/83	Rome Air Development Center, Griffiss Air Force Base, New York 13440 Writer—Office of Information Information Officer: Capt. Juventino R. Garcia, USAF
8/82 to 1/83	Utica College of Syracuse University, Utica, New York 13502 Resident Assistant, in charge of one floor of students in South Dormitory Dean of Students: Richard Caulk
5/81 to 5/82	The Student Press in America Archives Utica College, Utica, New York 13502 Editorial Assistant Curator: Prof. John Behrens

References
Raymond Simon, Professor of Public Relations, Utica College, Utica, New York 13502, (315) 792-3027
John Caponera, Writer/Editor, Office of Information, Northern Communications Area, Griffiss Air Force Base, New York 13440, (315) 336-6230
John C. Behrens, Professor of Journalism Studies, Utica College, Utica, New York 13502, (315) 792-3056

3. **Compile a list** of organizations where job openings might exist. If you intend to write directly to the person heading the public relations function, the best single source of names and addresses is the annual *Register* of the Public Relations Society of America, which lists the members of the society. Each member receives a copy of the Register and it may be possible to borrow a copy from a PRSA member who is nearby. Appropriate lists can be compiled by referring to the annual membership directories published by groups such as the American Hospital Association, the United Ways of America, the Boy and Girl Scouts of America, the Council for the Advancement of Education (college public relations and fund-raising directors), etc.

4. **Prepare a brief cover letter** individually typed and sent out with each resume mailed. Concentrate your mailing to organizations within a 200 to 300 mile radius of your location. Even though they may be interested in your application, organizations will not set up a personal interview if you're in New York and the position is in Los Angeles.

5. **Try to establish contact** and arrange for a personal interview with professionals in areas where there are a large number of public relations people. Even though the person who interviews you may not have a position available, he or she may know of openings elsewhere or may be able to direct you to someone who will in turn direct you to an opening.

   Make use of any contact that may steer you to job leads. For example, find out if there are any alumni of your college's public relations program in the city where you hope to find a position. Networking has become an acceptable part of the professional scene, so make use of your alumni network. An alum may not have a job but may be able to put you in touch with one.

6. **Do not get discouraged too easily.** Finding the right kind of position can take months of search, so explore all possibilities by reading the classified section of metropolitan papers, *Editor and Publisher*, the *Public Relations Journal*, and similar sources and by sending out letters and resumes and arranging for personal interviews. If a media job opens up, by all means consider it seriously because it will provide you with the kind of experience still considered invaluable by practitioners who themselves moved into the public relations field through this route.

SALARY AND OTHER EXPECTATIONS

Any discussion of salary levels for the first job in public relations has to be red-flagged by the notation that spiraling inflation has made figures outdated almost as soon as they're reported. Thus, in mid-1972 Dr. Frederick H. Teahan, education director of the PRSA, reported that a study of a sample of pre-associate (newly graduated) members of the society showed that their starting salaries ranged from $6,000 to $14,000 with the median salary at $7,500 and the average at $8,823. By mid-1983, when the author surveyed his school's May public relations graduates, he found that their salaries ranged from $9,500 to $18,500 with the median salary at $12,500 and the average at $13,500.

Several general observations can be made about entry salaries. First, they have consistently ranged between $1,000 and $3,000 above those of graduates who have taken newspaper jobs. Second, the highest starting salaries in public relations have been in business, industry, and counseling while the lowest have been in the social and health agency and hospital fields. Third, women's salaries have lagged behind men's salaries, though this gap is constantly being narrowed in public relations as in all fields.

As to expectations, all indications point to a continuance of two of the above three trends. The bulk of entry positions in the newspaper field continue to be on small town and small city dailies, while the bulk of entry positions in public relations are in large organizations situated in metropolitan areas; thus, salary levels of beginning newspaper positions will continue to be lower than those of beginning public relations positions.

Comparison of 1983 and 1982 Median Salaries of Top Level Public Relations/Public Affairs Practitioners in US and Canada, and by Type of Organization

Type of Organization	Median Salary 1983	Median Salary 1982	1983 Salary Range	Median Change*
All US Organizations	$42,000	$38,500	$ 9,700 – 180,000	+3,000
All Canadian Organizations	42,500	36,000	18,000 – 110,000	2,600
PR Firms	50,100	48,800	9,700 – 175,000	4,100
Advertising Agencies (PR Section)	36,000	35,500	18,000 – 100,000	3,000
Other Consulting	40,000	50,000	23,000 – 90,000	4,000
Banks	40,000	35,000	24,000 – 120,000	3,800
Insurance Companies	44,000	---	20,000 – 120,000	2,900
Other Fin'l Svc Organizations	43,000	37,500	18,000 – 95,000	3,900
Consumer Product Companies	44,000	44,000		4,000
Industrials	50,000	45,600	15,000 – 180,000	3,700
Conglomerates	51,000	44,000	18,400 – 125,000	4,000
Transportation	41,700	37,000	16,500 – 98,500	3,000
Utilities	43,500	42,300	19,500 – 155,000	3,900
Hospitals	31,800	29,300	18,500 – 100,000	3,000
Educational	37,000	32,000	18,800 – 85,000	2,000
Trade/Professional Assns	40,000	40,000	18,000 – 77,000	3,400
Other Nonprofits	31,100	32,000	14,500 – 90,000	2,500
Government: Federal	37,900 ⎫		19,400 – 67,200	2,000
State	34,000 ⎬ 37,500		22,500 – 57,000	2,000
Local	34,000 ⎭		22,100 – 22,100	3,100

*Calculated on the difference between 1983 and 1982 salaries as reported by *each respondent.*

Notes: 1) Total number of respondents is 1,060.
2) "Median Salary" and "Median Change" refer to the point on the scale at which—and correspondingly below which—50% of the respondents fall.

FIGURE 19.1

Reprinted with permission of *pr reporter.*

Entry-level public relations jobs in business, industry, and counseling will continue to offer higher salaries than similar entry-level public relations positions in other areas. However, because of governmental, legal, and activist pressures the gap between women's and men's entry salary levels in public relations, as in all fields, will become a thing of the past and will be covered over and deservedly buried.

What about salary levels of experienced practitioners? Figures compiled by *pr reporter* showed that the median salary of top-level public relations/public affairs practitioners—among the total number of 1,060 respondents filling out questionnaires—was $42,000 in 1983, an increase of $3,500 over the 1982 median salary. The lowest earner in the group (the head of a small public relations firm) made $9,700 and the highest (a vice-president of corporate relations of an industrial company) made $180,000. Figures 19.1 through 19.3 provide details as reported by *pr reporter.*

Median Salaries Related to Titles/Levels			Salary Groupings	
Title/Level	Median	Range	Below $20,000	32
President (of counseling			$20,000 – $24,999	62
firm)	$50,200	$ 9,700 – 125,000	25,000 – 29,999	58
Exec or senior vp	55,125	18,000 – 120,000	30,000 – 34,999	104
Vice president	55,000	22,000 – 180,000	35,000 – 39,999	95
2nd or asst vp	39,900	26,000 – 94,000	40,000 – 44,999	133
Top pr/pa position on			45,000 – 49,999	66
div'l, regional or plant			50,000 – 54,999	91
level	41,000	15,000 – 86,000	55,000 – 59,999	55
Director or manager	40,000	14,500 – 110,000	60,000 – 64,999	45
Coordinator/supv (of			65,000 – 69,999	25
section)	35,000	14,600 – 64,000	70,000 – 74,999	26
Professional specialist	30,000	14,000 – 100,000	75,000 – 99,999	47
Account executive	23,400	14,500 – 52,000	100,000 & over	34

FIGURE 19.2

Reprinted with permission of *pr reporter*.

FIGURE 19.3

Reprinted with permission of *pr reporter*.

DAILY WORK ROUTINES

Entry-level jobs in public relations tend to be involved with writing rather than with counseling for the simple reason that there are many writing but few counseling tasks that can be assigned to a relative newcomer to the field. Furthermore, the very act of counseling calls for the degree of maturity and experience that comes with age and time spent in the field. The young graduate may aspire to doling out sage advice, but is generally not going to be asked or paid for it until he or she gets a little older, a little wiser, and a bit more experienced.

We thus find the Public Relations Society of America describing "The Day" of the newcomer to the field in the following words:

The junior employee will answer calls for information from the press and the public, work on invitation lists and details for a press conference, escort visitors and clients, help research and write brochures, deliver releases to editorial offices, work up contact and distribution lists, scan newspapers and journals, paste scrap books of clippings, brief his superiors on forthcoming meetings, help write reports, speeches, presentations, articles and letters, research case histories, help produce displays and other audio-visual materials, do copy reading, select photographs for publication, arrange and guide plant tours, perform liaison jobs with advertising and other departments, arrange for holiday or other remembrances, conduct surveys and tabulate questionnaires, work with letter-shops and printers. The telephone, the typewriter, the mimeograph and addressograph machines, telegraph, postal and other message services are communication tools that are familiar features of the public relations man's (and woman's) work environment.[19]

On their first jobs graduates obviously won't be doing all things set forth by the PRSA occupational guide, but rather can be expected to do any one of them at some time or another. Much depends on the nature of the organization for which one works. In large organizations, public relations functions and activities tend to be compartmentalized; the beginner may well find himself or herself spending the work week writing for the employee publication or perhaps writing news releases, but not doing both. In small organizations, public relations functions or activities tend to be shared by a smaller number of professionals, and there is the opportunity to get involved in a variety of tasks. Finally, where the public relations function is the sole responsibility of one professional, this person will have to be versatile enough to handle graphics, write releases and features, deliver talks, hold press conferences, deal with printers, and counsel. Thus, although salary scales in social and health agencies and in hospitals are lower than in business and industry, the responsibilities assigned to the beginner tend to be greater and provide the opportunity to develop a wider range of skills and talents than is possible in large organizations with large public relations departments.

Next year, the year after that, or three years from now students who have used this text will be starting their first jobs in public relations. These jobs will be so varied that it's difficult to state explicitly the kind of tasks they'll be asked to handle. In concluding this last chapter, the author has selected at random excerpts from letters he has received from recent graduates. Here's what those graduates had to say:

1. From a graduate who's taken a government position:

Hope this letter finds you in good health and spirits. I am proud and happy to inform you that I have been employed by the City of _____ as a Communications Coordinator.

I am very pleased with the job. At this time I am simply handling basic publicity work and at other times filling in as a "temporary administrator" in hopes of restructuring some mismanaged departments.

The salary and benefits are excellent. My boss is very intelligent with very interesting plans for my talents. Suffice it to say, I am extremely happy with my new position.

2. From a graduate working for a public relations/advertising agency:

The work here has been interesting. I was sent to Chicago in January to talk to the editors of a new magazine that is the result of the merger of the top two publications in the research/development field. The agency's biggest client did a lot of advertising in both of these magazines, and is hoping to get a lot of press releases in the new one.

For two days at the end of February I attended the Pittsburgh Analytical Symposium which, for some strange reason, is held in Cleveland. I was able to meet some more of the agency's clients and some important editors. One of my most trying tasks here is following up press releases on the phone with selected magazines. I think meeting some of these editors face to face will improve my communications with them in the future.

3. From a graduate working in college public relations:

Well, my college education in public relations has paid off. I have just finished my first week of work as assistant to the director of public relations. My starting salary is an even $10,000, and I am quite delighted with it. My responsibilities run the entire range of public relations from writing press releases to suggesting new ideas. I have my own office, desk, secretary, and so on. Everything I do has to be approved by my boss and then by the president of the college before it goes out. There is a lot of work to do because we have several branches, and my boss and I are responsible for public relations for all of them.

P.S.: This is the first letter I've written since graduation, and no matter what grade you give me, it won't matter now.

4. From a graduate working for a trade association:

Since I changed jobs six months ago, the scope of my responsibilities and my employer's expectations of me have increased 500 percent. My title is public relations administrator, and I'm responsible for the entire $300,000-a-year public relations program for the association.

Here I get a chance to do it all—making a film; running a press room at the world's largest trade show; writing and placing institutional ads, television and radio public service announcements; interviewing and hiring freelancers and film producers and ad agencies; spending $10,000 to promote a single annual meeting; attending all board meetings to give public relations advice; setting up features with the largest circulation magazines in the business; running a national journalism awards contest; and, most importantly, advising our president.

I've never enjoyed a job more than I have this one. I work late and often go in on Saturdays, but that's only because I like it and can see a good chance to move up in the organization by doing so.

ENDNOTES

1. From talk given by Frank Wylie at the University of Maryland, April 22, 1975.
2. John C. Merrill and Ralph Lowenstein, *Media, Messages, and Men*, 2nd ed. (New York: Longman, 1979), p. 218.
3. David Finn, "Struggle for Ethics in Public Relations," *Harvard Business Review*, January-February 1959, p. 51.
4. John Cook, "PR Without the BS," *Public Relations Quarterly*, Spring 1974.
5. From transcript of remarks made by Dr. Lerner at a conference on responsibility in public relations sponsored by Ruder & Finn and held in New York City October 20-22, 1958.
6. See endnote 4.
7. From remarks made over the Educational Telephone Network, University of Wisconsin, January 6, 1975.
8. Michael Ryan and David L. Martinson, "The PR Officer as Corporate Conscience," *Public Relations Quarterly*, Summer 1983, p. 211.
9. Donald B. McCammond, "A Matter of Ethics," *Public Relations Journal*, November 1983, p. 46.
10. From regulations regarding the Grievance Board, Judicial Panels, and PRSA members charged with violations of the code as cited in the Bylaws of the PRSA and reported in the *PRSA 1983-84 Directory*, pp. 17-19 and 33-35.
11. Special Report, "Report and Recommendations of the Task Force on Stature and Role of Public Relations," *Public Relations Journal*, March 1981, pp. 21-44.
12. Frank A. Tennant, "Survey of Public Relations Division/AEJ Members on Licensing Public Relations Practitioners," paper presented at AEJ annual meeting, Madison, Wisconsin, August 25, 1977.
13. Luther Hodges, Jr., "The New Challenge for Public Relations," *Public Relations Journal*, August 1975.
14. Albert Walker, "End-of-Decade Survey Shows Academic Growth in Public Relations," *Public Relations Review*, Summer 1982, pp. 46-60.
15. *A Design for Public Relations Education.* Report of the Commission on Public Relations Education, cosponsored by the Public Relations Division of the Association for Education in Journalism and the Public Relations Society of America, 1975, pp. 8-12.
16. Gold Paper No. 4, *A Model for Public Relations Education for Professional Practice* (London: The International Public Relations Association, January 1982), p. 30.
17. *An Occupational Guide for Public Relations* (New York: Public Relations Society of America). Updated periodically.
18. From "Nineteenth Annual Survey of the Profession, Part 1," *pr reporter*, August 29, 1983, pp. 1-4.
19. See endnote 17.

PROJECTS, ASSIGNMENT, AND MINIS

1. A DAY IN THE LIFE OF THREE PRACTITIONERS: A MINI-CASE

At the request of the author of this textbook, three former students selected an arbitrary date and recorded their work routine for the day. At the time in their professional careers the three were: Robert Feldman, vice-president, Burson-Marsteller, New York City; Carol Garlick, assistant director of development, Middlesex Memorial Hospital, Middletown, Connecticut; and Anthony DeNigro, manager, media programs, Mobil Oil Corporation, New York City. Following are the "logs" they compiled and transmitted, along with some explanatory remarks.

ROBERT FELDMAN
Vice-President
Burson-Marsteller, Inc.
New York City

Wednesday, Sept. 21

8:00 am .... Take bus to work and read the New York *Times*.

8:30 .... Arrive at office; put material read last night (with my comments) in "out box" to go to appropriate people; review today's "To Do" list.

8:45 .... Walk around office; get coffee; see staff just to see what's going on.

9:00 .... Write a letter to client attaching the outline of a program presented last week.

9:10 .... Call another client contact (same company) re: approval status of several pending projects.

9:20 .... Receive call from company colleague; my boss and I are taking over an account he handled; he briefs me, per an earlier request, on status of a number of projects to prepare me (and my boss) for our trip to the client next week.

9:45 .... Receive a call from public relations agency in Florida that is doing work for one of our client's customers; they want authorization to quote our client in a press release they're developing; we give it.

9:55 .... Staff member asks me to preview a video merchandising tape we produced before he brings it to our client at a convention in San Diego; it looks good. (The tape merchandises much of the publicity we've generated for our client.)

10:30 .... Call Western Union to send telegram to a client who is getting married this weekend.

10:40 .... Meet with the staff member who is going to the San Diego convention (see 9:55); we review what we want to get out of the convention. He's to leave on a noon flight.

11:00 .... Meet with my boss to review details on the new account we're inheriting (see 9:20); I brief him on my earlier phone call; he briefs me on his recent conversation with the client; we're immediately put to work due to an overseas communications crisis the client is having; we put client in touch with our office in that country.

11:20 .... Meet with two staff members re: work to be done over the next few days while the person to whom they directly report will be out of town; decide there's a lot to discuss; we'll do it over lunch.

11:30	Meet with one of our art directors to go over graphic treatment of a marketing communications audit form we're developing for our client; we resolve the direction we want to take.
11:50	Receive phone call from client; he wants to review status of current press kit; a video news release we're producing; quality and quantity of our photo file; and other miscellaneous items. He also tells us his research department is doing some consumer research in a few weeks; asks us if we want to add some questions that might have some publicity value later on. We'll do that.
12:15 pm	Lunch with staff members to follow up on our earlier meeting (see 11:20).
1:30	Meet with colleague to discuss direction we want to take with an ongoing client program; the program's an annual event that's been running the last 12 years; we think it may be time to rethink the strategy; we decide research is in order so that we can (a) determine if the objectives of the program have been met, and (b) if so, what is now needed by the audiences that our client can help address.
2:00	Draft weekly activities report for our new client; give it to my secretary to type, distribute.
2:30	Return five phone calls from lunch.
3:00	Buy a soda.
3:05	Meet with staff member to review a speech he's preparing to deliver at a client meeting next month.
4:00	Call client to informally propose an idea for an upcoming convention important to the company; client approves idea, asks for specifics with budget.
4:30	Receive phone call from an energy consultant we've been talking to; we can't seem to set a meeting date; we see the opportunity of relationship between this firm and a client; this call still doesn't end with a confirmed date.
4:45	Receive phone call from staff member who's out of town at a client meeting; we review what's going on there and I confirm I am shipping out to him—via overnight mail—a prototype of a piece of collateral for the client's approval.
5:00	Write letter to client giving the specifics and budget for the convention idea (see 4:00). Will have it typed by my secretary tomorrow.
5:25	Meet with staff member who is going out of town day after tomorrow to arrange some media interviews we set up for our client. Staff member is relatively new here; the person to whom he directly reports is out of town (that person is getting the collateral from me tomorrow); so I review the details he needs to consider for his trip.
5:45	Prepare "To Do" list for tomorrow. Wife meets me at the office and we go home at 5:50.

Excerpt from cover letter: "Here it is, a day in the life. . . . This is a pretty accurate log of the day's activities. I was a little surprised my time was occupied with so many phone calls and meetings. Still, for the most part, that was time well spent. The log may be a little confusing in terms of how many staff members there are; FYI, there are six account people who directly or indirectly report to me.

"I suspect that if I did this log a few years ago it would have been simpler. I'd have been working on fewer projects and spending more time on each. Since I am now managing more business, I tend to spend a little bit of time on a lot of different things. . . ."

CAROL GARLICK
Assistant Director of Development
Middlesex Memorial Hospital
Middletown, Connecticut

8:00 am .... Arrive at work. Review projects for the day and coordinate activities with staff. Edit articles for community newsletter, written by public relations/development writer. Dictate letter to area service club presidents to ask support for a special hospital program. Dictate proposal for the Development Office's plan and objectives for the upcoming year.

9:30 .... Meet with Vice-President for Development regarding recognition dinner for the Development Fund's special giving club (donors at $500 and above).

10:00 .... Meet with volunteer chairperson of the Business Drive regarding follow-up on businesses which have not yet supported the current campaign.

11:00 .... Morning mail arrives. Review gifts that have come in. Draft merit evaluation for employee. Call community relations representative at local restaurant chain who is helping organize benefit for the hospital's Hospice Program.

12:00 noon ..... Have lunch with the hospital's Auxiliary president to discuss the group's fund-raising plans for the upcoming year.

1:00 pm .... Meet with public relations/development writer to plan the hospital's general information brochure, which will be mailed with a pledge card and cover letter to those prospects who have not yet supported the current campaign.

2:00 .... Work on draft of grant proposal for funds to support a program of the Social Work Department.

3:00 .... Hold monthly meeting with the executive council of the hospital's Management Club.

4:00 .... Afternoon mail arrives. Review it and read afternoon edition of the daily newspaper.

4:30 .... Dictate letters to thank volunteers and employees who helped organize a special program for the hospital's trustees. The hospital's president will sign the letters. Read national trade journal for hospital development. Review results of recent marketing survey, conducted over the telephone by an outside firm, for ideas on how the findings can be incorporated into Development Fund projects, such as brochures, and campaign emphasis.

6:00 .... Hold tour and dinner program for local company whose employees recently assisted in the hospital's phonathon.

9:00 .... Leave work for home.

Excerpt from cover letter: "I've tried to include the wide variety of activities this office handles into one day (well, at least a *taste* of the variety) and hope it meets your needs. Although 'public relations' isn't in my title, I'm hoping you'll note that it is obvious in my work. . . ."

ANTHONY J. DeNIGRO
Manager, Media Programs
Mobil Oil Corporation
New York City

8:30 am	....	Read day's Mobil/industry news clippings.
8:35	....	Read, route mail.
8:45	....	Order novel for vice-president's review re possible property for TV.
8:50	....	Assign vice-president speech to a speech writer.
9:00	....	Do final editing of a news release about a director-level appointment.
9:10	....	Check with vice-president re news coverage of Texas problem. Check with vice-president re the taping of radio commentaries.
9:15	....	Mobil Chemical Company public relations staffer called re inquiry from the Chicago *Tribune*; we discussed it. Reviewed with staffer the 9/26 meeting with energy writer from the *Economist* and Mobil president. Also reviewed with him the 10:15 meeting with general manager and the inquiry from *New York* magazine.
9:30	....	Interview an unemployed writer. No job here, but would recommend him to friends and associates.
10:00	....	Return three telephone calls.
10:15	....	Brief general manager on today's luncheon.
11:00	....	Have outside meeting with TV syndicator on the station lineup for the 1984 Mobil Showcase Network.
12:30	....	Lunch with New York City commissioner, Mobil Foundation president, Mobil vice-president, my general manager to review impact of grant for summer jobs program and ideas for next summer.
2:00	....	Return two telephone calls.
2:05	....	Give vice-president novel for possible TV property.
2:15	....	Select news clippings for weekly mailing to outside directors.
2:30	....	Receive final approvals on appointments news release, hand off to staffer for distribution Monday.
2:45	....	Read, route mail.
3:00	....	Brief manager of promotional and cultural affairs on the 11:00 am meeting.
3:15	....	Discuss personnel change in the department with general manager.
3:45	....	Review TV, newspaper coverage of Texas problem.
4:00	....	Read, route mail.
4:10	....	Have telephone discussion with TV syndicator re problems.
4:30	....	Set up recording time for vice-president's radio commentaries for Monday afternoon.
5:15	....	Went home.

Questions for Discussion

1. What similarities do you perceive in the daily activities of the three practitioners? What do you consider to be significant differences? What conclusions do you draw about these perceived similarities and differences?

2. How would you characterize the major areas of activities of the three? What kind of specific skills and attributes would you consider necessary to carry out these activities most effectively?

3. Which of the activities do you think you're now capable of handling and which do you think you couldn't handle? Why?

4. Did these descriptions of daily activities measure up to your expectations of what you might be doing after graduation? Explain.

2. PRACTITIONERS DISCUSS AN ETHICAL SITUATION: A MINI-CASE

To sharpen perceptions about ethical problems, staff members at Ruder & Finn met in a series of seminars with a group of theologians and philosophers to pursue the question of ethics and public relations. David Finn presented the following brief case for discussion:

> Company A decided to build an image of one of its major products as being purer than its competitors'. This was actually so. However, advertising claims of purity had been used and abused so heavily in the past by other companies that it decided to undertake a public relations program to get the story across. Accordingly, a complicated scheme was invented involving the development of an "independent" research report that was to provide the basis for newspaper and magazine articles.
>
> The trouble was that the research was engineered; in fact, it was not even to be paid for unless the publicity appeared in print. To ensure the success of the project, the man who arranged all this had some editors on his payroll as consultants for the research, thus almost guaranteeing eventual publication. It was a neat scheme—effective for the company and profitable for researcher, editor, and middleman.*

Questions for Discussion

1. What's your opinion of the method used to communicate the image of purity to the public?

2. If you had been asked to carry out the plan, and you were a member of the public relations firm earning $50,000 yearly, what would be your response?

3. Finn reports that one of the scholarly consultants participating in the seminars suggested as a "piece of litmus paper" test that one should never do anything he or she would not want to see published in tomorrow morning's newspaper. What's your opinion of this suggestion as a test of ethical behavior?

*David Finn, "Struggle for Ethics," *Harvard Business Review*, January-February 1959, p. 52.

APPENDIX A

PUBLIC RELATIONS SOCIETY OF AMERICA
Code of Professional Standards
For the Practice of Public Relations

This Code, adopted by the PRSA Assembly, replaces a similar Code of Professional Standards for the Practice of Public Relations previously in force since 1954 and strengthened by revisions in 1959, 1963 and 1977.

DECLARATION OF PRINCIPLES

Members of the Public Relations Society of America base their professional principles on the fundamental value and dignity of the individual, holding that the free exercise of human rights, especially freedom of speech, freedom of assembly and freedom of the press, is essential to the practice of public relations.

In serving the interests of clients and employers, we dedicate ourselves to the goals of better communication, understanding and cooperation among the diverse individuals, groups and institutions of society.

We pledge:

To conduct ourselves professionally, with truth, accuracy, fairness and responsibility to the public;

To improve our individual competence and advance the knowledge and proficiency of the profession through continuing research and education;

And to adhere to the articles of the Code of Professional Standards for the Practice of Public Relations as adopted by the governing Assembly of the Society.

ARTICLES OF THE CODE

These articles have been adopted by the Public Relations Society of America to promote and maintain high standards of public service and ethical conduct among its members.

1. A member shall deal fairly with clients or employers, past and present, with fellow practitioners and the general public.

2. A member shall conduct his or her professional life in accord with the public interest.

3. A member shall adhere to truth and accuracy and to generally accepted standards of good taste.

4. A member shall not represent conflicting or competing interests without the express consent of those involved, given after a full disclosure of the facts; nor place himself or herself in a position where the member's interest is or may be in conflict with a duty to a client, or others, without a full disclosure of such interests to all involved.

5. A member shall safeguard the confidences of both present and future clients or employers and shall not accept retainers or employment which may involve the disclosure or use of these confidences to the disadvantage or prejudice of such clients or employers.

6. A member shall not engage in any practice which tends to corrupt the integrity of channels of communication or the processes of government.

7. A member shall not intentionally communicate false or misleading information and is obligated to use care to avoid communication of false or misleading information.

8. A member shall be prepared to identify publicly the name of the client or employer on whose behalf any public communication is made.

9. A member shall not make use of any individual or organization purporting to serve or represent an announced cause, or purporting to be independent or unbiased, but actually serving an undisclosed special or private interest of a member, client or employer.

10. A member shall not intentionally injure the professional reputation or practice of another practitioner. However, if a member has evidence that another member has been guilty of unethical, illegal or unfair practices, including those in violation of this Code, the member shall present the information promptly to the proper authorities of the Society for action in accordance with the procedure set forth in Article XIII of the Bylaws.

11. A member called as a witness in a proceeding for the enforcement of this Code shall be bound to appear, unless excused for sufficient reason by the Judicial Panel.

12. A member, in performing services for a client or employer, shall not accept fees, commissions or any other valuable consideration from anyone other than the client or employer in connection with those services without the express consent of the client or employer, given after a full disclosure of the facts.

13. A member shall not guarantee the achievement of specified results beyond the member's direct control.

14. A member shall, as soon as possible, sever relations with any organization or individual if such relationship requires conduct contrary to the articles of this Code.

OFFICIAL INTERPRETATIONS OF THE CODE

Interpretation of Code Paragraph 2 which reads, "A member shall conduct his or her professional life in accord with the public interest."

> The public interest is here defined primarily as comprising respect for and enforcement of the rights guaranteed by the Constitution of the United States of America.

Interpretation of Code Paragraph 5 which reads, "A member shall safeguard the confidences of both present and former clients or employers and shall not accept retainers or employment which may involve the disclosure or use of these confidences to the disadvantage or prejudice of such clients or employers."

> This article does not prohibit a member who has knowledge of client or employer activities which are illegal from making such disclosures to the proper authorities as he or she believes are legally required.

Interpretation of Code Paragraph 6 which reads: "A member shall not engage in any practice which tends to corrupt the integrity of channels of communication or the processes of government."

1. Practices prohibited by this paragraph are those which tend to place representatives of media or government under an obligation to the member, or the member's employer or client, which is in conflict with their obligations to media or government, such as:

a. the giving of gifts of more than nominal value;
b. any form of payment or compensation to a member of the media in order to obtain preferential or guaranteed news or editorial coverage in the medium;
c. any retainer or fee to a media employee or use of such employee if retained by a client or employer, where the circumstances are not fully disclosed to and accepted by the media employer;
d. providing trips for media representatives which are unrelated to legitimate news interest;
e. the use by a member of an investment or loan or advertising commitment made by the member, or the member's client or employer, to obtain preferential or guaranteed coverage in the medium.

2. This Code paragraph does not prohibit hosting media or government representatives at meals, cocktails, or news functions or special events which are occasions for the exchange of news information or views, or the furtherance of understanding which is part of the public relations function. Nor does it prohibit the bona fide press event or tour when media or government representatives are given an opportunity for on-the-spot viewing of a newsworthy product, process or event in which the media or government representatives have a legitimate interest. What is customary or reasonable hospitality has to be a matter of particular judgment in specific situations. In all of these cases, however, it is or should be understood that no preferential treatment or guarantees are expected or implied and that complete independence always is left to the media or government representative.

3. This paragraph does not prohibit the reasonable giving or lending of sample products or services to media representatives who have a legitimate interest in the products or services.

Interpretation of Code Paragraph 13 which reads, "A member shall not guarantee the achievement of specified results beyond the member's direct control."

This Code paragraph, in effect, prohibits misleading a client or employer as to what professional public relations can accomplish. It does not prohibit guarantees of quality or service. But it does prohibit guaranteeing specific results which, by their very nature, cannot be guaranteed because they are not subject to the member's control. As an example, a guarantee that a news release will appear specifically in a particular publication would be prohibited. This paragraph should not be interpreted as prohibiting contingent fees.

AN OFFICIAL INTERPRETATION OF THE CODE AS IT APPLIES TO POLITICAL PUBLIC RELATIONS

Preamble

In the practice of political public relations, a PRSA member must have professional capabilities to offer an employer or client quite apart from any political relationships of value, and members may serve their employer or client without necessarily having attributed to them the character, reputation or beliefs of those they serve. It is understood that members may choose to serve only those interests with whose political philosophy they are personally comfortable.

Precepts

1. It is the responsibility of PRSA members practicing political public relations as defined above, to be conversant with the various statutes, local, state, and federal, governing such activities and to adhere to them strictly. This includes, but is not limited to, the various local, state and federal laws, court decisions and official interpretations governing lobbying, political contributions, disclosure, elections, libel, slander and the like. In carrying out this responsibility, members shall seek appropriate counseling whenever necessary.

2. It is also the responsibility of members to abide by PRSA's Code of Professional Standards.

3. Members shall represent clients or employers in good faith, and while partisan advocacy on behalf of a candidate or public issue may be expected, members shall act in accord with the public interest and adhere to truth and accuracy and to generally accepted standards of good taste.

4. Members shall not issue descriptive material or any advertising or publicity information or participate in the preparation or use thereof which is not signed by responsible persons or is false, misleading or unlabeled as to its source, and are obligated to use care to avoid dissemination of any such material.

5. Members have an obligation to clients to disclose what remuneration beyond their fees they expect to receive as a result of their relationship, such as commissions for media advertising, printing and the like, and should not accept such extra payment without their clients' consent.

6. Members shall not improperly use their positions to encourage additional future employment or compensation. It is understood that successful campaign directors or managers, because of the performance of their duties and the working relationship that develops, may well continue to assist and counsel, for pay, the successful candidate.

7. Members shall voluntarily disclose to employers or clients the identity of other employers or clients with whom they are currently associated and whose interests might be affected favorably or unfavorably by their political representation.

8. Members shall respect the confidentiality of information pertaining to employers or clients even after the relationships cease, avoiding future associations wherein insider information is sought

that would give a desired advantage over a member's previous clients.

9. In avoiding practices which might tend to corrupt the processes of government, members shall not make undisclosed gifts of cash or other valuable considerations which are designed to influence specific decisions of voters, legislators or public officials on public matters. A business lunch or dinner, or other comparable expenditure made in the course of communicating a point of view or public position, would not constitute such a violation. Nor for example, would a plant visit designed and financed to provide useful background information to an interested legislator or candidate.

10. Nothing herein should be construed as prohibiting members from making legal, properly disclosed contributions to the candidates, party or referenda issues of their choice.

11. Members shall not, through the use of information known to be false or misleading, conveyed directly or through a third party, intentionally injure the public reputation of an opposing interest.

AN OFFICIAL INTERPRETATION OF THE CODE AS IT APPLIES TO FINANCIAL PUBLIC RELATIONS

This interpretation of the Society Code as it applies to financial public relations was originally adopted in 1963 and amended in 1972 and 1977 by action of the PRSA Board of Directors. "Financial public relations" is defined as "that area of public relations which relates to the dissemination of information that affects the understanding of stockholders and investors generally concerning the financial position and prospects of a company, and includes among its objectives the improvement of relations between corporations and their stockholders." The interpretation was prepared in 1963 by the Society's Financial Relations Committee working with the Securities and Exchange Commission and with the advice of the Society's Legal Counsel. It is rooted directly in the Code with the full force of the Code behind it and a violation of any of the following paragraphs is subject to the same procedures and penalties as violation of the Code.

1. It is the responsibility of PRSA members who practice financial public relations to be thoroughly familiar with and understand the rules and regulations of the SEC and the laws which it administers, as well as other laws, rules and regulations affecting financial public relations, and to act in accordance with their letter and spirit. In carrying out this responsibility, members shall also seek legal counsel, when appropriate, on matters concerning financial public relations.

2. Members shall adhere to the general policy of making full and timely disclosure of corporate information on behalf of clients or employers. The information disclosed shall be accurate, clear and understandable. The purpose of such disclosure is to provide the

investing public with all material information affecting security values or influencing investment decisions. In complying with the duty of full and timely disclosure, members shall present all material facts, including those adverse to the company. They shall exercise care to ascertain the facts and to disseminate only information which they believe to be accurate. They shall not knowingly omit information, the omission of which might make a release false or misleading. Under no circumstances shall members participate in any activity designed to mislead, or manipulate the price of a company's securities.

3. Members shall publicly disclose or release information promptly so as to avoid the possibility of any use of the information by any insider or third party. To that end, members shall make every effort to comply with the spirit and intent of the timely disclosure policies of the stock exchanges, NASD, and the Securities and Exchange Commission. Material information shall be made available to all on an equal basis.

4. Members shall not disclose confidential information the disclosure of which might be adverse to a valid corporate purpose or interest and whose disclosure is not required by the timely disclosure provisions of the law. During any such period of non-disclosure members shall not directly or indirectly (a) communicate the confidential information to any other person or (b) buy or sell or in any other way deal in the company's securities where the confidential information may materially affect the market for the security when disclosed. Material information shall be disclosed publicly as soon as its confidential status has terminated or the requirement of timely disclosure takes effect.

5. During the registration period, members shall not engage in practices designed to precondition the market for such securities. During registration the issuance of forecasts, projections, predictions about sales and earnings, or opinions concerning security values or other aspects of the future performance of the company, shall be in accordance with current SEC regulations and statements of policy. In the case of companies whose securities are publicly held, the normal flow of factual information to shareholders and the investing public shall continue during the registration period.

6. Where members have any reason to doubt that projections have an adequate basis in fact, they shall satisfy themselves to the adequacy of the projections prior to disseminating them.

7. Acting in concert with clients or employers, members shall act promptly to correct false or misleading information or rumors concerning clients' or employers' securities or business whenever they have reason to believe such information or rumors are materially affecting investor attitudes.

8. Members shall not issue descriptive materials designed or written in such a fashion as to appear to be, contrary to fact, an indepen-

dent third party endorsement or recommendation of a company or a security. Whenever members issue material for clients or employers, either in their own names or in the name of someone other than clients or employers, they shall disclose in large type and in a prominent position on the face of the material the source of such material and the existence of the issuer's client or employer relationship.

9. Members shall not use inside information for personal gain. However, this is not intended to prohibit members from making bona fide investments in their company's or client's securities insofar as they can make such investments without the benefit of material inside information.

10. Members shall not accept compensation which would place them in a position of conflict with their duty to a client, employer or the investing public. Members shall not accept stock options from clients or employers nor accept securities as compensation at a price below market price except as part of an overall plan for corporate employees.

11. Members shall act so as to maintain the integrity of channels of public communication. They shall not pay or permit to be paid to any publication or other communications medium any consideration in exchange for publicizing a company, except through clearly recognized paid advertising.

12. Members shall in general be guided by the PRSA Declaration of Principles and the PRSA Code of Professional Standards for the Practice of Public Relations of which this Code is an official interpretation.

APPENDIX B

Corporate Reporting Requirements
Including SEC's Integrated Disclosure System, Effective May 24, 1982

Prepared by Robert W. Taft, APR, Senior Vice President, Hill and Knowlton, Inc.

Reporting Required For	Securities and Exchange Commission	New York Stock Exchange	American Stock Exchange	Generally Recommended Publicity Practice, All Companies
Accounting: Change in auditors	8-K; if principal auditor (or auditor for a subsidiary) resigns, declines to be re-elected, or is dismissed or if another is engaged. Disclose date of resignation, details of disagreements, comment letters to SEC by auditor on whether it agrees with reasons stated plus other disclosures detailed in 8-K. See also Regulation S-K, Item 304.	Prompt notice to Exchange, 8-K when filed. The NYSE recommends that the independent audit firm be represented at annual meeting to answer questions.	Same as NYSE.	Press release desirable at time of filing 8-K if differences are major. Consider clear statement in annual report or elsewhere on independence of auditors including their reporting relationship to Board's audit committee.

Reprinted with permission from April 1982 issue of *Public Relations Journal.* Copyright 1982.

Reporting Required For	Securities and Exchange Commission	New York Stock Exchange	American Stock Exchange	Generally Recommended Publicity Practice, All Companies
Accounting: Change in method	Independent public accountant must file letter indicating approval/ disapproval of "improved method of measuring business operations."	Prompt notification to Exchange required.	Notify Exchange before change is made and disclose the impact in succeeding interim and annual reports.	Statement of accounting policies is required in annual report. Give some publicity to accounting changes; illustrate how alternative accounting methods affect earnings. Special problems arise in changing LIFO/FIFO methods of accounting for inventory.
Amendment of charter or bylaws	Report if matter subject to stockholders' approval or if change materially modifies rights of holders of any class of registered securities.	Four copies of any material sent to stockholders in respect to proposed changes. Appropriately certified copy of changes when effective.	Ten copies of any material sent to stockholders must be filed with Exchange when effective with certified copy of (a) charter amendments; (b) directors' resolution as to charter or bylaws.	Recommend immediate publicity if change significantly alters rights or interests of shareholders. "Defensive" provision to make takeovers more difficult likely to receive very wide publicity.

Annual (or special) meeting of stockholders	10-Q following meeting including date of meeting, name of each director elected (if contested), summary of other matters voted on.	Four copies of all proxy material sent to shareholders. Prompt notice of calling of meeting; publicity on material actions at meeting. Ten days advance notice of record date or closing transfer books to Exchange.	Ten copies of all material sent to shareholders. Other requirements same as NYSE.	Press release at time of meeting. Competition for news space minimizes public coverage except on actively contested issues. Check NYSE schedules for competing meetings. Recommend wide distribution of post-meeting report to shareholders.
Annual report to shareholders: Contents	Required contents listed under Rule 14a-3 of the '34 Act. SEC still encourages "freedom of management expression."	Requirements are more than satisfied by compliance with SEC requirements.	Requirements are more than satisfied by compliance with SEC requirements.	Check printed annual report and appropriate news release to insure they conform to information reported on Form 10-K. News releases necessary if annual report contains previously undisclosed material information. Trend is to consider report a marketing tool.
Annual report to shareholders: Timing and distribution	Annual report to shareholders must precede or accompany delivery of proxy material. (Proxy material should *arrive* at least 30 days prior to annual meeting.) (Form 10-K must be filed within 90 days of close of year.)	Published and submitted to shareholders at least 15 days before annual meeting but no later than three months after close of fiscal year. PROMPTEST POSSIBLE ISSUANCE URGED. Recommend release of audited figures as soon as available.	Published and submitted to shareholders at least 10 days before meeting but no later than four months after close of fiscal year. PROMPTEST POSSIBLE ISSUANCE URGED. Recommend release of audited figures as soon as available.	Financial information should be released as soon as available; second release at time printed report is issued if report contains other material information. NYSE and Amex urge broad distribution of report to include statistical services so company information is available for "ready public reference."

Reporting Required For	Securities and Exchange Commission	New York Stock Exchange	American Stock Exchange	Generally Recommended Publicity Practice, All Companies
Annual report: Form 10-K	Required by Section 13 or 15 (d) of Securities Exchange Act of 1934 on Form 10-K. To be filed with SEC no later than 90 days after close of fiscal year. (Some schedules may be filed 120 days thereafter.) Extensive incorporation by reference from annual report to shareholders and from proxy statement now make integration of Form 10-K and report to shareholders more practical. (See general instructions G and H of Form 10-K.)	One signed copy must be filed with Exchange.	Three copies must be filed with Exchange. (See Company Guide, p. 253.)	Publicity usually not necessary unless 10-K contains previously unreported material information.
Bankruptcy or receivership	8-K immediately after appointment of receiver. Identify proceeding, court, date of event, name of receiver and date of appointment. Additional 8-K when order confirming a plan of reorganization is entered by court with information on court, date, details of plan, shares outstanding, assets and liabilities at date of order.	Immediate note to Exchange.	Same as NYSE.	Recommend press release at time of 8-K filing. Purpose is to tell creditors how to secure claims, not to notify stockholders of a material development. Further press releases and disclosures handled by receiver under court jurisdiction. Normally very limited.

Compensation	See Regulation S-K, Item 402 for exhaustive discussion of how information on management compensation must be presented in filings with SEC, including issuance of stock options and stock appreciation rights.	Not applicable.	Not applicable.	While not generally "material", information on executive compensation is widely reported when proxy statements issued; public relations issues should be discussed in advance of publication.
Control: Change in	Form 8-K. Disclose name of person acquiring control, amount and source of funds, basis of control, date and description of transaction, percent of voting shares held by new controlling person, identity of person from whom control acquired, terms of loans, terms of agreements with old and new management. Statement on Schedule 13D may be required by new controlling persons.	Prompt written notice to Exchange. Immediate release, if material. Recommends directors be identified in annual report.	Prompt written notice to Exchange. Immediate release, if material.	Recommend immediate announcement of any change in control of company. Normally announced by new controlling party.
Default upon senior securities	10-Q if actual material default in principal, interest, sinking fund installment, arrearage in dividends for preferred, registered or ranking securities not cured within 30 days of any stated grace period and if indebtedness exceeds 5 percent of total assets.	Immediate publicity and notice to the Exchange.	Immediate publicity and notice to the Exchange.	Immediate disclosure probably required at time default condition is known; include amount of default and total arrearage, date of default. Consider discussion of method and timing of curing default.

Reporting Required For	Securities and Exchange Commission	New York Stock Exchange	American Stock Exchange	Generally Recommended Publicity Practice, All Companies
Directors: Change in	8-K if director resigns or refuses to stand because of disagreement and if resigning director writes and requests disclosure of dispute. New directors and officers must personally file Form 3 upon election. Proxy rules require certain disclosures about votes cast for or withheld from individual directors; disclosure of vote on all directors if one or more directors receive 5 percent plus negative vote.	Prompt written notice to Exchange of any change. Immediate release, if material. Recommends Audit Committee for Board. Recommends directors be identified in annual report.	Prompt written notice to Exchange. Immediate release if material. Recommends that company with no outside directors nominate at least two independent directors.	Recommend immediate announcement of any contemplated change in directors. However, no technical requirement for publicity except where control of company changes or key person is added or lost.

Dividends	All issuers of publicly traded securities are required to give notice of dividend declarations pursuant to Rule 10B-17. Over-the-counter companies must provide advance notice of record date for subsequent dissemination to investors, extending comparable stock exchange requirements to OTC market. Failure to comply places issuer in violation of Section 10 (b) of the Securities Exchange Act of 1934.	Prompt notice to Exchange and immediate publicity. "Telephone Alert" to Exchange when the action is unusual and during market hours. "Immediate" means even while directors' meeting is still in progress. Ten days' advance notice of record date. NYSE manual implies announcement of management intention prior to formal board action may be required in case of a "leak" or rumor.	Same as NYSE. Notification to Exchange by telephone or telegram with confirmation by letter.	Prepare publicity in advance and release immediately by a designated officer on word of declaration. Publicity especially important when dividend rate changes. Statement of dividend policy now common in annual reports. Statements of "intention" to take dividend action also becoming common.
Earnings	Form 10-Q required within 45 days of close of each of first three fiscal quarters. Include information outlined in 10-Q, Part 1, Instruction 4, plus a narrative management analysis in form outlined in Form S-K, Item 303. Summary of quarterly results for two years in "unaudited" annual report footnote. Form 10-K required to report full year's earnings.	Quarterly. Publicity required. Shareholder mailing recommended. NYSE urges breakout of fourth quarter results for AP and UPI P/E ratio computation.	Quarterly. Should be published within 45 days after end of fiscal quarter for all four quarters.	Immediate publicity; do not hold data until printed quarterly report is published and mailed. Release no later than 10-Q filing; annual results as soon as available. Information in news release must be consistent with 10-Q. Breakout of current quarter results together with year-to-date totals desirable in 2nd, 3rd and 4th quarter releases.

Reporting Required For	Securities and Exchange Commission	New York Stock Exchange	American Stock Exchange	Generally Recommended Publicity Practice, All Companies
Employee stock purchase and saving plans	Form 11-K may be required under 15 (d) of '34 Act. Form S-8 may also be required.	No specific rules.	No specific rules.	Generally no publicity required or recommended. There is increasing trend to mention such programs in annual report.
Environmental matters	Reg. S-K; Item 103; Instruction 5. Disclosure in Forms 10-Q, 10-K and elsewhere under legal proceedings if a) material; b) involves claim for more than 10 percent of current assets; or c) government agency involved and amount likely to exceed $100,000.	No specific provision.	No specific provision.	SEC increasingly believes extensive environmental disclosure is "meaningless and confusing to investors"; has curtailed pressure for extensive timely press release reporting in favor of orderly filings. Handle conservatively.

	SEC	NYSE	AMEX	Public relations/financial community
Extraordinary charge or credit; charge to retained earnings	SEC expects discussion of nature of and reason for charge in "Management Discussion and Analysis."	Disclosure recommended for material provisions for future losses, discontinued operations, foreign operations, future costs. Include detail on amounts reserved, subsequently used and remaining available at year-end. Prior notice to Exchange required for any proposed substantial charge to retained earnings by company or by directly controlled subsidiary.	Same as NYSE for charge.	Generally material. Requires immediate disclosure. Press release should precede SEC filings. There is increasing "enterprise" reporting of impact of extraordinary items on earnings per share.
Float: Increase or decrease in	10-Q if an outstanding "class" of securities is changed more than 5 percent by issuance or purchase of securities, or payment of indebtedness. Include this information in 10-K. New rules specify timing and method for company to tender for own shares. See standard SEC treatment in Regulation S-K, Item 202.	Prompt notice when occasioned by actual or proposed deposit under voting trust agreements, etc., and brought to "official attention" of officers or directors. The NYSE requires prompt announcement of a program to purchase the company's own shares.	Prompt announcement upon establishing program to acquire the company's own shares.	Immediate publicity to extent permitted under registration restraints. Report details of statement of purpose required in 10-Q filing. Normally routine but will attract publicity if announcement signals major corporate repurchase program. Ads and releases where company tenders for own shares must conform with SEC filings. Publicity if there is sharp decrease in floating supply which could affect the market in the company's securities.

Reporting Required For	Securities and Exchange Commission	New York Stock Exchange	American Stock Exchange	Generally Recommended Publicity Practice, All Companies
Foreign currency translation	New FASB No. 52 requires report of foreign currency translation gains or losses as they occur (quarterly).	No requirement.	No requirement.	Recent adoption of FASB No. 52 should reduce or eliminate need for extended discussion of impact of foreign currency translation outside SEC filings except in extreme cases.
Inflation: Impact of	SEC requires adherence to FASB Statement No. 33. Report in two ways in a footnote: the effect of general inflation (constant dollar); the effect of changes in specific prices of materials (current costs). Discussion is still considered "experimental."	No requirement.	No requirement.	Publicity generally not necessary. However expect considerable shareholder and press interest in this section of annual report during periods of rapid inflation.

Legal proceedings	10-Q at start, termination of proceedings and in any quarter when material development occurs (generally damage claims in excess of 10 percent of current assets); also any suit against company by an officer, director or major stockholder. See Regulation S-K, Item 103.	No notice to NYSE required unless proceedings bear on ownership, dividends, interest or principal of listed securities, or start of receivership, bankruptcy, reorganization proceedings.	Public disclosure if material. Prompt notice to Exchange.	Public disclosure recommended if outcome of legal proceedings could have material effect on company and news of proceeding has not already become public. Court filings now commonly distributed to key business media with or without press release.
Listing: Initially or on another exchange	Involved and extensive legal work is required.	See listing requirements which are raised or revised frequently (NYSE Company Manual Section B). Dual listing now permitted.	See listing requirements. Dual listing now permitted.	Bulk of routine publicity handled by exchanges. Amex efforts particularly effective in electronic media. Discuss other special opportunities with legal and public relations counsel.
Management discussion and analysis	See Regulation S-K, Item 303 for complete discussion of presentation for both annual and quarterly financial reports.	Not applicable.	Not applicable.	Generally poorly written. SEC seeks greater discussion of liquidity. When well done, offers major opportunity for superior financial communications.
Market Information: Stock prices; Number of shareholders; Dividend payments; Markets where quoted	See Regulation S-K, Item 201, for standard treatment in all SEC filings.	Not applicable.	Not applicable.	Basic information rarely newsworthy in itself but valuable when presented in proper contexts.

Reporting Required For	Securities and Exchange Commission	New York Stock Exchange	American Stock Exchange	Generally Recommended Publicity Practice, All Companies
Merger: Acquisition or disposition of assets	8-K if company acquires or disposes of a significant (10 percent of total assets or whole subsidiary) amount of assets or business other than in normal course of business. Proxy soliciting material or registration statement may also be required. Check application of Rule 145(b) to any such transaction involving exchange of stock. (See also Tender Offers.)	8-K filed (where assets acquired). Immediate public disclosure. Prompt notice to Exchange where assets disposed of.	8-K filed, for acquisition or disposition of assets. Immediate public disclosure.	NYSE policy requires immediate announcement as soon as confidential disclosures relating to such important matters are made to "outsiders" (i.e., other than "top management" and their individual confidential "advisors"). Immediate publicity, especially when assets consist of an entire product line, division, operating unit or a "substantial" part of the business.
Policy statement on handling inside information	No rule.	No rule.	No rule.	Not specifically required by any regulatory authority. Cases involving insider information have turned on whether company had developed and implemented a written policy on disclosure of material, non-public corporate information. SEC requires submission of such statements as part of consent decree.

Prospectus and registration statement	Prospectus must be filed as part of registration statement. Copies distributed to underwriters and dealers in securities offerings, and in turn to investors. Photos of management, products, maps, other visuals permitted. Forecasts may be included in prospectuses and registration statements. See Regulation S-K, Item 500 for extensive discussion of contents.	Seven copies of final prospectus to Exchange. May be used as part of listing application covering the new securities.	Copy of complete registration filing to Exchange. Recent prospectus may be used as part of listing application covering the new securities.	News release, if issued at time of registration, must state from whom prospectus may be obtained. See SEC Rule 134 for permitted content of release at or after initial filing, and SEC Rule 135 for permitted content of release announcing intention to file.
Projection: Forecast or estimate of earnings	See Reg S-K General Policy (b). SEC policy encourages use of projections of future economic performance that have "a reasonable basis" and are presented in an appropriate format. Obligation to correct promptly when facts change. Should not discontinue or resume projections without clear explanation of action.	Immediate public disclosure when news goes beyond insiders and their confidential advisors.	Public disclosure not required initially, but if earnings forecast released, and later appears to be wrong, issuer must correct promptly and publicly.	Projections should be either avoided altogether or widely circulated with all assumptions stated. Projections by others may require correction by company if wrong but widely believed. Once having made projection, issuer has obligation to "update" it promptly if assumptions prove wrong. Press releases and other communications should include all information necessary to an understanding of the projection. Legal counsel should be consulted.

Reporting Required For	Securities and Exchange Commission	New York Stock Exchange	American Stock Exchange	Generally Recommended Publicity Practice, All Companies
Proxy material	Preliminary copies of proxy form and statement filed with SEC at least 10 days prior to shareholder mailing, finals when sent to holders and to each exchange where listed. SEC has broadened disclosure requirements to include additional information on directors, and has changed form of proxy to provide shareholders greater voice in corporate governance. Issuer must disclose in proxy final date for receipt of shareholder proposals.	Immediate newspaper publicity on controversial issues, especially when there is a contest. Four copies of definitive proxy material to Exchange. Ask for advance review in major matters, e.g., to determine Exchange policy; also whether brokers may vote "street name" shares without instructions from customers.	Same as NYSE. Ten copies of all proxy material are required when sent to shareholders.	Normally publicity not needed on routine matters. Press release at time proxy is mailed becoming more common. Press release may constitute "soliciting" material, so caution is advised. Special rules apply in contests; use caution. Corporate responsibility issues: no requirement to identify shareholder proposals by press release prior to meeting. Expanded information on executive compensation is widely used for round-up stories in spring. Review carefully prior to inquiries.
Questionable or illegal payments	Controversial "voluntary" program requires filing under miscellaneous item of Form 8-K. Guidelines for content published by SEC in May '76. Current policy in dispute.	No requirement.	No requirement.	Recommend press release conforming to 8-K at time 8-K is filed. However, no technical requirement for publicity. Recommend adoption of company policy statement on ethical business practices.

Redemption, repurchase, cancellation, retirement of listed securities	File 10-Q if amount of securities decrease is greater than 5 percent of amount outstanding. File 8-K and full general disclosure if the transaction is material. File Schedule 13E-4 on or prior to date of commencement of re-purchase offer. File Schedule 13E-3 if going private.	Immediate press publicity. Fifteen-day advance notice to Exchange prior to redemption. Prompt notice to Exchange of any corporate or other action affecting securities in whole or in part.	Fifteen-day advance notice to Exchange prior to redemption. Prompt notice of corporate action that will result in any of these.	Usually advertisement is required. Written notice to security holders. News release.
Rights to subscribe	Registration under the Securities Act of 1933. Prefiling notice covered by SEC Rule 135. Notice to NASD or exchanges 10 days before record date required under Securities Exchange Act antifraud provisions.	Preliminary discussion necessary. Immediate publicity. Important to work out time schedule with Exchange before any action taken. Notice to shareholders in advance of proposed record date.	Preliminary discussion necessary. Immediate publicity. Important to work out time schedule with Exchange before any action taken. Notice to shareholders in advance of proposed record date. Subscription period must extend at least 14 days after mailing date.	Immediate publicity and mailing to stockholders to give all adequate time "to record their interest and to exercise their rights," according to NYSE.
Securities: Change in, change in assets securing	10-Q if rights of holders are materially changed directly or through changes in another class of security. Separate item on Form 10-Q for withdrawal or substitution of assets.	Immediate notice to Exchange.	Immediate notice to Exchange. Timely disclosure if materially significant for investors.	Depends on terms. Occurs infrequently.

Reporting Required For	Securities and Exchange Commission	New York Stock Exchange	American Stock Exchange	Generally Recommended Publicity Practice, All Companies
Segment reporting: (line of business reporting)	See Regulation S-K, Item 101 for standard treatment in all SEC filings.	No requirement. However, "recommended" for inclusion in annual reports.	Same as NYSE.	SEC requirements have created significant opportunities to describe company in clear and detailed fashion. Evaluate filed information for use in all company presentations.
Stockholder proposals	Rule 14a-8 specifies when and under what circumstances company must include shareholder proposal in proxy materials.	No requirement.	No requirement.	SEC interest in "shareholder democracy" is declining. Current liberal rules may change. Publicity normally limited to special "advocacy" publications. General reporting likely at time of annual meeting only.
Stock split, stock dividend or other change in capitalization	10-Q required for increase or decrease if exceeds 5 percent of amount of securities of the class previously outstanding. Notice to NASD or Exchange 10 days before record date under Securities Exchange Act antifraud provisions.	Immediate public disclosure and Exchange notification. Issuance of new shares requires prior listing approval. "Telephone Alert" procedure should be followed.	Same as NYSE.	Immediate publicity as soon as proposal becomes known to "outsiders" whether formally voted or not. Discuss early whether to describe transaction as "split," "dividend" or both and use terminology consistently.

Tender offer	Conduct and published remarks of all parties governed by Sections 13(d), 13(e), 14(d), 14(e) of the '34 Act and regulations thereunder. Schedule 14D-1 disclosure required of raider. Target required to file Schedule 14D-9 for any solicitation or recommendation to security holders. (See also Hart, Scott Rodino requirements.)	Consult Exchange Stock List Department in advance. Immediate publicity and notice to Exchange.	Consult Exchange Securities Division in advance. Immediate publicity and notice to Exchange.	Massive publicity effort required; should not be attempted without thorough familiarity with current rules and constant consultation with counsel. Neither raider nor target should comment publicly until necessary SEC filings have been made. "Stop, look, listen" letter permitted under Rule 14d-9(e).
Treasury stock: Increase or decrease	Check Form 10-Q, items 5 and 6 for possible application. Note: Special rules apply during tender battle.	Notice within 10 days after close of fiscal quarter in which any transaction takes place. Prompt notice of any purchase above prevailing market price.	Same as NYSE. Companies required to notify Exchange on purchase above market price.	Normally no immediate publicity. Reason for action is normally given in annual or quarterly publication before or after event. However, see remarks under "Float," where applicable.

BIBLIOGRAPHY

100 BOOKS
FOR YOUR PUBLIC RELATIONS BOOKSHELF

Altschuler, Bruce E. *Keeping a Finger on the Public Pulse.* Westport, Conn.: Greenwood Press, 1982.

Arnoff, Craig E., and Baskin, Otis W. *Public Relations, The Profession and the Practice.* St. Paul, Minn.: West Publishing, 1983.

Baldwin, Thomas F., and McVoy, D. Stevens. *Cable Communication.* Englewood Cliffs, N.J.: Prentice-Hall, 1983.

Behrman, Jack N. *Discourses on Ethics and Business.* Cambridge, Mass.: Oelgeschlager, Gunn & Hain, 1981.

Berelson, Bernard, and Janowitz, Morris, eds. *Reader in Public Opinion and Communication*, 2nd ed. New York: The Free Press, 1966.

Berlo, David K. *The Process of Communication.* New York: Holt, Rinehart and Winston, 1960.

Bernays, Edward L. *Biography of an Idea.* New York: Simon & Schuster, 1965.

———. *Public Relations.* Norman, Okla.: University of Oklahoma Press, 1952.

———. *Crystallizing Public Opinion.* New York: Boni and Liveright, 1927.

Binn, Alec. *The 23 Most Common Mistakes in Public Relations.* New York: American Management Association, 1982.

Blankenship, A. B. *Professional Telephone Surveys.* New York: McGraw-Hill, 1977.

Bogart, Leo. *Silent Politics: Polls and the Awareness of Public Opinion.* New York: John Wiley & Sons, 1972.

Boorstin, Daniel. *The Image: A Guide to Pseudo-Events in America.* New York: Harper & Row, 1962.

Bradshaw, Thornton, and Vogel, David, eds. *Corporations and Their Critics.* New York: McGraw-Hill, 1981.

Bryson, Lyman, ed. *The Communication of Ideas.* New York: Harper & Brothers, 1948.

Budd, John F., Jr. *Corporate Video in Focus.* New York: Prentice-Hall, 1983.

Center, Allen, and Walsh, Frank. *Public Relations Practices,* 2nd ed. Englewood Cliffs, N.J.: Prentice-Hall, 1981.

Childs, Harwood. *An Introduction to Public Opinion.* New York: John Wiley & Sons, 1940.

Cole, R. S. *The Practical Handbook of Public Relations.* Englewood Cliffs, N.J.: Prentice-Hall, 1981.

Cutlip, Scott M., and Center, Allen H. *Effective Public Relations,* 5th ed. Englewood Cliffs, N.J.: Prentice-Hall, 1978.

Dillman, Dan. *Mail and Telephone Surveys—The Total Design Method.* New York: John Wiley & Sons, 1978.

Donaldson, Thomas, and Werhane, Patricia H. *Ethical Issues in Business.* Englewood Cliffs, N.J.: Prentice-Hall, 1979.

Douglas, George A. *Writing for Public Relations.* Columbus, Ohio: Charles E. Merrill, 1980.

Erdos, Paul L. *Professional Mail Surveys.* New York: McGraw-Hill, 1970.

Finn, David. *Public Relations Management.* New York: Reinhardt Publishing Co., 1960.

Franklin, Marc A. *The First Amendment and the Fourth Estate,* 2nd ed. Mineola, N.Y.: Foundation Press, 1981.

Free, Lloyd A., and Cantril, Hadley. *The Political Beliefs of Americans: A Study of Public Opinion.* New Brunswick, N.J.: Rutgers University Press, 1967.

Gallup, George H. *The Gallup Poll: Public Opinion 1972-77.* Wilmington, Del.: Scholarly Resources, 1978.

———. *The Sophisticated Poll Watcher's Guide.* Princeton, N.J.: Princeton Opinion Press, 1972.

Garbett, Thomas F. *Corporate Advertising: The What, the Why, and the How.* New York: McGraw-Hill, 1981.

Gillmor, Donald, and Barron, Jerome. *Mass Communications Law,* 3rd ed. St. Paul, Minn.: West Publishing, 1979.

Golden, L. L. L. *Only by Public Consent.* New York: Hawthorn Books, 1968.

Gordon, Reed, and Haroldsen, Edwin. *A Taxonomy of Concepts in Communication.* New York: Hastings House, 1975.

Greiner, Larry E. *Consulting to Management.* New York: Prentice-Hall, 1983.

Grunig, James E., and Hunt, Todd. *Managing Public Relations.* New York: Holt, Rinehart and Winston, 1983.

Hanson, James, and Abelson, Herbert I. *Persuasion: How Opinions and Attitudes Are Changed,* 3rd ed. New York: Springer Publishing, 1976.

Helm, Lewis, et al., eds. *Informing the People: A Public Affairs Handbook.* New York: Longman, 1981.

Hiebert, Ray E. *Courtier to the Crowd.* Ames, Iowa: Iowa State University Press, 1966.

Hill, John W. *The Making of a Public Relations Man.* New York: David McKay & Co., 1963.

Hudson, Howard Penn. *Publishing Newsletters.* New York: Charles Scribner's Sons, 1982.

Katz, Elihu, and Lazarsfeld, Paul. *Personal Influence.* New York: Free Press, 1964.

Katz, Ronald. *Cable: An Advertiser's Guide to the New Electronic Media.* Chicago: Crain Books, 1982.

Klapper, John T. *The Effects of Mass Communication.* Glencoe, Ill.: Free Press, 1960.

Key, V. O. *Public Opinion and American Democracy.* New York: Alfred A. Knopf, 1961.

Kotler, Philip. *Marketing for Nonprofit Organizations.* Englewood Cliffs, N.J.: Prentice-Hall, 1982.

Lane, Robert E., and Sears, David O. *Public Opinion.* Englewood Cliffs, N.J.: Prentice-Hall, 1964.

Latimer, Henry C. *Preparing Art and Camera Copy for Printing.* New York: McGraw-Hill, 1978.

Lazarsfeld, Paul, Berelson, Bernard, and Gaudet, Helen. *The People's Choice.* New York: Duell, Sloan and Pearce, 1944.

Lerbinger, Otto, and Sullivan, Albert. *Information, Influence, and Communication: A Reader in Public Relations.* New York: Basic Books, 1965.

Lesly, Philip. *The People Factor: Managing the Human Climate.* New York: Dow-Jones Irvin, 1974.

———, ed. *Lesly's Public Relations Handbook,* 3rd ed. Englewood Cliffs, N.J.: Prentice-Hall, 1983.

Lippmann, Walter. *Public Opinion.* New York: Macmillan Paperbacks, 1960.

Lovell, Ronald. *Inside Public Relations*. Boston: Allyn and Bacon, 1982.

MacDougall, Curtis D. *Understanding Public Opinion*. Dubuque, Iowa: Wm. C. Brown, 1966.

Marston, John. *Modern Public Relations*. New York: McGraw-Hill, 1979.

"Measuring the Effectiveness of Public Relations," Special Issue, *Public Relations Review*, Winter 1977.

Monroe, Alan D. *Public Opinion in America*. New York: Dodd, Mead, 1975.

Nagelschmidt, Joseph S., ed. *The Public Affairs Handbook*. New York: AMACOM, a Division of American Management Associations, 1982.

Naisbitt, John. *Megatrends*. New York: Warner Books, 1982.

Nelson, Harold L., and Teeter, Dwight L. *Law of Mass Communication*, 4th ed. Mineola, N.Y.: Foundation Press, 1982.

Newsom, Douglas, and Scott, Alan. *This Is PR/The Realities of Public Relations*, 2nd ed. Belmont, Calif.: Wadsworth, 1981.

Newsom, Douglas, and Siegfried, Tom. *Writing in Public Relations Practice*. Belmont, Calif.: Wadsworth, 1981.

Nimmo, Dan D., and Sanders, Keith R., eds. *Handbook of Political Communication*. Beverly Hills, Calif.: Sage, 1981.

Orlich, Donald C. *Designing Sensible Surveys*. Pleasantville, N.Y.: Redgrave Publishing Co., 1978.

Osgood, Charles, et al. *The Measurement of Meaning*. Urbana, Ill.: University of Illinois Press, 1957.

Overbeck, Wayne, and Pullen, Rick. *Major Principles of Media Law*. New York: Holt, Rinehart and Winston, 1982.

Patrick, Kenneth G. *Perpetual Jeopardy*. New York: Macmillan, 1972.

Pember, Don R. *Mass Media Law*, 2nd ed. Dubuque, Iowa: Wm. C. Brown, 1981.

Reilly, R. T. *Public Relations in Action*. Englewood Cliffs, N.J.: Prentice-Hall, 1981.

Public Affairs Profiles, 3rd ed. Washington, D.C.: Foundation for Public Affairs, 1982.

Reuss, Carol, and Silvis, Donn, eds. *Inside Organizational Communication*. New York: Longman, 1981.

Rice, Ronald E., and Paisley, William J., eds. *Public Communication Campaigns*. Beverly Hills, Calif.: Sage Publications, 1981.

Robinson, Edward J. *Public Relations and Survey Research*. New York: Appleton-Century-Crofts, 1969.

———. *Communication and Public Relations*. Columbus, Ohio: Charles E. Merrill, 1966.

Rogers, Everett M. *Diffusion of Innovations*, 3rd ed. New York: The Free Press, 1983.

Roll, Charles, Jr., and Cantril, Albert H. *Polls*. New York: Basic Books, 1972.

Ross, Irwin. *The Image Makers*. Garden City, N.Y.: Doubleday, 1959.

Ross, Robert. *The Management of Public Relations*. New York: John Wiley, 1977.

Rotman, Morris. *Opportunities in Public Relations*. Lincolnwood, Ill.: National Textbook Co., 1983.

Schramm, Wilbur, and Porter, William. *Men, Women, Messages, and Media*. New York: Harper & Row, 1982.

Schramm, Wilbur, and Roberts, Donald, eds. *The Process and Effects of Mass Communication*. Urbana, Ill.: University of Illinois Press, 1971.

Seitel, Fraser P. *The Practice of Public Relations*. Columbus, Ohio: Charles E. Merrill, 1980.

Selltiz, Claire, ed. *Research Methods in Social Relations*. New York: Holt, Rinehart, and Winston, 1962.

Sethi, S. Prakash. *Advocacy Advertising and Large Corporations*. New York: Lexington Books, 1977.

Sethi, S. Prakash, and Swanson, Carl L. *Private Enterprise and Public Purpose*. New York: John Wiley & Sons, 1981.

Shaw, Donald, and McCombs, Maxwell. *The Emergence of American Political Issues: The Agenda-Setting Function of the Press*. St. Paul, Minn.: West Publishing, 1977.

Simon, Morton J. *Public Relations Law*. New York: Appleton-Century-Crofts, 1969.

Simon, Raymond. *Publicity and Public Relations Worktext*, 5th ed. Columbus, Ohio: Grid, 1983.

———. *Public Relations Management*, 2nd ed. Columbus, Ohio: Grid, 1977.

———, ed. *Perspectives in Public Relations*. Norman, Okla.: University of Oklahoma Press, 1966.

Spitzer, Carton. *Raising the Bottom Line*. New York: Longman, 1982.

Steckmest, Francis W. *Corporate Performance: The Key to Public Trust*. New York: McGraw-Hill, 1982.

Steinberg, Charles. *The Creation of Consent: Public Relations in Practice*. New York: Hastings House, 1975.

The SEC, the Security Markets and Your Financial Communications, 4th ed. New York: Hill & Knowlton, 1979.

Voros, Gerald, and Alvarez, Paul. *What Happens in Public Relations*. New York: AMACOM, American Management Associations, 1982.

Walker, Albert. *Public Relations Bibliography*. College Park, Md.: Communications Research Associates, 1976-83.

Weiner, Richard. *Syndicated Columnists*. New York: Richard Weiner Associates, 1982.

————. *Professional's Guide to Publicity*, 2nd ed. New York: Richard Weiner, Inc., 1978.

————. *Professional's Guide to Public Relations Services*, 3rd ed. New York: Richard Weiner, 1975.

Yarrington, Roger. *Community Relations Handbook*. New York: Longman, 1983.

INDEX